T0340029

small arms survey
2013

everyday dangers

THE GRADUATE INSTITUTE | GENEVA

INSTITUT DE HAUTES ÉTUDES
INTERNATIONALES ET DU DÉVELOPPEMENT

GRADUATE INSTITUTE OF INTERNATIONAL
AND DEVELOPMENT STUDIES

CAMBRIDGE
UNIVERSITY PRESS

University Printing House, Cambridge CB2 8BS, United Kingdom

One Liberty Plaza, 20th Floor, New York, NY 10006, USA

477 Williamstown Road, Port Melbourne, VIC 3207, Australia

314-321, 3rd Floor, Plot 3, Splendor Forum, Jasola District Centre, New Delhi - 110025, India

103 Penang Road, #05-06/07, Visioncrest Commercial, Singapore 238467

Cambridge University Press is part of the University of Cambridge.

It furthers the University's mission by disseminating knowledge in the pursuit of education, learning and research at the highest international levels of excellence.

www.cambridge.org
Information on this title: www.cambridge.org/9781107041967

First published 2013

A catalogue record for this publication is available from the British Library

ISBN 978-1-107-04196-7 Hardback
ISBN 978-1-107-67244-4 Paperback

Cambridge University Press has no responsibility for the persistence or accuracy of URLs for external or third-party internet websites referred to in this publication, and does not guarantee that any content on such websites is, or will remain, accurate or appropriate.

FOREWORD

Wherever violence is a means to achieve a criminal objective, illegal firearms are usually involved—fuelling violence and empowering criminal groups worldwide. We are now confronting larger-scale, more systematic forms of violent crime, including those perpetrated by gangs and transnational criminal syndicates. Trade in illicit small arms and light weapons is also opening new markets, making firearms one of the main commodities to be exchanged in illegal markets. These dynamics shape an ever-evolving landscape, requiring constant cross-border action by law enforcement.

Reliable data and analysis, both national and international, are critical to the success of law enforcement action against violent crime involving the use of firearms. The *Small Arms Survey 2013: Everyday Dangers* offers valuable new information on the use of firearms around the globe. This includes domestic violence; the structured, rule-based use of firearms by organized crime groups; as well as the evolution of gang violence in response to internal and external factors. This volume also presents an analysis of illicit small arms and light weapons through selected case studies, casting new light on the kinds of weapons held by armed groups and their key role in driving armed violence.

Law enforcement must address and anticipate new trends in the illegal acquisition, use, and transfer of firearms to ensure the safety of our communities. Evidence-based research provided by the *Small Arms Survey 2013* can help us better understand the problem of violent crime involving the use of firearms. In turn, having a better understanding of the problem can bring law enforcement a step closer to meeting the challenges of fighting violent crime in the 21st century.

I invite all those organizations, authorities, and services tasked with preventing and combating crime worldwide to draw full benefit from this new edition of the *Survey*.

—Ronald K. Noble
INTERPOL Secretary General

CONTENTS

ABOUT THE SMALL ARMS SURVEY

The Small Arms Survey is an independent research project located at the Graduate Institute of International and Development Studies in Geneva, Switzerland. Established in 1999, the project is supported by the Swiss Federal Department of Foreign Affairs and current contributions from the Governments of Australia, Belgium, Canada, Denmark, Finland, Germany, the Netherlands, Norway, Sweden, the United Kingdom, and the United States. The Survey is grateful for past support received from the Governments of France, New Zealand, and Spain. The Survey also wishes to acknowledge the financial assistance it has received over the years from foundations and many bodies within the UN system.

The objectives of the Small Arms Survey are: to be the principal source of public information on all aspects of small arms and armed violence; to serve as a resource centre for governments, policy-makers, researchers, and activists; to monitor national and international initiatives (governmental and non-governmental) on small arms; to support efforts to address the effects of small arms proliferation and misuse; and to act as a clearinghouse for the sharing of information and the dissemination of best practices. The Survey also sponsors field research and information-gathering efforts, especially in affected states and regions. The project has an international staff with expertise in security studies, political science, law, economics, development studies, sociology, and criminology, and collaborates with a network of researchers, partner institutions, non-governmental organizations, and governments in more than 50 countries.

NOTES TO READERS

Abbreviations: Lists of abbreviations can be found at the end of each chapter.

Chapter cross-referencing: Chapter cross-references are fully capitalized in brackets throughout the book. One example appears in Chapter 2, which reviews the relationship between firearms and intimate partner violence: 'Stricter gun controls regulating general gun purchase and use were introduced in legislation in 2000, and more recent research suggests that the proportion of gun-related intimate partner homicides between 1999 and 2009 declined from 34 to 17 per cent, along with a similarly steep drop in all homicides (Abrahams et al., 2012; SOUTH AFRICA).'

Exchange rates: All monetary values are expressed in current US dollars (USD). When other currencies are also cited, unless otherwise indicated, they are converted to USD using the 365-day average exchange rate for the period 1 September 2011 to 31 August 2012.

Small Arms Survey: The plain text—Small Arms Survey—is used to indicate the overall project and its activities, while the italicized version—*Small Arms Survey*—refers to the publication. The *Survey,* appearing italicized, relates generally to past and future editions.

Small Arms Survey

Graduate Institute of International and Development Studies

47 Avenue Blanc

1202 Geneva, Switzerland

t +41 22 908 5777 **f** +41 22 732 2738

e sas@smallarmssurvey.org **w** www.smallarmssurvey.org

ACKNOWLEDGEMENTS

This is the 13th edition of the *Small Arms Survey*. Like previous editions, it is a collective product of the staff of the Small Arms Survey project, based at the Graduate Institute of International and Development Studies in Geneva, Switzerland, with support from partners. Numerous researchers in Geneva and around the world contributed to this volume, and it has benefited from the input and advice of government officials, advocates, experts, and colleagues from the small arms research community and beyond.

The principal chapter authors were assisted by in-house and external contributors, who are acknowledged in the relevant chapters. In addition, chapter reviews were provided by: Bibi Sheliza Ally, Rosemary Barbaret, James Bevan, Jurgen Brauer, Paolo Campana, Nick Cumming-Bruce, Paul Eavis, Shannon Frattaroli, Antonio Giustozzi, William Godnick, Chandre Gould, Sebastian Huhn, Roy Isbister, Thomas Jackson, Brian Jeffers, Holly Johnson, Gareth A. Jones, William Kullman, Sean Loughna, Fred Lubang, Salma Malik, Yeshua Moser-Puangsuwan, Richard Matzopoulos, Andrew Nicol, Silvia Ramos, Vincenzo Ruggiero, Gonzalo Saraví, Damien Spleeters, David Towndrow, Federico Varese, Achim Wennmann, Adrian Wilkinson, Joost van der Zwan, and the UN Office for Disarmament Affairs.

Anna Alvazzi del Frate, Eric G. Berman, Keith Krause, Emile LeBrun, and Glenn McDonald were responsible for the overall planning and organization of this edition. Alessandra Allen and Estelle Jobson managed the production of the *Survey*. Tania Inowlocki copy-edited the book; Jillian Luff produced the maps, with Dianna Targett; Richard Jones provided the design and the layout; Donald Strachan proofread the *Survey*; and Margaret Binns compiled the index. Jo Breeze, John Haslam, and Carrie Parkinson of Cambridge University Press provided support throughout the production of the *Survey*. Pablo Blum, Jovana Carapic, Natacha Cornaz, Olivia Denonville, Massimo Garsone, José Manuel Heredia González, Sarah Hoban, Mihaela Racovita, Pilar Reina, Christelle Rigual, Gideon Scher, Basma Al-Shami, Jordan Shepherd, and Cristina Tavares de Bastos fact-checked the chapters. Olivia Denonville and Martin Field helped with photo research. Cedric Blattner and Cristina Tavares de Bastos provided administrative support under the direction of Carole Touraine, who is responsible for the Survey's financial oversight.

The project also benefited from the support of the Graduate Institute of International and Development Studies, in particular Philippe Burrin and Monique Nendaz.

We are extremely grateful to the Swiss government—especially the Department for Foreign Affairs and the Swiss Development Cooperation—for its generous financial and overall support of the Small Arms Survey project, in particular Pierre von Arx, Serge Bavaud, Erwin Bollinger, Prasenjit Chaudhuri, Sabrina Dallafior, Alexandre Fasel, Thomas Greminger, Jasna Lazarevic, Armin Rieser, Paul Seger, Julien Thöni, Frédéric Tissot-Daguette, and Claude Wild. Financial support for the project is also provided by the Governments of Australia, Belgium, Canada, Denmark, Finland, Germany, the Netherlands, Norway, Sweden, the United Kingdom, and the United States.

The project further benefits from the support of international agencies, including the International Committee of the Red Cross, the UN Development Programme, the UN High Commissioner for Refugees, the UN Office for the Coordination of Humanitarian Affairs, the UN Office for Disarmament Affairs, UN Habitat, the UN Institute for Disarmament Research, the UN Office on Drugs and Crime, and the World Health Organization.

In Geneva, the project has benefited from the expertise of: Anthony Andanje, Silvia Cattaneo, Jesus 'Gary' Domingo, Gerfried Elias, Elsa Mouelhi-Rondeau, and Uglješa Zvekić.

Beyond Geneva, we also receive support from a number of colleagues. In addition to those mentioned above, and in specific chapters, we would like to thank: Abiodun Richards Adejola, Katherine Aguirre, Philip Alpers, Wolfgang Bindseil, Maria Brandstetter, Andrew Cooper, Steven Costner, Mathew Geertsen, Gillian Goh, Paul Holtom, Amber Jitts, Adèle Kirsten, Tsutomu Kono, Hideki Matsuno, Frank Meeussen, U. Joy Ogwu, Daniël Prins, Adam Ravnkilde, Jorge Restrepo, and Jeffrey Stirling.

Our sincere thanks go out to many other individuals (who remain unnamed) for their continuing support of the project. Our apologies to anyone we have failed to mention.

—**Keith Krause**, Programme Director
Eric G. Berman, Managing Director
Anna Alvazzi del Frate, Research Director

Small Arms Survey 2013

Editors	Emile LeBrun, Glenn McDonald, Anna Alvazzi del Frate, Eric G. Berman, and Keith Krause
Coordinators	Emile LeBrun and Glenn McDonald
Publication Managers	Alessandra Allen and Estelle Jobson
Designer	Richard Jones, Exile: Design & Editorial Services
Cartographer	Jillian Luff, MAP*grafix*, with Dianna Targett
Copy-editor	Tania Inowlocki
Proofreader	Donald Strachan

Principal chapter authors

Introduction	Emile LeBrun and Glenn McDonald
Chapter 1	Anna Alvazzi del Frate and Luigi De Martino
Chapter 2	Margaret Shaw
Chapter 3	Dennis Rodgers and José Luis Rocha
Chapter 4	Monica Massari
Chapter 5	Jennifer Hazen
Chapter 6	Natalie Jaynes
Chapter 7	Glenn McDonald
Chapter 8	Irene Pavesi and Christelle Rigual
Chapter 9	Pierre Gobinet
Chapter 10	Jeremy Binnie and Joanna Wright
Chapter 11	Nicolas Florquin
Chapter 12	Matt Schroeder

Police cordon off a woman's home after a murder-suicide in
Kansas City, Missouri, December 2012. © Dave Kaup/Reuters

Introduction

Many states are beset by forms of armed violence that do not rise to the level of armed conflict (war), but that never-theless generate serious health, social, and economic consequences. In fact, *non-conflict armed violence* claims far more lives worldwide than do ongoing wars. But it is a complex phenomenon, involving a mosaic of actors driven by diverse motivations and conditions. Curtailing its many manifestations requires tailored interventions developed from a sound evidence base.

CHAPTER HIGHLIGHTS

The 2013 edition of the *Small Arms Survey* explores different aspects of non-conflict armed violence, focusing on some broad categories as well as specific countries and regions. Individual chapters highlight, wherever possible, improving or deteriorating conditions and existing knowledge concerning the underlying drivers and dynamics of armed violence in those environments. This volume emphasizes that, while successes exist, policy outcomes are more mixed in many other contexts.

In South Africa, for example, the introduction of stronger gun laws following the end of the apartheid era appears to have helped drive down gun homicides and non-fatal assaults, although rates still remain high by global standards (SOUTH AFRICA). Law enforcement pressure is similarly a factor in the significant reductions in armed violence committed by Italian mafia groups in recent years. For many such groups, the use of violence has simply become too risky (MAFIA VIOLENCE).

The picture is more complex in some of the poorest neighbourhoods in Managua, Nicaragua, where original research suggests that barrio gangs' use of violence is influenced by a variety of factors. Changing policing practices and community interventions, combined with decisions by key gang leaders—or their arrest and incarceration—appear to have been important in the 'pacification' of *pandillas* (gangs). Another lesson is that gang violence fluctuates and security improvements may be erased, depending on the actions of influential actors, the rise of other armed actors, and changes in surrounding dynamics (GANG EVOLUTION).

Extending beyond country-specific examinations, two chapters look at types of armed violence that cut across borders. 'Land conflict' is a label that can be applied to different types of violent events, from fragmentary riots and protests, to community clashes and semi-organized conflict. In the African context, land conflict takes many forms, yet it is common across the continent and very often deadly. At the same time, while most violent conflicts in Africa have a land component, they tend to involve an array of other grievances (LAND CONFLICT IN AFRICA).

The victimization of women at the hands of intimate partners is widespread across many cultures and countries. Research reviewed in the 2013 *Survey* shows that the presence of guns in the home further increases the risk of serious injury and death. We are still at the early stages of understanding and addressing the many factors that underpin men's violence against women; yet it is clear that such danger is a daily fact for many women (INTIMATE PARTNER VIOLENCE). It is hardly surprising, then, that the Second Review Conference for the UN Programme of Action on Small Arms high-lighted the need both to combat violence against women and to facilitate their involvement in small arms policy-making (UN UPDATE).

The first six chapters of this volume—the 'non-conflict' section—generally emphasize that efforts to prevent and reduce armed violence need to take account of firearms types, characteristics, and sources. The following six chapters, which comprise the 'weapons and markets' section of the book, build on this observation by presenting new information on illicit guns and ammunition in certain countries. Some of the conclusions of this research challenge conventional wisdom.

A chapter analysing data on the prices of weapons in illicit markets in Lebanon, Pakistan, and Somalia finds that arms prices depend on more variables than ammunition prices. In Lebanon, ammunition prices tracked changes in regional security conditions particularly closely (ILLICIT MARKET PRICES).

A chapter on the sources of recovered illicit guns in Mexico and the Philippines provides surprising findings about the kinds of weapons criminals and armed groups hold and use in those countries. For example, while well-financed Mexican drug-trafficking organizations possess extensive arsenals, the types of weapons that they have acquired do not differ significantly from those in the hands of other, less wealthy groups—nor do they include the more sophisticated portable missiles used by governments and some state-sponsored groups (ILLICIT SMALL ARMS).

Improvised explosive devices (IEDs) comprise a weapon class developed and used almost exclusively by insurgent groups. Like land mines and cluster munitions, many types of IEDs are highly indiscriminate. Many of the victims of these weapons are civilians, especially in Iraq, where IEDs injured nearly 4,300 people and killed well over 1,000 in 2011—accounting for 41 per cent of the global civilian IED casualties that year (IMPROVISED EXPLOSIVE DEVICES).

One important way to limit the IED threat is to prevent access to the military ordnance used to create them, through effective stockpile management and security, disposal, and demilitarization of surplus and obsolete munitions. Ministries of defence typically engage private and public contractors to dispose of large quantities of surplus ammunition on an industrial scale, but this industry is not well understood by outsiders. A dedicated chapter opens industry processes and challenges up to examination for the first time (DEMILITARIZATION).

Definitions

The Small Arms Survey uses the term 'small arms and light weapons' to cover both military-style small arms and light weapons as well as commercial firearms (handguns and long guns). Except where noted otherwise, it follows the definition used in the *Report of the UN Panel of Governmental Experts on Small Arms* (UNGA, 1997):

Small arms: revolvers and self-loading pistols, rifles and carbines, sub-machine guns, assault rifles, and light machine guns.

Light weapons: heavy machine guns, grenade launchers, portable anti-tank and anti-aircraft guns, recoilless rifles, portable anti-tank missile and rocket launchers, portable anti-aircraft missile launchers, and mortars of less than 100 mm calibre.

The term 'small arms' is used in this volume to refer to small arms, light weapons, and their ammunition (as in 'the small arms industry') unless the context indicates otherwise, whereas the terms 'light weapons' and 'ammunition' refer specifically to those items.

'Armed violence' is defined as 'the use or threatened use of weapons to inflict injury, death, or psychological harm' (OECD, 2011, p. ii). When employing the term, the Survey focuses on the use of firearms by state and non-state actors.

Non-conflict section

Chapter 1 (Non-conflict violence): International attention to armed violence has tended to focus on interstate or civil wars. But the burden of *non-conflict* armed violence on people, societies, and states outstrips, by a wide margin, that generated by armed conflict and its aftermath. The opening chapter in the thematic section outlines some defining aspects of non-conflict armed violence, its forms, and it drivers, highlighting how different types of violence and violent actors overlap, interact, and change over time. It notes that addressing devastating forms of armed violence is often beyond the means of public sector institutions, especially where governance is weak. Multilateral and multisectoral initiatives for armed violence reduction are only now emerging.

Chapter 2 (Intimate partner violence): Between 40 and 70 per cent of female murder victims are killed by an intimate partner, often with a gun. In contrast, most male victims of gun violence die outside the home at the hands of individuals who are not their intimate partners. This chapter reviews how the possession of guns, personally and professionally, is strongly associated with particular notions of masculinity. It analyses data on the use of firearms in intimate partner violence, the gendered nature of firearm ownership and use, and the cultural underpinnings of gun possession by men. It underscores that the presence of guns in the home increases the risks of death, intimidation, and long-term abuse for female partners—as well as murder followed by suicide—and considers some of the policy options for reducing such risks to women in the home.

Chapter 3 (Gang evolution): Gangs are often considered a major security threat in Central America, but the specific dynamics of the gang threat are not well understood. This chapter offers an overview of the development of gangs in two *barrios* in Managua, Nicaragua. Gangs in these neighbourhoods arose in the aftermath of the 1980s Contra war, then institutionalized as they exerted control over local territory. Their subsequent development has not followed any simple trajectory, however. This chapter, based on original field research, shows how unique evolutionary dynamics affect gang use of firearms and violence. Internally, specific individuals can influence the way a gang evolves and how violent it becomes. Externally, the presence of other armed actors strongly influences gang use of firearms.

Chapter 4 (Mafia violence): Italian mafias have always used armed violence and intimidation to resolve disputes, strike at competitors, enhance their reputations, and seek advantage in both legal and illicit markets. The professionalized use of firearms and explosives represents one of their characteristic features. This chapter presents original research on patterns, rules, changes, and variations in the acquisition, storage, and use of firearms by traditional Italian mafia-type organizations during the past 20 years. Although quantitative data on firearm-related crime in Italy remains weak, this chapter indicates that mafia power rests on the availability of large arsenals and sophisticated weaponry as well as the ability to rely on specialized 'fire group' teams.

Chapter 5 (Land conflict in Africa): Land is the basis of security and survival for much of Africa's population. It is also intimately tied to national politics, community dynamics, and status, power, wealth, and security. Given its importance, as well as its scarcity, competition for land resources—and the inability of governments to manage competition effectively—has sown the seeds of violence for decades. This chapter reviews the factors that have contributed to the increasing costs of land conflict in Africa in recent years. It suggests that land disputes are most volatile, and most likely to erupt into violence, when grievances are high, security is threatened, mechanisms for adjudication are absent, and violence entrepreneurs are able to mobilize aggrieved populations.

Chapter 6 (South Africa): In the 19 years since South Africa's transition from apartheid to democracy, the country has made progress in a number of areas. Many South Africans are materially better off than they were in 1994 and certain aspects of public safety have improved; moreover, homicide rates in South Africa have dropped significantly. Yet, despite these gains, South Africa's income inequality and homicide rates remain among the world's highest. This chapter explores these problems, paying particular attention to the factors that drive or inhibit armed violence in the country, as well as the interventions that might further reduce levels of armed violence.

Weapons and markets

Chapter 7 (UN update): In 2012, at the Second Review Conference for the UN Programme of Action (PoA), UN member states reached consensus agreement on a substantive outcome that is designed, above all, to strengthen implementation of the PoA and its companion International Tracing Instrument over the coming years. This chapter analyses the substantive outcome of the Conference, but also the process that allowed it to succeed where the First Review Conference, convened in 2006, had failed—in particular, by giving a largely impracticable mandate a more forward-looking interpretation. The chapter also notes some of the missed opportunities at this latest UN small arms meeting, concluding that its legacy appears to be positive, although this largely depends on concrete follow-up.

Chapter 8 (Authorized trade): This chapter presents information on the largest exporters and importers of small arms and light weapons in 2010, based on UN Comtrade data. It identifies the top exporters in 2010 (those with annual exports of at least USD 100 million) as (in descending order) the United States, Germany, Italy, Brazil, Switzerland, Israel, Austria, the Russian Federation, South Korea, Sweden, Belgium, and Spain. Top importers in 2010 (those with annual imports of at least USD 100 million) were (in descending order) the United States, the United Kingdom, Canada, Germany, Australia, South Korea, France, and Thailand.

The chapter also includes the 2013 Transparency Barometer, which assesses the transfer reporting practices of the 55 countries that have been major exporters during at least one year since 2001. It identifies Switzerland, Romania, and Serbia as the most transparent of the major exporters, and Iran, North Korea, Saudi Arabia, and the United Arab Emirates as the least transparent for 2011 export-related activities.

Chapter 9 (Demilitarization): In many countries, excess stockpiles of obsolete or unserviceable munitions have reached a level requiring industrial demilitarization—that is, the process of safely dismantling or destroying large quantities of ammunition using industrial processes and recovering reusable materials. Since states rarely have the capacity to demilitarize all of the surplus ammunition stockpiles of their security forces, they turn to the demilitarization industry. US and Western European contractors routinely process significant amounts of conventional ammunition and are important participants in international, donor-funded arms control and ammunition demilitarization programmes. This chapter provides an introductory overview of the world's major industrial demilitarization contractors by examining their activities, technologies, and markets, along with some of the challenges they face.

Chapter 10 (Improvised explosive devices): Improvised explosive devices (IEDs) have had a devastating impact in recent years, with at least 13,000 civilians killed or injured in IED incidents across 44 countries in 2011, mostly in Afghanistan, Iraq, and Pakistan. The increase in civilian casualties over the past decade can be largely attributed to the use of larger IEDs and indiscriminate tactics. At the same time, the widespread use of improvised land mines in some parts of Afghanistan has restricted civilian access to governance, health care, markets, and education.

This chapter finds that it is possible to make it harder for militants to source the materials most commonly used to make large IEDs, but the necessary measures are expensive and difficult to implement. A more determined campaign to stigmatize the use of indiscriminate weapons and tactics, and a concerted effort to gather better data on the toll inflicted by IEDs, could complement such measures.

Chapter 11 (Illicit market prices): The prices of illicit firearms and their implications for security have attracted interest among journalists and researchers for some time. Most quantitative research has relied on second-hand reports, often prices quoted in media articles. Prices for illicitly sold ammunition are poorly documented. This chapter uses new data collected in Lebanon, Pakistan, and Somalia to refine our understanding of arms and ammunition prices at illicit markets. It shows that they generally follow similar trends, although arms prices often depend on a larger number of factors than ammunition prices, such as technical features and local perceptions. Notably, ammunition prices in Lebanon were strongly correlated with reported conflict casualties in neighbouring Syria.

Chapter 12 (Illicit small arms): This chapter presents the findings from the second instalment of the Small Arms Survey's multi-year study on illicit small arms and light weapons. The study, launched in 2012, seeks to improve public understanding of illicit small arms by acquiring and analysing new and hitherto under-utilized data on illicit weapons from a variety of countries. The chapter looks at illicit weapons in countries affected by high-intensity organized criminal violence and low-intensity armed conflict.

Information gleaned from more than 6,000 illicit small arms and light weapons in Mexico and the Philippines suggests that armed groups in these countries have acquired few, if any, technologically sophisticated light weapons, including portable missiles. Also notable is the large percentage of seized weapons of US design in the Philippines; meanwhile, in Mexico, authorities recovered only small quantities of what government officials and journalists often refer to as drug cartels' 'weapons of choice'.

CONCLUSION

Non-conflict armed violence holds many regions in the grip of insecurity, preventing development and undermining livelihoods. The *Small Arms Survey 2013* draws a number of strands together to assist states to better understand, and ultimately address, its many facets.

As the chapters in this volume show, the challenges are complex and progress to date is uneven. States working in isolation are bound to struggle. Multilateral frameworks and cooperation mechanisms to reduce armed violence, including initiatives such as the Geneva Declaration on Armed Violence and Development, have potential multiplier effects. The burden of armed violence is shared; so, too, are the likely solutions. ◼

—Emile LeBrun and Glenn McDonald

BIBLIOGRAPHY

OECD (Organisation for Economic Co-operation and Development). 2011. 'Breaking Cycles of Violence: Key Issues in Armed Violence Reduction.'
   Paris: OECD. <http://www.oecd.org/dac/incaf/48913388.pdf>

UNGA (United Nations General Assembly). 1997. *Report of the Panel of Governmental Experts on Small Arms.* A/52/298 of 27 August (annexe).
   <http://www.un.org/depts/ddar/Firstcom/SGreport52/a52298.html>

Roses bearing the faces of people killed in a shooting at Sandy Hook Elementary School, Newtown, Connecticut, January 2013. © Timothy Clary/AFP Photo

Everyday Dangers

NON-CONFLICT ARMED VIOLENCE

1

INTRODUCTION

In December 2011, Mitch Landrieu, the mayor of New Orleans, said that 'a student attending John McDonogh [one of the city's high schools] was more likely to be killed than a soldier in Afghanistan' (Robertson, 2011). His assessment, while partly rhetorical, pointed to an uncomfortable truth. With a homicide rate of 51 victims per 100,000 population, New Orleans residents faced greater risks than the populations of such war-torn countries as the Democratic Republic of the Congo (32 homicides per 100,000), Somalia (30 per 100,000), and Afghanistan (21 per 100,000) (Gilgen, 2011, p. 53).[1] As counterintuitive as it may seem, fatalities due to armed violence in non-conflict settings account for the overwhelming majority of violent deaths worldwide. Between 2004 and 2009, an average of 526,000 people died violently each year, but only 10 per cent of them qualified as direct conflict deaths (p. 70).

International attention, however, has traditionally focused on interstate or civil wars. Violence that is not captured by the terms 'armed conflict' or 'post-conflict'—and that does not violate international human rights law—is normally left to the relevant country to address as best it can. However, many states simply are not able to tackle the entrenched forms of non-conflict armed violence that affect them. The resulting human and economic costs to societies—and the frequent erosion of the state's legitimacy and monopoly on the use of force—have triggered a rethink of international and national policies designed to address armed violence.

Non-conflict armed violence is the theme linking the first six chapters of the *Small Arms Survey 2013*. This chapter, the first in that series, briefly reviews the concepts and ongoing debates about non-conflict armed violence among analysts and practitioners. It also touches on some of the manifestations of non-conflict violence, including principal dynamics and drivers, all of which are examined in greater detail in the following chapters.

What is 'armed violence'?

Armed violence is 'the use or threatened use of weapons to inflict injury, death, or psychosocial harm' (OECD, 2011, p. ii). It is perpetrated by a range of actors, from insurgents, gangs, and organized criminal groups to police forces and armies, militias, and armed individuals (Kaldor, 2007). Armed violence is used to assert supremacy, to intimidate opponents and civilians, to defend territory and other resources, to eliminate rivals, and to protect business operations. While the term calls to mind hostile engagements such as electoral violence, clashes over natural resources or contested areas, and fights between rival gangs or organized crime groups, it also encompasses interpersonal violence, including crimes of passion and 'honour'.[2] In addition, armed violence includes legal interventions as well as excessive use of lethal force by law enforcement (Geneva Declaration Secretariat, 2011).

The use of weapons is central to the definition of armed violence. But while 'weapons' may include blunt objects, knives, or any other tool used as a weapon, this thematic section uses the term 'armed violence' to refer primarily to

Box 1.1 Parsing conflict, post-conflict, and non-conflict armed violence

'Armed conflicts' can be defined on the basis of the identities of the belligerents, whether state or non-state, or according to their intensity, which is generally measured in terms of the number of casualties. Interstate violence and civil war represent the two 'classic' types of armed conflict. If at least one party involved is a non-state actor and a certain level of sustained intensity is reached, the conflict is labelled an 'intrastate armed conflict' or 'civil war'. Such conflicts become 'internationalized' when a foreign state intervenes, either directly or by proxy, to assist, finance, or provide operational support to a non-state belligerent (Vité, 2009, p. 71).

International humanitarian law is often used as a marker for the existence of an 'armed conflict'. It applies to the kinds of armed conflict just mentioned—but not to situations such as riots or isolated or sporadic acts of violence, which are character-ized by armed violence that is less intense or less sustained (Vité, 2009, p. 76). Similarly, much academic research distinguishes between low- and high-intensity armed conflicts on the one hand,[3] and crises—including situations that involve the sporadic use of violence—on the other.[4] Crises are not usually considered 'armed conflicts'.

Figure 1.1 shows that war between states accounts for only a small portion of all armed conflicts. The total number of armed conflicts peaked in 1992 and then started to decline; extra-systemic, or colonial, conflict disappeared by 1974[5] and interstate conflict has been relatively infrequent since 2004. In the period 2000–09, the total number of armed conflicts, the majority of which were intrastate, fluctuated between 30 and 40 per year. These figures are consistent with the estimates of the Conflict Barometer of Heidelberg University, which counts 28 high-intensity conflicts and as many as 126 crises for 2010 (HIIK, 2010, pp. 1, 88).

The notion of a *post-conflict* period gained currency at the end of the cold war, when the international community stepped up its efforts to stabilize and rebuild states following a number of armed conflicts around the globe (Collier, Hoeffler, and Söderbom, 2008, p. 462). Armed conflict, however, does not always produce a clear outcome—such as a military victory or a peace agreement—and it may be unclear when the post-conflict period begins. Significant fighting, often referred to as residual violence, may still occur between old or new belligerents in the period following the formal end of hostilities (UNODC, 2011b, p. 15).

Figure 1.1 Number of armed conflicts per year, 1946–2011

■ Extra-systemic (colonial) ■ Interstate ■ International intrastate ▨ Intrastate

NUMBER OF CONFLICTS

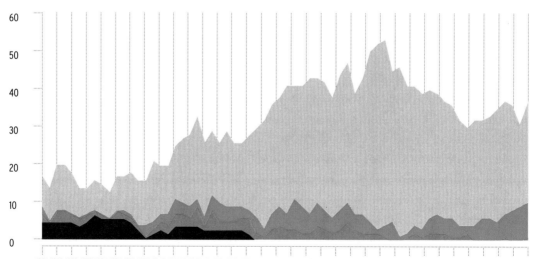

Source: Themnér and Wallensteen (2012, p. 568)

This section uses the term non-conflict to define situations of contemporary armed violence that are neither 'conflict' nor 'post-conflict' in nature. Cutting across a range of sectors, including criminal justice and public health, the concept is necessarily broad and thus overlaps with other notions, such as that of a crisis. Other labels have been developed to describe situations related to non-conflict armed violence; for example, the terms fragile situations and fragile states are increasingly being used to characterize countries or territories where armed violence has become an endemic problem.[6] When cross-border dimensions apply, non-conflict armed violence may be identified as a transnational threat. One such threat, transnational organized crime, is the subject of a UN framework convention (UNGA, 2000).

A perpetrator's motivations are relevant regardless of how an act of armed violence is defined. Incidents that are categorized according to their *nature* may be politically or economically motivated,[7] or they may be driven by hate or a perceived need to defend a sense of 'honour'. Violent events that are labelled according to their *setting* include cases of 'domestic violence' or 'urban violence'. Acts of violence may also be identified based on characteristics of the *victim*, such as 'gender-based violence', or of the *relationship* between the victim and the perpetrator, such as 'intimate partner violence'.

Any one incident may have multiple motivations, whether distinct or overlapping. An armed bank robbery may have terrorist roots. Armed groups may be engaged in a political struggle against or for the state and at the same time be involved in the trafficking of narcotics, as with insurgent forces in Colombia and Afghanistan.

Which approach is used to label or identify different types of armed violence depends largely on the outlook of the observer. While experts in international affairs or conflict studies may disregard—or even discard—information on the motivation behind the perpetration of a violent act, criminologists, sociologists, and, to some extent, public health professionals assess precisely that 'intention' to determine the nature of the violent act.

By examining various forms of armed violence under the broader 'non-conflict' umbrella, this section seeks both to provide a unified approach to armed violence and to facilitate the development of multi-sectoral responses to the challenges it poses.

Source: De Martino and Dönges (2012)

violence committed with firearms. On average, an estimated 42–60 per cent of lethal violence is committed with firearms worldwide (UNODC, 2011a, p. 10; Lozano et al., 2012, p. 2109; Geneva Declaration Secretariat, 2008, p. 67). For each person killed with a firearm, at least three more survive gunshot injuries (Alvazzi del Frate, 2012, p. 94). At the same time, the vast majority of violent deaths occur in countries and territories that are not considered conflict or post-conflict environments (Gilgen, 2011, p. 51). In short, most contemporary armed violence occurs in non-conflict settings.

One may expect the global distribution of firearms to reflect the global distribution of armed violence. The Small Arms Survey estimates that civilians hold some 650 million—or roughly 75 per cent—of approximately 875 million firearms possessed worldwide. Non-state armed groups and gangs hold a small proportion of these weapons—no more than 11.4 million. National armed forces and law enforcement agencies account for the remainder of the global stockpile, or less than a quarter (Karp, 2010, pp. 102–03). As discussed below, however, access to weapons does not, in and of itself, drive armed violence.

FLUID DYNAMICS: ARMED ACTORS AND VIOLENCE

Armed violence trends reflect complex relationships among different types of armed actors who engage in various forms of violence, which may evolve over time, along with motivations and objectives. Armed actors include

Table 1.1 **Conflict and non-conflict armed violence, examples by type of armed actor**						
	State security forces	(Pro-government) militias	Insurgent armed groups	Private security companies	Gangs and organized crime	Individuals
Interstate and civil war	✓	✓	✓			
(State) violence against civilians	✓	✓	✓	✓		
Terrorist attacks and violence		✓	✓		✓	✓
Community violence		✓	✓	✓	✓	
Gang and organized crime violence		✓	✓	✓	✓	
Violent assault and armed robbery		✓	✓		✓	✓
Domestic violence, violence against women	✓	✓	✓	✓	✓	✓

individuals as well as groups of varying sizes, affiliations, and structures, yet all of them have access to weapons (Hazen, 2010, p. 86).

While a distinct range of armed actors and types of armed violence may be identified, the relationships between them are complex. Table 1.1 provides a first attempt to plot these linkages. It does not imply an automatic relationship between different armed actors and various forms of armed violence, but instead provides examples of possible engagement of armed actors in violent acts. Often, these may be involved in various types of violence simultaneously. Furthermore, as the boundaries between different forms of violence may be blurred, different types of armed violence may overlap, interact, or mutually reinforce each other (Krause and Nowak, 2011, p. 34). In countries where armed violence is endemic, for instance, large-scale organized violence may coexist with criminal violence, human rights violations, terrorist attacks, and various forms of interpersonal violence (INTIMATE PARTNER VIOLENCE).

Uses of force: public and private

It is generally claimed that, in order to guarantee their citizens a certain level of physical security, including the security needed to pursue basic livelihoods, states must retain the monopoly on the legitimate use of force (van der Wilt, 2012, p. 1114). States sometimes decide to delegate or outsource the use of force to others, such as private security companies, if there are financial or other advantages to doing so (Bailes, 2007, p. 1).

In other cases, armed groups—including insurgents, separatists, vigilantes, and criminal organizations and gangs—may challenge the state's monopoly and its capacity to control violence in part or all of its territory. It is not uncommon for such actors to use armed violence simultaneously against the state and the civilian population. Thus, for example, a rebel group acting against state security forces may, at the same time, kidnap civilians in order to fund its military operations.

A man grieves for his brother who was killed in a bomb blast in Quetta, Pakistan, February 2013. © Naseer Ahmed/Reuters

Some states are ill equipped to respond to widespread non-conflict violence, particularly if they suffer from poor governance or pronounced ethnic and social divisions (Malby, 2011, p. 107; SOUTH AFRICA). Some governments abuse their monopoly on the use of force, using violence against their population for policy ends. Such is the case, for example, when police use excessive force to stop demonstrations, political leaders employ gangs to quash opponents, or security forces conduct violent civilian disarmament campaigns. Countries that have weak institutions or that routinely use violence against civilians generally report high homicide rates (Malby, 2011, p. 103).

Poor performance with respect to the rule of law damages a state's legitimacy and the population's trust (Malby, 2011, p. 88). If the people do not trust government institutions to protect them, they may pursue their own means of security, such as by procuring arms, supporting local vigilante-type defence forces, or refusing to disarm (LAND CONFLICT IN AFRICA and GANG EVOLUTION). In turn, these steps can lead to a downward spiral as violent private actors increase their power at the expense of governments.

The underlying drivers of armed violence

Although the use of weapons is one of the main vectors of armed violence, access to weapons—including to firearms—does not in and of itself determine whether armed violence will take place; multiple other factors also affect the likelihood, severity, and nature of armed violence. The relationship between *access* and *use* of weapons is complex. On the one hand, the presence of a gun in the home increases the risk of lethal violence in the case of domestic disputes (Hemenway, 2011, p. 7; INTIMATE PARTNER VIOLENCE); on the other hand, there is no clear link between access to firearms and overall levels of armed violence in a country. That said, high economic inequality, a history of conflict, violent events in neighbouring countries, and massive migration or repatriation flows have been associated with changes in levels of armed violence. In the past, a desire to secure access to land and natural resources—in situations of both resource abundance and scarcity—acted as a prime driver of many colonial wars, separatist insurgencies, and civil wars; today it continues to stoke non-conflict armed violence, such as violent communal clashes, in various parts of the world (SOUTH AFRICA and LAND CONFLICT IN AFRICA).

Non-conflict armed violence is often fuelled by the involvement of armed groups in legal and illegal economic activity as they use violence for political, as well as economic, ends (Cortright, 2012; Mulaj, 2010). Highly structured groups, such as gangs and organized criminal organizations, often employ violence in pursuit of profit and economic gain, or as a mechanism for resolving disputes (MAFIA VIOLENCE). Armed actors may use illicit economic activity to fund military operations or to expand their power, for example by increasing their control over territory (Hazen, 2010, p. 88; UNODC, 2010, p. 234).

> ### Box 1.2 The implications of definitions
>
> Whether violence is tied to an 'armed conflict', 'post-conflict', or 'non-conflict' situation is more than semantics. The populations involved in a clearly defined armed conflict can access international resources that may be denied in the absence of explicit labelling. More specifically, the armed conflict label can trigger UN Security Council interventions, the deployment of international peacekeeping missions, and the provision of relief aid.
>
> High levels of non-conflict violence can be as destructive in human and economic terms as a war, but affected countries typically benefit from little or no international support. Instead, these states are expected to respond using law enforcement, criminal justice, and public health tools. Yet in many countries the burden of non-conflict violence outweighs the capacity of state institutions to respond.
>
> Marked by their severity, such situations are now attracting more attention. Some countries, such as Mexico, have declared 'war' on organized crime groups and are using military tactics in an effort to curb the threat (Peterke, 2012, p. 2). Other countries—notably in Central America—have adopted *mano dura* (iron fist) strategies that are based exclusively on repression. These tactics often lead to an unintended escalation of violence (Lessing, 2012).
>
> In order to help affected populations, humanitarian agencies such as the International Committee of the Red Cross and Médecins Sans Frontières have recently started to deploy missions to countries such as Brazil, Honduras, and Mexico (IRIN, 2013).
>
> A new practice of granting refugee status to persons fleeing forced gang recruitment is also emerging, extending an important protection previously accorded only to persons fleeing armed conflicts (Cheng, 2011; Grayner, 2012).

In fact, the relationship between land, territory, and community appears crucial to understanding non-conflict violence. In general, the more a group is organized, the more likely it is to be interested in dominating territory, be it a rebel group, gang, or organized crime group (UNODC, 2012, p. 21). Such groups use violence to establish and preserve their power. Among them, groups that have close links to their communities, such as *pandillas* in Nicaragua, use violence more sparingly. They may function as security providers for the communities in which they operate—either formally, as private security companies, or informally, like the 'defence crews' in Jamaica (Small Arms Survey, forthcoming). In many cases, gangs or other non-state armed groups provide a social safety net that the state refuses, or is too weak, to offer (Williams and Godson, 2002, p. 316). In contrast to such community-based groups, those with transnational origins—such as the *maras* in Latin America—are often less constrained in their use of violence (GANG EVOLUTION).

CONCLUSION

As this chapter has discussed, non-conflict armed violence has many forms and causes. It severely burdens people, societies, and states worldwide, sometimes imposing costs that dramatically outstrip those generated by armed conflict and its aftermath. Nevertheless, countries afflicted with high levels of non-conflict armed violence must typically

Police seize a cache of weapons from alleged gang members in Tegucigalpa, Honduras, June 2012. © Orlando Sierra/AFP Photo

tackle the problem on their own. No peacekeepers are sent to assist the state in its efforts, which may be uncoordinated, focused exclusively on one sector, or generally limited if institutions are weak. Multilateral initiatives that aim to reduce armed violence in both conflict and non-conflict settings, such as the Geneva Declaration on Armed Violence and Development, remain underutilized (Geneva Declaration, 2006).

Non-conflict armed violence varies according to culture and country, but many 'local problems' are in fact shared by societies around the world. Relationships between actors and their use of violence are complex and can change over time. The following chapters flesh out the dense landscape of non-conflict violence in greater detail. ◼

ENDNOTES

1   These are average annual rates for the period 2004–09.

2   The World Health Organization defines *interpersonal violence* as violence between individuals, including family and intimate partner violence, as well as community violence (Krug et al., 2002, p. 6).

3   The Uppsala Conflict Data Program defines an *armed conflict* as 'a contested incompatibility which concerns government and/or territory where the use of armed force between two parties, of which at least one is the government of a state, results in at least 25 battle-related deaths. If a conflict generates more than 1,000 battle deaths a year, it is considered a war' (UCDP, n.d.).

4   The Heidelberg Institute for International Conflict Research defines a *crisis* as a 'tense situation in which at least one of the parties uses violent force in sporadic incidents' (HIIK, 2010, p. 88).

5   The Uppsala Conflict Data Program defines *extra-systemic conflict* as 'a conflict between a state and a non-state group outside its own territory. [. . .] This category basically contains colonial conflicts' (UCDP, n.d.).

6   The World Bank defines *fragile situations* as those with either: a) a harmonized average Country Policy and Institutional Assessment country rating of 3.2 or less; or b) the presence of a UN or regional peacekeeping or peace-building mission during the past three years. The list of fragile situations for 2013 includes some 35 countries (World Bank, 2013). The Organisation for the Economic Co-operation and Development defines *fragile states* as those 'failing to provide basic services to poor people because they are unwilling or unable to do so' (OECD, 2006, p. 147).

7   Political motivations include 'ethnic or religious hatred, political repression, political exclusion, and economic inequality' (Collier and Hoeffler, 2004, p. 570). Greed and profit-seeking are often cited among economic motivations; see Collier and Hoeffler (2004, pp. 564–65) and Arnson and Zartman (2005).

BIBLIOGRAPHY

Alvazzi del Frate, Anna. 2012. 'A Matter of Survival: Non-lethal Firearm Violence.' In Small Arms Survey, 2012, pp. 78–105.

Arnson, Cynthia and William Zartman. 2005. *Rethinking the Economics of War: The Intersection of Need, Creed, and Greed.* Washington, DC: Woodrow Wilson Center Press.

Bailes, Alyson. 2007. 'The Private Sector and the Monopoly of Force.' In Alyson Bailes, Ulrich Schneckener, and Herbert Wulf. *Revisiting the State Monopoly on the Legitimate Use of Force.* Policy Paper 24. Geneva: Geneva Centre for the Democratic Control of Armed Forces, pp. 1–9.

Cheng, Gracye. 2011. 'Gang Persecution as Grounds for Asylum in the US.' *Forced Migration Review*, No. 37, pp. 50–51.

Collier, Paul and Anke Hoeffler. 2004. 'Greed and Grievance in Civil Wars.' *Oxford Economic Papers*, Vol. 56, No. 4, pp. 563–95.

—, and Måns Söderbom. 2008. 'Post-Conflict Risks.' *Journal of Peace Research*, Vol. 45, No. 4, pp. 461–78.

Cortright, David. 2012. 'New Wars, Old Strategies.' *Peace Policy.* December.
    <http://peacepolicy.nd.edu/2012/12/10/new-wars-old-strategies/peacepolicy-dec-2012/>

De Martino, Luigi and Hanna Dönges. 2012. *Armed Conflicts: Defining the Concepts.* Unpublished background paper. Geneva: Small Arms Survey.

Geneva Declaration (Geneva Declaration on Armed Violence and Development). 2006. Geneva, 7 June.
    <http://www.genevadeclaration.org/the-geneva-declaration/what-is-the-declaration.html>

Geneva Declaration Secretariat. 2008. *Global Burden of Armed Violence.* Geneva: Geneva Declaration Secretariat.

—. 2011. *Global Burden of Armed Violence: Lethal Encounters.* Cambridge: Cambridge University Press.

Gilgen, Elizabeth. 2011. 'Trends and Patterns of Lethal Violence.' In Geneva Declaration Secretariat, 2011, pp. 43–86.

Grayner, Alexandra. 2012. 'Escaping Forced Gang Recruitment: Establishing Eligibility for Asylum after *Matter of S-E-G.' Hastings Law Journal,* Vol. 63, No. 5, pp. 1417–42.

Hazen, Jennifer. 2010. 'Gangs, Groups, and Guns: An Overview.' In Small Arms Survey, 2010, pp. 85–99.

Hemenway, David. 2011. 'Risks and Benefits of a Gun in the Home.' *American Journal of Lifestyle Medicine.* Vol. 5, No. 6. November, pp. 502–11.

HIIK (Heidelberg Institute for International Conflict Research). 2010. *Conflict Barometer 2010.* Heidelberg: University of Heidelberg.
    <http://www.hiik.de/en/konfliktbarometer/pdf/ConflictBarometer_2010.pdf>

IRIN (Integrated Regional Information Networks). 2013. 'Analysis: Urban Violence, New Territories for Aid Workers.' 10 January.
    <http://www.irinnews.org/Report/97188/Analysis-Urban-violence-new-territory-for-aid-workers>

Kaldor, Mary. 2007. *New and Old Wars: Organized Violence in a Global Era.* Stanford: Stanford University Press.

Karp, Aaron. 2010. 'Elusive Arsenals: Gang and Group Firearms.' In Small Arms Survey, 2010, pp. 101–27.

Krause, Keith and Matthias Nowak. 2011. 'A Unified Approach to Armed Violence.' In Geneva Declaration Secretariat, 2011, pp. 11–42.

Krug, Etienne, et al., eds. 2002. *World Report on Violence and Health.* Geneva: World Health Organization.

Lessing, Benjamin. 2012. 'When Business Gets Bloody: State Policy and Drug Violence.' In Small Arms Survey, 2012, pp. 41–72.

Lozano, Rafael, et al. 2012. 'Global and Regional Mortality from 235 Causes of Death for 20 Age Groups in 1990 and 2010: A Systematic Analysis for the Global Burden of Disease Study 2010.' *Lancet*, Vol. 380, No. 9859, pp. 2095–128.

Malby, Steven. 2011. 'Characteristics of Armed Violence.' In Geneva Declaration Secretariat, pp. 87–112.

Mulaj, Kledja. 2010. 'Violent Non-State Actors: Exploring their State Relation, Legitimation, Operationality.' In Kledja Mulaj, ed. *Violent Non-State Actors in World Politics.* London and New York: Columbia University Press, pp. 1–26.

OECD (Organisation for the Economic Co-operation and Development). 2006. *DAC Guidelines and Reference Series Applying Strategic Environmental Assessment: Good Practice Guidance for Development Co-operation.* Paris: OECD.

—. 2011. *Breaking Cycles of Violence: Key Issues in Armed Violence Reduction.* Paris: OECD.

Peterke, Sven. 2012. 'Regulating "Drug Wars" and other Grey Zone Conflicts: Formal and Functional Approaches.' HASOW Discussion Paper No. 2. Rio de Janeiro: Humanitarian Action in Situations Other Than War.

Robertson, Campbell. 2011. 'New Orleans Struggles to Stem Homicides.' *The New York Times.* 7 December.
    <http://www.nytimes.com/2011/12/08/us/new-orleans-struggles-to-stem-homicides.html?pagewanted=all>

Small Arms Survey. 2010. *Small Arms Survey 2010: Gangs, Groups, and Guns.* Cambridge: Cambridge University Press.

—. 2012. *Small Arms Survey 2012: Moving Targets.* Cambridge: Cambridge University Press.

—. Forthcoming. *Without a Ladder: Strategies to Counter Gang Culture in Jamaica.* Jamaica Armed Violence Assessment Issue Brief 2. Geneva: Small Arms Survey.

Themnér, Lotta and Peter Wallensteen. 2012. 'Armed Conflict, 1946–2011.' *Journal of Peace Research,* Vol. 49, No. 4, pp. 565–75.

UCDP (Uppsala Conflict Data Program). n.d. 'Definitions.' <http://www.pcr.uu.se/research/ucdp/definitions/>

UNGA (United Nations General Assembly). 2000. United Nations Convention against Transnational Organized Crime. Resolution 55/25, adopted 15 November. New York: UNGA.

UNODC (United Nations Office on Drugs and Crime). 2010. *The Globalization of Crime: A Transnational Organized Crime Threat Assessment.* Vienna: UNODC.

—. 2011a. *Global Study on Homicide.* Vienna: UNODC.

—. 2011b. *Criminal Justice Reform in Post-conflict States: A Guide for Practitioners.* Vienna: UNODC.

—. 2012. *Transnational Organized Crime in Central America and the Caribbean: A Threat Assessment.* Vienna: UNODC.

van der Wilt, Harmen. 2012. 'War Crimes and the Requirement of a Nexus with an Armed Conflict.' *Journal of International Criminal Justice,* Vol. 10, No. 5, pp. 1113–28.

Vité, Sylvain. 2009. 'Typology of Armed Conflicts in International Humanitarian Law: Legal Concepts and Actual Situations.' *International Review of the Red Cross,* Vol. 91, No. 873, pp. 69–94.

Williams, Paul and Roy Godson. 2002. 'Anticipating Organized and Transnational Crime.' *Crime, Law & Social Change,* Vol. 37, No. 4, pp. 311–55.

World Bank. 2013. 'Harmonized List of Fragile Situations FY13.'
    <http://siteresources.worldbank.org/EXTLICUS/Resources/511777-1269623894864/FCSHarmonizedListFY13.pdf>

ACKNOWLEDGEMENTS

Principal authors

Anna Alvazzi del Frate and Luigi De Martino

Contributors

Hannah Dönges, Christelle Rigual

Emergency services personnel assist a toddler, the survivor of a murder-suicide in a military housing complex, California, December 2011. © Richard Eaton/Corbis

Too Close to Home

GUNS AND INTIMATE PARTNER VIOLENCE

2

INTRODUCTION

Small arms policy and research have largely ignored the significance of gender in shaping attitudes and behaviour towards firearms, who owns and uses them, and the differential circumstances in which men and women become victims of firearm violence. The importance of gender differences in gun ownership and gun violence becomes strikingly clear when their role in non-conflict settings—such as family and domestic violence—is considered. Studies in a number of countries have shown that between 40 and 70 per cent of female murder victims are killed by an intimate partner (WHO, 2002, p. 93; UNODC, 2011a); in countries where guns are easily available, they are often the weapon used to commit such homicides. In stark contrast, most men who fall victim to gun violence are killed outside the home by people who are not their intimate partners.

In many cultures, the possession of guns, whether in a personal or a professional capacity, is strongly associated with traditional notions of masculinity that convey authority, privilege, prestige, and power. Yet the presence of guns in the home increases the risks of accidents, murder, and suicide for family members, and they play a significant role in the intimidation and long-term abuse of female partners. These realities have yet to significantly influence policy-making on gun violence prevention in many contexts.

This chapter highlights the relationships between guns, violence, and intimidation by intimate partners. It reviews what limited data exists on the use of firearms in intimate partner violence (IPV)—whether to kill, injure, or intimidate.[1] It also considers the gendered nature of firearm ownership and use, and the cultural supports for gun possession by men. The chapter finds that:

- While the majority of the victims and perpetrators of firearms-related homicides are male, many more women than men are killed, injured, and intimidated by firearms in the context of IPV.
- In countries with high levels of firearm violence, the risk that IPV against women will involve firearms is higher than elsewhere.
- Intimate partner murder followed by suicide ('murder–suicide') is primarily perpetrated by men, and firearms are the predominant weapon.
- Most gun owners are men, as are the majority of individuals in professions using guns—such as the armed forces, police, or private security; the risk of lethal IPV for women, as well as injury and intimidation, is increased by the presence of guns in the home, including work-related guns.
- Gender inequality, the tolerance and cultural acceptance of the use of violence against women, and common notions of masculinity that embrace firearms possession (which may be supported by both men and women) all combine to create a climate that places women at risk of IPV involving firearms.
- Withdrawal of gun rights following IPV incidents and the use of risk assessments for intimate partner homicide may help prevent subsequent violence, but only if cases are reported, which only a small minority are.

- Promising strategies to reduce gun-related IPV include stricter civilian gun possession regulations, broader prevention policies that raise awareness of the dangers of firearms in intimate partner settings, and interventions to change cultural attitudes to guns in relation to certain concepts of masculinity.
- Data that disaggregates victim–offender relationships and the type of weapon used in intimate partner violence and homicides is needed to track patterns and trends in firearm use, and to guide interventions and their evaluation.

This chapter has five main sections. This first considers the significant underreporting of intimate partner homicides, injury, and intimidation in comparison with most other forms of armed violence in conflict and non-conflict settings, and the importance of undertaking gendered analysis of firearms-related violence. It looks at some of the key challenges in identifying data within and between countries. The second section reviews existing data on the incidence and extent of intimate partner homicide in comparison with other homicides, and the marked gender imbalance of victims and perpetrators. It examines the use of firearms in intimate partner homicides, including those followed by the perpetrator's suicide, as well as in threats and intimidation of intimate partners. The third section explores the role of gender in gun ownership and access, in terms of both privately owned and work-related firearms. It examines research on the relationships between gun availability, guns in the home, and the risks of intimate partner homicide, as well as the normalization of gun carrying and its implications. The fourth section surveys the gendered cultural supports for firearms possession, including tolerance of violence in general and against women, and issues of power and masculinity associated with gun carrying and possession. The final section considers some of the policy responses to firearm use in intimate personal violence, in terms of the regulation of gun ownership and handling, court-ordered bans in cases of intimate partner violence, risk assessment, and the need for more fundamental changes in norms and attitudes towards guns and their use.

Research has not explored sufficiently the impacts of guns on men and women.

A GENDERED PERSPECTIVE ON ARMED VIOLENCE

Starting points

Given that the majority of gun-related fatalities and injuries globally occur outside the home, the role of firearms in intimate partner or domestic violence has received relatively little attention. In the great majority of cases in conflict and non-conflict settings, the victims of firearm-related violence—whether lethal or not—are young and adult men (UNODC, 2011a; WHO, 2002). This fact in itself underlines that gun violence is a highly gendered phenomenon, but research has not sufficiently explored the differential impacts of guns on women and men, or the role of gender in different contexts in which firearms are used.[2] Nor have women's experiences and understandings of violence generally been taken into account in policy discussions. Yet examining the ways in which the use of firearms is patterned, and how it affects men and women differently, offers important insight that can help guide policy and interventions (IFP, 2011; Farr, Myrttinen, and Schnabel, 2009; Bastick, Grimm, and Lazarevic, 2008).

Gun-related intimate partner violence is one part of the much wider problem of violence against women globally. In a recent analysis of femicides worldwide, the Geneva Declaration on Armed Violence and Development investigates some of these gender differences.[3] Based on data for 111 countries and territories, the study finds that around 66,000 women are killed violently each year around the world, representing some 17 per cent of all intentional homicides. These femicides generally occur in the domestic sphere, and the perpetrator is usually a current or former partner. About one in three of these femicides is committed with a firearm (Alvazzi del Frate, 2011, p. 114).

Firearms also play a significant role in non-fatal injury, threats, and intimidation by intimate partners, all of which are widespread and highly gendered (see Box 1). Whereas some men display or brandish weapons to threaten their female partners, the reverse is rare (Johnson and Dawson, 2011, p. 71; Tjaden and Thoennes, 2000, p. 11). A recent body of research identifies a range of types of intimate partner violence and threats, including with firearms; this behaviour forms part of a pattern of 'coercive controlling violence', which is characteristically used by men against their female partners (Ansara and Hindin, 2010).

Box 2.1 Terminology[4]

A number of different and overlapping terms are used to refer to violence in private settings–in the family or the home–and between adults in close personal relationships. Often used interchangeably, these terms sometimes reflect the distinct communities that use them. Throughout this chapter, 'gender' refers to characteristics of men and women that are shaped by culture and social norms, such as notions of masculinity and femininity, and the kinds of roles men and women play in public and private life; 'sex' denotes the biological categories of male and female.

Intimate partner violence is widely used at the international level to refer to violence perpetrated by current or former spouses, partners, or friends involved in a close personal or sexual relationship (WHO, 2002; 2010; UNGA, 2012). The term tends to be used by those working from a public health perspective and has largely replaced the term 'domestic violence' (WHO, 2005).

IPV includes not only violence against women, but also violence by women against men, between same-sex partners, and in dating relationships. The violence may be physical, sexual, or psychological, often involves a range of coercive and controlling behaviours, and tends to recur and increase in severity. Physical violence includes a range of actions such as slapping, kicking, hitting, or beating, as well as use of a weapon such as a knife, blunt object, or gun. Psychological violence includes intimidation, humiliation, and belittling; firearms may be used to intimidate and in threats to kill or injure intimate partners or someone close to them, including children (WHO, 2002).

While a number of studies, particularly those based on population surveys, have suggested that physical violence is used equally by men and women in intimate relationships,[5] there is strong evidence that women are more likely to experience long-term and serious injuries, and to be subjected to a range of controlling and threatening behaviours, including emotional, economic, and personal control by their male partners (Johnson, Nevala, and Ollus, 2008; Johnson and Dawson, 2011; Ansara and Hindin, 2010; 2011).

Some European countries and Australia, among other states, continue to use the gender-neutral term **domestic violence**. Until recently, the United Kingdom defined the term as:

> any incident of threatening behaviour, violence or abuse (psychological, physical, sexual, financial or emotional) between adults who are or have been intimate partners or family members, regardless of gender or sexuality (Home Office, 2012).

Following a recent consultation, the UK government expanded the definition to include coercive control and 16-17-year-olds. However, routine household crime surveys in the United Kingdom also use the term 'intimate violence' to refer collectively to intimate partner, family, and stranger sexual abuse (Home Office, 2012).

The US Centers for Disease Control and Prevention use the term 'intimate partner violence', while the US Department of Justice uses 'domestic violence', yet they define them in very similar ways (CDC, 2010; USDOJ, 2012). In Canada, most provinces use 'domestic violence' to refer to related policies, while the federal government uses **spousal abuse** to refer to abuse by a partner in a marriage or common-law or same-sex relationship. Spousal abuse forms part of the broader category of **family violence**, which includes violence against children and other family members (Statistics Canada, 2011).

Femicide is a term used especially since the 1970s to refer to the killing of women or girls who are specifically targeted because of their sex, and to highlight the gendered nature of the act (Bloom, 2008; Sagot and Carcedo, 2010). The term is now widely used to refer to any killing of a woman or girl, whether by an intimate partner, an acquaintance, or a stranger. In this way, it mirrors the term 'homicide'. Apart from intimate partner murders, it includes culturally specific forms of femicide, such as the murder of indigenous women and sex trade workers, the large-scale killing of women factory workers in Mexico and Central America, the execution of women in drug trafficking reprisals, dowry and 'honour' killings, female infanticide and sex selection practices, the killing of civilian women and girls in armed conflict, and as a weapon of war (UNGA, 2012). Firearms are involved in one-third of all recorded female homicides (Geneva Declaration Secretariat, 2011).

Data challenges

The widespread lack of focus on the gender dimensions of firearm violence and the differential impact of guns on men and women has meant that access to reliable information on both lethal and non-lethal firearm use in IPV is quite limited and, in many regions of the world, unreliable. Information on the range of gun-related IPV incidents—including lethal and non-lethal violence and intimidation—may come from police reports, victimization surveys, public health records, household surveys, court records, or specific studies of victims or perpetrators of intimate partner violence.

In the past two decades data on IPV has expanded considerably as more countries become compliant with international norms and standards on violence against women and as they begin to collect more standardized and disaggregated data.[6] However, states are often slow to implement and enforce new legislation and regulations, and setting up and maintaining a detailed national data collection system is expensive and time-consuming. A study of femicides in Mexico from 1985 to 2009, for example, looks at the registration of violent deaths of women following legislative changes in 2000 that required evidence of domestic violence to be recorded on death certificates. In 2009, reports on 88 per cent of female homicides recorded that year (1,858 cases) still had no information on whether they resulted from domestic violence (Echarri Cánovas and Ramírez Ducoing, 2011).

The underreporting and undercounting of intimate partner deaths is a significant issue in both developed and less developed countries. In some cases, the police classify intimate partner murders as accidents or suicides; in others, the deaths are systematically covered up or under-investigated, as has been the case in Mexico and Guatemala, as well as in Canada.[7] There are also social and cultural pressures on victims not to report incidents of intimate partner violence in many countries, so that official data on injuries caused by firearms, or their use to threaten or intimidate, is highly unreliable.

Reliable information on lethal and non-lethal firearm use in IPV is limited.

To overcome some of these problems, an increasing number of population-based IPV victimization surveys have been conducted and IPV-related components have been included in regular government household surveys.[8] These provide more accurate information on the extent of IPV and on non-lethal threats and intimidation with weapons, but not on intimate partner firearm deaths. Some information on intimate partner homicides has been collected by public health or household surveys conducted in a number of countries, for example by the Pan American Health Organization, the Small Arms Survey, and the World Health Organization (WHO).

Systematically assessing the role of firearms in IPV requires a considerable range of data to be collected and disaggregated, often from different sources; key details include the location where the firearm-related homicide or injury took place, who was involved, the relationship between victim and offender, and the type of weapon used. At each level of analysis, greater specificity is required, while the likelihood of error, differences in definitions, or missing information increases, and reliability and comparability decreases.

In the case of lethal violence, homicide data is available from 207 countries, of which 116 record firearms as instrument type, although many do not do so systematically.[9] In the United States, the US Bureau of Justice Statistics maintains updated information of intimate partner violence and murders (Catalano, 2007; 2012; Cooper and Smith, 2011); in addition, the Violence Policy Center uses federal data to compile an annual report that enables the tracking of the use of firearms in IPV (VPC, 2012a). Some European and other high-income countries such as Australia and Canada maintain data that is necessary to track firearms use in intimate partner homicides, but it is not always published routinely.

In middle- and low-income countries, however, reliable disaggregated information is much less common, and definitions of IPV vary. This makes it difficult to provide accurate estimates of the extent of firearms use in intimate settings in many countries, and to make comparisons between countries and across regions. Even in countries that track IPV, the definitions may vary. In the United States, for example, national homicide data and some states use a definition of 'intimate partner' that includes former spouses but not former boyfriends or girlfriends (Sorenson, 2006).[10] Moreover, the range of different data sources on IPV or firearms use, with variations in scope and questions asked, affect which incidents are captured and reported.[11]

Similar issues arise in relation to data on non-lethal firearms injury, threats, and intimidation; most such incidents go unreported (Johnson, Nevala, and Ollus, 2008). Even in countries such as the Netherlands, where hospital data on firearm-related admissions is routinely collected, information on the type of weapon or the relationship between victim and offender is not published (Alvazzi del Frate, 2012, p. 96). That said, many victimization surveys on violence against women are modelled on international surveys such as the International Violence against Women Survey, which includes questions on injuries, impact on health, intimidation, controlling behaviours, and frequency of violence. That survey also asks about the use of weapons to threaten or injure, but it does not disaggregate guns and knives (Johnson, Nevada, and Ollus, 2008). Similarly, the WHO Multi-country Study on Women's Health and Domestic Violence against Women uses six questions to assess the types of physical violence used by a partner, but it does not disaggregate by type of weapon (WHO, 2005).[12]

In the absence of national data, researchers often rely on information for individual states or provinces, or on small data sets from diverse sources such as hospitals and clinics, court records and programmes, or women's shelters. These studies may provide quantitative record data, or qualitative information from interviews and case studies. In some cases they offer vivid first-hand accounts of gun-related incidents and can serve as powerful documents for raising awareness of the dangers of guns in IPV.[13]

A crime investigator shows the jury a firearm used by Robert Ward to kill his wife, Florida, September 2011. © Red Huber/AP Photo

There is a clear need for enhanced routine data collection on the relationship between firearms and IPV in many countries. Internationally, indicators on violence against women could include specific information on firearm use. The Economic Commission for Europe and the UN Office on Drugs and Crime recently developed a model for disaggregating homicide statistics to take account of firearm use, the attributes of and relationship between the victim and the perpetrator, the location, and context (ECE and UNODC, 2011, p. 27). The femicide register established by the public prosecutor's office in Peru is a good example of a national system that includes specific information on firearm involvement in all circumstances (ECLAC, 2011, p. 14).

The overwhelming burden of partner violence is borne by women. The inclusion of modules on firearm possession and their use in IPV in routine household or victimization surveys would help to build a better picture of their role in society and on attitudes towards firearm possession. Better surveillance data would also enable some of the social and economic costs of firearm use in IPV to be estimated, which could help to inform policies and their evaluation.

PULLING TOGETHER DATA ON GUNS AND IPV

This chapter pulls together data, research, and publicly available information on the use of firearms in IPV from a variety of sources, including:

- studies and reports on homicides, IPV, firearms, gender, and related legislation and criminal justice interventions published by researchers and international or regional organizations such as the Council of Europe, the Economic Commission for Latin America and the Caribbean, the European Union, the Small Arms Survey, the Geneva Declaration Secretariat, the UN Office on Drugs and Crime, and WHO;
- the International Violence against Women Survey;
- national statistics databases such as those of Statistics Canada, the UK Home Office, and the US Bureau of Justice Statistics and Centers for Disease Control and Prevention;
- resource centres such as the US National Criminal Justice Reference Service and the US National Online Resource Center on Violence against Women; and
- criminal justice abstracts and medical databases.

The gendered nature of IPV

Over the past decade, a number of international comparative studies have demonstrated the prevalence of intimate partner violence in many different countries. By drawing on victimization surveys of selected populations, these studies show that IPV is common, universal, and highly gendered: 'the overwhelming burden of partner violence is borne by women at the hands of men' (WHO, 2002, p. 89). While population-based surveys often show that women also use violence against intimate male partners, extensive evidence reveals that women experience greater physical injury and emotional stress than male partners, and that the long-term health consequences are more serious.[14]

Some of this research has identified a number of types of IPV, such as coercive controlling, situational, violent resistance, and separation-instigated violence. In each case, gender is an important factor in terms of the relative involvement of men and women. Coercive controlling violence is primarily perpetrated by men against their female partners; it is chronic, more frequent, and more severe than other types of IPV, and it can include the use of firearms and other weapons (Ansara and Hinden, 2011; Johnson and Dawson, 2011).

Members of the Gulabi Gang, a women's movement founded in response to widespread violence against women, address a local man, Uttar Pradesh, India, February 2008. © G Akash/Panos Pictures

Homicide data provides particularly strong evidence of the gendered nature of IPV, showing that 'almost without exception [. . .] females are at greater risk than males, and that the majority of female homicide victims are killed by male intimate partners' (UNGA, 2012, p. 8). In the very small proportion of incidents in which women kill their male partners, they do so after prolonged violence and threats by those partners.[15] The Geneva Declaration Secretariat estimates a global ratio of one female to five male victims of homicide; the majority of those women are killed in the home (Alvazzi del Frate, 2011, pp. 117, 130).[16]

There are very wide regional variations. Based on the Global Burden of Armed Violence database, some 25 countries in southern Africa and Latin America and the Caribbean show 'high' or 'very high' rates of homicide and femicide compared to others. In countries where violence is widespread, women are at higher risk of being killed not only by their partners, but also by strangers, as well as in organized crime-related violence. In countries that exhibit low homicide rates, such as in Western Europe, domestic violence accounts for the great majority of intentional female deaths, including cases of homicide followed by suicide, which are primarily perpetrated by men. Figure 2.1 shows the percentage of women killed in private homes across a range of high- to low-homicide countries.

Figure 2.1 **Femicides committed in the home vs. total homicide rates, selected countries (latest available data)**

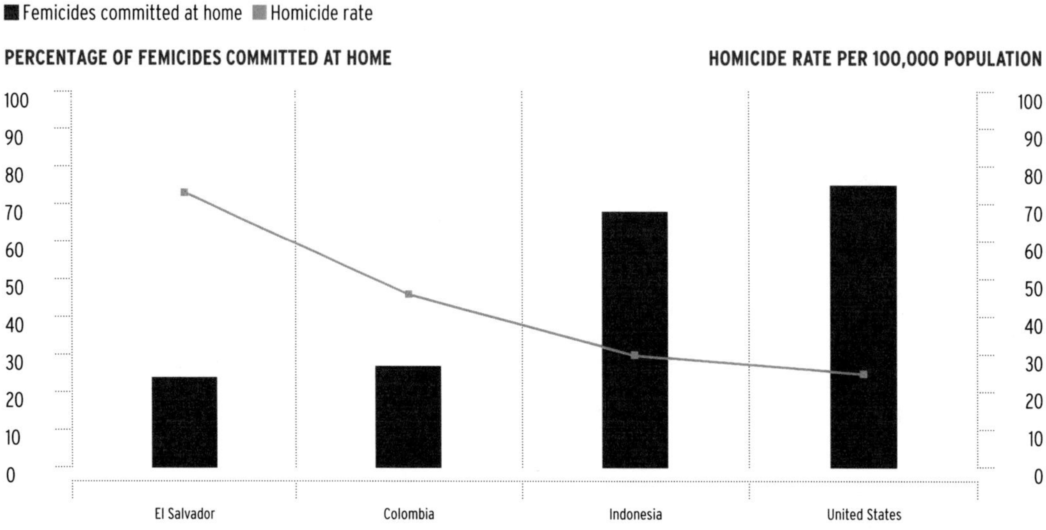

■ Femicides committed at home   ■ Homicide rate

PERCENTAGE OF FEMICIDES COMMITTED AT HOME   HOMICIDE RATE PER 100,000 POPULATION

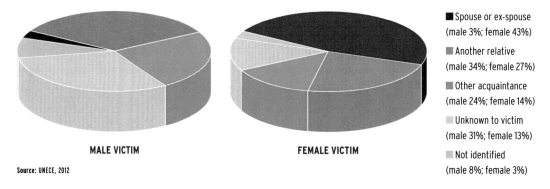

| | El Salvador | Colombia | Indonesia | United States |

Sources: Geneva Declaration Secretariat (2011); Ricaurte Villota (2011); Statistics Indonesia (2006); USDOJ (2000); Vaquerano (2011)

While some women also use violence against their male (or female) partners, this violence accounts for a very small proportion of intimate partner deaths overall. Data from selected European countries, for example, shows that 43 per cent of women were killed by a current or former intimate partner, compared with 3 per cent of men (see Figure 2.2).

A number of high-income countries, such as Canada and England and Wales, have experienced a decline in intimate partner homicides over the past three decades (Statistics Canada, 2011; Home Office, 2009). A similar decline is evident in the United States, whose Bureau of Justice Statistics shows a drop in the rate of IPV, homicides, and non-fatal injuries between 1980 and 2010, especially as regards male victims (Cooper and Smith, 2011; Catalano, 2012, p. 1; see Figure 2.3). Yet, despite the decline in intimate partner homicides, the proportion of female IPV victims has remained relatively stable, and four out of every five victims are female (Catalano, 2012). This underlines the huge challenges in reducing IPV against women.

Figure 2.2 **Relationship of perpetrators to homicide victims in 16 European countries, by sex of victim (latest available data)**

MALE VICTIM   FEMALE VICTIM

■ Spouse or ex-spouse
(male 3%; female 43%)

■ Another relative
(male 34%; female 27%)

■ Other acquaintance
(male 24%; female 14%)

■ Unknown to victim
(male 31%; female 13%)

■ Not identified
(male 8%; female 3%)

Source: UNECE, 2012

Figure 2.3 **Intimate partner homicides as a proportion of all US homicides, by sex of victim, 1980–2008**

■ Female intimate partners killed   ■ Male intimate partners killed

PERCENTAGE OF ALL HOMICIDES

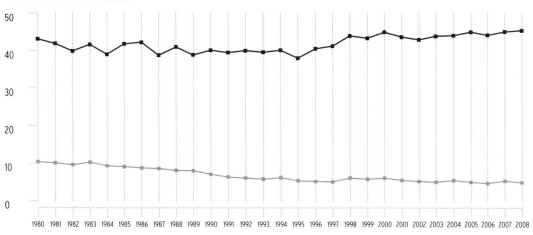

Source: Cooper and Smith (2011, p. 18)

The role of firearms in intimate partner homicides

Death and serious injuries are far more likely to occur with the use of firearms than with other violent methods (Liem and Oberwittler, 2012). In one US study, assaults with a firearm were found to be 12 times more likely to result in death than non-firearm assaults in family and intimate partner violence (Saltzman et al., 1992). In its *Global Study of Homicide,* the UN Office on Drugs and Crime shows that homicide rates are strongly associated with the level of firearm availability in a country (UNODC, 2011a, p. 10). This finding has been corroborated by a number of quantitative studies using data from criminal justice and public health sources.[17]

Globally, around half of all homicides are committed with firearms (UNODC, 2011a; Geneva Declaration Secretariat, 2008; 2011). Again, research reveals wide regional variations, with guns used in 74 per cent of all homicides in the Americas compared to 21 per cent in Europe, where gun ownership levels are relatively low (UNODC, 2011a, p. 40). Other methods, including force, knives, blunt objects, and strangulation, are more common in Europe (UNODC, 2011a, p. 40). The Global Burden of Armed Violence database estimates that one-third of all femicides are committed with guns; the rate is much higher in countries with high femicide rates, such as Brazil, Colombia, El Salvador, Guatemala, and Honduras. In those countries, more than 60 per cent of femicides are committed with firearms (Alvazzi del Frate, 2011, pp. 131, 132).

Evidence from a number of countries illustrates the significance of firearms in intimate partner deaths. Women are not only predominantly the victims, they are also more likely to be killed or threatened by firearms than men in such circumstances. Canada is a case in point. Even though the rate of spousal homicides has declined over the past 30 years, national data for 2000–09 shows that women are still 3–4 times more likely to be killed by their spouses than are men; in 26 per cent of these cases, women are killed with firearms, compared with 11 per cent of the men (Statistics Canada, 2011, pp. 33–35).

The first cross-national study of the relationship between firearm availability and female homicide was published in 2002 (Hemenway, Shinoda-Tagawa, and Miller, 2002). Using records from 25 high-income countries with populations exceeding two million, the study relies on data for the most recent available year between 1994 and 1999. The analysis reveals a very high correlation between firearm availability in a country and firearm femicides, with the United States appearing as 'an extreme case in terms of both gun prevalence and female homicide' (p. 102). The study finds no correlation with urbanization or income inequalities. Of the femicides whose perpetrators were identified, the majority were committed by intimate partners of the victims, leading the study to conclude that the availability of firearms is a major risk factor for women.

While the overall rates of homicide and IPV declined from 2004 to 2009 in the United States, recent statistics show that firearms are still heavily implicated in female intimate partner homicides. In 2010, 52 per cent of female homicide victims in the United States—849 of 1,622 femicides—were killed with a firearm, and two-thirds of them (574) by an intimate partner. Handguns were used in around 70 per cent of firearm femicides (VPC, 2012a, p. 7). The homicide rate for black women was nearly 2.5 times higher than for white women, although roughly similar proportions of black and white women were killed by an intimate partner and with a gun (pp. 7, 9).

> The majority of murder–suicides involve a male perpetrator and a female victim.

A national study of femicides in 1999 in South Africa estimates that half were intimate partner murders—a rate of 8.8 per 100,000.[18] The rate for 'coloured'[19] women was more than double that of black women, and six times that of white women. The study finds that the overwhelming majority of perpetrators were men (Mathews et al., 2004). The authors subsequently reviewed all femicides that were registered in 2009, ten years after the first study. Given an overall reduction in the number of homicides in South Africa over the previous ten years, the second study finds fewer intimate femicides and a lower rate: 5.5 per 100,000.[20] Yet it also reveals that a higher proportion of all femicides—57 per cent—were intimate partner deaths, making them the leading type of female homicide. The study also notes a significant decrease in gun-related intimate femicides, from 31 per cent in 1999 to 17 per cent in 2009 (Abrahams et al., 2012).[21] Another recent report estimates the rate of firearm-related intimate partner murders in South Africa to be 2.7 per 100,000 (Abrahams, Jewkes, and Mathews, 2010, p. 586).

A national study of violence against women and femicides perpetrated in 2010 in Brazil finds that 40 per cent of women were killed at home, compared with 15 per cent of male victims; 54 per cent of the women were killed with a firearm. Of the reported IPV cases, 65 per cent involved a partner or ex-partner (Waiselfisz, 2012, pp. 6, 7, 17).

In Peru, research shows that 70 per cent of femicides are perpetrated by intimate partners (UNGA, 2012, p. 9, n. 37). In 2010, the police recorded a total of 121 femicides and 47 attempted femicides. In 99 per cent of the cases, the aggressor was a man; most perpetrators were partners or ex-partners and 55 per cent of the femicides took place in the home. Ten per cent of the incidents were gun-related, while the most frequently used weapon was a knife or sharp object (Peru, 2010); that rate of firearm-related femicides appears to be much lower than in other countries (Small Arms Survey, 2012, ch. 1; Alvazzi del Frate, 2011, p. 129).

Firearms and intimate partner murder–suicide

Murder–suicides are generally defined as violent events in which the perpetrator kills one or more people and subsequently commits suicide within a short period of time.[22] While they are relatively rare events, available data suggests that the majority of murder–suicides are intimate partner incidents, with a male perpetrator and female victim, and sometimes their children as additional victims (Liem and Oberwittler, 2012; Liem et al., 2011; van Wormer, 2008).[23] Some studies in Canada, Sweden, and the United States report a high prevalence of prior physical abuse among intimate partner homicide–suicide cases (Liem and Oberwittler, 2012, p. 201). Jealousy, a recent or impending break-up, and financial problems are often factors in these events (van Wormer, 2008).

In the United States, studies based on online news reports have tracked murder–suicide cases since 2002. The Violence Policy Center estimates that more than 1,300 people died in murder–suicide incidents in the United States in 2011. The most recent figures report a total of 313 such events—defined as a suicide occurring within 72 hours of the initial murder—in the first six months of 2011 (VPC, 2012b);[24] 72 per cent of them were intimate partner incidents, of which 84 per cent were in the home and 94 per cent involved women killed by male perpetrators.[25] Children are often killed as well.[26] Guns are used frequently: 90 per cent of all incidents involved firearms (VPC, 2012b, p. 2). A report on 408 family murder–suicide cases recorded by the US National Violent Death Reporting System in participating states notes that 91 per cent of the perpetrators were men, and 88 per cent of the incidents were committed with a gun (Auchter, 2010).[27]

In Canada, based on homicide data covering more than 40 years—from 1961 to 2003—an estimated one in ten homicides was followed by the suicide of the perpetrator, amounting to 1,994 of all recorded homicides (Statistics Canada, 2005).[28] Three-quarters of the homicide–suicide victims were killed by a family member; of these, 57 per cent, or an average of 20 cases per year, involved spouses (857 cases in total). Of the spousal incidents, 97 per cent involved women killed by a husband who subsequently committed suicide, and 3 per cent involved men killed by a wife who then took her own life. Firearms were the most common method; some 74 per cent of all reviewed cases involved firearms used by a male perpetrator (Statistics Canada, 2005, p. 61). The same report also finds that firearms were the weapon most frequently used in murder–suicide cases in studies published in the 1990s in Australia and England and Wales (p. 61).

A subsequent review of data for England and Wales between 1997 and 2006 reports that an estimated 10 per cent of all intimate partner homicides, or 12 cases per year, were perpetrated by men and followed by suicide (van Wormer, 2008). The most recent data confirms that guns were the primary instrument used in homicide–suicides in England and Wales (Liem and Oberwittler, 2012).

In South Africa, 20 per cent of 1,349 intimate femicides in 1999 were classified as intimate murder–suicides—defined as a suicide occurring within one week of the murder (Mathews et al., 2008, p. 553). The perpetrators tended to be white, came mainly from professional or middle-class backgrounds, owned a gun legally, and frequently worked in the security sector as a police officer, member of the army, or guard (p. 5).

While firearms are less commonly used in IPV in Europe than in the Americas or South Africa, a comparative study of seven European countries shows that guns were the predominant weapon in murder–suicide incidents in 1990–2005 (Liem and Oberwittler, 2012).[29] In all seven countries under review, the perpetrators were almost exclusively men aged 25 to 64 and the large majority of victims were women in intimate partner relationships. In all countries except Poland, firearms were the primary means used for both the homicide and the suicide, and especially so in Finland, Germany, and Switzerland—all countries with relatively high rates of guns kept in the home. The authors conclude:

> *The observation that these three countries also have the highest rates of homicide–suicide lends support for the idea that the availability of firearms could play a decisive causal role in the frequency of homicide–suicide* (Liem and Oberwittler, 2012, p. 211).

Similar conclusions were reached in a cross-national study that compares murder–suicide deaths in the Netherlands, Switzerland, and the United States (Liem et al., 2011). Given that the presence of guns in the home is much higher in Switzerland and the United States[30] than in the Netherlands, where firearms possession is restricted and low, the substantially higher murder–suicide rates in those two countries, which primarily involve intimate partners, is partly attributed to the presence of firearms (p. 75).

In European countries, guns were the predominant weapon in murder-suicides in 1990-2005.

Non-lethal injuries and the use of guns to threaten intimate partners

As discussed earlier, intimate partner violence is defined as including a range of coercive and threatening behaviours that have physical, psychological, and emotional impacts on the victims. A consistent thread running through most research and commentary on IPV is that it is often chronic and enduring. In England and Wales, for example, domestic violence is associated with a very high rate of repeat victimization, with some 42 per cent of victims victimized more than once (Home Office, 2009, p. 14). Victimization survey findings from the British Crime Survey show that surveyed women experienced an average of 20 incidents per year, often increasing in severity (Home Office, 2009).

In Brazil, following the enactment of the Maria da Penha Domestic Violence Law of 2006, a women's hotline—the Central de Atendimento à Mulher—was set up. In the first ten months of 2008, 216,006 calls were received; some 64 per cent of callers said they were subject to aggression on a daily basis (Lemle, 2008).[31] A reported event of IPV is thus unlikely to be the first, and retrospective studies of intimate partner homicides generally show a history of violence and threatening behaviours. Indeed, reviews of more than 22 studies on the risk factors associated with spousal homicide indicate that, in all cases, previous violence was a precursor to homicide (Campbell, Webster, and Glass, 2009; Aldridge and Browne, 2003).

It is difficult to arrive at reliable estimates of the extent of non-fatal firearm injuries sustained by women in intimate partner violence, in part because incidents are not necessarily reported to the police or at hospitals. Nevertheless, as discussed above, it is likely that lethal incidents form a very small proportion of all events. Of the 8,000 women interviewed for the 2000 US National Violence against Women Survey, 22 per cent said they had experienced physical IPV in their lifetime, while only 1 per cent said a gun had been used in the assault (Tjaden and Thoennes, 2000, pp. 9, 11). Other US studies have shown that, while men are more likely to seek hospital treatment for gunshot wounds than women, women are more likely to have been shot and injured by an intimate partner than are men (Sorenson, 2006; Weibe, 2003).

A household survey of the incidence of non-fatal physical IPV undertaken by the California Department of Health Services finds that in 1998–99 nearly 6 per cent of the female population over 18 had experienced physical violence of some sort in the previous year—meaning that more than 620,000 women were affected. For 40 per cent of these women, the violence was serious; an estimated 25,000 had sought emergency hospital treatment (Lund, 2002).

Estimates of the use of guns to threaten and intimidate intimate partners are similarly difficult to make, primarily because most IPV events are not reported to the police (Johnson, Nevala, and Ollus, 2008; Tjaden and Thoennes, 2000). The threat that an intimate partner could use a gun may inhibit victims from making reports or taking any action that could provoke its use.

Table 2.1 Use of guns or knives in IPV events in nine countries	Percentage of women who reported the use of a knife or gun in the most serious IPV assault they ever experienced
Australia	15%
Costa Rica	26%
Czech Republic	8%
Denmark	10%
Hong Kong	8%
Mozambique	5%
Philippines	14%
Poland	19%
Switzerland	12%

Notes: The survey data was collected between 2002 and 2005 in the nine countries. The respondents reported on IPV assaults perpetrated by current and former partners.

Source: Johnson, Nevala, and Ollus (2008, pp. 45, 46)

The International Violence against Women Survey finds that the percentage of women who reported the use of guns or knives in the most serious intimate partner violence incident they experienced from current or former partners ranged from 5 to 26 per cent in the nine countries surveyed (see Table 2.1).

A number of specific population studies in the United States have found that guns are used to threaten and intimidate partners far more frequently that they are used to kill (van Wormer, 2008; Vetten, 2006; Rothman et al., 2005). One study finds the main risk factors associated with gun threats to be substance abuse, making threats with knives, and gun ownership in the preceding three years (Hemenway, Azrael, and Miller, 2000).

Another study was based on data for 8,529 men involved in court-ordered male batterers' programmes in Massachusetts between 1999 and 2003. It finds that 7 per cent of the sample reported owning a gun in the previous three years; these men were almost eight times more likely to have threatened intimate partners with guns than those in the sample who did not own guns. Yet the gun owners and the men who did not own guns were equally likely to have threatened their partner with a knife. The authors conclude that owning a gun is highly correlated with using it to threaten an intimate partner. They list four main types of threatening gun behaviour that had been used by the men: threatening to shoot their partner; cleaning, holding, or loading a gun during an argument; threatening to shoot a pet or person the victim cared about; and shooting a gun during an argument with a victim (Rothman et al., 2005).

Other US research has found that, when compared with a sample of women with a history of abuse, women killed by their partners were far more likely to have received death threats (73.6 per cent v. 7.6 per cent); to have been threatened with a weapon (55.3 per cent v. 4.7 per cent); and to have had a partner who used a gun (38.2 per cent v. 0.9 per cent) (Campbell et al., 2003). Threats to use a gun have also been associated with intimate partner stalking incidents (Campbell, Webster, and Glass, 2009; Tjaden and Thoennes, 2000).

Studies in Brazil and South Africa provide additional evidence of the use of firearms to threaten women in intimate relationships. In Rio de Janeiro in 2005, 60 per cent of 615 women reporting intimate partner abuse to the special police stations for women said their partner had a gun; 69 per cent of those women said it had been used to threaten them.[32] In addition, 73 per cent argued that the presence of a gun prevented them from reacting to the violence, and 68 per cent maintained that they felt unable to end the relationship for fear the partner might use the gun (IFP, 2011, p. 21).

> Intimate partner violence involving guns takes place primarily in the home.

In South Africa, the 1998 Domestic Violence Act made provisions for restrictions on gun ownership in cases of intimate partner violence. A study of all applications for protection orders conducted in 2000–01 (2,208 cases) finds that 37 per cent involved weapons, and, in 25 per cent of those cases, a gun. In 88 per cent of the cases firearms had been used to threaten a partner (Vetten, 2006, p. 88).[33]

GUN OWNERSHIP AND IPV

The preceding review of firearm-related intimate partner homicide and murder–suicide, non-lethal injury, and threats and intimidation shows that they are all highly gendered, and that women are primarily the victims and men the perpetrators. Intimate partner violence involving guns takes place primarily in the home, especially in countries where access to guns is relatively easy. It also appears that having a gun in the household places women at higher risk of injury or death caused by their partners. International and national data further suggests that women rarely use firearms in intimate personal violence, and that it is men, not women, who primarily own and use firearms.

This section reviews the gendered patterns of firearm ownership and use as an important underlying driver of risk for intimate partner violence, especially in the home.

The gendered nature of gun ownership

In 2007 the Small Arms Survey estimated that there were approximately 650 million civilian-owned firearms in the world, out of a total of some 875 million weapons (Small Arms Survey, 2007b, p. 39).[34] Based on the data available, most guns are owned and used by young and adult men. Women are underrepresented in professions that require the use of firearms, such as the police, military, or security; they are less likely than men to hunt and use guns for sport; and they are less likely to carry guns for self-defence.[35]

Even in the United States, where gun ownership is higher than in any other country, the proportion of women gun owners is relatively small. In a national survey conducted in 1994, only 9 per cent of adult women said they owned a gun (Cook and Ludwig, 1997); that figure has since risen, reaching 23 per cent in 2011 (Carroll, 2005; Saad, 2011; see Table 2.2). That rise may in part be due to the fact that, since the late 1980s, the US gun industry has been marketing guns to women for protection (VPC, 2001). Gun club membership among women, while small, has also reportedly increased, according to news articles and reports by gun shops, clubs, and organizations.[36]

The reasons men and women in the United States say they keep guns vary somewhat. In 2005, most gun-owning men said they used their guns for hunting (63 per cent), target shooting (68 per cent), and protection from crime (63 per cent). Women were more likely to say they owned them for protection (74 per cent), compared with 49 and 59 per cent for hunting and target shooting, respectively (Carroll, 2005). Protection appears to have remained the primary reason women buy guns since those surveys were conducted (*Washington Times,* 2010).

Table 2.2 **Proportion of civilian gun owners and applicants by sex and estimated civilian-held guns, selected countries**				
Country	**Category/year**	**Men**	**Women**	**Legally held guns***
Brazil	2010	'Almost a male monopoly'	n/a	7.6 million (43% of 17.6 million)
Canada	Gun owners, 2000	87% of all gun owners	13% of all gun owners	1.9 million (2012)
Portugal	Applicants for firearms licences, 2008-09	99% of all applicants	1% of all applicants	1.4 million (54% of 2.6 million)
South Africa	2006	'mainly a male phenomenon'	n/a	3.5-3.7 million
United States	'Personally own a gun', 1994	42% of male respondents	9% of female respondents	192 million
	'Personally own a gun', 2004	45% of male respondents	11% of female respondents	–
	'Personally own a gun', 2005	47% of male respondents	13% of female respondents	–
	'Personally own a gun', 2011	46% of male respondents	23% of female respondents	270 million (2007)

Note: * Estimates of legally held guns do not necessarily correspond with information in the 'Category/year' column.

Sources: Brazil: Dreyfus et al. (2010, p. 28); IFP (2011, p. 15); Canada: GPC Research (2001, p. 13); RCMP (2012); Portugal: Pureza et al. (2010, p. 68);[37] South Africa: Abrahams, Jewkes, and Mathews (2010, p. 586); Kirsten et al. (2006, p. 17); United States: Cook and Ludwig (1997, p. 2); Carroll (2005, p. 2); Hepburn et al. (2007, p. 15); Saad (2011, p. 3); Small Arms Survey (2011, p. 2)

Outside the United States, the International Crime Victimization Survey has tracked household firearm and handgun ownership since 1989; in 2004–05, firearms were kept in an average of 14 per cent of households in the 30 high-income countries surveyed (van Dijk, van Kesteren, and Smit, 2007, p. 279).[38] However, the survey does not provide rates for men and women. In Canada, 87 per cent of firearm owners interviewed in 2000 were men (GPC Research, 2001, p. 13). A study of firearms (*armas ligeiras*) in Portugal examined data from the national Department of Arms and Explosives on applications for firearms licences. The findings show that, in 2008–09, 99 per cent of the licence applications were from men (Pureza et al., 2010, p. 68).

In India, there are reports of an increase in gun carrying, including by women, for both status and protection. As the *Guardian* reports, 'Ownership levels per capita remain low—three guns for every 100 people in India—but there is strong anecdotal evidence that middle-class interest in firearms is rising fast' (Burke, 2012). Nearly 31,300 gun licences have been issued to women in the Punjab; 31,026 of them have actually purchased arms (Burke, 2012).

Table 2.2 lists the male–female ratio of civilian gun owners and the estimated number of civilian-held guns for selected countries. The information comes from a variety of sources and is not necessarily comparable.

A gun in the home, a threat to partners

As discussed above, most incidents of IPV take place in the home. The health risks of having guns in the home have been repeatedly explored by researchers over the past decade. There is evidence from the United States and other countries that the risks are elevated, particularly for intimate partner abuse, but also for male suicides and gun accidents. Much of the research has been conducted from a public health perspective, using health registry data and case control studies, or interviews with cohorts of victims of abuse. The research indicates that victims of abuse are more likely to come from households with guns than the general population; they are also at much higher risk of homicide or threats made with guns.[39]

The risks may be even greater for intimate partner murder–suicides. As the above-cited comparative studies show, such incidents, in which firearms play a significant role, were substantially more frequent in European countries with high rates of gun ownership, and in the United States, than in the Netherlands (Liem et al., 2011; Liem and Oberwittler, 2012).[40]

There has been ongoing debate, especially in the United States, about whether elevated risks in the home are offset by the protection that guns may provide homeowners against intruders or partners.[41] Yet there is little, if any, evidence that owning or having access to a gun protects a woman from attack by her partner—even when she lives apart from him (Campbell et al., 2003). US national data indicates there were 278 justifiable homicides committed by private citizens in 2010; only 34 of these homicides involved women killing men and, of those, 21 involved firearms—primarily a handgun.[42] In contrast, 575 women were killed by an intimate partner with a gun during the same period; that figure is six times higher than the number of women killed by male strangers using any weapon (98) (VPC, 2012a, p. 2).

A recent scientific literature review on the health risks and benefits of having a gun in the home in the United States concludes that the risks of keeping a gun outweigh the benefits, and that there are no credible studies showing otherwise:

The evidence is overwhelming that a gun in the home is a risk factor for completed suicide and that gun accidents are most likely to occur in homes with guns. There is compelling evidence that a gun in the home is a risk factor for intimidation and for killing women in their homes, and it appears that a gun in the home may more likely be used to threaten intimates than to protect against intruders (Hemenway, 2011, p. 7).

The risks of keeping a gun outweigh the benefits.

Work firearms and the normalization of gun carrying

Apart from privately owned guns, in many countries the possession of guns for professional reasons constitutes another source of risk for gun-related IPV. Professions in which guns are routinely used and sometimes brought into the home include the military, police, border guards, immigration and customs agents, and, increasingly, private security. The presence or availability of work-related firearms in the home has been linked to family violence, including intimate partner violence and intimidation in a number of countries, as well as to suicide (Mathews et al., 2008; Farr, Myrttinen, and Schnabel, 2009).

In addition to access to work guns, work-related post-traumatic stress appears to be a risk factor, especially for individuals serving in the military and police force (Johnson, Todd, and Subramanian, 2005; Knox et al., 2003). There is considerable evidence that male veterans suffering from post-traumatic stress, for example, are much more likely to use psychological and physical aggression against intimate partners than those without the disorder (Monson, Taft, and Fredman, 2009).[43]

Owning guns for professional reasons is a source of risk for IPV.

Private policing is rapidly expanding in many regions of the world, and private security companies now hold between 1.7 and 3.7 million firearms worldwide (Florquin, 2011). There is great regional variation in the arming of private security, however, with rates in Latin America ten times those in Western Europe (p. 102). In Brazil and other countries in the region, government offices, businesses, commercial centres, and private residences increasingly use on-site private security and surveillance. With a few exceptions, the great majority of armed private security guards are men.[44] In countries such as Afghanistan, Angola, Iraq, and Uganda, the number of private military security companies has also grown; these often recruit ex-military or ex-combatants who appear to be almost exclusively male.[45] Professional firearm users are typically subject to strict regulations about the storage of firearms when they are off duty, but controls over firearms and their use may be non-existent or poorly enforced in some contexts (UNODC, 2011b; Gumedze, 2008).

Men's work firearms inside and outside the home contribute to the wider 'normalization' of guns in public and private spaces, or to the 'militarization' of societies, with implications for women. This is especially evident in post-conflict situations in Israel, Northern Ireland, South Africa, and countries in Central America, for example (Farr, Myrttinen, and Schnabel, 2009; Hume, 2008). South Africa has been described as a country with a pervasive gun culture and marked gender inequalities, both of which contribute to the normalization of guns (Kirsten et al., 2006; Fish and Mncayi, 2009, p. 318). It has also seen a major expansion in private policing of both public and private space over the past decade. One study finds that 10 per cent of intimate partner femicides in South Africa were committed by men who had jobs with the police, armed forces, or security companies in 1999 (Abrahams, Jewkes, and Mathews, 2010, p. 587). As indicated above, murder–suicides in South Africa were also high among private security personnel (Mathews et al., 2008).

A study of gun licensing in Israel notes: 'Nearly 60% of the [58,690] new guns introduced into civic space in Israel [in 2000–04] were licensed to employees of private policing companies' (Mazali, 2009, p. 252). It suggests that the private security sector has incorporated 'the broader army and police cultures' of masculinity, has increased levels of sexual harassment, and led to an increase in the number of gun-related murders of intimate partners. At least nine female partners, ex-partners, or family members were murdered by security guards between 2002 and 2007, according to a review of news reports (p. 269).

CULTURE AND MALE VIOLENCE AGAINST WOMEN

Attitudes about acceptable gender roles, socially constructed concepts of masculinity and femininity, and the relative normalization of guns are underlying dynamics affecting violence broadly and gun-related IPV.[46] In Western culture, violence and firearms are glorified in films and images, and many boys are still socialized in ways that endorse controlling and violent behaviours. Yet, although attitudes to gun possession and violence against women are highly gendered in complex ways, they are not homogeneous across societies (Bastick, Grimm, and Lazarevic, 2008). Given that the majority of guns are owned and used by men, this section looks at gun use in IPV as part of a continuum of socially endorsed or tolerated attitudes and behaviours that includes violence against women as well as 'violent masculinities'. Gender inequality underlines all of these issues.

Tolerance of violence and violence against women

Countries with high rates of violence and gun possession also tend to have high rates of tolerance of violence against women in society generally (Alvazzi del Frate, 2011). In many contexts, women are unwilling to report IPV incidents to the police for fear that little action will be taken, that they may be revictimized by the justice system, or that they will suffer retribution for doing so, especially if their partner has a gun (Johnson, Nevala, and Ollus, 2008; AI, 2008). In cases that are reported, police and prosecutors are often very slow to investigate or pursue accusations, creating a context of impunity for perpetrators.[47]

The majority of guns are owned and used by men.

In Latin America and the Caribbean, the Pan American Health Organization looked at patterns of help-seeking by women who experienced IPV in five countries. The findings show that large percentages of women did not seek any help—not even from family members; the proportion ranged from 41 per cent in Nicaragua to 69 per cent in Haiti. The percentage of women who actually went to the police ranged from 2 per cent in Haiti to 16 per cent in Colombia (PAHO, 2005). Evidence from another study shows that family violence in El Salvador is still generally regarded as a private matter, and as the kind of violence that is normal, expected, and tacitly accepted (Hume, 2008).

In many societies, women themselves think it acceptable for men to use violence against their wives. In the nine-country study, the International Violence against Women Survey finds wide variations among women's views on whether intimate partner violence was a crime—rather than 'something that happens'—and whether they would report IPV to the police (Johnson, Nevala, and Ollus, 2008, pp. 141–42). The 2005 WHO multi-country study finds that in some countries 50–90 per cent of women felt that it was acceptable for a man to beat his wife under a number of circumstances (WHO, 2005, p. 39).[48] It also reveals a strong correlation between women's attitudes to the acceptability of wife beating and rates of IPV (p. 40).

Gender inequalities are also associated with notions of patriarchy and power exercised by men over women, and types of masculinity that reinforce the belief that men should control women (WHO, 2005; Johnson, Nevala, and Ollus, 2008; see Box 2.3, overleaf). These attitudes may be perpetuated by the socialization of boys and girls growing up, and actively or passively condoned by the wider cultural and religious contexts. Research on masculinity in a range of countries and regions has shown that men with non-equitable views are significantly more likely to have used gender-based violence than others (Barker et al., 2011a, p. 9). Similarly, studies of private military and security companies have shown them to endorse and encourage 'hyper-masculine' macho behaviours that reject 'feminine' approaches to problem solving (Via, 2010; Higate, 2009; Schulz and Yeung, 2008).

A member of one of the largest gangs in San Salvador shows off his gun, Las Victorias, January 2013. © Adam Hinton/Panos Pictures

Box 2.3 Power and masculinity

Gender inequality is often associated with concepts of power and masculinity as well as cultural attitudes that restrict the mobility and behaviour of women. Perceived transgressions of accepted roles on the part of women can provoke violent reactions by men. In India, for example, one member of a group of Hindu activist men who had attacked women for breaking cultural norms in 2009 provided this justification:

> These girls come from all over India, drink, smoke, and walk around in the night spoiling the traditional girls of Mangalore. [. . .] Why should girls go to pubs? Are they going to serve their future husbands alcohol? Should they not be learning to make chapattis? Bars and pubs should be for men only. We wanted to ensure that all women in Mangalore are home by 7 pm (Johnson, 2009).[49]

A wide range of norms—from the perception of men as socially superior to women, to the acceptance of violence as a legitimate way to discipline women—support the use of violence against women, making them vulnerable in the home and on the street.

The normalization of violence and weapons possession is also linked to guns as ways to achieve recognition, status, and power—especially among young men; normalization also extends to the concept of protection among men who perceive their role as protectors of their families. It is also strongly associated with gender inequalities in society. One observer argues that in post-conflict El Salvador, for example, violence has become 'a key expression of masculine behaviour and a mechanism for ensuring continued male privilege' (Hume, 2008, pp. 61, 62).

The symbolism and power associated with gun possession is very strong and persistent in many societies. A strong component of violence-endorsing masculinity and gun use is that they are often given both tacit and overt support by women and girls in many countries and cultural contexts.

Sources: AI, Oxfam International, and IANSA (2005, ch. 4); Barker (2005); Barker et al. (2011a); Bevan and Florquin (2006); Hume (2008); IFP (2011); Small Arms Survey (2010); WHO (2010, p. 53)

ADDRESSING GUN-RELATED IPV

What can be done to reduce the impacts of firearms on personal relationships, and female partners in particular? While it is important to address all forms of IPV, this section focuses specifically on some options for preventing gun-related intimate personal violence.

Recommendations found in the literature tend to suggest closer regulation of gun ownership, safe handling and storage, and the use of actuarial risk assessment instruments and court-mandated bans on gun possession in cases of known IPV. Other approaches include targeted and general public education campaigns to change attitudes towards gun possession and use. Overall, it is important to encompass both criminal justice and prevention approaches, and to work at the societal, community, and individual levels (WHO, 2010). Such a multi-level process can involve strengthening legislation, changing social norms and attitudes, and increasing protection and awareness at the local and individual levels.

National policy on IPV has improved around the world in recent years, with legislation enacted in many regions with high levels of firearm-related violence against women. In Latin American and the Caribbean, for example, the 1994 Inter-American Convention on the Prevention, Punishment, and Eradication of Violence against Women, also known as the Convention of Belém do Pará, has been ratified by 32 states parties; however, signatories have been very slow to implement its provisions on enacting and enforcing domestic violence legislation, providing services for victims, reducing impunity for IPV, and establishing data collection and training programmes associated with firearms and IPV for the police, judiciary, and health services (OAS, n.d.).[50] In Europe, one promising initiative is the Convention on Preventing and Combating Violence against Women and Domestic Violence, now signed by 27—although ratified by only three—of the 47 members states of the Council of Europe (Council of Europe, 2011).

There is some evidence from countries such as Australia, Canada, England and Wales, New Zealand, and South Africa that comprehensive reform of firearm legislation is associated with reductions of overall and intimate partner homicides.[51] In Canada, a universal licensing and registration system for all types of firearms was established in 1995.[52] This included registration of all rifles and shotguns, which are the firearms responsible for the majority of suicides and domestic homicides in Canada. Since 1995, there has been a reduction in both suicides and intimate partner homicides involving firearms (RCMP, 2010). Similar regulations governing purchase and safe handling and storage of firearms have been introduced in recent years in Australia, England and Wales, and Scotland, among other countries (Bricknell, 2012; Eder, 2011).

At the international level, the 2001 UN Firearms Protocol, the 2001 UN Programme of Action on small arms and light weapons, and related regional conventions and protocols are important for building consensus about the need to control and reduce illicit firearms proliferation (UN PoA–ISS, n.d.a; n.d.b).[53] Much of the associated action has focused on trafficking and supply, although the Nairobi Protocol and the South African Development Community Protocols both contain detailed obligations for states to reform and harmonize their laws and regulations on civilian firearms possession and use (Kytömäki, 2006, p. 58). There is still considerable scope for raising awareness of the dangers of firearm possession in domestic situations, and for developing stronger firearm controls in other contexts.

Restrictions on firearms ownership in IPV cases can help prevent future violence and homicide.

Separating abusers and guns

Legislation and court-ordered restrictions on firearms ownership and use in cases of IPV have become one of the main mechanisms to help prevent future intimate partner violence and homicides. In 1996 the US federal government passed the landmark Domestic Violence Offender Gun Ban as an amendment to earlier legislation prohibiting people under domestic violence restraining orders from purchasing or possessing a gun (Frattaroli, 2009). The 1996 legislation outlaws gun ownership and use for individuals who have been convicted of a misdemeanour domestic violence offence or who are subject to civil restraining orders against an intimate partner or the partner's child.[54] There are no exceptions, even for those using guns for professional purposes, such as the military or the police.

Many US states have since enacted additional legislation granting the police authority to remove guns when they respond to domestic violence calls, or the courts to demand the surrender of firearms by convicted offenders and impose other firearms restrictions (Frattaroli, 2009). In cases of domestic violence where a protective order is sought, the courts can variously impose a ban on the purchase of firearms or ammunition, revoke licences to carry a gun, and confiscate existing weapons. In a detailed review of state legislation, 27 states and the District of Columbia were found to have either police gun removal and/or court-ordered gun removal laws, while 23 states had neither (Frattaroli, 2009, p. 29).

Yet the effectiveness of police removal and court-ordered bans on firearms in cases of domestic abuse depends on the strength of the laws and the extent of their implementation and enforcement. Studies of the impact of such

A poster urges voters to 'Protect family' and vote yes in the 2011 referendum on tightening firearms laws in Zurich, Switzerland, January 2011.
© Walter Bieri/Associated Press

bans in the United States have shown that they can be effective (Vigdor and Mercy, 2006); however, state legislation varies considerably in terms of coverage. Frattaroli finds that both types of state laws varied in the strength of their conditions, including whether the police or judges were required ('shall') or had the discretion ('may') to remove firearms; whether an arrest was required; whether a gun had to have been used as an instrument of abuse; and whether the level of danger had to be considered. There was also variation regarding who had responsibility for the removal of guns, with some states leaving it to the offender to surrender firearms and others requiring law enforcement to confiscate them (Frattaroli, 2009).

Even when legislation is relatively strong, effective implementation still requires training of the police and judiciary— and enforcement. A number of studies have shown that the application of state legislation is sporadic. A report on women who sought domestic violence protection orders in North Carolina examines whether courts took appropriate action following the passage of new legislation; the law requires judges to ask plaintiffs whether their partner has a gun, and requires defendants to surrender their firearms within 24 hours. The results show that only 45 per cent of women were asked about firearms by judges, both before and after the passage of the legislation, and that of defendants required to surrender their firearms as a condition of the protection order, only 5 per cent were reported to have done so, and only 14 per cent had them confiscated by law enforcement (Moracco et al., 2006).

A similar study evaluates the impact of legislation requiring judges in California to order defendants in domestic violence protection order cases to surrender their guns and prohibiting the purchase of guns. It found that 48 per cent of the defendants were required to surrender their guns and prohibited from buying one, while 38 per cent were only prohibited from buying firearms (Sorenson and Shen, 2005, p. 925). Of further concern was that one in six restraining orders was not served, meaning that defendants were unaware of the conditions of the order (p. 929). Similar findings emerge from other studies, showing that judges do not order surrender in many cases and that law enforcement does not actively ensure that guns are surrendered (Webster et al., 2010; Frattaroli and Vernick, 2006). In addition, plaintiffs may not always know their rights.

South Africa's 1998 Domestic Violence Act allows individuals to request the removal of guns in their applications for protection orders in cases of domestic violence. A study of applications for protection orders in 2000–01 finds that a very small proportion of women requested the removal of guns from their perpetrators. While one in four cases involved a gun, only 2 per cent resulted in the removal of weapons, and only 3 per cent of applications requested their removal. The low rates may reflect the fact that women and magistrates were largely unaware of the legislation, that women were fearful of the consequences of such a request, or perhaps that they regarded gun possession as important in the context of high levels of community violence (Vetten, 2006). Stricter gun controls regulating general gun purchase and use were introduced in legislation in 2000, and more recent research suggests that the proportion of gun-related intimate partner homicides between 1999 and 2009 declined from 34 to 17 per cent, along with a similarly steep drop in all homicides (Abrahams et al., 2012; SOUTH AFRICA).

Risk assessment tools aid in calculating the risk of homicide in domestic violence.

In Canada, mandatory gun prohibition orders and revocations in domestic violence cases were introduced in 1995 (Johnson and Dawson, 2011, p. 91). In Australia, courts in domestic violence cases may suspend gun licences and remove guns, or revoke licences entirely. Nevertheless, many guns are reportedly returned to their owners if cases are withdrawn, suggesting ongoing risks for partners (Patty, 2011).

Most studies argue that, despite the conflicting evidence of their effectiveness due to poor implementation, police powers to remove firearms and court-ordered restrictions on gun ownership in intimate partner violence are valuable policy options; they call for greater public awareness and better implementation of these measures. Yet the removal of guns, suspension of licences, and prohibition of gun purchases all rely on cases of intimate partner violence being reported in the first place, and may be difficult if guns are illegally held.

Risk assessments

Possession of a firearm is only one of the factors placing women at risk of gun-related IPV. Intimate partner gun violence is often triggered by a range of individual, social, and economic factors—such as depression, jealousy, the threat of separation, alcohol abuse, or financial problems. Given the repetitive nature of much IPV, a number of studies have assessed the risk factors for further violence and homicide; some have developed actuarial risk assessment tools. These are intended to aid the police, medical, and social services in calculating the risks of homicide in domestic violence situations. Much of the work has been undertaken in the United States, building on studies of gun ownership among men sentenced for battering their wives; case control studies of intimate partner homicide victims and of women with non-fatal histories; and studies of women in shelters. Collectively, they have built a profile of attitudes to, and firearm use in, IPV in the United States (Campbell, 2005; Ventura et al., 2007).

The Danger Assessment is a 20-item tool developed by Jacquelyn Campbell over the past 25 years (Campbell et al., 2003; Campbell, Webster, and Glass, 2009, p. 655).[55] It is accompanied by a calendar to educate and enable women to track incidents and reduce the common tendency to minimize the number of violent incidents. Previous domestic violence by a male partner is a major and consistent risk factor, together with death threats, owning a gun, and unemployment. Apart from gun ownership, reviews of more than 22 empirical studies on risk factors for spousal homicide (primarily from the United States) have identified key risk factors: being a witness or victim of family violence; being in a de facto relationship (as opposed to being married); an age disparity between partners; having a non-biological child in the household; drug and alcohol abuse; sexual jealousy; separation or threat of separation; stalking; personality disorder; and previous domestic violence (Campbell, Webster, and Glass, 2009; Aldridge and Browne, 2003; Ansara and Hindin, 2010).

Risk assessment can be a valuable tool in preventing revictimization, but its use depends once again on the initial identification and reporting of abuse. Preventing abuse in the first place requires considerable public education and innovative interventions to increase awareness, provide alternative models, and begin to change attitudes.

Changing attitudes, norms, and behaviour

Preventing abuse requires public education to increase awareness and change attitudes.

A second major response to firearm use in IPV has been work to change attitudes towards the acceptance of guns as a normal part of society. One of the barriers to changing attitudes to violence against women has been the tendency to separate private violence from public violence, and to consider them separately. As a result, legislation, policies, and programmes on intimate partner violence have paid little attention to the links with sexual violence and harassment (and gun use against women) outside the home. Yet reducing IPV is intrinsically linked to broader social attitudes to the use of violence against women in all situations (Shaw, 2010). Listening to the experiences of victims and perpetrators to understand the wider use of guns in intimidation in IPV has been seen as important in understanding gendered attitudes and behaviours underlying firearm use (Sorenson and Weibe, 2004).

In relation to professional gun users, attitudes about the acceptability of violence are strong within the military, and preventing carry-over into the domestic sphere can be particularly challenging, but some approaches have shown success. One example is a multidisciplinary long-term project with US Air Force personnel. Launched in 1997, the project provided a range of supports and training to servicemen and their families. While it was designed primarily to reduce suicides, it also helped to reduce intimate partner abuse and child maltreatment. Rates of suicide were reduced by 33 per cent and severe and moderate family violence (intimate partner abuse and child maltreatment) by 54 and 30 per cent, respectively (Knox et al., 2003). There is a pressing need for greater attention to the problems of IPV among families in which one partner uses firearms professionally. Brazil is currently developing group programmes for men sentenced for IPV, many of whom are police or security professionals (Instituto NOOS, n.d.).

A number of programmes now engage at-risk populations—men, boys, women, and girls—to change attitudes to gun possession, and notions of masculinity that incorporate violence and weapon ownership (Barker et al., 2011b; Barker, Ricardo, and Nascimento, 2007; Harvey, Garcia-Moreno, and Butchart, 2007). Some seek to change perceptions of women and girls about what is 'normal' in relation to firearms and intimate violence. A Brazilian campaign developed by the NGO Viva Rio involved women and girls in Rio favelas—'mothers, sisters, girlfriends, wives, and cousins'—stressing that guns do not make men more manly or attractive (AI, Oxfam International, and IANSA, 2005).

CONCLUSION

The power of guns and cultural supports for gender inequalities are a lethal combination. While young and adult men are far more likely than other groups to die from firearm violence, women are overwhelmingly the victims of intimate partner homicides, and are at much higher risk in situations where their partner has access to a gun. In the places they should be the safest, women are at risk of lethal violence and ongoing threats and intimidation with firearms.

These gendered observations have not received the attention they deserve in wider discussions of guns and gun violence, nor have the economic and social costs of gun-related IPV violence to society—although this may be changing slowly. The impact of comprehensive gun law reform on intimate partner gun violence has been noted, although far more attention is directed to overall homicide rates following the implementation of such laws. In addition, in recent years specific laws that seek to separate abusive men from their firearms have been enacted in the United States and some other countries. This strategy, and the use of risk assessment instruments to guide court, police, and victim services to judge the risks of further lethal and non-lethal IP violence, including with firearms, also appear valuable.

However, preventing intimate partner gun violence before it occurs the first time requires not only legal reform but much deeper changes in cultural norms that influence men and women's attitudes and behaviours to each other, to the use of violence, and to firearms. These are long-term projects, but legal reform is often the beginning of a society's efforts to transform its norms of acceptability of violence. More widespread consideration of the risks to women associated with guns in the home would help to raise awareness, as would more public dialogue about men's gun use, gender inequality, and tolerance of violence against women.

In parallel with efforts to change social norms, there is a pressing need for better data on intimate partner gun violence. To date, the data has allowed us to see the general outline of the phenomenon, which is stark. But patterns of firearm use in intimate personal violence vary considerably across regions and countries, and more systematic data collection on the circumstances of gun violence and domestic violence incidents would improve our understanding of the many factors that influence gun-related IPV. At the same time, it would help to identify promising context-specific interventions, which are much needed since, for many women, the home is a more dangerous place than the street. ◼

LIST OF ABBREVIATIONS

| IPV | Intimate partner violence |
| WHO | World Health Organization |

ENDNOTES

1   The term 'intimate partner violence' is widely used to refer to violence between current or former spouses or partners, or close friends involved in a sexual relationship. It is often used interchangeably with the term 'domestic violence'. See Box 2.1 for a more detailed discussion.

2   Studying the behaviour of girls and young women as they grow up has shed considerable light on the differential cultural patterns and pressures that shape the behaviour and attitudes of young male offenders (Walklate, 2001). In the same way, exploring gender differences in perceptions of firearms and their use can promote a better understanding of the victimization of men and women.

3   The term 'femicide' in this chapter refers to any killing of a girl or woman, regardless of the relationship between the victim and the perpetrator. The term includes both intimate and stranger violence. See Box 2.1 for further information.

4   Broader terms are also in use. The UN Committee on the Elimination of Discrimination against Women defines 'gender-based violence' as 'violence that is directed against a woman because she is a woman or that affects women disproportionately' (CEDAW, 1992, para. 6). The UN

Declaration on the Elimination of Violence against Women defines 'violence against women' as 'any act of gender-based violence that results in, or is likely to result in, physical, sexual or psychological harm or suffering to women, including threats of such acts, coercion or arbitrary deprivation of liberty, whether occurring in public or in private life' (UNGA, 1993, art. 1). See also UNGA (2006, paras. 20, 31–33).

5   See, for example, Straus (2004).

6   Such international norms and standards are promulgated in the Convention on the Elimination of All Forms of Violence against Women of 1979 and the Declaration on the Elimination of Violence Against Women of 1993. See UNGA (2006).

7   See, for example, Beltran and Freeman (2007); NWAC (2010); Prieto-Carrón, Thompson, and MacDonald (2007); Sagot and Carcedo (2010).

8   A 2005 research guide identifies nearly 80 population-based studies on violence against women that were carried out between 1982 and 2004 in more than 50 countries (Ellsberg and Heise, 2005, p. 12).

9   The WHO International Classification of Diseases, which is used in many countries, features a code for homicides related to guns or explosives, but it does not differentiate between intimate partner homicide and other deaths.

10   Sorenson illustrates the practical implications of definitions by looking at the state of California, where intimate partners used to be defined as exclusively spousal (legal or common-law), with all former spouses and current and former boy- or girlfriends excluded. She estimates that a broadening of that definition would have nearly doubled the number of intimate partner homicides in California in 1990–99, from 1,192 to 2,313 (Sorenson, 2006). Other US studies have reported 13 per cent and 19 per cent of partner homicides miscategorized nationally, with the exclusion of former boy- and girlfriends in some states (Campbell et al., 2003; Campbell, Webster, and Glass, 2009).

11   For example, information may come from the Centers for Disease Control and Prevention, the General Social Survey, national household surveys, national firearms surveys, the Federal Bureau of Investigation *Supplementary Homicide Report,* injury and mortality reports, or Gallup Poll surveys.

12   To estimate the incidence and prevalence of physical violence, WHO asks a female respondent whether a current or former partner has ever: slapped her or thrown something at her that could hurt her; pushed or shoved her; hit her with a fist or something else that could hurt; kicked, dragged, or beaten her; threatened her with or actually used a gun, knife, or other weapon against her (WHO, 2005).

13   See, for example, AI, Oxfam International, and IANSA (2005) and AI (2008).

14   See, for example, Tjaden and Thoennes (2000) and Ansara and Hindin (2010; 2011).

15   See, for example, Ansara and Hindin (2011) and van Wormer (2008).

16   These findings are based on information from 111 countries for which reliable data was available, representing some 56 per cent of the world's female population. The database is one of the largest constructed to record female homicide.

17   Geneva Declaration Secretariat (2008; 2011); Hemenway, Shinoda-Tagawa, and Miller (2002); Hepburn and Hemenway (2004); Small Arms Survey (2012).

18   The study was based on mortuary and police records for 1999. The authors estimated that 1,349 women over the age of 14 were killed by male intimate partners that year (Mathews et al., 2004). An earlier study of intimate partner femicides in Gauteng province identifies 941 cases for the period 1990–99. The author refers to the figure as an underestimate, citing record-keeping problems. The percentage of gun-related deaths increased from 23 in 1990 to 41 by 1999 (Vetten, 2006).

19   In South Africa, 'coloured' refers to people of mixed racial ancestry.

20   The overall rate of homicide in South Africa decreased 50 per cent between 1995–96 and 2010–11 (SAPS, 2011).

21   There was also a drop in non-intimate femicides.

22   Van Wormer (2008) discusses the problems of assessing the extent of murder–suicide cases in many countries: data is rarely published and definitions of what constitutes a case vary.

23   The most common types of murder–suicide have been classified as spousal homicide–suicide, child homicide–suicide, familicide–suicide, and extra-familial homicide–suicide (Marzuk, Tardiff, and Hirsch, 1992). For a recent review of the literature, see Liem and Oberwittler (2012).

24   The Violence Policy Center had previously published reports in 2002, 2006, and 2008; the findings were consistent throughout the decade (VPC, 2008).

25   The other cases involved children and other family members as well as non-family incidents (VPC, 2012b).

26   Internet searches for IPV homicides in the United States overwhelmingly list murder–suicide cases that include children.

27   The National Violent Death Reporting System is maintained by the US Centers for Disease Control and Prevention.

28   They included cases initially categorized by the police as homicide incidents, but subsequently found to be suicides.

29   The seven countries and their rates of civilian firearms ownership per 100 people were: England and Wales (6.2), Finland (45.3), Germany (30.3), the Netherlands (3.9), Poland (1.3), Spain (10.4), and Switzerland (45.7). For additional ownership rates, see Small Arms Survey (2007a).

30   The rate of civilian firearm ownership in the United States is 88.8 per 100 people (Small Arms Survey, 2007a).

31   The cited figures are from the Secretary for Policies for Women in Brazil (Lemle, 2008).

32   See Soares (2006, p. 3) and IFP (2011, p. 20).

33   The use of guns to threaten victims is also strongly associated with rape cases in South Africa. In Gauteng province in 2003, 41 per cent of rapes of adult women reported to the police involved guns (Abrahams, Jewkes, and Mathews, 2010, p. 587).

34   See Small Arms Survey (2007b) for a more detailed discussion of the extent of gun ownership and the problems of estimation.

35   AI, Oxfam International, and IANSA (2005); Mathews et al. (2008); Pureza et al. (2010); and Saad (2011).

36   See, for example, Cafferty File (2012); CBS New York (2012); Gonzalez (2012); and Hawaii News Now (2012).

37   See also IANSA (n.d.).

38   The report includes data from the 2005 European Survey on Crime and Safety.

39   Hemenway (2011); Hemenway, Azrael, and Miller (2000); Sorenson (2006); Sorenson and Weibe (2004); Weibe (2003).

40   The percentages of homes that hold guns were estimated at 5 per cent in the Netherlands, 28 per cent in Switzerland, and 33 per cent in the
      United States.

41   See, for example, Kleck (1997) and Cook and Ludwig (1997).

42   The analysis uses data for single victim–single offender incidents.

43   The US Department of Veterans Affairs provides information and resources on post-traumatic stress and IPV (VA, n.d.).

44   For example, around a quarter of private security guards in the United States were female in 2008, but only some of them were armed (Strom
      et al., 2010).

45   Gumedze (2008); Higate (2009); Joras and Schuster (2008); Schulz and Yeung (2008).

46   Barker (2005); Bevan and Florquin (2006); Hume (2008); IFP (2011); Small Arms Survey (2010).

47   On impunity see, for example, Hume (2008); Prieto-Carrón, Thompson, and MacDonald (2007); UNGA (2006).

48   The countries surveyed were Bangladesh, Brazil, Ethiopia, Japan, Namibia, Peru, Samoa, Serbia and Montenegro, Tanzania, and Thailand.

49   Cited in Kapur (2012, p. 2).

50   See Shaw (2010).

51   Abrahams et al. (2012); AI, Oxfam International, and IANSA (2005); RCMP (2002; 2010); WHO (2008).

52   The 1995 Bill C-68 made the registration of shotguns (long guns) compulsory. Long guns are involved in the majority of firearm deaths in Canada,
      especially suicides and domestic homicides (RCMP, 2010). Nevertheless, the long gun registry was abolished by the Canadian government in 2012.

53   Regional protocols have been signed by countries in the Great Lakes region, the Horn of Africa, southern Africa, and the Organization of American
      States (Kytömäki, 2006).

54   A misdemeanour is a lower-level crime category, imposing a sentence of generally less than one year; in the United States, federal law already
      prohibited those convicted of felonies (typically more serious crimes) from owning and purchasing guns.

55   The initial Danger Assessment was a 15-item tool. The 20-item tool resulted from an 11-city study of 4,310 femicides, 194 near-femicides, and 414
      controls in the same cities, and has been used in other countries, including the United Kingdom.

BIBLIOGRAPHY

Abrahams, Naeemah, Rachel Jewkes, and Shanaaz Mathews. 2010. 'Guns and Gender-based Violence in South Africa.' *South African Medical Journal*,
      Vol. 100, No. 9, pp. 586–88.

Abrahams, Naeemah, et al. 2012. 'Every Eight Hours: Intimate Femicide in South Africa 10 Years Later!' *South African Medical Research Council
      Research Brief*. August.

AI (Amnesty International). 2008. *Picking up the Pieces: Women's Experience of Urban Violence in Brazil*. London: AI.

—, Oxfam International, and IANSA (International Action Network on Small Arms). 2005. *The Impact of Guns on Women's Lives*. Oxford: AI, Oxfam
      International, IANSA.

Aldridge, Mari and Kevin Browne. 2003. 'Perpetrators of Spousal Homicide: A Review.' *Trauma, Violence, and Abuse*, Vol. 4, No. 3, pp. 265–76.

Alvazzi del Frate, Anna. 2011. 'When the Victim Is a Woman.' In Geneva Declaration Secretariat, pp. 113–44.

—. 2012. 'A Matter of Survival: Non-lethal Firearm Violence.' In Small Arms Survey. *Small Arms Survey 2012: Moving Targets*. Geneva: Small Arms
      Survey, pp. 78–105.

Ansara, Donna and Michelle Hindin. 2010. 'Exploring Gender Differences in the Patterns of Intimate Partner Violence in Canada: A Latent Class
      Approach.' *Journal of Epidemiology and Community Health*, Vol. 64, pp. 849–54.

—. 2011. 'Psychological Consequences of Intimate Partner Violence for Women and Men in Canada.' *Journal of Interpersonal Violence*, Vol. 26, No. 8,
      pp. 1628–45.

Auchter, Bernie. 2010. 'Men Who Murder Their Families: What the Research Tells Us.' *NIJ Journal*, No. 266.
      <http://www.nij.gov/journals/266/murderfamilies.htm>

Barker, Gary. 2005. *Dying to be Men: Youth, Masculinity and Social Exclusion*. London: Routledge.

—, Christine Ricardo, and Marcos Nascimento. 2007. *Engaging Men and Boys in Changing Gender-based Inequity in Health*. Geneva: World Health
      Organization.

—, et al. 2011a. *Evolving Men: Initial Results from the International Men and Gender Equality Survey*. Washington, DC, and Rio de Janeiro: International
      Center for Research on Women and Instituto Promundo.

—, et al. 2011b. *What Men Have to Do with It: Public Policies to Promote Gender Equality*. Washington, DC, and Rio de Janeiro: International Center
      for Research on Women and Instituto Promundo.

Bastick, Megan, Karin Grimm, and Jasna Lazarevic. 2008. 'Armed Violence against Women.' In Geneva Declaration Secretariat. *Global Burden of Armed
      Violence*. Geneva: Geneva Declaration Secretariat, pp. 109–24.

Beltran, Adriana and Laurie Freeman. 2007. *Hidden in Plain Sight: Violence against Women in Mexico and Guatemala*. WOLA Special Report.
      Washington, DC: Washington Office on Latin America.

Bevan, James and Nicolas Florquin. 2006. 'Few Options but the Gun: Angry Young Men.' In Small Arms Survey. *Small Arms Survey 2006: Unfinished Business.* Geneva: Small Arms Survey, ch. 12.

Bloom, Shelah. 2008. *Violence against Women and Girls: A Compendium of Monitoring and Evaluation Indicators.* Chapel Hill, NC: MEASURE Evaluation.

Bricknell, Samantha. 2012. 'Firearms Trafficking and Serious and Organized Crime.' *Research and Public Policy Series 116.* Canberra: Australian Institute of Criminology.

Burke, Jason. 2012. 'Indian Women Turn to Firearms against Threat of Violence.' *Guardian.* 21 May.
<http://www.guardian.co.uk/world/2012/may/21/indian-women-take-up-firearms/>

Cafferty File. 2012. 'What's behind the Surge in Women Gun Owners?' 16 April.
<http://caffertyfile.blogs.cnn.com/2012/04/16/whats-behind-the-surge-in-women-gun-owners/>

Campbell, Jacquelyn. 2005. 'Assessing Dangerousness in Domestic Violence: History, Challenges and Opportunities.' *Criminology and Public Policy,* Vol. 4, No. 4, pp. 653–71.

—, Daniel Webster, and Nancy Glass. 2009. 'The Danger Assessment: Validation of a Lethality Risk Assessment Instrument for Intimate Partner Violence.' *Journal of Interpersonal Violence,* Vol. 24, No. 4, pp. 653–74.

—, et al. 2003. 'Risk Factors for Femicide in Abusive Relationships: Results from a Multisite Case Control Study.' *American Journal of Public Health,* Vol. 93, No. 7, pp. 1089–97.

Carroll, Joseph 2005. 'Gun Ownership and Use in America.' Gallup. 22 November.
<http://www.gallup.com/poll/20098/gun-ownership-use-america.aspx>

Catalano, Shannan. 2007. *Intimate Partner Violence in the United States.* Washington, DC: Bureau of Justice Statistics, United States Department of Justice.
<http://bjs.ojp.usdoj.gov/content/pub/pdf/ipvus.pdf>

—. 2012. *Intimate Partner Violence, 1993–2010.* Washington, DC: Bureau of Justice Statistics, United States Department of Justice.

CBS New York. 2012. 'New Research Shows Gun Purchases by Women on the Rise.' 6 February.
<http://newyork.cbslocal.com/2012/02/06/seen-at-11-new-research-shows-gun-purchases-by-women-on-the-rise/>

CDC (Centers for Disease Control and Prevention). 2010. 'Intimate Partner Violence: Definitions.' September.
<http://www.cdc.gov/violenceprevention/intimatepartnerviolence/definitions.html>

CEDAW (United Nations Committee on the Elimination of Discrimination against Women). 1992. General Recommendation No. 19.
<http://www.un.org/womenwatch/daw/cedaw/recommendations/recomm.htm>

Cook, Philip and Jens Ludwig. 1997. 'Guns in America: National Survey on Private Ownership and Use of Firearms.' *Research in Brief.* May. Washington, DC: National Institute of Justice.

Cooper, Alexia and Erica Smith. 2011. 'Homicide Trends in the United States, 1980–2008.' Washington, DC: Bureau of Justice Statistics, United States Department of Justice. <http://bjs.ojp.usdoj.gov/index.cfm?ty=pbdetail&iid=2221>

Council of Europe. 2011. Council of Europe Convention on Preventing and Combating Violence against Women and Domestic Violence.
<http://www.coe.int/t/dghl/standardsetting/convention-violence/default_EN.asp?>

Dreyfus, Pablo, et al. 2010. *Small Arms in Brazil: Production, Trade and Holdings.* Special Report No. 11. Geneva: Small Arms Survey.

ECE and UNODC (Economic Commission for Europe and United Nations Office on Drugs and Crime). 2011. *Principles and Framework for an International Classification of Crimes for Statistical Purposes.* ECE/CES/BUR/2011/NOV/8/Add.1. 11 October.
<http://www.unece.org/fileadmin/DAM/stats/documents/ece/ces/bur/2011/8Add1-crime_classification_report.pdf>

Echarri Cánovas, Carlos and Karla Ramírez Ducoing. 2011. *Feminicidio en México.Aproximación, tendencias y cambios, 1985-2009.* Mexico City: Cámara de Diputados et al. <http://www.equidad.scjn.gob.mx/IMG/pdf/LIBRO_FEMINICIDIO.pdf>

ECLAC 2011. *Annual Report 2011: Women's Autonomy from the Margins to the Mainstream.* Santiago: Economic Commission for Latin America and the Caribbean.

Eder, Simon. 2011. *Firearms Certificates in England and Wales.* Home Office Statistical Bulletin 05/11. London: Her Majesty's Stationery Office.

Ellsberg, Mary and Lori Heise. 2005. *Researching Violence against Women: A Practical Guide for Researchers and Activists.* Geneva: World Health Organization and Programme for Appropriate Technology for Health.

Farr, Vanessa, Henri Myrttinen, and Albrecht Schnabel, eds. 2009. *Sexed Pistols: The Gendered Impacts of Small Arms and Light Weapons.* New York: United Nations University Press.

Fish, Jennifer and Pumla Mncayi. 2009. 'Securing Private Spaces: Gendered Labour, Violence and Democratization in South Africa.' In Vanessa Farr, Henri Myrttinen, and Albrecht Schnabel, pp. 290–326.

Florquin, Nicolas. 2011. 'A Booming Business: Private Security and Small Arms.' In Small Arms Survey. *Small Arms Survey 2011: States of Security.* Cambridge: Cambridge University Press.

Frattaroli, Shannon. 2009. *Removing Guns from Domestic Violence Offenders: An Analysis of State Level Policies to Prevent Future Abuse.* Baltimore: John Hopkins Center for Gun Policy and Research.

— and John Vernick. 2006. 'Separating Batterers and Guns: A Review and Analysis of Gun Laws in 50 States.' *Evaluation Review,* Vol. 30, No. 3, pp. 296–312.

Geneva Declaration Secretariat. 2008. *Global Burden of Armed Violence.* Geneva: Geneva Declaration Secretariat.

—. 2011. *Global Burden of Armed Violence 2011: Lethal Encounters.* Geneva: Geneva Declaration Secretariat.

Gonzalez, John. 2012. 'She Can Shoot: A Women-only Gun Club.' ABC News. 11 July.

GPC Research. 2001. *Fall 2000 Estimate of Firearms Ownership*. Ottawa: GPC Research.
    <http://web.archive.org/web/20030419100209/http://www.cfc-ccaf.gc.ca/en/general_public/news_releases/GPC/survey.pdf>

Gumedze, Sabelo, ed. 2008. *The Private Security Sector in Africa*. ISS Monograph Series No. 146. Cape Town: Institute of Security Studies.

Harvey, Alison, Claudia Garcia-Moreno, and Alex Butchart. 2007. *Primary Prevention of Intimate Partner Violence and Sexual Violence*. Background
    paper. Geneva: World Health Organization.

Hawaii News Now. 2012 'Gun Registration in Hawaii Soars.' 18 April. <http://www.hawaiinewsnow.com/story/17520154/gun-registration-soars>

Hemenway, David. 2011. 'Risks and Benefits of a Gun in the Home.' *American Journal of Lifestyle Medicine*. 2 February.

—, Deborah Azrael, and Matthew Miller. 2000. 'Gun Use in the United States: Results from Two National Surveys.' *Injury Prevention*, Vol. 6, pp. 263–67.

—, Tomoko Shinoda-Tagawa, and Matthew Miller. 2002. 'Firearms Availability and Female Homicide Victimization Rates across 25 Populous High-
    income Countries.' *Journal of the American Medical Women's Association*, Vol. 57, pp. 100–04.

Hepburn, Lisa and David Hemenway. 2004. 'Firearm Availability and Homicide: A Review of the Literature.' *Aggression and Violent Behaviour*, Vol. 9,
    No. 4, pp. 417–40.

Hepburn, Lisa, et al. 2007. 'The US Gun Stock: Results from the 2004 National Firearms Survey.' *Injury Prevention*, Vol. 13, No. 1, pp. 15–19.

Higate, Paul. 2009. 'Putting "Mercenary Masculinities" on the Research Agenda.' Working Paper No. 03-09. Bristol: University of Bristol.
    <http://www.bristol.ac.uk/spais/research/workingpapers/.../higate0309>

Home Office. 2009. *Saving Lives, Reducing Harm, Protecting the Public: An Action Plan for Tackling Violence 2008–11*. London: Home Office.

—. 2012. *Cross-government Definition of Domestic Violence—A Consultation: Summary of Responses*. London: Home Office. September.
    <http://www.homeoffice.gov.uk/publications/about-us/consultations/definition-domestic-violence/domestic-violence-definition?view=Binary>

Hume, Mo. 2008. 'The Myths of Violence: Gender, Conflict and Community in El Salvador.' *Latin American Perspectives*, Vol. 35, No. 5, pp. 59–76.

IANSA (International Action Network on Small Arms). n.d. 'Portugal: Main Findings of "Violence and Small Arms: The Portuguese case" (2008–2010).'
    <http://www.iansa-women.org/node/440>

IFP (Initiative for Peacebuilding). 2011. *Women and Gun Violence: Key Findings from Rio de Janeiro (Brazil), San Salvador (El Salvador) and Maputo
    (Mozambique)*. Brussels: IFP.

Instituto NOOS. n.d. 'Paz em casa, paz no mundo.' <http://www.noos.org.br/portal/pazemcasa>

Johnson, Holly and Myrna Dawson. 2011. *Violence against Women in Canada: Research and Policy Perspectives*. Oxford: Oxford University Press.

Johnson, Holly, Sami Nevala, and Natalia Ollus. 2008. *Violence against Women: An International Perspective*. New York: Springer.

Johnson, Leanor, Michael Todd, and Ganga Subramanian. 2005. 'Violence in Police Families: Work–Family Spillover.' *Journal of Family Violence*, Vol. 20,
    No. 1, pp. 3–12.

Johnson, T. A. 2009. 'Mangalore's Metamorphosis.' *Indian Express*. 3 February.
    <http://www.indianexpress.com/news/mangalore-metamorphosis/418422/0>

Joras, Ulrike and Adrian Schuster, eds. 2008. *Private Security Companies and Local Populations: An Exploratory Study of Afghanistan and Angola*.
    Working Paper. Bern: swisspeace.

Kapur, Ratna. 2012. 'Pink Chaddis and SlutWalk Couture: The Postcolonial Politics of Feminism Lite.' *Feminist Legal Studies*, Vol. 20, No. 1, pp. 1–20.

Kirsten, Adèle, et al. 2006. *Islands of Safety in a Sea of Guns: Gun-free Zones in South Africa's Fothane, Diepkloof, and Khayelitsha*. Working Paper
    No. 3. Geneva: Small Arms Survey.

Kleck, Gary. 1997. *Targeting Guns: Firearms and Their Control*. Hawthorne, NY: Aldine de Gruyter.

Knox, Kerry, et al. 2003. 'Risk of Suicide and Related Adverse Outcomes after Exposure to a Suicide Prevention Program in the US Air Force: Cohort study.'
    British Medical Journal, Vol. 327, pp. 1376–80.

Kytömäki, Elli. 2006. 'Regional Approaches to Small Arms Control: Vital to Implementing the UN Programme of Action.' *Disarmament Forum*, No. 1,
    pp. 55–64.

Lemle, Marina. 2008. 'For an End to All Forms of Violence against Women.' Comunidad segura. 10 December.
    <http://www.comunidadesegura.org/?q=en/STORY-For-an-end-to-all-forms-of-violence-against-women>

Liem, Marieke and Dietrich Oberwittler. 2012. 'Homicide Followed by Suicide in Europe.' In Marieke Liem and W. A. Pridemore, eds. *Handbook of
    European Homicide Research: Patterns, Explanations and Country Studies*. New York: Springer, pp. 197–215.

Liem, Marieke, et al. 2011. 'Homicide–suicide and Other Violent Deaths: An International Comparison.' *Forensic Science International*, Vol. 207, pp. 70–76.

Lund, Laura. 2002. *Incidence of Non-fatal Intimate Partner Violence against Women in California, 1998–1999*. EPICgram Report No. 4. California:
    Epidemiology and Prevention for Injury Control Branch, California Department of Health Services.

Marzuk, Peter, Kenneth Tardiff, and Charles Hirsch. 1992. 'The Epidemiology of Murder–Suicide.' *Journal of the American Medical Association*, Vol. 267,
    pp. 3179–83.

Mathews, Shanaaz, et al. 2004. '"Every Six Hours a Women is Killed by Her Partner": A National Study of Female Homicides in South Africa.' *MRC Policy
    Brief*, No. 5, June.

—. 2008. 'Intimate Femicide–suicide in South Africa: A Cross-sectional Study.' *Bulletin of the World Health Organization*, Vol. 86, No. 7, July.
    <http://www.who.int/bulletin/volumes/86/7/07-043786.pdf>

Mazali, Rela. 2009. 'The Gun on the Kitchen Table: The Sexist Subtext of Private Policing in Israel.' In Vanessa Farr, Henri Myrttinen, and Albrecht
    Schnabel, pp. 246–89.

Monson, Candice, Casey Taft, and Steffany Fredman. 2009. 'Military-related PTSD and Intimate Relationships: From Description to Theory-driven Research and Intervention Development.' *Clinical Psychological Review,* Vol. 29, No. 8, pp. 707–14.

Moracco, Kathryn, et al. 2006. *Preventing Firearms Violence among Victims of Intimate Partner Violence: An Evaluation of a New North Carolina Law.* Doc. No. 215773, Award No. 2004-IJ-CX-0025. Washington, DC: United States Department of Justice.

NWAC (Native Women's Association of Canada). 2010. *What Their Stories Tell Us: Research Findings from the Sisters in Spirit Initiative.* Ottawa: NWAC. <http://www.nwac.ca/sites/default/files/reports/2010_NWAC_SIS_Report_EN.pdf>

OAS (Organization of American States). n.d. 'A-61: Inter-American Convention on the Prevention, Punishment and Eradication of Violence against Women—"Convention of Belém do Pará."' <http://www.oas.org/juridico/english/sigs/a-61.html>

PAHO (Pan American Health Organization). 2005. *Gender, Health, and Development in the Americas: Basic Indicators 2005.* Washington, DC: PAHO.

Patty, Anna. 2011. 'Guns Returned in Domestic Violence Cases'. *Sydney Morning Herald.* 19 September.

Peru. 2010. *Mujeras victimas de femicidio y tentativas a nivel nacional.* Lima: Ministerio de la Mujer y Desarrollo Social.

Prieto-Carrón, Marina, Marilyn Thompson, and Mandy MacDonald. 2007. 'No More Killings! Women Respond to Femicides in Central America.' *Gender and Development,* Vol. 15, No. 1, pp. 25–40.

Pureza, José Manuel, et al. 2010. *Violência e armas ligeiras: um retrato português.* Coimbra, Portugal: Centro de Estudos Sociais, Universidade de Coimbra. <http://www.ces.uc.pt/nucleos/nep/pages/pt/projectos-de-investigacao/concluidos/violencia-e-armas-ligeiras-um-retrato-portugues.php>

RCMP (Royal Canadian Mounted Police). 2002. *Research Summary: Domestic Violence Involving Firearms.* Ottawa: RCMP. <http://www.rcmp-grc.gc.ca/cfp-pcaf/res-rec/violence-eng.htm>

—. 2010. *RCMP Canadian Firearms Program: Program Evaluation.* Ottawa: RCMP. February. <http://www.rcmp-grc.gc.ca/pubs/fire-feu-eval/eval-eng.pdf>

—. 2012. *RCMP Facts and Figures (April–June 2012)—Canadian Firearms Program: Valid Licences as of June 2012.* Ottawa: RCMP. Accessed 8 August 2012. <http://www.rcmp-grc.gc.ca/cfp-pcaf/facts-faits/index-eng.htm>

Ricaurte Villota, Ana Inés. 2011. *Comportamiento del Homicidio.* Bogotá: Instituto Nacional de Medicina Legal y Ciencias Forenses. <http://www.medicinalegal.gov.co/images/stories/root/FORENSIS/2011/2-F-11-Homicidios.pdf>

Rothman, Emily, et al. 2005. 'Batterers' Use of Guns to Threaten Intimate Partners.' *Journal of the American Medical Women's Association,* Vol. 60, No. 1, pp. 62–68.

Saad, Lydia. 2011. 'Self-Reported Gun Ownership in the U.S. Is Highest Since 1993.' Gallup. 26 October. <http://www.gallup.com/poll/150353/Self-Reported-Gun-Ownershipp-Highest-Sinc-1993.aspx>

Sagot, Monserrat and Ana Carcedo. 2010. 'When Violence against Women Kills: Femicide in Costa Rica, 1990–1999.' In Rosa-Lina Fregosa and Cunthis Bejarano, eds. *Terrorizing Women: Femicide in Latin America.* Durham: Duke University Press.

Saltzman, Linda, et al. 1992.'Weapon Involvement and Injury Outcomes in Family and Intimate Assaults.' *Journal of the American Medical Association,* Vol. 267, No. 22, pp. 3043–47.

SAPS (South African Police Service). 2011. *Crime Report 2010/2011.*

Schulz, Sabrina and Christina Yeung. 2008. *Private Military and Security Companies and Gender.* Tool 10, Gender and SSR Toolkit. Vienna: Organization for Security and Co-operation in Europe.

Shaw, Margaret. 2010. *An International Overview of Violence against Women: Trends, Perspectives and Lessons for Latin America and the Caribbean.* Consultancy paper for the Inter-American Development Bank. June.

Small Arms Survey. 2007a. 'Annexe 4: The Largest Civilian Firearms Arsenals for 178 Countries.' <http://www.smallarmssurvey.org/fileadmin/docs/A-Yearbook/2007/en/Small-Arms-Survey-2007-Chapter-02-annexe-4-EN.pdf>

—. 2007b. *Small Arms Survey 2007: Guns and the City.* Cambridge: Cambridge University Press.

—. 2010. *Small Arms Survey 2010: Gangs, Groups, and Guns.* Cambridge: Cambridge University Press.

—. 2011. 'Estimating Civilian Gun Ownership.' Research Note No. 9. September. Geneva: Small Arms Survey.

—. 2012. *Small Arms Survey 2012: Moving Targets.* Cambridge: Cambridge University Press.

Soares, Barbara Musumeci. 2006. 'Guns: What Do Women Have to Fear?' *P@X Online Bulletin Peace Studies Group,* No. 6, June.

Sorenson, Susan. 2006. 'Firearm Use in Interpersonal Violence.' *Evaluation Review,* Vol. 30, pp. 229–36.

— and Haikang Shen. 2005. 'Restraining Orders in California: A Look at Statewide Data.' *Violence against Women,* Vol. 11, No. 7, pp. 912–33.

— and Douglas Weibe. 2004. 'Weapons in the Lives of Battered Women.' *American Journal of Public Health,* Vol. 94, No. 8, pp. 1412–17.

Statistics Canada. 2005. *Family Violence in Canada: A Statistical Profile.* Catalogue No. 85-224-IX. Ottawa: Statistics Canada.

—. 2011. *Family Violence in Canada: A Statistical Profile.* Catalogue No. 85-224-X. Ottawa: Statistics Canada.

Statistics Indonesia. 2006. 'The 2006 Survey of Violence against Women and Children in Indonesia.' <http://unstats.un.org/unsd/demographic/meetings/wshops/China_22-24Nov2010/Agenda item 6 Indonesia.ppt>

Straus, Murray. 2004. 'Women's Violence towards Men Is a Serious Social Problem.' In Richard Gelles and Donileen Loseke, eds. *Current Controversies on Family Violence,* 2nd edn. Newbury Park: Sage Publications, pp. 55–77.

Strom, Kevin, et al. 2010. *The Private Security Industry: A Review of the Definitions, Available Sources and Paths Moving Forward.* Research Report 2009-BJ-CX-K045 submitted to the US Department of Justice.

Tjaden, Patricia and Nancy Thoennes. 2000. *Extent, Nature and Consequences of Intimate Partner Violence: Findings from the First National Violence against Women Survey.* NCJ No. 181867. Washington, DC: National Institute of Justice, United States Department of Justice.

UNECE (United Nations Economic Commission for Europe). 2012. 'Statistical Database: Crime and Violence.' Accessed 20 November 2012.
<http://w3.unece.org/pxweb/database/STAT/30-GE/07-CV/?lang=1>

UNGA (United Nations General Assembly). 1993. Declaration on the Elimination of Violence against Women. A/RES/48/104 of 20 December.

—. 2006. *In-depth Study on All Forms of Violence against Women: Report of the Secretary-General*. A/61/122/Add.1 of 6 July.

—. 2012. *Report of the Special Rapporteur on Violence against Women, Its Causes and Consequences, Raschida Manjoo*. A/HRC/20/16 of 23 May.

UNODC (United Nations Office on Drugs and Crime). 2011a. *2011 Global Study on Homicide: Trends, Contexts, Data*. Vienna: UNODC.

—. 2011b. *Civilian Private Security Services: Their Role, Oversight and Contribution to Crime Prevention and Community Safety*. CCPCJ/EG.5/2011/CRP.1. Vienna: UNODC.

UN PoA–ISS (Programme of Action Implementation Support System). n.d.a. 'Firearms Protocol.'
<http://www.poa-iss.org/FirearmsProtocol/FirearmsProtocol.aspx>

—. n.d.b. 'Programme of Action.' <http://www.poa-iss.org/poa/poa.aspx>

USDOJ (United States Department of Justice). 2000. *Full Report of the Prevalence, Incidence, and Consequences of Violence against Women*. November.
<https://www.ncjrs.gov/pdffiles1/nij/183781.pdf>

—. 2012. 'Domestic Violence.' August. <http://www.ovw.usdoj.gov/domviolence.htm>

VA (United States Department of Veterans Affairs). n.d. 'Information on PTSD: Veterans, General Public & Family.'
<http://www.ptsd.va.gov/public/pages/fslist-family-relationships.asp>

van Dijk, Jan, John van Kesteren, and Paul Smit. 2007. *Criminal Victimisation in International Perspective: Key Findings from the 2004–2005 ICVS and EU ICS*. The Hague: Wetenschappelijk Onderzoek- en Documentatiecentrum.

van Wormer, Katherine. 2008. 'The Dynamics of Murder–Suicide in Domestic Situations.' *Brief Treatment and Crisis Intervention*, Vol. 8, No. 3, pp. 274–82.

Vaquerano, Fabio Molina. 2011. *Epidemiologia de los Homicidios en El Salvador: Año 2010*. El Salvador: Instituto de Medicina Legal. <https://sites.google.com/site/fabiomolinavaqueranoiml/documents/EPIDEMIOLOGIADELOSHOMICIDIOSA%C3%91O2010.pdf?attredirects=0&d=1>

Ventura, Lois, et al. 2007. 'Women and Men in Jail: Attitudes towards and Experiences of Domestic Violence.' *American Journal of Criminal Justice*, Vol. 37, pp. 37–48.

Vetten, Lisa. 2006. 'Mapping the Use of Guns in Violence against Women: Findings from Three Studies.' *African Security Review*, Vol. 15, No. 2, pp. 86–92.

Via, Sandra. 2010. 'Gender, Militarism, and Globalization: Soldiers for Hire and Hegemonic Masculinity.' In Laura Sjoberg and Sandra Via, eds. *Gender, War and Militarism: Feminist Perspectives*. Santa Barbara, CA: Praeger Security International, pp. 42–55.

Vigdor, Elizabeth and James Mercy. 2006. 'Do Laws Restricting Access to Firearms by Domestic Violence Offenders Prevent Intimate Partner Homicide?' *Evaluation Review*, Vol. 30, No. 3, pp. 313–46.

VPC (Violence Policy Center). 2001. *A Deadly Myth: Women, Handguns and Self Defense*. <http://www.vpc.org/studies/myth.htm>

—. 2008. *American Roulette: Murder–Suicide in the United States*, 3rd edn. Washington, DC: VPC.

—. 2012a. *When Men Murder Women: An Analysis of 2010 Homicide Data*. Washington, DC: VPC.

—. 2012b. *American Roulette: Murder–Suicide in the United States*, 4th edn. Washington, DC: VPC.

Waiselfisz, Julio Jacobo. 2012. *Mapa da Violencia 2012: Caderno Complementa 1—Homicidio de Mulheres no Brasil*. Brasilia: Ministry of Justice and Instituto Sangari.

Walklate, Sandra. 2001. *Gender, Crime and Justice*. Cullompton, Devon: Willan Publishing.

Washington Times. 2010. 'More Women May Be Turning to Firearms.' 30 March.
<http://www.washingtontimes.com/news/2010/mar/30/more-females-may-be-turning-to-firearms/>

Webster, Daniel, et al. 2010. 'Women with Protective Order Report Failure to Remove Firearms from Their Abusive Partners: Results from an Exploratory Study.' *Journal of Women's Health*, Vol. 19, No. 1, pp. 93–98.

Weibe, Douglas. 2003. 'Homicide and Suicide Risks Associated with Firearms in the Home: A National Case-control Study.' *Annals of Emergency Medicine*, Vol. 41, No. 6, pp. 771–82.

WHO (World Health Organization). 2002. *World Report on Violence and Health*. Geneva: WHO.

—. 2005. *WHO Multi-country Study on Women's Health and Domestic Violence against Women*. Geneva: WHO.

—. 2008. *Preventing Violence and Reducing Its Impact: How Development Agencies Can Help*. Geneva: WHO.

—. 2010. *Preventing Intimate Partner and Sexual Violence against Women: Taking Action and Generating Evidence*. Geneva: WHO.

ACKNOWLEDGEMENTS

Principal author

Margaret Shaw

After mugging a person, the pandilleros throw the victim's shoes onto telephone wires as a gesture
of triumph, Barrio Luis Fanor Hernández, Managua, November 2009. © Dennis Rodgers

Turning Points

GANG EVOLUTION IN NICARAGUA

3

INTRODUCTION

Gangs are widely considered to be among the most important security threats in post-cold war Central America, to the extent that they have been characterized as a 'new urban insurgency' aiming 'to depose or control the governments of targeted countries' (Manwaring, 2005, p. 2). As a result, policy-makers and the general public see them as a danger that has the potential to extend beyond the region, in particular to the United States and Canada. At the same time, however, branding gangs a 'national security threat' or a 'new urban insurgency' can significantly distort our understanding of the phenomenon (Hagedorn, 2008, p. xxx). The topic of gangs is often sensationalized, whether in media reports, academic studies, or policy documents, and the overwhelming majority of available information on Central American gangs is arguably flawed, with official statistics particularly inconsistent 'due to institutional weaknesses, deficient data collection, and the discretionary if not political use of crime data' (Wolf, 2012, p. 68).

Central American gangs are furthermore often considered generically, when it is critical to distinguish between the very different phenomena of *pandillas* and *maras*. The former are localized, home-grown gangs, while the latter are a hybrid social form with transnational roots.[1] Pandillas were initially present throughout the Central American region in the post-cold war period but have been largely supplanted by maras in El Salvador, Guatemala, and Honduras; today, they are only significantly present in Nicaragua.[2] Most of what has been written about gangs in Central America is actually about maras, but pandillas arguably constitute a globally more representative type of gang. Yet the dynamics of the latter remain poorly understood, especially with regard to the long-term logic of their violence.

This chapter draws on in-depth primary research to offer a comparative analysis of the post-cold war evolutionary trajectories of the pandillas associated with two specific *barrios* (neighbourhoods) in Managua, the capital of Nicaragua: Elías Blanco and Luis Fanor Hernández.[3] It focuses on shifting patterns of small arms use by gang members, exploring the different types of weapons employed at different points in time, the changing nature of the underground arms market, the rise and fall of armed actors, and the evolving relationship that gangs have with their local communities. The key findings of this chapter are:

- The spread and shape of Nicaraguan pandillas in the post-cold war period is linked to the aftermath of the 1980s Contra war, including in particular the demobilization of conscripted youths. Gangs, however, subsequently institutionalized on the basis of processes of local territorialization, and their development has not been linear or progressive.

- Gangs in different urban neighbourhoods can develop unique evolutionary dynamics that affect their use of firearms and resulting violence levels. These change over time due to both internal and external factors.

- Internally, one or two individuals can make a crucial difference to the way a gang evolves in Nicaragua, as well as how violent it becomes, particularly with regard to the acquisition of specialized knowledge about gun use.

- Externally, the changing availability of weapons and ammunition and the presence of other armed actors fundamentally influence the use of firearms by gang members, whose weapons acquisition tends to be more opportunistic than systematic.

- Gun use by pandilla members has not evolved in a linear manner; the use of firearms increased steadily during the 1990s, then declined during the following decade, before picking up again from around 2010.

- Manufactured firearms were more common in the 1990s than in the following decade, when home-made weapons became more widespread, to the extent that they are now the principal type of firearm associated with gangs.

This chapter is based principally on 30 in-depth interviews conducted with current and former gang members in barrios Elías Blanco and Luis Fanor Hernández in June–September 2012.[4] It also draws on ongoing, long-term, and regularly repeated longitudinal ethnographic research carried out by the authors since the late 1990s.[5]

The first section of the chapter provides a brief overview of violence in contemporary Nicaragua, situating gangs within it. The following section offers some background on barrios Elías Blanco and Luis Fanor Hernández before examining the respective evolutionary trajectories of the gangs in the two neighbourhoods during the past 25 years. It reviews the similarities and differences in their developmental paths, tracing the factors that pushed one type of transformation over another, as well as the way that these have had diverse consequences, whether in relation to the gang, other armed actors, or local communities. The next section considers the evolution of gang members' use of firearms, including the different types of weapon used by gang members at different points in time, how they were obtained, and the way they learned to use them. The concluding section offers a brief synthesis of findings and relates the local dynamics explored in the two neighbourhoods to the broader national context.

Nicaragua has long been linked to violence, enduring 'a continuous rite of blood'.

A BRIEF HISTORY OF NICARAGUAN GANG VIOLENCE

Nicaragua has long been associated with violence, to the extent that the novelist Salman Rushdie famously described the country as having endured 'a continuous rite of blood' (Rushdie, 1987, p. 18). It is notorious for having suffered the longest-running dictatorship in modern Latin American history, that of the Somoza dynasty, which was finally overthrown after 45 years of bitter struggle in 1979 by the Sandinista revolution. Although the new revolutionary regime promulgated a range of social programmes that benefitted the majority of the country's population for the first time in Nicaraguan history, the revolution was soon overshadowed by a bitter civil war against the US-sponsored 'Contras'.[6] This conflict had a devastating effect on the country's economy, destroying and disrupting communication and economic infrastructure, and terrorizing and demoralizing the population, particularly in the countryside. More than 30,000 people—almost 1 per cent of the country's population—were killed, and the war was a primary reason for the Sandinista revolutionary regime's electoral defeat in February 1990 (Walker, 2003, p. 56).

Rather than leading to peace, regime change marked a shift in Nicaragua's geography of violence, the logic of which was well summarized by Eduardo Galeano, who remarked that, 'while the streets of Nicaragua's cities were peaceful during the years of formal conflict, once peace was declared, the country's streets became scenes of war' as a result of a dramatic explosion in urban crime and delinquency (Galeano, 1998, pp. 322–24, authors' translation).[7] According to official Nicaraguan National Police statistics, crime levels rose steadily by an annual average of more than 10 per cent during the 1990s, compared to just under 2 per cent during the 1980s, with the absolute number of crimes almost quadrupling between 1990 and 2000. Crimes against persons—including homicides, rapes, and assaults—increased especially significantly (Cajina, 2000, pp. 185–87).

Figure 3.1 **Inconsistent homicide data for Nicaragua, 2000-11**

■ Nicaraguan National Police   ■ Instituto de Medicina Legal (Institute of Forensic Medicine)
■ Pan American Health Organization   ▪ World Health Organization

HOMICIDE RATE PER 100,000 POPULATION

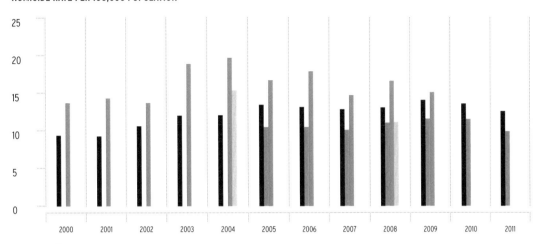

Source: Nowak (2012)

While this overall trend of increasing urban crime is undoubtedly accurate, official Nicaraguan crime statistics are problematic. The inefficiency and weakness of Nicaraguan state institutions[8] clearly affects their reporting capacity,[9] and official crime statistics are also manipulated,[10] as successive post-revolutionary governments have sought to project Nicaragua as 'the safest country in Latin America', partly in order to attract foreign investment.[11] All post-1990 governments in Nicaragua, but especially that of Enrique Bolaños (2002–06), also attempted to project successful crime-fighting initiatives as a major element of their government policy; consequently, they have generally preferred to release 'positive'—that is, low—crime statistics.[12] The problem is particularly evident with regard to homicide statistics, as highlighted by the discrepancies between different data sources (see Figure 3.1).

Poor official statistics notwithstanding, ethnographic studies carried out in the past two decades or so confirm crime and delinquency as critical social concerns in urban Nicaragua.[13] Gangs are frequently described as the major source of insecurity in these investigations, and they have also regularly been identified as such in various Nicaraguan opinion polls on the topic. A 1999 survey conducted by the Nicaraguan NGO Ética y Transparencia, for example, found that 50 per cent of respondents identified gangs as the principal threat to their personal security (Cajina, 2000, p. 177). More than a decade later, the 2011 Citizen Security Perception Survey carried out by the Managua-based Institute for Strategic Studies and Public Policy[14] found that almost 60 per cent of respondents considered gangs the most important security threat in Nicaragua (Orozco, 2012, p. 8). More generally, Nicaraguan media regularly carries reports of gangs being involved not only in a range of petty crimes, including theft and mugging, but also in armed robbery and murder.[15]

Gangs before 1990

Gangs (pandillas) are by no means new features of Nicaraguan society. They can be traced back to the country's large-scale urbanization, when Managua grew from some 50,000 inhabitants in 1940 to more than 250,000 in 1963 (Kates et al., 1973, p. 982). These first gangs were little more than spontaneous groups of youths that emerged organically in urban slums and only lasted as long as the peer group underpinning it stayed together. They were never prominent; indeed, gangs are not mentioned at all in Reinaldo Antonio Téfel's seminal study of urban poverty in Nicaragua (Téfel Vélez, 1976). The number of gangs declined significantly during the 1980s due to universal military service, the age of conscription being 16, and also because of the highly developed grassroots organization that was a hallmark of the Sandinista revolution, which included youth work brigades and extensive local neighbourhood watches.

Pandillas disappeared almost completely from view during the first half of the 1980s, before beginning to re-emerge towards the middle of the decade due to the war-fuelled erosion of the Sandinista welfare state, declining levels of local organization, the decreasing legitimacy of the revolutionary regime, and increasing numbers of youths deserting their military service (Lancaster, 1992, p. 132). These new gangs principally involved groups of young men[16] who had been conscripted together and who joined forces in order to protect their families and friends from the rising crime and insecurity, thereby displaying something of a vigilante ethos.

Gangs from 1990 to 2005

By the mid-1990s, a full-blown gang culture had become institutionalized.

From the early 1990s onwards, gangs began to proliferate exponentially, becoming a ubiquitous feature of poor urban neighbourhoods in all of the country's major cities. By 1999, the Nicaraguan National Police estimated that there were 110 gangs incorporating 8,500 youths in Managua, double the number recorded in 1996, and five times that documented in 1990 (Rodgers, 2006a, p. 273).[17] These figures are undoubtedly underestimates,[18] but they do provide a sense of the growth of the phenomenon in the first decade of the post-revolutionary period.

By the mid-1990s, a full-blown gang culture had become institutionalized. Gang members engaged in a wide range of petty delinquency, while rival gangs collectively fought each other for control over territory, in particular their local neighbourhoods, but also adjacent no-man's lands, roads, and other public spaces. These conflicts principally revolved around protecting local neighbourhood inhabitants from rival gangs; due to their fixed nature and their adherence to processes of regular escalation, they arguably provided a measure of predictability within an otherwise chaotic and highly insecure broader social context. In that sense, this new wave of gangs may be seen as continuing the original vigilante ethos of the first post-war generation, despite gang membership turnover due to gang members 'maturing out' between the ages of 19 and 22 (Rocha, 2000a; Rodgers, 2006a; 2007a).

Pandillas changed radically in nature around the turn of the century, however. In particular, they shifted from displaying solidarity with their local neighbourhood communities and offering localized forms of protection and social order to being much more parochial, predatory, and feared organizations. This shift was largely linked to the spread of cocaine in Nicaragua. The drug began to move through the country in substantial quantities from 1999 onwards,[19] and its consumption in the form of crack rapidly became a major element of gang culture. Although gang members in the early and mid-1990s did consume drugs, cocaine was practically unknown then, and they mainly smoked marijuana or sniffed glue.

Unlike those drugs, however, crack makes its users extremely aggressive, violent, and unpredictable; its consumption thus led to a rise in spontaneous, random attacks by addicted gang members looking to obtain money for their next fix. Contrary to the past, these gang members actively targeted local residents, generating a widespread and tangibly heightened sense of fear in urban neighbourhoods in Managua and other Nicaraguan cities, including Chinandega, Diriamba, and Estelí, starting from around 2000. In other words, crack consumption fundamentally changed the nature of the relationship between gangs and their local communities (Rocha, 2007a).

In some neighbourhoods, gang members integrated into the emergent Nicaraguan drug economy as street dealers, further increasing insecurity in those areas. For the most part, dealers worked independently, selling irregularly on street corners in their neighbourhood and sourcing their crack cocaine from one of a small number of neighbourhoods in the city, where it was being distributed initially by individuals on a rather ad hoc basis (Rodgers, 2010). Distributors were often ex-gang members who drew on their historical links to their local gang to enrol current members as their security apparatus. In these neighbourhoods, gang activities shifted from territorial protection to ensuring the proper functioning of the drug economy, which they achieved by collectively imposing local regimes of terror that went far beyond the more diffuse crack consumption-related violence. In order to reduce the risk of denunciation, these drug-dealing gangs created a climate of chronic fear by repeatedly threatening and committing arbitrary acts of violence against community inhabitants. At the same time, gang wars ceased because these would have impeded potential clients from coming to buy drugs (Rodgers, 2006a; 2007b; Rocha, 2007a).

Gangs from 2005 to the present

From the beginning of the 21st century—but most visibly around 2005—the number of pandillas in Nicaraguan cities began to decline, even disappearing completely in some neighbourhoods (Rocha, 2007a). The trend was attributable partly to the atomizing effect of crack consumption and partly to the emergence of more professional drug-dealing groups, often referred to as *cartelitos* (little cartels). These groups generally involved individuals from several different neighbourhoods, and even different parts of Nicaragua. Cartelitos imposed localized regimes of terror on the local communities in which they based their operations, brutally repressing local gangs to prevent them from becoming challengers.

This violence reached a peak around 2009–10, after which it eased up significantly as many cartelitos either fell apart due to internecine fighting or were taken over by rivals. Those that remained began to reduce their involvement in local drug dealing and refocused on drug trafficking, largely in the hopes of making much higher profits. Instead of dominating local communities, cartelito members began to minimize their visibility,

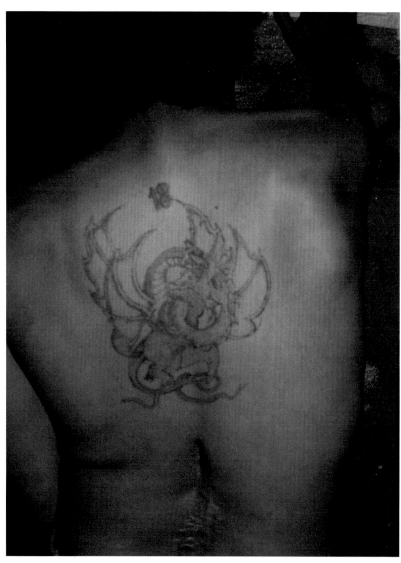

Former gang member showing his tattoo and the scar of a machete wound, Barrio Luis Fanor Hernández, Managua, July 2007.
© Dennis Rodgers

which led to improvements in local security in the urban neighbourhoods where they had previously operated. While drug dealing continues to be widespread in Nicaraguan cities, it has become much smaller in scale, disorganized, and more individualized, although those engaging in it are often gang members or ex-gang members.

Changes in urban policing in Nicaragua, 1990–2012

Changing forms of urban policing also transformed the panorama of Nicaraguan gang violence, particularly in Managua. During the early and mid-1990s, the police rarely entered poor urban neighbourhoods, largely in view of the fact that the violence there remained localized and tended not to spill over into richer areas, but also because gangs frequently out-gunned the police (Hernández, 2001). From the late 1990s until about 2005, however, the drug business led gang violence to spread throughout the city.

To contain this growth, the police began to implement what might be termed 'spectacular' policing, entering poor neighbourhoods in an arbitrary and intimidating manner, heavily armed and wearing riot gear, and more often than not specifically targeting youths (Rodgers, 2006b).[20] This approach led to a decline in gangs in some neighbourhoods, but increasing engagement with drug dealers in others. The police were initially confrontational but rapidly became accommodating, with some cartelitos even paying corrupt police officers to bust rival drug-dealing groups as they jostled for market domination.[21]

Predominant patterns of policing changed again around 2005, partly as a result of the institutionalization of corruption between some cartelitos and the police. In Managua, policing became more indirect in response to the conclusion of a range of urban infrastructural developments that isolated poor neighbourhoods; police now principally patrolled roads surrounding slums and poor neighbourhoods—rather than the poor areas themselves.[22]

Dynamics changed again as the ruling Sandinista National Liberation Front (FSLN) party co-opted gangs in a number of poor neighbourhoods from November 2008 onwards, actively hiring gang members to disrupt opposition marches and paint slogans around the city (Rocha, 2008, p. 28). The characteristic patrolling pattern in poor urban neighbourhoods consequently became rather desultory and non-interventionist perambulations by very lightly armed two-officer teams on a single motorcycle two or three times per day, except for Sundays. While this approach proved ineffective in terms of containing or managing violence, it permitted significant information gathering about local gangs to facilitate recruitment by FSLN activists.[23] A similar pattern pertains to the handful of new police substations set up in neighbourhoods that have been particularly notorious for their gang activity.

> Gangs feature in poor neighbourhoods, but not as much as previously.

The emergence of new actors?

Gangs continue to be a feature of many poor urban neighbourhoods in present-day Nicaragua, but not to the same degree as during the 1990s and the early years of the following decade. Yet, as detailed in the next section, there is evidence that a new generation of territorial gangs is emerging, as well as new armed actors. Media reports and recent high-profile drug-trafficking cases suggest that the cartelitos' monopoly over trafficking routes in Nicaragua are coming to an end, not least because Colombian and Mexican cartels may be encroaching upon them.[24]

In 2010, Nicaragua saw the first drug cartel execution-style killings, which were widely blamed on Mexican contract killers (Quintero, 2010a; 2010b). Towards the end of 2011 the Nicaraguan government deployed 1,000 soldiers into the Nicaraguan countryside (Stone, 2011). The troops were ostensibly meant to deal with gangs—even though gangs are a fundamentally urban phenomenon; their more likely goal was to address the increasing territorialization of drug-trafficking groups, which reportedly control large swathes of the Nicaraguan countryside in the northern Caribbean region (Romero, 2010). How this development might affect the potential re-emergence of gangs and the broader political economy of violence in Nicaragua remains to be seen.

COMPARING DIVERGENT GANG TRAJECTORIES

Barrios Elías Blanco (EB) and Luis Fanor Hernández (LFH) are both poor settlements located in south-east Managua. EB is part of a conglomerate of purpose-built low-income neighbourhoods, the first of which—Barrio de Pescadores— was constructed in 1963 to provide housing for a group of flood-displaced lakeside slum dwellers. A few years earlier, migrants from rural areas had established LFH as an illegal squatter community, one of many such informal settlements that mushroomed on the edge of Managua at that time. In view of its inhabitants' extreme poverty, the settlement came to be known as *La Sobrevivencia* (Survival),[25] but during the 1980s it benefitted from a Sandinista state housing development project and was renamed LFH.[26] EB continues to be very poor, but socio-economic conditions in LFH have improved significantly, albeit unequally, for reasons detailed below. In 2005, EB had a population of some 2,100, while LFH had approximately 3,000 inhabitants.[27]

EB and LFH have both long been notorious for their high levels of insecurity—and especially their gang activity. Taxi drivers will typically refuse to enter LFH, particularly at night, while EB is located in an area that the Nicaraguan National Police considers among the most dangerous in Managua due to its high concentration of pandillas.[28] Gangs in these two neighbourhoods, however, have experienced markedly different evolutionary trajectories over the past two decades. Although these may appear similar at first glance—given that both can be broken down into five distinct phases (see Table 3.1)—contextual differences between the two neighbourhoods led the gangs to develop in distinct ways, with critical consequences for their practices of violence as well as their broader social environment.

Table 3.1 **Pandilla evolutionary phases in two urban neighbourhoods**			
Phase	**Elías Blanco**	**Luis Fanor Hernández**	**Predominant form of violence associated with the pandillas**
Pre-institutional	1990-92	1989-92	Vigilantism; drunken fighting at bars; some individual crime and delinquency
Golden era	1993-99	1993-98	Gang warfare; both individual and group crime and delinquency
Atomization (EB) vs. drug dealing (LFH)	2000-04	1999-2005	EB: drug-fuelled individual crime and delinquency; personal vendettas LFH: collective violence to support local drug economy; drug-fuelled individual crime and delinquency; personal vendettas
Pacification	2005-09	2006-11	Low levels of individual crime and delinquency (mainly drug-fuelled); diminishing personal vendettas
Revival	2010-present	2012-present	Increasing individual crime and delinquency; renewed collective forms of gang violence, including gang warfare

Even if the gangs in the two neighbourhoods experienced similar initial phases—regardless of the small differences in timing—they underwent distinct third phases, with the EB gang going through a process of 'atomization' while the LFH gang delved into 'drug dealing'. The fourth phase—'pacification'—is common to the two gangs but underpinned by different actors in the two neighbourhoods; similarly, the current 'revival' is happening for different reasons in the two barrios. That said, the predominant forms of violence associated with the different evolutionary phases also reveal significant similarities between the gangs of each neighbourhood.

The pre-institutional phase

The first of the five evolutionary phases is called 'pre-institutional' because the gangs that emerged then did not display any structural continuity or autonomy, even if some gang members moved on to the next phase of gang development on an individual basis. During this initial period, gangs in EB and LFH generally came together more or less organically but often lasted only for a year or two. Their membership drew on particular peer and social groups rather than a spatially defined youth population. The first such gang emerged in EB in 1990 and remained active until 1992. Its members hailed from EB but also from other neighbourhoods in the vicinity. A similar type of gang emerged in LFH in 1989 and lasted until 1992.

During this period, many of the gang members in EB and LFH were demobilized Sandinista Popular Army conscripts.[29] These individuals systematically identified three basic reasons for joining a gang. First, the change of regime in 1990 had led to an abrupt reduction of their social status as conscripts, whereas 'defending the nation' had previously

Pandilleros simulating a fight, Barrio Carlos Fonseca Amador, Managua, September 2002. © José Luis Rocha

been held very high in their communities; becoming gang members thus offered a means of reaffirmation vis-à-vis a wider society that seemed to be forgetting them rapidly. Second, becoming gang members was a way for them to recapture some of the adrenaline-charged energy of war, while also reconstituting a comradeship and solidarity reminiscent of their wartime experience as conscripts. But perhaps most importantly, these young men saw becoming gang members as a natural continuation of their previous role as soldiers. The early 1990s were highly uncertain times, marked by political polarization, violence, and spiralling insecurity, and these youths felt they could better 'serve' their families and friends by joining a gang than attempting to 'protect' them as individuals (Rodgers, 2006a, pp. 283–84).

Pre-institutional gangs tended to be relatively small, generally comprising no more than a dozen members. Most were between 18 and 22 years old, although the LFH gang also involved a few younger members who took on mascot-like roles. Most of the violence of these first gangs, whether in EB or LFH, was vigilante in nature and involved beating up individuals who had robbed, attacked, or threatened the friends or family of gang members. This brutality occurred principally in the gangs' local neighbourhoods, but they also rapidly began to fight other gangs at popular local nightclubs and bars on Friday and Saturday nights, for reasons unrelated to their vigilante ethos but rather tied to drinking and macho posturing. These fights generally only involved fists but could also escalate to include knives and broken bottles; firearms were used occasionally, although their role in such brawls often became mythologized. Many gang members also began to engage in crime and delinquency on an individual basis or in small groups of two or three, but they generally tended to do so outside their neighbourhood, to avoid being recognized.

The golden era[30]

By the mid-1990s, a persistent and full-blown territorial gang culture had developed in both EB and LFH, significantly changing predominant patterns of gang violence. In particular, gangs became exclusively associated with a specific urban neighbourhood and began to engage regularly in forms of gang warfare that aimed to extend or defend their territory. Although this activity often had highly deleterious consequences for residents, it generally involved an ordered, predictable logic. The first battle of a gang war typically featured fighting with fists and stones, but each new battle involved an escalation of weaponry, first to sticks, then to knives and broken bottles, and eventually to home-made mortars, guns, and AK-47s.

> Gangs provided an 'early warning system' that was recognized and appreciated by local inhabitants.

Although the rate of escalation varied, the sequence did not—that is, gangs did not begin their wars with firearms (Rodgers, 2006a, p. 276). The fixed nature of gang warfare acted as a restraining mechanism, with each stage of the escalation process calling for greater but definite intensity of action, while always remaining under the actors' control. It also provided an 'early warning system' for local neighbourhood inhabitants, thereby offering them a means of circumscribing what Hannah Arendt called the 'all-pervading unpredictability' of violence (Arendt, 1969, p. 5).

This function was widely recognized and appreciated by local inhabitants, who frequently talked approvingly about their local gang. They often provided assistance to gang members, for example by hiding them if the police chased them into the neighbourhood because of their delinquent activities. Gang members returned the favour by going out of their way to protect residents of their local neighbourhood, especially if they were threatened by outsiders. They also frequently provided free bodyguard services and generally watched out for people's property. Gang members in LFH declared that the motivation behind such practices was that they wanted to show their 'love' (*querer* in the Nicaraguan vernacular) for their local neighbourhood. As a gang member named Miguel claimed, 'We show our love for the neighbourhood by fighting other gangs.'[31] One of his peers, Julio, concurred:

You show the neighbourhood that you love it by putting yourself in danger for people, by protecting them from other gangs [. . .]. You look after the neighbourhood in that way, you help them, keep them safe.[32]

As Zygmunt Bauman has contended, 'in an ever more insecure and uncertain world the withdrawal into the safe haven of territoriality is an intense temptation' (Bauman, 1998, p. 117). He argues that 'the defence of the territory—the 'safe home'—becomes the pass-key to all doors which one feels must be locked to stave off the [. . .] threat to spiritual and material comfort' (p. 117). This 'pass-key' was critical to underpinning gang culture institutionally, as it moved from being based on peer groups to being based on territory. Gangs thus developed a certain structural autonomy, which was subsequently consolidated through conflict, independent of individual membership. As a result, the gangs of the golden era were also larger and more organized than their predecessors. In EB, the gang mobilized between 40 and 80 gang members, while the LFH gang had about 100 members. The overwhelming majority of members were new recruits, although a small number of individuals remained from the previous phase in both neighbourhoods, often as leaders.

Atomization vs. drug dealing

The spread of crack cocaine fundamentally changed the nature of the gangs.

Gang dynamics in both EB and LFH changed dramatically around 1999–2000. In both cases, the spread of crack cocaine fundamentally changed the nature of the gangs, which shifted from displaying a sense of social solidarity with the local community to becoming more exclusive and predatory organizations. This was partly due to the fact that gang members became crack consumers, many to the point of full-blown addiction. Users became aggressive and unpredictable, and regularly attacked, stole from, burgled, and threatened local neighbourhood inhabitants in order to secure their next fix. This behaviour significantly increased insecurity in both EB and LFH, leading to a breakdown of the gangs' relationships with their respective local communities. In LFH, levels of insecurity deteriorated even further as the gang became involved in drug dealing.

Although drug dealing became a feature of many neighbourhoods in Managua after 2000, it was generally a small-scale business that a few individual gang members carried out in an ad hoc manner. This was the case in EB, for example. In contrast, LFH was one of a small number of neighbourhoods through which cocaine arrived into the city (from Nicaragua's Caribbean coast) and from which it was then distributed.[33] The trade's impact on the way LFH gang members became involved in drug dealing was significant. In particular—and in contrast to EB—they did so as part of a highly organized drug economy that not only integrated them as individual street dealers, but also collectively, as a security infrastructure. The gang as a group enforced contracts and guarded drug shipments whenever they entered or left the neighbourhood; more generally, gang members engaged in a campaign of terror to intimidate local inhabitants, not only to prevent denunciations, but also to ensure that drug dealing could occur unimpeded. In doing so, the gang violently underpinned a process of localized capital accumulation that enabled a small group of drug dealers to flourish in an otherwise impoverished environment with few economic opportunities, while also generating significant insecurity for local neighbourhood inhabitants (Rodgers, 2007c; 2009; 2010).

The changing patterns of gang violence in EB and LFH also affected the gangs structurally; for one, their membership became older. In the 1990s, gang members in both neighbourhoods had been as young as 7 but rarely older than 22; by the beginning of the next decade, however, their age range had risen to 16–25, although it should be noted that the majority had been gang members in the previous phase. In part, this trend towards older gang membership reflected the growing role of crack consumption, as younger consumers suffered more from the drug's effects and were therefore unable to 'keep up' with the gang. In the case of LFH, the trend also took hold since it was function-ally necessary to be of a certain size and strength to be an effective street dealer.

The EB and LFH gangs also reduced significantly in size, to about 15–20 members. In EB, this downsizing was principally a consequence of crack consumption, which is generally a solitary activity. From around 2000 onwards, gang members began to hang out less and less together as a group and internecine fights became increasingly com-mon. These clashes were often organized around individual vendettas, or *traidos,* which stood in stark contrast to the collective conflicts of the 1990s (Rocha, 2005). In LFH, the gang's reduction in size also occurred mainly for func-tional reasons, even though many who had been gang members in the mid- and late 1990s also said that they left the gang because they no longer identified with its new predatory ethos (Rodgers, 2007b). The fact that the LFH gang became the security apparatus of the emergent drug trade meant that it needed to be a well-coordinated and tight-knit group, which its previous incarnation as a fluid group of approximately 100 members would not have been able to be. This difference was critical, which is why this phase of the EB gang's evolutionary development is called 'atomization' and that of the LFH gang 'drug dealing'.

Pacification

Starting in 2005, the gang's atomization in EB gave way to a process of 'pacification', whereby the pandilla was increasingly controlled and regulated. This shift reflected generally changing forms of policing in Managua, and more specifically an increased police presence in EB due to the establishment of a police substation in a nearby neighbour-hood. The pacification was also spurred by a rise in NGO and civil society interventions. The Centro de Prevención de la Violencia (Centre for the Prevention of Violence), for instance, developed a series of initiatives. It arranged for regular visits by psychologists to gang member families; organized workshops for gang members on practical issues, such as how to seek and secure employment; and created an association of gang member 'peace leaders', whose aim was to retain the social dynamism of the gang but move it towards more positive forms of collective action (Bellanger, 2006).[34]

These interventions significantly reduced gang violence in EB between 2005 and 2009, and gang members restricted themselves to petty and generally individualized criminality. But NGO initiatives came to an abrupt end when inter-national funding to Nicaragua suffered significant cuts following government-imposed restrictions on its distribution. By the end of 2009, most NGOs and civil society organizations had ceased operating in EB. Combined with a decreas-ing law enforcement presence due to further changes in police patrolling patterns, these cuts brought an end to the process of gang pacification in the neighbourhood.

The LFH gang underwent a pacification phase starting in 2006. Although it may seem similar to that experienced by the EB gang, this phase actually occurred for very different reasons, and in a distinct manner. In EB, external actors—namely the police, NGOs, and civil society organizations—were the key factors in the gang's pacification. In contrast, the LFH process was associated with an internal actor that emerged from the local drug trade.

Drug sales had initially been organized in an informal manner around a single individual known as el Indio Viejo (the Old Indian). He had been a member of the first neighbourhood gang and had originally drawn on a network of both former and current gang members in order to run his drug dealing business (Rodgers, 2010). Over time he began to professionalize and became more selective in picking his partners. By 2005, he was leading a shadowy group involving both youths and adults, not all of whom had gang experience and not all of whom came from LFH, although their main base remained in the neighbourhood. This group was locally referred to as the *cartelito,* or 'little cartel'.

Gang members restricted themselves to petty and generally individualized criminality.

In response to the gang members' increasing crack consumption, concomitant unreliability, and amateur nature, the cartelito rapidly began to develop its own security infrastructure. In doing so, it clashed with the LFH gang. The pandilla was no match for the cartelito, which was both better armed and more professional (members of the cartelito did not consume the drugs they sold, for example). The pandilla also grew weaker as a number of its older members retired, and two other members quit to join the cartelito. In 2006, after a series of violent confrontations that led several gang members to be critically injured and one killed, the pandilla effectively ceased to exist as a collective unit. Although youths still hung out individually in the neighbourhood streets and consumed crack, local inhabitants generally identified them as *chavalos vagos* (delinquent youths) rather than *pandilleros* (gang members). Personal conflicts, or traidos, persisted between individuals and were the principal vectors of violence associated with former gang members, beyond minor individualized crime and delinquency.

After breaking up the gang, the cartelito sought to consolidate its domination of LFH and to expand its operations beyond the neighbourhood. Paradoxically, levels of post-cold war insecurity in LFH reached their peak in 2007–10, when the pandilla was no longer operating. During this period, armed individuals associated with the cartelito randomly patrolled the neighbourhood on motorbikes, arbitrarily intimidating local residents—'to train us', as one inhabitant called Doña Yolanda put it.[35] In particular, they violently prevented local youths from congregating on street corners to keep them from coalescing into a gang that might eventually challenge the cartelito. As it professionalized, the cartelito also fought against equivalent organizations in Managua and beyond, largely to secure an increased share in the drug market. Shoot-outs in and around the neighbourhood became common occurrences, although the cartelito sometimes employed the police as a proxy, particularly against other drug-dealing groups.

Current teen gangs are involved in a variety of petty criminal activity.

Revival

By 2009 the LFH cartelito had begun to reduce its involvement in local drug-dealing activities, refocusing instead on drug trafficking, partly because it was much more lucrative. Moreover, law enforcement personnel had arrested el Indio Viejo, who subsequently blamed the visibility of drug dealing for his arrest and decided to change tactics following his release. As a consequence, local violence dynamics underwent a major transformation. The cartelito no longer sought territorial control in order to manage sales, but generally avoided attracting attention, using the neighbourhood only as a residence and transit point. Nevertheless, el Indio Viejo was arrested again in 2011, along with a number of other members of the cartelito. A rival whose group had developed close links to certain members of the Nicaraguan government was reportedly able to supersede the bribes that el Indio Viejo had regularly paid the police to be left alone. What remained of the cartelito subsequently reorganized in a much reduced manner around his number two, who was also an ex-gang member from the first post-war generation and was known as 'Pac-Man' (due to his voracious appetite).

These developments radically improved the local security situation in LFH. Around 2010, a group of 4–6 youths who had previously been pandilla members, and who were all crack addicts, emerged as the main source of local violence. They would sit together at a nearby pedestrian bridge, waiting to mug passers-by; they generally did not bother local inhabitants and were mostly active at night. In mid-2012, however, about a dozen 14–15-year-olds came together as a new gang, hence the label 'revival' for this phase. They hang out together as a group on LFH street corners, effectively occupying the sociological vacuum left by the cartelito's withdrawal (and the prior disappearance of the earlier pandilla). These teens are involved in a variety of petty criminal activities, although they sometimes act collectively. In July 2012, for example, this new gang attacked the gang in a nearby neighbourhood. Although they were repelled with several members injured, two of them critically, this instance of collective violence by the group signalled the beginning of a new cycle of gang warfare.

EB witnessed a similar gang revival phase, although it started earlier, around the beginning of 2010. On the one hand, it coincided with the decline in NGO and civil society organization interventions in the neighbourhood. On the other hand, it also followed a process of politicization of the local pandilla that had begun in 2008 and whereby the ruling FSLN party regularly hired both active and retired EB gang members—whom they provided with ammunition, transportation, and immunity—to disrupt opposition marches 'spontaneously' (Rocha, 2008). As a result, a new generation of EB gang members, along with some previous members, began to hang out together as a group, and were regularly contracted by the FSLN. Although this process of instrumental politicization is not solely responsible for the revival, it played an important role in connecting individuals who had been gang members from about 2005 to 2010 with a new generation of 14–16-year-old youths; by providing a common group activity, it also helped the gang reoccupy the sociological space from which it had withdrawn during the pacification phase.

GANGS AND GUNS

Although not all gangs are necessarily associated with gun violence, it is often claimed that the widespread availability of firearms increases the likelihood of their use by gang members (Yablonsky, 1997, p. 5). In many ways, this connection is not surprising; as Hannah Arendt famously pointed out, violence 'always needs *implements*' (Arendt, 1969, p. 4). That said, the evolutionary trajectories of the pandillas in EB and LFH display distinct shifts and fluctuations in their levels of violence and use of firearms. In general terms, gun use by gang members increased steadily during the 1990s, but then declined in EB during the following decade and in LFH from about 2005; by about 2008, something of a revival had begun, marked by a critical change in the types of firearm used. At first glance this trend would seem to correspond closely to that of the EB and LFH gangs' institutional evolutions, but closer analysis reveals that it was less determined by the gangs' institutionalization than by a mixture of general and specific contextual factors, including the gangs' changing practices of violence; the variable availability of different types of firearm; the intervention of other violent actors; and evolving knowledge about firearm use.

> 'Violence always needs *implements*.'
>
> –Hannah Arendt

Patterns of weapon use

Gang members in EB and LFH have used a wide range of weapons over the past 25 years. These have included a variety of manufactured firearms, such as pistols and revolvers (Makarov and Tokarev TT, Smith & Wesson, Taurus, and Glock), shotguns (both break- and pump-action), assault rifles (AK-47s), submachine guns (Thompson and Uzi), and military weapons such as grenades. They have also used home-made weapons—mainly mortars, but also pistols and pump-action shotguns. There are no rules governing firearm ownership in either the EB or the LFH gangs, however. As one LFH pandilla member called Mayuyu put it, 'here any old cat can wander around with a gun'.[36] Gang members' weapons are also generally their individual property, in both EB and LFH.[37]

By all accounts, manufactured firearms were more common in the 1990s than during the following decade, while the opposite trend applies to home-made weapons, which are now the principal type of firearm associated with pandillas. The types of manufactured firearms and military weapons that were more common during the 1990s were Makarov and Tokarev TT pistols as well as AK-47s and grenades, most of which were leftover weapons from the 1980s war against the Contras. An exception to the general trend is the home-made mortar, which has been a staple gang weapon in Nicaragua since the early 1990s.

The functionality of guns

As an EB gang member called el Revoliático asserted, 'The gang with the most powerful weapons is usually the one that wins.'[38] Indeed, firearms and military weapons such as mortars and grenades constitute the pinnacle of gang members' armoury in Nicaragua. At the same time, it is often claimed that youths 'typically seek guns for the status they confer, rather than as inputs into a crime production function' (Cook et al., 2007, p. F562). In this respect, even if small arms can clearly bestow a certain aura of power to individual gang members in both EB and LFH—while some weapons can increase the collective prestige of an entire gang—gun ownership by gang members in Nicaragua is primarily functional. Gang members in EB and LFH acquired and used firearms first and foremost in order to better carry out criminal and delinquent activities, as is highlighted in Box 3.1, which details the guns acquired by Milton, an LFH gang member who was active in the early and mid-1990s.[39]

Although firearms played a significant role in gang members' individual delinquency in EB and LFH right from the re-emergence of gangs in the early 1990s, they only became a major feature of collective gang warfare during the mid-1990s. This is particularly true of the AK-47, which served as one of the primary firearms of the Sandinista Popular Army in the 1980s; the revolutionary regime also distributed many of these assault rifles among the general population to prepare against a potential US invasion. Following the end of the Contra war, 142,000 small arms were destroyed between 1991 and 1993 in Nicaragua (Small Arms Survey, 2002, p. 74). Many AK-47s were destroyed during that period, but many more remained in circulation and found their way into the hands of gang members. They initially used them mainly in their criminal and delinquent activities during the early 1990s, before expanding their usage to gang warfare during the mid-1990s.[40] In particular, AK-47s often constituted the most common means by which a gang war's escalation process reached its final point of intensification.

Box 3.1   Milton's guns

My first firearm was a Makarov handgun, which I got from a retired policeman in 1991. I'd just started mugging, and he came to find me one day, and said, 'I hear that you're a quick-thinking kind of guy, and I wondered whether you didn't want to rent a gun. It would make your business much easier, you know.' I asked him what he wanted in return, and he told me 50 per cent of whatever I made. I thought about it, and said, 'Sure, let's see how it works out.' So he taught me how to use it–how to take off the security, how to maintain it, oil it, take it apart, and put it together again–and then he'd give it me loaded with ten shots every time I decided to go out on *bisnes*.

It worked well, and so a couple of years later I bought my own gun, from a guy in another barrio, for NIO 300 [USD 50], which was a lot of money at the time. A cousin of mine who lives there put us in touch with each other. It was a .22 revolver. I did all sorts of shit with that one.

One time I went to a party with my mate Lencho, and there was a guy there wearing the new Nike trainers–well, you know, new at the time. Lencho saw them, and said, 'Fuck, I'd love to have those,' and so I said to him, 'No worries, *maje*, I'm going to give them to you as a present.' Lencho was a good mate, always willing to help me whenever I asked him, so I wanted to do him a good turn. I waited until the guy with the shoes left and followed him out, and then I pulled the gun on him in a side street and told him to give me the shoes. He also had 20 dollars on him, which was a bonus, so we were able to go and get completely wasted afterwards [. . .].

I had to sell that gun cheaply when my first son was born, in 1995, because I needed money to buy milk and other stuff for the baby [. . .]. I thought about buying a new one, but Lencho had acquired a TT handgun, which he would lend me no problem, although that was the gun that jammed on me, and because of that I got caught while mugging an old lady and spent a few weeks in jail in 1997.

After that I left the gang, and I went to Costa Rica for a few years and worked picking coffee. When I came back the gang had changed, so I no longer hung out with it, and I set up my food business, which keeps me busy, and for which I don't need a gun.

Source: Dennis Rodgers interview with Milton, LFH, 17 July 2012; authors' translation

Starting around 2000, gang members in both EB and LFH diminished their use of AK-47s as well as surplus 1980s military weapons such as grenades. They stopped using grenades because they were not reusable weapons and their supply was finite. The decline of AK-47s, however, came about because many of them ceased to function, even though the assault rifle is one of the most durable ever made. According to Bismarck, who had been a member of the first LFH gang in the early 1990s, 'They're old weapons, from the [Contra] war, and also gang members today don't know how to care for them, so they break down.'[41] Gang members in EB echoed this sentiment, including with reference to other firearms from the 1980s, such as Makarov pistols. As summarized by El Cofla, an EB gang member: 'The firearms we always avoid using are Makarov pistols, those with the magazines, because they fuck up too much [. . .]. They jam, and the bullet stays inside [. . .]. There's only old Makarovs left.'[42] Milton in LFH also suggested that the decline in the use of AK-47s was due to the fact that many gang members became crack addicts around 2000–02 and sold their AKs to buy drugs because they were weapons for which they could get a good price.[43]

The impact of other armed actors

Between 2000 and 2005, gang members in both EB and LFH continued to employ other firearms, including new ones such as Taurus and Smith & Wesson pistols, as well as break- and pump-action shotguns. Indeed, these were used more often and were much more visible than previously, not only because crack consumption bred more intense violence, but also, in the case of the LFH gang, because of its developing role as the security apparatus of the then emergent drug trade. Local drug dealers, and particularly el Indio Viejo, often sold such guns to LFH gang members.

From about 2005 onwards, however, gang members in EB and LFH began to use firearms much less frequently. In EB, NGO, civil society, and police pacifying interventions generally reduced gang activity. In LFH, another armed entity significantly influenced the gang, namely the cartelito. This critical difference between the EB and LFH gangs was starkly reflected in the evolving political economy of weapons in the two neighbourhoods. AK-47s were the only type of assault rifles ever mentioned by gang members in EB. They were the most common firearm in LFH and, as in EB, became less common around 2000. Starting around 2005, the rise of the cartelito led to the emergence of new firearms. A gang member known as Mayuyu recalled: 'One guy in the cartelito, Mungo, has an Uzi submachine gun, which el Indio Viejo got for him through his Colombian contacts a few years ago.'[44]

Mungo, a former LFH gang member, was one of a small number who joined the cartelito in 2005. He served as one of the cartelito's main 'enforcers' when they violently broke up the LFH gang. Having access to firearms such as Uzis was one reason Mungo and others were able to do so with relative ease. Although most of the LFH gang members were armed with pistols and revolvers at the time, they were no match for Uzis. Between 2006 and 2010, Mungo and other members of the cartelito patrolled the neighbourhood and dispersed any group of youths known to be associated with the gang, generally by shooting to scare them, while also killing one gang member in 2006. After successfully breaking up the pandilla, Mungo and others then systematically confiscated weapons from LFH youths, generally violently. Not surprisingly, perhaps, it is around this time that home-made guns, known as *armas hechizas,* began to emerge in significant quantities in LFH. Their use also increased in EB during this period, primarily because these were the only firearms that EB gang members could get their hands on and knew how to use at the time.

Home-made weapons

Nicaraguan gang members have long used home-made weapons. This is particularly true of home-made mortars (*morteros caseros*), which were a ubiquitous feature of gang warfare during the golden era, but which are also used at political demonstrations and sometimes fired at New Year's parties. They consist of a metal tube—usually a piece of water

Nicaraguan gang members have long used home-made weapons.

piping—that is sealed at one end and to which two handles are welded (see Figure 3.2). They can shoot either a double powder load, with the first providing the propulsion, and the second exploding a few seconds later, or a single powder load, to propel small stones, nails, bits of glass, or—and this was a particularly popular variant in LFH during the 1990s—cut-up rubber sandals (*chinelas*), the pieces of which would then start melting on expulsion, burning anyone they hit.

Many gang members make their own mortars, paying a local metalwork shop NIO 50–60 (USD 4–5) to allow them to use their soldering tools; others buy their mortars from the La Caimana firework company, where they also purchase the powder loads. The price of a mortar was NIO 150–200 during the mid-1990s, and NIO 250–300 during the following decade (due to exchange rate inflation, both price ranges remained approximately equivalent to USD 15–20).

The other home-made firearms used by gang members are shotguns and pistols (see Figure 3.3). Shotguns, or *chimbas*, fire manufactured bullets, generally either .38 or .22 calibre, but also AK-47 7.62×39 mm cartridges and 12- or 16-gauge shotgun shells. These weapons are more complicated to make than mortars. Daimaku, who was a gang member in EB around 2008–10, described how to make a particular type of home-made pistol known as a Xica da Silva:

> *The name comes from a Brazilian soap on TV that was called Xica da Silva, where people used a particular kind of gun, quite long, and since that's the way those we make are, too, that's the name. These guns shoot AK, Makarov, and .38-calibre bullets, but we make them in an artisanal manner [. . .]. What you do is you take two tubes and attach one to the handle, while the other one is hollow. To this one, you then weld two ringlets on the sides, to hold down the slingshot. After that, you get a pin, which you sharpen on a whetstone, to get a very fine point, and you attach it to the slingshot, and then you get the bullet, which you put in the tube. You adjust the pin, you check the slingshot, and then you let go of the pin and it detonates the bullet.*[45]

Figure 3.2 **A home-made mortar being shot**

© Dennis Rodgers

Figure 3.3 **A home-made shotgun (chimba) and a home-made pistol (Xica da Silva)**

© José Luis Rocha

Compared to manufactured firearms, home-made weapons are quite inaccurate and take more time to reload, which is highly problematic in conflict situations. But perhaps the single biggest issue with home-made guns is that they are prone to malfunction. An LFH gang member called Felix commented:

> Home-made guns are improvised, makeshift weapons. [They're] dangerous because these guns are not made with any degree of precision, so if the calibre is not appropriate to the size of the piping, then it blows up, and this happens a lot.[46]

Not surprisingly, perhaps, hand injuries from exploding hand-made guns became very common among gang members in both EB and LFH around 2007–10.[47] Having said this, as Julio, an LFH gang member, noted: 'A home-made gun breaks down a lot, but it's also easier to fix than a real gun'[48]—which was potentially a major advantage over manufactured guns, as gang members could mend defective home-made weapons themselves. Whereas many gang members produced mortars, only a few actually made their own home-made pistols or shotguns from scratch, however, and the rest bought their home-made firearms from, or had them mended by, these or gang members in other neighbourhoods. Charola, who was an LFH gang member, bought his home-made shotgun from another neighbourhood gang member for NIO 350 (USD 21) in 2006, while in EB prices reportedly oscillated between NIO 250 and 500 (USD 10–22) in 2012.

Weapon sources and prices

Prior to the mid-1970s, gang members' access to firearms was limited, and so they were rarely used. Gun use increased with the intensification of the FSLN-led insurrection during the second half of the 1970s, although it is unclear whether this increase was due to the greater availability of weapons as a result of the insurrection or the fact that many gang members joined the FSLN (Rocha, 2006b, p. 25). The Contra war of the 1980s, however, had a clear and direct impact on gangs and, more specifically, on their use of firearms. As described above, many of the first-generation gang members in both EB and LFH were youths who had served in the military. Almost all of them brought a range of weapons back with them, including Makarov and Tokarev TT pistols, AK-47s, and grenades. Picapollo, a member of the first gang that emerged in EB in 1990 and who became a leader of the gang in the mid-1990s, recalled in an interview:

> I stole [two AK-47s] from the battalion I did my military service with, but then everybody was doing it—some guys were even robbing grenades and bazookas! Don't ask me how we got it all out, but we did [. . .]. That's why all the gangs had that kind of shit then.[49]

The practice extended beyond the gang, and many gang members who had not served in the military also had access to such weapons through relatives who had been conscripted.

The proliferation of such weapons in the early 1990s is one reason why the post-conflict gangs in EB and LFH were more violent than their historical predecessors. But the post-war flood of small arms was a one-off event, with only short-term impacts. While Table 3.2 must be taken as indicative rather than comprehensive, it shows a definite trend away from war weapons after the 1990s, and a gradual turn to newer firearms. This shift was partly due to the fact that older weapons broke down, were lost, or were confiscated.

At the same time, gang members reported that newer weapons were more difficult to obtain. In LFH, this lack of availability coincided with the rise of the cartelito, which actively impeded gang members from obtaining firearms. Having said this, the most common sources of weaponry for gang members, across all epochs but particularly in the 1990s, were other gang members, whether in the same neighbourhood or elsewhere. Most of them had, at least initially,

Prior to the mid-1970s, gang members' access to firearms was limited.

Table 3.2 Types, prices, and sources of manufactured firearms in LFH, 1990–2012

Period	Type of weapon	Price	Source	Status
Early 1990s	.38 Smith & Wesson	Unknown	Private security guard (friend of brother-in-law)	Given to another gang member
	Makarov pistol	Rented for 50% of profits of delinquency	Retired policeman	Policeman took it back
	.22 Smith & Wesson	NIO 300 (USD 50)	Gang member from another barrio (friend of a friend)	Sold for NIO 700 (USD 75) in 1995
	Tokarev TT pistol	Not applicable	Brought back from military service by brother	Broke down and then was lost
	AK-47 assault rifle	Not applicable	Brought back from military service by brother	Sold for USD 350 in 2000
Mid-1990s	Makarov pistol	NIO 800 (USD 90)	Older gang member from neighbourhood	Confiscated by police when caught committing a robbery
	Tokarev TT pistol	Not applicable	Stolen from policeman	Lost during botched mugging
	.22 Smith & Wesson	Unknown	Bought from retired army personnel living in neighbourhood	Sold for NIO 700 (USD 75) in 1995
	AK-47 assault rifle	Not applicable	Brought back from military service by father	Stolen from home

been selling weapons that they or a relative had brought back from the army. Such stockpiles were obviously finite, and the supply gradually dwindled.

Over time, gang members thus turned to different firearms suppliers. They particularly reported that, starting around 2005, private security guards became a major source of both firearms and ammunition. Certainly, private security has boomed in Nicaragua over the past decade and a half. In 1995, the country only had eight private security companies, but the number increased to 56 by 2003 and to 98 by 2009. The number of armed private security guards similarly increased from some 9,000 in 2003 to almost 20,000 in 2009—compared to 9,630 police officers in this same year (Silva, 2003; PNUD, 2011, pp. 55–68). Many gang members in both EB and LFH reported stealing guns from private security guards, including shotguns (*escopetas*), the guards' primary weapons. Several gang members in LFH also described buying both weapons and ammunition from private security guards whom they knew, either because these lived in the neighbourhood or, in one case, because the guard was employed at the gang member's workplace.[50]

Table 3.2 **Cont.**				
Period	**Type of weapon**	**Price**	**Source**	**Status**
Late 1990s–2003	Thompson submachine gun	NIO 3,000 (USD 250)	Unknown	Attempted to sell it to local drug dealer (el Indio Viejo), who refused to buy it
	.22	NIO 2,500 (USD 195)	Gang member in other neighbourhood (friend of a friend)	Unknown
	Taurus Special	NIO 5,000 (USD 360)	Local drug dealer (el Indio Viejo)	Still in possession of gang member
	9 mm Smith & Wesson	NIO 4,500 (USD 320)	Gang member from another barrio (cousin)	Sold for NIO 7,500 (USD 465) in 2004
2004–09	.38	NIO 3,500 (USD 170) in 2009	Unknown	Given to another gang member in another neighbourhood (cousin)
	9 mm Taurus	NIO 7,000 (USD 330)	Gang member from another barrio (friend of a friend)	Still in possession of gang member
	.38 Smith & Wesson	NIO 4,000 (USD 190)	Gang member from another barrio (friend of a friend)	Still in possession of gang member
	Shotgun	Not applicable	Stolen from private security guard	Still in possession of gang member
	.40 Glock	USD 150	Son of an army officer	Still in possession of gang member
2010–present	.38 Taurus	NIO 3,000 (USD 125)	Police officer (brother of a work colleague)	Still in possession of gang member

A number of gang members in both EB and LFH also claimed that corrupt police officers began to resell weapons that they had confiscated from gang members or drug dealers around the beginning of the pacification phase in 2005. With one exception, however, none of the gang members interviewed had actually bought a weapon this way. On the other hand, according to Daimaku in EB, the police and the army became major sources of ammunition around this time:

> We buy bullets illegally, we know which bróderes have connections to the police or the army, and we can buy however many we want from them, normally for NIO 2–3 [USD 0.10–0.15] per bullet, whether for an AK-47 or a .22. We also buy [shells] for our shotguns, but these are more expensive, like NIO 10 [USD 0.45] per [shell].[51]

This type of interaction probably reflects the fact that a number of police officers lived in EB and had ties of kinship or friendship to gang members. A gang member known as el Pelón described the situation:

Police officers live here, and they're cool with us. They only ask that we respect them, and if we're fighting with another gang, they don't intervene or call other police officers. They even sell us bullets for our guns, sometimes even giving them to us for free! [52]

By all accounts, gang members in EB and LFH found it relatively easy to source ammunition in the 1990s, as there were major stockpiles left over from the war, many of which were not controlled properly. It only took a few informal inquiries in most of Managua's markets to be able to find individuals who were selling all sorts of different calibre bullets and slugs in the mid-1990s. During the late 1990s, however, those with guns began to source their ammunition differently, through connections. Jader, in LFH, explained that he had sourced his ammunition at a local market for a number of years but that, by 2012, he had had to develop a different approach:

Now I buy from the guy who has the billiards hall in the next neighbourhood. He's got the same gun as me, but legally, and so he can buy bullets in proper shops, and he then sells me a case or two on the side whenever I want, but he doesn't sell them cheaply. [53]

Another LFH gang member called Spencer explained that licensed firearms shops would also sell ammunition illegally, but usually at a high mark-up: 'Normally a bullet costs between NIO 3 and 12 [USD 0.15–0.60] legally, but if you buy them illegally, it's at least NIO 20 [USD 0.95] a bullet.' [54]

Price inflation is by no means unusual (ILLICIT MARKET PRICES); 'substantial transaction costs' often exist in underground gun markets, including 'large mark-ups over legal prices, substantial search times, uncertainty about product quality, and [. . .] physical risk[s] associated with exchange' (Cook et al., 2007, p. F561). These costs can vary across different contexts, although neither EB nor LFH witnessed significant price increases or decreases. The prices reported in Table 3.2, however, are higher than those recorded in a study on average underground market prices carried out in 2009 by the Nicaraguan Institute for Strategic Studies and Public Policy. That study finds that a 9 mm automatic pistol cost NIO 2,000–2,500 (USD 95–120), a 12- or 16-gauge shotgun around NIO 4,000 (USD 190), an AK-47 about NIO 4,500–5,000 (USD 215–240), and an Uzi submachine gun roughly NIO 9,000 (USD 430) (Tórrez González, 2010). Having said this, weapon prices fluctuated significantly, even within phases, and were only partly determined by the source of the weapon. Similarly, the resale price clearly varies tremendously.

Knowledge and training

The use of firearms requires some specialized knowledge. The first gang members in EB and LFH either obtained this knowledge directly during their military service or were taught by somebody who had done so, whether gang members or others. Bismarck, who had no military experience, described the learning process: 'We were taught how to use firearms by the gang members who had done their military service [. . .]. They showed us how to load guns, how to shoot them, how to strip and clean them.' [55] Most of the members of the first LFH gang matured out by 1992, but Bismarck and Milton, who were younger, made the transition to the next gang; as a result, they were critical for the transmission of this specialized knowledge. This was also the case in EB, where a gang member called Picapollo played a similar role.

Although the transmission of this specialized knowledge continued across successive generations of gang members, there was something of a 'Chinese whispers' effect in both EB and LFH as the temporal distance from the generation that had had professional training increased. The fact that the knowledge had been diluted over time became particularly apparent by the late 1990s, with the number of accidents involving manufactured firearms soaring in both EB and LFH. [56]

As Bismarck explained in an interview in 2002, in LFH the accidents were linked to an increasing number of defective weapons, largely due to improper or deficient care. He also confirmed that gang members did not always understand how to use their weapons and thus often unintentionally shot themselves or others. In his words: 'Gang members nowadays don't take proper care of their weapons, so they're breaking down all the time, sometimes even blowing up in their face.' He went on to discuss the case of a young gang member who had recently shot himself in the foot:

> He had no idea what he was doing. He'd got this pistol, and thought that made him a poderoso (big man), but you know, you've got to know how to use a gun to be able to do something with it. He shot himself because he put it in his belt without the security turned on [. . .]. The problem was that he hadn't had proper training, because there's nobody left in the gang who really knows, and so he'd only half understood things, or hadn't been told properly, and that's why he shot himself.[57]

A critical difference between EB and LFH—and one of the reasons why the gang in the latter was more violent than that in the former after 2000—was that LFH saw a renewal of gang member knowledge about the use of firearms. This was due to a single individual, an ex-gang member from the mid-1990s called Jhon, who had spent five years in the Nicaraguan Army and had been extensively trained in a variety of weapons systems. He had joined the neighbourhood gang in 1994 at the age of 13 but was sent to the Army by his family in 1997 because they could no longer cope with him and hoped that it would educate him. After he returned to the neighbourhood in 2002, Jhon's expertise in weapons became crucial to raising the level of knowledge within the LFH gang about how to use guns safely and with more strategic effect (see Box 3.2). This was the primary reason why the LFH gang became one of the most feared in the district during this period, as it was one of the most effective in its deployment of violence.

Interviews with gang members confirm that, once Jhon retired from the gang in 2004, knowledge acquisition about guns in LFH lost focus once again. Some gang members subsequently reported learning informally from a better-informed peer, while others claimed to have been taught by professional criminals; in both cases, however, training was very informal and often off the cuff.

Box 3.2 Jhon's military training

[The Army is] where I learnt to use firearms, the AK-47, the sniper rifle, the RPG–which is a rocket-launcher–all kinds of weapons! I had classes, it was like school, and they taught us to shoot, to strip and clean our weapons, and there were also exams. I can strip and re-assemble any kind of weapon–I know everything, I tell you! The basic weapon in the Army was the AK-47, but because I could shoot really well, I became a sniper, and so used a special rifle. I went and trained in Martinique and Marie-Galante, they're French islands, and I trained with the French Army and also the Venezuelan Army. [. . .] All of this helped me when I came back to the neighbourhood afterwards. [. . .]

During my service I'd come back every 15 days, and whenever I came, all the bróderes would say, 'bring me a gun, mon, bring me an AK', but I'd just say to them, 'oye maje, do you know how to use a gun?' I'd tell them that I wasn't going to bring anything if they didn't know how to take care of their guns, if they couldn't strip and re-assemble them. I told them that they needed to learn all of this, and so they asked me to teach them.

So after a while, I brought back an AK-47 and taught them all, in groups of five. [. . .] You see, an AK-47 isn't complicated, but there's a specific order you have to follow to strip it in order to be able to clean it. The first thing you do is release the magazine catch, then you remove the magazine, then you cock the rifle, and–then–you take off the receiver cover and the recoil mechanism [. . .]. Then you remove the bolt carrier and then the bolt, and then you release the catch on the right side of the rear sight, and take off the hand guard, and then all that's left is the skeleton, which you clean. Afterwards, to re-assemble it, you just put everything back together in the reverse order.

Source: Dennis Rodgers interview with Jhon, LFH, 16 July 2012; authors' translation

CONCLUSION

At first glance, contemporary Nicaraguan gang dynamics seem to exemplify the 'democratization' of violence that Latin America is widely perceived to have undergone since the end of the cold war (Koonings and Kruijt, 1999; 2004). Along with cartelitos and private security firms, gangs are among a range of violent actors that have come to the fore in recent years, superseding more traditional ones such as authoritarian states or guerrilla movements. Beyond generally increasing levels of insecurity, this state of affairs also has a potential impact on illegal firearms markets, not least by increasing demand.

The evolutionary trajectory of Nicaraguan gangs suggests that the reality is more complex, however. The spread of Nicaraguan gangs in the immediate post-cold war period can be linked to the aftermath of the 1980s Contra war and the demobilization of conscripted youths; as such, it could be interpreted as linked to a process of violence 'democratization'. Yet gangs subsequently institutionalized on the basis of a process of local territorialization that owed little to geopolitical factors.

Specific gangs also developed unique evolutionary dynamics that affected their use of firearms and resulting violence levels, both of which have changed over time in non-linear ways. Ultimately, these patterns show that gangs are not just reflections of 'macro' structural conditions, but that their dynamics are also the result of a range of 'micro' internal and external factors. This is particularly clear with regard to gang member firearms use, which is not dependent solely on availability. A critical internal factor, for example, concerns the transmission of knowledge about gun use.

In both EB and LFH, firearms know-how was initially transmitted in the late 1980s and early 1990s by youths who had been military conscripts; subsequently, something of a 'Chinese whispers' effect caused this knowledge to become increasingly diluted. By the turn of the century, there were rising numbers of firearm accidents in both neighbourhoods, and guns were also breaking down in increasing numbers due to deficient care. This trend came to a halt in LFH when a single individual who had served in the army between 1997 and 2002 refreshed LFH gang members' knowledge, with major implications for the gang's violence levels and perceptions of security.

More generally, the trajectories of both the EB and LFH gangs during the 1990s highlight the importance of individual leader figures, and in particular how these contributed significantly to institutionalizing the gangs and their particular practices of violence. Leader figures declined over the following decade, but rather than resulting in less violent gangs, this trend made them more unpredictable and more prone to manipulation and domination by external actors. By 2008, the EB gang had been co-opted by the ruling FSLN party to disrupt opposition rallies. Similarly, in LFH, the cartelito began to co-opt leading gang members around 2005, significantly facilitating its subsequent brutal repression of the gang, which also increased general levels of insecurity in the neighbourhood. Such developments are relevant for anti-gang strategies based on attempts to 'decapitate' gangs by arresting (or killing) their leaders, as this approach can result in greater violence and insecurity than the more predictable and generally managed brutality of a clearly led organization.

Externally, the fact that leftover weapons from the 1980s began to break down in the late 1990s meant that it became more difficult for gang members to find weapons. This led them to source their firearms from new suppliers such as private security guards or the police; the fact that these guns were more difficult to access clearly contributed to reducing levels of gang violence between 2005 and 2010.[58] At the same time, the presence of other armed actors also impeded access to weapons. The rise of the cartelito in LFH was a key factor in the neighbourhood gang's decline, as it sought to both disarm and suppress the gang.[59] In EB, on the other hand, this process was mainly due to the interventions of NGOs and civil society organizations.

This contrast between LFH and EB highlights how processes of gang 'pacification'—which are effectively about closing up the spaces within which gangs can emerge—do not necessarily have to occur violently. That lesson is relevant to the entire Central American region, where repressive anti-gang policies popularly known as *mano dura* have clearly failed.[60] The most effective non-violent policy interventions remain context-driven, however, and must be informed by close qualitative understandings of specific gang dynamics. ◾

LIST OF ABBREVIATIONS

EB	Elías Blanco
FSLN	Frente Sandinista de Liberación Nacional (Sandinista National Liberation Front)
LFH	Luis Fanor Hernández
NIO	Nicaraguan córdoba

ENDNOTES

1   The emergence of maras in the region is partly linked to the mass deportation of Central American refugees from the United States in the mid-1990s, including almost 46,000 Central American convicts deported between 1998 and 2005, although not all were gang members (UNODC, 2007, pp. 40–42). Maras do not represent a transplanted US gang culture, however, but rather an amalgamation with local pandilla culture. They are quite different from US gangs; the number of deportee gang members has been declining steadily since the mid-1990s, such that they now constitute a minority of contemporary Central American *mareros* (Demoscopía, 2007, p. 49). Due to their transnational origins, maras are less embedded within local social and cultural norms than pandillas, and therefore less constrained in their brutality. This partly explains why Nicaragua is less violent than its northern neighbours, although its levels of brutality are higher than generally reported. See Rodgers (2009; 2012a).

2   Although pandillas still operate in El Salvador, Guatemala, and Honduras, they are much less visible, and also much less extensive, than maras. For an explanation as to why there are no maras in Nicaragua, see Rocha (2006a).

3   These names are pseudonyms.

4   See note 27 for more on the interviewees, their characteristics, and interview methods.

5   See Rodgers (1997; 2000; 2006a; 2007a; 2007b; 2010; 2012a) and Rocha (2000a; 2000b; 2003; 2005; 2007a; 2007b; 2008), as well as Rocha and Rodgers (2008). Assertions made in this chapter that are not directly referenced or associated with a specific interview, particularly with regard to developments in barrios Elías Blanco and Luis Fanor Hernández, are based on knowledge acquired by the authors during previous research, or represent a synthesis of information obtained from interviews with both gang members and non-gang members in these neighbourhoods.

6   The term 'Contras' comes from the Spanish word *contrarevolucionarios* (counter-revolutionaries).

7   Although armed groups of ex-Sandinista Popular Army military personnel and Contra guerrillas continued to plague rural areas in the north of the country well into the 1990s, these were generally local in scope and never constituted a major threat to the Nicaraguan state. See Rocha (2001).

8   Since 1990, a process of depoliticization and reductions in both size and budget have severely affected the operational capacity of the Nicaraguan National Police, which has limited patrolling capacity and is completely absent in 21 per cent of the country's 146 municipalities (Cajina, 2000, p. 174).

9   The Pan American Health Organization estimates that more than 50 per cent of all mortalities in Nicaragua in 1995 were not registered due to deficient record keeping by hospitals and morgues (PAHO, 1998, p. 384).

10 There are, for example, marked discrepancies between Nicaraguan police statistics and those of other organizations, including the International Criminal Police Organization. The latter recorded that 1,157 homicides were 'known to the police' in Nicaragua in 1998, compared to official figures of 381 homicides and 180 assassinations (INTERPOL, 1999; Policía Nacional de Nicaragua, 2000, p. 34).

11 This particular association is explicit in many of former president Enrique Bolaños' speeches, including for example the one delivered to the Association of American Chambers of Commerce in Latin America on 9 May 2002 (Bolaños, 2002).

12 This approach has sometimes led officials to contradict themselves, as when they prioritize crime suppression despite official data suggesting that the problem is not significant, or when they simultaneously proclaim the country safer than the rest of Central America but make regional citizen security a key policy focus. See GoN (2002a; 2002b).

13 Bolognesi (2009); Rocha (2007a); Rodgers (2000; 2006a; 2007b); Vermeij (2006).

14 Instituto de Estudios Estratégicos y Políticas Públicas.

15 It should be noted that media reporting on crime and insecurity is not necessarily accurate. See Huhn, Oettler, and Peetz (2009).

16 Although female gang members are not completely unknown in Nicaragua, they are not the norm (Rodgers, 2006a, p. 286).

17 By comparison, Managua's population reportedly grew by just under 4 per cent between the 1995 and 2005 censuses, from 903,100 to 937,085 (GoN, 2006, p. 26).

18 Although it is not clear whether he defined gangs in the same way as the police, Juan Carlos Núñez recorded the existence of a total of 13 pandillas just in the two Managua barrios San Luis and Altagracia in the early 1990s. At that time, both of these were relatively typical examples of poor urban neighbourhoods in the city, which had more than 400 such neighbourhoods (Núñez, 1996, pp. 245–50).

19 On the reasons for this particular trend, see Rodgers (2006a, pp. 278–79).

20 The Nicaraguan National Police often claims that the decline in gangs is related to its putatively 'preventative' violence-reduction policies, which it argues are more enlightened than the repressive *mano dura* (iron fist) policies put in place in El Salvador, Guatemala, and Honduras (Granera, 2012). Based on research conducted in the Nicaraguan juvenile justice sector, Rocha has found such policies to be more symbolic than substantive; he highlights that repression remained the guiding principle for police action against gangs on the ground, even if this approach did not reach the same levels of brutality as those associated with mano dura in other Central American countries (Rocha, 2007c). See also Jütersonke, Muggah, and Rodgers (2009).

21 On the issue of collusion between drug dealers and police, see Dudley (2012).

22 See Rodgers (2004; 2012b). At the same time, a limited number of new police substations were also established in certain Managua neighbourhoods, as a consequence of the implementation of a range of international aid-funded programmes aiming to improve citizen security. José Luis Rocha interview with Jimmy Javier Maynard, police general commissioner and national police sub-director, Managua, 18 April 2012.

23 Dennis Rodgers interview with the Luis Fanor Hernández Sandinista youth organization coordinator, Managua, 30 October 2009.

24 See Fox (2012) and O'Neill McCleskey (2012).

25 This name is a pseudonym.

26 See Rodgers (forthcoming).

27 This section relies on primary research conducted in the two barrios. The two authors conducted a total of 14 interviews in EB and 16 in LFH. Interviewees were all male and between 14 and 42 years old; they were deliberately selected to obtain a representative spread of gang members from different gang epochs in each neighbourhood. Interviews were cross-referenced and also compared with information provided by individuals who were not gang members, including family members and other neighbourhood residents, to avoid taking gang member discourse at face value. Unattributed assertions are either based on knowledge acquired from the authors' previous field research or they represent a synthesis of information obtained from interviews with gang members and non-gang members. All individual gang member names mentioned in this chapter are pseudonyms.

28 José Luis Rocha interview with Hamyn Gurdián, police commissioner, Managua, 17 March 1999.

29 In other neighbourhoods demobilized Contra youths also formed gangs, although they were generally a minority (Rodgers, 2006a, p. 283). Not all demobilized youths joined gangs, partly because the overwhelming majority were from rural areas. A clear majority of youths who came from poor urban neighbourhoods ended up joining gangs, however.

30 This study uses the term 'golden era' because it was an expression frequently used by post-2000 gang members in both EB and LFH to describe the 1990s.

31 Dennis Rodgers interview with Miguel, LFH, 4 November 1996.

32 Dennis Rodgers interview with Julio, LFH, 4 November 1996.

33 Street dealers in EB actually often sourced their crack in LFH.

34 For the history of such initiatives, see Rocha and Bellanger (2004).

35 Dennis Rodgers interview with Doña Yolanda, resident, LFH, 2 November 2009.

36 Dennis Rodgers interview with Mayuyu, LFH, 13 July 2012.

37 Individual ownership was particularly common with respect to firearms, which gang members systematically claimed they never lent to anybody, except sometimes to their closest friends within the gang. Yet several gang members in LFH did report that some collective weapons existed during the 1990s, although these weapons had generally been stolen by small groups of two or three gang members, who shared them among themselves; in EB, some gang members said that they regularly held collections among themselves to buy ammunition, which they then shared.

38 José Luis Rocha interview with el Revoliático, EB, 5 July 2012.

39 Some gang members also reported obtaining firearms for 'personal protection'. This was especially the case if they were engaged in long-term personal vendettas.

40 Gang members generally acquired the firearms they used in gang warfare individually and not as a group; indeed, they tended to be the same weapons that they used for their delinquency.

41   Dennis Rodgers interview with Bismarck, LFH, 13 July 2012.

42   José Luis Rocha interview with El Cofla, EB, 1 July 2012.

43   Dennis Rodgers interview with Milton, LFH, 17 July 2012.

44   When asked how he knew that it was an Uzi, Mayuyu replied: 'Because I know what Uzis look like, I've seen them on television.' Dennis Rodgers interview with Mayuyu, LFH, 13 July 2012. His identification was, however, confirmed by Jhon, another gang member who was familiar with Uzis following a stint in the Nicaraguan Army.

45   José Luis Rocha interview with Daimaku, EB, 5 July 2012.

46   Dennis Rodgers interview with Felix, LFH, 15 July 2012.

47   This observation is made on the basis of information from 2012 interviews as well as the long-term longitudinal investigations being carried out by the authors in EB and LFH.

48   Dennis Rodgers interview with Julio, LFH, 14 July 2012.

49   José Luis Rocha interview with Picapollo, EB, 9 September 2012.

50   Dennis Rodgers interview with el Gordo sucio, LFH, 21 July 2012.

51   José Luis Rocha interview with Daimaku, EB, 5 July 2012.

52   José Luis Rocha interview with el Pelón, EB, 5 April 2006.

53   Dennis Rodgers interview with Jader, LFH, 13 July 2012.

54   Dennis Rodgers interview with Spencer, LFH, 13 July 2012.

55   Dennis Rodgers interview with Bismarck, LFH, 13 July 2012.

56   This observation is based on information from 2012 author interviews as well as their long-term longitudinal investigations in EB and LFH.

57   Dennis Rodgers interview with Bismarck, LFH, 26 February 2002.

58   Overall, though, it must be stressed that Nicaraguan gang members generally show a relatively low level of sophistication in their firearm use, exhibiting more opportunistic than systematic approaches to weapons acquisition. This suggests that gangs are not a primary source of demand for firearms or an illegal market of weapons and ammunition in Nicaragua.

59   The cartelito's relationship with the LFH gang goes against the grain of much current thinking about the relationship between gangs and organized criminality insofar as much of the literature casts gangs as institutional channels to organized crime. See, for example, Lo (2012).

60   See Jütersonke, Muggah, and Rodgers (2009).

BIBLIOGRAPHY

Arendt, Hannah. 1969. *On Violence*. New York: Harcourt Brace.

Bauman, Zygmunt. 1998. *Globalization: The Human Consequences*. Cambridge: Polity.

Bellanger, Wendy. 2006. 'La sociedad civil ante la violencia juvenil en Nicaragua.' In José Miguel Cruz, ed. *Maras y pandillas en Centroamérica: las respuestas de la sociedad civil organizada*. San Salvador: UCA Editores.

Bolaños, Enrique. 2002. 'Palabras del Presidente de la República Enrique Bolaños Geyer ante la Asociación de Cámaras de Comercio Americanas en Latinoamérica, Washington, D.C., 9 de mayo de 2002.'

    <http://www.enriquebolanos.org/discursos_pdf/Washington%20-%20EBG%20en%20AMCHAM%20-%2009%20May%2002.pdf>

Bolognesi, Paola. 2009. 'Il Recupero dei Pandilleros da Parte di una Chiesa Evangelica Pentecostale a Managua, Nicaragua.' Ph.D. thesis, Department of Political Science, University of Bologna, Italy.

Cajina, Roberto. 2000. 'Nicaragua: de la seguridad del estado a la inseguridad ciudadana.' In Andrés Serbin and Diego Ferreyra, eds. *Gobernabilidad democrática y seguridad ciudadana en Centroamérica: el caso de Nicaragua*. Managua: CRIES.

Cook, Philip, et al. 2007. 'Underground Gun Markets.' *Economic Journal*, Vol. 117, No. 524, pp. F558–88.

Demoscopía. 2007. *Maras y pandillas: comunidad y policía en Centroamérica*. San José: Demoscopía.

Dudley, Steven. 2012. 'Folk Singer's Death Shines Light on Nicaragua Police Corruption.' *InSight Crime*. 9 July.

    <http://www.insightcrime.org/nicaragua-a-paradise-lost/folk-singers-death-shines-light-on-nicaragua-police-corruption>

Fox, Edward. 2012. 'Nicaraguan at Center of Cabral Murder Case Convicted of Drug Trafficking.' *InSight Crime*. 27 September.

    <http://www.insightcrime.org/news-briefs/nicaraguan-farinas-cabral-murder-convicted>

Galeano, Eduardo. 1998. *Patas arriba: la escuela del mundo al revés*, 4th edn. Madrid: Siglo Veintiuno.

GoN (Government of Nicaragua). 2002a. 'Diagnóstico de seguridad ciudadana en Nicaragua.' 29 July. Managua: GoN.

    <http://enriquebolanos.org/ministerios_informes_pdf/Diagnostico%20%20Seg%20Ciudadana.pdf>

—. 2002b. 'Resumen ejecutivo: diagnóstico de seguridad ciudadana en Nicaragua.' 23 September. Managua: GoN.

<http://www.enriquebolanos.org/discursos_pdf/Washington%20-%20EBG%20en%20AMCHAM%20-%2009%20May%2002.pdf>

—. 2006. *Cifras oficiales: censos nacionales 2005—VIII censo de población y IV de vivienda.* Managua: GoN. <http://www.nicaragua.unfpa.org.ni/

publidoc/Pob%20y%20Desarrollo%20Estudios%20e%20investigaciones/Censo%20Pob.%20Cifras%20Oficiales.pdf>

Granera, Aminta. 2012. 'Seguridad ciudadana en Centroamérica.' Presentation to the Center for Strategic and International Studies, Washington, DC, 18 June.

<http://csis.org/files/attachments/120618_Granera_Presentation_1.pdf>

Hagedorn, John. 2008. *A World of Gangs: Armed Young Men and Gangsta Culture.* Minneapolis: University of Minnesota Press.

Hernández, Paul Baker. 2001. Nicaragua News Service, Vol. 9, No. 6. 5–11 February.

<http://www.tulane.edu/~libweb/RESTRICTED/NICANEWS/2001_0205.txt>

Huhn, Sebastian, Anika Oettler, and Peter Peetz. 2009. 'Contemporary Discourses on Violence in Central American Newspapers.' *International Communication Gazette*, Vol. 71, No. 4. June, pp. 243–61.

INTERPOL (International Criminal Police Organization). 1999. *International Crime Statistics 1998.* Saint-Cloud: INTERPOL.

<http://www.interpol.int/Public/Statistics/ICS/1998/Nicaragua1998.pdf>

Jütersonke, Oliver, Robert Muggah, and Dennis Rodgers. 2009. 'Gangs, Urban Violence, and Security Interventions in Central America.' *Security Dialogue*, Vol. 40, Nos. 4–5. August–October, pp. 373–97.

Kates, Robert, et al. 1973. 'Human Impact of the Managua Earthquake.' *Science*, Vol. 182, No. 7. December, pp. 981–90.

Koonings, Kees and Dirk Kruijt, eds. 1999. *Societies of Fear: The Legacy of Civil War, Violence and Terror in Latin America.* London: Zed Books.

—. 2004. *Armed Actors: Organised Violence and State Failure in Latin America.* London: Zed Books.

Lancaster, Roger. 1992. *Life Is Hard: Machismo, Danger, and the Intimacy of Power in Nicaragua.* Berkeley: University of California Press.

Lo, T. Wing. 2012. 'Triadization of Youth Gangs in Hong Kong.' *British Journal of Criminology*, Vol. 52, No. 2. December, pp. 556–76.

Manwaring, Max. 2005. *Street Gangs: The New Urban Insurgency.* Carlisle: United States Army War College.

Nowak, Matthias. 2012. 'Inconsistent Homicide Data for Nicaragua, 2000–11, based on the Global Burden of Armed Violence 2011 Database.' Unpublished background paper. Geneva: Geneva Declaration Secretariat.

Núñez, Juan Carlos. 1996. *De la ciudad al barrio: redes y tejidos urbanos en Guatemala, El Salvador y Nicaragua.* Guatemala City: Universidad Rafael Landívar.

O'Neill McCleskey, Claire. 2012. 'Colombia Arrests Trafficker Who Helped Facundo's Alleged Killer Escape.' *InSight Crime.* 18 October.

<http://www.insightcrime.org/news-briefs/colombia-dismantles-gang-linked-to-author-of-cabral-murder>

Orozco, Roberto. 2012. *IV encuesta sobre percepción de la seguridad ciudadana.* Managua: Instituto de Estudios Estratégicos y Políticas Públicas.

PAHO (Pan American Health Organization). 1998. *Health in the Americas*, vol. 2. Washington, DC: PAHO.

PNUD (Programa de las Naciones Unidas para el Desarrollo—United Nations Development Programme). 2011. *Seguridad ciudadana 1998–2010—Nicaragua: riesgos, retos y oportunidades.* Managua: PNUD.

Policía Nacional de Nicaragua. 2000. *Anuario estadístico 1999.* Managua: Policía Nacional.

Quintero, Lésber. 2010a. 'Tres ejecutados.' *El Nuevo Diario.* 10 October. <http://www.elnuevodiario.com.ni/nacionales/85307>

—. 2010b. 'Una nueva ejecución.' *El Nuevo Diario.* 31 October. <http://impreso.elnuevodiario.com.ni/2010/10/31/nacionales/135021>

Rocha, José Luis. 2000a. 'Pandilleros: la mano que empuña el mortero.' *Envío*, Vol. 216, pp. 17–25.

—. 2000b. 'Pandillas: una cárcel cultural.' *Envío*, Vol. 219, pp. 13–22.

—. 2001. 'Breve, necesaria y tormentosa historia del FUAC.' *Envío*, Vol. 232, pp. 10–22.

—. 2003. 'Tatuajes de pandilleros: estigma, identidad y arte.' *Envío*, Vol. 258, pp. 42–50.

—. 2005. 'El traido: clave de la continuidad de las pandillas.' *Envío*, Vol. 280, pp. 35–41.

—. 2006a. 'Mareros y pandilleros: ¿nuevos insurgentes, criminales?' *Envío*, Vol. 293, pp. 39–51.

—. 2006b. 'Pandilleros del siglo XXI: con hambre de alucinaciones y de transnacionalismo.' *Envío*, Vol. 294, pp. 25–34.

—. 2007a. *Lanzando piedras, fumando 'piedras': evolución de las pandillas en Nicaragua 1997–2006.* Cuaderno de Investigación No. 23. Managua: UCA Publicaciones.

—. 2007b. 'Del telescopio al microscopio: hablan tres pandilleros.' *Envío*, Vol. 303, pp. 23–30.

—. 2007c. 'Mapping the Labyrinth from Within: The Political Economy of Nicaraguan Youth Policy Concerning Violence.' *Bulletin of Latin American Research*, Vol. 26, No. 4. October, pp. 533–49.

—. 2008. 'La Mara 19 tras las huellas de las pandillas políticas.' *Envío*, Vol. 321, pp 26–31.

— and Wendy Bellanger. 2004. 'Pandillas juveniles y rehabilitación de pandilleros en Nicaragua.' In Equipo de Reflexión, Investigación y Comunicación et al., eds. *Maras y pandillas en Centroamérica: políticas juveniles y rehabilitación.* Managua: UCA Publicaciones.

— and Dennis Rodgers. 2008. *Bróderes descobijados y vagos alucinados: una década con las pandillas Nicaragüenses, 1997–2007.* Managua: Envío.

Rodgers, Dennis. 1997. 'Un antropólogo-pandillero en un barrio de Managua.' *Envío*, Vol. 184, pp. 10–16.

—. 2000. *Living in the Shadow of Death: Violence,* Pandillas, *and Social Disintegration in Contemporary Urban Nicaragua.* Unpublished Ph.D. thesis, Department of Social Anthropology, University of Cambridge.

—. 2004. 'Disembedding the City: Crime, Insecurity, and Spatial Organisation in Managua, Nicaragua.' *Environment and Urbanization,* Vol. 16, No. 2. October, pp. 113–24.

—. 2006a. 'Living in the Shadow of Death: Gangs, Violence, and Social Order in Urban Nicaragua, 1996–2002.' *Journal of Latin American Studies,* Vol. 38, No. 2. April, pp. 267–92.

—. 2006b. 'The State as a Gang: Conceptualising the Governmentality of Violence in Contemporary Nicaragua.' *Critique of Anthropology,* Vol. 26, No. 3. September, pp. 315–30.

—. 2007a. 'Joining the Gang and Becoming a *Broder:* The violence of Ethnography in Contemporary Nicaragua.' *Bulletin of Latin American Research,* Vol. 26, No. 4. October, pp. 444–61.

—. 2007b. 'When Vigilantes Turn Bad: Gangs, Violence, and Social Change in Urban Nicaragua.' In David Pratten and Atreyee Sen, eds. *Global Vigilantes.* London: Hurst, pp. 349–70.

—. 2007c. 'Managua.' In Kees Koonings and Dirk Kruijt, eds. *Fractured Cities: Social Exclusion, Urban Violence and Contested Spaces in Latin America.* London: Zed, pp. 71–85.

—. 2009. 'Slum Wars of the 21st Century: Gangs, Mano Dura, and the New Urban Geography of Conflict in Central America.' *Development and Change,* Vol. 40, No. 5. September, pp. 949–76.

—. 2010. 'Génèse d'un gangster? De la *pandilla* au *cartelito* au Nicaragua post-Sandiniste.' *Problèmes d'Amérique Latine,* Vol. 76, pp. 61–76.

—. 2012a. 'Nicaragua's Gangs: Historical Legacy or Contemporary Symptom?' *NACLA Report on the Americas,* Vol. 45, No. 1. Spring, pp. 66–69.

—. 2012b. 'Haussmannization in the Tropics: Abject Urbanism and Infrastructural Violence in Nicaragua.' *Ethnography,* Vol. 13, No. 4. December, pp. 411–36.

—. Forthcoming. '*Bróderes, Vagos,* and *Compadres* in the *Barrio:* Kinship, Politics, and Local Territorialization in Urban Nicaragua.' In Brodwyn Fischer, Bryan McCann, and Javier Auyero, eds. *Cities from Scratch: The Informal City in Latin America.* Durham: Duke University Press.

Romero, Elízabeth. 2010. 'General Avilés dice que controlan territorio.' *La Prensa.* 20 March.
<http://www.laprensa.com.ni/2010/03/20/nacionales/19664-general-aviles-dice-que>

Rushdie, Salman. 1987. *The Jaguar Smile: A Nicaraguan Journey.* New York: Penguin.

Silva, José Adán. 2003. 'Policía en desventaja ante seguridad privada.' *La Prensa.* 3 March.
<http://archivo.laprensa.com.ni/archivo/2003/marzo/03/nacionales/nacionales-20030303-18.html>

Small Arms Survey. 2002. *Small Arms Survey 2002: Counting the Human Cost.* Oxford: Oxford University Press.

Stone, Hanna. 2011. 'Nicaragua Deploys 1,000 Soldiers to Tackle Rural Crime.' *InSight Crime.* 19 December.
<http://www.insightcrime.org/news-briefs/nicaragua-deploys-1000-soldiers-to-tackle-rural-crime>

Téfel Vélez, Reinaldo Antonio. 1976. *El infierno de los pobres: diagnóstico sociológico de los barrios marginales de Managua.* Managua: El Pez y la Serpiente.

Tórrez González, Fátima. 2010. 'Armas artesanales: el "juguete mortal" de los pandilleros.' *El Nuevo Diario.* 26 December.
<http://impreso.elnuevodiario.com.ni/2010/12/26/sucesos/138399>

UNODC (United Nations Office on Drugs and Crime). 2007. *Crime and Development in Central America: Caught in the Crossfire.* Vienna: United Nations.

Vermeij, Peter-Jan. 2006. 'That's Life: Community Perceptions of Informality, Violence and Fear in Two Spontaneous Human Settlements in Managua, Nicaragua.' Master's thesis, Department of Social Sciences, Utrecht University, Netherlands.

Walker, Thomas. 2003. *Nicaragua: Living in the Shadow of the Eagle,* 4th edn. Boulder: Westview Press.

Wolf, Sonja. 2012. 'Mara Salvatrucha: The Most Dangerous Street Gang in the Americas?' *Latin American Politics and Society,* Vol. 54, No. 1. Spring, pp. 65–99.

Yablonsky, Lewis. 1997. *Gangsters: Fifty Years of Madness, Drugs, and Death on the Streets of America.* New York: New York University Press.

ACKNOWLEDGEMENTS

Principal authors

Dennis Rodgers and José Luis Rocha

A police officer stands next to graffiti portraying mafia boss Matteo Messina Denaro, Palermo, Sicily, April 2008. © Alessandro Fucarini/AP Photo

Guns in the Family
MAFIA VIOLENCE IN ITALY

4

INTRODUCTION

In the span of 52 days in 1992, two horrific bomb attacks in Palermo killed Sicilian judges Giovanni Falcone and Paolo Borsellino, Falcone's wife Francesca Morvillo, and eight police agents who were part of their armed escorts. The murders provoked mass demonstrations against the mafia in Italy and marked the beginning of a stunning escalation of violence by the Sicilian mafia against the Italian state. Tensions culminated with a terrorist bombing campaign on the mainland in 1993, when bombs planted in Florence, Milan, and Rome killed ten people and wounded more than 70 (CPIFCOMS, 2010a, pp. 10–11). The impressive amount of explosives used in these 'military-style' actions provoked public astonishment and harsh law enforcement countermeasures, unprecedented in the contemporary history of Italian mafia operations.

The Sicilian mafia, like similar organized crime groups based in Italy, has always adopted violence as a last resort, namely when preferred alternatives—such as non-violent displays of strength or threats—cannot achieve the same results. Yet the professionalized use of firearms and explosives remains a characteristic feature of mafia organizations. The use of violence and intimidation against competitors and opponents enables these groups to enhance their reputation and acquire privileged positions in the markets in which they operate, whether legal or illegal. Thus, mafia-type organizations have generally relied on the availability of weapons.

This chapter examines patterns, rules, changes, and variations in the use of armed violence by organized crime groups across Italy, focusing specifically on traditional mafia-type organizations. It also reviews available information on firearm acquisition, storage, and use by these groups. Key findings include:

- Organized crime groups tend to make 'economical' use of violence, and deliberate killings are typically the last resort. This principle varies by group, however, with some acting less restrainedly than others in the use of armed violence to solve disputes, overcome problems related to their businesses, and maintain territorial control.

- The Camorra group, historically rooted in Naples and surrounding areas, is responsible for almost half (48 per cent) of all mafia homicides documented in Italy over the period 1992–2010 (see Table 4.1). A greater availability of firearms in the region, a stronger presence of organized crime members, and recurrent conflicts among clans may partly explain the group's predominance in violence.

- Mafia homicides declined by some 43 per cent from 2007 to 2010 (see Table 4.1). Analysts suggest that organized crime groups have entered a submersion phase, moving further into legal markets in which the use of violence and firearms is increasingly counterproductive to business operations.

- Most mafia clans maintain their own arsenals of collectively held firearms, with selected members in charge of procuring, storing, maintaining, and distributing firearms in response to requests or circumstances.

- The level of sophistication and the variety of firearms among mafia clans have increased since the 1970s. Most mafiosi (mafia members) currently rely on machine guns, revolvers, pistols, and AK-pattern assault rifles, although they even use World War II-era firearms or modified toy guns.

- Mafia groups procure firearms through robberies from firearms shops; thefts from the military, police forces, and private citizens; and in exchange for drugs and other illicit commodities.

- Criminal groups in the former Yugoslavia, Albania, and other Eastern European countries are key sources of firearms for Italian organized crime groups.

In view of the fact that no systematic data is currently available on the use of firearms by organized crime groups in Italy, this chapter provides an initial attempt at a qualitative analysis of this under-researched and relatively hidden phenomenon. The first part presents an overview of the main actors comprising the multifaceted Italian organized crime scene and provides a summary of the structure, internal organization, and modes of operation of the four main traditional mafia-type organizations: the Cosa Nostra, the 'Ndrangheta, the Camorra, and the Sacra Corona Unita (United Holy Crown, or SCU). The second section analyses organized crime and armed violence with a special focus on mafia homicides in Italy over the past 20 years and the changes and variations in the use of armed violence across the country. The final section explores characteristics, patterns, and rules of firearms procurement, possession, storage, and use by these groups. Thematic text boxes examine the role played by Italian organized crime groups in the illegal firearms trade and the presence of adolescents specialized in the use of armed violence inside some mafia groups.

The organized crime scene is dominated by the Cosa Nostra, the 'Ndrangheta, the Camorra, and the Sacra Corona Unita.

THE ORGANIZED CRIME SCENE

In the Italian debate, the expression 'organized crime' is a broad concept covering different offences and actors. Based on Article 416 of Italy's penal code, criminal organizations composed of at least three members who repeatedly get involved in serious crimes usually fall into this category; however, Article 416bis defines a mafia-type criminal association as relying on the intimidating power of the bonds of association, the condition of subjugation, and *omertà* (the code of silence), as enforced by intimidation (Italy, 2007, arts. 416, 416-bis).[1] Thus 'mafia' refers to a specific type of organized criminal organization that has the capacity to exercise power through systematic intimidation or political influence.[2]

Three major mafia-type organizations whose origins date back to the second half of the 19th century dominate the Italian organized crime scene: the confederation of groups comprising the Sicilian Cosa Nostra, the Calabrian 'Ndrangheta, and the Campanian Camorra (Lupo, 2009; Ciconte, 1992; Sales, 1993). Though originally rooted in regions of southern Italy, since the post-war period these organizations have expanded towards north-central areas—where they have acquired strong economic interests—and abroad, where they have the support of well-established settlements (Sciarrone, 2009; Varese, 2011). Beginning in the late 1970s, Apulia also witnessed the expansion of organized crime with the emergence of a so-called 'fourth mafia', the Sacra Corona Unita (Massari, 1998; see Map 4.1).

In addition to these four traditional mafia-type organizations,[3] Italy has faced increasing activity from several foreign criminal groups since the mid-1990s. Whether ethnically homogeneous or mixed, these groups were originally at the margins of the Italian criminal underworld but have since become increasingly active in several illegal markets (DNA, 2011). Italy's geopolitical position in drugs and human trafficking was a major factor in the emergence of these groups,

Map 4.1 **Mafia strongholds in Italy**

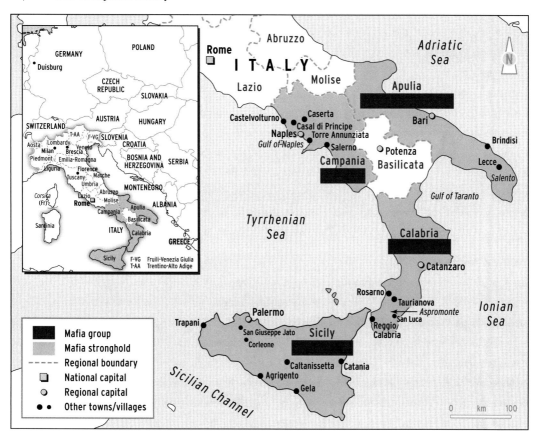

with countries in Eastern Europe and the former Yugoslavia acting as the source for illegal goods and services intended for Western markets. Among the principal foreign criminal organizations operating in Italy, law enforcement agencies note Balkan, Chinese, and Nigerian syndicates, as well as Russian and North African organized crime groups. These are mostly involved in smuggling illegal immigrants, trafficking humans and drugs, prostitution, counterfeiting, and money laundering (DNA, 2011, pp. 151–60). Although the outcomes of investigations confirm growing cooperation between Italian mafia-type groups and foreign criminal organizations in the management of illegal markets such as drugs, the latter tend to operate within specific sectors of criminal activities and in areas where mafia control is less intense (p. 152).

Traditional mafia structures

The word 'mafia' has appeared continuously since the mid-19th century, be it in political debates, judicial investigations, journalistic commentary, fiction, or parliamentary enquiries. While the term was originally used in Italian to refer exclusively to the Sicilian group, its meaning has since expanded to connote organized crime and various criminal phenomena. Until the 1980s, the word 'mafia' also defined a way of life, a form of behaviour, and an expression of traditional society. This view was largely based on the ideological representation mafiosi provided of themselves as mediators, resolvers of disagreements, and protectors of the weak (Lupo, 2009, p. 12).

Statements made by *pentiti* (former mafiosi who cooperate with the judiciary) have helped to separate such ideological representations from the real situation. Most of them provide insight into the mafia's hierarchical structure, careful vetting of members, division of territory, and syndicate-wide coordination mechanisms. The statements also reveal that mafia groups tend to outlive their individual members (Lupo, 2009).

Academic debate on the mafia among Italian scholars has generated a wide array of definitions that focus mostly on structure, activities, and resources (Varese, 2010, pp. 1–33). This chapter defines 'mafia' as an organized crime group characterized by the capacity to take root in certain areas, exert social control over society, rely on economic and military resources, and secure a certain degree of social support (Sciarrone, 2009, pp. 44–45).[4]

In order to understand its complexity, the mafia may be seen, as Santino suggests, as 'a system of violence and illegality aimed at accumulating wealth and gaining power, which also uses a cultural code and enjoys a certain level of popular support' (Santino, 1995, p. 130). In this sense, the groups exhibit political, cultural, and social features in addition to criminal and economic aspects. According to this approach, the mafia cannot be separated from official, legal society and should be considered within its wider social context (Ruggiero, 1996).

The Cosa Nostra

'Cosa Nostra' (Our Business) is the expression used by mafiosi to refer to the Sicilian mafia. Its structure was disclosed in 1984 in statements made by *pentito* Tommaso Buscetta and other former mafia members who decided to collaborate with law enforcement agencies (Stajano, 1992; Arlacchi, 1992; 1994).

This organization still represents a sort of paradigm for other organized crime groups. It is composed of various units, called *famiglie* or *cosche* (families), which usually take their name from the territory where they operate, be it a neighbourhood, as in the city of Palermo, or a village. Although Cosa Nostra *famiglie* operate in each Sicilian province— where they exercise a sort of totalitarian control—Palermo 'is and still remains the place where the criminal organization most greatly expresses its vitality at both the decisional and (mostly) operational levels' (DNA, 2011, p. 51).

A *famiglia* may contain a varying number of members, from ten to as many as 100; called *uomini d'onore* (men of honour) or *soldati* (soldiers), they are usually organized in *decine* (groups of ten) supervised by a *capodecina* (head of a group of ten). Each *famiglia* is run by a *capofamiglia* (family head) or representative—elected by the members of the family—a *consigliere* (adviser), and a *sottocapo* (deputy). Several families operating in the same area form a larger unit called a *mandamento*, whose own chief is appointed by the various *capifamiglia*. In the past, two governing bodies operating at the provincial and regional levels—the *Commissione provinciale* (provincial commission) and *Commissione regionale* (regional commission)—supervised the activities of the various families, though no evidence is currently available on their actual existence. Today a more restricted committee composed of few trusted *capomandamenti* (heads of mandamentos) seems to manage overall Cosa Nostra businesses (Ingroia, 2008, p. 164–65).

Law enforcement operations have had a strong impact on the Cosa Nostra since the mid-1990s, leading to the imprisonment of major bosses such as Totò Riina, Bernardo Provenzano, and Salvatore Lo Piccolo, and sparking the emergence of a new generation of *uomini d'onore,* who are significantly younger than the former leaders.

After the 'terror strategy' adopted during the early 1990s—with the killings of judges Giovanni Falcone and Paolo Borsellino, and the 'massacre strategy' with bomb attacks in Florence, Milan, and Rome in 1993,[5] through which the Cosa Nostra openly challenged the state—the organization went through a 'submersion phase', aimed at avoiding the attention of law enforcement. Since then, the Cosa Nostra has been enduring a 'transition phase' characterized by the selection of new leadership and the adoption of new organizational patterns and strategies (DNA, 2011, p. 52).

The Cosa Nostra represents a sort of paradigm for other organized crime groups.

'Ndrangheta

The 'Ndrangheta (group of brave men) is the mafia-type association historically rooted in the area of Reggio Calabria, in the southern part of the province of Calabria.[6] Over the past 20 years, this organization has steadily grown in prominence; today it is well established across the entire region, as well as in the north-central part of the country and abroad.

Its structure is divided into basic units called *'ndrine* (families), composed of one or more groups with deep local roots, whether in a neighbourhood or a village. Each *'ndrina* relies largely on blood ties between members. The biological family almost always overlaps with the criminal family and represents the cornerstone of the *'ndrina*'s internal structure. A group of several *'ndrine* comprises a *locale* (a federation of groups), which operates in broader areas as large as an entire province. Each *'ndrina* is led by a *capobastone*, the highest rank a 'Ndrangheta affiliate can achieve after having moved up through the internal hierarchy (Gratteri and Nicaso, 2009, pp. 65–66).

The most recent investigations suggest that 'Ndrangheta structure has undergone significant changes over the past few years. In Calabria, the group is mostly divided into three main regional components—the Tyrrhenian, the City, and the Ionian. The entire organization is overseen by a corporate body called the *Provincia* (Province) or *Crimine* (Crime), which deliberates and endorses most important decisions involving groups operating in Calabria, as well as those active in other regions and abroad (DNA, 2011, p. 99; CPIFCOMS, 2010b, pp. 11–12).

Camorra

The term Camorra refers to a wide array of criminal groups based in Naples and other cities in the Campania province, such as Caserta and Salerno. These groups are often highly fragmented and hardly comprise a homogenous syndicate

Men linked to the Camorra stand in a street in Scampia, Naples, February 2009. © Samuel Aranda/Corbis

(Sales, 2008, p. 100). The latest official reports indicate that the Camorra is currently characterized by 'the extraordinary fluidity of changes inside the main criminal groups historically rooted in certain areas', mostly due to the effects of law enforcement operations as well as conflicts between major clans (DNA, 2011, p. 78). As opposed to both the 'Ndrangheta and the Cosa Nostra, the rather flexible structure of this organization does not currently rely on governing bodies or other coordinating mechanisms aimed at managing the activities of the various clans.

The Camorra cannot be reduced to a single, unified criminal configuration (DNA, 2011, p. 73); nevertheless, major differences can be identified among groups operating in the city of Naples, those active in the province, and others mostly based in the area of Caserta. More than half the criminal groups active in Campania are based in the city of Naples, where criminal density is very high and the balance of power between the various clans is especially fragile (Brancaccio, 2009, p. 78). Often relying on blood ties, these clans tend to operate as a sort of criminal elite, well established at the social, economic, and even political–institutional levels.[7] In the areas surrounding Naples, clans are more tightly structured, tend to manage all illegal activities in their territory, and display a strong tendency towards reinvestment of their illegal profits in the legal market (Brancaccio, 2009, p. 78). The area in and around Caserta is managed by the so-called Casalesi clan, a cartel of clans that emerged in the late 1980s (Cantone, 2012, pp. 20–21). Although still dangerous, this cartel has been heavily affected by major law enforcement operations and the arrest of several bosses.

Sacra Corona Unita

More than half the criminal groups of the Camorra are based in Naples.

The SCU, an Apulian mafia-type organization based largely in the southern part of the region, was founded in the early 1980s and drew heavily on the model furnished by robustly structured organized crime syndicates such as the 'Ndrangheta and the Camorra. The SCU's internal organization reflects a hierarchical structure and strong symbolism based on old 'Ndrangheta statutes and codes—such as tattoos and other visual identifiers of group affiliation.[8] Particularly during the late 1980s and 1990s, this organization experienced internal conflicts among various clans, leading to heavy reliance on violence as a tool for solving disputes and imposing authority over the local underworld (Massari, 2009, pp. 246–47). Other characteristics of the 'fourth mafia' include a low level of internal cohesion and a strong utilitarian approach, which led several bosses to accord priority to economic gain over the consolidation of power.

Over the past ten years, the SCU has undergone a significant transformation, since the incarceration of most of its bosses made space for a new generation, composed largely of the sons and relatives of the original leaders. The new elite has maintained a low profile while consolidating business through large, diversified investments in the legal economy. Moreover, the proximity to the Balkans, particularly Albania and Montenegro, has encouraged renewed interest in drug trafficking activities, as well as involvement in more traditional crimes such as robbery and extortion (Massari, 2009, p. 247).

ARMED VIOLENCE: CHARACTERISTICS AND TRENDS

Functions and meanings of violence

An account from the second half of the 19th century describes the Sicilian mafia as 'the violence industry' because of its ability to extort protection money and guarantee monopolies, and mafiosi as 'violence entrepreneurs' in view of their ability to use force in a professionalized way (Franchetti, 1993; Gambetta, 1993; Dickie, 2007, pp. 52–53).

More than a century later, scholarly debates and findings still cast violence as the qualifying characteristic of mafia power. Violence is one of the main resources used by mafia families to maintain their market position and increase the competitiveness of their businesses (Paoli, 2000, p. 212). Organized criminals use it not only to enforce contracts, but also to defy them; not just as a means of aggression, but also as a means of defence (Gambetta, 2009, p. 78).

Moreover, beyond the extensive use of violence, merely the credible *threat* of its use often grants criminal organizations a powerful monopoly over legal and illegal markets. A violent reputation—not necessarily linked to the actual use of violence—represents a sort of calling card that allows mafiosi to impose their own rules, solve disputes, and claim respect. Both the use and the threat of violence, however, can be drastically minimized if other options, such as corruption, are available, especially when organized criminals forge partnerships with official actors.

As already noted, the Italian penal code recognizes the use of intimidation as a distinctive feature of any mafia group. The effects of this tactic are particularly visible in the subjugation of local communities, especially in southern Italy, but also increasingly elsewhere.[9] In these areas, criminal organizations often exercise strong social control and tend to poison many aspects of daily life through threats, blackmail, and intimidation as they attempt to impose strict control over all activities that fall into their area of interest. Although homicides, assaults, and injuries are the most visible manifestations of the ability of organized crime groups to perpetrate wide-scale violence, subtler strategies also exist; based on the systematic use of terror and threats, these organizations increase group cohesion and efficiency, secure a certain level of social support, and challenge the ability of the state to enforce law and order.

Box 4.1 Mafias in Italy: key events

1962 Anti-mafia Parliamentary Committee appointed.

1962–63 First mafia war in Sicily.

10 December 1969 The Viale Lazio massacre in Palermo and the rise of the Corleonesi clan.

1974 Corleonesi boss Luciano Liggio arrested in Milan.

1974–80 First 'Ndrangheta war in Calabria.

1978–83 Second mafia war in Sicily.

1980 Piersanti Mattarella, president of Sicilian Regional Assembly, and prosecutor Gaetano Costa killed in Palermo.

1982 Pio La Torre, secretary of the Communist Party in Sicily, and Gen. Carlo Alberto dalla Chiesa killed in Palermo.

1979–83 Camorra war in Campania.

1983 Judge Bruno Caccia killed in Turin by 'Ndrangheta.

1984 Tommaso Buscetta turned state's witness.

1985–91 Second 'Ndrangheta war in Calabria.

1986 Palermo trial against 474 Cosa Nostra members.

1989–91 Taurianova *faida* (feud) in Calabria.

1991 Beginning of the San Luca *faida* in Calabria.

23 May 1992 Judge Giovanni Falcone killed in the Capaci massacre.

19 July 1992 Judge Paolo Borsellino killed in the Via D'Amelio massacre.

15 January 1993 Cosa Nostra boss Totò Riina arrested.

27 May 1993 Beginning of Cosa Nostra terror strategy with a car bomb in Florence.

27 July 1993 Car bomb in Milan; two bombings on the same night in Rome.

19 March 1994 Father Giuseppe Diana killed in Campania by the Camorra.

24 June 1995 Cosa Nostra boss Leoluca Bagarella arrested.

Mid-1990s Beginning of Cosa Nostra submersion phase.

2004–05 First Scampia *faida* in Naples.

16 October 2005 Francesco Fortugno, vice-president of the Regional Council of Calabria, killed.

11 April 2006 Cosa Nostra boss Bernardo Provenzano arrested and end of the submersion phase.

15 August 2007 Duisburg (Germany) massacre by the 'Ndrangheta.

18 September 2008 Castelvolturno massacre in Campania.

2010 Operation 'Crimine' against 300 'Ndrangheta members.

2012 Second Scampia *faida* begins in Naples.

In this regard, the analysis of the functions and meanings of mafia activity suggests that the organizations employ two types of violence. *Instrumental* violence is aimed at achieving concrete goals, such as a certain position in the marketplace or the elimination of obstacles, competitors, or dangers. Yet violence can also play a more *symbolic* role, such as when it is intended to enhance the reputation of the clans, deepening their sphere of respect and securing a certain level of impunity. These two functions are not always distinct and often overlap. In both cases, violence may be carried out inside the criminal organization—as in the case of inter-mafia conflicts or disciplinary action against group members—as well as outside, as in the so-called 'terror strategy' adopted by the Cosa Nostra during the early 1990s (see Box 4.1).[10]

This chapter focuses on the most tangible expressions of organized criminal violence, namely the violence committed with firearms. Despite the high profile of mafia and other Italian criminal organizations both inside and outside Italy, the use of firearms by these groups has not been studied closely. The findings presented in this chapter are based on a qualitative analysis of information collected through author interviews with anti-mafia prosecutors based at the Direzione Nazionale Antimafia (National Anti-mafia Directorate, or DNA) in Rome and local Direzione Distrettuale Antimafia (District Anti-mafia Directorate) offices in the provinces of Lecce and Reggio Calabria, law enforcement officers in Rome, and mafia experts; content analysis of judicial files and police reports concerning major anti-mafia operations provided by interviewees; an examination of DNA reports on organized crime in Italy issued from 2006 to 2011; a study of reports and hearings issued by the Anti-mafia Parliamentary Committee from 2002 until April 2012; and a review of news reports in the Italian newspaper *La Repubblica* from 2002 to June 2012. Since most of the official sources lack detailed information on the use of firearms by organized crime groups, primary sources, such as author interviews, comprise the most relevant empirical basis for this research.

The four traditional mafia-type organizations show heterogeneous patterns in the use of armed violence.

Organized crime and firearm-related offences

Organized crime groups often employ armed violence as a last resort, when less risky strategies are not viable. Prudence guides such use of firearms, with criminals generally evaluating related risks to avoid drawing the attention of law enforcement agencies and raising concern among the population. Depending on the situation, violence is used in different degrees, ranging from a simple threat, or act of intimidation, to the infliction of injuries or the commission of homicide. The four traditional mafia-type organizations show heterogeneous patterns in the use of violence, as some are more inclined to resort to weapons, while others are more cautious.

In attempting to understand the role of armed violence in the organized crime world, it is important to consider its effect on the local population. Indeed, demonstrative acts of violence may sometimes reinforce a group's image of invincibility among local communities, thus weakening any opposition to the organization. Such acts include the use of firearms or explosives in the commission of crimes, including robberies, extortions, homicides, and kidnappings. That said, little data is currently available on the number of crimes committed with the use of weapons and on the types of weapon used.[11]

Local Italian newspapers often report on acts of mafia violence and intimidation involving the use of firearms and explosives against shopkeepers, entrepreneurs, political administrators, and private citizens. Most of these incidents are related to protection rackets (Gambetta, 1993). Mafia groups usually generate a demand for security and protection by causing a high level of insecurity and uncertainty in the marketplace as well as society (Grasso and Varano, 2002). Extortion may also be presented as a form of taxation on local production activities and a way to assert political power over a territory. Bullet holes in shop and car windows, explosions near commercial centres, and intimidating letters containing bullets are all common mafia methods of communication. These methods are also used outside of the southern areas where mafia groups are historically rooted. Recent judicial files concerning the 'Ndrangheta in Lombardy, for example, show evidence of more than 70 incidents of intimidation using firearms, ammunition, and explosives against the local business and trade sectors (*La Repubblica*, 2012).[12]

Law enforcement agencies have not released systematic, detailed information on the use of weapons in the commission of these types of crimes, making rigorous quantitative analysis impossible. Nevertheless, information collected for this chapter provides a qualitative overview of the major trends and dynamics concerning the use of firearms in homicides committed by organized crime groups.

Mafia homicides

Murder is the paradigmatic expression of mafia power. Mafiosi use it to eliminate opponents and competitors, as well as ordinary citizens who may be completely outside criminal enterprises and law enforcement operations. In areas where traditional mafia-type groups are deeply rooted, they tend to vie against the state for the monopoly over the use of force; in a similar vein, they are generally intolerant of other criminal gangs or individual criminals who carry out illegal activities in the areas where they operate. As a consequence, ordinary criminals may need to request authorization from the local mafia clan (Tribunale di Caltanissetta, 2005, pp. 236–37). As already noted, organized crime groups tend to make 'economical' use of violence, seeking to balance the risks of overt displays of armed violence with the need to maintain a violent reputation essential to securing respect from the local population and partnerships with official actors.

During periods of intense conflict, such as the mafia wars that occur cyclically inside

Table 4.1	**Mafia homicides in Italy, by group, 1992–2010**				
Year	**Cosa Nostra**	**'Ndrangheta**	**Camorra**	**SCU**	**Total**
1992	152	53	126	9	340
1993	53	41	59	5	158
1994	83	34	60	4	181
1995	95	38	131	17	281
1996	90	45	138	11	284
1997	48	43	135	21	247
1998	51	28	131	34	244
1999	39	33	80	29	181
2000	17	45	86	26	174
2001	31	39	68	25	163
2002	18	30	54	23	125
2003	13	33	77	37	160
2004	17	45	122	19	203
2005	18	42	72	7	139
2006	14	23	77	8	122
2007	12	16	85	4	117
2008	12	22	59	9	102
2009	19	11	49	7	86
2010	10	24	18	15	67
Totals	**792**	**645**	**1,627**	**310**	**3,374**

Notes: This table combines data from two sources. The Ministero dell'Interno-Direzione Centrale Polizia Criminale (Ministry of Interior-Central Criminal Police Directorate) provides mafia homicide data for the period 1992-2006, broken down by individual organized crime group. Mafia homicide data for 2007-10 is drawn from reporting by the Istituto Nazionale di Statistica (National Institute of Statistics, ISTAT), which disaggregates homicides by region (Apulia, Calabria, Campania, and Sicily, plus one 'other' category). According to ISTAT, mafia homicides in each region mostly correspond to the specific organized crime group dominant in them. In this table, therefore, the regional figures for 2007-10 are applied to each of the four major mafia groups. The table does not include an additional 12 mafia homicides that were recorded outside of the main areas of operation over the four-year period.

Sources: 1996-2006: MI-DCPC (2007); 2007-10: ISTAT (2008; 2009; 2010; 2012); author communication with ISTAT, December 2012

the organized crime world, the use of firearms is usually high, especially in the commission of homicides. During Sicily's 'second mafia war' alone, more than 1,000 people were killed (Dino, 2008, pp. 297–98). In the same period, from 1979 to 1983, the war between the two main groups comprising the Neapolitan Camorra—the Nuova Camorra Organizzata led by Raffaele Cutolo and the Nuova Famiglia—claimed around 900 lives (Brancaccio, 2009, p. 66). In Calabria a few years later, between 1985 and 1991, the 'Ndrangheta killed more than 700 people using mostly its own powerful, sophisticated weapons arsenal (Gratteri and Nicaso, 2009, p. 61). No precise information is available on the types of firearm used in the commission of these homicides.

During the 1990s, mafia homicides showed irregular trends. The highest peak was reached in 1992, with 340 homicides nationally. A general decline followed, with exceptions in 1995 (281 homicides), 1996 (284 homicides), and 1997 (247 homicides). In 1999, 181 mafia homicides were recorded (see Table 4.1).

From 2000 onwards, the overall number of mafia homicides began to decline.

From 2000 onwards, the overall number of mafia homicides began to decline, although there was a peak in 2004 with 203 mafia homicides; given the explosion of the first Scampia *faida* (feud)[13] at that time, the Camorra accounted for more than half of those deaths. Declines accelerated from 2005, dropping almost 52 per cent by 2010. Of a total of 69 mafia-type homicides reported in 2010 throughout Italy, 24 occurred in Calabria, 18 in Campania, 15 in Apulia, and 10 in Sicily, meaning that only 2 homicides—or 3 per cent of the total—were registered outside of the areas under the control of the major mafia groups (ISTAT, 2012). Although the declining number of mafia homicides over the past decade may elicit cautious optimism, a qualitative analysis of data concerning the main organized crime groups operating in the country leads to more complex evaluations.

While the rate of mafia homicides reported by law enforcement in 2010 was 0.1 per 100,000 inhabitants at the national level and 0.3 in the Mezzogiorno—or southern—regions, it was 1.2 per 100,000 in Calabria, the highest among the four traditional mafia regions, with a peak of 3.3 in the city of Catanzaro (ISTAT, 2012).[14] One prosecutor interviewed for this study stressed that, in Calabria, the widespread availability of weapons belonging to the 'Ndrangheta, together with a large percentage of mafiosi out of the total population, may have led to more frequent use of firearms, especially in the area of Reggio Calabria.[15] As he put it: 'the more firearms are available, the more they are used'.[16] While no detailed data is currently available on the actual number of firearms at their disposal, law enforcement officials generally share the view that mafiosi have no shortage of weapons. Traditional cultural codes related to revenge and *faida* may also have contributed to the region's high incidence of violent crime (see Box 4.2).

In addition to being prevalent, mafia homicides in Calabria are often marked by excessive cruelty. One of the most dramatic episodes—perhaps the most brutal in contemporary mafia history—occurred in May 1991, when, during the so-called Taurianova *faida,* which involved several 'Ndrangheta clans, a man was killed and decapitated. His head was subsequently used as a target in a shooting contest improvised by his killers in the middle of the city's main square, in front of almost 20 people who witnessed the macabre scene (Sergi, 1992, p. 20).

The case of the Camorra demonstrates the sometimes very close relationship between violence and cruelty among Italian organized crime groups. The so-called Scampia *faida* in the Naples area in 2004–05 was characterized by an unprecedented level of ferocity—which may be explained on the basis of the perceived need to strengthen, in those exceptional circumstances, the reputation of the clans involved and to impose a climate of terror. The period witnessed many acts of indirect revenge against relatives or people who happened to be close to a clan associate on the run.[17]

One of the cruellest homicides during this *faida* occurred in November 2004, when a 22-year-old woman named Gelsomina Verde was kidnapped, tortured, and shot in the back of the head; her body was subsequently burned inside

Box 4.2 **The Duisburg massacre**

On the night between 14 and 15 August 2007, in the city of Duisburg, Germany, six young Calabrian men were killed by 54 shots fired by two 9 mm pistols a few metres away from an Italian restaurant that belonged to one of the men. The victims were between 17 and 39 years old and all had been somehow connected to a 'Ndrangheta clan based in the remote Calabrian village of San Luca, in the inland area of Aspromonte. For more than 15 years, that clan had been engaged in a brutal conflict with another clan that had originally been based in the same village (Bolzoni, 2008; Colaprico, 2007). As the Anti-mafia Parliamentary Committee states in its report, San Luca could be considered:

> a strategic place in the past and current history of the 'Ndrangheta, a crucial area for the control of drug trafficking [. . .] and the location of a long and bloody *faida* between two family groups belonging to Calabrian mafia aristocracy (CPIFCOMS, 2008, pp. 11-12).

The two clans counted around 100 members each, out of a total population of around 4,000 inhabitants (Baldessero, 2007).

The *faida* arose from an apparently trivial matter. In 1991 in San Luca, during Carnival, a group of boys close to one of the families threw rotten eggs at the windows of a bar owned by a member of the other clan, making fun of the owner's protests and curses. A few days later, in the same village, two young members of the egg-throwing boys' family were killed and two injured. This event marked the beginning of a conflict that saw several deaths and reached its peak at Christmas 2006, when the wife of a boss involved in the *faida* was killed as well (CPIFCOMS, 2008, pp. 11-12).

Although all these events took place in Calabria, the Duisburg massacre occurred because one of the boys shot there was thought to be the custodian of the firearms used to kill the woman a year before; he had been marked for death for this reason. As the parliamentary report states, this 'tribal *faida* mixed with ruthless mafia modernity' sent shockwaves through both Italian and German public opinion (CPIFCOMS, 2008, p. 10). This was the first, and so far probably the only, visible manifestation of bloody violence expressly planned and carried out by a commando belonging to a mafia-type organization sent for that purpose outside the national territory. This massacre exposed the power of a criminality that had originated in the most remote areas of Calabria but was now spreading worldwide 'through the obscure underworld of globalization' (p. 11).

A police inspector holds up a photo of a weapon linked to the Duisburg massacre during a press conference, Duisburg, Germany, March 2009.
© Frank Augstein/AP Photo

Box 4.3   Myths and stereotypes: the mafia code of honour

Traditional mafia-type organizations have often used subtle communication strategies to enhance their mystique (Dino, 2002). The expression *uomini d'onore* (men of honour) used by mafiosi to define members of the group is quite revealing of their long-standing self-perception as men committed to the pursuit of morality and justice. Tommaso Buscetta, one of the first Sicilian turncoat informants, remembered how in the past the Cosa Nostra 'was born to protect weak people from the abuse of the powerful and affirm values such as friendship, family [...], solidarity, *omertà* (the code of silence), in a word, the sense of honour' (Arlacchi, 1994, p. 11). All these values were deeply rooted in the traditional Sicilian sub-cultural system, in which the value of a man was mainly assessed through his ability to defend personal and family honour and avenge offences.

Within the mafia world, these values inform the strategy of the group and the individual alike. Thus, the mafia often represents itself as a sort of brotherhood committed to fighting injustice and protecting the poor. The belief that mafiosi operate according to a code of honour still shapes the widespread popular image of the mafia; in turn, mafiosi exploit that notion to legitimize their use of violence and the management of political functions in local communities (Paoli, 2000, p. 123).

According to this code of honour, mafiosi are not to engage in any disreputable illegal activities—such as prostitution or, at least until the early 1970s, the distribution of drugs[18]—and should protect women and children from violent acts. The latter is one of the most glaring myths the mafia has tried to disseminate, as mafia clans have killed more than 150 women since the end of the 19th century (Associazione daSud, 2012). Women have been killed in the context of indirect revenge or because they were trapped inside perverse family relationships; others were targeted because of their political activism and some lost their lives as innocent bystanders in shootouts. Many others were victims of so-called 'honour homicides' because they had dared to challenge mafia rules, such as by denouncing a mafioso, convincing a relative or husband to collaborate with law enforcement agencies, or choosing a partner who did not share the same mafia background.

Recently released information on suicides committed by women who had collaborated with prosecutors in Calabria in 2011 raised several disturbing questions. In at least two cases these women had decided—or were forced—to kill themselves by drinking hydrochloric acid, which is not only extremely painful, but also peculiar from a symbolic perspective. Celeste Costantino of the anti-mafia organization daSud stresses the ambivalent feelings that may have induced these women—who were profoundly influenced by their socialization to mafia disvalues—to take such a dramatic decision:

from the mouth some revelations came out, and through the same mouth one washes away the temptation to continue this, the desperation of having tried to do this, and the dishonour of having already done this (Associazione daSud, 2012, p. 5).

her car. A few months before the murder, she had dated a man who had been 'sentenced to death' by the clan and had thus gone into hiding (Saviano, 2006, pp. 94–97). The mafiosi had aimed to find out his whereabouts from the young woman. That homicide was clearly an extreme and symbolic act of violence. As Roberto Saviano notes in his book on the Camorra, which delves into accounts of this *faida*, 'people may become maps on which messages are inscribed' (Saviano, 2006, p. 97; see Box 4.3).

Among the traditional mafia-type organizations, the Camorra stands out for resorting to violence, seemingly indifferent to the general rule of parsimony observed by the Cosa Nostra and the 'Ndrangheta and to the possible effects of the uneconomical use of violence.[19] One Camorra defector, for example, stated that his boss was so 'bloodthirsty' that he did not consider the consequences of his violent acts. While driving a car in a residential district of Naples, the boss had told him that he felt disappointed because there were no police cars he could shoot at to provide 'another signal' (*La Repubblica*, 2011). The Camorra committed an estimated 3,500 homicides between 1980 and 2008 (Brancaccio, 2009, p. 72).

Mafia groups also fall back on homicides to address internal conflicts and non-compliance with the rules of the organization, such as when members abuse drugs or flirt with the wives of imprisoned clan members.[20] No data is available on mafia homicides related to internal disputes.

Similar characteristics in the use of violence have been recorded in the Apulian SCU. Since its beginnings at the end of the 1980s, this criminal group has frequently employed armed violence to exert hegemony over the local underworld. The area of Salento—the southern part of the region where the SCU maintains its base—witnessed 118 mafia homicides in 1989 and 145 the following year. Violence and terror became common tools for achieving power and securing a reputation (Dino, 2008, p. 293).

From the late 1990s until 2005, the SCU was almost decapitated by tough law enforcement operations in the areas of Lecce and Brindisi, several court trials, and the incarceration of most of the bosses. This period also saw an increase in an Albanian criminal presence in the region and, along with it, trafficking activities mostly related to the drug trade (Massari, 2008, p. 503). Fear of attracting further attention from police convinced leading SCU clans to adopt a much lower profile.

One of the most recent important SCU homicides occurred in 2003, in the area of Lecce, when a boss was killed in a bar, in front of many witnesses, with the express aim of sending a clear message to his affiliates to squash their attempts at establishing control over a number of illegal activities in the area.[21] The SCU is currently implementing a more subtle strategy, aware that:

> *any mafia that can manage to ensure order in the areas where it operates, without using conspicuous forms of violence, ends up being more easily tolerated and in turn seen as a subject that may offer alternative services to the state* (DNA, 2011, p. 149).

Cosa Nostra boss Bernardo Provenzano enters a police building in Palermo escorted by hooded police officers, April 2006. © Luca Bruno/AP Photo

In this regard, the Apulian criminal organization more closely resembles the Sicilian model, which is currently characterized by stricter internal secrecy due in part to the adoption of new rules, such as only allowing membership to individuals from the same village (DNA, 2011, p. 149).

With respect to the Cosa Nostra, one prosecutor stated that the general strategy is to employ homicide as a tool for solving a problem without creating additional problems.[22] Nino Giuffrè, a defector from the Sicilian mafia, corroborated this point by referring to what his boss Bernardo Provenzano once told him: 'It should be evaluated whether somebody causes more harm dead or alive.'[23]

Overall, the Cosa Nostra prefers a gradual increase in the use of violence. The first step is usually a threat, at times indirect rather than explicit; if that threat is not heeded, it may be followed by the actual use of violent methods.[24] After a relatively calm phase in Sicily, the Cosa Nostra appears to have reintegrated the use of homicide as a tool for solving internal problems.[25] The five murders that took place in the Palermo area in 2011 confirm that the Sicilian organization still employs homicide as a governing tool; that approach may set the tone for future strategies as the organization emerges from a transition phase that began with the arrest of Bernardo Provenzano in April 2006 (DNA, 2011, p. 52).

There is a specific reason why homicide statistics may be undercounts, especially in Sicily. The preferred mafia killing method is referred to as *lupara bianca*, which calls for the elimination of all physical evidence of the victim. The victim is usually strangled or suffocated and the body dissolved in acid. Although this practice is still in evidence in Sicily—where four cases were recorded in 2011—and in Calabria, it is mostly used during relatively calm phases, during which homicides can be planned far in advance.[26] One prosecutor remarked that, whenever possible, the Cosa Nostra prefers to use hands and acid rather than firearms.[27]

Each organized crime family usually relies on its own firearm arsenal.

CHARACTERISTICS OF GUN USE BY ORGANIZED CRIME GROUPS

Acquisition of and access to weapons

Italian law requires licensed firearms dealers to verify the eligibility of purchasers and maintain records of gun purchases, which must be forwarded to the police on a monthly basis (Italy, 2010). Ineligible buyers, such as members of criminal groups, tend to obtain guns from the legitimate market through 'straw purchasers'—relatives, friends, or ordinary citizens with a gun licence who buy firearms on their behalf and then usually report them stolen. Serial numbers on these firearms are usually obliterated. As a straw purchaser is not likely to be able to acquire more than one gun in this way, mafiosi seem to rely on more structured sources of supply to maintain their arsenals.

Mafiosi have also made use of explosives, as when the Cosa Nostra employed TNT during the terror strategy between 1992 and 1993. Investigators recently accused a fisherman from the Palermo area of providing explosives recovered from sunken mines, torpedoes, unexploded ordnance, and aerial bombs left over from World War II (Selvatici, 2012).

Each organized crime family usually relies on its own firearm arsenal, which represents the collective property of the group. Results from several investigations show that each criminal group, particularly in the Cosa Nostra, has members who, because of their expertise and contacts, are in charge of procuring firearms, which are stored and distributed to other members based on the circumstances or specific requests (Tribunale per i Minorenni di Caltanissetta, 2003, p. 27). In some cases, these arsenals consist of very old firearms that are stored, regularly oiled, and maintained by members expressly devoted to these tasks. In others, they expand continuously as the group uses family funds to buy new or second-hand 'pieces', depending on their availability.[28]

There are some exceptions to these arrangements. The Brancaccio family, the Palermo-based group charged with most of the killings in the area during the 1990s, relied on firearms stored and provided by another Cosa Nostra family, which managed one of the largest arsenals ever discovered in Sicily, the Misilmeri arsenal (Corte di Assise di Palermo, 2001, pp. 12–21). In 1992, Leonardo Messina, one of the first Cosa Nostra turncoat informants, also explained that the Campofranco family based near Caltanissetta was the main firearms supplier for other groups operating in that area (Tribunale di Caltanissetta, 2012, p. 183). As another defector puts it: 'providing firearms [to other groups] is considered a sort of customer service' (Tribunale di Caltanissetta, 2004, p. 125).

Such family-wide ownership may have developed in an effort to withstand any scarcity of firearms at the local level as well as to meet internal demand for specific types of weapons. This approach may also facilitate safe storage, away from the area where both the mafia group and law enforcement units usually operate. In these cases, members usually return firearms to the family in charge of storing them after their use (Corte di Assise di Caltanissetta, 2000, p. 191).

If a group decides to commit a homicide outside its own territory, it must abide by certain guidelines. Cosa Nostra rules, which some other organized crime groups also follow, require that the group request authorization from the local family and use firearms borrowed from that family (Tribunale di Caltanissetta, 2004, p. 125). Similarly, when professional killers are hired, their employers must provide the firearms needed for the crime.

Although firearms are usually considered group property, research suggests that individual members may also own personal guns. Firearms are sometimes given as a gift to affiliates as a sign of friendship or trust or just to mark special occasions. One Camorra turncoat, employed as a hit man by the Gionta clan,[29] described how the clan boss gave him a pistol as a gift immediately after his formal affiliation. Afterwards, he was invited to choose any guns he liked from a big bag; he recounted selecting 'the flashiest guns' (Tribunale di Torre Annunziata, 2009, p. 69).

The ability to shoot is among the top qualities of a man of honour.

Camorra clans display a high level of firearms exchange among members. Guns often circulate from one clan to another after being adequately modified to avoid traceability. Thus there is a large availability of old firearms for use in the management of various crimes.[30]

Another important factor in the use of firearms is a mafioso's ability to shoot. The 'Ndrangheta has always considered marksmanship an important skill and a testing ground for new members.[31] One of the cruellest killers in the Corleonesi family, called 'Scarpuzzedda', was a Cosa Nostra legend because of his excellent firearm skills. As one prosecutor put it, from Bernardo Provenzano on down, 'the ability to shoot is among the top qualities of a man of honour'.[32]

Arsenal sizes and distribution

Assessing the size and quality of current organized crime arsenals is not an easy task; indeed, available information is highly fragmented because there is no systematic collection of data. Most of the details have come to light as a result of law enforcement seizures, which often take place in response to information provided by mafia turncoats. Indeed, police tend to test the reliability of *pentiti* by asking them to locate hidden arsenals. Given the strict territorial organization of major mafia groups, each one usually relies on its own arsenal. Thus, information provided to the police will help to dismantle just that single arsenal. A turncoat is highly unlikely to have any details on other arsenals, given that each family jealously guards such information. That said, several arsenals were found as a result of ad hoc investigations in the area of Caltanissetta, Sicily, in 2011–12.[33]

Since the number of arsenals discovered in a certain area is not necessarily an indicator of the availability of firearms to a certain group, data derived from seizures cannot simply be generalized to produce broader findings. Nevertheless, interviews suggest that, in the case of both the Camorra and the 'Ndrangheta, the areas where these criminal organizations traditionally operate—Campania and Calabria—are 'flooded' with large numbers of weapons.[34]

In contrast, Cosa Nostra arsenals in Sicily seem to be mainly composed of 'old' firearms that have been in storage for many years. Given the sophisticated technology of pistols and assault rifles produced up to 50 years ago, some organized crime groups may not perceive a need to update their stock regularly in order to remain competitive (UNODC, 2010, p. 129). Nevertheless, the Sicilian mafia is currently 'starved' for weapons and trying to buy whatever the illicit market may offer.[35]

As mentioned earlier, a mafia family that owns its own arsenal usually stores its own firearms. An important exception emerged in 2001 with the seizure of one of the largest Cosa Nostra arsenals. Some of the weapons in the so-called Balistreri arsenal, run by a group associated with the Misilmeri mafia family, belonged to another group—the Brancaccio family, based in Palermo—for whom the local clan acted as trusted manager (Corte di Assise di Palermo, 2001, pp. 163, 180–81).[36]

In both Sicily and Calabria, most arsenals are discovered in rural areas, close to old houses, inside farm stalls, behind double walls, in bunkers, or in underground caches or wooden boxes.[37] The firearms may be individually wrapped in cellophane to avoid the effects of humidity, or they may be placed in sacks and then wrapped in large plastic bags. Another creative form of storing firearms was recently discovered in Naples, where seven pistols and ammunition had been hidden behind the altar in a church whose entrance was monitored through a video surveillance system (Quotidiano.Net, 2012).

Generally, two people are in charge of arsenals, a guardian and a trustee; if one of them is arrested, the other one can immediately move the weapons elsewhere.[38] Results from several investigations show that these custodians occasionally dig up, check, and clean the weapons (Corte di Assise di Palermo, 2001, p. 181). In Calabria, especially along the Tyrrhenian coast, authorities have discovered

Weapons confiscated by police from members of the Camorra, Scampia, Naples, December 2004. © Silvia Morara/Corbis

several arsenals guarded mostly by farmers.[39] As stated by a prosecutor interviewed, the Camorra usually appoints people with no links to the criminal group as firearm keepers. The group tends to select individuals with no criminal record or known offences, so that they do not attract attention. In exchange, the guardians receive a monthly payment from the organization.[40]

Weapon types and procurement patterns

The image of a mafioso with a *lupara*—a homemade sawn-off shotgun—has become a ubiquitous symbol of Italian organized crime in the public imagination. Traditionally used in wolf hunting—the word 'lupara' means 'for a wolf'—this weapon has a shortened barrel, allowing easier concealment, and the lack of a choke allows for a wider spread of shot when the weapon is fired. Especially in the past, mafiosi preferred to use this unsophisticated hunting weapon as it was not likely to attract police attention and because its ammunition, once fired, could not be easily identified. Its use was particularly widespread in the Sicilian countryside, such as the areas surrounding the cities of Agrigento, Caltanissetta, and Trapani.[41] Nevertheless, during the past few decades, the use of the lupara has continually

declined, especially in Sicily and Calabria, where it was most popular in the past.[42]

Since the 1970s and early 1980s, the level of sophistication in mafia weaponry has increased, as has the variety of firearms available in mafia arsenals. Thanks to greater financial resources, the Cosa Nostra, for example, started using short-barrel guns, such as .38-calibre and .357 Magnum handguns. Assault rifles, such as AK-pattern rifles, and rocket and grenade launchers have been introduced in more difficult assaults (Sagramoso, 2001, p. 22). One prosecutor argued that the Cosa Nostra first began to avail itself of AK-pattern assault rifles in the early 1980s, testing them against bullet-proof jewellery store windows to gauge their power; the group later used the weapons in homicides, such as the 'Palermo ring road massacre', which claimed five lives in June 1982, and the homicide of Gen. Carlo Alberto dalla Chiesa, his wife, and a police agent a few months later.[43]

During the mid-1990s, the increased availability of cheap, yet powerful, weapons that mostly originated in Belgium and the

Balkans—including AK-pattern rifles, machine guns, pistols, hand grenades, and anti-tank rocket launchers—created a growing demand among Italian criminal organizations for new kinds of equipment. During this period, the bosses of the Cosa Nostra's dominant Corleonese family and other clans based in Catania significantly increased their arsenals (Sagramoso, 2001, pp. 22–23).

Some of the newly acquired firearms were found by Italian police in 1996, when, in just a few months, large numbers of weapons were discovered in San Giuseppe Jato, a village 40 km from Palermo, and Mala Tacca, a rural area near the highway between Palermo and the local airport (Lodato, 1996, p. 8). At that time, the San Giuseppe Jato arsenal was the largest that had ever been discovered by law enforcement in Italy. Police seized two underground bunkers that contained, among other weapons, 10 missiles, 10 bazookas, 50 AK-pattern rifles, 35 pistols, 7 sub-machine guns, 10 anti-tank bombs, 400 kg of explosives, and some bulletproof jackets; most of these weapons originated in Eastern Europe, the former Yugoslavia, Iran, and Afghanistan (Viviano, 1996, p. 20).

These seizures occurred during the relatively calm period following the 1992–93 'killing season', when the Cosa Nostra decided to adopt a lower profile. The fact that the seized weapons were mostly new and in perfect working order suggests that the Sicilian syndicate had maintained its 'military' potential despite its attempt to avoid escalations of violence. As demonstrated through a recent flurry of homicides, this behaviour has remained intact, indicating that violence continues to be a viable option for these groups, as long as its use is planned according to the circumstances and in line with specific rules.

Criminal organizations face hardly any problems in securing their own weapons sources. Some organized crime groups have access to large stockpiles of sophisticated weaponry, including military firearms and—as several *pentiti* have argued with reference to the Sicilian Cosa Nostra—even bazookas. They generally prefer to use 7.65 mm machine guns and revolvers,[44] as well as 9 × 21 mm pistols—the model used by Italian police. AK-pattern assault rifles are also widely used, since they seldom misfire, cost less than their market equivalent (the M16), and are best known by members.[45] Yet, on the whole, the choice of weapon is driven by pragmatism and weapons are usually destroyed after the commission of a crime.[46] Still, some mafiosi may select specific types of firearm for comfort and reliability. During shortages, they may even use surviving wartime firearms or modified toy guns.

To date, law enforcement has not been able to shed much light on mafia firearm procurement practices. It is not clear whether each organization relies on one single supply source or many. In the past, the Camorra was considered the most successful in opening and securing reliable procurement channels, thanks to strong links with Eastern European criminal organizations.[47] Although no steady supply channels have emerged so far, most *pentiti* confirm that criminal organizations face hardly any problems in securing their own weapons sources.[48]

In terms of firearm procurement, four main patterns can be identified:

- robberies from firearm shops;
- theft of firearms from military or police forces;
- theft of firearms from private citizens; and
- exchange of illegal goods (such as drugs) for firearms.[49]

As with terrorist groups during the 1970s, thefts from firearm shops have always been one of the most popular mafia procurement patterns. However, some firearm shopkeepers have colluded with certain mafia clans. One interviewee remarked that in Sicily there have always been 'Cosa Nostra armouries' that provided firearms to both hunters and mafiosi.[50] In addition, the use of firearms stolen from police officers allowed some Camorra groups in particular to expand and diversify their arsenals, as evidenced during the 1990s, when large numbers of firearms stolen from Naples police headquarters ended up in the hands of the Casalesi clans.[51]

In some cases, such procurement was facilitated by individuals who were nominally on the right side of the law. In fact, a major international firearms trafficking operation discovered in 2006 was actually run by a carabinieri marshal who had supplied new arms—especially AK-pattern rifles—to several Casalesi clans (Tribunale di Napoli, 2010, p. 44). In addition, almost 70 per cent of the 'thefts' of legally owned civilian-held firearms in Campania had been faked; the guns were not stolen but voluntarily given to mafiosi. This type of procurement represents an important channel used by organized crime to secure 'clean' weapons for homicides and other crimes.[52]

Mafiosi also procure weapons through drug-trafficking and other channels used by networks and suppliers based in Eastern Europe and the Balkans. In this context, arms are often paid for with drugs—especially cocaine, whose trafficking and wholesale distribution in Europe are largely supervised by the Calabrian 'Ndrangheta—or cash, given the enormous cash flows provided by drug trafficking.[53] Criminal gangs operating in Rome—some of which were involved in homicides that have sparked widespread social outrage—use the same procurement approach. They invest part of the large flow of drug money in the purchase of firearms. For members of these gangs, the availability and use of large numbers of weapons secures them high criminal status in the greater underworld system.[54]

Gun trafficking

Almost 30 years ago, in a speech on firearms at a conference in Brescia,[55] the Sicilian judge Giovanni Falcone warned his audience about the crucial role of the illegal firearms trade in facilitating connections between apparently distinct sectors of criminal activity—such as drug trafficking. He also called attention to emerging partnerships between criminal organizations and legitimate partners operating in different countries (Falcone, 1984). He referred to a number of investigations that had provided some evidence on how Italian organized crime groups exchanged firearms for other illicit commodities—at that time mostly heroin from the Middle East—emphasizing the significant international financial flows created by these activities. He also mentioned the strong, though neglected, links between mafiosi and white-collar criminals, who are mostly specialized in money-laundering activities, in terms of both firearms and drugs, calling them the most worrying trend and a true danger for democratic institutions. Years later, criminologist Vincenzo Ruggiero described these links as the 'dirty economy', an area characterized by 'the exchange of services and mutual entrepreneurial promotion between conventional organized crime and official actors' (Ruggiero, 1997, p. 35).[56]

> Western Balkans, the Russian Federation, and Eastern Europe are key sources of firearms trafficked into the EU.

Since then, in Italy, no comprehensive investigation of the illegal firearms trade has successfully shed light in a systematic way on the characteristics of this market, its actors, routes, or trafficking methods, even though large numbers of weapons have been readily available to major mafia groups since the late 1970s (Sagramoso, 2001, p. 22).[57]

Based on information released in official reports and the few available studies, as well as data provided by interviewees, Italian criminal organizations appear to be active as traffickers, buyers, and intermediaries in the international illegal firearms trade. Since the end of the conflicts of the 1990s, large illegal stockpiles have remained beyond the control of authorities, leaving the Western Balkans, as well as the Russian Federation and Eastern European countries, as key sources of firearms trafficked into the European Union (Europol, 2011, p. 38). The geographical proximity of Italy to the former Yugoslavia and Albania has allowed domestic criminal groups to buy weapons at relatively low prices (Sagramoso, 2001, p. 21). Of the networks based in Italy, Europol finds that the 'Ndrangheta and the Albanian criminal groups are most involved in the illegal arms trade (Europol, 2011, p. 38).[58]

During the Balkan conflicts of the mid-1990s in particular, the Apulian SCU also established close links with new partners operating on the other side of the Adriatic Sea (Jamieson and Silj, 1998, p. 22; DNA, 2008, p. 803).[59] According to the Anti-mafia Investigative Directorate, the number of seizures of ammunition and explosives in Apulia in 1998 was 50 per cent above the national average (Sagramoso, 2001, p. 25). Today, most weapons available to the SCU still come from Albania and the former Yugoslavia; these include Tokarev pistols, AK-pattern rifles, and Chinese grenades trafficked through Albania.[60]

During the 1990s, mafiosi smuggling routes that had traditionally been used for cigarettes and drugs were easily converted to channel the growing flow of illegal immigrants from Albania. In a report released in 2003, the Anti-mafia Parliamentary Committee stresses that, during the 1990s, firearms and ammunition, along with immigrants, also travelled in small, fast boats along the same routes. The strong partnership established between mafia groups and foreign criminal organizations facilitated a specific type of service exchange; Italian organizations requested drugs and firearms in order to allow Balkan organized crime groups to manage the business of irregular immigration by sea along the Italian coast (CPIFCOMS, 2003, p. 304). In this way, the Committee concludes, Italy became the main hub in the international illicit firearms trade managed by Albanian and Montenegrin criminals along routes previously used by Apulian tobacco smugglers (p. 275).

From the Balkans, smuggled weapons still cross the Adriatic by boat or travel by land through northern Italy. They are often concealed in legitimate loads, carried in trucks or jeeps, or transported in small quantities in private cars, often temporarily hidden in sheds near highways before they reach their final destination (Sagramoso, 2001, p. 23; Europol, 2011, p. 38). Although no systematic information is currently available on illicit arms flows from the Balkans to or through Italy, the country is considered a major transit point for smuggled weapons headed to northern and eastern Europe (Sagramoso, 2001, p. 21).

Each mafia clan relies on its own fire group.

Gruppi di fuoco (fire groups)

Italian organized crime groups assign the use of violence inside and outside the group to members expressly chosen for that purpose. As suggested by their Italian designation, *gruppi di fuoco* (fire groups), these individuals form units in charge of carrying out a wide array of violent acts, ranging from physical assaults to killings, although homicides are by far the most frequent.

Each clan typically relies on its own fire group. In cases such as the Secondigliano Alliance, based in the area of Naples and composed of a federation of several Camorra groups, each clan may provide its own killers for the Alliance's fire group.[61] In other cases, professional hit men are lent out to other clans for assignments. This strategy helps ensure a higher level of anonymity and wider freedom of movement; moreover, it reduces the chances that law enforcement agencies will be able to identify the authors of crime (Tribunale di Torre Annunziata, 2009, p. 159).

Although marksmanship is among the most appreciated skills in gruppi di fuoco, larger fire groups tend to comprise members who perform various tasks besides shooting. Especially in the case of the Cosa Nostra, investigations have shown that these members provide services such as stealing motorbikes for use in attacks, riding them during attacks, and destroying (usually burning) them immediately after a homicide in order to erase all possible traces left by the killers. These groups may also contain as many as six or seven people who—as asserted during an interview—operate as 'commandos', sometimes without even knowing the target they are meant to hit.[62] Membership in a fire group can also serve to test one's personal ability or to create a strong bond among clan members.[63]

Key homicides by fire groups, such as the one in 2007 in Palermo, tend to be precisely planned. Selected members follow the victims to be able to predict their movements and patterns, such as when they leave work or when they usually go to their favourite bar, and others prepare the overall strategy and provide support during and immediately after the act.[64]

Particularly in the past, the Camorra's more structured clans tended to adopt strict selection criteria regarding the composition of fire groups. As has been reported about the Cosa Nostra, membership in a fire group has often allowed mafiosi to advance in the group's internal hierarchy; indeed, it functions as one of the main channels of upward mobility inside criminal organizations. Both Antonio Iovine and Michele Zagaria—two powerful bosses in

---

Box 4.4 Becoming a mafia soldier: the case of minors

In the bestseller *Gomorrah,* Roberto Saviano tells of his encounter–probably fictitious but quite plausible–with Pikachu, a 14-year-old boy from Secondigliano, a socially deprived area in the northern part of Naples and one of the main battlefields in the so-called Scampia *faida* that exploded among Camorra clans in 2004. Pikachu–a nickname taken from a Japanese cartoon–guides Saviano through the streets of Secondigliano, where they meet Tonino Kit Kat, a boy who is already affiliated with the so-called *System* (the name given by Camorra members to their criminal organization).

Although reluctant to answer his questions, Tonino shows the novelist the big bruises on his chest. Those large, livid spots on his adolescent body were the signs left by gunshots to his flak jacket during his training in the use of firearms. As Saviano puts it:

> in order to train them not to fear firearms, [Camorra members] ask them to wear flak jackets and then they shoot at them [. . .]. Kit Kat had been trained, with others, to receive shots, a training for death, indeed, *almost* death (Saviano, 2006, pp. 118-19).

The Italian Interior Ministry reports that from 1990 to 2002, 147 minors were charged with membership in a mafia-type organization in Apulia and Campania while an additional 167 were charged in Sicily and Calabria (Ministero della Giustizia, 2004, pp. 19-20). The most represented age group was that of 16-17-year-olds; more than 79 per cent of minors in Apulia and Campania had a previous criminal record and around 40 per cent had family members already charged with the same crime (pp. 24-26).

Children who have relatives involved in mafia businesses risk greater exposure to violence and may be more likely to participate in criminal activities than their peers. While social deprivation may lead some youths to join mafia groups, others pursue membership to gain a sense of belonging to what they perceive as a mysterious and powerful world. The mythical self-representation the mafia tends to disseminate captivates these boys.[65] One Sicilian 'baby hit man' explained why there were so many adolescent members in his clan: 'No problem at all, because . . . I don't know, probably because Sicily is like that, but there is this prestige thing' (Tribunale per i minorenni di Caltanissetta, 2003, p. 26).

Mafia-type organizations usually choose their members based on their abilities and capacities, rather than simple blood ties, which are important but not crucial. Minors may be particularly sought-after since they attract less attention and can be used as killers without alarming the victim. As one former member of the Sicilian Stidda group told the judge who interviewed him, 'a mafioso does not care about a 13- or 14-year-old boy. He does not expect him to put a gun to his head and fire as soon as his back is turned' (Tribunale per i minorenni di Caltanissetta, 2003, p. 26).[66] The same goes for law enforcement agencies, since minors rarely attract their attention. Furthermore, adolescents are 'cheap merchandise'; they are paid less than adults, work long hours, are always available on the streets, and can be easily replaced (Dino, 2012, p. 160; Saviano, 2006, p. 119).

The Camorra has always used adolescents for different tasks, not necessarily as killers, but often as sentries at entrances to areas of the city where retail drug markets flourish or as lookouts during the commission of robberies and other crimes.[67] Currently, the so-called Secondigliano System relies largely on the availability of adolescents; as formal mafia members, these youths have been entrusted with important roles, including in fire groups that are responsible for recent homicides (Cantone, 2012, p. 41). In the past, these boys would have had to go through a sort of apprenticeship, which would gradually have allowed them to ascend the mafia social ladder. Nowadays, they can play leading roles by the time they turn 20. This trend is also in evidence in more structured, traditional mafia-type organizations, such as the Cosa Nostra, where one of Palermo's emerging bosses is thought to be in his twenties.[68]

the Casalesi cartel arrested between 2010 and 2011—began their careers as hit men in a fire group (Cantone, 2012, p. 28). In the case of the Camorra, members used to be able to advance gradually thanks to individual abilities and merits, yet nowadays criminal careers appear to be shorter than in the past. This shift could be related to the high level of violence affecting the Campanian criminal organization since the late 1990s and the related fragmentation and conflicts within the group (see Box 4.4).

The approach adopted by Camorra fire groups during some of the cruellest massacres in the past decade is similar to heavy combat strategy. During the 30-second raid in Castelvolturno in September 2008, when six African immigrants were killed, the use of firearms was so utterly disproportionate—considering that none of the victims were able to defend themselves—that at least 125 bullets were found on the ground, fired from two AK-pattern assault rifles, one 9 mm sub-machine gun, and four semi-automatic pistols (della Valle, 2009). According to investigators, this strategy—which led prosecutors to charge the group with the aggravating circumstance of terrorism—may also be linked to widespread cocaine use among Camorra members. Such drug abuse has also led to a marked decline in the professionalism of fire groups, leaving the Camorra reliant on at most three or four reliable killers in all of Campania.[69]

CONCLUSION

In a first step towards bridging the information gap on the use of firearms by organized crime groups in Italy, this chapter presents original research and analyses relevant information available from official, academic, and media sources. It finds that, to maintain their power and strategic resources, mafia-type organizations under review prioritize the availability of large arsenals and sophisticated weaponry as well as the ability to rely on members who are specialized in the use of firearms—such as the fire groups.

Since 2007, most criminal organizations—especially the Cosa Nostra and the SCU—appear to have entered a submersion phase, confirmed by a 43 per cent decrease in the number of homicides through 2010 (see Table 4.1). This submersion is most probably strategic, aimed at avoiding law enforcement attention as the groups consolidate their hold on legal markets. They have similarly tended to minimize the use of firearms in recent years. But emerging trends, such as the case of the latest Camorra *faida* or the return of mafia homicides in Palermo, indicate that the use of armed violence remains an available option.

While important strides have been made in understanding patterns of firearm acquisition, possession, and storage, as well as mafia groups' deployment of firearm violence, quantitative data remains weak and further research on firearm-related crimes in Italy is clearly needed. As of this writing, researchers had not yet been granted access to a considerable pool of existing official data, including on firearms seizures and the type of crimes committed with firearms by mafia clans. Once this important information becomes public, it will help present a much more focused picture of the actual dimensions and characteristics of mafia-related violence—and of ways to contain and reduce it. ◼

LIST OF ABBREVIATIONS

DDA	Direzione Distrettuale Antimafia (District Anti-mafia Directorate)
DNA	Direzione Nazionale Antimafia (National Anti-mafia Directorate)
ISTAT	Istituto Nazionale di Statistica (National Institute of Statistics)
SCU	Sacra Corona Unita

ENDNOTES

1   Issued in 1982, Law No. 646, also known as the Rognoni–La Torre Law, introduced Article 416bis into the Italian penal code, criminalizing membership in mafia-type associations. It also informed the definition of the term 'organized crime group' adopted in the United Nations Convention against Transnational Organized Crime (Italy, 1982; UNODC, 2004).

2   Although the terms 'mafia' and 'organized crime' are often used as synonyms, they are analytically distinct; in the Italian context, they are usually employed to distinguish between traditional, mostly autochthonous criminal groups that are often characterized by a hierarchical structure—referred to as mafia-type associations—and more recent, loosely organized, and sometimes exogenous criminal organizations—which are generally defined as organized crime groups.

3   The expression 'traditional mafia-type organizations' was coined in 1994 by the Anti-mafia Parliamentary Committee in reference to the Cosa Nostra, the 'Ndrangheta, the Camorra, and the Sacra Corona Unita (CPIFCOMS, 1994, p. 9).

4   Most foreign criminal organizations active in Italy would fall outside this definition because of the lack of social control outside the boundaries of their ethnic communities or the inability to take root locally.

5   Although most Cosa Nostra affiliates involved in these crimes were sentenced—and the criminal responsibility of these massacres clearly identified—there is still a vacuum in the so-called 'hidden agents' of these acts; that is, the secret architects behind that strategy. As several investigations have already shown, in the early 1990s the Cosa Nostra was actively looking to establish close partnerships with politicians and members of various agencies who could have provided benefits if that 'massacre strategy' stopped. This sensitive yet crucial topic—referred to as the *trattativa* (negotiation) between the mafia and the state—was the object of great debate in Italy in 2012.

6   The word 'Ndrangheta resembles the Greek term *andragatia*, which refers to virile virtues, courage, and rectitude (CPIFCOMS, 2008, p. 15).

7   According to the chief prosecutor of the Direzione Distrettuale Antimafia (Anti-mafia District Directorate, or DDA) of Naples, in 2009 almost 30 per cent of Neapolitan politicians and local representatives were in collusion with the Camorra (Barbagallo, 2010, pp. 239–40).

8   Furthermore, the promotion of members to various ranks within the internal hierarchy usually takes place through rituals based on traditional codes and statutes from old secret criminal associations rooted in southern Italy (Massari, 1998).

9   As clearly stated in several reports issued by the Anti-mafia Parliamentary Committee since the mid-1990s, and as recently confirmed by major investigations—such as those code-named 'Infinito' and 'Crimine', which concluded in 2010 and 2011, respectively, shedding light on 'Ndrangheta activity in Lombardy—traditional mafia-type organizations have also successfully managed to impose their control in various north-central Italian regions (Sciarrone, 2009; Varese, 2011; CPIFCOMS, 2010b).

10   As Alessandra Dino notes, 'the massacre strategy of the early 1990s […] was planned by counting on the echo effect that the media would produce and on the impact that this wave of homicides and attacks would have on the population' (Dino, 2002, p. 163).

11   Neither the Direzione Investigativa Antimafia (Anti-mafia Investigative Directorate) nor the Direzione Centrale della Polizia Criminale (Central Directory of the Criminal Police)—institutional agencies in charge of analysing mafia crime trends—currently collects systematic data on the use of firearms by organized crime groups. Author phone interview with an officer of the Direzione Investigativa Antimafia, Rome, 11 September 2012.

12   These files are part of the 'Infinito' investigation, carried out between 2006 and 2010 by the DDA of Milan in cooperation with the DDA of Reggio Calabria (Tribunale Ordinario di Milano, 2010, p. 61).

13   The word *faida* usually refers to conflicts that affect two mafia clans operating within a limited area. These conflicts tend to revolve around issues of honour and personal revenge. They typically fluctuate in intensity, often going through latent phases only to suddenly explode again (Brancaccio, 2009, pp. 74–75).

14   That same year, the mafia homicide rate was 0.3 in Campania, 0.4 in Apulia, and 0.2 in Sicily (ISTAT, 2012).

15   The 'Ndrangheta currently relies on an estimated 10,000–15,000 affiliates and includes approximately 170 member clans. Yet, as stated by the former chief prosecutor for the DDA in Reggio Calabria, these figures may be significant underestimates. He added that, in a small village such as Rosarno, one of the 'Ndrangheta strongholds in Calabria, the number of affiliates is around 250, out of a total population of 15,000 inhabitants. If relatives, friends, and acquaintances are factored in, that number can swell to 1,500–2,000 related adults. Not even in Palermo does the Cosa Nostra rely on such a large proportion of affiliates (CPIFCOMS, 2010b, p. 5).

16   Author interview with an adjunct prosecutor, DDA, Reggio Calabria, 24 August 2012.

17   Author interview with a deputy national anti-mafia prosecutor, Rome, 9 July 2012. Roberto Saviano describes this *faida* as the cruellest in southern Italy in the past ten years (Saviano, 2006, p. 91). According to the latest DNA report, in December 2011 this *faida* had not yet concluded (DNA, 2011, p. 80).

18   As one member of the Cosa Nostra from the Agrigento area in Sicily replied to questions posed by the judge interrogating him: 'I consider myself not guilty of the crime of both membership in a criminal association and a mafia-type association, since I have never committed a crime, nor have I joined others for this purpose. But I should say that I was born and will die mafioso, if mafia means, as I understand it, doing good to others, providing for those in need, finding a job for the unemployed […]. I think that those who hurt others and, in particular, those in the drug trafficking business are not mafiosi, but just ordinary delinquents. They are damaging the younger generations. When I come into contact

with somebody who traffics drugs, I move away from him because I feel disgusted' (Paoli, 2000, p. 126). This member was actually far from being this altruistic; yet the powerful role of traditional cultural codes in backing his identity as a mafioso and legitimizing his power must be recognized (p. 126).

19   Author interview with a deputy national anti-mafia prosecutor, Rome, 9 July 2012.

20   Author interview with a deputy national anti-mafia prosecutor, Rome, 9 July 2012.

21   Author interview with the chief prosecutor, DDA, Lecce, 5 July 2012.

22   Author interview with a deputy national anti-mafia prosecutor, Rome, 28 June 2012.

23   Author interview with an adjunct prosecutor, DDA, Reggio Calabria, 24 August 2012.

24   Author interview with a deputy national anti-mafia prosecutor, Rome, 28 June 2012.

25   The last major homicide that affected internal Cosa Nostra power strategies occurred in June 2007 (DNA, 2011, p. 52).

26   The perpetrators of such murders can display inconceivable callousness. One former Cosa Nostra member confessed that, after having strangled a thief and placed his body in acid, he and his companion became hungry and decided to eat some sandwiches. Referring to his companion, Gaspare Spatuzza, he explained: 'He ate the sandwich with one hand, while he stirred the tibia and thighbones of the man he was dissolving in acid with the other' (Bolzoni, 2009).

27   Author interview with a deputy national anti-mafia prosecutor, Rome, 28 June 2012.

28   Author interview with a deputy national anti-mafia prosecutor, Rome, 28 June 2012.

29   This clan traditionally operates in the area of Torre Annunziata on the Gulf of Naples.

30   Author interview with a judge, Ufficio del Massimario della Suprema Corte di Cassazione, Naples, 27 June 2012.

31   Author interview with the chief of the Police Department's Flying Squad, Rome, 10 July 2012.

32   Author interview with a deputy national anti-mafia prosecutor, Rome, 28 June 2012.

33   Author interview with a deputy national anti-mafia prosecutor, Rome, 28 June 2012.

34   Author interviews with a deputy national anti-mafia prosecutor, Rome, 9 July 2012, and an adjunct prosecutor, DDA, Reggio Calabria, 24 August 2012.

35   Author interview with a deputy national anti-mafia prosecutor, Rome, 28 June 2012.

36   The fire group (a group expressly formed for implementing violent acts) belonging to the Brancaccio family played a crucial role in the 1992 massacres, which led to the death of judges Giovanni Falcone and Paolo Borsellino, and others (CPIFCOMS, 2012, p. 7). The arsenal contained explosives that were very similar to the ones used in the 1992 massacres, as well as rocket and missile launchers (Corte di Assise di Palermo, 2001, p. 13). Author interview with an adjunct prosecutor, DDA, Reggio Calabria, 24 August 2012.

37   Author interview with the chief of the Police Department's Flying Squad, Rome, 10 July 2012.

38   Author interview with a deputy national anti-mafia prosecutor, Rome, 28 June 2012.

39   Author interview with an adjunct prosecutor, DDA, Reggio Calabria, 24 August 2012.

40   Author interview with a judge, Ufficio del Massimario della Suprema Corte di Cassazione, Naples, 27 June 2012.

41   Author interview with a deputy national anti-mafia prosecutor, Rome, 28 June 2012.

42   In March 2012 a homicide with a lupara in the area of Reggio Calabria was filmed by an anonymous video-maker who sent a flash drive containing the video to the Carabinieri (Il Quotidiano della Calabria, 2012).

43   Author interview with a deputy national anti-mafia prosecutor, Rome, 28 June 2012.

44   Author interviews with a deputy national anti-mafia prosecutor, Rome, 28 June 2012; with the chief of Police Department's Flying Squad, Rome, 10 July 2012; and a deputy national anti-mafia prosecutor, Rome, 9 July 2012.

45   Author interview with a deputy national anti-mafia prosecutor, Rome, 28 June 2012.

46   Author interview with a deputy national anti-mafia prosecutor, Rome, 28 June 2012.

47   Author interview with a judge, Ufficio del Massimario della Suprema Corte di Cassazione, Naples, 27 June 2012.

48   Author interview with a judge, Ufficio del Massimario della Suprema Corte di Cassazione, Naples, 27 June 2012.

49   Author interview with a judge, Ufficio del Massimario della Suprema Corte di Cassazione, Naples, 27 June 2012.

50   Author interview with a deputy national anti-mafia prosecutor, Rome, 28 June 2012.

51   Author interview with a judge, Ufficio del Massimario della Suprema Corte di Cassazione, Naples, 27 June 2012.

52   Author interview with a judge, Ufficio del Massimario della Suprema Corte di Cassazione, Naples, 27 June 2012. Such procurement also happens elsewhere. In Rome, for example, some of the firearms used for the commission of several homicides in 2011 and 2012, though mostly related to conflicts between criminal gangs, had been stolen from the apartments of private citizens. Author interview with the chief of Police Department's Flying Squad, Rome, 10 July 2012.

53   Author interview with a judge, Ufficio del Massimario della Suprema Corte di Cassazione, Naples, 27 June 2012.

54   Author interview with the chief of Police Department's Flying Squad, Rome, 10 July 2012.

55   The area of Brescia, in the northern part of the country, is currently home to almost 150 firms that are involved in firearm manufacturing, such as Beretta. These account for almost 90 per cent of national production (Eurispes, 2008a, p. 49).

56   International arms traffickers often rely on corrupt officials and professionals, including for fraudulent paperwork and transportation services (UNODC, 2010, p. 144).

57   Most of the prosecutors interviewed for this study stressed this point. It should also be mentioned that during the early 1980s Judge Carlo Palermo attempted to carry out a major investigation on drugs and arms trafficking between Turkey and Italy, via Austria and Yugoslavia; most of those accused were acquitted (Palermo, 1988; Cecchetti, 1988).

58   According to the research institute Eurispes, profits made by the 'Ndrangheta from illegal arms trafficking in 2007 amounted to EUR 2,938 million (USD 3,900 million). Although this data is quoted in several reports, no information is available on the methodology or sources used to produce this figure (Eurispes, 2008b, p. 3). The crucial role played by the 'Ndrangheta in supplying sophisticated weapons to other organized crime groups has been confirmed by Cosa Nostra turncoat Gaspare Spatuzza, who provided information on a stockpile of weapons, including a surface-to-air missile, bought by his clan in order to kill anti-mafia judge Giancarlo Caselli, who, for security reasons, was often transported by helicopter while he was chief prosecutor for the DDA in Palermo (Viviano and Ziniti, 2009).

59   A note that was drafted by a boss of the SCU in March 1991, given to his wife during a colloquium in prison, and seized by the police contained a shopping list with precise indications on the weapons sought by the organization. These included three FAMAS assault rifles, two M16 grenade launchers, three AK-47s, three Ingram MAC-10 machine pistols, Beretta and Wildey semi-automatic pistols, and one ATIS shotgun, among others. Document provided to the author by the chief prosecutor of the DDA, Lecce, 5 July 2012.

60   Author interview with the chief prosecutor, DDA, Lecce, 5 July 2012.

61   Author interview with a deputy national anti-mafia prosecutor, Rome, 9 July 2012.

62   Author interview with a deputy national anti-mafia prosecutor, Rome, 28 June 2012.

63   Author interview with the chief of Police Department's Flying Squad, Rome, 10 July 2012.

64   Author interview with a deputy national anti-mafia prosecutor, Rome, 28 June 2012.

65   This ambivalent mix of truth and mystery allows mafias to secure consensus from certain sectors of the population and to structure their power (Siebert, 2010). It allows them to mask and dissimulate the actual criminal nature of their organizations, with the result that some people perceive the mafia as a sort of benefactor. Demonstrations of indebtedness and allegiance to the mafia include public tributes, such as when the Sicilian football team dedicated victories to mafia bosses, or when the picture of a recently imprisoned boss was displayed close to the symbol of the patronal festival in a village near Naples (similar cases were recorded in Calabria), or when elaborate fireworks criss-cross the Neapolitan sky to celebrate the release of Camorra or SCU bosses.

66   *Stidda* ('star' or 'constellation' in Sicilian) is the name of a mafia-type organization that emerged in the early 1980s in the southern part of Sicily. In the late 1980s, the city of Gela became a recruitment centre for adolescents who would be employed as killers or in extortion rackets (Massari, 2004).

67   Author interview with a judge, Ufficio del Massimario della Suprema Corte di Cassazione, Naples, 27 June 2012.

68   Author interview with a deputy national anti-mafia prosecutor, Rome, 28 June 2012.

69   Author interview with a judge, Ufficio del Massimario della Suprema Corte di Cassazione, Naples, 27 June 2012.

BIBLIOGRAPHY

Arlacchi, Pino. 1992. *Gli uomini del disonore: La mafia siciliana nella vita del grande pentito Antonino Calderone*. Milan: Mondadori.

—. 1994. *Addio Cosa Nostra: La vita di Tommaso Buscetta*. Milan: Rizzoli.

Associazione daSud, ed. 2012. *Sdisonorate: Le mafie uccidono le donne*. Rome: daSud. <http://www.dasud.it/sdisonorate/>

Baldesserro, Giuseppe. 2007. 'E il boss rifiutò la tregua: "Piuttosto muoriamo tutti".' *La Repubblica*. 19 August.

Barbagallo, Francesco. 2010. *Storia della camorra*. Rome and Bari: Laterza.

Bolzoni, Attilio. 2008. 'La strage rimossa.' *La Repubblica*. 31 July.

—. 2009. 'Dagli omicidi a pentito anti-premier: "U' Tignusu" adesso studia teologia.' *La Repubblica*. 3 December.

Brancaccio, Luciano. 2009. 'Guerre di camorra: i clan napoletani tra faide e scissioni.' In Gabriella Gribaudi, ed. *Traffici criminali: Camorra, mafie e reti internazionali dell'illegalità*. Turin: Bollati Boringhieri, pp. 65–89.

Cantone, Raffaele. 2012. *Operazione Penelope*. Milan: Mondadori.

Cecchetti, Giorgio. 1988. 'Traffico d'armi: Poche le condanne, tante le assoluzioni.' *La Repubblica*. 2 February.

Ciconte, Enzo. 1992. *'Ndrangheta dall'Unità ad oggi*. Rome and Bari: Laterza.

Colaprico, Piero. 2007. 'Duisburg, diffuso un identikit dell'autista: Dieci killer per la strage di Ferragosto.' *La Repubblica*. 17 August.

Corte di Assise di Palermo. 2001. *Sentenza contro Benigno Salvatore + 13*. 1 June.

Corte di Assise di Caltanissetta. 2000. *Procedimento contro Annaloro Francesco + 22*. 29 February.

CPIFCOMS (Commissione parlamentare d'inchiesta sul fenomeno della mafia e sulle altre associazioni criminali similari). 1994. *Relazione sulle risultanze dell'attivitá del gruppo di lavoro incaricato di svolgere accertamenti su insediamenti e infiltrazioni di soggetti ed organizzazioni di tipo mafioso in aree non tradizionali.* Rome: Tipografia del Senato.

—. 2003. *Relazione annuale.* Rome: Tipografia del Senato.

—. 2008. *Relazione annuale sulla 'Ndrangheta.* Rome: Tipografia del Senato.

—. 2010a. 'Comunicazioni del Presidente sui grandi delitti e le stragi di mafia degli anni 1992–1993.' Rome: Tipografia del Senato.

—. 2010b. *Audizione del Procuratore distrettuale antimafia di Reggio Calabria, Dottor Giuseppe Pignatone.* 21 September. Rome: Tipografia del Senato.

—. 2012. *Audizione del Procuratore della Repubblica presso il Tribunale di Caltanissetta, Dottor Sergio Lari.* 26 March. Rome: Tipografia del Senato.

della Valle, Nazareno. 2009. 'Caserta, nuovo arresto per Setola e altri tre per la strage di Castelvolturno anche per odio razziale.' L'ecodicaserta.it. 15 June. <http://www.ecodicaserta.it/index.php?option=com_content&view=article&id=4717:caserta-nuovo-arresto-per-setola-e-altri-3-per-la-strage-di-castelvolturno-anche-per-odio-razziale&catid=28:cronaca&Itemid=34>

Dickie, John. 2007. *Cosa Nostra: A History of the Sicilian Mafia.* London: Hodder and Stoughton.

Dino, Alessandra. 2002. *Mutazioni: Etnografia del mondo di Cosa Nostra.* Palermo: La Zisa.

—. 2008. 'Guerre di mafia.' In Manuela Mareso and Livio Pepino, pp. 290–300.

—. 2012. 'Attrazioni fatali: genitori e figli nel quotidiano mafioso.' In Monica Massari, ed. *Attraverso lo specchio: Scritti in onore di Renate Siebert.* Cosenza: Luigi Pellegrini Editore, pp. 153–75.

DNA (Direzione Nazionale Antimafia). 2008. *Relazione annuale sulle attività svolte dal Procuratore nazionale antimafia e dalla Direzione nazionale antimafia nonché sulle dinamiche e strategie della criminalità organizzata di tipo mafioso nel periodo 1° luglio 2007–30 giugno 2008.* December. Rome: DNA.

—. 2011. *Relazione annuale sulle attività svolte dal Procuratore nazionale antimafia e dalla Direzione nazionale antimafia nonché sulle dinamiche e strategie della criminalità organizzata di tipo mafioso nel periodo 1° luglio 2010–30 giugno 2011.* December. Rome: DNA.

Eurispes. 2008a. 'Il mercato delle armi: il contesto italiano.' In Eurispes. *Rapporto Italia 2008.* Rome: Eurilink Editori, pp. 48–49.

—. 2008b. *'Ndrangheta Holding: Dossier 2008.* Rome: Eurispes.

Europol. 2011. *OCTA 2011: EU Organised Crime Threat Assessment.* The Hague: European Police Office.

Falcone, Giovanni. 1984. 'Criminalità ed armi.' Paper presented at primo Congresso sulla disciplina delle armi, Ateneo di Brescia and Camera di commercio, industria, artigianato e agricoltura. Brescia, 17–18 February.

Franchetti, Leopoldo. 1993. *Condizioni politiche e amministrative della Sicilia.* Rome: Donzelli.

Gambetta, Diego. 1993. *The Sicilian Mafia: The Business of Private Protection.* Cambridge: Cambridge University Press.

—. 2009. *Codes of the Underworld: How Criminals Communicate.* Princeton: Princeton University Press.

Grasso, Tano and Aldo Varano. 2002. *U Pizzu: L'Italia del racket e dell'usura.* Milano: Baldini e Castoldi.

Gratteri, Nicola and Antonio Nicaso. 2009. *Fratelli di sangue.* Milan: Mondadori.

Il Quotidiano della Calabria. 2012. 'Il sicario con la lupara in mano: Poi arrivano gli spari—Video.' 25 March. <http://www.ilquotidianocalabria.it/news/il-quotidiano-della-calabria/349552/Il-sicario-con-la-lupara-in-mano—Poi-arrivano-gli-spari—VIDEO.html>

Ingroia, Antonio. 2008. 'Cosa Nostra.' In Manuela Mareso and Livio Pepino, pp. 162–72.

ISTAT (Istituto Nazionale di Statistica). 2008. *Delitti denunciati dalle Forze dell'Ordine: Anno 2007.* <http://giustiziaincifre.istat.it/jsp/dawinci.jsp?q=pl02a0010014000&an=2007&ig=1&ct=342&id=4A|18A>

—. 2009. *Delitti denunciati dalle Forze di Polizia all'Autorità Giudiziaria: Anno 2008.* <http://www.istat.it/it/archivio/13980>

—. 2010. *Delitti denunciati dalle Forze di Polizia all'Autorità Giudiziaria: Anno 2009.* <http://www.istat.it/it/archivio/20189>

—. 2012. *Delitti denunciati dalle Forze di Polizia all'Autorità Giudiziaria: Anno 2010.* <http://www.istat.it/it/archivio/50144>

Italy. 1982. Law No. 646 ('Rognoni–La Torre Law'). 13 September.

—. 2007. Penal Code. Libro II, Titolo V, as amended 7 December 2012. <http://www.altalex.com/index.php?idnot=36766>

—. 2010. Decreto Legislativo 26 ottobre 2010 No. 204: Attuazione della direttiva 2008/51/CE, che modifica la direttiva 91/477/CEE relativa al controllo dell'acquisizione e della detenzione di armi. *Gazzettta Ufficiale,* No. 288. 10 December 2010.

Jamieson, Alison and Alessandro Silj. 1998. *Migration and Criminality: The case of Albanians in Italy.* Ethnobarometer Programme Working Paper No. 1. Rome: Ethnobarometer.

La Repubblica. 2011. 'I Casalesi volevano uccidere magistrati e carabinieri.' 1 December. <http://napoli.repubblica.it/cronaca/2011/12/01/news/i_casalesi_volevano_uccidere_magistrati_e_carabinieri-25902693/?ref=search>

—. 2012. ''Ndrangheta, ecco come i boss avevano in mano la Lombardia.' 4 June. <http://milano.repubblica.it/cronaca/2012/06/04/news/_ndrangheta_ecco_come_i_boss_avevano_in_mano_la_lombardia-36528811/>

Lodato, Saverio. 1996. 'La santabarbara della mafia.' *L'Unità.* 18 July, p. 8.

Lupo, Salvatore. 2009. *History of the Mafia.* New York: Columbia University Press.

Mareso, Manuela and Livio Pepino, eds. 2008. *Nuovo dizionario di mafia e antimafia.* Turin: Edizioni del Gruppo Abele.

Massari, Monica. 1998. *La Sacra Corona Unita: Potere e segreto*. Rome and Bari: Laterza.

—. 2004. 'L'evoluzione della criminalità organizzata e le dinamiche della violenza.' In Stefano Becucci, ed. *La città sopsesa: Legalità, sviluppo e società civile a Gela*. Turin: Edizoni del Gruppo Abele, pp. 51–82.

—. 2008. *Sacra Corona Unita*. In Manuela Mareso and Livio Pepino, pp. 498–504.

—. 2009. 'La Sacra Corona Unita: storie, culture, identità.' In Gabriella Gribaudi, ed. *Traffici criminali: Camorra, mafie e reti internazionali dell'illegalità*. Turin: Bollati Boringhieri, pp. 241–64.

MI–DCPC (Ministero dell'Interno–Direzione Centrale Polizia Criminale). 2007. *N° omicidi di mafia consumati e scoperti, distinti per organizzazione criminale: Anni 1992–2006*. <http://www.camera.it/_bicamerali/leg15/commbicantimafia/documentazionetematica/28/schedabase.asp>

Ministero della Giustizia. 2004. *Mafia Minors: Final Report*. Rome: Ministero della Giustizia.

Palermo, Carlo. 1988. *Armi & droga: l'atto d'accusa del giudice Carlo Palermo*. Rome: Editori Riuniti.

Paoli, Letizia. 2000. *Fratelli di sangue: Cosa Nostra e 'Ndrangheta*. Bologna: Il Mulino.

Quotidiano.Net. 2012. 'Napoli, armi nascoste dietro l'altare e droga in comunità: due arresti.' 18 October.
<http://qn.quotidiano.net/cronaca/2012/10/18/788520-napoli-armi-altare-droga-comunita-recupero-camorra.shtml>

Ruggiero, Vincenzo. 1996. *Organized and Corporate Crime in Europe: Offers that Can't Be Refused*. Aldershot: Dartmouth.

—. 1997. 'Criminals and Service Providers: Cross-national Dirty Economies.' *Crime, Law & Social Change*, Vol. 28, No. 1, pp. 27–38.

Sagramoso, Domitilla. 2001. *The Proliferation of Illegal Small Arms and Light Weapons in and around the European Union: Instability, Organized Crime and Terrorist Groups*. London: Centre for Defence Studies, King's College, University of London, and Saferworld.

Sales, Isaia. 1993. *La camorra, le camorre*. Rome: Editori Riuniti.

—. 2008. 'Camorra.' In Manuela Mareso and Livio Pepino, pp. 98–111.

Santino, Umberto. 1995. *La mafia interpretata: dilemmi, stereotipi, paradigmi*. Soveria Mannelli: Rubbettino.

Saviano, Roberto. 2006. *Gomorra: Viaggio nell'impero economico e nel sogno di dominio della camorra*. Milan: Mondadori.

Sciarrone, Rocco. 2009. *Mafie vecchie, mafie nuove: Radicamento ed espansione*. Rome: Donzelli.

Selvatici, Franca. 2012. 'Stragi di mafia, arrestato l'uomo del tritolo.' *La Repubblica*. 13 November, p. 18.

Sergi, Pantaleone. 1992. 'Con la testa mozzata fecero tiro al bersaglio.' *La Repubblica*. 17 March, p. 20.

Siebert, Renate. 2010. 'Resoconti dal mondo accanto: quotidianità e criminalità.' In Mario Schermi, ed. *Crescere alle mafie*. Milan: Franco Angeli, pp. 13–69.

Stajano, Corrado, ed. 1992. *Mafia: L'atto d'accusa dei giudici di Palermo*. Rome: Editori Riuniti.

Tribunale di Caltanissetta, Ufficio del Giudice per le Indagini Preliminari. 2004. *Ordinanza di custodia cautelare in carcere nei confronti di Madonia Giuseppe + 9*. 6 July.

—. 2005. *Ordinanza di custodia cautelare in carcere nei confronti di Amarù Massimo + 44*. 15 November.

—. 2012. *Ordinanza di custodia cautelare in carcere nei confronti di Carruba Maurizio + 4*. 14 June.

Tribunale di Napoli, Sezione del Giudice per le indagini preliminari, Ufficio V. 2010. *Ordinanza applicativa di misura cautelare nei confronti di Schiavone Francesco + 73*. 17 April.

Tribunale di Torre Annunziata, Sezione Penale. 2009. *Sentenza contro Gionta Pasquale + altri*. 17 December.

Tribunale Ordinario di Milano, Ufficio del Giudice per le Indagini Preliminari. 2010. *Ordinanza di applicazione di misura coerctiva nei confronti di Agostino Fabio + 159*. 5 July.

Tribunale per i Minorenni di Caltanissetta. 2003. *Sentenza contro Iannì Simon*. 27 March.

UNODC (United Nations Office on Drugs and Crime). 2004. *United Nations Convention against Transnational Organized Crime*. New York: United Nations.

—. 2010. *The Globalization of Crime: A Transnational Organized Crime Threat Assessment*. Vienna: UNODC.

Varese, Federico. 2010. 'General Introduction: What is Organized Crime?' In Federico Varese, ed. *Organized Crime*. London: Routledge, Vol. 1, pp. 1–35.

—. 2011. *Mafias on the Move: How Organized Crime Conquers New Territories*. Princeton. Princeton University Press.

Viviano, Francesco. 1996. 'Missili e lanciarazzi nell'arsenale della mafia.' *La Repubblica*. 28 February.
<http://ricerca.repubblica.it/repubblica/archivio/repubblica/1996/02/28/missili-lanciarazzi-nell-arsenale-della-mafia.html>

— and Alessandra Ziniti. 2009. 'I segreti di Spatuzza: "Così uccide la mafia".' *La Repubblica*. 9 December.

ACKNOWLEDGEMENTS

Principal author

Monica Massari

A member of the Dinka tribe protects his cattle from raiders, Rumbek, South Sudan. January 2009. © Joerg Boethling

Survival at Stake

VIOLENT LAND CONFLICT IN AFRICA

5

INTRODUCTION

In Africa, land is not only an economic good, but also the very basis of security and survival for much of the population. A primary source of livelihood for many, land is not only directly linked to agriculture and production, but also intimately tied to the politics of the countries, the social dynamics of the people, and the status, power, wealth, and security of those who control it. Access to land increases security and reduces the vulnerability of the individual, the family, and the community. Yet competition for scarce resources, the political manipulation of access to land through ethnic, religious, and economic discrimination, and the forced removal of the poor from productive lands have sown the seeds of violence for decades. Violent land conflict—historically and today—revolves around questions of land use, land access, land ownership, and ultimately who benefits from the land and what it produces.

Examples of violent land conflict abound in Africa. *Resource conflicts* became the catch phrase of the 1990s, when civil wars erupted across the continent in places such as Angola, Côte d'Ivoire, the Democratic Republic of the Congo (DRC), Liberia, and Sierra Leone, fuelled by diamonds, timber, oil, and other natural resources (Klare, 2002). Resource conflicts are not always civil wars; they also include localized violence over particular resources, as in the Niger Delta, where armed clashes and kidnapping were commonplace in 2003–09, and in the Kivus of eastern DRC, where the most recent violence has involved the killing and raping of dozens of civilians, the forceful recruitment of hundreds, and the displacement of hundreds of thousands.

Other forms of land conflict, such as *communal clashes,* are frequent in pastoral areas of East Africa; these include clashes between farming and herding populations as well as cattle raiding among pastoralist communities. Some land conflicts percolate for decades, only to come to international attention in the most violent ways. The disputed 2007 Kenyan elections, for instance, spurred weeks of violence, killing more than 1,100, injuring at least 3,500, and destroying at least 115,000 homes. The election violence in Kenya can be traced back to the land policies of the colonial era and the ethnic politics of the post-independence period. Even *social conflicts*—such as protests and riots—have erupted due to contests over land and land resources, and the costs have been high. Despite the frequency and significant costs of violent land conflict, efforts to address the violence are often reactive and short-term in nature, rarely addressing the underlying causes of insecurity and conflict.

This chapter reviews the types and characteristics of conflicts in Africa that are either the direct result of land-related disputes, or that have important land issue components. These include resource conflicts, communal clashes, and social conflicts. The discussion considers the risk factors that can lead land disputes to escalate into armed violence, and the consequences of these conflicts for affected populations. Among the chapter's key conclusions are the following:

- Violent land conflict in Africa is common, widespread, and deadly.
- Almost every armed conflict in Africa has had a land dimension to it, but very few are concerned solely with land issues. In almost all cases, land is one of many contributing factors—such as economic inequality, political competition, discrimination, and exclusion—that fuel violence.
- Violent land conflict in Africa—including resource conflicts, communal clashes, and social conflicts—has resulted in tens of thousands of direct conflict deaths and the displacement of hundreds of thousands over the past decade.
- Violent land conflict is more than just fighting over a plot of land. It includes community clashes over ways of life, political struggles for power, and economic struggles for wealth.
- Land disputes are most volatile, and at highest risk of violence, when grievances are high, security is threatened, mechanisms for adjudication are absent, and violence entrepreneurs are able to mobilize aggrieved populations.
- The failure to manage communal conflicts over land, the inability of states to provide basic security, the resulting cycles of retaliatory violence, and the availability of small arms are all factors that have contributed to increasing the costs of violent land conflict over the past decades.

This chapter begins with an examination of the importance of land in the African context. The second section defines violent land conflict and identifies the primary factors that contribute to land disputes and raise the risk of disputes escalating into violence. The third section discusses three manifestations of violent land conflict in Africa: resource conflicts; communal clashes; and social conflicts over land-related resources. This chapter emphasizes that violent land conflict can take many forms, but in all of its guises it remains a widespread, common, and deadly phenomenon in Africa.

Land is crucial for the livelihoods of large portions of the population.

LAND: A VITAL RESOURCE

In order to understand land disputes in Africa, and why they can serve as a critical driver of violent conflict, it is important to recognize the centrality of land in most African societies. Land has specific economic, social, and political meanings in the different African contexts, which affect the various permutations of how land plays an integral role in the daily lives of Africans. This section reviews some of these roles and meanings in an effort to enhance our understanding of how land disputes can become violent conflicts.

Land as an economic resource

Land is an essential economic resource in Africa. It is necessary for housing and a fundamental element of household wealth. As one Sierra Leonean put it: 'The soil is our bank' (Moore, 2010). In Uganda, one observer noted that 'land constitutes between 50 and 60 percent of the asset endowment of the poorest households' (Deininger, 2003, p. xx). Through agricultural and pastoral practices, land is crucial for the livelihoods of large portions of the population. Indeed, the majority of the African population depends on working the land and on land-based resources as primary sources of income and food (van der Zwan, 2011, p. 2). An estimated 85 per cent of Acholi households in Uganda sustain themselves through agricultural activities (McKibben and Bean, 2010, p. 23). Even in cases where populations have switched to non-agricultural employment, land and subsistence farming remain their safety net in tough economic times (Oxfam, 2011, p. 9).

The availability of arable land is particularly important for agriculture-based societies. In African countries, agricultural land accounts for anywhere from 3.7 per cent of national land (Egypt)—or 8.4 per cent (Central African Republic) if only sub-Saharan Africa is considered—to 83.7 per cent (Burundi), with the continental average hovering around 45 per cent (see Map 5.1).[1] The importance of land as an economic resource underscores the necessity of *access* to land for the security of the population, especially for those surviving on subsistence agriculture or pursuing pastoral livelihoods, while the inability to access land increases insecurity and vulnerability. However, the availability of useable land and access to this land do not necessarily correspond. The various possible and competing uses of land—housing, grazing, farming, tourism, mining—as well as the threats to land availability and quality through changing weather patterns, expanding desertification, mechanized farming, growing populations, and declining access to water—all add to the pressures on land use and increase the likelihood of disputes over how any particular parcel of land is used.[2]

Map 5.1 **Agricultural land in Africa, as a percentage of the national area, 2009**

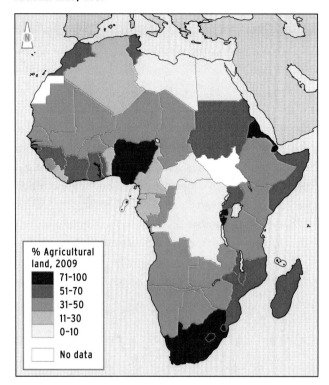

% Agricultural land, 2009
- 71-100
- 51-70
- 31-50
- 11-30
- 0-10
- No data

Source: World Bank (2012)

The symbolic meaning of land

In Africa, land holds special social or cultural significance for particular groups. The significance may be related to the cultural practices or history of a group. In Uganda, for example, the Acholi fear that, if a deceased family member is not buried on ancestral land, his or her spirit will not pass on and will haunt them forever (McKibben and Bean, 2010, p. 23). For some groups a particular parcel of land is important because it is where generations of ancestors have lived, or where particular ceremonial or cultural events can be held, or traditional or religious beliefs can be practised (Oxfam, 2011, p. 9). Access to land is often secured by tradition, rather than by title, and an estimated 90 per cent of the population in rural Africa still access land that their ancestors accessed (Moore, 2010).

Land may have a cultural or psychological significance to a group based on ethnicity or religion (van der Zwan, 2011, p. 2). Certain regions in Guinea are identified with particular ethnic groups. In Nigeria, the population views the northern half of the country as predominantly Muslim land ruled by sharia law, whereas most see the south as Christian land. These defining characteristics of the population living on a particular piece of land or in a specific region have been used to identify those who belong, and those who do not, thereby enabling the identification of 'indigenous' people and discrimination against non-natives, even when those non-natives are nationals of the same country.

While competition over land will persist, it can threaten to escalate into violence when land is viewed as 'indivisible'— something that cannot be shared or parcelled out to different groups or individuals. When emotion interferes with attachment to the land, this may foment dissent. Many secessionist wars, ethnic conflicts, and religious clashes are characterized by these attachments. When land is linked to a specific identity, such as ethnicity, the situation tends to be more volatile, and small disputes can escalate into larger, more violent clashes because defending the land is perceived as defending the group and ensuring its survival (Putzel, 2009, p. 4). The combination of land, ethnicity, and politics has driven conflict in countries such as the DRC, Kenya, and Rwanda, while the explicit use of political mechanisms to avoid the 'ethnicization' of land has helped to reduce the frequency of violent incidents over land in Tanzania and Zambia (pp. 5–9, 11–13).

Land as a political resource

Land is an important political resource: 'It's power; it's status; it's security. It's the most powerful asset people have' (Moore, 2010). In part, the political importance of land relates to its economic function, since those who control the means of production and sources of extraction benefit most financially from the ownership of land. In many African countries economic power equates to political power, and vice versa.

Land ownership bestows traditional authority upon the owner (van der Zwan, 2011, p. 2). In many areas of Africa, lands are communally owned, and authority over land is vested in the traditional ruler of the community, often a traditional chief. The chief determines who can use the land, how it can be used, and whether it can be sold. Other community members can be granted the right to use the land and can sell the rights to work the land, but they cannot sell the land itself. In a number of rural communities, land rights are based on a chief's oral agreements. If the chief dies or is displaced by war, confusion over land rights may ensue, throwing this system into disarray.

Increasingly, traditional rights are being challenged by more modern concepts of land rights as private rights. Governments have implemented privatization programmes, and many parties seek private land ownership rights for

Orma men stand around the remains of Pokomo people killed during a raid on Kipao village in the Tana Delta, Kenya. December 2012. © Ivan Lieman/AFP Photo

the security they can offer. But privatization threatens traditional power bases in many communities, leading to resistance by traditional rulers (van der Zwan, 2011, p. 2). Privatization has disrupted pastoralist traditions as well, through the parcelling out of land and redrawing of borders in ways that restrict the traditional transit routes of pastoral communities and their access to grazing areas. Political elites and entrepreneurs, among others, have capitalized on privatization efforts to purchase communal lands, effectively displacing poor families that lack legal statutory rights to their land. While privatization can offer more secure tenure to individuals when it is backed by the enforcement of legal rights, it has also been a source of violent conflict when it has benefited a small percentage of a country's elite.

The authority to grant land rights is an important political power that can be used to manipulate or reward supporters and punish opponents. This has occurred in areas of traditional governance, as well as in modern governance systems. Politicians have manipulated political boundaries, altered borders, and reallocated land to gain supporters and win elections (see Box 5.1).

Box 5.1 Kenya's land disputes: the intertwining of land, ethnicity, and politics

Although Kenya fought a war of independence over land issues, the country still faces the pressing challenges of resolving the inequalities of the system and removing politics from the land question (Oucho, 2010, p. 4). As analysts have pointed out, 'The land questions are rooted in the colonial period and its attempts to polarize land relations around class, ethnic factors, and political affiliations' (Kanyinga, Lumumba, and Amanor, 2008, p. 101). The politicization has continued under the post-colonial regimes (Murunga, 2011, pp. 9–17; Wepundi, 2012, pp. 2–3). Land reform policies initiated in the 1950s only exacerbated tensions and generated disputes, rather than remedying them.

The main problem is that the system remains 'open to abuse by those involved in defining the existing structure of rights' (Kanyinga, Lumumba, and Amanor, 2008, p. 105). The consolidation of power in the central government following decolonization resulted in both the presidency and land becoming 'increasingly intertwined in the exercise of political power at the expense of popular democratic institutions' (p. 107). This trend became evident in the emergence of ethnic-based political parties, which had particular land interests and supported different approaches to resolving the land question, while also being deeply divided over land reform policies.

The Jomo Kenyatta regime (1964–78) generally tried to avoid the land question. In contrast, the Daniel Arap Moi regime (1978–2002) used regional conflicts over land and the unresolved land question as a political tool to build a support base and deny the opposition (Kanyinga, Lumumba, and Amanor, 2008, p. 114). Land became an ethnic patronage resource and a means of rewarding loyal ethnic elites, while land grabbing enabled the accumulation of political power (pp. 115–16; see Box 5.3). As pressures for liberalization mounted, the pace of patronage and land grabbing accelerated, concentrating land ownership in the elite and intensifying landlessness among the poor. Like Kenyatta's government, the Mwai Kibaki government (2002–present) has skirted around the land issue. The Kibaki administration reduced the use of patronage to gain the loyalty of the elite, merely shifting its focus to politically significant ethnic communities (p. 123). Patronage continues in a modified, but no less risky, form.

Electoral violence has occurred since the first multi-party election in 1992, characterized by protests, vigilante violence, the use of political thugs to intimidate opposition supporters, and large clashes between ethnic groups leading up to elections. Post-election violence has involved spontaneous, premeditated, and state-directed violence, including the killing and maiming of people and livestock, looting and destruction of property, and arson (Murunga, 2011, p. 24; Oucho, 2010, p. 1). The post-election violence in 2007–08 reached staggering heights, with the death toll topping 1,100. The ethnic groups with the highest number of deaths included the Luo (278 killed), Gikuyu (268), Luyia (168), and Kalenjin (158), with the police bearing the greatest responsibility for these deaths; 405 died from gunshot wounds. The police mainly targeted Nyanza province, where some 80 per cent of victims died from gunshots, followed by the Western province (73 per cent), the Rift Valley (26 per cent), and Nairobi (18 per cent) (Murunga, 2011, p. 39).

Several violent events took place in the lead-up to the March 2013 general elections. In September 2012, mass graves were uncovered in the village of Kilelengwani, in the Tana Delta region, the centre of recent violence. At least 100 people were killed with guns, machetes, and spears in clashes in a long-running conflict between the Pokomo—mostly farmers—and the Orma—semi-nomadic cattle herders (BBC News, 2012a; 2012b; 2012c). The clashes are over land and water, but also have their roots in politics. Kenyan officials have been able to use their positions to broker lucrative land deals, leasing extensive tracts of land for large-scale cultivation. As elections approached, tensions were rising and concerns growing that the volatile situation could erupt into a repeat of the widespread violence seen following the December 2007 polls.

Sources: BBC News (2012a; 2012b; 2012c); Kanyinga, Lumumba, and Amanor (2008); Murunga (2011); Oucho, (2010); Wepundi (2012)

VIOLENT LAND CONFLICT

Land disputes are ubiquitous in Africa as a result of competition for land use, poorly understood means of ownership, inadequate legal frameworks, unequal distribution of access, and the politicization of land; in addition, modernization and population pressures bring new constructions of ownership and force together competing users of land. Non-violent land disputes tend to be underreported because they are typically local concerns managed through local adjudication mechanisms. Disputes rarely make the news unless they turn violent, and even violent communal clashes may be reported only when they reach a significant scale, as with the aftermath of the 2007 elections in Kenya. One reason for low reporting is that, by the time land-based conflicts reach high levels of violence, they are usually characterized as political, economic, or ethnic conflicts, and the role that land plays in contributing to the eruption of violence is often minimized (Moore, 2010).

Defining land conflict

Almost every major episode of violence in Africa has had a land dimension.

There is no broad consensus on a definition of land conflict.[3] The term can include everything from non-violent land disputes and interstate border disputes to intrastate secessionist conflicts. In this chapter, violent land conflict includes any instance of armed violence that occurs between individuals or groups resulting from disputes over land access, land ownership, or the spoils of land cultivation. This definition is sufficiently broad to include resource conflicts, communal clashes, and social conflicts.

Most violent land conflicts emerge from land disputes, such as disagreements over how land is owned, used, or distributed. Land disputes occur in many countries in Africa, but they are not inherently violent. Although land—its management, access, and use—is one factor that can contribute to violent conflict, not all countries with land scarcity challenges or issues of unequal access suffer from violent conflict (Huggins and Clover, 2005, p. 6). Most major violent conflicts result from not just land issues, but a mixture of underlying grievances, including economic inequality, political competition, discrimination, and exclusion. This can make it difficult to determine which violent conflicts result from land disputes, or to what extent such disputes played a role in an emerging armed conflict. Despite this difficulty, research suggests that almost every major episode of violence in Africa has had a land dimension to it (Putzel, 2009, p. 16). That said, focusing excessively on land issues can oversimplify the complexity of violent conflict and the multiple drivers that contribute to it.

While land disputes are usually only one factor in a violent conflict, they can provide an important indicator of future violent land conflicts. But not all African countries maintain comprehensive records of land disputes, making it difficult to track incidents over time and to determine which disputes turned violent and why. Increasingly, organizations such as the Norwegian Refugee Council have started documenting land disputes in post-conflict countries, tracking their frequency and identifying their characteristics while also contributing to effective dispute management systems (McKibben and Bean, 2010; NRC, 2011).[4] These monitoring activities recognize that land disputes are an important part of the post-conflict environment and that, if not handled properly through legal and administrative means, they can turn into violent conflicts, as has happened in Côte d'Ivoire, Liberia, and Uganda (see Box 5.2).

Causes of violent land conflict

Four important factors contribute to the emergence of violent land conflict. First, poor governance and the lack of institutional mechanisms to adjudicate disputes fairly and manage grievances through non-violent means leave some populations marginalized by discriminatory policies. Second, the failure of states to provide basic security to populations

Box 5.2 Land-related post-conflict armed violence

While land disputes can contribute to armed violence, and even war, it is also true that civil wars can aggravate land disputes and perpetuate violent land conflict in the post-conflict period (OECD-DAC, 2001; Pantuliano and Elhawary, 2009). Indeed, civil wars have sown the seeds for post-conflict land violence in many ways. Wars frequently displace populations, sometimes for years or decades at a time. Refugees and internally displaced persons often return to find their homes and fields destroyed or occupied by settlers. Communal ownership of land can contribute to confusion over claims but, even in systems with individual titles, documents are often lost or destroyed during wars and documentation systems no longer function or lack the capacity to resolve conflicting claims.

Exacerbating the situation are animosities between groups that may have supported or fought on different sides during the war and that fear and distrust one another in the insecure post-conflict environment. Moreover, post-conflict governments, often struggling to manage numerous challenges at once, may not pay enough attention to land issues in the early post-war years.

Angola, Côte d'Ivoire, Liberia, Sudan, and Uganda, among other African countries, have been facing post-conflict challenges in managing land disputes and preventing violent land conflict. In Uganda, more than 30 northern districts face the prospects of land wars as a result of land grabs during and after the war, boundary disputes, lack of documentation, and insufficient attention to and management of the disputes (Mabikke, 2011, pp. 1, 5-7).

In Liberia, where as many as 90 per cent of civil cases in the court system involve land disputes, violent land conflict persists as one of the top five security concerns (see Figure 5.1 overleaf). Liberian residents claim that, if they fight a war again, it will be over land (Gilgen and Nowak, 2011, p. 10). Another study of post-conflict land disputes in Liberia indicated that in the three counties studied—Grand Gedeh, Lofa, and Nimba—at least 40 per cent of survey respondents reported violence taking place in relation to disputes over land that had been appropriated during the war; between 35 and 50 per cent of respondents reported violence taking place in relation to a boundary conflict; and at least 40 per cent reported violence taking place in relation to other types of land disputes, such as inheritance or rent issues (Hartman, 2010, pp. 24, 28, 32).

In Côte d'Ivoire, land disputes that began in the 1990s were exacerbated by the civil war (2002-10) and continue to be aggravated by widespread displacement and weak dispute mechanisms. As wartime refugees and displaced persons return to their homes, contradictory legislation hampers the resolution of increasing numbers of land disputes. Despite the 1935 law rescinding customary land rights, 98 per cent of rural land is still subject to management by customary law, the basic premise of which holds that land is communal and rights to use it can be bought and sold, whereas the land itself cannot be sold.

Land use is usually granted by the traditional ruler in exchange for some form of compensation by the user. Over time, the price of compensation has increased to the point that many believe they are buying the land, not leasing it (IDMC, 2009). This has led to numerous disputes between leasers and renters, which have been increasingly portrayed as disagreements between indigenous people and migrants, or between the young and the old. This characterization has brought ethnic and nationalistic dimensions into land disputes, tying them into a broader and highly contentious national dialogue about who is Ivorian.

Côte d'Ivoire's government has responded by beginning to implement the 1998 law to settle disputes by formalizing and privatizing land rights. But the law allows only citizens to own land, and its implementation would disenfranchise the large migrant population that had been enticed to immigrate in the 1950s, 1960s, and 1970s to work on large plantations. In the west of the country, less than a quarter of the population is indigenous. The strict implementation of the 1998 law would create widespread confusion and contestation of land ownership. Many are concerned that the land issue could be a source of serious violence if not managed in a way that is deemed both fair and largely free of the ethnic and nationalistic rhetoric that has long divided the country (IDMC, 2009, p. 11).

Sources: Gilgen and Nowak (2011); Hartman (2010); IDMC (2009); Mabikke (2011); OECD-DAC (2001); Pantuliano and Elhawary (2009)

Figure 5.1 **Common security concerns in Liberia, 2010**

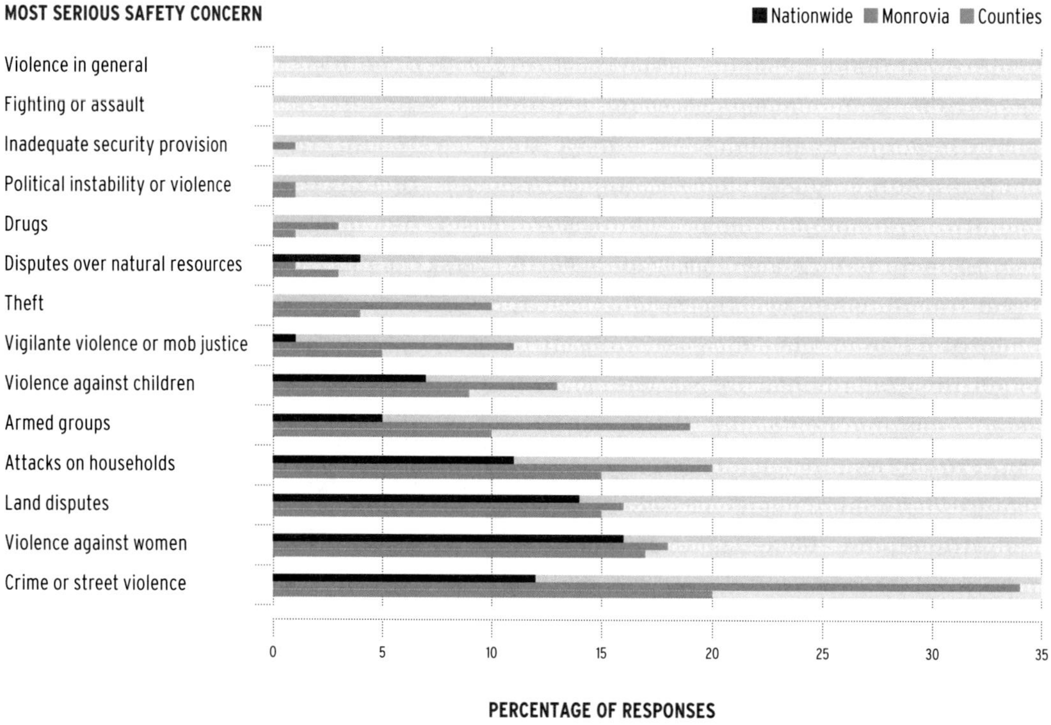

MOST SERIOUS SAFETY CONCERN   ■ Nationwide ■ Monrovia ■ Counties

PERCENTAGE OF RESPONSES

Source: Gilgen and Nowak (2011, p. 8)

increases insecurity and the likelihood that communities will resort to self-help mechanisms, including armed violence. Third, unresolved grievances over land access and use create fertile ground for land disputes. Fourth, the presence of violence entrepreneurs who are able to take advantage of opportunities for economic and political gain by mobilizing popular grievances about land issues raises the risk of violence (Huggins and Clover, 2005, p. 6). Such mobilization is more likely in areas where there is a history of poor group relations and of land distribution based on ethnicity, as well as the marginalization of particular groups. When these conditions occur, the 'ethnic card' and 'us versus them' rhetoric can easily inflame communities. These factors can be seen as additive in that poor governance and the lack of state-provided security generate popular grievances that can then provide opportunities for violence entrepreneurs to mobilize disaffected populations. These four factors are discussed briefly below.

Insufficient governance and adjudication mechanisms

Good governance entails the creation, implementation, and enforcement of fair laws, and the effective and unbiased adjudication of disputes. Customary law and formal statutes, and their implementation, provide a framework for land rights and land use, determining the distribution of land within a population and across users. In some cases, policies clarify the rules and the rights clearly. In other cases, statutory and customary laws contradict one another. Furthermore, competing centres of authority between national and local governments can create confusion and conflict. The insecurity of tenure systems in many countries can leave families and communities at constant risk of losing their lands.

Governments must address competition for land, a scarce resource, while also managing competing claims for its use. Competition for access to land occurs not just between farmers and herders, but also between industrialists and

Box 5.3 Land grabbing

Sales of large parcels of agricultural land–a relatively recent development in Africa–has only exacerbated problems of access to land and inequality in the distribution of land rights. Greed has encouraged land grabbing by politicians, elites, and international companies. Land grabbing is defined as 'the acquisition of land by a public or private enterprise or individual in a manner that is considered to be illegal, underhanded or unfair' (McKibben and Bean, 2010, p. 4). The practice has involved the forceful removal of communities from their lands, as was the case in Uganda, where more than 20,000 were forcefully evicted, and even beaten in the process, between 2006 and 2010. In some instances, communities may agree to leave after being told they have no legal right to remain or because they are compensated in minor ways (Oxfam, 2011, pp. 3, 15-16, 21).

Limited domestic production capacity and the food price crisis of 2007-08 have driven some states to purchase land in Africa and elsewhere for production. Rather than relying on buying food on international markets, which may be prohibitively expensive or too unreliable an option, wealthy countries that lack arable land at home–such as China, India, Kuwait, and Saudi Arabia–are purchasing large plots of land in countries such as Kenya, Mozambique, Sudan, and Tanzania to ensure access to both food crops and biofuel production. Map 5.2 (overleaf) indicates some of the countries that have sold large plots of land to foreign entities. Due to the secrecy of many land deals, it is difficult to ascertain the extent and nature of many land deals.[7] In some cases, land has been expropriated by the state to be sold to the highest international bidder (Deininger and Byerlee, 2011).

Since 2001, more than 30 million hectares–an area almost the size of Germany–have been leased or sold in Africa (Oxfam, 2011, p. 5). While some observers argue this is a good deal for poor countries, which benefit from the investment of resources and new technologies, others suggest these are simply 'land grabs', an expression of neo-colonialism, that push poor farmers off their lands, line the pockets of corrupt politicians, and contribute to already volatile situations (*Economist*, 2009a; 2009b; von Braun and Meinzen-Dick, 2009; Oxfam, 2011; 2012). The majority of land deals for agricultural production yield export commodities, which do little to address local demand for food and can exacerbate food security challenges in African countries (Oxfam, 2011, p. 10).

Sources: Deininger and Byerlee (2011); Economist (2009a; 2009b); von Braun and Meinzen-Dick (2009); McKibben and Bean (2010); Oxfam (2011; 2012)

Maasai protesters demand that land leased to British settlers be given back to them, Uhuru park, Nairobi, Kenya, August 2004. © Radu Sigheti/Reuters

Map 5.2 **Examples of land grabbing in Africa since 2000**

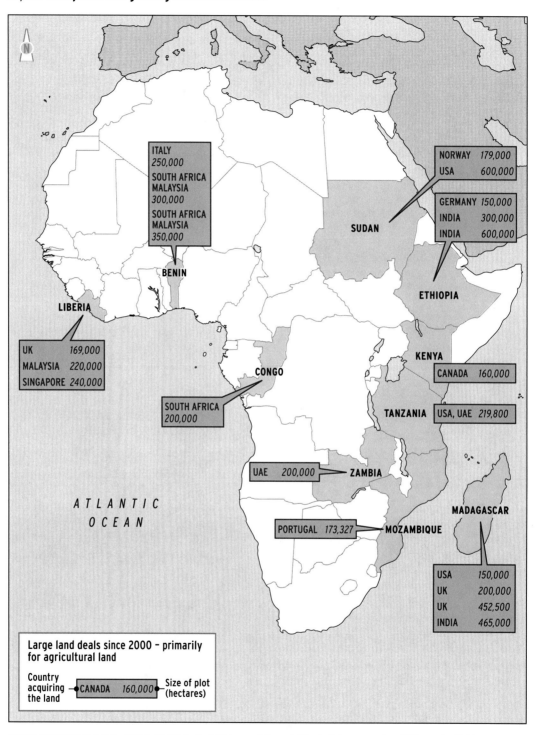

Notes: This map shows deals concluded since 2000 that entail: 1) the transfer of rights to use, control, or own land through sale, lease, or concession; and 2) the conversion of land from local community use or important ecosystem service provision to commercial production.

Source: Land Portal (n.d.)

entrepreneurs focused on mining, tourism, and other potential business ventures; increased land competition contributes to the volatility of areas struggling to satisfy the demands of various actors (van der Zwan, 2011, p. 3). Governments can regulate competition through policies and land management, but poor management can lead to inequalities in access and distribution, as well as discrimination against particular groups based on ethnicity, religion, origin, wealth, or political leanings. Corrupt or greedy politicians can use policies to serve their own purposes, rather than the needs of the population (see Box 5.3). When poorly implemented, policies—whether fair or ill-conceived—can result in confusion, create competing claims on land, and exacerbate difficulties inherent in enforcing the rule of law.

When competing claims arise, various mechanisms can be used to adjudicate disputes through non-violent means; these include customary rules and practices and the formal legal system. In many countries, however, government institutions and laws are inadequate to respond to the task. Weak institutions offer few (or poor) mechanisms to adjudicate disputes or settle ownership issues in cases of competing or unclear ownership. Judiciaries are often slow, and the poor typically lack access to formal courts. Legal titles may have been lost or issued multiple times for the same plot of land. Official land records, often still kept only in hard-copy paper format, may be missing or in some cases not even maintained. In areas far from cities and with weak local governance structures, individuals are more likely to pursue local remedies to their land disputes, often through traditional chiefs, as they are the most familiar and most accessible.[5] Yet such mechanisms are not always able to end disputes or to settle them in ways deemed fair by complainants.[6] Without reliable adjudication mechanisms, individuals and communities can be left on their own to resolve their land disputes; at times, they may resort to violence to ensure the security of both their persons and of their land.

The inability of government forces to provide security can leave communities vulnerable.

Failure to provide security

The inability of government forces to provide security can leave communities vulnerable to attack and dispossession of their land or their livestock. This vulnerability, especially in areas where cyclical attacks are common, heightens feelings of insecurity and inspires communities to pursue their own means of security, often by procuring arms, supporting local defence forces, or refusing to disarm (Bevan, 2008, pp. 26–27; Kingma et al., 2012, pp. 29, 33–41). These steps are important contributing risk factors for violent land conflict.

In some cases, security forces are incapable of providing security. They may lack sufficient resources—salaries, food, housing, vehicles, personnel, or arms—to conduct patrols and enforce laws across the country. This is especially true in rural areas, where greater resources to patrol or establish a police presence may be required. Providing security for mobile populations, such as pastoral communities, imposes even greater costs and difficulties for security forces. Poorly trained, under-equipped, and under-resourced, security forces in many countries may simply lack the ability to confront raiding or other armed forces, and may be overwhelmed when intervening against them. When these conditions apply, communities are less likely to trust government forces to provide security.

In other cases, security forces actually heighten insecurity and instability, for instance by backing one community against another or by arming one community and not another. A number of governments have armed local defence forces as a way of providing security in communities that cannot be secured by the national security forces. Some governments have exacerbated poor security situations by committing human rights abuses while carrying out their duties, intervening in raids, or disarming communities. In particular, East African governments have conducted a number of forced and violent disarmament campaigns to remove weapons from communities.[8] Moreover, some disarmament programmes have reduced community security and even promoted localized arms races, especially if they were forced, conducted in some communities and not others, or not complemented by the provision of state-led security. The failure of governments to provide security not only heightens insecurity, but also pushes communities to devise their own solutions. In many cases, this entails arming themselves.

Grievances

In many cases the main challenge is not sheer scarcity, but rather the perception that access to and distribution of land are unfairly and unequally granted (Huggins and Clover, 2005, p. 2; van der Zwan, 2011, p. 3). Discriminatory policies and poor governance can produce popular grievances. Unequal access and distribution of land—by family, tribal affiliation, ethnic group—can be linked back to local and national policies of allocation, distribution, and ownership; to whether scarce land is properly managed, protected, and controlled; and to how economic opportunities are granted. When groups believe they are being intentionally harmed by government policies, grievances against the government grow. When groups believe these policies specifically benefit other groups, at their expense, grievances against other communities grow. These grievances provide fertile ground for mobilization.

Grievances also arise from perceptions of insecurity. Groups that believe they have been mistreated or simply left to their own fates by governments that are unwilling or unable to provide security are likely to lack trust in the government and view discriminatory policies as targeting them and their livelihoods. Insecurity contributes to poor relationships between communities and governments as well as between communities. Histories characterized by grievances among groups, fuelled by decades of discrimination and violence, increase the sense of insecurity, lead communities to take measures to protect their livelihoods and families, and form the basis of retaliatory attacks. Examples of cycles of violence can be seen among the pastoral communities engaged in cattle rustling and at the intersection of pastoral and agricultural communities. The fact that both governments and development agencies have largely overlooked land disputes has provided unmonitored space for related grievances to grow and fuel violent conflict (Putzel, 2009, pp. 14–16).

> Land represents a lucrative prize and an important tool in violent political struggles.

Violence entrepreneurs

While institutional mechanisms for dispute resolution, fair policies, and good governance are important, there is also a need to curb the intentional manipulation of land management for political advantage and the instrumental use of land for economic gain. Violence entrepreneurs—whether elites, politicians, or businessmen—are those who capitalize on situations of instability and insecurity to mobilize aggrieved populations for political or economic gain. Examples of such entrepreneurship abound. Land represents a lucrative prize and an important tool in violent political struggles between elites in places such as Kenya, South Africa, and Zimbabwe (USAID, 2005, p. 19). Politicians have not only granted land to those whose votes they need, but have also given weapons to those communities to defend that land, increasing the risk of violence and enhancing the capacity to injure (Huggins and Pottier, 2005, p. 384). This goes beyond bad policy. It is the intentional mobilization of groups to commit violence in order to achieve political ends. On the economic side, businessmen have capitalized on the poor economic prospects of young men living in pastoral communities by offering them opportunities to engage in commercial cattle raiding and other illicit activities that utilize the young men's warrior skills for economic gain.

Violent conflict is more likely when localized disputes are linked to broader patterns of political, social, and economic exclusion and discrimination (UN, 2010, p. 6). This linking of the local with the national often expands the nature of the conflict beyond the simple issue of a plot of land to that of broader injustices against communities. Violence entrepreneurs are able to link the local to the national and mobilize aggrieved populations. The risk of widespread violence increases as conflicts involve groups of people, rather than just individuals (Bruce, 2011, p. 1). Violence is most likely when these injustices appear targeted at particular groups, when they threaten the survival and future prospects of that group, and when non-violent, legal action is no longer perceived as a viable path to remedying injustices or delivering security to threatened communities. The confluence of these factors can escalate minor, localized conflicts into large-scale armed conflicts with devastating consequences (OECD–DAC, 2005, p. 1; Deininger, 2003, p. 157).

VIOLENT LAND CONFLICT IN AFRICA

'Violent land conflict' is treated in the literature in a number of ways: as armed conflicts between countries over borders; armed conflicts within countries over natural resources or secessionist goals; and armed clashes at the community or neighbour level.[9] Armed conflicts over identified pieces of territory—border wars and secessionist wars—are clearly violent land conflicts but with political and economic considerations. Civil wars tend to offer less obvious external indicators of the role land plays in the conflict. In some cases, land may be at the core of the dispute—as in Rwanda; in other cases, it may be one of many drivers—as in Sudan and Mozambique. In cases where civil wars are clearly fuelled by natural resources—diamonds, oil, gold—the link to land is more evident, while in other cases the role of land may be less apparent, though not necessarily a less important driver of conflict. Clashes at the community level between pastoral and agricultural communities are easily identifiable as violent land conflicts, but many community conflicts may not have evident links to land. In addition, numerous short-lived but violent events erupt over disputes about land and land-related issues, such as food, water, subsistence, environmental degradation, and access to natural resources.

This section focuses on three types of violent land conflict: resource conflicts, which take place at the national and local levels; communal conflicts, which are more localized conflicts; and social conflict events, which include protests and riots. This discussion focuses on violent conflicts that have a clear relationship to land but that are not typically considered *wars* or *armed conflicts* in the traditional sense (NON-CONFLICT VIOLENCE).

A Congolese miner bags raw chunks of cassiterite, the base element of tin, which is exported daily, July 2004, Mubi, Democratic Republic of Congo.
© Finbarr O'Reilly/Reuters

Resource conflicts

Resource conflicts tend to occur either at the national level or at the local level (see Table 5.1). At the national level, resource wars are typically intrastate armed conflicts fought between the government and at least one organized non-state armed group (UCDP, 2012b). In these conflicts, the goal of the armed group is often to overthrow the government. These wars are highlighted here because the conflict parties—both the government and the armed groups—fight over access to valuable land resources, which they also use to finance their wars. Such resources include diamonds in Angola, Côte d'Ivoire, the DRC, Liberia, and Sierra Leone; oil in Angola; cocoa in Côte d'Ivoire; and timber in Liberia. While some resource wars have resulted from land-related issues, land is usually only one of the underlying drivers of the conflict.[10]

National-level wars have often been of long duration, or they have recurred numerous times over a decade or more. While estimates of battle- and conflict-related deaths are often unreliable, they suggest that these conflicts have claimed tens of thousands of lives in battle and many more in war-related circumstances such as disease or lack of water, food, or shelter (Geneva Declaration Secretariat, 2008, chs. 1, 2; HSRP, 2012, p. 194).

In addition to being extremely costly in terms of the numbers killed, injured, and displaced, these wars have also had a negative impact on development, the health of the population, and the infrastructure and economy of the afflicted country. The widespread availability of small arms—and the capacity of armed groups to purchase weapons using substantial profits from the natural resource trade—arguably contributed to the high death tolls and costs of these wars.

Table 5.1 Resource-related conflicts, 1975–present

Country	Natural resource(s)	Type of conflict	Dates
Angola	Oil, diamonds	Civil war	1975–2002
Angola (Cabinda)	Oil	Secession	1975–2006
Côte d'Ivoire	Cocoa, diamonds, cotton	Civil war	2002–11
Democratic Republic of the Congo	Diamonds, gold, timber, coltan, cassiterite, copper, cobalt	Civil war; localized armed conflict	1996–97, 1998–2003, 2004–09, 2012–present
Guinea-Bissau	Illicit drug trade	Coups	1998–99 Coups: 2003, 2004, 2009, 2012
Liberia	Timber, diamonds	Civil war	1989–97, 1999–2003
Nigeria (Niger Delta)	Oil	Localized armed conflict	2003–09
Republic of the Congo	Oil	Civil war	1997–99
Senegal (Casamance)	Cashews	Secession	1982–2004
Sierra Leone	Diamonds	Civil war	1991–2002
Sudan	Oil	Civil war	1983–2005

Notes: This table only includes African conflicts that were clearly fought over or fuelled by natural resources. In some cases, the sale of the natural resource provided financing; in other cases, it was the taxation of the growing, harvesting, transportation, or sale of the resource that provided financial gain to one or both of the warring parties.

Years are approximations of start and end dates. Consulted databases list different dates depending on battle-related death levels, periods of inactivity, and cease-fires and peace agreements.

Sources: Hazen (2013); Klare (2002); Le Billon (2005); UCDP (2012a)

Box 5.4 The Kivus: land conflict and armed groups

The Democratic Republic of the Congo provides an important reminder of the challenges of managing natural resources, the legacy of colonialism, and the need to address long-standing grievances and conflicts over land rights. This is especially true in the eastern part of the country, the Kivus, which have suffered bouts of extreme violence since before colonial times (see Map 5.3 overleaf). The chronic instability in the Kivus has its roots in local disputes over land, citizenship, power, and identity, which over time have been tied to local, national, and regional political dynamics, exacerbating existing grievances and spurring more violent conflict.

The colonial practices of the Belgians in the Congo provided a basis for altering the ethnic balance in the east and the political balance among local groups. The Belgians implemented policies that reduced the role of customary law, expropriated large tracts of land deemed 'vacant' for settler farming, and facilitated the mass migration of Rwandans for labour on plantations and in mines (Huggins, 2010, p. 13; Stearns, 2012b, pp. 10-16). As a result, indigenous populations such as the Hunde were displaced. The Hunde refused to work for the colonialists and became a minority population, while the Tutsi population grew in size and status. The Hunde resented their loss of land and power; these grievances and the resulting tensions between the Hunde and immigrant populations (mainly the Banyarwanda Tutsi) served as the foundation for decades of conflict (Stearns, 2012b, p. 17).

Independence and democratization exacerbated fears among the population. For indigenous groups, these changes stoked fears of repression by immigrant communities; in contrast, the immigrant populations feared the loss of citizenship rights and with them access to and ownership of land. Through elections and decentralization indigenous groups, such as the Hunde, increased their power through control over administrative functions. Indigenous leaders proposed various measures to limit the rights of the Banyarwanda and went so far as to propose their expulsion from North Kivu, where they had been living for generations. A May 1965 uprising, dubbed the Kanyarwanda War and characterized by Hunde-Banyarwanda clashes, led to the labeling of Banyarwanda as rebels and drew further calls for their expulsion.

Policies under President Joseph Mobutu Sese Seko (1965-97) exacerbated the tensions between local groups, sometimes to the advantage of the Banyarwanda, and sometimes to their disadvantage, depending on the political goals of Mobutu (Stearns, 2012b, pp. 23-26). In 1972 he granted citizenship to anyone who had immigrated before 1960, enabling the Banyarwanda to amass large tracts of land. In 1981 Mobutu reversed this law, granting citizenship to those who had arrived in the country before 1885, thereby raising doubts about the land ownership of some 500,000 Banyarwanda. In 2004, the law would once again return to the 1960 reference point, but only after massacres in 1992, the 1994 genocide in neighbouring Rwanda, and the civil wars of 1996-98 and 1998-2003. Contestation over citizenship and deep-seated communal tensions persist and the continuation of ethnic discrimination and a weak state presence contribute to the ongoing instability in the east.

More recently, the Tutsi-dominated National Congress for the Defence of the People (CNDP) fought a rebellion from 2004 to 2009. The CNDP imposed control over much of North Kivu and enabled the return and migration of Tutsi to the region. These population movements generated concerns among the indigenous population that the CNDP was trying to shift the demographics in the area to favour the Banyarwanda-Tutsi population. The arrival of thousands of returnees and economic refugees exacerbated the existing competition over land resources and revived long-standing questions over land access and tenure (Bafilemba, 2010; Huggins, 2010, pp. 25-26). The CNDP signed a peace agreement with the government in 2009, but this did little to address the concerns in the region.

The latest rebellion began in April 2012, when the March 23 Movement (M23) emerged. The group consists primarily of ex-CNDP fighters who had been integrated into the DRC's national army as part of the 23 March 2009 peace agreement, from which the group takes its name. The M23 is Tutsi-dominated and operates mainly in the mineral-rich North Kivu province.

While the ethnic orientation of the group is important, given the region's history of ethnic tensions and anti-Tutsi sentiment, the current rebellion may be less about ethnicity than economics. There are different views on why the rebellion began. One argument is that the push to arrest the former CNDP leader, Gen. Bosco Ntaganda, who has two open International Criminal Court indictments against him, sparked the rebellion. Another holds that the split was prompted by the decision to rotate the Congolese troops out of the resource-rich area, which soldiers, including former rebels, had controlled and exploited. Rwanda, which reportedly turns a profit of USD 100-300 million per year from the mineral trade, allegedly supports the M23 rebellion with weapons, ammunition, and training, as well as troops, for security reasons but also to ensure a continuation of the resource flow (Hogg, 2012).

The M23 rebellion has taken a deep toll on the population. By September 2012 fighting had displaced at least a half million people (News24, 2012). Their abuses of the local population include summary executions, dozens of rapes, forced recruitment of several hundred people, and the abduction and use of children as soldiers (HRW, 2012). It remains unclear what the rebels want—stated goals have ranged from implementation of the 2009 peace agreement to the stepping down of President Joseph Kabila to the creation of a new state in the east—but the group is clearly capable and willing to continue fighting to obtain concessions. Meanwhile, the population continues to suffer from the lack of security and governance in the region.

Sources: ACAC (2010); Al Jazeera (2012); Bafilemba (2010); Gouby (2012); Hogg (2012); Huggins (2010); HRW (2012); Jones (2012); Marysse (2002); News24 (2012); Stearns (2012a; 2012b); UN (2012a; 2012b); Webb (2012)

Map 5.3 **The Kivus and M23 areas of operation, September 2012– January 2013**

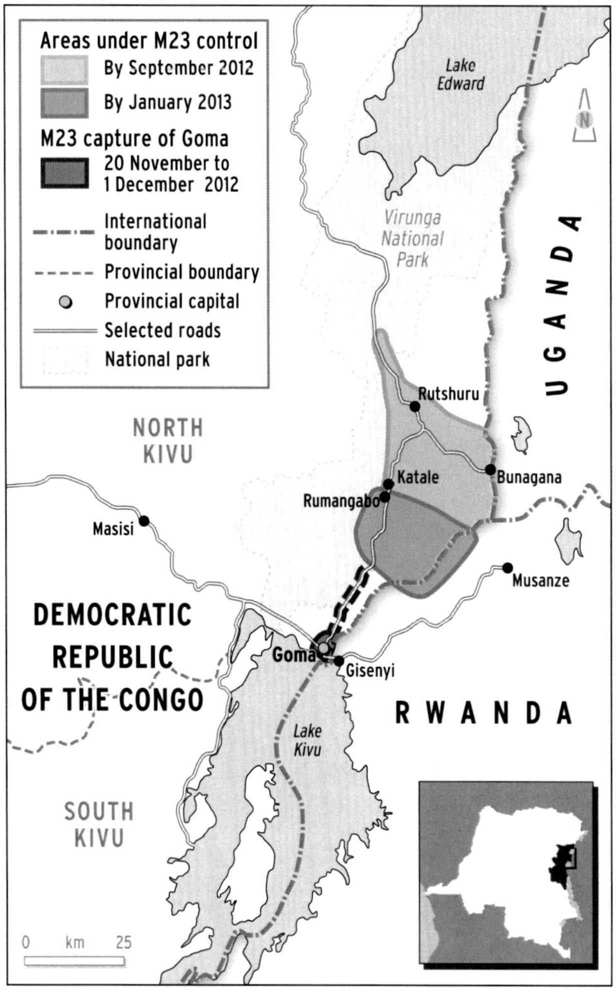

Areas under M23 control
By September 2012
By January 2013

M23 capture of Goma
20 November to
1 December 2012

– - – International boundary
– – – Provincial boundary
○ Provincial capital
—— Selected roads
National park

Lake Edward

Virunga National Park

U G A N D A

NORTH KIVU

Rutshuru

Katale   Bunagana

Rumangabo

Masisi

Musanze

DEMOCRATIC REPUBLIC OF THE CONGO

Goma
Gisenyi

R W A N D A

Lake Kivu

SOUTH KIVU

0   km   25

The DRC is among the countries that have witnessed recurring resource-related conflict. It has experienced recurring armed violence since 1996, including civil wars (1996–98 and 1998–2003) and regional violence (2004–09). The majority of the violence has taken place in the eastern part of the country, an area rich in mineral resources. Although the last civil war officially ended in 2003 with the Lusaka Peace Agreement, violent clashes have continued in the Kivus, including the most recent 2012 rebellion by the M23 rebels (see Box 5.4).

Resource conflicts do not always rise to the level of widespread civil wars. There are numerous cases of localized or regional violence, with groups fighting one another or natural resources and related profits. In addition to the Kivus, the struggle over oil profits in the Niger Delta is a prime example (see Box 5.5). The groups fighting these conflicts often claim to represent aggrieved populations, but in many cases their primary aim is to control the extraction and profits of natural resources, or at least to gain a greater percentage of the profits. Natural resources play an important role in fuelling these conflicts, but political factors play a strong role as well.

Local resource conflicts vary in severity. While the conflict in the Kivus has led to mass displacement and numerous deaths, the conflict in the Niger Delta has created an atmosphere of insecurity through kidnapping and armed clashes, but the majority of the costs have been economic, through oil sabotage, oil bunkering, and limits on the ability of oil companies to operate. While the death toll has been lower in the Delta, the conflict has had far-reaching economic effects.

Violent land conflict among communities

Community conflicts over land are often related to the security of a group, whether in terms of economic security, political power, or the basic survival of a group that may be displaced from its lands. Violent clashes between farming and pastoral communities over land use have been common for decades in Central and East Africa, but their increasing frequency and persistence have turned regions into areas of low-intensity conflict (IRIN, 2012b). In some instances the

Box 5.5 The Niger Delta: a fight for more than just oil

A range of factors fuel armed violence in Nigeria, including politics and elections, democratization and political liberalization, the emergence of armed groups, natural resource competition, inter-group political wrangling over ethnicity and religion, and poverty. But at the heart of many conflicts is a struggle for access to resources and the distribution of benefits (Hazen, 2007, p. 6).

The Niger Delta offers a microcosm of Nigerian national politics. Political patronage remains at the core of local governance and determines the distribution of power and resources (Hazen, 2007, p. 22). Political power remains concentrated in the hands of a few elites who, with their access to money, arms, and private militias, can manipulate elections; in this political system, widespread corruption offers the opportunity to access vast government coffers for personal gain (p. 7). The enormous sums of money available to local, state, and national politicians explain the intensity with which candidates vie for public positions, including by spending considerable amounts on pre-election activities and engaging in violence and intimidation (p. 17). Winning an election, in some cases, is not unlike winning the lottery.

Elections have demonstrated the strong role of political godfathers and the willingness to use any means necessary and available to win elections, including violence. The 2003 elections marked an important shift in political violence. Candidates armed local youth groups as their personal militias, often referred to as *political thugs* among locals (HRW, 2007, p. 33). These private militias 'encouraged' support for the candidate, and 'discouraged' support for opposition candidates through intimidation and violence, including clashes with the militias of opposing candidates (Hazen, 2007, p. 6).

The militarized nature of politics combined with the prevalence of armed groups has allowed for an easy marriage between politics and violence. Armed groups are not new in Nigeria, but they are increasingly well armed and trained, and sophisticated in their tactics. After 2003, armed groups, hired for political purposes, were set free without being disarmed and have since evolved into economically independent and more politically savvy entities (Hazen, 2007, p. 79). As a result, some groups have tried to engage in and influence the political process themselves. Increased access to funding from oil bunkering and the access to arms by militant groups strengthened the militants' position. The military's heavy-handed response to militant activity and the failure of the government to address the underlying grievances of the population—even though the majority of the Delta residents still live in poverty, without reliable access to good roads, health care, education facilities, or employment—turned many civilians against military intervention (Hazen, 2007, p. 10).

While the grievances in the Delta are well founded, not all of the violence can be attributed to the fight for justice, development, or the equitable distribution of oil revenue. The Delta has played host to numerous armed groups over the past decade. Some groups agitate for political change and democratic governance, but many others fight for resource control. In some instances, groups simply take advantage of the uncertain situation to engage in criminal activities and oil bunkering for profit (Hazen, 2007, p. 10).

By 2008, mounting violence had reduced oil production by more than 50 per cent (Thurston, 2010). The government stepped in to offer an amnesty programme in 2009, essentially paying militants to stop the violence. The amnesty has held, for the most part, but many fear the end of the amnesty programme in 2014 will result in a return of violence in the Delta because little has been done to address the underlying grievances of the population.

Sources: Hazen (2007; 2009); Thurston (2010)

violence is short-lived and the damage minimal, while in other cases the active violence persists for weeks and months, leadings to thousands of deaths. Histories of inter-group violence feed cycles of revenge, occasionally with months passing between attacks.

Community clashes take place not only over agricultural and grazing lands, but also over ancestral lands and access to natural resources. In Liberia, for example, disputes in rubber plantations in 2008 brought about the killing of at least 20, while riots over ancestral lands in Uganda left at least 20 dead in 2009 (Moore, 2010). The interlinking of community clashes with larger political conflicts, as in the eastern DRC, has inflamed already volatile situations. The current episode of violence at the hands of the M23 rebellion can be traced back to land disputes between ethnic groups, but the nature of the conflict has evolved over time, increasing in intensity and involving external patrons, as participants to the violence seek to control not only land but also the rich mineral wealth extracted from

Map 5.4 **Non-state communal conflicts over land in Africa, 1989–2011**

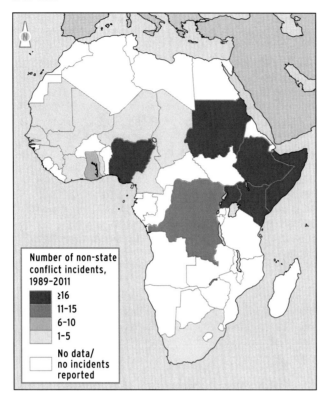

Number of non-state conflict incidents, 1989–2011

- ≥16
- 11–15
- 6–10
- 1–5
- No data/ no incidents reported

Source: UCDP (2012d)

it. Similar dynamics can be found in other pastoral communities in Ethiopia, Kenya, Somalia, Sudan, and Uganda, where bows and arrows have been traded in for more powerful weapons and violence has escalated as localized conflicts become fodder for national politics (Mkutu, 2001, p. 8).

Map 5.4 illustrates patterns of non-state communal conflict in Africa, meaning conflicts between non-state groups within a country.[11] It does not provide exhaustive coverage, but instead represents the best estimate of the number of communal armed conflicts over land resources, based on reports of violent clashes, or incidents, between communities.[12]

There is no comprehensive database that collects figures of those killed, injured, or displaced by violent land conflicts between pastoral and agricultural communities or between ethnic groups. A review of some of the available estimates suggests the impact of these conflicts has been high (see Table 5.2).

Violent communal conflicts over land and resources such as cattle have taken place for generations among various groups, including pastoralists (see Box 5.6). Yet their tactics and intensity are changing. Traditional bows and arrows, while still used in conflicts today, are now often accompanied by small arms, increasing the devastation of attacks. For example, while cattle rustling and clashes over farm land are common in East Africa, the availability of small arms across Kenya's borders, particularly from war-torn Somalia, has exacerbated an already conflict-prone situation, making it more violent (Akwiri, 2012). The Karimojong conflicts—stretching from Uganda into South Sudan and Kenya—have become more lethal and more protracted with the widespread availability of small arms (Bevan, 2008, pp. 26–27; Kingma et al., 2012, pp. 27–30). Bevan (2008) traces the evolution of the conflicts in Karamoja and the role of small arms in increasing violence and weakening the capacity of local authorities to manage the situation (see Box 5.7).

These conflicts are also changing in terms of their scale, frequency, and level of destruction. Historically, attacks focused more on cattle rustling than on attacking communities. This has changed in some areas, with attacks now focused more directly on civilians, including children, women, and the elderly; indeed, attackers have not refrained from killing, abducting, and raping victims while also decimating villages by arson (Burnett, 2012; Small Arms Survey, 2012, pp. 6–7). The escalation of clashes suggests a potential for an arms race among communities that view their security as threatened and their governments as unwilling or unable to protect them.

Box 5.6 Pastoralist communities and the struggle for land and livelihoods

East Africa–including Ethiopia, Kenya, Somalia, and the two Sudans–is home to the largest group of pastoralists in the world. A pastoral life involves more than the economic activity of raising livestock, even if these animals are at the centre of the economic, social, and political organization of pastoral communities. The ability of the pastoral system to survive depends on access to water and pasture lands. The drive to access water and land has brought pastoralists into conflict with agricultural communities, other pastoralist groups, and state security forces.

Pastoralists are semi-nomadic, moving their herds during dry seasons and times of drought to areas where there is better access to water and land. This movement has brought them into conflict with sedentary farming populations. Shifts in land ownership and changing state and national borders have made pastoral activities more difficult and led to increased conflict over land use. The privatization of land rights has led to the marginalization of pastoral areas and the weakening of traditional authority.

The privatization of rights has shifted land ownership from communal to private. This counters past practices of communal ownership among pastoral communities, which allowed for broader grazing areas, as well as negotiations among communities for grazing rights. The implementation of borders between plots of land effectively reduced the ability of pastoralists to move their herds. It also made communal land available for purchase, further displacing pastoralists. For example, the West Pokot district in Kenya has lost much of its pastoral land to agricultural activities (Mkutu, 2003, p. 11). The expansion of agricultural activities and the creation of national parks using traditional pastoral lands have reduced the amount of land available for pastoral activities, while also exacerbating the tensions between agricultural and pastoral communities, and between pastoralists and the state.

Pastoralists have been largely marginalized in the political and economic systems of these African states. Pastoral areas are among the poorest and receive less representation in government and economic assistance than other regions. This means they have fewer options for protecting their way of life or coping with droughts that threaten their livelihoods. These are also areas that have received limited attention from governments, including the provision of law and order, leaving responsibility for security to the traditional authorities. The Karimojong in Uganda have responded to the lack of state-provided security by making their own guns (Mkutu, 2003, pp. 12–13).

The increase in private land rights and the shift to modern governance structures have weakened traditional governance structures, and at times placed traditional laws in contravention of national laws. Traditional governance provided means of distributing access to resources and mechanisms for resolving disputes, and imposed controls over cattle raiding. The weakening of these controls has reduced the ability to manage land conflicts and provided the opportunity for more frequent and deadlier raids. In Karamoja, Uganda, the impact of widespread raiding on pastoral communities has been devastating, depleting the key form of currency and livelihood (cattle) to such a point as to drive young men towards criminality, where economic opportunities appear better (Bevan, 2008, pp. 27–28).

Cattle raiding is an age-old activity, conducted to replenish lost stock, to expand grazing lands, or to obtain the costs of bride payments, an important cultural practice among pastoral communities. Traditionally, cattle rustling focused on the theft of livestock, but a number of factors have contributed to the changing nature of raiding and violent land conflict. Pastoralist communities have armed themselves with small arms in order to protect their cattle, defend their land, and even engage in cattle raiding themselves. Traditional authorities are no longer able to control raiding practices, and young men have demonstrated a willingness to conduct armed raids in order to acquire cattle and thereby enhance their stature in the community. There is also evidence of the commercialization of cattle raiding by businessmen who invest in the practice as a means of making money. In Samburu district in Kenya, the theft of more than 25,000 cattle during 1996–99 suggests that cattle raiding has become more organized, with few of the stolen livestock being recovered, and reports of the meat being sold as far away as South Africa and Saudi Arabia (Mkutu, 2003, p. 16). Raids have resulted not only in the loss of cattle, but also in the deaths of women and children, the destruction of homes, and the displacement of hundreds of thousands.

Ugandan and Kenyan authorities have responded in various ways. They have deployed the police to enhance security, but the police have often proved inadequate to the task, or in some cases complicit in the activities. They have provided arms to communities and minimal training to create volunteer forces to protect communities, but this has led to an arms race among affected communities and attracted armed vigilantes who conduct their own raids for profit. Governments in the region have also tried disarmament campaigns, but the forced disarmament programmes were marred by human rights violations, while the voluntary amnesty programmes produced few results (Mkutu, 2003, pp. 13–14, 28–30; Sheekh, Atta-Asamoah, and Sharamo, 2012, pp. 6–7). Insecurity in pastoralist areas and the inability of the state to provide security have left those communities feeling insecure without their arms, and unwilling to give them up. Without putting in place mechanisms for managing land disputes, measures to provide security, and programmes to address the economic needs of these communities, removing the arms will simply create more insecurity and increase the market for new arms acquisition.

Sources: Africa Confidential (2012); Bevan (2008); IRIN (2012a); Mkutu (2001; 2003); Sheekh and Mosley (2012); Sheekh et al. (2012)

Box 5.7 Cattle raiding, small arms, and violent conflict

Cattle raiding is an old tradition in the pastoral communities of Africa, such as in Ethiopia, Kenya, Sudan, and Uganda (see Box 5.6). Pastoral groups conducted raids in order to replenish depleted stocks after droughts, to recover cattle stolen in raids, to expand grazing areas, or to acquire new cattle for bride prices. Since the 1970s, armed violence in pastoral communities has expanded. It is now more frequent and more violent, and involves more than just traditional cattle raiding.

A number of factors have contributed to the escalation of armed violence in pastoral communities, which is most frequently expressed through community raids, commercial raiding, and criminal activities. These factors include:

- the reduction in available grazing lands;
- weak state presence;
- poor governance;
- a lack of security;
- few economic opportunities for young pastoralists who have lost cattle through drought and raids;
- the pursuit of economic profits by urban entrepreneurs who have turned cattle raiding into a formalized, albeit illegal, economic venture;
- the weakening of traditional dispute mechanisms; and
- the proliferation of small arms.

While small arms play an important role in the escalation of violence, they are a symptom, not a cause, of the violent conflict taking place in pastoral areas. The causes of the violent conflict are complex and not suited to simple prescriptive solutions.

Pastoralist communities have acquired small arms not only to protect their cattle and their land, but also to engage in cattle raiding themselves. Initially, raids focused on the cattle as the prize, and revenge raids often attempted to recapture stolen livestock. The cattle thus stayed within the pastoral community, providing opportunities for repeated thefts. In addition, there were strong traditional constraints on violence. Deaths were taken seriously, and those responsible were required to undergo ceremonial cleansing rituals and compensate the families of those killed. As pastoral communities have adapted to changing conditions, so have the traditions of cattle raiding and of the communities as a whole, contributing to more violent activities.

Today, many raids are conducted against communities that are far away or with minimal ties to the raiding party's community, reducing constraints on actions, and increasing the toll of raids as women and children are abducted or killed and homes are burned. The weakening of traditional authorities, who traditionally oversaw ritual cleansings and compensation, further reduces the accountability of raiding parties. Commercial raiding, conducted by pastoralists who are paid by urban entrepreneurs to steal cattle, has not only increased the economic incentive for raids, but has also led to a reduction in the overall stock in grazing areas as these cattle are not swapped among pastoral groups, but are sold on the market. The reduction in cattle has exacerbated the plight of pastoral communities, and desperation has spurred more frequent raids. It has also driven the traditional warriors into other economic activities, such as commercial raids or service as hired thugs.

From colonial times pastoralists gradually replaced traditional weapons with more modern ones. They initially used simple single-shot rifles, but in the late 1970s assault rifles became more common, and today they are the most widely used. Pastoralists have sourced weapons from Kenya, the Sudans, and Uganda, using established trade routes (Bevan, 2008; Mkutu, 2006). Yet they have also obtained weapons through domestic sources, including markets, barter, and state security forces. Groups obtain weapons during raids, by stealing the weapons of the communities they attack. Civil wars and unrest in neighbouring countries contribute to the influx of small arms into the region. The cost of small arms—although it varies based on location and demand—has dropped over time, making small arms affordable to many. The cost of ammunition, by contrast, has generally increased, though it is still affordable, and relatively easy to smuggle in small quantities.

The availability of small arms and their frequent use in violence have not only generated fear among communities but have also created a demand for weapons. The acquisition of weapons has been far from uniform. The strength of some groups, such as the Karimojong, has spurred victimized communities to seek to arm themselves. Governments have responded in some areas by arming local defence groups. Yet state security forces have been largely absent from conflict resolution efforts and, where they have intervened, they have often been outnumbered and outgunned. This has left communities to their own devices to ensure their security. The insecurity in the region has many causes, but the commonality is that communities are seeking to defend themselves through the possession of small arms.

Sources: Bevan (2008); Bainomugisha, Okello, and Ngoya (2007); Kingma et al. (2012); Mkutu (2006); Small Arms Survey (2012)

Table 5.2 Examples of communal conflicts over land or land-related resources, Africa, 1999–2011[13]

Country	Year	Groups	Number killed in clashes
Democratic Republic of the Congo	1999	Hema, Lendu	5,000–7,000
	2002–03	Hema, Lendu	4,269
	2007	Bena Kapuya, Bena Nsimba	25
Ethiopia	2002	Afar, Issa	75
		Anuak, Dinka	35
		Dizi, Surma	35
		Ogaden, Sheikhal	435
	2009	Borana, Gehri	300
Kenya	2010	North-eastern groups	179
	2011	North-eastern groups	370
	2012	Orma, Pokoma	>100
Sudan	2007	Didinga, Toposa	>50
		Dongotono, Logir	67
	2009	Lou Nuer, Murle	>1,000
	2011	Lou Nuer, Murle	>600
Uganda	2003	Bokora Karimojong, Pian Karimojong	30
	2003, 2007	Bokora Karimojong, Jie Karimojong	133
	2009	Karimojong groups	>50

Sources: HIU (2009a); Petrini (2010)

Violent social conflict related to land and resources

In addition to resource conflicts and communal clashes, various types of violent events can be considered 'social conflict'; these are not normally counted in mainstream armed conflict datasets. Social conflict events include demonstrations, riots, protests, and strikes. Map 5.5 indicates which African countries experienced violent social conflict over three land-related issues:

1) food, water, and subsistence;
2) environmental degradation; and
3) economic resources (usually land-based).[14]

Map 5.5 **Social conflict over land and natural resources in Africa, 1990–2011**

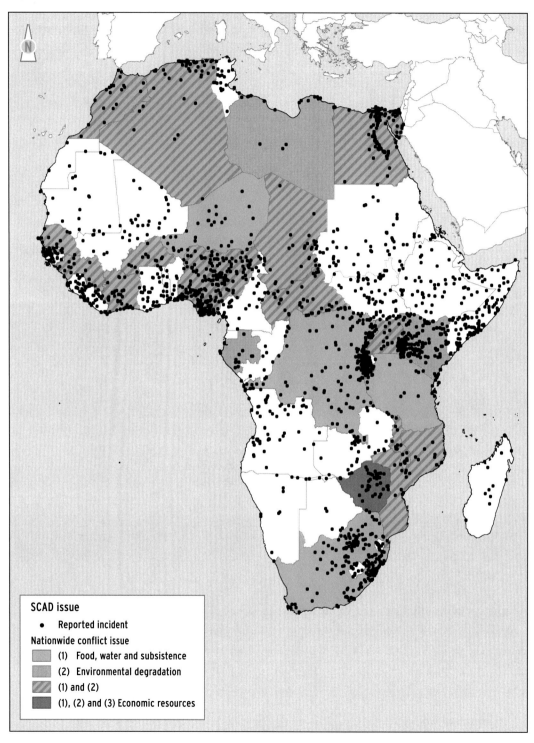

SCAD issue

• Reported incident

Nationwide conflict issue

(1) Food, water and subsistence

(2) Environmental degradation

(1) and (2)

(1), (2) and (3) Economic resources

Note: Shaded countries have experienced nationwide conflict over the identified issues; dots indicate the locations of incidents that erupted over any of these issues.

Source: SCAD (2012)

Ugandan soldiers watch over Karamojong pastoralists rounded up in a 'cordon and search' operation to secure weapons in Looyakaromwae village, Uganda, March 2007. © Euan Denholm/Reuters

While these incidents can all be considered social conflict events, not all of them resulted in violent deaths, which is often the barometer for inclusion in conflict datasets. The Social Conflict in Africa Database includes 7,473 reports of social conflict based on land-related issues. The vast majority of these events lasted only one day, while just a handful lasted more than one year. In the majority of these incidents, nobody was killed, yet a small percentage resulted in tens, hundreds, and even thousands of deaths (see Figure 5.2 overleaf).

The incidents with the highest number of fatalities resulted from land disputes, cattle rustling, and protests or clashes over economic resources. Land disputes and cattle rustling have occurred for decades in the DRC, Kenya, Nigeria, Sudan, and Uganda. Some long-standing communal conflicts have become cycles of revenge violence, fed by retaliatory attacks that have escalated in intensity over the years; such conflicts exist between the Hema and Lendu, the Nyanga and the Hunde, and the Munzaya and Eyele in the DRC; between the Murle and Lou Nuer in Sudan; among the Karimojong in Uganda; and between the Ogoni and Andoni in Nigeria. Many of the incidents that claimed the highest number of lives lasted several months, although some events that lasted only a few days resulted in hundreds of deaths.

Figure 5.2 **Incidents resulting from land-related issues in Africa, per number of deaths, 1990-2011**

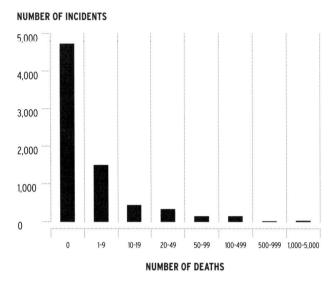

NUMBER OF INCIDENTS

NUMBER OF DEATHS

Source: SCAD (2012)

CONCLUSION

Land disputes are most at risk for turning violent when grievances are high, when mechanisms for adjudication are absent or produce biased resolution, and when violence entrepreneurs, often politicians, take advantage of the situation to encourage and finance violence for personal gain. These conflicts are fuelled by previous cycles of violence between communities engaging in revenge and retaliatory attacks. A history of inter-group violence, grievances, and fear reduce the sense of security and encourage resort to self-help tactics.

Violent land conflict takes the form of family feuds, communal clashes, and cattle rustling, as well as regional and national armed conflicts. The death tolls range from tens to thousands killed, sometimes over long periods, but sometimes within days or weeks. In addition to loss of life, communities that experience land conflict also suffer injuries, kidnapping, the destruction of housing and land, the marginalization of conflict areas, and rising insecurity. The situation is likely to worsen as populations grow, resources become scarcer, competition over land increases, and small arms become more widely available.

Land issues are a pervasive characteristic of African society and governance challenges, but they are just one facet of the problem. They are often intertwined with many other factors that contribute to armed violence, making it difficult to disentangle the role of land grievances. A better understanding of the role of land in armed violence is required, as are informed policies to address the root causes of unrest. Unless land grievances are resolved, the politicization of land is reduced, and mechanisms are put in place to fairly adjudicate disputes and provide basic security to populations, violent land conflict will remain a risky and deadly phenomenon across Africa. ▪

LIST OF ABBREVIATIONS

CNDP	Congress for the Defence of the People
DRC	Democratic Republic of the Congo
M23	March 23 Movement
UCDP	Uppsala Conflict Data Program

ENDNOTES

1   According to the World Bank and the Food and Agriculture Organization of the United Nations, 'Agricultural land refers to the share of land area that is arable, under permanent crops, and under permanent pastures' (World Bank, 2012).

2   Bruce (2011); Moore (2010); Obioha (2008); Oxfam (2011); van der Zwan (2011).

3   Some authors speak of land-related violent conflict, rather than 'land conflict'; see van der Zwan (2011) and OECD–DAC (2005). The United States Agency for International Development distinguishes between 'land disputes', which involve competing claims over land rights to a particular piece of land that can be addressed within existing legal frameworks, and 'land conflict', which arises when legal frameworks are not sufficient to resolve competing claims, claims are between groups over large areas of land, and tension and danger of violence are implied, but violence is not necessarily occurring (Bruce, 2011, p. 1).

4   For a discussion of recommendations for managing land disputes and preventing violent land conflict, see Bruce (2011); OECD–DAC (2005); and Oxfam (2011; 2012).

5   See Hartman (2010, pp. 8–15).

6   See Hartman (2010) and Mabikke (2011).

7   The Land Matrix is an online public database designed to let users contribute data on land deals. For details, see Land Portal (n.d.).

8   For a discussion of the recent civilian disarmament campaign and its repercussions in Jonglei, South Sudan, see Small Arms Survey (2012, pp. 8–9).

9   An *armed conflict* is 'a contested incompatibility which concerns government and/or territory where the use of armed force between two parties, of which at least one is the government of a state, results in at least 25 battle-related deaths'; a conflict reaches the intensity of a *war* when it results in 1,000 battle-related deaths. See UCDP (2012b).

10 The 1990s witnessed a long debate in the literature about the motivations for civil wars. The 'greed versus grievance' debate posited that the civil wars were fought either over money and resources (greed) or for the rectification of grievances. Key authors included Paul Collier, David Keen, Will Reno, and Michael Ross; see Berdal and Malone (2000) and Ballentine and Sherman (2003) for edited volumes on the debate. The debate has largely waned with the recognition that both greed and grievance play a role in civil wars, and that resources more often play a role in fuelling conflicts, rather than starting them. See, for example, Ballentine and Sherman (2003, pp. 3–6) and Hazen (2013). The debate did succeed in bringing economic factors back into the discussion of civil wars and prompted a shift away from a focus on political factors.

11 The Uppsala Conflict Data Program (UCDP) defines non-state conflict as 'the use of armed force between two organized armed groups, neither of which is the government of a state, which results in at least 25 battle-related deaths in a year' (UCDP, 2012b).

12 The data used for this map was derived from the UCDP non-state conflict database (UCDP, 2012d). The data was first sorted so that only events in Africa were included; it was then further sorted into only those labeled *informally organized groups*, which includes: 'Groups that share a common identification along ethnic, clan, religious, national or tribal lines. These are not groups that are permanently organized for combat, but who at times organize themselves along said lines to engage in fighting. This level of organization captures aspects of what is commonly referred to as "communal conflicts", in that conflict stands along lines of communal identity' (UCDP, 2012c). This incorporates the conflicts that are most likely to involve community conflicts over land, as opposed to political conflicts or rebel movements. A review of the data suggests that land is at least one factor in these conflicts.

13 See also IRIN (1999) on the 1999 DRC conflict; Asaka (2012) and Sheekh and Mosley (2012) on the 2012 Kenya conflict; IRIN (2012a) on the 2010 and 2011 Kenya conflicts; HIU (2009b) on the 2009 Uganda conflict; and Small Arms Survey (2007, p. 2) on the 2007 Sudan conflicts.

14 'Land' is not among the categories available for clustering data in the Social Conflict in Africa Database (SCAD, 2012). In creating Map 5.5, the author has thus used the three categories most closely associated with land issues.

BIBLIOGRAPHY

ACAC (Africa Canada Accountability Coalition). 2010. *Land, Citizenship, and Conflict in the Kivus*. Issue Brief. Vancouver: University of British Columbia. July. <http://www.africacanada.org/wp-content/uploads/2010/06/Land_Citizenship_and_Conflict_in_the_Kivus_1.pdf>

Africa Confidential. 2012. 'Kenya: Kilelengwani Burns.' Vol. 53, No. 19. 21 September.

Akwiri, Joseph. 2012. 'Raiders Kill 38 in Latest Land Clashes in Kenya.' Reuters. 10 September.
   <http://www.reuters.com/article/2012/09/10/us-kenya-clashes-idUSBRE88912W20120910>

Al Jazeera. 2012. 'Congo's M23 Rebels Threaten to Take Goma.' 11 July. <http://www.aljazeera.com/news/africa/2012/07/2012711172138525791.html>

Asaka, Jeremiah. 2012. 'Water and Land Conflict in Kenya in the Wake of Climate Change.' *News Security Beat*. 28 September.
   <http://www.newsecuritybeat.org/2012/09/water-land-conflict-kenya-wake-climate-change/#.URoTnejlE7A>

Bafilemba, Fidel. 2010. 'North Kivu: Controversy as Refugee Returns Exacerbate Land Conflicts.' Washington, DC: Enough Project. 16 July.
   <http://www.enoughproject.org/publications/north-kivu-controversy-refugee-returns-exacerbate-land-conflicts>

Bainomugisha, Arthur, Julius Okello, and John Bosco Ngoya. 2007. *The Tragedy of Natural Resources Dependent Pastoral Communities: A Case of Teso–Karamoja Border Land Conflict.* ACODE Policy Research Series No. 23. Kampala: Advocates Coalition for Development and Environment. <http://www.acode-u.org/documents/TESO.pdf>

Ballentine, Karen and Jake Sherman, eds. 2003. *The Political Economy of Armed Conflict: Beyond Greed and Grievance.* Boulder: Lynne Rienner.

BBC (British Broadcasting Corporation) News. 2012a. 'Kenya's Tana Clashes: President Kibaki Imposes Curfew.' 11 September. <http://www.bbc.co.uk/news/world-africa-19556387>

—. 2012b. 'Kenya Tana River Delta Massacres Raise Election Violence Fear.' 17 September. <http://www.bbc.co.uk/news/world-africa-19621246>

—. 2012c. 'Mass Graves Found in Kenya's Tana River Delta Region.' 18 September. <http://www.bbc.co.uk/news/world-africa-19634076>

Berdal, Mats and David Malone, eds. 2000. *Greed and Grievance: Economic Agendas in Civil Wars.* Boulder: Lynne Rienner.

Bevan, James. 2008. *Crisis in Karamoja: Armed Violence and the Failure of Disarmament in Uganda's Most Deprived Region.* Occasional Paper 21. Geneva: Small Arms Survey. <http://www.smallarmssurvey.org/fileadmin/docs/B-Occasional-papers/SAS-OP21-Karamoja.pdf>

Bruce, John. 2011. *Land and Conflict: Land Disputes and Land Conflicts.* Property Rights and Resource Governance Briefing Paper No. 12. Washington, DC: United States Agency for International Development. April.
<http://usaidlandtenure.net/sites/default/files/USAID_Land_Tenure_Land_and_Conflict_Issue_Brief.pdf>

Burnett, John. 2012. 'In South Sudan, Cows Are Cash and Source of Friction.' National Public Radio. 16 August.
<http://www.npr.org/2012/08/16/158776225/in-south-sudan-cows-are-cash-and-source-of-friction>

Deininger, Klaus. 2003. *Land Policies for Growth and Poverty Reduction.* World Bank Policy Research Report. Washington, DC: World Bank and Oxford University Press. <http://siteresources.worldbank.org/EXTARD/Resources/336681-1295878311276/26384.pdf>

— and Derek Byerlee. 2011. *Rising Global Interest in Farmland: Can It Yield Sustainable and Equitable Benefits?* Washington, DC: World Bank.
<http://siteresources.worldbank.org/INTARD/Resources/ESW_Sept7_final_final.pdf>

de Wit, Paul, Christopher Tanner, and Simon Norfolk. 2009. *Land Policy Development in an African Context: Lessons Learned from Selected Experiences.* Land Tenure Working Paper 14. New York: Food and Agriculture Organization. October. <ftp://ftp.fao.org/docrep/fao/012/ak547e/ak547e00.pdf>

Economist. 2009a. 'Buying Farmland Abroad: Outsourcing's Third Wave.' 21 May. <http://www.economist.com/node/13692889>

—. 2009b. 'Land Deals in Africa and Asia: Cornering Foreign Fields.' 21 May. <http://www.economist.com/node/13697274>

Geneva Declaration Secretariat. 2008. *Global Burden of Armed Violence.* Geneva: Geneva Declaration Secretariat.
<http://www.genevadeclaration.org/fileadmin/docs/Global-Burden-of-Armed-Violence-full-report.pdf>

Gilgen, Elisa and Matthias Nowak. 2011. *A Legacy of War? Perceptions of Security in Liberia.* Liberia Armed Violence Assessment Issue Brief No. 1. Geneva: Small Arms Survey. September. <http://www.smallarmssurvey.org/fileadmin/docs/G-Issue-briefs/Liberia-AVA-IB1.pdf>

Gouby, Melanie. 2012. 'Congo M23 Rebels Accused of Forming Parallel Gov't.' Associated Press. 22 September.
<http://bigstory.ap.org/article/congo-m23-rebels-accused-forming-parallel-govt>

Hartman, Alexandra. 2010. *Comparative Analysis of Land Conflicts in Liberia: Grand Gedeh, Lofa and Nimba Counties.* Oslo: Norwegian Refugee Council. November. <http://www.nrc.no/arch/_img/9536779.pdf>

Hazen, Jennifer M. 2007. *Small Arms, Armed Violence, and Insecurity in Nigeria: The Niger Delta in Perspective.* Occasional Paper No. 20. Geneva: Small Arms Survey. December. <http://www.smallarmssurvey.org/fileadmin/docs/B-Occasional-papers/SAS-OP20-Nigeria.pdf>

—. 2009. 'From Social Movement to Armed Group: A Case Study from Nigeria.' *Contemporary Security Policy*, Vol. 30, No. 2. August, pp. 281–300.

—. 2013. *What Rebels Want: Resources and Supply Networks in Wartime.* Ithaca, NY: Cornell University Press.

HIU (Humanitarian Information Unit). 2009a. 'Conflicts without Borders Dataset, 2009.' Washington, DC: United States Department of State. Accessed September 2012. <https://hiu.state.gov/Pages/CWOB.aspx>

—. 2009b. 'Africa: Conflict Without Borders, Sub-national and Transnational Conflict-Affected Areas January 2009–July 2009.' Accessed January 2013.
<https://hiu.state.gov/Products/Africa_ConflictsWithoutBorders_2009Jul_HIU.pdfY>

Hogg, Jonny. 2012. 'Insight: Ethnic, Economic Interests Entangle Rwanda in Congo.' Reuters. 17 October.
<http://in.reuters.com/article/2012/08/22/us-congo-democratic-east-idINBRE87L06P20120822>

HRW (Human Rights Watch). 2007. *Chop Fine: The Human Rights Impact of Local Government Corruption and Mismanagement in Rivers State, Nigeria.* New York: HRW. <http://www.hrw.org/reports/2007/01/30/chop-fine>

—. 2012. 'DR Congo: M23 Rebels Committing War Crimes.' 11 September.
<http://www.hrw.org/news/2012/09/11/dr-congo-m23-rebels-committing-war-crimes>

HSRP (Human Security Report Project). 2012. *Human Security Report 2012: Sexual Violence, Education, and War: Beyond the Mainstream Narrative.* Vancouver: Human Security Press. <http://www.hsrgroup.org/human-security-reports/2012/overview.aspx>

Huggins, Chris. 2010. *Land, Power and Identity: Roots of Violent Conflict in Eastern DRC.* London: International Alert. November.
<http://www.international-alert.org/resources/publications/land-power-and-identity>

— and Jenny Clover. 2005. 'Introduction.' In Chris Huggins and Jenny Clover, eds. *From the Ground Up: Land Rights, Conflict and Peace in Sub-Saharan Africa*. Pretoria: Institute for Security Studies. June, pp. 1–23. <http://www.iss.co.za/pubs/Books/GroundUp/contents.htm>

— and Johan Pottier. 2005. 'Land Tenure, Land Reform and Conflict in Sub-Saharan Africa: Towards a Research Agenda.' In Chris Huggins and Jenny Clover, eds. *From the Ground Up: Land Rights, Conflict and Peace in Sub-Saharan Africa*. Pretoria: Institute for Security Studies. June, pp. 383–92. <http://www.iss.co.za/pubs/Books/GroundUp/contents.htm>

IDMC (Internal Displacement Monitoring Centre). 2009. *Whose Land Is This? Land Disputes and Forced Displacement in the Western Forest Area of Côte d'Ivoire*. Geneva: IDMC, Norwegian Refugee Council. October.
<http://www.internal-displacement.org/countries/cotedivoire/reports/CDI_SCR_Nov09.pdf>

IRIN (Integrated Regional Information Network). 1999. 'DRC: IRIN Focus on Hema–Lendu Conflict.' 15 November.
<http://www.irinnews.org/Report/10506/DRC-IRIN-Focus-on-Hema-Lendu-conflict>

—. 2012a. 'Kenya: Politics, Pastureland and Conflict.' 29 August. <http://www.irinnews.org/report/96201/KENYA-Politics-pastureland-and-conflict>

—. 2012b. 'Kenya: Situation Tense after Renewed Tana River Clashes.' 14 January.
<http://www.irinnews.org/Report/29740/KENYA-Situation-tense-after-renewed-Tana-River-clashes>

Jones, Pete. 2012. 'In Democratic Republic of the Congo: Fear of New Ethnic Conflict Is Tangible.' *Guardian*. 22 June.
<http://www.guardian.co.uk/world/2012/jun/22/congo-fear-new-conflict-m23-rebels>

Kanyinga, Karuti, Odenda Lumumba, and Kojo Sebastian Amanor. 2008. 'The Struggle for Sustainable Land Management and Democratic Development in Kenya: A History of Greed and Grievances.' In Kojo Sebastian Amanor and Sam Moyo, eds. *Land & Sustainable Development in Africa*. London: Zed Books, ch. 4.

Kingma, Kees, et al. 2012. *Security Provision and Small Arms in Karamoja: A Survey of Perceptions*. Special Report No. 17. Geneva: Small Arms Survey and Danish Demining Group. <http://www.smallarmssurvey.org/fileadmin/docs/C-Special-reports/SAS-SR17-Karamoja.pdf>

Klare, Michael. 2002. *Resource Wars: The New Landscape of Global Conflict*. New York: Owl Books.

Land Portal. n.d. 'Land Matrix.' Accessed September 2012. <landportal.info/landmatrix>

Le Billon, Philippe. 2005. 'Resources and Armed Conflicts.' *Adelphi Papers*, No. 373, Vol. 45. London: Routledge, pp. 29–49.

Mabikke, Samuel. 2011. 'Escalating Land Grabbing in Post-Conflict Regions of Northern Uganda: A Need for Strengthening Good Land Governance in the Acholi Region.' Paper presented at the International Conference on Global Land Grabbing, University of Sussex, United Kingdom. April.

Marysse, Stefaan. 2002. 'Plunder, Criminalization of the State and Decline in the World System: The Case of D.R. Congo.' Paper presented at the 10th General Conference of the European Association of Development Research and Training Institutes, 19–21 September.
<http://www.eadi.org/fileadmin/WG_Documents/Reg_WG/marysse.pdf>

McKibben, Gareth and James Bean. 2010. *Land or Else: Land-Based Conflict, Vulnerability, and Disintegration in Northern Uganda*. Kampala: International Organization for Migration, Norwegian Refugee Council, and the United Nations Development Programme. August. <http://www.internal-displacement.org/8025708F004CE90B/(httpDocuments)/7139454B01EC0D2DC1257814003F2E6B/$file/Uganda+-+Land+or+Else.pdf>

Mkutu, Kennedy. 2001. *Pastoralism and Conflict in the Horn of Africa*. Bradford, UK: Bradford University.
<http://www.saferworld.org.uk/downloads/pubdocs/WebLaikipia.pdf>

—. 2003. *Pastoral Conflict and Small Arms: The Kenya–Uganda Border Region*. London: Saferworld. November.
<http://www.saferworld.org.uk/downloads/pubdocs/Pastoral%20conflict.pdf>

—. 2006. 'Small Arms and Light Weapons among Pastoral Groups in the Kenya–Uganda Border Areas.' *African Affairs*, Vol. 106, No. 422, pp. 47–70.

Moore, Jina. 2010. 'Africa's Continental Divide: Land Disputes.' *Christian Science Monitor*. 30 January.
<http://www.csmonitor.com/World/Africa/2010/0130/Africa-s-continental-divide-land-disputes>

Murunga, Godwin. 2011. 'Spontaneous or Premeditated? Post-Election Violence in Kenya.' Discussion Paper 57. Uppsala: Nordiska Afrikainstitutet.
<http://www.isn.ethz.ch/isn/Digital-Library/Publications/Detail/?ots591=0c54e3b3-1e9c-be1e-2c24-a6a8c7060233&lng=en&id=133996>

News24. 2012. 'DRC Rebels Form "Mini State".' 19 September. <http://www.news24.com/Africa/News/DRC-rebels-form-mini-state-20120919>

NRC (Norwegian Refugee Council). 2011. *Searching for Soap Trees: Norwegian Refugee Council's Land Dispute Resolution Process in Liberia*. Oslo: NRC.
<http://www.nrc.no/arch/_img/9546544.pdf>

Obioha, Emeka. 2008. 'Climate Change, Population Drift and Violent Conflict over Land Resources in Northeastern Nigeria.' *Journal of Human Ecology*, Vol. 23, No. 4, pp. 311–24. <http://www.krepublishers.com/02-Journals/JHE/JHE-23-0-000-000-2008-Web/JHE-23-4-000-000-2008-Abst-PDF/JHE-23-4-311-08-1759-Obioha-E-E/JHE-23-4-311-08-1759-Obioha-E-E-Ab.pdf>

OECD–DAC (Organisation for Economic Co-operation and Development–Development Assistance Committee). 2001. *The DAC Guidelines: Helping Prevent Violent Conflict*. Paris: OECD. <http://www.oecd.org/development/conflictandfragility/1886146.pdf>

—. 2005. *Land and Violent Conflict*. Issues Brief. Paris: OECD. <http://www.sdc.admin.ch/ressources/resource_en_92766.pdf>

Oucho, John. 2010. 'Undercurrents of Post-Election Violence in Kenya: Issues in the Long-term Agenda.' In Karuti Kanyinga and Duncan Okello, eds. *Tensions and Reversals in Democratic Transitions: The Kenya 2007 General Elections*, ch. 13. Nairobi: Society for International Development and Institute for Development Studies, University of Nairobi.
<http://www2.warwick.ac.uk/fac/soc/crer/afrobrain/oucho/publications/john_oucho.pdf>

Oxfam. 2011. *Land and Power: The Growing Scandal Surrounding the New Wave of Investments in Land.* Oxfam Briefing Paper 151. Oxford: Oxfam. 22 September. <http://www.oxfam.org/en/grow/policy/land-and-power>

—. 2012. *'Our Land, Our Lives': Time Out on the Global Land Rush.* Oxfam Briefing Note. Oxford: Oxfam. October.
<http://www.oxfam.org/en/grow/policy/%E2%80%98our-land-our-lives%E2%80%99>

Pantuliano, Sara, ed. 2009. *Uncharted Territory: Land, Conflict and Humanitarian Action.* Rugby: Practical Action.
<http://www.odi.org.uk/sites/odi.org.uk/files/odi-assets/publications-opinion-files/5556.pdf>

— and Samir Elhawary. 2009. *Uncharted Territory: Land, Conflict and Humanitarian Action.* Humanitarian Policy Group Policy Brief 39. London: Overseas Development Institute. November. <http://www.odi.org.uk/resources/docs/5301.pdf>

Petrini, Benjamin. 2010. 'Violent Conflict Dataset, 1991–2008.' Washington, DC: World Bank. Accessed December 2012.
<http://siteresources.worldbank.org/EXTCPR/Resources/407739-1267651559887/Violent_Conflict_Dataset_combined.pdf>

Pons-Vignon, Nicolas and Henri-Bernard Solignac Lecomte. 2004. *Land, Violent Conflict and Development.* Working Paper No. 233. Paris: Organisation for Economic Co-operation and Development.
<http://www.oecd-ilibrary.org/fr/development/land-violent-conflict-and-development_717151268534;jsessionid=1bu4sg7q4oilt.delta>

Putzel, James. 2009. 'Land Policies and Violent Conflict: Towards Addressing the Root Causes.' London: Crisis States Research Centre, London School of Economics and Political Science. <http://www.fig.net/pub/fig_wb_2009/papers/acc/acc_1_putzel.pdf>

SCAD (Social Conflict in Africa Database). 2012. 'Social Conflict in Africa Database Version 3.0.' Austin: University of Texas. Accessed September 2012.
<http://strausscenter.org/scad.html>

Sheekh, Nuur Mohamud, Andrews Atta-Asamoah, and Roba Sharamo. 2012. *Kenya's Neglected IDPs: Internal Displacement and Vulnerability of Pastoralist Communities in Northern Kenya.* Johannesburg: Institute for Security Studies and Internal Displacement Monitoring Centre. 8 October.
<http://www.issafrica.org/pgcontent.php?UID=31819%263>

Sheekh, Nuur Mohamud and Jason Mosley. 2012. 'Kenya: Tana Delta Violence—Is There Worse to Come?' *African Arguments.* Royal African Society blog. Accessed November 2012. <http://africanarguments.org/2012/11/06/kenya-tana-delta-violence-%E2%80%93-is-there-worse-to-come-%E2%80%93-by-nuur-mohamud-sheekh-and-jason-mosley/>

Small Arms Survey. 2007. *Responses to Pastoral Wars: A Review of Violence Reduction Efforts in Sudan, Uganda, and Kenya.* HSBA Issue Brief No. 8. Geneva: Small Arms Survey. September. <http://www.smallarmssurvey.org/publications/by-type/sudan-hsba/sudan-issue-briefs.html>

—. 2012. *My Neighbour, My Enemy: Inter-tribal Violence in Jonglei.* HSBA Issue Brief 21. Geneva: Small Arms Survey. October.
<http://www.smallarmssurveysudan.org/fileadmin/docs/issue-briefs/HSBA-IB21-Inter-tribal_violence_in_Jonglei.pdf>

Stearns, Jason. 2012a. 'Fact-checking the M23 Rebellion.' Congo Siasa Blog. 1 July.
<http://congosiasa.blogspot.de/2012/07/fact-checking-m23-rebellion.html>

—. 2012b. *North Kivu: The Background to Conflict in North Kivu Province of Eastern Congo.* Nairobi: Rift Valley Institute Usalama Project.
<http://www.humansecuritygateway.com/documents/RVI_NorthKivu_TheBackgroundtoConflictinNKivuProvinceofECongo.pdf>

Thurston, Alex. 2010. 'Recent Violence Prompting Questions about Niger Delta Strategy.' *Christian Science Monitor.* 27 October.
<http://www.csmonitor.com/World/Africa/Africa-Monitor/2010/1027/Recent-violence-prompting-questions-about-Niger-Delta-strategy>

UCDP (Uppsala Conflict Data Program). 2012a. 'UCDP/PRIO Armed Conflict Dataset, v. 4-2012, 1946–2011.' Accessed December 2012.
<http://www.pcr.uu.se/research/ucdp/datasets/ucdp_prio_armed_conflict_dataset/>

—. 2012b. 'Definitions.' Accessed January 2013. <http://www.pcr.uu.se/research/ucdp/definitions/>

—. 2012c. 'UCDP Non-State Conflict Codebook, v. 2.4-2012, 1989–2011.' Accessed January 2013.
<http://www.pcr.uu.se/digitalAssets/120/120457_ucdp-non-state-conflict-dataset-codebook-v2.4_2012.pdf>

—. 2012d. 'Non-State Conflict Dataset, v.2.4-2012, 1989–2011.' Accessed January 2013.
<http://www.pcr.uu.se/research/ucdp/datasets/ucdp_non_state_conflict_dataset_/>

UN (United Nations). 2010. *Land and Conflict: Guidance Note for Practitioners.* New York: Interagency Framework Team for Preventive Action.
<http://www.un.org/en/events/environmentconflictday/pdf/GN_Land_Consultation.pdf>

—. 2012a. 'Addendum to the Interim Report of the Group of Experts on the Democratic Republic of the Congo (S/2012/348) Concerning Violations of the Arms Embargo and Sanctions Regime by the Government of Rwanda.' S/2012/348/Add.1 of 27 June.
<http://www.un.org/ga/search/view_doc.asp?symbol=S/2012/348/Add.1>

—. 2012b. *Interim Report of the Group of Experts on the Democratic Republic of the Congo.* S/2012/348 of 21 June.
<http://www.un.org/ga/search/view_doc.asp?symbol=S/2012/348>

USAID (United States Agency for International Development). 2005. *Conducting a Conflict Assessment: A Framework for Strategy and Program Development.* Washington, DC: USAID. April.
<http://www.securitymanagementinitiative.org/index.php?option=com_docman&task=doc_details&gid=356&lang=en&Itemid=28>

van der Zwan, Joost. 2011. 'Conflict-Sensitive Land Policy and Land Governance in Africa.' Strengthening the Economic Dimensions of Peacebuilding Practice Note 7. London: International Alert. <http://www.international-alert.org/sites/default/files/publications/PracticeNote7.pdf>

von Braun, Joachim and Ruth Meinzen-Dick. 2009. *'Land Grabbing' by Foreign Investors in Developing Countries: Risks and Opportunities.* Policy Brief 13. Washington, DC: International Food Policy Research Institute. April. <http://www.ifpri.org/sites/default/files/publications/bp013all.pdf>

Webb, Malcolm. 2012. 'Thousands Flee Renewed Violence in DRC.' Al Jazeera. 18 May.
<http://www.aljazeera.com/indepth/features/2012/05/2012517105421722232.html>

Wepundi, Manasseh. 2012. 'Political Conflict and Vulnerabilities: Firearms and Electoral Violence in Kenya.' Armed Violence Issue Brief 2. Geneva: Small Arms Survey. December. <http://www.smallarmssurvey.org/fileadmin/docs/G-Issue-briefs/SAS-AV-IB2-electoral-violence-kenya.pdf>

World Bank. 2012. 'Agricultural Land (% of Land Area).' World Bank dataset. Accessed September 2012.
<http://data.worldbank.org/indicator/AG.LND.AGRI.ZS>

ACKNOWLEDGEMENTS

Principal author

Jennifer M. Hazen

Illegal electricity wiring running through the informal settlement, Imizamo Yethu, Cape Town, March 2010. © Ariadne Van Zandbergen

Trend Lines

ARMED VIOLENCE IN SOUTH AFRICA

6

INTRODUCTION

On 27 April 1994 the first democratic elections were held in South Africa, marking the country's official transition from more than 300 years of authoritarianism and institutionalized racism to a free and democratic society. In the 19 years since, the country has made progress in improving rule of law, governance, and public health. South Africa now ranks well above its neighbours in sub-Saharan Africa in economic and human development indicators (UNDP, 2011). Yet, despite localized economic growth, South Africa experiences persistently high levels of unemployment (an average of 25 per cent in 2000–12),[1] income inequality, systemic corruption, and unequal economic and social transformation. These challenges are so severe that they risk undoing recent gains.

Similarly, South Africa's health outcomes remain much lower than those of other middle-income countries that are not at war—in fact, lower than in many poorer countries (Coovadia et al., 2009, p. 817). The nation continues to struggle with high levels of armed violence, with a homicide rate about four times the global average—among the world's highest (Geneva Declaration Secretariat, 2011, pp. 51–53). Research suggests that persistently high levels of armed violence and underperformance in health and development are related (Bellis et al., 2010; OECD, 2009; Geneva Declaration Secretariat, 2008). South Africa appears to be a case in point.

This chapter explores South Africa's dilemma, namely that its incremental progress and growth are undermined by ongoing and systemic armed violence and inequality. It applies the emerging optic of armed violence prevention, which focuses on understanding and addressing the contributing and inhibiting drivers of armed violence. The main conclusions include the following:

- Since 1994, homicide rates in South Africa have remained among the highest in the world despite a consistent decline.
- There appears to be a positive correlation between the partial implementation of the Firearms Control Act (FCA) of 2000 and a reduction in firearm homicides. Better implementation of the law could further reduce levels of firearm homicides.
- Despite stated commitments and a legal obligation to address armed violence, the South African Police Service (SAPS) still faces serious challenges related to reforming its own practices, including police use of force and firearms.
- Armed violence prevention efforts are undermined by the lack of data on the causes and circumstances of armed violence. Enhanced availability and public access to relevant data on armed violence would strengthen evidence-based armed violence reduction and prevention (AVRP) programming.
- The South African government's national policies to address and reduce levels of inequality have shown only modest results. Based on evidence of a strong association between high levels of inequality and high levels of armed violence, inequality may be viewed as an important driver of armed violence in South Africa.
- AVRP programming in South Africa tends to focus on violence drivers, such as gender inequality and alcohol abuse. Outcome evaluations demonstrate that some of these efforts have positive impacts, but these remain small in scale.

This chapter is divided into two main sections. The first provides an overview of trends in armed violence since 1994, focusing on the most recent available data, covering 2011–12. It also draws on research from other contexts to highlight some of the factors that appear to contribute to or inhibit armed violence generally. The second section concentrates on factors that appear most relevant to the South African context and assesses national policies to prevent gun violence, policing challenges, and civil society armed violence prevention efforts. It closes with reflections on the possible directions for future research and prevention activities.

ARMED VIOLENCE IN CONTEMPORARY SOUTH AFRICA

From apartheid to democracy

This chapter uses the term 'armed violence' to mean 'the use or threatened use of weapons to inflict injury, death or psychosocial harm, which undermines development' (OECD, 2009, p. 13). This definition recognizes a broad spectrum of consequences, ranging from emotional trauma to death and injury. In the South African context, the current experience of armed violence cannot be properly assessed without understanding the country's violent past.[2]

Map 6.1 **South Africa**

South Africa's history of violence is long and complex, extending back to the arrival of the Portuguese in the 1400s. Dutch colonists came in the 17th century, followed by the British. This period saw the violent abuse of the indigenous population and the establishment of the foundations of the systemic violence that would give rise to the apartheid system.

Under apartheid (1948–94), institutionalized discrimination forced black South Africans to live under inhumane conditions. As the struggle against this system intensified, the state embarked on a brutal path of repression against black South Africans and others who opposed it (TRC, 1998). The anti-apartheid struggle initially responded to this state-led violence with non-violent direct action, and later with armed resistance. Since the success of the anti-apartheid movement in 1994, the country has pursued transitional justice, prioritizing healing and reconciliation over retribution (Tutu, 2000). Nearly 20 years since the advent of the country's democratic transition, the country still faces violence, but of a different nature.

Democracy brought not only political changes but also massive institutional upheaval. The entire government bureaucracy and infrastructure rapidly shifted from serving only about 10 per cent of the population to serving the entire population (Coovadia et al., 2009, p. 817). The previously excluded semi-independent 'homelands' or 'bantustans' of Bophuthatswana, Ciskei, Gazankulu, KaNgwane, KwaNdebele, KwaZulu, Lebowa, Qwaqwa, Transkei, and Venda were officially absorbed into the state, enlarging the population of citizens and the administrative responsibility of the state to serve them (Schönteich and Louw, 2001; SAHO, n.d.). It is no understatement to say the nation was reborn in 1994.

Police-recorded homicides

The transition has led to some remarkable gains in security. According to the SAPS and the Institute for Security Studies, homicides decreased from 66.9 per 100,000 in 1994 to 30.9 in 2011–12 (see Figure 6.1). Nevertheless, the current rate remains elevated by international standards; South Africa had the eighth-highest violent death rate among 186 countries and territories in 2011 (Geneva Declaration Secretariat, 2011, p. 53). Rates above 30 per 100,000—which the Geneva Declaration Secretariat labels 'very high'—are typically observed in countries at war or with serious ongoing crises (p. 58).

Figure 6.1 **Homicide rate per 100,000, 1994–2012**

RATE PER 100,000 POPULATION

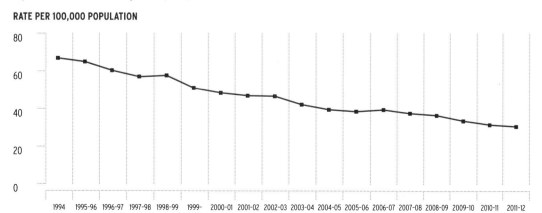

Sources: 1994: ISS (2012); 1995-2003: UNODC (2011a); 2004-12: SAPS (2012a)

Figure 6.2 **Number of homicides and percentage committed with firearms, 1995-2012**

■ Homicide   ■ Percentage of homicides by firearm

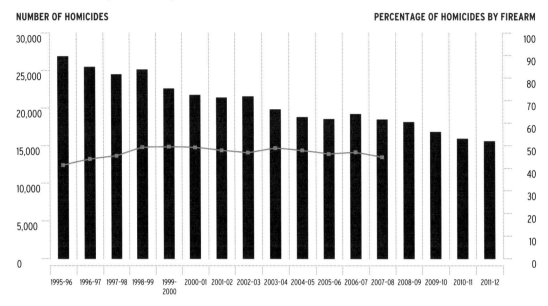

NUMBER OF HOMICIDES   **PERCENTAGE OF HOMICIDES BY FIREARM**

Sources: UNODC (2011a; 2011b)

The distribution of homicides across the country is uneven, however. Homicide rates in 2011–12 were highest in the areas of the Eastern and Western Cape provinces, followed by the 'belt' of Northern Cape, Free State, and KwaZulu Natal. In these five provinces homicide rates were above the national average, with a peak of 48 per 100,000 in the Eastern Cape. Lower rates were observed in Gauteng, Mpumalanga, and North West, as well as Limpopo, where the rate was lowest, at 13.2 homicides per 100,000 (SAPS, 2012a).

In 2000 the SAPS stopped providing data on the percentage of homicides and other forms of lethal violence committed with firearms (Shaw and Gastrow, 2001, p. 237; Lamb, 2008; Burton et al., 2004, p. 22). Still, prior to 2007, South Africa submitted some relevant data to the UN Office on Drugs and Crime indicating that fewer than half of annual homicides were committed with a firearm (UNODC, 2011a, p. 114). Figure 6.2 shows the annual number of homicides recorded by the SAPS over the period 1995–2012 and the percentage committed with firearms, which dramatically increased between 1995 and 1998 (roughly from 40 to 50 per cent) and then stabilized at just under 50 per cent.

Fatal injury data

Other data sources complement the picture of levels of gun violence, though they must be consulted with caution. The National Injury Mortality Surveillance System (NIMSS) collects data on fatal injuries from medico-legal laboratories and state forensic laboratories (NIMSS, 2009b, p. 2).[3] The information includes the intent and the mechanism of injuries, coded using the International Classification of Diseases-9 system,[4] as well as demographic information of victims, such as age and sex (NIMSS, 2009b, p. 2). Yet, because NIMSS coverage has changed over time—from 15 mortuaries in 5 provinces in 2000 to 62 mortuaries in 7 provinces in 2008—national trend analysis has become impossible (p. vii). The current coverage is estimated at 39–52 per cent of all injury deaths (p. vii).

Figure 6.3 **Weapons used in homicides, 2008[5]**

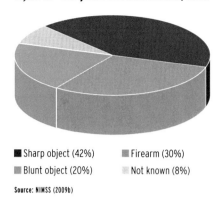

■ Sharp object (42%)   ■ Firearm (30%)
■ Blunt object (20%)   ■ Not known (8%)

Source: NIMSS (2009b)

Despite these limitations, NIMSS data provides a snapshot of intentional gun deaths at the national level for 2008 (the latest available data). Firearms are involved in 30 per cent of homicides documented by NIMSS (see Figure 6.3). More than half of all homicides (52 per cent) and homicides committed with firearms (54 per cent) involved victims aged 20–34; men are six times more likely to be killed than women (NIMSS, 2009b).

NIMSS provincial data shows declines in violent deaths, both firearm-related and by other methods, in Gauteng and Mpumalanga from 2008 through 2010, but rates remain very high at 43 and 26 per 100,000 inhabitants, respectively.[6] The proportion of deaths committed with firearms declined by almost five per cent in both provinces, yet the use of sharp (bladed) weapons rose slightly in Gauteng and increased by 8 per cent in Mpumalanga (see Figure 6.4).[7]

CONTRIBUTING AND INHIBITING FACTORS

Recent multi-disciplinary research on armed violence—as advanced by the Geneva Declaration on Armed Violence and Development initiative, the World Health Organization (WHO), the United Nations Development Programme, and others—has generated a measure of consensus about the drivers of armed violence as well as its inhibiting factors. The emerging framework, rooted in violence prevention concepts and practice, has gradually influenced the policies and programmes of states and development assistance donors. While the field has benefitted from contributions and

Figure 6.4 **Weapons used in fatal injuries, Gauteng and Mpumalanga, 2008–10**

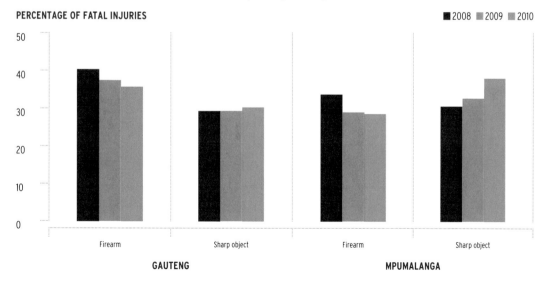

PERCENTAGE OF FATAL INJURIES   ■2008 ■2009 ■2010

Source: NIMSS (2009a; 2012a; 2012b)

Boys play with a toy gun in Alexandra township, Johannesburg, January 2006.
© Jon Hrusa/Keystone

expertise from areas as diverse as security sector reform, peace-building, criminology, and arms control, it has been particularly guided by the public health approach and the social-ecological model.

The public health approach is premised on the understanding that strategies to prevent other negative health outcomes—such as lifestyle-related disease, motor vehicle injuries, falls, and burns—can be usefully applied to prevent violent injuries, including intentional violence.[8] The social-ecological model provides a complementary tool for identifying risk and resilience factors by distinguishing four different 'levels' of influence—individual, relationship, community, and societal (see Table 6.1). The model sees violence and violence prevention as 'the product of [these] multiple levels of influence on behaviour' (Krug et al., 2002, p. 12).

Armed violence prevention is a relatively new field, and much of the debate and discussion among researchers and practitioners draws on and adapts the public health approach and social-ecological model, which have traditionally been applied to violence prevention more broadly. For example, armed violence literature and discourse modifies the public health conception of *risk and protective factors*, using a more general notion of *contributing and inhibiting factors*. This adaptation is prompted by the recognition that armed violence is both 'a cause and consequence of a range of risk factors such as horizontal inequalities, poverty, socio-political exclusion, and governance challenges' (OECD, 2009, p. 28). While the discussion below assumes that violence and armed violence share many of the same contributing and inhibiting factors, more research is needed to disentangle these phenomena and identify the specific factors that are most relevant to each category.

While not exhaustive, Table 6.1 captures the breadth of factors that can be taken into account in efforts to reduce and prevent armed violence. Of the contributing and inhibiting factors identified above, at least five distinct elements of armed violence prevention can be distilled. These are introduced briefly below.

Table 6.1 **Selected contributing and inhibiting factors for armed violence**		
Level	**Contributing factors**	**Inhibiting factors**
Individual factors	Substance abuse	Positive self-esteem
	History of or exposure to violence; psychosocial trauma	Access to psychosocial support
Relationship factors	Poor parent-child bonding	Safe, stable, and nurturing relationships between children and parents or caregivers
	Association with delinquent peers, such as gang membership	Association with positive peer groups
Community factors	Social isolation	Access to social support
	High levels of unemployment	Access to economic opportunities
	High density of alcohol outlets	Limited availability of alcohol
	Availability of weapons	Limited access to lethal means
	High rates of gun ownership	Rigorous gun licensing procedures
Societal factors	Ineffective criminal justice system	Effective criminal justice system
	Social norms that accept violence	Social norms that do not tolerate violence
	Unequal gender relations	Values that promote gender equity
	Policies that perpetuate economic, social, and political inequalities	Policies that promote economic, social, and political equality
	Legacy of violence; emergence from armed conflict; mistrust within society	Social cohesion and trust
	Resource scarcity and competition	Basic needs met
	Little to no information about the nature and extent of armed violence	A functioning armed violence monitoring system

Sources: Bellis et al. (2010); Geneva Declaration Secretariat (2008); OECD (2009, pp. 33-34; 2011, pp. 25-26); WHO (2008)

Armed violence legislation. Evidence from middle- and high-income countries suggests that the effective implementation of legislation and regulations to limit access to lethal means can reduce armed violence (Bellis et al., 2010). To take only one example, in the Colombian cities of Bogotá and Cali, the enforced ban on carrying firearms on weekends after paydays, on holidays, and on election days contributed to a significant drop in homicide rates in both cities (Villaveces et al., 2000).

Policing practices. Evidence from high-income countries suggests that policing strategies that promote community engagement can contribute to reductions in youth homicides and firearm assaults (Bellis et al., 2010). Stringent rules on the use of force and firearms by police, firearm equipment and training standards, weapons storage, and police oversight mechanisms have also been associated with violence reduction.[9]

Government socio-economic policy. The extent to which government policies promote social, political, and economic equality can strongly influence levels of violence. The link between income inequality and homicide rates has been documented in the international crime and violence prevention literature (Hsieh and Pugh, 1993, p. 198). As Wilkinson notes, 'the most well established environmental determinant of levels of violence is the scale of income differences between rich and poor' (Wilkinson, 2004, p. 1).

AVRP programming. Well-designed and -implemented programming that focuses on one or more of the contributing or inhibiting factors has shown promise in reducing armed violence. WHO has identified ten key prevention strategies that could help to reduce armed violence (WHO, 2008, p. 3). Table 6.1 covers many of these strategies, including: strengthening relationships between children and caregivers; developing life and social skills; promoting gender equality and addressing cultural norms that support violence; reducing access to and harmful use of alcohol; reducing access to lethal means; disrupting illegal drug markets; and reducing inequalities (p. 27).

Data and monitoring of armed violence. Studies have shown that 'effectively reducing and preventing armed violence requires diagnosing its patterns and understanding its nature, extent and associated harms' (Bellis et al., 2010, p. 4). Available evidence suggests that the establishment of armed violence monitoring systems has positively contributed to armed violence reduction efforts.[10] Reliable data is needed for effective monitoring and evaluation of armed violence reduction programming.

> Reliable data is needed for effective monitoring and evaluation of armed violence reduction programming.

The following sections discuss how these five elements of armed violence prevention have been developed and applied in the South African context.

ARMED VIOLENCE LEGISLATION

The Domestic Violence Act and the Firearms Control Act

Following the end of apartheid the government undertook an array of legislative reforms to bring the country's laws into alignment with the new democratic framework and to signal a break with the past. The drafters of the South African Constitution of 1996 ensured a departure from apartheid-era jurisprudence by giving prominence to the right to life and security of the person, codified in various laws. Two wide-ranging laws form the cornerstone of the government's legislative approach to armed violence reduction: the Domestic Violence Act (DVA) of 1998 and the Firearms Control Act of 2000.

The DVA establishes the legal framework for the detection, reporting, and prosecution of domestic violence. At the time of drafting, a number of submissions were made to highlight the role of firearms in situations of domestic violence (Combrinck et al., 1998). The drafters of the legislation incorporated these concerns by making special provision for the removal of a firearm as part of the court's powers to issue a protection order (RSA, 1998b, ss. 7(2)(a); 9(1–2)). The use of the instruction 'may' in the Domestic Violence Bill was strengthened to 'must' in the final Act, placing a clear obligation on the SAPS to remove a firearm or dangerous weapon in situations of domestic violence (RSA, 1998a, s. 7(1); 1998b, s. 9(1); INTIMATE PARTNER VIOLENCE).

The FCA replaced the apartheid-era Arms and Ammunition Act of 1969. The promulgation of the FCA was the result of a lengthy public consultation process involving a cross-section of interested parties (Kirsten, 2008). Like the DVA, the final text of the FCA was influenced by the public submission process. Many of the key AVRP provisions in the legislation are the result of effective lobbying from groups, including ones that focus on violence against women and child safety. Implementation of the FCA was phased in from 2000 to 2004; however, critics have argued that further implementation is needed, especially with respect to the work of the central regulatory authority, as discussed in the next section.

The FCA requires both firearm registration and owner licensing for all gun owners in South Africa. Under the FCA, prospective gun owners must first obtain a competency certificate following training at an accredited training facility. The law also stipulates that applicants meet certain requirements; they must be at least 21 years old, they must submit proof of being a 'fit and proper person' of 'stable mental condition', and they may not be 'dependent on any substance which has an intoxicating or narcotic effect' (RSA, 2000, ch. 5, ss. (9)(2)(a)–(e)). Convictions in a range of offences disqualify prospective applicants; these include firearm misuse and violence, sexual abuse, fraud, alcohol and drug abuse, sabotage, terrorism, public violence, arson, intimidation, rape, and kidnapping (ss. (9)(2)(f)–(o)). Competency certificates are valid for five years and must be renewed (s. 10 (2)). In addition to the renewal process, other provisions in the Act allow for a person to be declared 'unfit to possess a firearm' in the event of a domestic violence charge or conviction or after expressing an intention to inflict harm (to him- or herself or someone else), among other conditions (ss. 102–05).

The FCA requires that all firearms be properly stored in an approved gun safe (RSA, 2004a, ss. 67(1–4); 86(1)(12)). Guns may be carried in public but 'must be completely covered' and the person carrying should be able to 'exercise effective control' over the firearm (RSA, 2000, ch. 9, s. 84(2)). FCA-mandated penalties for violating any of the requirements range from fines to imprisonment for periods from two to 25 years, depending on the offence (RSA, 2000, Schedule 4).

> Reduced firearm homicide rates are linked to the partial implementation of the FCA.

According to research published by South Africa's Medical Research Council, the FCA has made a positive contribution to reducing armed violence. In a 2010 *South African Medical Journal* article, Abrahams, Jewkes, and Mathews review NIMSS data to assess whether there was a significant difference between the rates of firearm homicides and non-firearm homicides for the period 2001–04 (Abrahams, Jewkes, and Mathews, 2010, pp. 586–88). The authors find that, 'although a decline in both homicide rates is shown, there is a significantly faster decline for the firearm homicide group' (p. 588). Without establishing strict causality, the authors identify a correlation between the reduced firearm homicide rates and the gradual implementation of the FCA (p. 587).

A follow-up study published in 2012 confirms this assessment. It compares femicide rates for the years 1999 and 2009, finding a significant decrease in gun-related femicides, with '529 fewer women killed by gunshot in 2009 compared to 1999' (Abrahams et al., 2012, p. 3; INTIMATE PARTNER VIOLENCE). As in the earlier study, the authors find a strong association with the FCA. Other research has suggested additional benefits in reduced firearm violence targeting children (Campbell et al., 2011; Alvazzi del Frate, 2012). If implementation of the FCA is further enhanced, as many have suggested, there may be further positive results to accrue.

Implementation challenges

A central critique of the FCA relates to the inadequate functioning of the regulatory body within the SAPS that oversees firearm-related administration and monitoring. The mandate of the Central Firearms Register (CFR) is clearly set out in the Act (RSA, 2000, ch. 17, ss. 123–27). After complaints from both gun control and pro-gun lobby groups, the minister of police established a task team to investigate problems with the CFR and advise on remedial action (SAPS, 2010b). The gun lobby's complaints highlighted delays in acquiring a firearm licence, while gun control groups complained that the CFR did not conduct physical inspections of prospective gun owners' premises. The findings of the task team reveal some cases of firearm licences being awarded without due process and, in some instances, licences being awarded for prohibited firearms, such as AK-47s (Civilian Secretariat for Police, n.d.).[11] Over and above alleged corruption and fraudulent licensing, the task team report criticizes the CFR data system as inherently flawed, pointing out that it does not allow for any meaningful quantitative assessment of South African firearm stockpiles (Civilian Secretariat for Police, n.d.).

Two studies have identified problems in the implementation of the DVA's requirement that guns be removed from the homes of domestic abusers and those facing protection orders. The first study, conducted in 2000–01, examines applications for protection orders at one urban and one semi-urban court. The study finds that, although 25 per cent of the applications referred to firearms, orders for police to remove the weapons were made in only 2 per cent of urban cases and 1 per cent of semi-urban cases (Schneider and Vetten, 2006). The second study, conducted in 2006–07 in rural and peri-urban areas, also examines applications for protection orders (Vetten et al., 2009). It reveals that fewer than five per cent of final protection orders requisitioned the removal of weapons, even though 37 per cent of the applications stated that a weapon had been used during an incident of abuse to either threaten (63 per cent) or hurt (50 per cent) the applicant (TLAC and Ceasefire Campaign, 2009, p. 9).

Another problem area relates to the implementation of FCA-defined firearm-free zones. These zones are areas in which guns are prohibited and where it is a criminal offence to keep or carry a firearm or ammunition (RSA, 2000, s. 140). In alignment with this provision and in response to a spate of shootings at schools, the then minister of safety and security issued an official notice of 'intention to declare all schools and other learning institutions, including institutions for higher education and Universities, as firearm-free zones, in terms of section 140 of the Firearms Control Act, 2000' (RSA, 2004b). To date, however, not one school has actually been declared a firearm-free zone, despite repeated calls from civil society (Gun Free South Africa, 2010).

No school has been declared a firearm-free zone, despite repeated calls from civil society.

POLICING PRACTICES

Use of force and firearms

The SAPS is legally mandated to play a role in preventing and reducing crime and violence in South Africa. Although police leadership has translated this mandate into commitments to address armed violence, the strength of these commitments has been uneven since 1994.

Immediately following the political transition, a range of reform mechanisms were put in place to foster democratic policing practices and signal a break with the apartheid-era mode of policing (Cawthra, 1992; Bruce, 2002). In terms of AVRP, these include SAPS commitments to good practice in the use of force and firearms. Because apartheid-era policing was marked by the excessive use of force with little to no accountability or oversight, reform efforts placed a premium on establishing legislative obligations to control and limit police use of force and improve police oversight and accountability for abuses (Tait and Marks, 2011).

In post-apartheid South Africa, police use of force and firearms is governed by the SAPS Act (No. 68 of 1995), the FCA, and the Criminal Procedure Act (No. 51 of 1977). This legal framework places an obligation on the state and on police to protect citizens and exercise caution and restraint when using force. The SAPS Act articulates this obligation clearly: 'Where a member who performs an official duty is authorised by law to use force, he or she may only use the minimum force which is reasonable in the circumstances' (SAPS, 1995, s. 13(3)(b)). In addition, particular legislative provisions concern safe storage of firearms and types of weapon and ammunition to be used, all with the intention of limiting irresponsible use of firearms and unnecessary use of force (RSA, 2000, s. 120(3)(a–b); Operational Response Services, 2004; State President's Office, 1994, s. 9(2)).

For example, the Criminal Procedure Act governs the use of force in effecting an arrest. Following an incident in 1999 in which a civilian shot and killed a fleeing burglary suspect, the law was challenged in the courts and was eventually found to fall short of constitutional muster (CCSA, 2002). The Constitutional Court ruled that the Criminal Procedure Act needed to be amended to reflect more clearly the principles of proportionality and least degree of force possible in effecting arrests. The proposed amendments were debated in Parliament and ultimately included in the Criminal Procedure Amendment Bill (B26-2012).

The SAPS has internal accountability mechanisms as well as two external oversight bodies that are mandated to ensure compliance with legislation and the human rights standards enshrined in the constitution. The oversight bodies are the Civilian Secretariat for Police and the Independent Police Investigative Directorate (IPID). Among other roles, IPID is tasked with investigating every case of irregular discharge of a SAPS firearm (IPID, 2012a, s. 6).

Uneven reform

While the 1994–99 period saw a strong push to institutionalize democratic policing practices, this momentum has not been sustained, and some have argued that positive efforts have even been reversed since 1999 (Rauch, 2000; Bruce, 2012b). At the leadership level, two of the four post-apartheid national police commissioners were found guilty of fraud and corruption between 2009 and 2011.[12] In addition, the head of SAPS Crime Intelligence was suspended in 2011 after being charged with murder and fraud.[13] There are also criminal investigations under way into the activities of an elite unit within the SAPS known as the 'Cato Manor Hit Squad'. Thirty SAPS members from the Cato Manor unit are facing charges of murder, theft, defeating the ends of justice, and unlawful possession of firearms and ammunition (Hofstatter, Afrika, and Rose, 2011; Nair, 2012).

Efforts to institutionalize democratic policing practices have not been sustained.

A disconnect has also been apparent between the legislative commitments to democratic policing and statements by police and other government leaders (Bruce, 2012b). In 2008 Deputy Minister of Safety and Security Susan Shabangu made headlines when she addressed an anti-crime summit and instructed police:

> *You must kill the bastards [criminals] if they threaten you or the community. You must not worry about the regulations. [. . .] You have been given guns, now use them. I want no warning shots. You have one shot and it must be a kill shot. If you miss, the criminals will go for the kill* (Hosken, 2008).

Shabangu's statement was endorsed a few days later by President Jacob Zuma, who has used similar rhetoric in the past (Webb, 2008).[14]

The current minister of police, Nathi Mthethwa, and former national police commissioner Bheki Cele have also used inflammatory language. Soon after taking office, Mthethwa called on police to 'teach those people a lesson—to fight fire with fire' (Hartley, 2008). Cele gained notoriety when he entered office and suggested that the laws governing police use of force be changed (Goldstone, 2009). In addition to introducing 'shoot to kill' rhetoric, Mthethwa and Cele also reinstituted the military ranking system, which had been a marker of the apartheid-era police (SAPS, 2010a). This behaviour suggests that the old mentality and approach to policing remain ingrained.

Since 2011, the SAPS has come under growing public scrutiny of its use of force and firearms. In April 2011, for instance, police beat and shot a schoolteacher during a protest march in Ficksburg in the Free State Province; the teacher subsequently died (*Mail and Guardian,* 2011; *Daily Maverick,* 2011). The public outcry following the Ficksburg shooting led the South African Human Rights Commission to investigate. In November 2012, the Human Rights

Protesting miners shot dead by police outside a South
African mine in Rustenburg, August 2012.
© Siphiwe Sibeko/Reuters

Commission released its report, which concludes that the SAPS had used excessive force,
had violated the applicable legislative pre-
scriptions, and had failed to deploy sufficiently trained and equipped members. The
report recommends that the SAPS improve
training of its members in the management of
public gatherings (SAHRC, 2012).

Prior to the release of the Commission
findings, the SAPS' use of force made international headlines when police opened fire on
striking miners, killing some 34 and wound-
ing 78 at the Lonmin-owned Marikana mine
(Polgreen, 2012; Bruce, 2012b). The incident
led to the establishing of an official commission of inquiry into the events (DOJCD, 2012).
While the scale of the Marikana incident
warrants attention, the problem of excessive
and unjustified use of police force has been
documented in numerous other cases prior
to Marikana.[15]

Police shootings

Recent IPID data shows a sharp increase in
fatal police shootings, from 282 in 2005–06 to
460 in 2011–12 (IPID, 2012b; Bruce, 2012a). The number of people fatally shot during police investigations has also
increased, from 9 in 2005–06 to 34 in 2011–12 (IPID, 2012b). Very few of these shootings have been prosecuted. In
the 2011–12 reporting period, the IPID made 162 recommendations for prosecution of SAPS members for deaths as
a result of police action; only 18 of those recommendations resulted in convictions (IPID, 2012b, pp. 32, 38). The frequency and scale of excessive use of force points to a fundamental and systemic problem within the SAPS (Bruce, 2012b).

In addition to incidents of excessive use of police force on duty, there are also growing concerns about off-duty
police officers using their service firearms in domestic violence and murder–suicide. In fact, these kinds of incidents
became so frequent as to lead to an official investigation in 2009. The results show that, in 80 per cent of the cases
investigated, the murder weapon was an SAPS member's service firearm (ICD, 2009, p. 19).[16] The study attributes the
high prevalence of femicides committed by SAPS members to the high stress levels involved in their day-to-day
working conditions and notes the lack of psychosocial support available for SAPS members (pp. 21–31). The report
singles out the easy access to firearms as 'the most worrying factor in femicides committed by SAPS members' (ICD,
2009, p. 39; INTIMATE PARTNER VIOLENCE).

Firearm proficiency also appears to be an issue in the SAPS' ability to inculcate good practice in the use of force and firearms. SAPS members' firearm proficiency came under public scrutiny in March 2012, when the media cited a leaked internal audit report stating that SAPS members were not competent to use firearms. The report finds that, of the more than 157,700 armed SAPS members who participated in firearms training, nearly 27,400 members had failed firearms proficiency tests (Govender, 2012). The broader SAPS training process has also received criticism for its heavy-handed and militarized approach, which has been linked to the generalized problem of police brutality (Gumede-Johnson, 2011).

At the community level, public confidence in the SAPS has varied over time but has generally improved. While only 38 per cent of respondents to the National Victims of Crime Survey said they were satisfied with the police in 1998, the satisfaction rating had risen to 62 per cent by 2012 (Statistics South Africa, 1998; 2012b, p. 31). But support is uneven, and some communities are deeply unsatisfied. For example, residents and civil society organizations from the Khayelitsha area in the Western Cape lobbied the government to establish a commission of inquiry into the allegations of police inefficiency and the general breakdown in relations between the community and the police (SJC, 2012). Community members were eventually successful, and a commission was established in September 2012 (Western Cape Government, 2012a). This victory was short-lived, however. Immediately after the commission was set up, the national minister of police lodged a court application to halt its work (SAPS, 2012b).

GOVERNMENT SOCIO-ECONOMIC POLICY

The inequality-armed violence link

The psychosocial consequences of inequality are thought to play an important role in driving violence, including armed violence, in South Africa (CSVR, 2008; Ward et al., 2012, p. 217). Inequality generates feelings of 'insecurity and inadequacy as well as frustration, hopelessness and anger' (CSVR, 2008, p. 4); these can influence violent behaviour.

Bruce traces the roots of this phenomenon to apartheid and the way black South Africans internalized institutionalized racism; he suggests that the resulting low self-esteem has been compounded by ongoing social and economic inequality in the post-apartheid period, confirming feelings of inferiority, powerlessness, and marginalization (Bruce, 2006, p. 34). In addition to these 'internalized' factors, other research suggests that inequality between areas of wealth and poverty also drives crime and violence (O'Donovan, 2011, p. 32).

The government has initiated a range of developmental policies with the intention of addressing the deep socio-economic inequalities that resulted from the apartheid era.[17] These have emphasized access to essential services such as health, education, sanitation, housing, water, and communication (NPC, 2012). Socio-economic measures have included the creation of the Industrial Development Corporation, the Job Fund, and the New Growth Path Framework. Other policy initiatives intended to reduce inequality include the Broad-Based Black Economic Empowerment Act, the Women Empowerment and Gender Equality Bill, and the Green Paper on Land Reform. Government socio-economic policy has also focused on assisting the most vulnerable groups in society through a massive social grant system that provides pensions, foster care, child support, and disability grants to roughly 16 million people (SASSA, 2012). The next section reviews socio-economic improvements achieved in the post-apartheid era, while describing where gains remain limited.

Socio-economic gains

South Africans are significantly better off materially than ten years ago.

According to the most recent census data, South Africans are significantly better off materially than at the time of the last census ten years earlier (Statistics South Africa, 2012a). In 2001 approximately 18 per cent of people who were at least 20 years old had reported no schooling; by 2011, that figure had shrunk to less than 9 per cent (Statistics South Africa, 2012a, p. 7). Moreover, 46 per cent of South Africans reported having access to piped water in their homes, while another 27 per cent had access to piped water in their yards. Sixty per cent said they had flush toilets, and nearly 85 per cent were using electricity for lighting (pp. 8–10). Refuse was removed by a local authority at least once a week for about two-thirds of the population (Statistics South Africa, 2012c, p. 97). These figures represent significant material improvements.

A report compiled by the South African government and the United Nations Development Programme suggests that the country is on track to meet Millennium Development Goals 1 and 2: combating extreme poverty and hunger and achieving universal primary education (RSA, 2010). Yet South Africa is lagging behind in terms of reaching other Millennium Development Goals, most notably regarding child and maternal mortality, both of which have worsened (RSA, 2010, pp. 59–73; AUC et al., 2012, p. 68). The National Committee on Confidential Enquiries into Maternal Deaths reports that, for each year in the period 2005–07, 1,400 mothers died in the neonatal period, representing a 20 per cent increase in maternal deaths in comparison with the period 2002–04. Meanwhile, an estimated 60,000 children die each year in South Africa. For the period 2005–09, malnutrition and the Human Immunodeficiency Virus (HIV) were the main underlying causes of child mortality (Department of Health, 2009; CoMMiC, 2011).

Persistent challenges

South Africa's uneven performance in reaching the Millennium Development Goals is not the only indication that the country continues to struggle with high levels of inequality. Indeed, its level of inequality is often cited as one of the highest in the world, based on its Gini coefficient ratings (Bertelsmann Stiftung, 2012, p. 18; Bloomberg Businessweek, 2012). The Gini coefficient is a measure of inequality, with 0 reflecting perfect equality and 100 reflecting high levels of inequality. Since 1994 South Africa has had a Gini rating within the range of 56.59 to 63.14 (Trading Economics, 2012a).

The country's high levels of inequality are emphasized by South African sources.[18] In 2010 the South African government established the National Planning Commission to undertake a critical review of the country's progress and to develop a plan for the next 20 years. In 2011 the Commission identified nine key challenges 'in fighting poverty and inequality and in achieving the objectives set out in [the] Constitution' (NPC, 2011, p. 1):

- too few South Africans are employed;
- the quality of education for poor black South Africans is sub-standard;
- poorly located and inadequate infrastructure limits social inclusion and faster economic growth;
- South Africa's growth path is highly resource-intensive and hence unsustainable;
- spatial challenges continue to marginalize the poor;
- the ailing public health system confronts a massive disease burden;
- the performance of the public services is uneven;
- corruption undermines state legitimacy and service delivery; and
- South Africa remains a divided society (NPC, 2011, pp. 9–29).

Two markers cut across these challenges: income inequality and education inequality. Household income diverges significantly by race group. According to 2011 census data, the household income reported by whites grew faster than that of any other racial group, and white households reported bringing in almost six times the average income of black households (Statistics South Africa, 2012a; 2012d). This income disparity is also discussed in the most recent World Bank South Africa Economic Update, which suggests that the richest 10 per cent of the population earn 58 per cent and the poorest 10 per cent of the population earn just 0.5 per cent of national income (Im et al., 2012).

> Easy access to alcohol is strongly linked to increased risk of armed violence.

Education inequality is a matter of growing public concern in South Africa. Popular media campaigns highlight the persistent disparities regarding access to textbooks, toilets, and electricity.[19] These claims are borne out in research. Each year the University of Cape Town's Children's Institute produces a 'Child Gauge' to assess progress among the country's young people. The 2012 Child Gauge concludes that, unless the inequality situation changes dramatically, many of the apartheid-era inequalities will be reproduced (Children's Institute, 2012). Even as access to education has improved, the quality of education remains uneven, with historically black schools still lagging behind in terms of equipment, infrastructure, and teaching capacity. This discrepancy was illustrated when, in 2009, all sixth graders (ages 11–13) in the Western Cape took standard numeracy tests; whereas 60 per cent of the schoolchildren in former 'white' schools passed, only 2 per cent in black township schools did so (Isaacs, 2012).

CIVIL SOCIETY AVRP PROGRAMMING

AVRP programming is an important component of reducing and preventing armed violence. As noted earlier in this chapter, research has identified a range of contributing and inhibiting factors that can be approached through AVRP (OECD, 2011). For example, studies have found that there is a strong connection between easy access to alcohol and increased risk of armed violence (Ramsoomar and Morojele, 2012; WHO, 2006; Sánchez et al., 2011). In response to this finding, various programmes have been developed in South Africa and globally to reduce armed violence by limiting access to alcohol.[20] The international experience demonstrates that it is possible to develop programmes that can effectively tackle the key drivers of armed violence, but that the long-term sustainability and efficacy of these programmes 'requires investing in institutional capacity, infrastructure and good governance' (Bellis et al., 2010, p. 5).

Men participate in a community march opposing violence against women, Gugulethu, February 2012. © Sonke Gender Justice

Box 6.1 Assessing AVRP in South Africa

In 2009 the Centre for the Study of Violence and Reconciliation undertook an audit to gauge the extent of armed violence programming in South Africa. It investigated the work of 58 programmes doing armed violence prevention work in South Africa as part of a broader exercise of the Geneva Declaration on Armed Violence and Development to assess promising practices in armed violence prevention and reduction programming in a variety of contexts (Bruce, Kirsten, and Masuku, 2009; Eavis, 2011). The audit identifies *direct* programmes–those that 'seek to address the instruments, actors, and institutional environments enabling or protecting against armed violence, e.g. arms collection [and] the demobilization of armed groups' (Eavis, 2011, p. 12). It distinguishes those direct programmes from the *indirect* approaches, which include efforts that 'address proximate and structural risk factors giving rise to armed violence, e.g. youth programming schemes [and] targeted education interventions' (p. 12).

The audit reveals that the majority of the surveyed organizations were engaged in 'indirect' programming. That is, they did not frame their work as armed violence reduction specifically, but rather in terms of the risk factors their work seeks to address. Of the 58 organizations interviewed, only eight were involved in 'direct' AVRP programming (Bruce, Kirsten, and Masuku, 2009, p. 2).

The findings suggest that organizations are paying attention to key risk factors and social determinants of armed violence. Study respondents identified the following risk factors (in descending order of importance): gender-based discrimination; marginalized youth; legacies of violence; trauma; rising inequality; availability of weapons; family or parenting role model issues; norms, beliefs, and practices that perpetuate violence; substance abuse; inequitable conceptions of masculinity; lack of early childhood development; and domestic violence (Bruce, Kirsten, and Masuku, 2009, p. 28).

While most of the organizations interviewed reported including monitoring and evaluation components in their programmes, the monitoring was mostly at the activity level, without sufficient attention to the outcomes and impact of the programmes (Bruce, Kirsten, and Masuku, 2009, pp. 30–33). Three exceptions emerged. Two of them–'Stepping Stones' and 'One Man Can'–have demonstrated tangible results in addressing the gender norms that drive violence. A third, recently piloted alcohol reduction intervention called 'Booza TV' is also showing positive results. Brief descriptions of all three follow:

Stepping Stones

The Stepping Stones programme is a 50-hour intervention that uses participatory learning approaches 'to equip participants to build better, safer, and more gender equitable relationships' (Jewkes, Wood, and Duvvury, 2010, p. 1075). Topics include gender-based violence, behaviour motivation, and risk-taking (p. 1075). The programme has been implemented in 40 countries and translated into 13 languages. According to a randomized control trial of the programme as implemented in South Africa, 'Stepping Stones instilled a clear and new perception of risk and desire to avoid it' (p. 1083). Another evaluation uses a cluster randomized controlled trial and finds that:

> Stepping Stones significantly improved a number of reported risk behaviours in men, with a lower proportion of men reporting perpetration of intimate partner violence across two years of follow-up (Jewkes et al., 2008, p. 1).

One Man Can

The Sonke Gender Justice Network's One Man Can campaign has been noted as an example of emerging best practices in promoting gender equality (OECD, 2011, p. 28). Sonke is an NGO that works across the African continent to build the capacity of government, civil society organizations, and populations to achieve gender equality, prevent gender-based violence, and reduce the spread of HIV and the impact of AIDS. One Man Can–Sonke's flagship intervention–is 'a broad campaign that tries to mobilize men to become involved in civil movements around gender, violence, and health' (Sonke, n.d.a). The campaign utilizes traditional forms of activism, such as marches, workshops, drama, song, video, sport, and art, to raise awareness on gender equality. The aim of One Man Can is to 'support men and boys to take action to end domestic and sexual violence and to promote healthy, equitable relationships' (Sonke, n.d.b).

A 2009 assessment of One Man Can documents significant changes in the short-term behaviour of participants in the weeks following the workshops, with 50 per cent reporting taking action to address gender-based violence in their communities (Colvin, Human, and Peacock, 2009, p. 127). Another evaluation finds that participants reflected improved perceptions on gender equity following their involvement in One Man Can activities (Dworkin et al., 2012, p. 115).

Booza TV

Booza TV is a multimedia campaign that challenges social norms around drinking (Booza TV, n.d.). The campaign consists of a series of six 30-minute edutainment documentaries that cover different topics relating to alcohol norms. The film clips feature interviews with academics, law enforcement personnel, students, local celebrities, and bar staff. The aim of Booza TV is to 'encourage a well-informed debate about alcohol abuse and what to do about it' (Western Cape Government, 2012b). The results from pilot screenings of the series are positive, indicating that 'the series [is] effective in challenging the views, attitudes and opinions of viewers' (Western Cape Government, 2012b).

South Africa's AVRP programming has been uneven over time. During the apartheid era, civil society energy was focused almost exclusively on ending apartheid. In the years following apartheid some of this energy fed into violence prevention efforts, including AVRP. For example, the very first firearm amnesty was held in December 1994; although it lasted only 24 hours, it led to the recovery of some 900 firearms and raised awareness of the issue (Kirsten, 2008, p. 33). Subsequent amnesties in 2004–05 and 2010 recovered about 100,000 and 42,000 guns, respectively (South African Parliament, 2012; Kirsten, 2007).

The past 19 years have seen a shift in the focus and character of South African civil society. The reasons for this shift are partly contextual and partly donor-driven, as changes in the socio-political environment helped to shape donor priorities. South Africa has enjoyed substantial donor support since 1994, especially in the areas of health—specifically with respect to HIV and the Acquired Immune Deficiency Syndrome, or AIDS—and, more recently, education. Yet violence prevention strategies, and AVRP programming in particular, have largely been under-funded (Habib and Maharaj, 2008). Notwithstanding the limited funding pool, the violence prevention sector has advanced in terms of advocacy, programming, and building an evidence base (Bruce, Kirsten, and Masuku, 2009).

In general, however, civil society efforts remain small-scale and focus on 'indirect' armed violence risk factors, such as alcohol abuse and gender inequality (see Box 6.1 previous page). Some have shown promise, while others remain unevaluated in terms of their impact on armed violence. Yet funding shortages prevent successful projects from being scaled up and untested interventions from being monitored. Given the scale of armed violence in South Africa and its negative effects on development, however, investment in prevention could make good economic sense in the long term.

Guns are handed in at the entrance to a sports event, north of Johannesburg, August 2007. © Jerome Delay/AP Photo

DATA AND MONITORING OF ARMED VIOLENCE

Access to disaggregated data on violent incidents can help to inform armed violence research and prevention efforts. Such access relies partly on ongoing data collection of incident details, including the type of weapon used, the time of death or injury, sex of victim and perpetrator, and their blood alcohol levels at the time of death or injury. Based on demonstrated violence prevention successes, WHO has called for improved quality and access to data and monitoring on armed violence. The organization emphasizes surveillance as an important priority in its 2002 *World Report on Violence and Health* and reiterates that point in its Global Campaign for Violence Prevention Plan of Action (Krug et al., 2002; VPA, 2012).

In South Africa, however, homicide data generated by the SAPS and NIMSS remains the primary indicator of armed violence levels. While the reporting of both agencies places South Africa ahead of most other African countries,[21] many relevant violent event characteristics remain unrecorded or unpublished.[22] The question of quality and access to better health and injury data needs to be viewed against the massive changes brought about by the transition to democracy. The transformation of the public sector has had an impact on the existence, collection, recording, and, ultimately, reliability of data. Quality and transparency remain challenges in both police and health data systems.

Police homicide data is not disaggregated and has been subject to allegations of manipulation prior to release (SAPA, 2011b). The lack of disaggregated police homicide data means that it is not possible to know, for example, characteristics of victims and perpetrators, the context and location of incidents, or how many homicides were committed per weapon type.

At the same time, the quality of data generated by the current cause of death registration system is compromised due to uneven coverage. Public access to the data is also restricted. Ideally, the entities that serve as data custodians would respond to reasonable data requests from violence prevention practitioners. It appears that capacity constraints currently make this impossible.[23]

The lack of coordination between the Department of Health and the police also affects mortuary data quality. In April 2006 the South African government shifted the running of mortuaries from the SAPS to the Department of Health (*Mail and Guardian,* 2012). This transfer has resulted in poor coordination of data and, ultimately, a discrepancy between police and mortuary data. In practice, this means that autopsy reports from the mortuary do not reach the investigating police officer; the quality of investigations is compromised as a result. A 2012 report on child homicide notes that post-mortem investigations were conducted by the health authorities but that the information did not lead to further police investigation, with the

Box 6.2 The value of better data for programming

The utility of strong data and monitoring for armed violence prevention has been convincingly illustrated. One prominent example is the Cure Violence model (formerly known as CeaseFire) from the United States. Cure Violence views violence as a learned behaviour that can be prevented using disease and injury control methods. Concentrating interventions on communities that are most severely affected by violence, the model uses data to identify and detect potentially violent events, interrupt and intervene in situations that are likely to result in a shooting or killing, and change the behaviour and social norms that perpetuate violence.

An evaluation of the programme roll-out in Chicago shows that it contributed to reductions in armed violence (shootings) and was associated with clear declines of actual and attempted shootings, with drops ranging from 17 to 24 per cent in surveyed areas (Skogan et al., 2008, p. 17). A more recent roll-out in Baltimore is associated with '5.4 fewer homicide incidents and 34.6 fewer nonfatal shooting incidents during 112 cumulative months of intervention' (Webster et al., 2012, p. 41).

Preliminary efforts are under way to replicate the Cure Violence model in Cape Town, but it is too early to assess the programme's full scope or effects.[24]

result that perpetrators were not apprehended (Mathews et al., 2012). For these reasons, the overall assessment of the state of data and monitoring on armed violence in South Africa is decidedly mixed. While public access to data on crime and violence had improved, Safety and Security Minister Steve Tshwete announced a moratorium in 2000 on the release of crime statistics (Burton et al., 2004, p. 22). Since the lifting of the moratorium in 2001, the quality of and access to both police and health data has also improved. But the challenge remains that the lack of data on the causes and circumstances of armed violence prevents more targeted policies and programming and better evaluation efforts (see Box 6.2). This dilemma has been well articulated by researchers and academics but has yet to translate into a change in the status quo (Small Arms Survey, 2008; CSVR, 2007; Ward et al., 2012).

CONCLUSION

It has been argued that armed violence and systemic poverty and inequality are linked and that countries that experience entrenched forms of armed violence risk getting trapped in cycles of under-development. This review suggests that the chances of breaking out of the cycle of armed violence and under-development are improved when efforts are made on both fronts. Improving socio-economic equality addresses some of the conditions that give rise to violence and can pay dividends in improved health, well-being, and security. It is incumbent upon the state to reflect this fundamental relationship in policy and programming.

South Africa has seen significant gains in armed violence reduction. Homicides, including gun homicides, have been in steady decline since 1994, and national legislation appears to be partly responsible, though further action is needed. Some socio-economic indicators are similarly improving. But South Africa's income inequality and homicide rates are still among the world's highest, and available evidence suggests that inequality remains an important driver of armed violence (CSVR, 2008, pp. 36–50).

While the SAPS should be central in armed violence prevention efforts, its ability to serve this function has been constrained by a range of serious internal problems. Apartheid-era policing practices have been suppressed but not fully transformed, and significant work remains to ensure that the SAPS serves to reduce, rather than exacerbate, levels of armed violence. Implementing further reform and enforcement procedures related to police use of force and firearms is an important step the government can take in this regard.

More broadly, perceptions of corruption, misconduct, and a lack of transparency across a number of state agencies persist. By publishing disaggregated fatal and non-fatal violence data annually, the government can demonstrate commitment to transparent democratic norms. Doing so would also assist researchers and health professionals in developing firearm violence-specific interventions and evaluating existing programmes that focus on contributing factors for violence, such as alcohol abuse and gender inequality. Such measures are more than symbolic in a country that remains deeply divided and where the weight of history is heavy. ▪

LIST OF ABBREVIATIONS

AIDS	Acquired Immune Deficiency Syndrome
AVRP	Armed Violence Reduction and Prevention
CFR	Central Firearms Register

DVA	Domestic Violence Act
FCA	Firearms Control Act
HIV	Human Immunodeficiency Virus
IPID	Independent Police Investigative Directorate
NIMSS	National Injury Mortality Surveillance System
SAPS	South African Police Service
WHO	World Health Organization

ENDNOTES

1　This average figure is calculated using South African labour force survey data (Trading Economics, 2012b).

2　For comprehensive accounts of South Africa's history, see the seven reports compiled by the South African Truth and Reconciliation Commission (TRC, n.d.). The Commission was tasked with investigating 'the causes, nature and extent' of individual gross human rights violations perpetrated in South Africa between 1 March 1960 and 10 May 1994 (TRC, 1998, p. 57).

3　Single data is collated from four sources: post-mortem reports, SAP 180 forms, chemical pathology laboratory results, and criminal justice system reports (NIMSS, 2009b).

4　This World Health Organization classification system, now in its tenth revision (2007), is the global standard diagnostic tool for epidemiology, health management, and clinical purposes. See WHO (n.d.).

5　Percentages are based on cases for which the age of the victim was known. Age was unknown in 7 per cent of the cases (NIMSS, 2009b, p. 8).

6　According to NIMSS, age-standardized injury mortality rates were calculated using population data from the 2001 national census (NIMSS, 2012a, p. 12; 2012b, p. 16).

7　The intent of injury was undetermined in 31.4 per cent of the cases. One-third of the victims were in the 20–34 age group and another third were in the 35–54 age group.

8　See Small Arms Survey (2008) for more on the public health approach to armed violence and the concepts of risk and resilience.

9　For a full discussion on police use of force and firearms, see Small Arms Survey (2004).

10　Two notable examples are the Cure Violence (formerly CeaseFire) model and the Scottish Violence Reduction Unit (Cure Violence, n.d.; VRU, n.d.; VPA, n.d.). See Box 6.2 for more details on the Cure Violence model.

11　Author telephone interview with a member of the task team, Pretoria, 2 November 2012.

12　Jackie Selebi was national police commissioner in 2000–08. He was discharged from his duties in 2009 in the wake of corruption charges. In 2010 he was found guilty of corruption and sentenced to 15 years in prison (Smith, 2010). Selebi's successor, Bheki Cele, was national police commissioner from 2009 to 2011, when he was found guilty of fraud and tender irregularities. He was dismissed the same year (BBC, 2012).

13　In March 2011 crime intelligence chief Richard Mdluli was charged with the murder of his former lover's husband (SAPA, 2011a). In September 2011 he was charged with fraud and corruption for allegedly using SAPS funds to purchase luxury vehicles (Prince, 2011).

14　Zuma is also known for singing the liberation struggle song, *Awuleth' Umshini Wami* (Bring Me My Machine Gun), in public appearances (Foster, 2009).

15　In October 2009 a hairdresser was mistaken for a hijacker and shot and killed by the SAPS (Otto, 2009). In November 2009 a three-year-old boy was shot and killed by SAPS while sitting in a car that contained a pipe the police thought suspicious (Berger, 2009). In April 2011 a woman was shot and killed by a SAPS member as she mistakenly bumped into a police vehicle while trying to reverse out of a parking bay (Laing, 2011).

16　Storing a service weapon at home represents a breach of section 98(5)(b) of the FCA, which states that SAPS members should return their weapons at the end of their shift (RSA, 2000, s. 98(5)(b)). Yet respondents in the 2009 study argued that a firearm that had been returned after a shift could easily be stolen from the police station (ICD, 2009, p. 30).

17　See Terreblanche (2002) for a thorough account of how apartheid entrenched inequality in South Africa.

18　See Nattrass and Seekings (2010) and the Presidency of the Republic of South Africa (2009).

19　The NGO Equal Education campaigns for quality education for all. One of the campaigns calls on the South African government to implement minimum norms and standards for school infrastructure in all schools in the country. See the online petition at Equal Education (n.d.).

20　Two case studies—Diadema in Brazil and Cali in Colombia—illustrate how reducing alcohol availability helps to reduce homicide rates. See Duailibi et al. (2007) and Sánchez et al. (2011).

21 The only African countries that carry out emergency room surveillance activities on a regular basis are Ethiopia, Ghana, Kenya, Mozambique, South Africa, and Uganda (Gilgen, Krause, and Muggah, 2010, p. 17).

22 These characteristics include the type of firearm used in assaults, the location of violent events (home, street, public place), and the relationship between victim and perpetrator.

23 The NIMSS website bears the following note: 'Important notice: Due to current human resources pressures the Crime, Violence and Injury/Safety and Peace Promotion Research Unit is unable to process requests for data and customised reports' (MRC, n.d.).

24 Author correspondence with Jalon Arthur, Cure Violence, Chicago, 18 January 2013.

BIBLIOGRAPHY

Abrahams, Naeemah, Rachel Jewkes, and Shanaaz Mathews. 2010. 'Guns and Gender-based Violence in South Africa.' *South African Medical Journal*, Vol. 100, No. 9. September, pp. 586–88.

Abrahams, Naeemah, et al. 2012. 'Every Eight Hours: Intimate Femicide in South Africa 10 Years Later!' *South African Medical Research Council Research Brief*. August, pp. 1–4. <http://www.mrc.ac.za/policybriefs/everyeighthours.pdf>

Alvazzi del Frate, Anna. 2012. 'A Matter of Survival: Non-lethal Firearm Violence.' In Small Arms Survey. *Small Arms Survey 2012: Moving Targets*. Cambridge: Cambridge University Press.

AUC (African Union Commission) et al. 2012. *MDG Report 2012: Assessing Progress in Africa toward the Millennium Development Goals*. <http://www.afdb.org/fileadmin/uploads/afdb/Documents/Publications/MDGReport2012_ENG.pdf>

BBC (British Broadcasting Corporation). 2012. 'South Africa Police Chief Bheki Cele Fired by Jacob Zuma.' 12 June. <http://www.bbc.co.uk/news/world-africa-18414786>

Bellis, Mark, et al. 2010. *Preventing and Reducing Armed Violence: What Works?* Background paper for the Oslo Conference on Armed Violence. New York and Oslo: United Nations Development Programme and Norwegian Ministry of Foreign Affairs. <http://www.preventviolence.info/showResourcespdf.aspx?id=18a25404-4a63-4353-8055-cbb3ceb116ff >

Berger, Sebastien. 2009. 'South African Boy, 3, Shot Dead by Police.' *Telegraph*. 10 November. <http://www.telegraph.co.uk/news/worldnews/africaandindianocean/southafrica/6539648/South-African-boy-3-shot-dead-by-police.html>

Bertelsmann Stiftung. 2012. *Bertelsmann Transformation Index 2012: South Africa Country Report*. Gütersloh: Bertelsmann Stiftung.

Bloomberg Businessweek. 2012. 'South Africa's Brewing Class War.' 6 September. <http://www.businessweek.com/articles/2012-09-06/bloomberg-view-south-africas-brewing-class-war>

Booza TV. n.d. Website. <http://boozatv.com/>

Bruce, David. 2002. 'New Wine from an Old Cask? The South African Police Service and the Process of Transformation.' Paper presented at John Jay College of Criminal Justice, New York. 9 May.

—. 2006. 'Racism, Self-Esteem and Violence in SA: Gaps in the NCPS' Explanation?' *SA Crime Quarterly*, No. 17. September.

—. 2012a. 'Police Shootings: Compilation of IPID Figures.' Unpublished paper.

—. 2012b. 'Marikana and the Doctrine of Maximum Force.' *Mampoer Shorts*. Johannesburg: Parktown Publishers.

—, Adèle Kirsten, and Themba Masuku. 2009. *Armed Violence and Armed Violence Reduction Programming in South Africa*. Unpublished background paper. Johannesburg: Centre for the Study of Violence and Reconciliation.

Burton, Patrick, et al. 2004. *National Victims of Crime Survey: South Africa 2003*. Pretoria: Institute for Security Studies. <http://www.iss.co.za/pubs/monographs/no101/contents.html>

Campbell, Nathan, et al. 2011. 'Gunshots of Children in Cape Town: Did the Introduction of the New Firearm Bill in 2004 Have Any Effect?' Paper presented at the 1st Safety and Violence Initiative Conference, Cape Town, 8–9 September. Cape Town: Trauma Unit Red Cross Children's Hospital Cape Town, Childsafe South Africa, and Department of Paediatric Surgery, University of Cape Town.

Cawthra, Gavin. 1992. *South Africa's Police: From Police State to Democratic Policing?* London: Catholic Institute for International Relations.

CCSA (Constitutional Court of South Africa). 2002. 'Ex Parte Minister of Safety and Security and Others: In Re S v Walters and Another. Case CCT 28/01. 21 May. <http://www.saflii.org/za/cases/ZACC/2002/6.html>

Children's Institute. 2012. *South African Child Gauge 2012: Children and Inequality—Closing the Gap*. Cape Town: University of Cape Town.

Civilian Secretariat for Police. n.d. 'Enquiry into the Functioning of the Central Firearms Registry and the Implementation of Related Aspects of the Firearms Control Act, 2000 (Act 60 of 2000).' <http://www.gunownerssa.org/documents/EnquiryFunctioningCFRandFCA2000.pdf>

Colvin, Christopher, Oliver Human, and Dean Peacock. 2009. *'It Looks Like Men Are Competing with Rights Nowadays': Men's Perceptions of Gender Transformation in South Africa*. Cape Town: Sonke Gender Justice Network. 16 July.
<http://genderjustice.org.za/resources/reports.html?view=docman>

Combrinck, Helene, et al. 1998. 'Domestic Violence Bill [B75-98].' Submission to the Justice Portfolio Committee and the Safety and Security Portfolio Committee hearings. Cape Town: Women and Human Rights Project, Community Law Centre, University of the Western Cape.

CoMMiC (Committee on Morbidity and Mortality in Children under Five Years). 2011. *1st Triennial Report of the Committee on Morbidity and Mortality in Children Under 5 Years*. <http://www.doh.gov.za/docs/reports/2011/morbreport.pdf>

Coovadia, Hoosen, et al. 2009. 'Health in South Africa 1—The Health and Health System of South Africa: Historical Roots of Current Public Health Challenges.' *Lancet*, Vol. 374. 5 September, pp. 817–34.

CSVR (Centre for the Study of Violence and Reconciliation). 2007. *The Violent Nature of Crime in South Africa: A Concept Paper for the Justice, Crime Prevention and Security Cluster*. Johannesburg: CSVR. <http://www.csvr.org.za/docs/crime/compatibility_mode.pdf>

—. 2008. 'Adding Injury to Insult: How Exclusion and Inequality Drive South Africa's Problem of Violence.' Johannesburg: CSVR.
<http://www.csvr.org.za/docs/study/4.Book_SocioEconomic_20_03_2009.pdf>

Cure Violence. n.d. 'Fidelity to the Cure Violence (CeaseFire) Model: Why Picking and Choosing Doesn't Work.'
<http://cureviolence.org/news/fidelity-to-the-cure-violence-ceasefire-model-why-picking-and-choosing-doesnt-work/>

Daily Maverick. 2011. 'Remembering Andries Tatane, Not Forgetting Police Brutality.' 18 April.
<http://dailymaverick.co.za/article/2011-04-18-remembering-andries-tatane-not-forgetting-police-brutality>

Department of Health. 2009. *Report of the Maternal Child and Women's Health Summit*.
<http://www.mspsouthafrica.org/about_rrhf/pmtct/mch_summit/>

DOJCD (Department of Justice and Constitutional Development). 2012. 'Establishment of a Commission of Enquiry into the Tragic Incident at or near the Area Commonly Known as the Marikana Mine in Rustenburg, North West Province, South Africa.'
<http://www.justice.gov.za/legislation/notices/2012/20120912-gg35680-nor50-marikana.pdf>

Duailibi, Sergio, et al. 2007. 'The Effect of Restricting Opening Hours on Alcohol-Related Violence.' *American Journal of Public Health*, Vol. 97, pp. 2276–80.

Dworkin, Shari, et al. 2012. 'Men's Perceptions of Women's Rights and Changing Gender Relations in South Africa: Lessons for Working with Men and Boys in HIV and Anti-Violence Programs.' *Gender & Society*, Vol. 26, No. 1, pp. 97–120.

Eavis, Paul. 2011. *Working against Violence: Promising Practices in Armed Violence Reduction and Prevention*. Geneva: Geneva Declaration Secretariat.

Equal Education. n.d. 'Show Government You Care: Sign Our Petition and Be Counted!'
<http://www.equaleducation.org.za/show_government_you_care_petition>

Foster, Douglas. 2009. 'Jacob's Ladder.' *Atlantic*. June.
<http://www.theatlantic.com/magazine/archive/2009/06/jacobs-ladder/307442/?single_page=true>

Geneva Declaration Secretariat. 2008. *Global Burden of Armed Violence*. Geneva: Geneva Declaration Secretariat.

—. 2011. *Global Burden of Armed Violence: Lethal Encounters*. Cambridge: Cambridge University Press.

Gilgen, Elisabeth, Keith Krause, and Robert Muggah. 2010. *Measuring and Monitoring Armed Violence: Goals, Targets, and Indicators*. New York and Oslo: United Nations Development Programme and Norwegian Ministry of Foreign Affairs.

Goldstone, Carvin. 2009. 'Police Must Shoot to Kill, Worry Later—Cele.' IOL News. 1 August.
<http://www.iol.co.za/news/south-africa/police-must-shoot-to-kill-worry-later-cele-1.453587#.UPaHe6z0fTo>

Govender, Prega. 2012. 'Menace to Society: 27000 Cops Fail Firearm Test.' *Sunday Times* (South Africa). 4 March.
<http://www.timeslive.co.za/sundaytimes/2012/03/04/menace-to-society-27000-cops-fail-firearm-test>

Gumede-Johnson, Kamvelihle. 2011. 'Police Training: Brutality Exposed.' *Mail and Guardian* (South Africa). 3 June.
<http://mg.co.za/article/2011-06-03-saps-the-strong-arm-of-force>

Gun Free South Africa. 2010. 'Gun Free South Africa Demand that All Schools be Declared Firearm Free Zones.' Press release. 18 November.
<http://www.gca.org.za/Home/tabid/1120/ctl/Details/mid/7475/ItemID/922/language/en-US/Default.aspx>

Habib, Adam and Brij Maharaj, eds. 2008. *Giving and Solidarity: Resource Flows for Poverty Alleviation and Development in South Africa*. Cape Town: HSRC Press.

Hartley, Wyndham. 2008. 'South Africa: Police will Fight Fire with Fire—Minister.' *Business Day*. 13 November.
<http://allafrica.com/stories/200811130134.html>

Hofstatter, Stephan, Mzilikazi Wa Afrika, and Rob Rose. 2011. 'Shoot to Kill: Inside a South African Police Death Squad.' *Times* (South Africa). 11 December.
<http://www.timeslive.co.za/local/2011/12/11/shoot-to-kill-inside-a-south-african-police-death-squad>

Hosken, Graeme. 2008. 'Kill the Bastards, Minister Tells Police.' IOL News. 10 April.
<http://www.iol.co.za/news/south-africa/kill-the-bastards-minister-tells-police-1.395982#.UMhr4qz0fTo>

Hsieh, Ching-Chi and M.D. Pugh. 1993. 'Poverty, Income Inequality, and Violent Crime: A Meta-analysis of Recent Aggregate Data Studies.' *Criminal Justice Review*, Vol. 18, No. 2. Autumn, pp. 182–202.

ICD (Independent Complaints Directorate). 2009. 'Femicide: A Case Study on Members of the South African Police Service.'
<http://www.info.gov.za/view/DownloadFileAction?id=124571>

Im, Fernando, et al. 2012. *South Africa Economic Update: Focus on Inequality of Opportunity*. The World Bank Group Africa Region Poverty Reduction and Economic Management No. 3. Washington, DC: World Bank. July.
<http://documents.worldbank.org/curated/en/2012/01/16561374/south-africa-economic-update-focus-inequality-opportunity>

IPID (Independent Police Investigative Directorate). 2012a. 'Regulations for the Operation of the Independent Police Investigative Directorate.' Government notice. 10 February.

—. 2012b. *IPID Statistical Report 2011/12*.

Isaacs, Doron. 2012. 'Incomes-Based Education?' Speech delivered at Institute for Justice Reconciliation conference on 'Economic Justice for the Next Generation.' <http://reconciliationbarometer.org/newsletter/volume-ten-2012/incomes-based-education/>

ISS (Institute for Security Studies). 2012. 'Fact Sheet: Explaining the Official Crime Statistics for 2011/12.' Pretoria: ISS. 20 September.

Jewkes, Rachel, Katharine Wood, and Nata Duvvury. 2010. '"I Woke up after I Joined Stepping Stones": Meanings of an HIV Behavioural Intervention in Rural South African Young People's Lives.' *Health Education Research*, Vol. 25, No. 6. 11 October, pp. 1074–84.

Jewkes, Rachel, et al. 2008. 'Impact of Stepping Stones on HIV and HSV-2 and Sexual Behaviour in Rural South Africa: Cluster Randomised Controlled Trial.' *British Medical Journal*, Vol. 337, pp. 1–11.

Kirsten, Adèle. 2007. 'Simpler, Better, Faster: Review of the 2005 Firearms Amnesty.' ISS Paper 134. Pretoria: Institute for Security Studies. April.

—. 2008. *A Nation Without Guns? The Story of Gun Free South Africa*. Scottsville: University of KwaZulu-Natal Press.

Krug, Etienne, et al., eds. 2002. *World Report on Violence and Health*. Geneva: World Health Organization.

Laing, Aislinn. 2011. 'Woman "Shot Dead by Police after Driving into Force Car".' *Telegraph*. 28 April. <http://www.telegraph.co.uk/news/worldnews/africaandindianocean/southafrica/8481483/Woman-shot-dead-by-police-after-driving-into-force-car.html>

Lamb, Guy. 2008. 'Under the Gun: An Assessment of Firearm Crime and Violence in South Africa.' Report compiled for the Office of the President. Pretoria.

Mail and Guardian (South Africa). 2011. 'Who Was Andries Tatane?' 21 April. <http://mg.co.za/article/2011-04-21-who-was-andries-tatane>

—. 2012. 'Hellish Mortuary Scenes Haunt the Memories of Loved Ones.' 13 July.
<http://mg.co.za/article/2012-07-12-hellish-mortuary-scenes-haunt-the-memories-of-loved-ones>

Mathews, Shanaaz, et al., 2012. 'Child Homicide Patterns in South Africa: Is There a Link to Child Abuse?' *South African Medical Research Council Research Brief*. August, pp. 1–4.

MRC (South African Medical Research Council). n.d. 'Our Research.' Accessed February 2013. <http://www.mrc.ac.za/crime/nimms.htm>

Nair, Nivashni. 2012. 'Cato Manor Cops Demand Disciplinary Hearings Take Place.' 30 October. *Times* (South Africa).
<http://www.timeslive.co.za/thetimes/2012/10/30/cato-manor-cops-demand-disciplinary-hearings-take-place>

Nattrass, Nicoli and Jeremy Seekings. 2010. *The Economy and Poverty in the Twentieth Century in South Africa*. CSSR Working Paper No. 276. Rondebosch: Centre for Social Science Research, University of Cape Town. July. <http://cssr.uct.ac.za/sites/cssr.uct.ac.za/files/pubs/wp276.pdf>

NIMSS (National Injury Mortality Surveillance System). 2009a. *A Profile of Fatal Injuries in Mpumalanga: The 2nd Annual Report of the Provincial Injury Mortality Surveillance System 2008*. <http://www.mrc.ac.za/crime/fatal_inj08.PDF>

—. 2009b. 'A Profile of Fatal Injuries in South Africa: 10th Annual Report of the National Injury Mortality Surveillance System 2008.'
<http://www.mrc.ac.za/crime/nimss2008.pdf>

—. 2012a. 'A Profile of Fatal Injuries in Gauteng: 2010.' <http://www.mrc.ac.za/crime/NIMSSGauteng2010.pdf>

—. 2012b. 'A Profile of Fatal Injuries in Mpumalanga: 2010.' <http://www.mrc.ac.za/crime/NIMSSMpumalanga2010.pdf>

NPC (National Planning Commission). 2011. 'Diagnostic Overview.' <http://www.npconline.co.za/pebble.asp?relid=33>

—. 2012. 'Our Future—Make it Work: National Development Plan 2030.' <http://www.info.gov.za/view/DownloadFileAction?id=172306>

O'Donovan, Michael. 2011. 'Crime, Poverty and Inequality in South Africa: What the Data Shows.' In Chandré Gould, ed. *National and International Perspectives on Crime and Policing*. Pretoria: Institute for Security Studies.

OECD (Organization for Economic Co-operation and Development). 2009. 'Armed Violence Reduction: Enabling Development.' 24 March.

—. 2011. *Investing in Security: A Global Assessment of Armed Violence Reduction Initiatives*.
<http://www.oecd.org/dac/conflictandfragility/48927716.pdf>

Operational Response Services. 2004. Standing Order (General) 262: Crowd Management During Gatherings and Demonstrations. Issued on 2004-09-16 by Consolidation Notice 13/2004.

Otto, Hanti. 2009. 'Cops Not to Blame for Kekana's Death.' *IOL News*. 19 October.
<http://www.iol.co.za/news/south-africa/cops-not-to-blame-for-kekana-s-death-1.461899#.URjQTPKzlCR>

Polgreen, Lydia. 2012. 'Mine Strike Mayhem Stuns South Africa as Police Open Fire.' *The New York Times*. 16 August.
<http://www.nytimes.com/2012/08/17/world/africa/south-african-police-fire-on-striking-miners.html>

Presidency of the Republic of South Africa. 2009. 'Development Indicators.' <http://www.thepresidency.gov.za/learning/me/indicators/2009/indicators.pdf>

Prince, Chandré. 2011. 'Richard Mdluli Bust for Fraud.' *Times* (South Africa). 23 September.
<http://www.timeslive.co.za/politics/2011/09/23/richard-mdluli-bust-for-fraud>

Ramsoomar, Leane and Neo Morojele. 2012. 'Trends in Alcohol Prevalence, Age of Initiation and Association with Alcohol-related Harm among South African Youth: Implications for Policy.' *South African Medical Journal*, Vol. 102, No. 7, pp. 609–12.

Rauch, Janine. 2000. 'Police Reform and South Africa's Transition.' Paper presented at the South African Institute for International Affairs conference.

RSA (Republic of South Africa). 1998a. 'Domestic Violence Bill B75-98.' <http://www.info.gov.za/view/DownloadFileAction?id=71541>

—. 1998b. 'Domestic Violence Act.' *Government Gazette*, Vol. 402. <http://www.info.gov.za/view/DownloadFileAction?id=70651>

—. 2000. 'Firearms Control Act 2000.' *Government Gazette*, Vol. 430. <http://www.info.gov.za/view/DownloadFileAction?id=68229>

—. 2004a. 'Firearms Control Regulations 2004.' <http://www.saps.gov.za/crime_prevention/firearms/legislation/gov_notice_english.pdf>

—. 2004b. 'Notice 749 of 2004: Ministry for Safety and Security.' *Government Gazette*, No. 26305. 7 May.

—. 2010. 'Millennium Development Goals: Country Report 2010.' <http://www.statssa.gov.za/news_archive/Docs/MDGR_2010.pdf>

SAHO (South African History Online). n.d. 'The Homelands.' Accessed 23 January 2013. <http://www.sahistory.org.za/special-features/homelands>

SAHRC (South African Human Rights Commission). 2012. 'Report on the Findings of the Investigation into the Killing of Free State Activist, Andries Tatane.' <http://www.sahrc.org.za/home/21/files/Report%20Comm%20%20SA%20Police%20Service%20301012.pdf>

Sánchez, Álvaro, et al. 2011. 'Policies for Alcohol Restriction and Their Association with Interpersonal Violence: A Time Series Analysis of Homicides in Cali, Colombia.' *International Journal of Epidemiology*, Vol. 40, pp. 1037–46.

SAPA (South African Press Association). 2011a. 'Mdluli in Court on Murder Charge.' 31 March.
<http://www.news24.com/SouthAfrica/News/Mdluli-in-court-on-murder-charge-20110331>

—. 2011b. 'Cops Held for Manipulating Crime Stats.' 12 December.
<http://www.news24.com/SouthAfrica/News/Cops-held-for-manipulating-crime-stats-20111212>

SAPS (South African Police Service). 1995. 'South African Police Service Act, 1995.' No. 68 of 1995.

—. 2010a. 'Military Ranks for SAPS to Take Effect April 1—Mthethwa.' 12 March.
<http://www.politicsweb.co.za/politicsweb/view/politicsweb/en/page71656?oid=165613&sn=Detail>

—. 2010b. 'Remarks by Minister of Police, E. N. Mthethwa, MP to the National Press Club on the Current Challenges Affecting the South African Police Service Firearms Application and Licensing Processes, Sheraton Hotel, Pretoria.' 2 November.
<http://www.info.gov.za/speech/DynamicAction?pageid=461&sid=14225&tid=23633>

—. 2012a. 'Murder in RSA for April to March 2004/2005 to 2011/2012.'
<http://www.saps.gov.za/statistics/reports/crimestats/2012/categories/murder.pdf>

—. 2012b. 'Minister Nathi Mthethwa to File Court Papers Challenging the Khayelitsha Commission of Inquiry.' 31 October.
<http://www.info.gov.za/speech/DynamicAction?pageid=461&sid=31893&tid=89025>

SASSA (South African Social Security Agency). 2012. 'A Statistical Summary of Social Grants in South Africa.' 30 September.
<http://www.sassa.gov.za/Portals/1/Documents/90081a2d-c3c8-4329-a0ce-d2e5a04d0ee2.pdf>

Schneider, Vera and Lisa Vetten. 2006. *Going Somewhere Slowly? A Comparison of the Implementation of the Domestic Violence Act (No. 116 of 1998) in an Urban and Semi-urban Site*. Johannesburg: Centre for the Study of Violence and Reconciliation.

Schönteich, Martin and Antoinette Louw. 2001. 'Crime in South Africa: A Country and Cities Profile.' ISS Occasional Paper No. 49. Pretoria: Institute for Security Studies.

Shaw, Mark and Peter Gastrow. 2001. 'Stealing the Show? Crime and Its Impact in Post-Apartheid South Africa.' *Daedalus*, Vol. 130, No. 1. Winter.

SJC (Social Justice Coalition). 2012. 'Premier Zille: Act Now to Restore Faith in Khayelitsha Police and Courts.'
<http://www.sjc.org.za/posts/premier-zille-act-now-to-restore-faith-in-khayelitsha-police-and-courts>

Skogan, Wesley, et al. 2008. 'Evaluation of CeaseFire–Chicago'. Evanston, IL: Northwestern University.
<http://www.ipr.northwestern.edu/publications/ceasefire_papers/executivesummary.pdf>

Small Arms Survey. 2004. *Small Arms Survey 2004: Rights at Risk*. Oxford: Oxford University Press.

—. 2008. *Small Arms Survey 2008: Risk and Resilience*. Cambridge: Cambridge University Press.

Smith, David. 2010. 'South Africa's Former Police Chief Jackie Selebi Sentenced.' *Guardian*.
    <http://www.guardian.co.uk/world/2010/aug/03/jackie-selebi-south-africa-corruption-sentence>

Sonke (Sonke Gender Justice Network). n.d.a. 'Case Study: One Man Can Campaign.'
    <http://www.genderjustice.org.za/issue-1/resources/sonke-newsletter/issue-1/issue-1-articles/case-study-one-man-can-campaign>

—. n.d.b. 'One Man Can Campaign Toolkit.' <http://www.genderjustice.org.za/one-man-can-toolkit/tools/one-man-can-toolkit>

South African Parliament. 2012. 'Police: Question No. 2127.' <http://www.pmg.org.za/node/33761>

State President's Office. 1994. Regulation of Gatherings Act. No. 205 of 1993. <http://www.info.gov.za/acts/1993/a205-93.pdf>

Statistics South Africa. 1998. *Victims of Crime Survey 1997*. Pretoria: Statistics South Africa.
    <https://www.statssa.gov.za/Publications/VictimsOfCrime/VictimsOfCrime1997.pdf>

—. 2012a. *Census 2011: Key Results*. Pretoria: Statistics South Africa.

—. 2012b. *Victims of Crime Survey 2012*. Pretoria: Statistics South Africa.
    <http://www.statssa.gov.za/Publications/statsdownload.asp?PPN=P0341&SCH=5343>

—. 2012c. *Census 2011: Census in Brief*. Pretoria: Statistics South Africa.

—. 2012d. 'Income and Expenditure Survey (IES) 2010/2011.' Press statement. 6 November.
    <http://www.statssa.gov.za/news_archive/press_statements/IES_%202010_2011_Press%20Statement_6_November_2012.pdf>

Tait, Sean and Monique Marks. 2011. 'You Strike a Gathering, You Strike a Rock: Current Debates in the Policing of Public Order in South Africa.'
    South African Crime Quarterly, No. 38. December. <http://www.issafrica.org/uploads/CQ38Tait_Marks.pdf>

Terreblanche, Sampie. 2002. *A History of Inequality in South Africa, 1652–2002*. Pietermaritzburg: University of Natal Press and KMM Review Publishing.

TLAC (Tshwaranang Legal Advocacy Centre) and Ceasefire Campaign. 2009. 'Submission to the Portfolio Committee and Select Committee on Women,
    Youth, Children and People with Disabilities.'
    <http://www.tlac.org.za/wp-content/uploads/2012/01/Firearms-and-the-Domestic-Violence-Act.pdf>

Trading Economics. 2012a. 'Gini Index in South Africa.' <http://www.tradingeconomics.com/south-africa/gini-index-wb-data.html>

—. 2012b. 'South Africa Unemployment Rate.' <http://www.tradingeconomics.com/south-africa/unemployment-rate>

TRC (Truth and Reconciliation Commission). 1998. *Truth and Reconciliation Commission of South Africa Report*, vol. 1. Cape Town: Juta & Company.
    <http://www.justice.gov.za/trc/report/finalreport/Volume%201.pdf>

—. n.d. 'The TRC Report.' <http://www.justice.gov.za/trc/report/index.htm>

Tutu, Desmond. 2000. *No Future without Forgiveness*. New York: Random House.

UNDP (United Nations Development Programme). 2011. 'South Africa—Country Profile: Human Development Indicators.'
    <http://hdrstats.undp.org/en/countries/profiles/ZAF.html>

UNODC (United Nations Office on Drugs and Crime). 2011a. *2011 Global Study on Homicide: Trends, Context, Data*. Vienna: UNODC.

—. 2011b. 'Homicide Statistics 2011.' <http://www.unodc.org/documents/data-and-analysis/statistics/crime/Homicide_statistics2012.xls>

Vetten, Lisa, et al. 2009. 'Implementing the Domestic Violence Act in Acornhoek, Mpumalanga.' Tshwaranang Legal Advocacy Centre to End Violence
    against Women Research Brief No. 2. February.
    <http://www.tlac.org.za/wp-content/uploads/2012/01/Research-Brief-implementing-the-Domestic-Violence-Act-in-Acornhoek.pdf>

Villaveces, Andrés, et al. 2000. 'Effect of a Ban on Carrying Firearms on Homicide Rates in 2 Colombian Cities.' *Journal of the American Medical Association*,
    Vol. 283, No. 9, pp. 1205–09.

VPA (Violence Prevention Alliance). 2012. 'Global Campaign for Violence Prevention: Plan of Action for 2012–2020.'
    <http://www.who.int/violence_injury_prevention/violence/global_campaign/gcvp_plan_of_action.pdf>

—. n.d. 'Scottish Violence Reduction Unit.' <www.who.int/violenceprevention/about/participants/vru_scotland/en/index.html>

VRU (Violence Reduction Unit). n.d. 'About Us.' <http://www.actiononviolence.com/about-us>

Ward, Catherine, et al. 2012. 'Violence, Violence Prevention and Safety: A Research Agenda for South Africa.' *South African Medical Journal*, Vol. 102,
    No. 4. April, pp. 215–18.

Webb, Boyd. 2008. 'You Will Die, Shabangu Warns.' IOL News. 17 April.
    <http://www.iol.co.za/news/south-africa/you-will-die-shabangu-warns-1.396878?ot=inmsa.ArticlePrintPageLayout.ot>

Webster, Daniel, et al. 2012. *Evaluation of Baltimore's Safe Streets Programme: Effects on Attitudes, Participants' Experiences, and Gun Violence*. Baltimore:
    Johns Hopkins Bloomberg School of Public Health. <http://www.jhsph.edu/sebin/u/p/2012_01_11.SafeStreetsEval.pdf>

Western Cape Government. 2012a. 'Commission of Inquiry into Allegations of Police Inefficiency in Khayelitsha and of a Breakdown in Relations between the Community and the Police in Khayelitsha.' <http://www.westerncape.gov.za/text/2012/8/Terms%20of%20Reference.pdf>

—. 2012b. 'Booza TV: A Sobering Look into the Dangerous Drinking Habits of Western Cape Citizens.' <http://www.westerncape.gov.za/eng/pubs/public_info/B/243677>

WHO (World Health Organization). 2006. *Interpersonal Violence and Alcohol.* WHO Policy Briefing.

—. 2008. *Preventing Violence and Reducing Its Impact: How Development Agencies Can Help.* Geneva: WHO. <http://whqlibdoc.who.int/publications/2008/9789241596589_eng.pdf>

—. n.d. 'International Classification of Diseases (ICD).' <http://www.who.int/classifications/icd/en/>

Wilkinson, Richard. 2004. 'Why Is Violence More Common Where Inequality Is Greater?' *Annals of New York Academy of Sciences,* Vol. 1036, pp. 1–12.

ACKNOWLEDGEMENTS

Principal author

Natalie Jaynes

Contributors

Anna Alvazzi del Frate and Irene Pavesi

A federal firearms specialist searches gun records on microfiche, Martinsburg, WV, USA, March 2010.
© Ricky Carioti/The Washington Post/Getty Images

Second Wind

THE POA'S 2012 REVIEW CONFERENCE

7

INTRODUCTION

All fired up. Nothing to do. The Second Review Conference (RevCon) for the UN Programme of Action (PoA)[1] faced the same problem that had helped to sink its predecessor, namely how to make sense of a mandate that required it 'to review progress made' in PoA implementation when there was no mechanism to do so.[2]

This chapter explains how the Second Review Conference, despite such uncertainty, managed to achieve a result that holds out the promise of a strengthened PoA. Drawing on relevant UN documents and the author's own observations of the meeting and its preparatory phase, the chapter examines the principal features of the Review Conference process and outcome. Its main conclusions include the following:

- The Second Review Conference avoided many of the problems that plagued the First Review Conference, largely through the use of a working method that contributed to the success of UN small arms meetings after 2006.
- The Review Conference outcome is forward-looking, setting out a series of measures intended to bolster implementation of the PoA and the International Tracing Instrument (ITI)[3] during the next six-year meeting cycle.
- While the Review Conference text draws on the conclusions of preceding PoA meetings, overall it has little to say about 'progress made' in PoA and ITI implementation, reflecting the lack of formal monitoring tools.
- The Review Conference outcome raises the possibility of increased attention to longer-term trends in small arms proliferation and misuse, including the related question of PoA and ITI effectiveness.
- The challenges associated with the proliferation and misuse of small arms remain acute, yet UN member states have now laid the foundations for sustained and effective solutions to the problem.

The chapter begins by analysing the difficulties inherent in the Review Conference mandate, as initially formulated, before presenting the main features of Conference preparations. A section covering the main developments at the Conference itself then paves the way for a more detailed analysis of Review Conference achievements—in terms of process as well as substance. The conclusion recaps the chapter's main themes, including the Conference's potentially positive, but as yet unconfirmed, legacy.

CONFERENCE MANDATE

In preparing for the Second Review Conference, UN member states were, in a sense, starting from scratch. The PoA's First Review Conference, convened in June–July 2006, had failed to produce a substantive outcome, largely because states could not agree what its formal mandate—'to review progress made' in PoA implementation (UNGA, 2001, para. IV.1.a)—meant exactly.[4] Nevertheless, the subsequent meeting cycle proved quite productive. In contrast to the first two Biennial Meetings of States (BMSs), held in 2003 and 2005, BMS3 and BMS4 (held in 2008 and 2010) produced substantive outcomes covering a range of subjects.[5] There was nothing very new in these discussions, but the meeting outcome documents, negotiated by diplomats, did offer useful elaboration of many existing (often vague) PoA provisions. An Open-ended Meeting of Governmental Experts (MGE), convened in May 2011, resulted in a Chair's Summary that recapped discussions of specific challenges states were encountering in their implementation of the ITI and means of overcoming the same (New Zealand, 2011).[6]

These meetings were designed to clarify the practical implications of fulfilling PoA and ITI commitments in specific areas and to share experiences in meeting associated implementation challenges. They did not, however, attempt to assess the extent to which states, individually or collectively, were fulfilling their commitments under these instruments. BMS4 considered the question of PoA follow-up, producing a recommendation for 'a comprehensive assessment of progress in the implementation of the Programme of Action [. . .] as an input for the 2012 Review Conference', which, in a subsequent General Assembly resolution, became an invitation to 'Member States to communicate [. . .] their views' on such progress (UNGA, 2010a, para. 40;[7] 2010b, para. 29). The result, a short report compiling the submissions of seven states, fell far short of 'a comprehensive assessment' of progress in implementing the PoA and ITI, but it did contain useful information on national implementation by the seven countries, their assessment of implementation challenges, and their priorities for the future, including for the Second Review Conference (UNGA, 2012d).

In short, the second PoA meeting cycle (2006–12), though far more productive than the first, did not examine 'progress made' in PoA implementation. Nor did it establish any mechanism that would, for example, analyse the information contained in national reports on PoA and ITI implementation. That left the Second Review Conference to grapple with the question of how to give effect to its formal mandate. The General Assembly resolutions that preceded the Conference offered little help in this regard, most often simply echoing the PoA's original formulation of the Review Conference mandate.[8] Resolution 66/47, however, also encouraged states 'to explore ways to strengthen [PoA] implementation' at the Conference, suggesting that the Conference would, to some extent, look to the future (UNGA, 2011, para. 14).

The PoA process lacked a mechanism for examining 'progress made' in PoA implementation.

RUN-UP TO REVCON

Notwithstanding the uncertainties surrounding its mandate, the Review Conference was able to look to the UN small arms meetings that preceded it for guidance as to how to go about its work. BMS3 established a set of principles for the preparation and organization of UN small arms meetings that broke with earlier, relatively unstructured practice and guided BMS3, as well as BMS4 and the 2011 MGE, to greater success.[9] A key element of this approach was the early designation of the meeting chair.

The chair takes the reins

In May 2011, Ambassador U. Joy Ogwu of Nigeria was designated chair of the Second Review Conference and of its Preparatory Committee (PrepCom).[10] As preceding meeting chairs had done, she took advantage of this early nomination to consult with member states on procedural and substantive questions relating to the Conference well before it, or its PrepCom, convened.[11]

Joy Ogwu, Permanent Representative of Nigeria to the UN and President of the Review Conference, addresses delegates at the Second Review Conference on the UN PoA, New York, August 2012. © UN Multimedia

At an early stage in her consultations, Ambassador Ogwu floated the possible adoption of another element of the BMS3 working method, namely limiting the number of meeting topics (Nigeria, 2011a; 2011b). This option was rejected in favour of a comprehensive approach; there would be no culling of topics from the broader PoA and ITI menu when developing the Review Conference agenda (Nigeria, 2011c). That obviously put a premium on effective time management at the two-week Review Conference and its one-week PrepCom session.

The idea of conducting parallel Review Conference sessions was explored during the consultations, but dropped due to a lack of available meeting space and the difficulty smaller delegations would have had in covering simultaneous meetings (Nigeria, 2012a). Instead, Ambassador Ogwu adopted two further components of the BMS3 approach that had helped make the most of scarce meeting time. The first was the use of facilitators, employed at both BMS3 and BMS4 to shepherd the development of specific sections of meeting outcome documents (Nigeria, 2011a; 2011b). The second component was to dispense with—or, in the case of the Review Conference, limit—general statements in order to focus meeting discussions on the contents of the outcome documents (Nigeria, 2011c; 2012a).[12]

In order to prepare for the Review Conference, it was important to make good use of the PrepCom, something states had failed to do before the First Review Conference.[13] In general terms, this implied some discussion of, and agreement on, substantive components of the Review Conference at the PrepCom (Nigeria, 2011b; 2011c). To help steer the meeting in this direction, in early March Ambassador Ogwu issued a set of 'indicative non-papers', listing 'possible areas of focus' in the PrepCom discussions (Nigeria, 2012b).

The March 2012 PrepCom

The PrepCom for the Second Review Conference convened from 19 to 23 March 2012. The key issue facing the meeting was the same that had confronted the UN membership since the start of Conference preparations, namely how to carry out the Conference's formal mandate 'to review progress made' in PoA implementation when the UN membership had established no mechanism for measuring such progress.

At the outset of the PrepCom, Ambassador Ogwu emphasized the need for the meeting to focus on substance. She asked national delegations to indicate which topics, in their view, the Review Conference should address and to limit the length of their interventions.[14] There was no 'general debate' or 'general exchange of views'—UN language for a wide-ranging discussion of any and all aspects of a particular subject. Instead, upon completion of initial formalities that included the adoption of the meeting agenda, the PrepCom moved immediately to a 'thematic debate' consisting of five topics mirroring the structure of the PoA and a sixth relating to the ITI as a whole (UNGA, 2012a).[15]

The PrepCom moved immediately to a thematic debate consisting of six topics. Throughout the week, PrepCom discussions proceeded at a relatively brisk pace, with most countries mentioning specific issues they wanted the Review Conference—and the subsequent six-year meeting cycle—to address. On 22 March, the second-to-last day of the PrepCom, Ambassador Ogwu distributed a Chair's Summary that sought to distil the range of views states had expressed regarding Review Conference priorities (Nigeria, 2012c).[16] In essence, for each of the six PrepCom topics, the document presented some of the steps states had taken to implement the PoA and ITI and, at the same time, it listed 'suggested themes for the Second Review Conference' (Nigeria, 2012c). To some extent, the document looked backwards in that it 'noted' specific examples of progress in PoA and ITI implementation that states had cited at the PrepCom. Yet, in its enumeration of suggested Review Conference themes, which were largely priorities for work after the Conference, it also looked to the future. Overall, however, the focus was not on introducing new issues to the existing PoA–ITI framework, but rather on strengthening implementation of this framework.

On the final day of the PrepCom, states could not agree whether to annex the Chair's Summary to the formal (procedural) report of the meeting. Instead, the Summary was issued as a 'conference room paper'—officially, one input, among others, to the Review Conference, 'prepared under [the chair's] own responsibility' (UNGA, 2012b, para. 10). Nevertheless, almost all states that spoke on the issue at the end of the PrepCom said they considered the Chair's Summary a good basis for the upcoming Review Conference discussions. In practice, the document was to provide a rough template of the Conference outcome structure, as well as much of the raw material that would fill that structure.

From PrepCom to RevCon

Early in her consultations, and again at the PrepCom, Ambassador Ogwu indicated she wished to use the period between the March PrepCom and the August–September Review Conference to prepare and discuss a draft outcome document of the Conference; the Review Conference would largely concern itself with negotiations on the draft (Nigeria, 2011c; 2012a).[17] On 6 June, as an annexe to a letter she addressed to UN member states, Ambassador Ogwu distributed a set of 'zero drafts' of the Review Conference outcome, comprising:

- a '2012 Declaration';
- an implementation plan for the PoA;
- an implementation plan for the ITI; and
- a schedule of meetings covering the 2012–18 period (Nigeria, 2012d; UNGA, 2012c).

The zero drafts sought to translate the PrepCom discussions into draft outcome form (Nigeria, 2012d). They included many of the points contained in the Chair's Summary that Ambassador Ogwu produced at the end of the PrepCom and used the PrepCom meeting structure. The implementation plan for the PoA contained four separate sections covering implementation at the national, regional, and global levels, plus international cooperation and assistance. While tackling the question of what meetings to convene during the 2012–18 cycle, the separate schedule of meetings document also included other points relating to PoA and ITI follow-up.

The zero drafts were discussed at informal consultations that Ambassador Ogwu convened at the UN's New York headquarters on 14 and 29 June 2012. Thereafter, the main work of developing the draft outcome shifted to the four facilitators she had appointed:

- Claire Elias (Australia) for the 2012 Declaration;
- Amr Aljowaily (Egypt) for the ITI implementation plan;[18]
- Bibi Sheliza Ally (Guyana) for the PoA implementation plan; and
- Tomoaki Ishigaki (Japan) for the schedule of meetings.

As the Conference on the Arms Trade Treaty occupied UN arms control diplomats for almost all of July, the facilitators conducted most of their consultations on the zero drafts in August, releasing a new set of draft outcome documents the week before the Review Conference (UNGA, 2012e).[19] The 21 August drafts retained the structure and much of the content of the zero drafts. In an effort to address competing national proposals, however, some parts of the new text were unclear[20] or went so far as to dilute existing PoA or ITI commitments.[21] That conjured up the ghost of the First Review Conference, which at times had seemed determined to call the existing normative framework into question.[22] The challenge for the Second Review Conference, then, building on the 21 August drafts, was to find ways of adding value to—not subtracting it from—existing PoA and ITI norms, while staying within the bounds of the politically feasible.

States had nine days to negotiate the Review Conference outcome.

THE SECOND REVIEW CONFERENCE

The PoA's Second Review Conference was convened at UN headquarters in New York from 27 August to 7 September 2012. With a UN holiday on 3 September removing one working day from the schedule, states had nine days to negotiate the Conference outcome. As described above, the UN membership had made a reasonably good start on this task, with Ambassador Ogwu preparing an initial draft of the Review Conference texts after the PrepCom and following up in August with revised versions that took account of the facilitators' pre-Conference consultations. Success was not guaranteed, however. Formally, no part of the draft outcome was, or would be, agreed by the UN membership until the last day of the meeting;[23] meanwhile, important challenges remained—not least, the fact that certain parts of the 21 August drafts weakened existing PoA–ITI norms.

At the first session of the Review Conference, Ambassador Ogwu reiterated the need to make optimal use of the limited time available. She encouraged states to utilize the 'general exchange of views' segment of the Conference to indicate the kind of Review Conference outcome they sought, using their national reports to convey information on implementation (UNGA, 2012g).[24] In the event, the Review Conference breezed through the initial 11 points of its agenda at its first meeting on 27 August. These involved organizational matters, such as the election of Ambassador Ogwu as Conference president, as well as the—sometimes more contentious—adoption of the Conference agenda and rules

The representative of Australia addresses delegates at the Second Review Conference, New York, August 2012. © UN Multimedia

of procedure (UNGA, 2012g; 2012f). Most of the first meeting was, in fact, devoted to item 12 of the agenda, the 'general exchange of views'.

Agenda item 12 was largely wrapped up by the second day of the Conference, with statements by intergovernmental organizations and NGOs taking up part of the second and third days.[25] This was in stark contrast to the PoA's First Review Conference, during which statements by all groups, but especially states, took up almost the entire first week.[26] Equally important, during the opening phase of the Second Review Conference, most countries followed Ambassador Ogwu's suggestion and set out their objectives for the Conference outcome; only exceptionally did their statements focus on past implementation.

On the morning of the third day of the Conference, 29 August, attention shifted to the 21 August drafts (UNGA, 2012e). Starting with the PoA implementation plan, states reviewed these texts, usually paragraph by paragraph, making specific comments and requests for amendments. Beginning on Friday, 31 August, plenary meetings were supplemented by informal meetings; open to all states, these were convened during lunchtime or in the evening in smaller rooms and without UN language interpretation. By the end of the first week, the Review Conference had completed one or more readings of each draft outcome document, with the exception of the 2012 Declaration.

On Tuesday morning, 4 September, the start of the Conference's second week, the president issued revised versions of the PoA and ITI implementation plans, and of the 'follow-up' section,[27] all of which took account of the discussions held in week one (UNGA,

2012h). On 4–5 September, states considered the 2012 Declaration and the three other documents in plenary and informal meetings, which were frequently chaired by the four facilitators.[28] On Thursday morning, 6 September, the second-to-last day of the Conference, Ambassador Ogwu issued a new set of outcome documents, comprising an 'Annex 1', with revised versions of the 2012 Declaration, the PoA implementation plan, and the follow-up section, and an 'Annex 2' incorporating the revised ITI implementation plan (UNGA, 2012i). In consolidating the four outcome texts into two, the President sought to balance the demands of some states for a single outcome document and of others for the initial four-document structure.

States considered the two-annexe text—as a whole—in a plenary meeting on Thursday morning. While many states said they could accept the document as it stood, others raised objections to certain parts of the text. By this time, although issues that had prompted much debate at the Conference, such as ammunition, border controls, gender, and conflict tracing, had been settled, other sticking points remained. These included: language on international transfer controls, in particular UN arms embargoes (PoA implementation plan); the topics of future UN small arms meetings (follow-up section); and a possible study on the implications for ITI implementation of recent developments in small arms manufacturing, technology, and design (ITI implementation plan). On Thursday afternoon and evening, the facilitators chaired successive, informal meetings that attempted to resolve these and other outstanding issues.

UN member states broke the spell that had doomed the 2006 Conference.

The disagreement on arms embargoes saw the European Union pushing for clear references to such measures in the Conference outcome and Iran and North Korea strongly resisting the same. The dispute was settled by replacing a provision that repeated PoA language on embargoes with general reaffirmations of PoA undertakings, including those on arms embargoes, at the national and global levels.[29] Language fixes were also found for the provisions on future meeting topics[30] and the ITI technical study.[31]

These and other revisions were incorporated in new versions of the two outcome documents that the president issued on the morning of the last day of the Conference, Friday, 7 September (UNGA, 2012j). Final amendments to the Declaration and to transfer controls language in the PoA implementation plan were required before the Conference outcome documents could be adopted, by consensus, on Friday afternoon (UNGA, 2012l; 2012m), as annexes to the formal Conference report (UNGA, 2012k).

UN member states had broken the spell that had doomed the First Review Conference, but what was gained—or lost—as a result? The next sections consider the specific achievements, and some of the missed opportunities, of the Second Review Conference in terms of process, as well as substance.

PROGRESS MADE: PROCESS

At both the beginning and the end of the Second Review Conference, states noted its importance to the broader UN arms control agenda.[32] Discussions on an Arms Trade Treaty had stalled.[33] After more than a decade, the Conference on Disarmament in Geneva remained at an impasse. Not only did the Review Conference result set a positive precedent for the PoA's Third Review Conference, but it also demonstrated that the UN's 193 member states could still reach agreement on arms and security matters. Some of the structural reasons for this outcome are mentioned above; this section recaps these points and calls attention to several others that, together, contributed to the relatively positive Review Conference result.

Overall, the Review Conference, including its preparatory phase, was characterized by incremental, visible progress towards a final (consensual) outcome. At an early stage, Ambassador Ogwu was nominated as the chair-designate of the Review Conference and its PrepCom. Her initial consultations allowed for the timely development of the key parameters of the Review Conference process. Prominent among these was the optimal use of scarce meeting time at both the PrepCom and the Review Conference. PrepCom discussions were substantive in nature, allowing Ambassador Ogwu to identify a list of 'elements' for the Conference and, in early June, table a set of 'zero drafts' that served as the basis for subsequent, focused discussions on, and revisions to, Conference outcome text (Nigeria, 2012c; UNGA, 2012c).

The pre-Conference drafts presented, at least implicitly, the solution to the problem of the Review Conference's ambiguous—and, to some extent, impracticable—mandate 'to review progress made in the implementation of the Programme of Action' (UNGA, 2001, para. IV.1.a). These documents acknowledged, in general terms, the efforts states had undertaken to give practical effect to the PoA and ITI. Fundamentally, however, they were forward-looking in nature, identifying measures to strengthen implementation in various areas during the period leading to the Third Review Conference in 2018.

By and large, the process was inclusive, transparent, and structured. At the Conference itself, the president, with the assistance of the facilitators, produced four new versions of the Review Conference outcome. Language was sharpened. Text that weakened existing PoA and ITI norms was brought into conformity with those instruments. Issues that, for some, went beyond the text of the PoA and ITI were subjected to caveats (such as 'when appropriate'), yet since these provisions typically sought to enable action, not compel it, they largely retained their value. Many issues, though important to some states, were left by the wayside in the drive towards consensus. Successive drafts of the Review Conference outcome retained only those points and language formulations that were broadly acceptable to all other states—mostly as discussed during meetings attended by all states, but sometimes as elaborated by smaller groups of states with an interest in the relevant issue. Even in the latter case, however, the Conference president and the facilitators identified such groups and invited interested countries to join their discussions.

By and large, the Review Conference process was inclusive, transparent, and structured. As noted above, UN member states took on board many elements of the working method that had initially been applied at BMS3 and that had helped put the UN small arms process back on track after the First Review Conference. Yet they also avoided several other hazards that had contributed to the failure of the 2006 Conference. Among them, perhaps the most important was the resolution of the uncertainty surrounding the Review Conference mandate at an early stage. By the time the Conference started, states seemed comfortable with an outcome document that, while forward-looking, was rooted squarely in the implementation of existing PoA and ITI norms.

Ambassador Ogwu also maintained control of the process, for example by avoiding the use of rolling text (the submission of a draft to line-by-line amendment), something that had gobbled up scarce time at the First Review Conference. Last, but not least, there was a spirit of compromise at the Second Review Conference that had been largely absent at its 2006 predecessor. Positions that met serious opposition were usually sacrificed in favour of commonly acceptable language. Overall there were fewer 'red lines' at play at the Second Review Conference than in 2006. When states reached an apparent impasse, for example on the issue of arms embargoes, compromises were promptly found. The Second Review Conference also saw states focusing largely on substance—rather than on the kinds of political considerations that had bedevilled the First Review Conference.[34] At the end of the day, this is arguably the key test of any multilateral process—whether it enables consideration of, and action on, the substantive matters at hand.

PROGRESS MADE: SUBSTANCE

The Review Conference outcome comprises two documents. The first—the PoA outcome—focuses on the Programme of Action but also includes provisions that apply to the ITI, such as those relating to international cooperation and assistance or to future UN meetings. The second document focuses exclusively on the ITI. The next sections analyse the contents of these documents, beginning with the three sections of the PoA outcome.

The 2012 Declaration

The 2012 Declaration (UNGA, 2012l, s. I) acts as the springboard for the other components of the Review Conference outcome. With greater specificity than anywhere else in the outcome, it notes several areas where 'progress [. . .] has been made in implementing' the PoA and ITI (paras. I.7–8). At the same time, however, the Declaration emphasizes 'that implementation remains uneven', while illicit small arms continue to threaten individuals and societies around the world (paras. I.4–5, I.9). As a result, states 'reaffirm [their] support and commitment to implement all the provisions' of the PoA and ITI, both by following up on previous PoA meetings and through 'the further strengthening and development of norms and measures at the national, regional and global levels' (paras. I.1, I.10–11). The core objective of the Declaration, and of the Review Conference outcome, is 'to achieve clear and tangible results over the next six years that will improve the security, safety and livelihoods of our people' (para. I.18).[35] Fundamentally, then, the Declaration, like the Review Conference outcome as a whole, looks to the future.[36]

> The PoA implementation plan highlights opportunities for enhanced application of the PoA framework.

In addition to providing the above 'mission statement', the 2012 Declaration introduces many of the issues that, as developed in other parts of the Conference outcome, constitute its substantive added value. Reflecting the conclusions of small arms research, the Declaration highlights 'the different concerns and needs' of those affected by illicit small arms, defining such groups by gender, age, and the presence of a disability (para. I.14). The Declaration fills a gap in the PoA by making specific reference to 'international human rights law' (para. I.4).[37] The same paragraph, concerning the effects of illicit small arms, also mentions 'certain natural resources' in place of the PoA's more restrictive reference to 'precious minerals' (UNGA, 2012l, paras. I.4, I.17; 2001, preamble, para. 7). Further, the 2012 Declaration acknowledges the 'close links' between the illicit small arms trade and armed violence (UNGA, 2012l, para. I.17);[38] it also foreshadows text in the PoA implementation plan concerning, for example, national action plans, border controls, and international cooperation and assistance (paras. I.7, I.9, I.12–13).

The PoA implementation plan

The PoA implementation plan (UNGA, 2012l, s. II) recaps existing PoA language in some areas,[39] but in several others it elaborates on basic PoA norms in order to take account of past implementation experience and highlight opportunities for the enhanced application of the PoA framework. For example, the provision on national points of contact with its commitment 'to share and update this information regularly' responds, at some level, to independent reports that such information is frequently out of date (UNGA, 2012l, para. II.2.d; Parker, 2011, pp. 22–27). Similarly, the plan notes the importance of involving arms transfer licensing authorities, among other actors, in intra-governmental coordination on small arms issues (UNGA, 2012l, para. II.2.c).[40]

In comparison with the PoA, the implementation plan puts more emphasis on 'the participation and representation of women in small arms policymaking' (para. II.2.i).[41] This language, however, represents only a small step forward for a large number of countries that had pushed for broader references to 'gender'. Further added value can be found in the document's encouragement 'to develop and implement national action plans' (para. II.2.l), which some states have

An officer of the Indian Border Security Force speaks to journalists at the India-Pakistan border where heroin, fake currency, and weapons were allegedly seized, Thatha Koda, India, January 2009. © Altaf Qadri/AP Photo

used to coordinate their PoA implementation even though the instrument is silent on such plans. Significantly, Review Conference language on border controls is not limited to 'information-sharing' (UNGA, 2001, para. II. 27), but includes the concepts of 'cooperation [and] coordination' (UNGA, 2012l, para. II. 3.e).[42] The implementation plan also stresses enhanced 'synergies between the Programme of Action and relevant subregional and regional instruments' (para. II.3.b), one example of the greater attention the Review Conference outcome pays to the relationship between the PoA and other initiatives.[43] In addition, the plan highlights the potential role of industry in tackling the illicit small arms trade (para. II.4.e),[44] an important feature of the 2011 MGE discussions.[45]

The Review Conference commitments on international cooperation and assistance, contained in the PoA implementation plan and applicable to both the PoA and the ITI,[46] are generally quite strong. For example, PoA language calling upon states to 'seriously consider rendering assistance' reads, in the implementation plan, as an undertaking '[t]o render' such assistance—provided, as both texts specify, states are 'in a position to do so' (UNGA, 2001, para. III.3; 2012l, para. II.5.b).[47] The other salient feature of the section is its incorporation of concepts, discussed at BMS3 and BMS4 and reflected in their outcome documents, including 'the identification, prioritization and communication of [. . .] assistance needs' (para. II.5.c); 'matching needs and resources' (para. II.5.h); increasing the 'measurability and effectiveness of international cooperation and assistance' (para. II.5.d);[48] and 'ensuring the sustainability of assistance' (para. II.5.e).[49]

The PoA implementation plan also encourages the building of national capacity 'to monitor and analyze the consequences' of small arms proliferation and misuse (para. II.5.c). This provision focuses on the impacts of illicit small arms, presumably measured as physical, social, and economic costs. Yet, read in conjunction with references to armed violence elsewhere in the PoA outcome,[50] it also suggests a possible link to the Geneva Declaration process and its 'measurability' pillar.[51] Looking past immediate impacts to longer-term trends and their causes, the language of paragraph II.5.c also raises the question of whether the PoA and ITI have been effective in curbing small arms proliferation and misuse.

The follow-up section

At the Review Conference, the main subject of debate in relation to follow-up was the number and character of meetings that were to be convened during the 2012–18 cycle. States generally argued against convening too many meetings, but also expressed a strong preference for further MGEs. Nevertheless, there was no consensus to replace one or more BMSs with one or more MGEs. The follow-up section of the PoA outcome (UNGA, 2012l, s. III) therefore *adds* an MGE to the cycle, in 2015, while, as before, scheduling two BMSs in advance of the next Review Conference, in 2014 and 2016 (para. III.1). It schedules the PoA's Third Review Conference for 2018, at the end of the next six-year cycle, and elects to follow the practice of the Second (not First) Review Conference in opting for a one-week (not two-week) PrepCom (para. III.2). While states did not agree to identify the topics of any of these meetings in advance—with the exception of international cooperation and assistance, which will continue to feature in all meetings (para. III.3)—a reference to 'physical security measures' (para. III.4) reflects the preference many states expressed for discussing stockpile management, specifically at a future MGE.

The follow-up section recalls the BMS4 'recommendation to clearly define and distinguish the mandates of Programme of Action meetings' (s. III, preamble, para. 3), but offers only select hints as to what this means in practice. By mentioning the need to consider the 'political and technical aspects' of PoA meeting topics and by noting the importance of ensuring 'to the extent possible, the participation of appropriate experts/officials from States' (para. III.4), the UN membership appears to be moving towards a clearer distinction between political, diplomat-led BMSs and technical, expert-driven MGEs, but it has yet to express this clearly.

Other parameters of PoA follow-up, many of which were first articulated in the BMS4 outcome, are nailed down with greater precision. These include:

* linking and ensuring 'the complementarity of, meeting mandates and outcomes' (s. III, preamble, para. 3);[52]
* identifying the topics of PoA and ITI meetings well in advance (para. III.4);[53]
* designating meeting chairs early, if possible one year in advance of the meeting (para. III.5);[54]

- synchronizing national implementation reports with BMSs and review conferences (biennial reporting) (para. III.9);[55] and

- providing financial assistance 'to enable States that are otherwise unable to do so to participate in' PoA meetings (para. III.10).[56]

The PoA implementation plan also encourages the use of a template for national reports prepared by the UN Office for Disarmament Affairs (para. II.2.k).[57] Finally, building on discussions at BMS3,[58] the follow-up section devotes some space to the question of enhanced linkages between the global (PoA) and regional levels, including the possible alignment of regional small arms meeting schedules with their global counterparts (paras. III.6–7).

The ITI implementation plan

The ITI outcome, which takes the form of an 'Implementation Plan 2012–2018', provides important diplomatic fuel for the UN tracing process (UNGA, 2012m). The BMS3 and BMS4 outcomes regarding the ITI added little to the existing framework, their normative elements consisting largely of reminders to states to follow up on their ITI commitments.[59] As the 2011 MGE dealt with the nuts and bolts of ITI implementation in far greater depth, the 2012 ITI outcome takes its lead from the MGE in articulating specific implementation measures. These include:

- strengthening measures against efforts by traffickers to remove or alter weapons markings (para. 2.a);
- training relevant personnel for weapons identification and record-keeping (para. 2.b);
- strengthening coordination between government agencies to facilitate timely responses to tracing requests (para. 2.c); and
- exchanging tracing results, both within government and with other states, to help prevent diversion (para. 2.d).

A police officer handles a weapon marked as belonging to the armed forces of Venezuela, seized from a gang allegedly involved in drug trafficking, Medellin, Colombia, September 2008. © Luis Benavides/AP Photo

At the Review Conference, there was no agreement on a proposal, made at the MGE, to establish a technical committee composed of government and industry representatives for the purposes of drafting recommendations for ITI implementation in light of new developments in weapons manufacture and design.[60] Instead of establishing such a committee, the ITI outcome requests that the UN Secretary-General report on such questions, 'drawing on views of States' (para. 3.g)—although presumably not limited to them, given the need for industry inputs on such matters.

The ITI outcome contains its fair share of reminders regarding the fulfilment of basic ITI commitments, such as ensuring that the laws, regulations, and administrative procedures needed to support ITI implementation are in place (para. 3.a)[61] and sharing information on national marking practices (para. 3.e).[62] Regarding the designation of national point(s) of contact, the ITI outcome goes so far as to set a (modest) deadline for this task, namely the Third Review Conference (para. 2.f).[63]

In addition, the ITI outcome adds flesh to the bones of the Tracing Instrument's brief mention of its application to 'conflict situations' (UNGA, 2005, preamble, para. 2). Under paragraph 2.e of the document, UN member states undertake to 'cooperate, when appropriate [with UN] bodies, organs and missions', as well as regional organizations, in tracing small arms and light weapons in accordance with ITI rules. The Review Conference discussions on this provision related mainly to multilateral peace operations deployed in conflict or post-conflict settings, but the agreed language would also bring UN political missions, tribunals, and sanctions monitoring groups within its scope.

CONCLUSION

The Second Review Conference marks an important step forward in the UN small arms process. Avoiding many of the problems that plagued the First Review Conference, UN member states reached consensus agreement on a substantive outcome, committing themselves to a series of measures designed to bolster implementation of the PoA and ITI during the period up to 2018. While some of these measures simply repeat PoA or ITI text, many of them, drawing on earlier meeting discussions, fill out the existing framework. The Review Conference outcome also consolidates recent moves towards a more structured process, sketching out the broad outlines of the 2012–18 meeting cycle.

Despite these gains, important gaps remain. First, although the UN small arms process is more structured than before, states have not really heeded the BMS4 recommendation 'to clearly define and distinguish the mandates of Programme of Action meetings' (UNGA, 2010a, para. 34; 2012l, s. III, preamble, para. 3). Crucially, it remains impossible to say much about 'progress made' in the implementation of the PoA and ITI in the absence of mechanisms that independently assess the extent to which states are meeting their commitments under these instruments. The Review Conference outcome does point to the possible consideration of longer-term trends in small arms proliferation and misuse, along with the question of PoA and ITI effectiveness (UNGA, 2012l, para. II.5.c), but this chapter of the PoA story has yet to be written.

Implementation aside, there is still room for normative development. Among the many issues that states tried, and failed, to include in the Review Conference outcome—often because of the opposition of a small number of states[64]—the exclusion of the word 'ammunition' from the final texts is perhaps the most puzzling omission. Neither excluded from, nor included in, the PoA, given the latter's failure to define 'small arms and light weapons', ammunition remains in some kind of political limbo, notwithstanding its pivotal role in fuelling crime and conflict around the world. Such omissions will not, however, decide the legacy of the Second Review Conference. The Conference outcome, despite its gaps, remains an important diplomatic achievement. Language on border controls, women (though not 'gender'), and conflict tracing, although contentious at past UN meetings, found expression in the final outcome. Moreover, despite the apparent preference of a few states for a weaker PoA and ITI, there was no dilution of existing norms.

With or without an Arms Trade Treaty, the PoA will remain the only comprehensive global framework for small arms control, covering almost all stages of the small arms life cycle from cradle (manufacture) to grave (final disposal). 'Control' is more difficult than prohibition. The long life span and complex ownership chains of many small arms make the task harder. Yet, building on preceding UN meetings and taken together with the PoA and ITI themselves, the Second Review Conference offers an extensive road map for meeting these challenges.

What is essential, obviously, is not simply to have the map, but to use it to move forward. Given the UN membership's continuing reluctance to countenance formal monitoring of 'progress made' in PoA and ITI implementation, the depth and breadth of commitment to these instruments remains unclear. As they indicated quite clearly at the Second Review Conference, a small number of states view UN small arms norms with considerable suspicion. Yet, at the end of the day, it was the determination of the vast majority of states to wrest something useful from the Conference that proved decisive. While a future embracing 'the full and effective implementation' of the PoA and ITI[65] remains to be written, for the moment the UN small arms process has a spring in its step. ■

LIST OF ABBREVIATIONS

BMS	Biennial Meeting of States to Consider the Implementation of the Programme of Action to Prevent, Combat and Eradicate the Illicit Trade in Small Arms and Light Weapons in All Its Aspects
ITI	International Instrument to Enable States to Identify and Trace, in a Timely and Reliable Manner, Illicit Small Arms and Light Weapons
MGE	Open-ended Meeting of Governmental Experts
PoA	Programme of Action to Prevent, Combat and Eradicate the Illicit Trade in Small Arms and Light Weapons in All Its Aspects
PrepCom	Preparatory Committee
RevCon	United Nations Conference to Review Progress Made in the Implementation of the Programme of Action to Prevent, Combat and Eradicate the Illicit Trade in Small Arms and Light Weapons in All Its Aspects

ENDNOTES

1   Full name: Programme of Action to Prevent, Combat and Eradicate the Illicit Trade in Small Arms and Light Weapons in All Its Aspects. See UNGA (2001).

2   That mandate is set out in UNGA (2001, para. IV.1.a).

3   Full name: International Instrument to Enable States to Identify and Trace, in a Timely and Reliable Manner, Illicit Small Arms and Light Weapons. See UNGA (2005).

4   See McDonald (2007, pp. 118–21).

5   The subjects were: international cooperation and assistance; illicit brokering; stockpile management and surplus disposal; border controls; and PoA follow-up. Each outcome included a separate section on the International Tracing Instrument. See UNGA (2008a; 2010a).

6   See also McDonald (2012).

7   See also UNGA (2010a, para. 36).

8   See, for example, UNGA (2008b, para. 14).

9   See Čekuolis (2008, p. 23).

10 This was also the deadline suggested by the UN General Assembly. See UNGA (2010b, para. 19).

11 In advance of the March 2012 session of the PrepCom, Ambassador Ogwu held six informal consultations at UN headquarters in New York, one set of consultations in Geneva, and several consultations at the regional level.

12 Regarding both components, see Čekuolis (2008, p. 23).

13 See McDonald (2007, pp. 118, 120).

14 Unpublished remarks made at the PrepCom, United Nations headquarters, New York, 19 March 2012.

15 The PrepCom topics were: national, regional, and global-level implementation of the PoA (topics 1–3), implementation, international coopera-tion, and assistance (topic 4), PoA follow-up (topic 5), and all aspects of the ITI (topic 6). See UNGA (2012a).

16 Unpublished remarks made at the PrepCom, United Nations headquarters, New York, 22 March 2012.

17 Unpublished remarks made at the PrepCom, United Nations headquarters, New York, 21 and 23 March 2012. See also UNGA (2012b, s. V, Decision I).

18 To acknowledge the distinct nature of the PoA and ITI processes, Amr Aljowaily was also appointed ITI 'moderator', continuing a practice that had started at BMS3.

19 Ambassador Ogwu initially issued the revised draft outcomes as an attachment to her letter of 21 August 2012 (Nigeria, 2012e). In addition to their publication as UN document L.4/Rev.1 (UNGA, 2012e), the same drafts were released as a Review Conference 'conference room paper' (UN doc. A/CONF.192/2012/RC/CRP.2).

20 See, for example, UNGA (2012e, annexe II, paras. 2.e, 3.d).

21 For example, the provision on ITI reporting, by associating mandatory ITI reporting with voluntary PoA reporting, appeared to nullify the firm commitment to report under the ITI (UNGA, 2012e, annexe III, para. 3.g; 2005, para. 36; 2001, para. II.33).

22 See McDonald (2007, p. 119).

23 In the language of diplomacy, 'nothing is agreed, until everything is agreed'.

24 Unpublished remarks made at the Review Conference, United Nations headquarters, New York, 27 August 2012.

25 For a list of the interventions made by states, intergovernmental organizations, and NGOs, see UNGA (2012k, paras. 12–14). Many of the statements are posted on UN (n.d.).

26 See McDonald (2007, p. 120).

27 The same section had earlier been called 'Schedule of meetings, 2012–2018' (UNGA, 2012e).

28 States reviewed the L.4/Rev.1 version of the Declaration and the CRP.3 versions of the other documents.

29 See UNGA (2012i, annexe 1, para. II.17; 2012l, paras. II.2.a, II.4.a).

30 Compare UNGA (2012i, annexe 1, para. III.4) with UNGA (2012l, para. III.4).

31 Compare UNGA (2012i, annexe 2, para. 11) with UNGA (2012m, para. 3.g).

32 See, for example, CARICOM (2012, p. 5).

33 States failed to reach agreement on a treaty at a July 2012 conference but subsequently elected to hold an additional negotiating conference in March 2013 (UNGA, 2012n).

34 See McDonald (2007, pp. 118–21).

35 See also paras. I.2–3, I.6, I.9.

36 See UNGA (2012l, paras. I.1, II.1; 2012m, para. 1).

37 The PoA makes no reference to 'human rights' (UNGA, 2001).

38 See also UNGA (2012l, paras. I.4, I.10); Geneva Declaration (2006).

39 Examples include provisions relating to stockpile management and international transfer control. See UNGA (2012l, paras. II.2.e–f, II.2.h).

40 See also para. I.13.

41 See also para. I.14.

42 See also para. II.2.c.

43 Concerning related UN General Assembly initiatives, see para. I.10.

44 See also para. I.15.

45 See New Zealand (2011).

46 The ITI outcome includes relatively strong ITI-specific provisions on international cooperation and assistance. See UNGA (2012m, paras. 3.b–d).

47 The Declaration also calls for enhanced international cooperation and assistance. See UNGA (2012l, paras. I.9, I.13).

48 See also para. I.13.

49 Regarding all these points, see UNGA (2008a, s. I; 2010a, s. II).

50 See UNGA (2012l, paras. I.4, I.10, I.17).

51 See Geneva Declaration (2006); Geneva Declaration Secretariat (n.d.).

52 See UNGA (2010a, para. 34).

53 See UNGA (2010a, para. 34).

54 See UNGA (2010a, paras. 34, 45).

55 See UNGA (2010a, paras. 35, 38).

56 This is also mentioned in para. II.5.g. See also UNGA (2010a, paras. 37, 43).

57 See UNGA (2010a, paras. 35, 41).

58 See UNGA (2008a, paras. 6, 7.n, 29.c).

59 See, for example, UNGA (2008a, annexe, para. 9.b; 2010a, annexe, para. 10.c).

60 See New Zealand (2011, p. 4).

61 See UNGA (2005, para. 24).

62 See UNGA (2005, para. 31).

63 See UNGA (2005, paras. 25, 31).

64 See RCW et al. (2012).

65 This is the basic goal formulated by both the PoA and ITI outcomes (UNGA, 2012l, para. II.1; 2012m, para. 1).

BIBLIOGRAPHY

CARICOM (Caribbean Community). 2012. 'Republic of Guyana Statement on Behalf of the Caribbean Community (CARICOM) by H.E. Mr. George Talbot, Permanent Representative.' 27 August.
<http://www.poa-iss.org/RevCon2/statements/20120828Statements/20120828Guyana%20(OBO%20CARICOM)-E.pdf>

Čekuolis, Dalius. 2008. 'Tackling the Illicit Small Arms Trade: The Chairman Speaks.' *Arms Control Today*, Vol. 38, No. 8. October, pp. 19–24.
<http://www.armscontrol.org/act/2008_10/Cekuolis>

Geneva Declaration (Geneva Declaration on Armed Violence and Development). 2006. Geneva, 7 June.
<http://www.genevadeclaration.org/the-geneva-declaration/what-is-the-declaration.html>

Geneva Declaration Secretariat. n.d. 'Measurability.' Accessed 4 February 2013. <http://www.genevadeclaration.org/measurability.html>

McDonald, Glenn. 2007. 'Back to Basics: Transfer Controls in Global Perspective.' In Small Arms Survey. *Small Arms Survey 2007: Guns and the City.* Cambridge: Cambridge University Press, ch. 4.
<http://www.smallarmssurvey.org/fileadmin/docs/A-Yearbook/2007/en/full/Small-Arms-Survey-2007-Chapter-04-EN.pdf>

—. 2012. *Precedent in the Making: The UN Meeting of Governmental Experts.* Small Arms Survey Issue Brief No. 5. Geneva: Small Arms Survey. March.
<http://www.smallarmssurvey.org/fileadmin/docs/G-Issue-briefs/SAS-IB5-Precedent-in-the-making.pdf>

New Zealand. 2011. *Summary by the Chair of Discussions at the Open-ended Meeting of Governmental Experts on the Implementation of the Programme of Action to Prevent, Combat and Eradicate the Illicit Trade in Small Arms and Light Weapons in All Its Aspects, 9 to 13 May 2011, New York.* A/66/157 of 19 July (Annexe). <http://www.poa-iss.org/mge/Documents/MGE-ChairLetter/A-66-157-MGE-E.pdf>

Nigeria. 2011a. Letter dated 30 November from U. Joy Ogwu, Permanent Representative of Nigeria to the United Nations.
<http://www.poa-iss.org/RevCon2/Documents/RevCon-ChairLetters/Letter1-30Nov2011.pdf>

—. 2011b. Letter dated 15 December from U. Joy Ogwu, Permanent Representative of Nigeria to the United Nations.
<http://www.poa-iss.org/RevCon2/Documents/RevCon-ChairLetters/Letter2-15Dec2011.pdf>

—. 2011c. Letter dated 30 December from U. Joy Ogwu, Permanent Representative of Nigeria to the United Nations.
<http://www.poa-iss.org/RevCon2/Documents/RevCon-ChairLetters/Letter3-30Dec2011.pdf>

—. 2012a. Letter dated 24 January from U. Joy Ogwu, Permanent Representative of Nigeria to the United Nations.
<http://www.poa-iss.org/RevCon2/Documents/RevCon-ChairLetters/Letter4-24Jan2012.pdf>

—. 2012b. Letter dated 6 March from U. Joy Ogwu, Permanent Representative of Nigeria to the United Nations.
<http://www.poa-iss.org/RevCon2/Documents/RevCon-ChairLetters/Letter5-14March2012.pdf>

—. 2012c. *Chair's Summary: Elements for the Second Review Conference.* 23 March. A/CONF.192/2012/PC/CRP.13.
<http://www.poa-iss.org/RevCon2/Documents/PrepCom/Chair-summary-Elements-CRP13.pdf>

—. 2012d. Letter dated 6 June from U. Joy Ogwu, Permanent Representative of Nigeria to the United Nations.
<http://www.poa-iss.org/RevCon2/Documents/RevCon-ChairLetters/Letter6-6June2012.pdf>

—. 2012e. Letter dated 21 August from U. Joy Ogwu, Permanent Representative of Nigeria to the United Nations.
<http://www.poa-iss.org/RevCon2/home/Pres-d%20letter%20of%20transmittal.pdf>

Parker, Sarah. 2011. *Analysis of National Reports: Implementation of the UN Programme of Action on Small Arms and the International Tracing Instrument in 2009–10.* Occasional Paper No. 28. Geneva: Small Arms Survey.
<http://www.smallarmssurvey.org/fileadmin/docs/B-Occasional-papers/SAS-OP28-Analysis-of-National-Reports.pdf>

RCW (Reaching Critical Will) et al. 2012. *Small Arms Monitor*, Vol. 5, No. 10. 10 September.
<http://www.reachingcriticalwill.org/disarmament-fora/salw/2012revcon/sam>

UN (United Nations). n.d. 'Review Conference 2012: Statements.' <http://www.poa-iss.org/RevCon2/statements/>

UNGA (United Nations General Assembly). 2001. Programme of Action to Prevent, Combat and Eradicate the Illicit Trade in Small Arms and Light Weapons in All Its Aspects ('UN Programme of Action'). Adopted 21 July. A/CONF.192/15 of 20 July. <http://www.poa-iss.org/PoA/PoA.aspx>

—. 2005. International Instrument to Enable States to Identify and Trace, in a Timely and Reliable Manner, Illicit Small Arms and Light Weapons ('International Tracing Instrument'). Adopted 8 December. A/60/88 of 27 June (Annexe).
<http://www.poa-iss.org/InternationalTracing/InternationalTracing.aspx>

—. 2008a. Outcome of the Third Biennial Meeting of States to Consider the Implementation of the Programme of Action to Prevent, Combat and Eradicate the Illicit Trade in Small Arms and Light Weapons in All Its Aspects. Adopted 18 July. A/CONF.192/BMS/2008/3 of 20 August (s. IV).
<http://www.poa-iss.org/DocsUpcomingEvents/ENN0846796.pdf>

—. 2008b. Resolution 63/72, adopted 2 December. A/RES/63/72 of 12 January 2009.
<http://www.un.org/ga/search/view_doc.asp?symbol=A/RES/63/72&Lang=E>

—. 2010a. Outcome of the Fourth Biennial Meeting of States to Consider the Implementation of the Programme of Action to Prevent, Combat and Eradicate the Illicit Trade in Small Arms and Light Weapons in All Its Aspects. Adopted 18 June. A/CONF.192/BMS/2010/3 of 30 June (s. V).
<http://www.poa-iss.org/BMS4/Outcome/BMS4-Outcome-E.pdf>

—. 2010b. Resolution 65/64, adopted 8 December. A/RES/65/64 of 13 January 2011. <http://www.un.org/ga/search/view_doc.asp?symbol=A/RES/65/64>

—. 2011. Resolution 66/47, adopted 2 December. A/RES/66/47 of 12 January 2012.
<http://www.poa-iss.org/RevCon2/Documents/A-RES-66-47-Small-Arms/A.RES.66.47%20%28e%29.pdf>

—. 2012a. 'Draft Provisional Agenda.' Adopted 19 March. A/CONF.192/2012/PC/L.1 of 14 March.
<http://www.poa-iss.org/RevCon2/Documents/PrepCom/L1-ProvisionalAgenda/L1-ProvisionalAgenda-E.pdf>

—. 2012b. *Report of the Preparatory Committee for the United Nations Conference to Review Progress Made in the Implementation of the Programme of Action to Prevent, Combat and Eradicate the Illicit Trade in Small Arms and Light Weapons in All Its Aspects.* Adopted 23 March. A/CONF.192/2012/RC/1 of 27 March. <http://www.poa-iss.org/RevCon2/Documents/RevCon-DOC/A-Conf192-2012-RC-1-PCreport-E.pdf>

—. 2012c. *Draft Outcome Documents of the United Nations Conference to Review Progress Made in the Implementation of the Programme of Action to Prevent, Combat and Eradicate the Illicit Trade in Small Arms and Light Weapons in All Its Aspects.* 6 June. A/CONF.192/2012/RC/L.4 of 28 June.
<http://www.reachingcriticalwill.org/images/documents/Disarmament-fora/salw/2012revcon/documents/draft-outcome-L4.pdf>

—. 2012d. *Progress Made on the Implementation of the Programme of Action to Prevent, Combat and Eradicate the Illicit Trade in Small Arms and Light Weapons in All Its Aspects, 10 Years following Its Adoption: Report of the Secretary-General.* A/67/113 of 25 June.
<http://www.poa-iss.org/CASAUpload/ELibrary/A-67-113-E.pdf>

—. 2012e. *Draft Outcome Documents of the United Nations Conference to Review Progress Made in the Implementation of the Programme of Action to Prevent, Combat and Eradicate the Illicit Trade in Small Arms and Light Weapons in All Its Aspects.* 21 August. A/CONF.192/2012/RC/L.4/Rev.1 of 30 August. <http://www.reachingcriticalwill.org/images/documents/Disarmament-fora/salw/2012revcon/documents/draft-outcome-L4-rev1.pdf>

—. 2012f. 'Provisional Rules of Procedure of the Conference.' Adopted 27 August. A/CONF.192/2012/RC/L.2 of 14 August.

—. 2012g. 'Provisional Agenda.' Adopted 27 August. A/CONF.192/2012/RC/L.1 of 14 August.
<http://www.un.org/ga/search/view_doc.asp?symbol=A/CONF.192/2012/RC/L.1>

—. 2012h. Untitled (draft outcome documents). United Nations Conference to Review Progress Made in the Implementation of the Programme of Action to Prevent, Combat and Eradicate the Illicit Trade in Small Arms and Light Weapons in All Its Aspects. [4 September.] A/CONF.192/2012/RC/CRP.3.
<http://www.poa-iss.org/RevCon2/documents/>

—. 2012i. Untitled (draft outcome documents). United Nations Conference to Review Progress Made in the Implementation of the Programme of Action to Prevent, Combat and Eradicate the Illicit Trade in Small Arms and Light Weapons in All Its Aspects. [6 September.] A/CONF.192/2012/RC/CRP.3/Rev.1. <http://www.poa-iss.org/RevCon2/documents/Outcome/Draft-Outcome-CRP3-Rev1.pdf>

—. 2012j. Untitled (draft outcome documents). United Nations Conference to Review Progress Made in the Implementation of the Programme of Action to Prevent, Combat and Eradicate the Illicit Trade in Small Arms and Light Weapons in All Its Aspects. [7 September.] A/CONF.192/2012/RC/CRP.3/Rev.2. <http://www.poa-iss.org/RevCon2/Documents/RevCon-DOC/Rev1/Draft-Outcome-CRP3-Rev2.pdf>

—. 2012k. *Report of the United Nations Conference to Review Progress Made in the Implementation of the Programme of Action to Prevent, Combat and Eradicate the Illicit Trade in Small Arms and Light Weapons in All Its Aspects.* Adopted 7 September. A/CONF.192/2012/RC/4 of 18 September.
<http://www.poa-iss.org/RevCon2/Documents/RevCon-DOC/Outcome/PoA-RevCon2-Outcome-E.pdf>

—. 2012l. Outcome Document on the Programme of Action to Prevent, Combat and Eradicate the Illicit Trade in Small Arms and Light Weapons in All Its Aspects. Adopted 7 September. A/CONF.192/2012/RC/4 of 18 September (Annexe I).
<http://www.poa-iss.org/RevCon2/Documents/RevCon-DOC/Outcome/PoA-RevCon2-Outcome-E.pdf>

—. 2012m. Outcome Document on the International Instrument to Enable States to Trace, in a Timely and Reliable Manner, Illicit Small Arms and Light Weapons. Adopted 7 September. A/CONF.192/2012/RC/4 of 18 September (Annexe II).
<http://www.poa-iss.org/RevCon2/Documents/RevCon-DOC/Outcome/PoA-RevCon2-Outcome-E.pdf>

—. 2012n. Resolution 67/234, adopted 24 December. A/RES/67/234 of 4 January 2013. <http://www.un.org/ga/search/view_doc.asp?symbol=A/RES/67/234>

ACKNOWLEDGEMENTS

Principal author

Glenn McDonald

Metal handgun mouldings in a production line at the Zastava Arms factory, in Kragujevac, Serbia, June 2010. © Oliver Bunic/Bloomberg/Getty Images

Trade Update

AUTHORIZED SMALL ARMS TRANSFERS

8

INTRODUCTION

This chapter presents information on states with the largest aggregate values of authorized small arms exports and imports in 2010, as captured by the United Nations Commodity Trade Statistic Database (UN Comtrade), noting changes since the previous year's report covering 2009 activities. It also includes the latest edition of the Small Arms Trade Transparency Barometer—normally covering transfers conducted in 2011 and not limited to UN Comtrade data—designed to assess countries' transparency in reporting on their small arms exports.

The main findings of the chapter include:

- In 2010 the top exporters of small arms and light weapons (those with annual exports of at least USD 100 million), according to available customs data, were (in descending order) the United States, Germany, Italy, Brazil, Switzerland, Israel, Austria, the Russian Federation, South Korea, Sweden, Belgium, and Spain.

- In 2010 the top importers of small arms and light weapons (those with annual imports of at least USD 100 million), according to available customs data, were (in descending order) the United States, the United Kingdom, Canada, Germany, Australia, South Korea, France, and Thailand.

- The 2013 edition of the Barometer identifies Switzerland, Romania, and Serbia as the most transparent of the major exporters, and Iran, North Korea, Saudi Arabia, and the United Arab Emirates as the least transparent.

AUTHORIZED SMALL ARMS TRANSFERS: ANNUAL UPDATE

Since 2001, the Small Arms Survey has relied on state reporting to UN Comtrade to identify the largest exporting and importing states based on annual aggregate values of small arms transferred.[1] This year, the authorized transfers update presents data provided by states for transfer activities in 2010.[2]

In 2010, top exporters (exporting at least USD 100 million of small arms and light weapons annually) were, in descending order of export value, the United States, Germany, Italy, Brazil, Switzerland, Israel, Austria, the Russian Federation, South Korea, Sweden, Belgium, and Spain (see Table 8.1).[3] Compared to the previous year, the number of top exporting countries remained steady at 12, and major exporting countries declined slightly from 38 in 2009 to 35 in 2010.

Among the top exporting countries, the United States is consistently the largest, and it increased its exports from USD 706 million in 2009 to USD 821 million in 2010. Two countries joined the list of top exporters in 2010: Israel (whose exports climbed from USD 98 million in 2009 to USD 183 million in 2010) and Sweden (whose exports jumped from USD 38 million to USD 132 million). For the first time since 2001, Denmark was among the list of major exporters—

Table 8.1 Exporters of small arms based on UN Comtrade, 2010

Category		Value (USD)	Countries (listed in descending order of value exported)
Top exporters	Tier 1	≥500 million	1: United States
	Tier 2	100–499 million	11: Germany, Italy, Brazil, Switzerland, Israel, Austria, Russian Federation, South Korea, Sweden, Belgium, Spain
Major exporters	Tier 3	50–99 million	9: Turkey, Czech Republic, China, Japan, Canada, United Kingdom, Finland, Croatia, Taiwan
	Tier 4	10–49 million	14: Norway, France, Portugal, Mexico, Serbia, Singapore, Philippines, Argentina, India, Hungary, Cyprus, Australia, Romania, Denmark

Table 8.2 Importers of small arms based on UN Comtrade, 2010

Category		Value (USD)	Countries (listed in descending order of value imported)
Top importers	Tier 1	≥500 million	1: United States
	Tier 2	100–499 million	7: United Kingdom, Canada, Germany, Australia, South Korea, France, Thailand
Major importers	Tier 3	50–99 million	15: Colombia, Netherlands, Spain, Norway, Saudi Arabia, Singapore, Italy, Belgium, Russian Federation, Israel, Mexico, Estonia, Denmark, Switzerland, Indonesia
	Tier 4	10–49 million	33: Lebanon, Austria, Afghanistan, Malaysia, Portugal, Poland, Pakistan, Qatar, Peru, Sweden, Turkey, Philippines, Iraq, Japan, Venezuela, United Arab Emirates, Brazil, Kuwait, Finland, Czech Republic, Argentina, Jordan, New Zealand, Ukraine, Morocco, South Africa, Botswana, Greece, Cyprus, Chile, Ireland, Bulgaria, Slovakia

countries that export at least USD 10 million of small arms and light weapons annually—while Bosnia and Herzegovina, the Netherlands, and Poland were dropped from the list.

The top importers (importing at least USD 100 million of small arms and light weapons annually) in 2010 were, in descending order of import value, the United States, the United Kingdom, Canada, Germany, Australia, South Korea, France, and Thailand (see Table 8.2). Overall, the number of top importers increased slightly, from seven countries in 2009 to eight in 2010, while major importers increased from 47 to 48 over the same period. Two countries moved up from the major importers to the top importers category: Thailand (whose imports rose from USD 83 million in 2009 to USD 104 million in 2010) and South Korea (whose imports increased more than sevenfold, from USD 17 million to USD 130 million).

The aggregate value of exports by top and major exporters in 2010 decreased slightly, from USD 4.5 billion in 2009 to USD 4.4 billion. This is the first time that UN Comtrade has recorded a drop in small arms transfers since 2005. As reflected in the Transparency Barometer that follows, however, UN Comtrade covers only a portion of the authorized small arms trade.

THE 2013 TRANSPARENCY BAROMETER

This section presents the 2013 edition of the Small Arms Trade Transparency Barometer, designed to assess countries' transparency in reporting on their small arms and light weapons exports. The Barometer examines countries that claim—or that are believed—to have exported at least USD 10 million worth of small arms and light weapons, including their parts, accessories, and ammunition, during at least one calendar year between 2001 and 2011. The three main sources used to score state transparency in the Barometer are: (1) national arms export reports;[4] (2) the UN Register of Conventional Arms (UN Register); and (3) UN Comtrade (see Table 8.3 overleaf). The Barometer does not assess the veracity of the data states provide.

This year, delays in publishing national submissions to the UN Register for 2011 activities have affected the scoring of several states (see notes to Table 8.3). Once all submissions to the UN Register are published, a revised and authoritative 2013 Transparency Barometer will be posted online.[5]

The current edition of the Transparency Barometer assesses national transparency in small arms export activities in 2011, normally based on state reporting in 2012.[6] It reviews 55 countries' reporting practices: the 52 countries covered in the previous year's Barometer plus Colombia, Egypt, and Malawi, which are scored for the first time this year.

This year's Barometer identifies Switzerland, Romania, and Serbia as the three most transparent countries. Switzerland has led the ranking since the 2009 Barometer, while Serbia entered the top three for the first time.[7] Croatia broke into the top ten, advancing from 15th to 7th place, and Denmark moved down from 7th to 11th place. The least transparent countries are Iran, North Korea, Saudi Arabia, and the United Arab Emirates, all scoring zero points out of a possible 25.00 points. Compared to the last edition, the average score decreased by 5 per cent (0.57 points—from 11.22 to 10.65) while the average score of the top ten countries remained constant at 18.00 points.

Improvements in transparency were observed for 14 countries. Croatia experienced the greatest point increase, rising by 2.00 points due to the introduction of detailed information on licences refused in its national report. Poland increased its score by 1.50 points by providing information on brokering licences, both granted and refused, to the EU Annual Report on military exports. Finally, Serbia increased its score by 1.00 point because its national report featured more detailed information on entities registered for exports.

Country-specific declines were experienced by Montenegro (which dropped by 6.00 points), Bosnia and Herzegovina (4.75 points), Saudi Arabia (2.75 points), and Taiwan (1.75 points). Montenegro submitted data to the UN Register in 2012 for 2011 activities, its first time since 2007, but lost points because its contribution has not yet been published. Bosnia and Herzegovina lost points because it did not issue its national arms export report for two successive years; nor did it report to UN Comtrade.[8] Saudi Arabia did not report to any of the reporting instruments considered in this analysis; hence its score decreased to zero points. Finally, Taiwan reported to UN Comtrade, but on fewer categories than previously.[9]

Overall, the reporting practices reviewed show a high level of transparency for timeliness, with the vast majority of countries (91 per cent) providing information to at least one reporting tool. Transparency was poorer for the parameters of access and consistency, clarity, comprehensiveness, and deliveries—for which countries earned an average of 40–60 per cent of available points. Countries scored the lowest on information on licences granted and refused, with more than half scoring zero points in both parameters. The only tool for reporting on these parameters is a national arms export report. ■

Table 8.3 Small Arms Trade Transparency Barometer 2013, covering major exporters*

	Total (25.00 max)	Export report**/ EU Annual Report***	UN Comtrade	UN Register	Timeliness (1.50 max)	Access and consistency (2.00 max)	Clarity (5.00 max)	Comprehensiveness (6.50 max)	Deliveries (4.00 max)	Licences granted (4.00 max)	Licences refused (2.00 max)
Switzerland	20.75	X	X	X(10)^A	1.50	1.50	4.00	5.00	3.00	4.00	1.75
Romania	19.75	X/EU Report	–	X	1.50	2.00	2.75	4.50	3.50	3.50	2.00
Serbia[1]	19.75	X(10)	X	X(10)	1.50	1.50	3.75	5.00	3.50	2.50	2.00
Netherlands	19.25	X/EU Report	X	X	1.50	2.00	4.50	4.75	2.50	3.00	1.00
United Kingdom	19.25	X/EU Report	X	X	1.50	2.00	4.00	4.75	3.00	2.50	1.50
Germany[2]	18.25	X/EU Report	X	X	1.50	1.50	3.75	3.25	3.00	3.50	1.75
Croatia	16.75	X	X	X	1.50	1.00	3.25	3.50	3.00	3.00	1.50
Belgium	16.00	X/EU Report	X	X^A	1.50	2.00	3.00	2.50	2.50	2.50	2.00
Italy	16.00	X/EU Report	X	–	1.50	1.50	3.25	5.00	2.50	2.00	0.25
Spain	16.00	X/EU Report	X	–	1.50	2.00	2.50	3.50	3.50	1.50	1.50
Denmark	15.50	X/EU Report	X	X	1.50	1.50	4.25	3.25	2.50	1.50	1.00
Sweden	15.50	X/EU Report	X	X	1.50	2.00	4.00	4.00	2.50	1.50	0.00
Norway	15.00	X	X	X	1.50	1.50	3.75	3.00	3.00	2.00	0.25
United States[3]	15.00	X	X	X(10)^A	1.50	1.50	2.75	4.25	3.00	2.00	0.00
Czech Republic	14.75	X/EU Report	X	X	1.50	1.50	2.50	3.50	3.00	2.00	0.75
Austria[4]	14.25	X(10)/EU Report	X	X	1.50	1.50	2.25	3.75	3.00	2.00	0.25
Finland	14.25	X/EU Report	X	X	1.50	1.50	3.25	3.25	2.50	2.00	0.25
France	14.25	X/EU Report	X	X	1.50	1.50	4.00	3.00	2.50	1.50	0.25
Poland	14.25	X(10)/EU Report	X	X	1.50	1.00	2.25	3.75	3.00	1.50	1.25
Slovakia[5]	14.25	X/EU Report	X	X	1.50	1.50	2.50	3.75	2.50	2.00	0.50
Hungary	12.25	X/EU Report	X	X(10)^A	1.50	1.50	2.75	2.50	2.50	1.50	0.00
Bulgaria	12.00	X/EU Report	–	X	1.50	1.50	2.25	2.00	3.00	1.50	0.25
Canada	11.75	X(07–09)	X	X(10)	1.50	0.50	2.75	4.00	3.00	0.00	0.00
Greece	11.50	EU Report	X	X	1.50	0.50	2.00	3.25	3.00	1.00	0.25
Portugal	11.00	EU Report	X	X(10)^A	1.50	1.00	1.75	2.25	3.00	1.50	0.00
Australia	10.25	–	X	X	1.50	1.00	1.50	3.25	3.00	0.00	0.00
Luxembourg	10.25	EU Report	X	–	1.50	0.50	1.75	2.50	2.50	1.50	0.00
Lithuania	10.00	EU Report	X	X(10)^A	1.50	1.00	1.75	1.75	2.50	1.50	0.00

	Total (25.00 max)	Export report** / EU Annual Report***	UN Comtrade	UN Register	Timeliness (1.50 max)	Access and consistency (2.00 max)	Clarity (5.00 max)	Comprehensiveness (6.50 max)	Deliveries (4.00 max)	Licences granted (4.00 max)	Licences refused (2.00 max)
South Korea	9.75	-	X	X(10)^Δ	1.50	1.00	1.50	3.25	2.50	0.00	0.00
Thailand	9.75	-	X	X^Δ	1.50	0.50	1.50	3.25	3.00	0.00	0.00
Israel	9.25	-	X	-	1.50	0.50	1.50	3.25	2.50	0.00	0.00
India	9.00	-	X	X(10)	1.50	0.50	1.50	2.50	3.00	0.00	0.00
Mexico	9.00	-	X	X(10)^Δ	1.50	1.00	1.50	2.50	2.50	0.00	0.00
Pakistan	9.00	-	X	X(10)	1.50	0.50	1.50	3.00	2.50	0.00	0.00
Colombia	8.75	-	X	X(10)	1.50	0.50	1.50	2.25	3.00	0.00	0.00
Turkey	8.75	-	X	X(10)	1.50	0.50	1.50	2.75	2.50	0.00	0.00
Montenegro	8.50	-	X	X^Δ	1.50	0.50	1.50	2.00	3.00	0.00	0.00
Philippines	8.25	-	X	-	1.50	0.50	1.50	2.25	2.50	0.00	0.00
Argentina	8.00	-	X	X	1.50	1.00	1.50	1.50	2.50	0.00	0.00
Cyprus	8.00	-	X	X	1.50	0.50	1.00	2.50	2.50	0.00	0.00
Ukraine	8.00	X	-	X(10)^Δ	1.50	1.50	1.00	2.00	2.00	0.00	0.00
Brazil	7.50	-	X	X(10)	1.50	0.50	1.00	2.00	2.50	0.00	0.00
Japan	7.50	-	X	X	1.50	1.00	1.25	1.25	2.50	0.00	0.00
China	6.50	-	X	X	1.50	0.50	1.00	1.00	2.50	0.00	0.00
Singapore	6.00	-	X	X	1.50	0.50	1.00	1.00	2.00	0.00	0.00
Taiwan	5.75	-	X	-	1.50	0.50	1.00	0.75	2.00	0.00	0.00
Russian Federation	5.50	-	X	X(10)^Δ	1.50	1.00	0.50	0.50	2.00	0.00	0.00
Malawi	4.50	-	X	-	1.50	0.00	0.75	0.75	1.50	0.00	0.00
Egypt	4.25	-	X	-	1.50	0.50	0.50	0.25	1.50	0.00	0.00
Bosnia and Herzegovina	4.00	-	-	X (10)	1.00	0.00	0.50	1.00	1.50	0.00	0.00
South Africa	2.00	X	-	X^Δ	1.50	0.50	0.00	0.00	0.00	0.00	0.00
Iran	0.00	-	-	-	0.00	0.00	0.00	0.00	0.00	0.00	0.00
North Korea	0.00	-	-	-	0.00	0.00	0.00	0.00	0.00	0.00	0.00
Saudi Arabia	0.00	-	-	-	0.00	0.00	0.00	0.00	0.00	0.00	0.00
United Arab Emirates	0.00	-	-	-	0.00	0.00	0.00	0.00	0.00	0.00	0.00

Note: The online version of the Transparency Barometer incorporates updates and corrections, and fills in reporting gaps, all of which affect states' scores as well as their rankings for current and previous years. For these reasons, the online editions–rather than the printed version–should be considered definitive. See Small Arms Survey (n.d.).

Notes

* Major exporters are countries that export–or are believed to export–at least USD 10 million worth of small arms, light weapons, their parts, accessories, and ammunition in a given year. The 2013 Barometer includes all countries that qualified as a major exporter at least once during the 2001–11 calendar years.

** X indicates that a report was issued. X(years) indicates that a report was not issued by the cut off-date; in that case, the country is evaluated on the basis of its most recent submission, covering activities in the period reported in brackets.

*** The Barometer assesses information provided in the EU's *Fourteenth Annual Report* (CoEU, 2012), reflecting military exports by EU member states in 2011.

Δ The country submitted data to the UN Register for its 2011 activities but its contribution was not available for analysis by the cut-off date due to delays in the release of a further addendum to the reports of the UN Secretary-General on the UN Register (UNGA, 2012a; 2012b). As a result, it is evaluated on the basis of its most recent submission, covering activities in 2010, when available.

Scoring system

The scoring system for the 2013 Barometer remains the same as in 2012. The Barometer's seven categories assess: timeliness, access and consistency in reporting, clarity, comprehensiveness, and the level of detail provided on actual deliveries, licences granted, and licences refused. For more detailed information on the scoring guidelines, see Small Arms Survey (n.d.).

Explanatory notes

Note A: The Barometer is based on each country's most recent arms export report, made publicly available between 1 January 2011 and 31 December 2012.

Note B: The Barometer takes into account national reporting to the UN Register from 1 January 2011 to 21 January 2013 as well as information states have submitted to UN Comtrade for their 2011 exports up to 8 January 2013.

Note C: The fact that the Barometer is based on three sources–national arms export reports, reporting to the UN Register, and UN customs data–works to the advantage of states that publish data in all three outlets. Information provided to each of the three sources is reflected in the scoring. The same information is not credited twice, however.

Country-specific notes

1. Serbia published a national arms export report in 2012 that was limited to data from 2010.

2. Germany submitted data to the UN Register for its 2011 activities but its full contribution on small arms and light weapons transfers was not available by the cut off-date.

3. The US report is divided into several documents. For the purposes of the Barometer, the US annual report refers to the State Department report pursuant to Section 655 on direct commercial sales, and the report on foreign military sales, which is prepared by the US Department of Defense.

4. Austria published a national arms export report in 2012 that was limited to data from 2010.

5. Slovakia submitted data to the UN Register for its 2011 activities but its contribution on small arms and light weapons transfers was not available by the cut-off date.

Source: Small Arms Survey (2013)

LIST OF ABBREVIATIONS

NISAT	Norwegian Initiative on Small Arms Transfers
UN Comtrade	United Nations Commodity Trade Statistic Database
UN Register	United Nations Register of Conventional Arms

ENDNOTES

1   UN Comtrade does not provide full coverage of the small arms and light weapons trade. See Dreyfus, Marsh, and Shroeder (2009, pp. 8–11, 28–31) for a discussion of the strengths and limitations of UN Comtrade data and Lazarevic (2010, pp. 16–24) for an overview of the reporting tools on small arms and light weapons transfers.

2   The Small Arms Survey relies on the analysis of UN Comtrade data provided by the Norwegian Initiative on Small Arms Transfers (NISAT) project at the Peace Research Institute, Oslo. NISAT considers countries' self-reported exports as well as 'mirror data'—reported imports by destination countries. See Marsh (2005). For this chapter, NISAT downloaded data from the UN Comtrade on 8 January 2013, giving exporting and importing states at least 24 months to report on 2010 transfers.

3   See the online annexes to this chapter for a complete list of the major importers and exporters, along with the values transferred, the main partners, and categories of weapons traded.

4   This category includes information that European Union (EU) states have contributed to the EU Annual Report on military exports (CoEU, 2012).

5   See Small Arms Survey (n.d.).

6   There are important exceptions to these yearly timeframes. See Lazarevic (2010) for full details on the scoring methodology and a description of the changes to the Transparency Barometer scoring system since its introduction in 2004.

7   For comparisons with previous rankings and scores, please consult the online versions of the Transparency Barometer (Small Arms Survey, n.d.).

8   Bosnia and Herzegovina and Montenegro did provide information on their 2010 activities to the South Eastern and Eastern Europe Clearinghouse for the Control of Small Arms and Light Weapons, which published data in its *Regional Report on Arm Exports* in 2012 (SEESAC, n.d.); however, these reports are not included among the sources monitored for the purposes of the Transparency Barometer.

9   Taiwan's score was generated using the data it submits to UN Comtrade, as published by the International Trade Centre in its TradeMap database. Taiwan did not report on the UN Comtrade category 930200, which includes pistols and revolvers.

BIBLIOGRAPHY

CoEU (Council of the European Union). 2012. *Fourteenth Annual Report According to Article 8(2) of Council Common Position 2008/944/CFSP Defining Common Rules Governing Control of Exports of Military Technology and Equipment.* 2012/C 386/01. 14 December. <http://eur-lex.europa.eu/LexUriServ/LexUriServ.do?uri=OJ:C:2012:386:0001:0431:EN:PDF>

Dreyfus, Pablo, Nicolas Marsh, and Matt Shroeder. 2009. 'Sifting the Sources: Authorized Small Arms Transfers.' In Small Arms Survey. *Small Arms Survey 2009: Shadows of War.* Cambridge: Cambridge University Press, pp. 7–59.

Lazarevic, Jasna. 2010. *Transparency Counts: Assessing States Reporting on Small Arms Transfers, 2011–08.* Occasional Paper No. 25. Geneva: Small Arms Survey.

Marsh, Nicholas. 2005. *Accounting Guns: The Methodology Used in Developing Data Tables for the Small Arms Survey.* Unpublished background paper. Oslo: Norwegian Initiative on Small Arms Transfers, Peace Research Institute, Oslo. 14 November.

SEESAC (South Eastern and Eastern Europe Clearinghouse for the Control of Small Arms and Light Weapons). n.d. 'Regional Reports: Online Database.' Accessed 15 January 2013. <http://www.seesac.org/arms-exports-reports/regional-reports/1/>

Small Arms Survey. 2013. *Small Arms Trade Transparency Barometer 2013: Sources.* Unpublished background paper. Geneva: Small Arms Survey.

—. n.d. 'The Transparency Barometer.' <http://www.smallarmssurvey.org/weapons-and-markets/tools/the-transparency-barometer>

UNGA (United Nations General Assembly). 2012a. *Report of the Secretary-General: United Nations Register on Conventional Arms.* A/67/212 of 30 July 2012. <http://www.un.org/ga/search/view_doc.asp?symbol=A/67/212>

—. 2012b. *Report of the Secretary-General: United Nations Register on Conventional Arms.* A/67/212.Add.1 of 21 September 2012.

ANNEXES

Online annexes at <http://www.smallarmssurvey.org/publication/by-type/yearbook/small-arms-survey-2013.html>

Annexe 8.1. Annual authorized small arms and light weapons exports for major exporters (yearly exports of at least USD 10 million), 2010

Annexe 8.2. Annual authorized small arms and light weapons imports for major importers (yearly imports of at least USD 10 million), 2010

ACKNOWLEDGEMENTS

Principal authors

Irene Pavesi and Christelle Rigual

Contributors

Thomas Jackson

Warheads are transported to be detonated in controlled explosions in a dedicated facility 800 m below ground, Lökken Verk, Norway, 2012. © Nammo Demil Division

Burning the Bullet
INDUSTRIAL DEMILITARIZATION OF AMMUNITION

9

INTRODUCTION

States procure more conventional[1] ammunition than they use. To avoid depot congestion with obsolete ammunition and to reduce storage costs, they dispose of part of their stockpiles via foreign military sales and increase the use of ammunition for training purposes.[2] Despite these disposal initiatives, a large part of a nation's surplus ammunition stockpile will ultimately require *demilitarization*—a process by which ammunition is safely dismantled or destroyed while, ideally, its valuable materials are recovered.

In many countries, excess stockpiles of obsolete or unserviceable munitions have reached a level requiring demilitarization on an industrial scale, often in a race against time as the ammunition tends to become unsafe with age. Since states rarely have the capacity to demilitarize the surplus ammunition stockpiles of their collective security forces, they often turn to the demilitarization industry.

Policy-makers and programmers tend to be poorly informed about the demilitarization industry's markets, challenges, and techniques, for several reasons. Data pertaining to ammunition demilitarization is just as sensitive as ammunition design and procurement information. Hence, policy-relevant information is rarely distributed publicly and resides predominantly within individual ministries of defence (MoDs), their contractors, and some international bodies such as NATO ammunition working groups. Furthermore, contractors fear that discussing their activities and capacities publicly may put them at a commercial disadvantage. Finally, academia has not traditionally covered this activity.

Yet this chapter shows that US and Western European contractors routinely process significant amounts of conventional ammunition, much of which is foreign. They design, manufacture, market, and operate complex technologies that are simply outside the traditional prerogatives of most MoDs. They are also prime actors, stakeholders, and potential facilitators of international donor-funded arms control and ammunition demilitarization programmes.

This chapter provides an introductory snapshot of the world's major industrial demilitarization contractors by examining their activities, technologies, markets, and challenges. It relies on the results of industry questionnaires[3] sent out in early 2012, unclassified and declassified NATO documents, and interviews with key demilitarization stakeholders in the industry, governments, and international organizations. The chapter focuses on Western and Central Europe as well as on the United States and Canada, which account for the vast majority of industrial demilitarization activity worldwide.

Among the chapter's key findings are the following:

- The demilitarization industry is currently centred in Western Europe and the United States.
- The industry operates under standard competitive tendering rules.
- While the technology exists to destroy the vast majority of ammunition types, it may not be available in the timeframe required and is generally lacking in countries that need it most.

- Aside from the United States, where a few contractors struggle to reduce the massive conventional ammunition stockpile, many NATO nations' industrial facilities have underutilized demilitarization capacity.

- Cluster munitions, especially multiple-launch rocket system (MLRS) rockets, still account for a significant part of the demilitarization activity in the United States and Western Europe.

- Most nations' ammunition destruction regimes involve a combination of both open burning and open detonation (OB/OD) as well as industrial demilitarization methods.

- The costs involved in transporting and demilitarizing large quantities of ammunition can be significant and are a heavy burden on an MoD's budget.

- There is currently no common international or European standard, legislation, or compliance mechanism that specifically addresses ammunition demilitarization by commercial contractors.

- MoDs are not automatically involved in the commercial ammunition demilitarization sector's activities, unless munitions from their national armed forces are concerned.

- In countries where industrial demilitarization is less developed and contractors do not meet prevailing safety standards, the potential for accidents is much higher during industrial processes.

This chapter begins by describing the industry's actors and the markets in which they compete, as well as opportunities that are likely to emerge in the foreseeable future. The section that follows identifies the industry's activities, its core industry processes, and its general capabilities and capacities. The third section details the industry's complex regulatory and compliance regime as well as its logistical and safety constraints. The final section highlights the ongoing debate on environmental considerations versus cost-effectiveness, discussing the advantages and drawbacks of OB/OD as well as the relevance of recover, recycle, and reuse (R3) policies.

A limited number of capable companies occupy the international market.

INDUSTRY ACTORS AND MARKETS

Industry actors

The demilitarization industry's main contractors are currently based in Western Europe and the United States. In Europe, the end of the cold war triggered dramatic reductions in force levels, a build-up of surplus ammunition stockpiles, and advances in demilitarization. Most notably, the new government of the reunified Germany inherited a significant stockpile of ammunition from the East German National People's Army (Nationale Volksarmee), leading German firms to develop industrial-scale demilitarization processes to reduce it (RTO, 2010, pp. 3-22, 3-23). More recently, the Convention on Cluster Munitions (CCM) spurred the development of new processing and disassembly equipment. In the United States, research and development of industrial demilitarization capacity developed mainly in response to increasing environmental restrictions, the will to reduce reliance on OB/OD, and the federal government's push for enhanced waste prevention and recycling (MSIAC, 2006, p. 2).

A limited number of capable companies occupy the international market. Broadly speaking, the US and European demilitarization industry consists of a core group of approximately 30 major contractors that compete against, but also contract and sub-contract, each other. Table 9.1 lists a selection of European and US demilitarization companies' headquarters and processing plants that appeared regularly during the author's research as (i) international contractors with proven operational capability, (ii) equipment manufacturers, (iii) tender applicants, or (iv) potential regional demilitarization service providers.

Table 9.1 Major European and US demilitarization companies, processing plants, and/or equipment providers		
Country	**Company**	**Location**
Albania	ULP Mjekes	State-owned enterprise near Elbasan*
Bulgaria	EXPAL Bulgaria JSC	Gabrovo*
France	Alsetex	Précigné
	MBDA	Bourges
Germany	EST Energetics GmbH	Steinbach
	Nammo Buck GmbH	Pinnow (near Berlin)
	SAB (Sonderanlagenbau) Nord GmbH	Elmshorn
	sonUtec GmbH	Sonneberg
	Spreewerk Lübben GmbH	Lübben
Greece	Soukos Robots S.A.	Larissa
Israel	Red Wings Ltd.	Rehovot
Italy	Esplodenti Sabino Srl	Processing plant in Casalbordino (Chieti)
Norway	Nammo NAD	Løkken Verk
Poland	JAKUSZ SZ Bogdan Jakusz	Kościerzyna
	Mesko SA	Skarzysko-Kamienna
Serbia	TRZ Kragujevac	Kragujevac*
Slovakia	KONSTRUKTA-Industry	Trencin
Spain	EXPAL	Madrid
Sweden	Dynasafe Demil Systems AB	Karlskoga
	Nammo Vingåkersverken	Vingåker
Turkey	AKANA Engineering and Trade Ltd.	Ankara
	MKE (Pirinç Fabrikası)	Kırıkkale
	ROKETSAN	Ankara
United Kingdom	EOD Solutions Ltd.	Rayleigh, Essex
	QinetiQ	Shoeburyness, Essex
United States	DynCorp International	Falls Church, Virginia
	El Dorado Engineering, Inc.	Salt Lake City, Utah
	General Atomics	San Diego, California
	Gradient Technology	Elk River, Minnesota
	General Dynamics Ordnance and Tactical Systems	Saint Petersburg, Florida
	U.S. Demil, LLC	Buffalo, New York
	UXB International, Inc.	Blacksburg, Virginia

Note: * See Gobinet (2012).

There is a clear link between ammunition production and demilitarization activities. Industrial demilitarization providers are often former or active ammunition producers. Nammo Buck GmbH in Germany was an ammunition factory before reunification, and has been involved in demilitarization since 1991 (Nammo, 2012, p. 2). The Spanish company EXPAL, which comprises a demilitarization division, is a subsidiary of the MAXAM group, founded by Alfred Nobel in 1872. The group develops, manufactures, and sells explosives, chemicals, and ammunition for the international civilian and defence industries. MKE, a leading company in the Turkish defence industry and supplier of the Turkish Armed Forces, also dedicates one of its 11 factories to demilitarization, reuse, and recycling processes (NIAG, 2010, p. 73). For companies that still actively produce ammunition, demilitarization seems to represent only a small part of gross income. For example, Nammo's demilitarization activity represents less than 10 per cent of the group's total turnover (Nammo, 2012, p. 2). While major demilitarization providers also manufacture their own machinery, some companies, such as Spreewerk Lübben GmbH,[4] Dynasafe Demil Systems AB, Sonderanlagenbau Nord GmbH, and El Dorado Engineering, mainly focus on manufacturing and marketing demilitarization equipment. They then sell or lease 'turnkey' equipment to other client companies, MoDs, and international outfits that carry out the actual demilitarization contracts.

Industrial demilitarization providers are often former or active ammunition producers.

Industrial demilitarization contractors operate under private, government, or mixed ownership. In Eastern and South-east Europe, the companies are often fully or partially state-owned and MoD-operated. Nevertheless, many are revenue-generating operations, which allows them to cover expenses (TRZK, 2012). In Western Europe and the United States, some of the major industrial contractors are state-owned but operate as any private company in the business. For instance, the Nordic Ammunition Company (Nammo) is jointly owned by Norway's Ministry of Trade and Industry and by the Finnish security and aerospace group Patria Holding Oyj.[5] In 2002 the group created a demilitarization division that now comprises three processing sites: Nammo Vingåkersverken in Sweden, Nammo NAD in Norway, and Nammo Buck GmbH in Germany (Perala, 2002). Other major contractors and equipment providers—such as General Atomics, Dynasafe Demil Systems AB, DynCorp International, El Dorado Engineering, Inc., and Sonderanlagenbau Nord GmbH—are privately held corporations.[6]

Public–private partnerships are common. In some countries, the MoD (and not the industry) undertakes much of the stockpile demilitarization tasks via 'organic'—that is, state-owned, MoD-operated—facilities (Van Baalen and Honey, 2011, pp. 10-11). The military continues to rely heavily on OB/OD. Commercial contractors, on the other hand, use automated industrial demilitarization and high production rates, with a focus on R3 (see below). In practice, cost and technical efficiency require that both processes be used; therefore, commercial contractors usually work in cooperation with organic facilities (Boyer, 2012, slide 14). Within the US Armed Forces, for instance, the US Army has been the only service manager for conventional ammunition since 1997. As such, the Army conducts the majority of the ammunition demilitarization and disposal for all military services, performing this work at army storage depots and manufacturing plants. Yet commercial contractors are frequently involved as well (RTO, 2010, p. 3-24).

Markets

Contracts and tenders

Industry contractors demilitarize all types of ammunition under normal competitive tendering rules. They seek to optimize their profits, invest in new demilitarization technology, and maintain their customer base. The extent of the 'competition' largely depends on the type and quantity of ammunition to be destroyed and on the number of companies that possess the technology and equipment required to destroy the spectrum of ammunition identified by the tender, in accordance with the country's relevant regulations. The contracts usually cover receipt, storage, internal move-ment, demilitarization processes, the processing of by-products, such as explosives and metals, and the disposal of all scrap materials. They can also include transportation costs from military storage to civilian demilitarization locations.

National procurement and logistics agencies publish requests for proposals (RfPs). In Germany, for instance, the Federal Office of Bundeswehr Equipment, Information Technology and In-Service Support[7] plays an important role in the tendering process. For public tenders in the European Union (EU), procurement rules[8] set out specific threshold values for supplies and service contracts. Consequently, oversight of routine small-scale disposal remains at the national level. Contracts within the EU that exceed threshold values go to international tender (Nammo, 2012, p. 15). Many national authorities use regional organizations to issue RfPs for large disposal programmes. This procedure frames the tenders qualitatively by ensuring that contractors operate certified quality and environmental management systems or meet specific requirements, for instance with regard to the capability of the pollution control system associated with an incinerator.

Over time, this competition can also streamline demilitarization costs (see below) and encourage contractors to innovate where commercially viable. The NATO Support Agency (NSPA),[9] for example, manages RfPs for the disposal of surplus ammunition holdings on behalf of NATO Ammunition Support Partnership and Partnership for Peace (PfP) countries,[10] monitoring these contracts until completion. NSPA handles aspects such as preparing and auditing state-ments of work, issuing calls for tenders, reviewing tenders and awarding contracts, and submitting progress reports as well as certificates of destruction to the sponsor nation or customer (Towndrow, 2011b).[11]

> Some regional organizations coordinate RfPs for large disposal programmes.

Contracts are negotiated on a case-by-case basis but seem to follow certain regional patterns. In the United States, the contracts involve much larger quantities of ammunition than in Western Europe, yet there appears to be limited domestic commercial competition for high-tonnage stockpile items; large corporations form consortiums to bid on big, multi-year contracts, effectively precluding competition from smaller companies.[12] In European contracts, the smaller volumes of ammunition and much lower demand limit the amount of explosives that can be recycled and sold for civilian purposes, which also results in shorter contracts and fewer incentives to invest in specialized machinery. The European demilitarization market is more fragmented, yet consequently more competitive. One consultancy report confirms this view, recommending that the US demilitarization industry continue partnering with NSPA while seeking commercial demilitarization companies outside the contiguous United States to increase competition (Boyer, 2012, slide 11).

Ammunition demilitarization costs

Several factors have a direct impact on demilitarization costs. Open-source NSPA presentations provide a good estimate of the range of contract values, revealing that they vary largely according to ammunition types (Courtney-Green, 2007, pp. 3–4). To a significant degree, the nature and quantity of the ammunition determines the technology requirements for its demilitarization. Risk and costs increase when the demilitarization process necessitates extra handling, manipu-lation, and the use of multiple technologies. To achieve economies of scale, contractors prefer to spread expenditures over a large quantity of ammunition of the same type, which allows the plant to optimize the demilitarization process and reduce costs. The need to comply with different states' environmental and ammunition disposal legislation also creates variations in the cost of destruction (see below).

Pricing is a sensitive topic. Open-source literature gives generic pricing examples in gross tonnes ('all-up weight'),[13] which includes packaging but not transportation (Courtney-Green, 2005, p. 22; Peugeot, 2009, p. 22). The UN Office for

Table 9.2 **Indicative ammunition demilitarization costs, 2011**	
Ammunition type/component	**Indicative costs (EUR/tonne)**
Small arms ammunition* (<20 mm calibre)	101-529 (USD 132-691)
Fuses	237-1,039 (USD 310-1,357)
Propellants**	856 (USD 1,118)
Warheads (high-explosive)***	564-610 (USD 737-797)
Cannon and medium calibre (20-105 mm)	419-757 (USD 547-989)
Pyrotechnics	1,654 (USD 2,160)

Notes:

* Dependent on technique and economy of scale.

** Conversion to commercial explosives may lead to cost recovery.

*** Costs after removal and destruction of cartridge cases.

Source: UNODA (2011b)

Disarmament Affairs' International Ammunition Technical Guidelines note indicative demilitarization costs for Western Europe (see Table 9.2).

Contract prices are usually expressed per item of ammunition and are confidential so as not to undermine contract negotiations or otherwise put a company at a competitive disadvantage. The unit price usually reflects a net price in which the cost of processing is offset by the cash return from the sale of valuable scrap metals and other materials. Prices often include transportation from military storage to the processing plant and can represent a significant proportion of the overall cost. For this study, some contractors provided rough-order-of-magnitude demilitarization prices per item in US dollars. The price ranges for each ammunition family were extremely broad, always context-specific, and rarely generically representative of the marketplace. NATO has yet to develop a unit cost basis for specific munitions types processed through specific demilitarization processes (NIAG, 2010, p. 172), yet it is generally accepted that open competition is the most effective way to control pricing.

The costs of demilitarization may be increasing. In 2004, an ammunition consultancy firm estimated the average cost of ammunition demilitarization at a European facility at approximately USD 800–1,200 per tonne depending on the type of ammunition (UNDP and Threat Resolution Ltd., 2004, p. 5.3). In 2007 the US Army estimated the average demilitarization cost of all conventional ammunition at approximately USD 1,400 per ton (Gonzalez, 2010, p. 8). One year later, a French MoD report estimated that, for complex munitions, missiles, and torpedoes, demilitarization costs ranged from EUR 1,000 to 5,000 per tonne (USD 1,350–6,700) (France, 2008, p. 10); the US Army estimated the average demilitarization cost of conventional ammunition at approximately USD 1,800 per ton, with projections over USD 2,000 per ton for 2012 (Raftery, 2008; Gonzalez, 2010, p. 8). Recent estimates put the average cost of demilitarizing a tonne of ammunition in the United States and Western Europe at approximately USD 1,600 (RTO, 2010, p. 3-3).[14]

Demilitarization is reportedly less expensive in Eastern Europe, where several countries receive external funding for this activity. Recent Small Arms Survey research carried out in the framework of the Regional Approach to Stockpile Reduction (RASR) initative shows that in such contexts additional factors influencing the demilitarization price include: (i) the economic level of the host nation, (ii) local capacity, (iii) the training levels of local staff, and (iv) donor priorities. Given these variables, it is difficult to make direct comparisons. Donor-funded demilitarization projects often include weapons and ammunition and are negotiated at an overall fixed cost, applicable to all ammunition types (Lazarevic, 2012, p. 24). In most cases, start-up costs per tonne are high; subsequent destruction is much less expensive as economies of scale take effect and national capacity is built (Wilkinson, 2006).

In 2011, for example, the Albanian facility ULP Mjekes estimated that processing more than 31,000 tonnes of various munitions cost the plant less than EUR 11 million (USD 14.5 million). This would imply an average cost of approximately EUR 350 (USD 460) per tonne (Sina, 2011). TRZ Kragujevac estimates its demilitarization costs on behalf of the

Serbian MoD at EUR 780 (USD 1,000) per tonne, and claims that they will fall below EUR 500 (USD 650) per tonne following the upcoming installation of an explosive waste incinerator and new disassembly machines (TRZK, 2012).

Market opportunities

Industrial demilitarization contractors unanimously point to the United States as the largest market and argue that it will almost certainly remain so for the foreseeable future. The US demilitarization stockpile is not decreasing. In the year 2000 the US Department of Defense (DoD) had more than 500,000 short tons[15] of excess, obsolete, and unserviceable munitions in its demilitarization stockpile (Hsu, Pruneda, and Kwak, 2000). In 2010 the US conventional ammunition demilitarization stockpile was still estimated at 450,000–600,000 tons, representing approximately a sixth of the total stockpile (RTO, 2010, p. 3-24; NIAG, 2010, p. 82; Gibbs, 2010).[16] The current annual demilitarization budget of more than USD 150 million is not diminishing the stockpile, 'but rather keeps it at the same level' (Nammo, 2012, p. 15). Although large quantities of the surplus munitions are disposed of each year, a similar quantity is declared surplus, largely as a leftover from remaining cold war stockpiles.

Few European companies have accessed the US demilitarization market. One that has, Nammo Inc., established a subsidiary called Nammo Demil LLC in 1999 to serve as the programme manager for US commercial demilitarization requirements. Since 1999 Nammo Demil LLC has worked as the principal contractor on US contracts or as subcontractor to General Dynamics–Ordnance and Tactical Systems in the framework of several five-year commercial demilitarization contracts (Nammo, 2012, p. 14).

In Western Europe, the large stockpiles of surplus cold war-era munitions have mostly been dealt with, and current stockpiles are growing at a much slower rate, except for more recent classes of munitions such as those fired by multiple-launch rocket systems, as discussed below (NIAG, 2010, p. 82). A 2008 French MoD report estimates that approximately 2,000 tonnes of conventional munitions would require demilitarization annually in France from 2009 to 2014, not including a total of 7,500 tonnes of missiles, (mostly MLRS) rockets, and torpedoes over the same period (France, 2008, p. 17).

Eastern European and Commonwealth of Independent States countries, which still harbour significant stockpiles of conventional ammunition surpluses, are seldom mentioned by Western European and US contractors as future demilitarization markets. In some of these countries, demilitarization remains a domestic activity largely inaccessible to open, international tender competition. In 2012, for example, the Russian MoD declared its intention to decommission 11 ammunition storage areas and dispose of three million tonnes of ammunition by the end of 2013 (Voice of Russia, 2012; IANS and Ria Novosti, 2012). It is unclear whether the Russian Federation has a credible national demilitarization capacity to achieve this, what quantity will be disposed by OB/OD, and whether the country will open the domestic market to international demilitarization providers.[17]

In similar contexts, international donor-funded demilitarization programmes are instrumental in shedding light on a country's demilitarization capacity by promoting local processing facilities wherever possible. Such is the case in Ukraine, for instance, where NSPA is currently using four Ukrainian plants[18] to demilitarize 1.5 million small arms and light weapons and more than 130,000 tonnes of obsolete ammunition in the framework of a 12-year (four-phase) PfP Trust Fund project.[19]

Very little information on other regional markets is available. There seems to be a high demand for Western technology and capacity in Asia and the Middle East, where the industrial demilitarization market is reportedly underdeveloped. However, Western European companies need to use local contractors in order to reduce shipping and logistics costs to remain competitive, and it is unclear whether they are meeting the regional demand. African countries

International donor-funded programmes help shed light on a country's demilitarization capacity.

have requirements for explosive ordnance disposal, mine clearance, and mine disposal activities. Many states on this continent need to dispose of outdated stockpiled munitions, yet African defence budgets for industrial demilitarization tend to be quite restricted (Nammo, 2012, p. 15).

Cluster munitions

Cluster munitions, especially MLRS rockets, currently represent a significant part of the demilitarization activity in the United States and Western Europe.[20]

The capability for disposal of the cluster munitions existed before the signature of the Convention on Cluster Munitions in 2008. Western countries started destroying cluster munitions around 2000. In 2001, for instance, Nammo Buck GmbH demilitarized 8,000 BL-755 cluster bombs in a three-year, USD 2.5 million contract for the German government (Perala, 2001). In anticipation of the CCM, around 2005, governments and contractors developed automated disassembly equipment to separate bomblets from their dispensers (Zaugg et al., 2007). The United States reportedly destroyed around 7,000 tons of cluster munitions per year in 2000–10, at an average annual cost of USD 6.6 million (Bohle, 2010).

However, the CCM process—and entry into force in August 2010—generated a spike in the volume of surplus cluster munitions that exceeded most NATO nations' immediate demilitarization capacity (NIAG, 2010, p. 97). In several NATO countries, the number of surplus MLRS rockets[21] illustrated this vividly. In 2007, several hundred thousand M26 rockets in Europe and the United States had reportedly reached the end of their lifetime and were awaiting

CBU bomblets undergo an automated demilitarization process at Joplin, Missouri, USA, 2012. © General Dynamics Ordnance and Tactical Systems (GD-OTS)

disposal within the coming ten years (Herbst, 2007). A 2008 French MoD report estimates that, after sub-munitions were prohibited by the CCM, approximately 160,000 MLRS became obsolete in Western Europe. The report states that most of the European demilitarization capacity for MLRS was in Germany, and that there was doubt as to whether it could absorb the European MLRS rocket stockpiles—including those of US forces stationed in Europe (France, 2008, p. 10).

In Europe, NSPA consolidated MLRS rocket demilitarization requirements on behalf of its NATO customers to achieve economy of scale. In 2007, NSPA contracted Nammo Buck, Nammo NAD, Esplodenti Sabino, and Spreewerk on behalf of the Netherlands and the United Kingdom to demilitarize 60,000 M26 MLRS rockets containing more than 38 million sub-munitions. The contract was spread over the period 2007–13 and is valued at approximately EUR 49 million (Towndrow, 2010, p. 20; 2011a, p. 8). Rough-order-of-magnitude demilitarization prices reportedly average EUR 600–700 (USD 800–950) per rocket[22] (Courtney-Green, 2007, p. 21). In November 2011, NSPA also awarded a contract to MBDA in France for the destruction of 36,000 complex munitions, including 1,000 missiles, 22,000 M26 rockets—each containing 644 sub-munitions—and 13,000 155-mm projectiles, each containing 63 sub-munitions; all in all, more than 15 million sub-munitions are set for destruction by 2017 (MBDA, 2011; Lucas, 2012). As of late 2012, experts estimated that 95 per cent of the Western European MLRS stockpiles had been destroyed or were on contract to be processed by 2018.[23]

The CCM appears to have affected the demilitarization activities of non-states parties as well. As of December 2011, six of the top ten items of the US ammunition demilitarization stockpile contained sub-munitions. The 155 mm M483 howitzer shell, a type of dual-purpose improved conventional munition,[24] represented the largest tonnage of the stockpile, with approximately 120,000 tons (Boyer, 2012, slide 7). In particular, the disposition of the large inventory of the MLRS pods that are reaching the end of their shelf life will reportedly be the US Army missile demilitarization programme's largest challenge over the next several years (Wright, Lee, and Gunter, 2011). In 2010 the US Army expected approximately 50,000 to 60,000 MLRS to enter the demilitarization programme, starting in the year 2012 (Dillard, 2010).

European and US governments contract the industry to demilitarize large MLRS stockpiles.

In the United States, the Army Aviation and Missile Life Cycle Management Command (AMCOM) contracts the industry to demilitarize MLRS. As of May 2012, General Dynamics–Ordnance and Tactical Systems had reportedly processed more than 51,000 rockets during the first four years of a five-year contract with AMCOM to demilitarize more than 89,000 MLRS (Meyer and Winkler, 2012, p. 2). Government-owned facilities such as the recent MLRS recycling facility at the Anniston Defense Munitions Center were also designed and built to address the MLRS demilitarization stockpile (Dillard, 2010; Wright, Lee, and Gunter, 2011). In July 2012, in Canada, media sources reported that the Department of National Defence was planning to dispose of more than 12,000 dual-purpose improved conventional munition projectiles containing more than one million bomblets in a CAD 2 million tender (USD 2 million) (Carlson, 2012).

ACTIVITIES

Core processes

Demilitarization is defined as 'the complete range of processes that render weapons, ammunition and explosives unfit for their originally intended purpose' (UNODA, 2011a, p. 8). It involves 'removing or otherwise neutralizing the military potential' of ammunition (MSIAC, 2006). The term applies equally to serviceable and to unserviceable surplus material or equipment.

Many demilitarization techniques are available,[25] categorized by the stage of the demilitarization process in which they are applied. Table 9.3 illustrates the basic process and applicable techniques. Demilitarization is considered complete

Table 9.3 Summary of the ammunition demilitarization process and techniques

Process stage	Description	Examples of techniques and equipment
1. Transport	Compliance with dangerous goods or hazardous waste regulations that apply to the transportation of ammunition and explosives earmarked for demilitarization.	Delivery by road, air, or sea.
2. Storage until demilitarization	Compliance with relevant quantity–distance standards.	Storage in self-contained, partially buried bunkers designed to send any blast upward and not outward to minimize damage.
3. Manual unpacking and preparation	Sorting and unpacking.	Removal of non-explosive elements for recycling.
4. Pre-processing and disassembly	Separation of projectiles, propellants, and casings; exposure of energetic material prior to removal.	Techniques include manual disassembly; delinking; defusing and depriming; automatic and semi-automatic disassembly; crushing; cryofracture; laser cutting; hydro-abrasive cutting; mechanical cutting; robotic disassembly. Equipment includes grenade shearing machines; bullet disassembly machines; fuse disassembly machines; and metal part disassembly machines.
5. Energetics* removal	Physical removal of energetic materials from their housing or casing.	Meltout: the use of autoclaves and hot water or steam to heat and melt the energetic material in munition to aid or cause its removal from casings. The process is used to remove cast high explosives such as TNT, Comp B, and Tritonal, but compositions such as RDX, HMX, and PBXs cannot be readily melted. Equipment includes US Ammunition Peculiar Equipment (APE) 1300 and 1401 (autoclave and steam meltout).
		Washout: the use of a high-pressure jet to abrade the energetic material.
6. Energetics disposal (primary destruction)	Decommissioning or destruction of energetic materials.	Open burning (OB): material is burned in the open, without control of the gasses.
		Open detonation (OD): typically, items are stacked for destruction and then a donor charge is used to initiate the items. The key requirements are the detonation of all items and the reduction of projection hazards.
		Controlled detonation chamber: material is detonated by a donor charge in a cold chamber that allows the pressure, fragmentation, and noise effects to be controlled and the emissions to be treated.

Process stage	Description	Examples of techniques and equipment
		Static detonation chamber (SDC, also called static kilns): hot detonation chambers heat the contents to induce burning, deflagration, or detonation without using a donor charge. Examples include Dynasafe SDC 1000, SDC 1200 CM (for chemical munitions), SDC 1500, and SDC 2000.
		Rotary kiln (explosive waste incinerator): these furnace incinerators are rarely used for disposal of propellants or explosives. The most common rotary kiln design worldwide is the US APE 1236. Rotary Kiln 418 is used for energetics, explosives, ammunition up to 12.5 mm calibre, fuses, boosters, and air bag devices.
		Oxidation processes that undergo development or validation: a) molten salt oxidation; b) alkaline hydrolysis (also known as caustic or base hydrolysis); c) supercritical water oxidation.
7. Energetics disposal (secondary destruction)	Production of scrap material 'free from explosives'.	Thermal decontamination (open flame or contained).
8. Pollution control system	Compliance with regional or national environmental regulations covering noise, air, water, and land emissions, as well as waste management and recovery.	Dry ceramic filtration: used for the removal of particulates.
		Afterburner: used immediately after the kiln, these generally operate in the 850–1,200ºC range to destroy volatile organic compounds and dioxins.
		Baghouse system: this approach is still predominant in the United States. The system uses Gore-Tex/Teflon filter bags.
		Scrubber system: uses water with an alkaline salt added to absorb, remove, and neutralize acidic gases (including chlorine, hydrogen chloride, and sulphur dioxide) from the off-gas.
		Granulated activated carbon or active carbon filter: absorbs nitrogen-based compounds, removes heavy metals (including mercury), and treats 'pink' waste water.

Notes: * This chapter defines energetic materials as the explosive compounds and chemicals used in military explosives and propellants. The most common chemicals are '2,4,6-trinitrotoluene (TNT), 1,3,5-hexahydro- 1,3,5-trinitrotriazine (RDX), and 1,3,5,7-tetrahydro- 1,3,5,7-tetranitrotetrazocine (HMX), which are used as high explosives, and nitrocellulose (NC), 2,4-dinitrotoluene (DNT), nitroglycerin (NG), and nitroguanidine (NQ), which are used in propellants' (Johnsen et al., 2011, pp. 22-1–22-2).

Sources: Dynasafe Demil Systems AB (2012); MSIAC (2006); Nammo (2012); NIAG (2010); author correspondence with Thomas Stock, managing director, Dynasafe Germany GmbH, 10 December 2012

Box 9.1   R3: recovery, recycling, and reuse

Demilitarization contractors seek to maximize the amount of recovered material that can then be sold to offset processing costs and thus reduce the overall cost of demilitarization. This promotes a culture of recovery, recycling, and reuse, known as R3 (Van Baalen and Honey, 2011, p. 10-9). R3 methods strip the ammunition down to its basic, recyclable component parts and compounds.

One of the easiest forms of resource recovery is the reuse of scrap metal from munitions casings. Metals such as iron, steel, copper, brass, tin, lead, and tungsten are valuable and can be recovered and recycled for commercial purposes. Approximately 240 kg of aluminium, 90 kg of copper, and 1,000 kg of steel can be recycled as scrap metal for every MLRS pod[26] (Wright, Lee, and Gunter, 2011). But the scrap metal must be safe for reuse. Typically, scrap metal is 'flashed'–that is, heated to approximately 400°C in an incinerator to remove traces of energetic materials or toxic substances–before it is qualified as 'free from explosives' and sold (MSIAC, 2006, p. 74).

Contractors can also reclaim the propellants, explosives, and pyrotechnic ingredients for reuse in commercial applications. The difficulty of explosive recovery resides in limiting contamination and controlling the quality of the recovered explosives. There are two major non-energetic, end-use applications:

- First, energetic materials can be processed into other materials, typically fertilizers or components of fertilizers, because of their high nitrogen content. Explosive D (ammonium picrate), which has no commercial use, can be converted 'into the commercially viable products Picric Acid and Ammonium Nitrate, which are used in the leather dye and fertilizer industries, respectively' (Schmit, 2009).
- A second example is the conversion of white phosphorus (WP) into phosphoric acid, which can be sold to the soft drinks industry (RTO, 2010, p. 3-27).

Since 1989, the US military has been decommissioning WP ordnance at the Crane Army Ammunition Plant using a facility called the Ammunition Peculiar Equipment 1400 White Phosphorus-Phosphoric Acid Conversion Plant. The plant can process 5,240 kg of WP and can produce 21,800 kg of phosphoric acid per day; the resulting phosphoric acid and scrap metal are sold commercially (Peske, 2010; Walsh, Walsh, and Collins, 2011). In Europe, facilities for recovery of phosphoric acid include Alsetex, which has a modern plant in France (MSIAC, 2006, p. 76).

Recovered energetic materials are also used for energetic end-use applications, such as in the production of a wide range of commercial explosives and blasting devices for mining and quarrying. Importantly, the fact that there are examples of commercially viable uses for these materials does not mean that there is a potential market for all the materials or in all quantities.

once all residues from the reverse engineering or destruction process have been destroyed or recycled (see Box 9.1).

Not all of these steps are systematically required. For example, munitions could be destroyed without prior disassembly or removal of energetics, and some steps can be combined. For each of these processes, the industry has developed specific equipment. A single type of equipment does not, in and of itself, represent a complete demilitarization line; rather, the systems complement each other. Contractors also modify technologies to be mobile (not fixed to a permanent installation) so that they can be moved from stockpile to stockpile, or they develop modular, transportable technologies that are temporarily fixed to a platform so that they can operate in one country or region before being transferred to another (Gobinet, 2013).

The best option is seldom a single approach, but rather a combination of them. Many contractors thus use a mixture of OB/OD and other, more environmentally friendly methods that aim to recover valuable materials. The decision to choose any particular technique is based on cost, safety, environmental considerations, customer preference and time-frame, logistics, availability, the type and quantity of ammunition being destroyed, the physical or chemical condition of the ammunition, and the value of recovered material.

Capabilities and capacities

Within NATO countries, the technology exists to destroy the vast majority of ammunition types (Van Baalen and Honey, 2011, p. 10–11). Demilitarization contractors process ordnance, regardless of whether it is clearly labelled or

Photo (left): A projectile's nose fuse being removed remotely during the automated disassembly process, Kirikkale, Turkey, September 2007.
© NATO Support Agency (NSPA)

Photo (right): The saw-cutting of high-explosive projectiles to expose their energetic content; after which, the components travel on a conveyor belt to the next station to melt out the explosives, Lübben, Germany, 2012. © Spreewerk Lübben GmbH

stored in suitable conditions. This includes a wide range of conventional ammunition, from small arms ammunition to aircraft bombs, sea mines, torpedoes, and cluster munitions.

Capacities vary. Equipment capacity is dependent on the type of ammunition processed. Small arms ammunition destruction rates are highest. Destruction rates are slower for TNT-filled medium- and heavy-calibre shells, and slower still for more modern RDX- or HMX-filled shells and for guided missiles.

There is no standard unit of measurement for industrial demilitarization processing capacities (Van Baalen and Honey, 2011, p. 10-14; NIAG, 2010, p. 171). Comparing production rates is thus difficult. Since OB/OD long served as the preferred demilitarization method, weight is often used as a unit of measurement. Large differences appear when comparing unpacked with packaged munition weight. To measure maximum load rates, NATO and contractors typically use all-up weight and net explosive quantity.[27] Contractors also base their standard throughput rates upon clearly defined ammunition types and typically express these rates in 'rounds of specified ammunition type' per time unit. Generally speaking, a company such as TRZK can process more than 3,000 tonnes of conventional ammunition per year (TRZK, 2012); companies such as ROKETSAN Missiles Industries Inc. in Turkey and Yuzhmash missile factory in Ukraine can reportedly process around 6,000 tonnes of conventional ammunition per year. Nammo Vingåkersverken in Sweden can reportedly handle 15,000–20,000 tonnes of conventional ammunition per year (NIAG, 2010, p. 71).

Capacity is an issue in the United States, where the amount of surplus ammunition grows faster than it is being demilitarized. US figures from the 2010 Demilitarization Symposium in Tulsa indicate that, between fiscal years 1980 and 2010, US forces generated a 2.2 million-ton surplus, whereas only 1.5 million tons were demilitarized. Although 70,000 tons of ammunition were processed in the year 2010, DAC estimates that doubling the demilitarization funding of USD 146 million would only reduce the surplus ammunition stockpile by 6 per cent per year.[28]

In contrast, most NATO nations have underutilized industrial demilitarization capacity (Van Baalen and Honey, 2011, p. 10-11). In Europe, most of the large demilitarization contractors have redundant infrastructure in the form of high-throughput equipment and multiple production lines. Nammo and Spreewerk confirm that their facilities are seldom running at full capacity (Nammo, 2012, p. 7; Spreewerk Lübben GmbH, 2012, p. 3). It could be argued that these capabilities are rarely located where they are most needed; that is, in 'client' countries in Eastern Europe with significant surplus ammunition stockpiles but no funds to address them (RTO, 2010, pp. 1-2, 4-1).

REGULATIONS, STANDARDS, AND OVERSIGHT

There is currently no common international or European standard, legislation, or compliance mechanism that *specifically* addresses ammunition demilitarization by commercial contractors.

This may complicate, and in some cases prevent, the development of a systematic, multinational approach to ammunition demilitarization.[29] Within NATO, Standardization Agreement 4518 provides a brief—and outdated—overview of the demilitarization process and available techniques, but it was not written to provide industry standards (NIAG, 2010, p. 171). National legislation usually does not regulate the destruction of military ammunition by civilian industrial contractors. To process military ammunition, industrial contractors must therefore apply a patchwork of civilian explosives industry legislation and for certain activities, such as OB and OD, they may adapt military guidance.

Seemingly unrelated legislation and civilian regulations affect the demilitarization industry indirectly. Changes to regulations in the areas of environment, safety, and staff training requirements can have effects on demilitarization practices. There is also a complex framework of regional, national, and even local rules subjecting demilitarization activities to various local permits and licences. In the United States, for example, the demilitarization of munitions requires compliance with numerous local, state, and federal regulations, most of which require air emissions permits and chemical release reports (Thompson, Kennedy, and Nordquist, 2004).

Logistics can account for half of the cost of some demilitarization contracts. US and Western European contractors usually know these constraints well because they have a direct impact on their business. However, client governments and national programmers may find this regulatory framework complex and opaque. The following sections highlight three key regulatory areas—transport controls, compliance and oversight, and safety and physical security—that are not often scrutinized by the policy-maker.

Transport controls

Transporting ammunition and managing cross-border cooperation are key activities of the demilitarization industry. Surplus ammunition can be shipped to dedicated storage and demilitarization locations by road, rail, ship, or air. Transport can be a significant logistical undertaking. In 2010, for example, the EXPAL Bulgaria JSC plant in Gabrovo won two tenders from an Asian country for the demilitarization of 8,000 tonnes of ammunition in 2010 and for 4,000 tonnes (including more than 400 different types of ammunition) in 2011. In the case of the second Asian contract, 215 ISO containers were brought from Asia to the Black Sea, delivered to Burgas, then transported by road to Gabrovo. The Bulgarian police reportedly provided transport security and the transfer was made in accordance with European regulations on the transport of hazardous goods (Gobinet, 2012, p. 90).

Ammunition transport—and logistics in general—represent a large expense. In the United States, average packaging, crating, handling, and transportation costs represent an estimated 35 per cent of total demilitarization costs (Boyer, 2012, slide 6). Worldwide, it is estimated that logistics can represent as much as 50 per cent of the total cost of some demilitarization contracts. This may exclude expensive and complex insurance policies for transported weapons and ammunition, as well as additional expenses to ensure transport security (Spreewerk Lübben GmbH, 2012, p. 5).

Transportation of ammunition and explosives is principally governed by international and national legislation relating to the movement of dangerous goods. Munitions classified as dangerous goods are transported by rail and road in accordance with national legislation based on comprehensive directives and regulations such as: (i) the European Agreement concerning the International Carriage of Dangerous Goods by Road; and (ii) the UN Recommendations on the Transport of Dangerous Goods, also known as the 'Orange Book' (UNECE, 2009; 2011b). In a number of former Warsaw Pact countries, whose massive ammunition stockpiles have not formally been tested or classified under the UN system, this represents a major hurdle to the demilitarization enterprise; the ammunition cannot be transported legally across borders unless it is officially classified under the UN Globally Harmonized System of Classification and Labelling of Chemicals (UNECE, 2011a). This requires a range of expensive tests.

Where the ammunition is being transported for the purpose of demilitarization, some nations have additionally applied legislation and procedures for the control of hazardous waste. Transportation and storage of ammunition classified as hazardous waste are subject to further regulation and permit requirements typically administered by national environmental agencies. Those involved in issuing permits are rarely familiar with explosives or the demilitarization industry and the permitting process can become a significant burden. A boundary between the two regimes is usually easy to determine: is the ammunition both properly packaged and labelled (that is, safe to move), or does the transport involve some other material, no longer classified as ammunition, that may thus be subject to hazardous waste legislation? For example, the transport of explosive-contaminated material to be incinerated at another facility may be subject to hazardous waste legislation and procedures. Another consequence of classifying munitions as hazardous waste is the application of the Basel Convention on the Control of Transboundary Movements of Hazardous Wastes and Their Disposal, which restricts the export of hazardous waste, in particular from developed countries to developing countries (UNEP, 1989).

Demilitarization contractors and other stakeholders need to understand whether and when obsolete ammunition is categorized as hazardous waste. In the United States, the 1997 Environmental Protection Agency Military Munitions Rule provides clarification by stating that serviceable ammunition earmarked for disposal is not considered waste until it is actually demilitarized. Ammunition storage and transportation by the DoD are thus exempt from the US Environmental Protection Agency's Resource Conservation and Recovery Act[30] requirements, but they remain subject to strict DoD regulations. Under EU law, the definition of waste is broader; obsolete munitions or expended munitions can more easily be considered hazardous waste. However, with the reported exception of Sweden, current EU regulations[31] do not apply to military munitions being transported for demilitarization in Europe because, as in the United States, there is an assumption that such munitions are regulated more strictly than hazardous waste. In contrast to the United States, however, there is no 'Munitions Rule' to make this understanding explicit (MSIAC, 2006, p. 23).

> Demilitarization companies do not own the ammunition until a certificate of destruction is delivered.

Compliance and oversight

Contractors must demonstrate to customers that they have management systems in place to cover aspects such as budgeting, health and safety, and quality. Internationally recognized certifications for quality management standards (ISO 9001:2008), environmental management systems (ISO 14001:2004), occupational health and safety assessment standards (OHSAS 18000),[32] and NATO contracts quality assurance requirements (AQAP 2130)[33] are routinely accepted as evidence of a mature management system, but they do not necessarily guarantee compliance with a particular technical standard.

Industrial demilitarization implies the withdrawal of the weapons or ammunition from service and a transfer of responsibility, and eventually ownership, to the demilitarization industry. As a rule, demilitarization companies do not own the ammunition until they deliver a certificate of destruction. The original owner of the ordnance can monitor its destruction, or delegate verification to a government quality assurance representative. After demilitarization, ownership of the remaining material normally passes to the contractor. The certificate of demilitarization, duly signed by the nominated quality assurance representative, is typically considered as effective proof of transfer of property from the country's armed forces to the contractor. However, this transfer of property is not automatic. National authorities may request ownership of any recyclable material, such as metallic scrap and explosive residues, and decide whether to destroy them or sell them to fund future demilitarization programmes.

Various national authorities and ministries oversee the activities of demilitarization contractors. While MoDs usually have oversight of the disposal of their own armed forces' munitions, they are not systematically involved in all of the industrial demilitarization contractors' activities. Research for the RASR initiative shows that the activities of demilitarization firms are usually overseen by ministries of industry, trade, or interior, which accredit and monitor them, but less often by MoDs (Gobinet, 2012). Indeed, while MoDs usually have oversight whenever munitions from national armed forces are concerned, they are otherwise not systematically involved in the private demilitarization sector's activities. Consequently, the MoDs are not always aware of the capabilities and capacities of commercial demilitarization facilities operating in their country.

This is especially true for the cross-border transport—that is, import and export—of surplus and excess ammunition. A written contribution by Nammo gives an idea of the complexity and variety of interlocutors. For Nammo Vingåkersverken Sweden, exports are overseen by the Inspectorate of Strategic Products, and imports are overseen by the Swedish Contingencies Agency MSB. The MoD is involved only when handling national demilitarization contracts. Otherwise oversight is provided by audit by national authorities regarding environmental, energetic, and site permission

Dynasafe's SDC 1500 for the destruction of conventional ammunition with a capacity of 4.5 kg NEO per feed, Abu Dhabi, 2011. © Dynasafe Demil Systems AB

compliance. For Nammo Norway NAD, exports and imports are overseen by the Directorate for Civil Protection and Emergency Planning and by the Ministry of Foreign Affairs. The Norwegian MoD is only involved in ammunition from the Norwegian armed forces; audits are performed by agencies other than the MoD. Meanwhile, Nammo Buck GmbH's main interlocutors are the Bundesministerium für Wirtschaft und Technologie (Ministry for Economics and Technology) and Bundesamt für Wirtschaft und Ausfuhrkontrolle (Federal Office for Economy and Export). The MoD is not involved for ammunition but oversees weapons and military systems. Oversight is executed by the Federal Office of Bundeswehr Equipment, Information Technology and In-Service Support acting as the MoD's procurement agency (Nammo, 2012).

Safety and physical security

When appropriate risk management processes are applied, dismantling ammunition is not inherently risky. Industrial demilitarization lines tend to expose the minimum number of people to the smallest quantity of explosives for the shortest period of time, consistent with operational needs. When built to NATO standards, facilities confine all explosive damage to the workshop where an incident occurrs.

Explosions can occur during processing, even in NATO-standard facilities.

Yet the nature of demilitarization means that explosions can occur during processing, even in NATO-standard facilities. In its reply to the Survey's 2012 questionnaire, Spreewerk Lübben GmbH reported one accident causing four deaths (date unspecified) (Spreewerk Lübben GmbH, 2012, p. 8). Nammo reported four accidents. Its Swedish subsidiary, Nammo Vingåkersverken, suffered an explosion in 2000 during a clean burning operation. The plant reported only material damage. Nammo Buck GmbH reported three accidents that claimed two lives (Nammo, 2012, p. 18).[34] More recently, on 2 January 2012, a blast killed four persons at the NSPA-commissioned demilitarization plant in the Turkish province of Kırıkkale.[35] On 11 January 2012, one woman died and a man was injured during an explosion at the EXPAL-operated plant in Gabrovo, Bulgaria, while processing anti-personnel landmines.[36]

Explosions can also occur during storage. Since demilitarization facilities also need to store large amounts of ammunition before processing it, they must meet strict quantity–distance standards, such as those in the *Manual of NATO Safety Principles for the Storage of Military Ammunition and Explosives*, in the US Army's Ammunition and Explosives Safety Standards, and in the International Ammunition Technical Guideline 02.20 Safety and Quantity Distances (NATO, 2010; USDA, 2011; UNODA, 2011c). The bunkers used to store explosives are self-contained, partially buried, and designed to send any blast upwards and not outwards to minimize damage.

In countries where industrial demilitarization is less developed, involving contractors that do not meet Western European or US standards, there is greater potential for accidents. Poor MoD oversight over inexperienced private demilitarization companies may result in them developing, selling, or using non-functional or unsafe demilitarization equipment. Another risk is that ammunition storage, handling, and operating areas are not kept free of debris. Other procedures that are designed to prevent the ignition and spread of explosive materials are not always applied. Risks are heightened when demilitarization companies are also producers; production accidents can spread to storage areas or demilitarization lines if the two processes are not properly separated.

There are several examples of accidents in situations of substandard storage and demilitarization practice. It is not always clear whether the explosion occurred during the ammunition manufacturing, storage, or demilitarization process. Much of the information remains restricted and details of follow-up investigations are legally and politically sensitive. One example occurred in Niksic, Montenegro, in July 2006, with the explosion of 200 tonnes of military explosives that a private contractor had imported and intended to transform into explosives for civilian use.[37] An enormous blast occurred in March 2008 at a demilitarization site near Gërdec, Albania, killing 26 people and injuring more than 300. A series of explosions also rocked VIDEX JSC's Midzhur factory, located near Gorni Lom, Bulgaria, in February 2010. When a depot containing ten tonnes of ammonite accidentally ignited, a large part of the factory was destroyed and the blast spread to a nearby compound where Greek anti-personnel mines awaited demilitarization. The Gerdëc and Midzhur explosions are the object of detailed case studies (Lazarevic, 2012).

While demilitarization may involve the risk of an accident, failure to demilitarize or destroy aged and surplus ammunition stockpiles can—and does—lead to significant unplanned explosions. The Survey's Unplanned Explosion at Munitions Sites database reveals that more than 400 ammunition depot explosions[38] were recorded from 1987 to 2012, affecting almost half of all UN member states (Small Arms Survey, 2012).

Demilitarization plants are vulnerable to the theft and diversion of weapons and ammunition during storage and transport. To date, accounts of demilitarization contractors breaking their contracts and reselling expired ammunition elsewhere remain anecdotal and unverifiable. Nevertheless, surplus stockpiles are an easy source of diversion in many countries (Gobinet and Gramizzi, 2011).

Surprisingly, this subject is not often discussed among demilitarization practitioners. This may reflect the fact that in the United States and Western Europe demilitarization contractors are confident that they exercise good stewardship of the ammunition and explosives under their control. Large contractors have clearly implemented security operating procedures, such as regular inventory checks of ammunition and components. They invest in perimeter security infrastructure and employ specialized security personnel (Nammo, 2012). Some contractors also rely on host nation security forces to secure and safeguard munitions during demilitarization activities.

ENVIRONMENTAL CONSIDERATIONS VERSUS COST EFFECTIVENESS

Many munitions and propellants are harmful to the environment (see Figures 9.1 and 9.2). Demilitarizing large quantities of ammunition requires the rigorous control and processing of toxic substances such as ammonium perchlorate, mercury fulminate, WP, and lead compounds.[39] The packaging material can also require handling and treatment to contain the heavy metals and persistent organic pollutants that were often used as preservatives in wooden ammunition packaging before it was banned. Some of the demilitarization processes themselves generate additional environmental hazards, such as air pollutants, pink water, and other hazardous secondary

Figure 9.1 Environmental hazards from industrial demilitarization

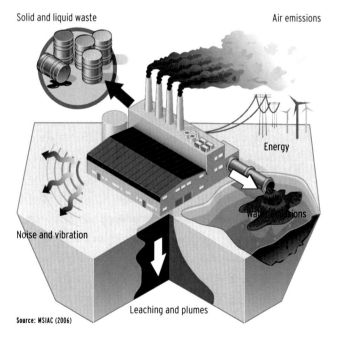

Solid and liquid waste

Air emissions

Energy

Water emissions

Noise and vibration

Leaching and plumes

Source: MSIAC (2006)

Figure 9.2 **Demilitarization waste products generated by a 66 mm M72 lightweight anti-armour weapon (LAW) high-explosive anti-tank (HEAT) rocket**

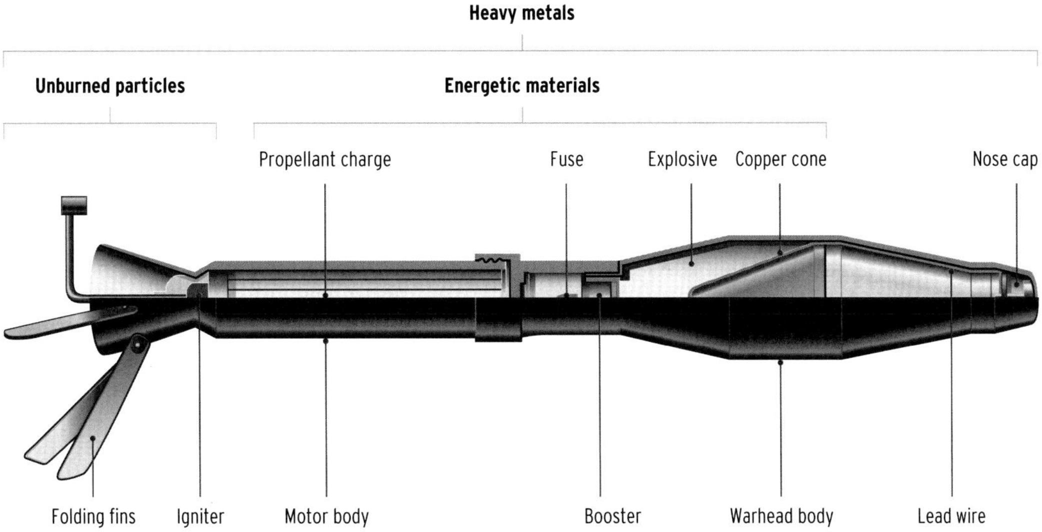

materials.[40] Any demilitarization process must ensure that there is appropriate control of the materials at all stages, and particularly the final disposition of any hazardous waste stream.

All of these substances have been the subject of regional or national environmental regulation covering noise, air, water, and land emissions, as well as waste management and recovery. Concerning air emissions, for example, the EU Waste Incineration Directive, which is also implemented in Canada, sets common emissions standards for incinerators in EU countries (EU, 2000; MSIAC, 2006). NSPA incorporates this legislation into all its demilitarization contracts awarded in EU countries and aims to achieve similar standards in contracts awarded in PfP countries; that said, strict adherence to these standards is not always possible given these countries' local demilitarization capacities and national legislation, which may be less demanding.[41]

The EU Industrial Emissions Directive superseded the EU Waste Incineration Directive on 6 January 2011 and was to be ratified by member states by January 2013 (EU, 2000; 2010). The equivalent US regulations are the Standards for Hazardous Waste Incinerators (United States, 2004). These regulations are broadly similar to their EU counterparts, although significant differences exist in a number of areas, such as destruction efficiency, categorization of metal emissions, and nitrogen oxides and sulphur dioxide threshold emissions (MSIAC, 2006, p. 17).

The relationship between the industry and environmental legislation has both stimulated and limited demilitarization activities. Environmental legislation has largely spurred the development of R3 demilitarization processes to reduce the reliance on OB/OD but has also made demilitarization systems more complex and expensive to develop and operate. The environmental compliance process itself is costly. In the United States, the major demilitarization facilities must operate under Resource Conservation Recovery Act Subpart X and Clean Air Act Title V permits. Securing these permits has reportedly cost some demilitarization sites, especially incinerators, USD 2–5 million, and permits must be renewed every five to ten years (Thompson, 2007; Thompson and Holkum, 2011a, p. 28-14; El Dorado Engineering, Inc., 2012).

The conflicting priorities of environmental compliance and cost effectiveness lie at the heart of the OB/OD debate as well as the effectiveness of R3 processes.

The OB/OD debate

Demilitarization uses two main methods: OB/OD and industrial demilitarization. Most nations' demilitarization regimes involve a combination of both. Each method has its advantages and disadvantages (King and Diaz, 2011, pp. 37–42). Environmental considerations are a decisive factor and in that respect OB/OD remains controversial.

Disadvantages

In the past years, OB/OD has fallen out of favour with many demilitarization practitioners who consider it a source of uncontrolled soil, groundwater, and air pollution. The public also views OB/OD in a negative light, citing noise and vibrations, and claiming health risks as a result of the dispersion of chemicals in the surrounding air and groundwater (RTO, 2010, p. 3-18). While industrial contractors use these arguments as well, they are also aware that OB/OD competes directly with industrial dismantling.

The principal environmental impacts of OB/OD are air emissions,[42] residual material (either energetics or toxic materials such as heavy metals), and noise. When carried out on a large scale over an extended period in one location, significant quantities of hazardous materials may accumulate on or near the site. The literature also emphasizes surface and subsurface contamination with heavy metals and unexploded explosives, which results from incomplete consumption of energetics, even during high-order detonation[43] (RTO, 2010, p. 3-18). This is accentuated if poor techniques are used, which may leave large quantities of unexploded materials. Similarly, incomplete detonation may occur if the

Albanian EOD soldiers preparing a mixed demolition pit of about one tonne of munitions deemed unsuited for industrial demilitarization, Bize demolition range, Albania, September 2009. © David Towndrow, NATO Support Agency (NSPA)

wrong procedure is used, with the result that energetic materials are released into the environment; this type of problem may arise during the destruction of insensitive munitions, which, by design, react less violently to thermal effects than conventional munitions.

Detractors of OB/OD also point to the dangers caused by shockwaves, projected fragments, and kick-outs[44] ejected by the explosions over a wide area. Open burning, although rarely used with ammunition today, is still used for propellants and some pyrotechnics. Even when done properly, the deflagration process is incomplete. If done incorrectly, raw propellant tends to scatter from the burn point, often leaching into the surrounding soil (RTO, 2010, p. 3-18).

Some demilitarization specialists also find the OB/OD process inefficient. OB/OD is considered wasteful of resources, since nothing can be recycled. The process is slow, labour-intensive—particularly in heavily populated regions where explosive limits are low—and its safe execution depends on daylight and good weather. Although it can be argued that OB/OD is appropriate for high-explosive rounds, it is less suitable for munitions with less energetic material content (such as countermeasure ammunition and low-vulnerability ammunition), as they are filled with insensitive high explosives that require significant preparation to ensure complete detonation. In addition, beyond a certain quantity, OB/OD may not be cost-effective. The destruction of large stockpiles of ammunition in non-conflict environments often requires the building of industrial demilitarization facilities, which, once amortized, are more effective and less costly.

Beginning in 2000, some countries progressively moved away from OB/OD. That year, the Canadian Department of National Defence instituted severe restrictions on OB/OD operations as a result of reports of environmental contamination at several Canadian Forces bases and ammunition depots (Park, Eng, and Garrard, 2011, p. 1.2). Between 2000 and 2006, it appears the United States sought to replace OB/OD methods with alternate, environmentally approved methods. The DoD's reliance on OB/OD reportedly dropped from 80 per cent in the 1980s to 32 per cent in 2010.[45] A number of countries, notably Germany, the Netherlands, and Sweden, have banned OB/OD if alternative processes are available (MSIAC, 2006).

Some countries have re-examined OB/OD and its environmental impacts.

Advantages

Although the demilitarization industry is very vocal about the need to phase out OB/OD, opinions are more nuanced among 'organic' demilitarization practitioners, or MoD representatives, and among the mine action and explosive ordnance disposal community.

One argument is cost. Many industrial demilitarization methods use complex and expensive pollution control systems. El Dorado Engineering estimated the cost of providing EU-standard nitrogen oxide control at USD 1 million in the United States, where the substance is not regulated (MSIAC, 2006). In a 2009 proposal, NSPA estimates the cost of shipping, installation, training, commissioning, and spare parts for a pollution control system at EUR 1.4 million (USD 1.9 million) (NAMSA, 2009, annexe D). This has obvious repercussions on the per unit demilitarization price. One observer finds that a 750-pound bomb costs USD 225 per ton to destroy using OB/OD, but more than USD 1,000 per ton to demilitarize using R3 processes (Raftery, 2007, p. 14). Countries that have entirely banned OB/OD have no choice but to use more environmentally friendly options, regardless of how costly they are.

Due to the high costs of industrial demilitarization, some countries have re-examined OB/OD, seeking to quantify its environmental impacts more precisely. Much of this research has been carried out in the United States, where OB and OD are subject to a permit system, regulated by the Environmental Protection Agency. Studies conducted by the Naval Air Weapons Center at China Lake, California, concluded in 2004 that, if ammunition items were properly prepared prior to OD, the metal from the ammunition casing tended to fragment, rather than vaporize, and therefore did not contribute to air emissions. The resultant emission plume did not contain sufficient quantities of toxic or hazardous pollutants to pose a significant danger to human health or the environment. The studies also concluded that the levels of dioxins from the OD of explosive waste were significantly less than the emissions typically generated by a medical waste incinerator.[46] In 2004, the South Eastern and Eastern Europe Clearinghouse for the Control of Small Arms and Light Weapons confirmed and used many of these findings (SEESAC, 2004, p. 25).

From 2008 onwards, some practitioners in the demilitarization community progressively reinstated OD as a sensible method for use on particular munitions in appropriate locations. Based on test results indicating that the impact on the environment due to OB and OD operations is much less severe than previously believed, the US DoD progressively requalified OB and OD methods as an indispensable, safe, efficient, and environmentally acceptable means of clearing large quantities of obsolete military munitions (Nordquist, Cramer, and Williams, 2009; DoD OB/OD Workgroup, 2008).[47] In the United Kingdom in 2008, the open burning of 170,000 barmines,[48] 20 miles outside of London, was considered the most environmentally friendly option due to the lack of industry interest in buying the RDX/TNT by-products of industrial demilitarization, and due to the cost[49] and CO_2 footprint associated with transporting the mines to Europe for industrial processing (Emerson and Towndrow, 2008; RTO, 2010, p. 3-3). More recently, the Finnish and Canadian defence forces conducted similar soil sampling studies, both of which pointed to relatively modest environmental impacts of OB and OD (Park, Eng, and Garrard, 2011, pp. 1-12–13; MSIAC, 2006). Efforts are under way to characterize and quantify air emissions from OB/OD, mostly through the creation of dispersion models and the updating of emissions factors databases (Nordquist, Cramer, and Williams, 2009; Williams, 2010).

OB/OD remains the primary destruction method for many armed forces, including within NATO.

Regardless of cost and environmental issues, field practitioners consider OB/OD indispensable in situations that involve the disposal of:

- munitions in insufficient quantity to justify setting up an industrial production line;
- munitions that are not safe to move or safe to process industrially;
- surplus propellant and explosive materials that cannot easily be recycled or reused;
- munitions in countries where logistics are poor and the shipping of large equipment is not cost-effective; and
- stockpiled munitions in-theatre following a conflict.

As a result, OB/OD remains the primary 'institutional' or 'organic' ammunition and explosives disposal method for many armed forces, including within NATO. In the UK, for example, propellants and explosives are currently destroyed by OB/OD. QinetiQ at Shoeburyness processes small items through an explosive waste incinerator, but the bulk of the propellants and explosives, as well as a large range of munitions, are burned or detonated in the open (Stalker, 2011b, p. 17-1). International organizations issuing RfPs usually acknowledge the need for MODs to retain OB/OD capacity, but will nevertheless prohibit the use of OB/OD in most demilitarization contracts to avoid litigation and to standardize tenders. For instance, NSPA endorses OB/OD where it is demonstrably safe and environmentally responsible to use—such as in most of its PfP projects (NAMSA, 2009, annexe G).

The effectiveness of R3 processes

The R3 philosophy of recovery, recycling, and reuse is the staple of the demilitarization industry. Proceeds from the sale of recyclable munitions materials derived from demilitarization are used to offset the processing costs. Yet there are technical and commercial challenges.

Not all munitions are suited to R3. Ammunition designers have traditionally focused their product development and design on performance, not on ease of demilitarization at the end of the munitions' life cycle (Mescavage, 2010).

In particular, modern munitions containing plastic-bonded explosives (PBXs) are more difficult to recycle than conventional explosives. Conventional melt-cast explosives,[50] based on TNT, are vulnerable to unplanned stimuli, such as bullet attacks and sympathetic detonations. In order to reduce accidental initiation during storage, transportation, and handling, ammunition manufacturers increasingly use insensitive munitions that are 'less susceptible to shock and other external stimuli' (Temple and Hooper, 2011, p. 21.3). These munitions use PBXs instead of TNT. Most of the insensitive formulations are not recyclable or are 'at least more difficult to demilitarize at the end of their shelf life' (Ampleman, 2011, p. 31.3). 'Design for demilitarization'—US DoD policy that aims to factor disposal considerations 'that do not impact performance' into ammunition procurement—has yet to gain comparable traction outside the United States (Mescavage, 2010; Stalker, 2011a, p. 14.2) .

Other circumstances may complicate the application of R3 processes. In some cases, the quantity to be demilitarized is insufficient to develop an economically sustainable industrial process line. The history of munitions is often unknown, and identification of chemicals, components, and materials present in munitions can be difficult to establish when no records are available.[51] This makes the reuse of components or materials difficult in the military environment, which has exacting performance requirements.

Donor-funded demilitarization projects report that the recycling of scrap metal is where most of the money is made. For some lines, typically the large-calibre and mortar lines, the returns from sales of scrap are reportedly similar to the total processing costs (Towndrow, 2012, p. 8). According to NSPA, the current costs for the demilitarization (excluding

Factory workers preparing to thermally treat bulk explosives recovered during the demilitarization process at EST Energetics GmbH, Steinbach, Germany, 2011.
© NATO Support Agency (NSPA)

transport) of 120 mm mortars in Albania are almost matched by the returns on the scrap metal. For 122 mm artillery shells, the demilitarization cost of EUR 7.29 (USD 9.53) per shell is exceeded by the scrap value EUR 8.59 (USD 11.23) per shell.[52] In general, however, the costs of processing and transport are still higher than the return from the recovered material.

The situation is different for the recycling of explosives for commercial, energetic end-use applications. This activity is largely market-driven and only viable when relevant quantities are significant. The main challenge is identifying a suitable and sustainable market for the end-use material (Van Baalen and Honey, 2011, p. 10-13). However, the explosive industry is very competitive and TNT is a fairly low-value explosive.[53] As far as the civil demilitarization industry is concerned, the amounts of energetic material that it can supply are trivial and the cost of recovery and conversion high with respect to the market value of recycled materials (RTO, 2010, p. 3-23; NIAG, 2010, pp. 83–88).

In most cases, R3 offsets the cost of demilitarization, but makes no profit.

Some examples illustrate the problem. In 2003 the US Army Aviation and Missile Research, Development, and Engineering Center established a Missile Recycling Capability at the Anniston Defense Munitions Center to recycle up to 15,000 TOW missiles annually. It was initially estimated that '98 percent of the missile hardware, warhead explosives and propellant ingredients could be reused or recycled into various industrial applications' (Gustafson, 2003). Yet the reuse and recycling of the TOW's energetic materials into commercial explosives, such as booster charges for the mining industry, yielded limited results because the US economic downturn severely limited market demand for reuse of this material. Currently, the disassembled TOW launch and flight motors are being disposed of through OB/OD. Similar concerns affect the demilitarization of the MLRS. While the US Army reuses components and recycles scrap metal, energetics are processed by closed disposal thermal treatment processes (Wright, Lee, and Gunter, 2011, pp. 6.4, 6.5).

The potential for recovery and reuse of military explosives for military applications is unclear. In the United States a programme was initiated in 2001 to requalify TNT recovered from demilitarization operations and reuse it to load munitions and bombs. Since TNT production capabilities in the United States and Canada were scarce or nonexistent, it was estimated that the process would be cost-effective (Anderson, 2001). Yet a recent report indicates that recovered TNT is not normally suitable for military applications (RTO, 2010, p. 3-28).

Although practitioners often disagree on the extent to which R3 revenues can offset operational costs, there is general agreement that in most cases R3 will partially offset the cost of demilitarization rather than produce an overall profit. In other words, demilitarization will not generate revenue overall, but the use of R3 can help reduce costs considerably (RTO, 2010, p. 3-28).

CONCLUSION

Most Western countries have 'organic'—that is, state-owned, MoD-operated—demilitarization facilities to process ammunition that has been declared unsafe for operational use by security forces. The routine disposal can amount to a significant volume over a year, and can comprise many different types of munitions. These categories are typically destroyed by the military using simple dismantling techniques or by OB/OD.

The end of the cold war created vast surplus ammunition stockpiles, which this 'organic' demilitarization capacity could not address. Because of the large tonnages involved and given time pressure—as ammunition tends to become unsafe with age—industrial dismantling became a cost-effective and efficient option. These complex processes require specialized, automated machinery, flexible lines, and high production rates that only industry can provide. The large, post-cold war ammunition stockpiles in the United States and Europe provided the necessary economies of scale for this industry to thrive.

Predominantly headquartered in the United States and Western Europe, a limited number of industrial demilitarization contractors transport, store, and demilitarize significant amounts of ordnance on behalf of client governments under normal competitive tendering rules. Importantly, they are also prime actors, stakeholders, and potential facilitators of international donor-funded arms control and ammunition demilitarization programmes.

Industrial demilitarization contractors operate under a complex regulatory framework, blending classified military ammunition standards with general civilian legislation aimed at controlling large continuous processing operations. Among other factors, compliance with international, regional, and national environmental legislation has influenced the development of industrial demilitarization technologies for disassembly, incineration, and contained detonation of conventional ammunition. Increasingly strict environmental emission limits—especially in the EU—have mandated the inclusion of complex pollution control systems at the end of the demilitarization lines, as well as the recovery, recycling, and reuse of ammunition components. This remains an important requirement in the industry.

Yet the requirements of environmental compliance are often at odds with the international community's push for speedy surplus destruction at reasonable cost. For example, multiple licensing requirements slow demilitarization programmes, while the need to comply with environmental legislation increases the costs of demilitarization for client governments. The current debates surrounding the environmental impact of OB/OD and the extent to which R3 revenues can offset overall demilitarization costs reflect the underlying struggle between environmental imperatives and the need for cost-effectiveness in industrial ammunition demilitarization.

At this writing, significant surplus stockpiles remained in the United States, Europe, and elsewhere. In Europe, many of the surplus cluster munitions and MLRS are already on contract for disposal over the next few years but, once this backlog has been dealt with, it seems likely that these countries' demand for industrial demilitarization services will drop. It is generally believed that manufacturers currently produce significantly less ammunition for current weapon systems than they did during the cold war, and therefore that MoDs are generally procuring much smaller quantities of ammunition. In the short and medium term, the quantities that will require demilitarization are thus likely to be far lower, yet the complexity of the dismantling process may increase (Van Baalen and Honey, 2011, p. 10-8; NIAG, 2010, p. 160). If these predictions are accurate and demilitarization needs fall, the commercial market is likely to consolidate around an even smaller number of operators. ◼

LIST OF ABBREVIATIONS

AMCOM	United States Army Aviation and Missile Life Cycle Management Command
APE	Ammunition Peculiar Equipment
CCM	Convention on Cluster Munitions
DAC	Defense Ammunition Center (United States Army)
DoD	Department of Defense
EU	European Union
MLRS	Multiple-launch rocket system
MoD	Ministry of defence
NATO	North Atlantic Treaty Organization

NSPA	North Atlantic Treaty Organization Support Agency
OB/OD	Open burning/open detonation
PBX	Plastic-bonded explosive
PfP	Partnership for Peace
R3	Recover, recycle, and reuse
RASR	Regional Approach to Stockpile Reduction
RfP	Request for proposal
SDC	Static detonation chamber
WP	White phosphorus

ENDNOTES

1   This chapter does not discuss: (i) the demilitarization of chemical or nuclear weapons; or (ii) the removal of unexploded ordnance or explosive remnants of war by commercial companies or NGOs (a distinct market with its own regulatory framework).

2   Artillery and mortar rounds, which often make up the bulk of a nation's surplus conventional ammunition tonnage, are procured in such large quantities that disposing of them exclusively through increased training would exceed barrel wear limitations. Author correspondence with Adrian Wilkinson, ammunition specialist, December 2012.

3   Many companies did not fill out the Survey's industry questionnaire, invoking such reasons as proprietary procedures, pricing, and individual market share. The following companies did reply: Dynasafe Demil Systems; DynCorp International; El Dorado Engineering; EST Energetics/Spreewerk; EXPAL; Nammo; NIRAS/DEMEX; SAB (Sonderanlagenbau) Nord GmbH; and TRZ Kragujevac.

4   The annual turnover of a company like Spreewerk Lübben GmbH, for instance, is approximately EUR 12 million (USD 16 million) (Spreewerk Lübben GmbH, 2012, p. 3).

5   Author correspondence with Sissel Solum, senior vice president of communications, Nammo Raufoss, 10 December 2012.

6   Dynasafe Demil Systems AB (2012); El Dorado Engineering, Inc. (2012); Follin (2012); DynCorp International (2012); author correspondence with Karsten Wohlert, managing director, Sonderanlagenbau Nord GmbH, 6 December 2012.

7   This agency replaced the Federal Office of Defense Technology and Procurement as of 2 October 2012.

8   For public supply and service contracts, the threshold is currently set at EUR 400,000 (USD 525,000) (European Commission, 2012).

9   At the NATO Lisbon Summit on 19–20 November 2010, heads of state and government agreed to merge three agencies—the NATO Maintenance and Supply Agency, the NATO Airlift Management Agency, and the Central Europe Pipeline Management Agency—into a single body, the new NATO Support Agency, or NSPA, which became operational on 1 July 2012.

10 A well-documented PfP Trust Fund case study is Albania (Gobinet, 2012, p. 37).

11 To sponsor weapons and ammunition disposal programmes, the United Nations Development Programme, the Organization for Security and Co-operation in Europe, the EU, and the European Community also coordinate the procurement of high-value items such as explosive waste incinerators.

12 Author correspondence with a demilitarization contractor, July 2012.

13 Demilitarization figures can reflect short tons (US), tons (UK), or metric tonnes, for either the gross weight of the ammunition or the gross weight of the ammunition including packaging (which is referred to as tonnes all-up weight). This ambiguity makes accurate estimation of capacities and capabilities difficult. Logistics planning for demilitarization, for example, traditionally uses tonnes all-up weight. This chapter reflects, for each figure, the unit of measurement used in the corresponding source.

14 US figures from the 2010 Demilitarization Symposium in Tulsa indicate an average cost of USD 1,570 per tonne. Author correspondence with the US Army Defense Ammunition Center (DAC), 20 November 2012.

15 The short ton is a unit of mass equal to 2,000 pounds (about 907 kg). In the United States it is often called simply 'ton' and is not distinguished from the metric ton (or tonne, 1,000 kg, roughly 2,205 pounds) or the long ton (2,240 pounds or roughly 1,016 kg).

16 US figures from the 2010 Demilitarization Symposium in Tulsa indicate a demilitarization stockpile of 587,000 tons, with annual funding of approximately USD 146 million. Author correspondence with DAC, 20 November 2012.

17 NSPA recently participated in high-level staff talks with deputy director-level representatives of the Russian demilitarization industry. These talks may result in a cooperative effort between NATO and the Russian Federation in the area of ammunition demilitarization, initially as an exchange of technical information (author correspondence with NSPA, October 2012).

18 The four plants are state enterprise Ukroboronservice (demilitarization capacity of 12,000 tonnes of ammunition per year, including use of domestically produced explosive waste incinerator); state enterprise Ukroboronleasing (demilitarization capacity of 33,000 small arms and light weapons per month); Shostka State Research Institute for Chemical Products (demilitarization capacity of 20,000 tonnes of ammunition per year);

Donetsk governmental plant of chemical products (demilitarization capacity of an explosive waste incinerator procured by NSPA from El Dorado Engineering, Inc., 22,000 7.62 mm rounds per hour, plus 440 fuses per 8-hour shift). Author correspondence with NSPA, October 2012.

19 The Ukraine State Demilitarization Programme foresees the demilitarization of 474,000 tonnes of ammunition by the end of 2017. Author correspondence with NSPA Project Office, Ukraine, 13 November 2012.

20 The Geneva International Centre for Humanitarian Demining defines cluster munitions as 'conventional munitions each of which is designed to disperse or release multiple submunitions (in some cases called "bomblets") over an area that may extend to several hundred square metres. The general definition of this weapon describes both the container (also called a dispenser or "parent munition") and the submunitions it holds' (GICHD, 2009, p. 8).

21 An MLRS artillery rocket such as the M26 contains a warhead that delivers 644 M77 sub-munitions. The disposal of MLRS warheads poses challenges in terms of the massive number of bomblets that must be handled.

22 In contrast, the destruction of a BL755 cluster bomb reportedly costs anywhere from EUR 250 to EUR 400 (USD 350–550), depending on the degree of material recycling (Towndrow, 2010; Bohle, 2010, p. 18).

23 Author correspondence with NSPA and Brian Jeffers, director, marketing division, Nammo, December 2012.

24 Dual-purpose improved conventional munitions are dispensed in large numbers using projectiles or artillery rockets, such as MLRS (GICHD, 2009, p. 13).

25 For a preliminary overview of these techniques, see Wilkinson (2006, annexe 1).

26 One launch pod contains six standard MLRS rockets.

27 The measurement is sometimes referred to as net explosive content, net explosive mass, or net explosive weight (in US pounds). Net explosive quantity, expressed in kilograms, is 'the total explosive content present in a container, ammunition, building etc, unless it has been determined that the effective quantity is significantly different from the actual quantity. It does not include such substances as white phosphorous, smoke or incendiary compositions unless these substances contribute significantly to the dominant hazard of the hazard division concerned' (UNODA, 2011a, p. 20).

28 Author correspondence with DAC, 20 November 2012.

29 Aside from the biannual US DoD Global Demilitarization Symposium, there is no international trade body to give voice to or represent the demilitarization industry.

30 The Act gives the Environmental Protection Agency the authority to control the generation, transportation, treatment, storage, and disposal of hazardous waste (USEPA, n.d.).

31 Concerning waste management, an EU directive specifically excludes decommissioned explosives from its scope, but the text does not define what 'decommissioned' means (EU, 2008). Industry representatives report that they consider decommissioned explosives to be those 'destined for demilitarization'. The exclusion provides significant advantages for those involved in demilitarization, as much of the legislation relating to waste and stemming from the directive no longer applies. However, the products of disposal, packaging waste, and other by-products are not exempted from EU environmental requirements (Honey, 2011, p. 11.3; Stalker, 2011b, p. 17.4).

32 OHSAS 18000 is an international series of occupational health and safety management system standards.

33 AQAP stands for Allied Quality Assurance Publications; AQAP 2130 is the NATO quality assurance requirement for inspections and tests.

34 In 2000 an operator died during the start-up of a 155 mm improved conventional munition projectile demilitarization process in the Lindesberg facility; in 2006 an operator died during the demilitarization process utilizing a detonation chamber; and an explosion occurred during the fully automatic disassembly of MLRS M26—the plant reported only material damage (Nammo, 2012).

35 Author correspondence with NSPA, 3 January 2012.

36 Author correspondence with an EXPAL product manager for demilitarization, January 2012.

37 Survey researchers' notes taken during the 3rd RASR workshop, 2–4 November 2010, Sarajevo.

38 Explosions that occur during industrial demilitarization do not qualify as unplanned explosions at munitions sites. However, the database definition covers explosions of ammunition that is being stockpiled in a plant's depot prior to demilitarization.

39 Ammonium perchlorate is the oxidizer and primary ingredient in solid propellant for most large rocket motors, including MLRS. White phosphorus is used in ammunition such as mortar projectiles, artillery shells, and grenades as an obscurant and incendiary to screen, shield, or protect troops, to blind or isolate the enemy, or to mark their targets (Voie, 2011; Karsrud, Voie, and Longva, 2011; Walsh, Walsh, and Collins, 2011).

40 Air pollutants include volatile organic compounds, acidic gases (such as nitrogen oxides and sulphur dioxide), particulate matter, heavy metals, and dioxins. Pink water refers to water contaminated with TNT, RDX, HMX, or the by-products of these explosives (MSIAC, 2006).

41 Author interview with David Towndrow, NSPA, 23 July 2012.

42 Notably, one of the products of burning TNT is nitric oxide, a major air pollutant.

43 High-order detonations occur when a round fully functions as designed. Specialists define a high-order detonation as 'the consumption of a minimum of 99.99% of the explosive load during detonation' and low-order detonation as 'a detonation that propagates incorrectly, fragmenting most of the ordnance and consuming around 75% to 99.99% of the [high-explosive] load' (Walsh et al., 2011).

44   Kick-out is the ejection of undetonated devices and can be minimized by the proper placement of multiple charges.

45   R3 processes account for the other 68 per cent. Author correspondence with DAC, 20 November 2012.

46   MSIAC (2006); Nordquist, Cramer, and Williams (2009); Park, Eng, and Garrard (2011); Thompson and Holkum (2011a, p. 28.14).

47   As many of the alternative (and high-tech) methods proved economically unsustainable in the United States, the country adopted the existing, simpler methods of mechanical cutting and melt-out that had served Europe so well (see Table 9.3).

48   A barmine is a long, rectangular anti-tank landmine.

49   The United Kingdom estimated that the open burning of 170,000 barmines would cost GBP 1 (USD 1.60) per barmine, as opposed to GBP 13 (USD 20) per barmine by industrial processing in Europe (RTO, 2010, p. 3-23). Extensive work was reportedly carried out to determine and monitor the environmental impact, and to inform regulators and local populations.

50   Trinitrotoluene (TNT) is a crystal that melts at around 81°C. In the melt-cast process, explosive mixtures based on TNT are liquefied by raising the temperature above 81°C, then cast inside of shells. The temperature is subsequently lowered to let the explosives solidify (Ampleman, 2011).

51   In order to characterize the chemicals, components, and materials present in munitions, some nations have established databases. The largest of these is the Munition Items Disposition Action System (MIDAS) database managed by the US Army Defense Ammunition Center. Originally established in the early 1990s to identify alternatives to OB/OD, the system now encompasses virtually the entire US inventory of munitions (Thompson and Holkum, 2011a; 2011b).

52   Author interview with David Towndrow, NSPA, 23 July 2012.

53   TNT yields approximately EUR 400 (USD 520) per tonne. Author correspondence with Adrian Wilkinson, ammunition specialist, December 2012.

BIBLIOGRAPHY

Ampleman, Guy. 2011. 'Development of New Insensitive and Greener Explosives and Gun Propellants.' Presentation made at the RTO-MP-AVT-177 Symposium on Munition and Propellant Disposal and Its Impact on the Environment, 17–20 October, Edinburgh.

Anderson, Curtis. 2001. 'Qualification of Recycled TNT for Use in the Production of HE Loaded Projectiles and Bombs.' *JOCG Demil Express*, Vol. 9. Spring. <https://tpm.dac.army.mil/events/Docs/DemilExpress/Vol09.pdf>

Bohle, Vera. 2010. 'Implementation Aspects of Stockpile Destruction.' *Disarmament Forum*, Vol. 1, pp. 13–24. Geneva: United Nations Institute for Disarmament Research. <http://www.unidir.org/pdf/articles/pdf-art2928.pdf>

Boyer, Travis. 2012. 'US Mobile Demilitarization Investment Study Overview for NATO Maintenance and Supply Agency (NAMSA).' Presentation made at the NAMSA conference on Mobile Equipment for Ammunition Demilitarization, Capellen, Luxembourg, 31 May.

Carlson, Kathryn Blaze. 2012. 'DND's $23M cluster bomb stockpile will cost $2M to junk.' *National Post*. 19 July. <http://news.nationalpost.com/2012/07/19/dnds-23m-cluster-bomb-stockpile-will-cost-2m-to-junk/>

Courtney-Green, Peter. 2005. 'Effective Disposal of Surplus Munitions Stockpiles.' Presentation made at Defence Logistics 2005, London, 8 February. <http://www.namsa.nato.int/Demil/docs/Defence_Logistics_2005.pdf>

—. 2007. 'Demilitarization Developments in NATO.' Paper presented at the 15th Annual Global Demilitarization Symposium and Exhibition, Reno, Nevada, 15 May. <http://www.dtic.mil/ndia/2007global_demil/GeneralSessionTuesday/T1420CourtneyGreen.pdf>

Dillard, David. 2010. 'MLRS Recycling Facility Coming to Anniston.' *JOCG Demil Express*, Vol. 27. Spring. <https://tpm.dac.army.mil/events/Docs/DemilExpress/Vol27.pdf>

DoD OB/OD Workgroup. 2008. 'Development of Emission Factors to Sustain Conventional OB and OD Operations at DOD Facilities.' *JOCG Demil Express*, Vol. 24. Fall. <https://tpm.dac.army.mil/events/Docs/DemilExpress/Vol24.pdf>

Dynasafe Demil Systems AB. 2012. 'Small Arms Survey Questionnaire for Industrial Demilitarization Contractors.' Unpublished questionnaire.

DynCorp International. 2012. 'Small Arms Survey Questionnaire for Industrial Demilitarization Contractors.' Unpublished questionnaire.

El Dorado Engineering, Inc. 2012. *Capabilities and Experience*. Brochure.

Emerson, Steve and David Towndrow. 2008. 'Barmine Disposal.' Presentation made at the 16th Annual Global Demilitarization Symposium, Salt Lake City, Utah, 5–8 May.

EU (European Union). 2000. Directive 2000/76/EC of the European Parliament and of the Council of 4 December 2000 on the Incineration of Waste. <http://eur-lex.europa.eu/LexUriServ/LexUriServ.do?uri=OJ:L:2000:332:0091:0111:EN:PDF>

—. 2008. Directive 2008/98/EC of the European Parliament and of the Council of 19 November 2008 on Waste and Repealing Certain Directives. <http://eur-lex.europa.eu/LexUriServ/LexUriServ.do?uri=OJ:L:2008:312:0003:0030:en:PDF>

—. 2010. Directive 2010/75/EU of the European Parliament and of the Council of 24 November 2010 on Industrial Emissions (Integrated Pollution Prevention and Control). <http://eur-lex.europa.eu/LexUriServ/LexUriServ.do?uri=CELEX:32010L0075:EN:NOT>

European Commission. 2012. 'Current Rules, Thresholds, and Guidelines.' <http://ec.europa.eu/internal_market/publicprocurement/rules/current/index_en.htm>

Follin, John. 2012. 'Transportable Cryofracture Process for the Destruction of Munitions.' Presentation made at the NAMSA conference on Mobile Equipment for Ammunition Demilitarization, Capellen, Luxembourg, 31 May.

France. 2008. *Synthèse du rapport sur le démantèlement des matériels d'armement.* Paris:
   Ministry of Defence. <http://www.relec.es/RECICLADO_ELECTRONICO/GestionRAEEs/Franciaresiduosmilitares.pdf>

Genov, Borislav Georgiev, Hristo Ivanov Hristov, and Hristo Petrov Hristov. 2011. 'Bulgarian Defence Institute Future Environmental Initiatives.' Presentation made at the RTO-MP-AVT-177 Symposium on Munition and Propellant Disposal and Its Impact on the Environment, 17–20 October, Edinburgh.

Gibbs, Larry. 2010. 'My Perspective on Enterprise Challenges.' *JOCG Demil Express*, Vol. 28. Fall.
   <https://tpm.dac.army.mil/events/Docs/DemilExpress/Vol28.pdf>

GICHD (Geneva International Centre for Humanitarian Demining). 2009. *A Guide to Cluster Munitions*, 2nd edn.
   <http://www.gichd.org/publications/subject/cluster-munitions>

Gobinet, Pierre. 2012. *Capabilities and Capacities: A Survey of South-east Europe's Demilitarization Infrastructure.* Special Report No. 15. Geneva: Small Arms Survey. April. <http://www.smallarmssurvey.org/fileadmin/docs/C-Special-reports/SAS-SR15-South-East-Europe-Demilitarization.pdf>

—. 2013. 'Dynamic Disposal: An Introduction to Mobile and Transportable Industrial Ammunition Demilitarization Equipment.' RASR Issue Brief No. 3. Geneva: Small Arms Survey.

— and Claudio Gramizzi. 2011. 'Scraping the Barrel: The Trade in Surplus Ammunition.' Issue Brief No. 2. Geneva: Small Arms Survey. April.
   <http://www.smallarmssurvey.org/fileadmin/docs/G-Issue-briefs/SAS-IB2-Scraping-the-barrel.pdf>

Gonzalez, Jose. 2010. *Office of the Secretary of Defense (OSD) Perspective.* Presentation for the 18th Annual Global Demilitarization Symposium and Exhibition, Tulsa, 11 May. <https://midas.dac.army.mil/Symposium/2010/10_Proceedings/A2_Gonzalez.pdf>

Gustafson, Joan. 2003. 'Missile Recycling Center (MRC) Now a Reality.' *JOCG Demil Express*, Vol. 13. Spring.
   <https://tpm.dac.army.mil/events/Docs/DemilExpress/Vol13.pdf>

Herbst, Eduard. 2007. 'Nammo Contract.' *JOCG Demil Express*, Vol. 22. Fall.

Honey, Peter. 2011. 'NIAG Study Group 139 Report on Regulatory Aspects Relating to Demilitarisation and Disposal of Munitions.' Presentation made at the RTO-MP-AVT-177 Symposium on Munition and Propellant Disposal and Its Impact on the Environment, 17–20 October, Edinburgh.

Hsu, Peter, César Pruneda, and Solim Kwak. 2000. 'The Integrated Molten Salt Oxidation Plant.' *JOCG Demil Express*, Vol. 8. Fall.
   <https://tpm.dac.army.mil/events/Docs/DemilExpress/Vol08.pdf>

IANS (Indo Asian News Service) and Ria Novosti. 2012. 'Russia to Scrap 3 mn tonnes of Ammunition.' 2 February.
   <http://www.thaindian.com/newsportal/world-news/russia-to-scrap-3-mn-tonnes-of-ammunition_100594885.html>

Johnsen, Arnt, et al. 2011. 'Contamination of Energetic Materials in the Norwegian Firing Ranges.' Presentation made at the RTO-MP-AVT-177 Symposium on Munition and Propellant Disposal and Its Impact on the Environment, 17–20 October, Edinburgh.

Karsrud, Tove Engen, Øyvind Voie, and Kjetil Sager Longva. 2011. 'Environmentally Responsible Smoke Munitions.' Presentation made at the RTO-MP-AVT-177 Symposium on Munition and Propellant Disposal and Its Impact on the Environment, 17–20 October, Edinburgh.

King, Benjamin and F. David Diaz. 2011. 'Preparing PSSM Programmes: Avoiding the Inevitable Problems?' In Benjamin King, ed. *Safer Stockpiles: Practitioners' Experiences with Physical Security and Stockpile Management (PSSM) Assistance Programmes.* Geneva: Small Arms Survey, pp. 8–47.
   <http://www.smallarmssurvey.org/fileadmin/docs/B-Occasional-papers/SAS-OP27-Safer-Stockpiles.pdf>

Lazarevic, Jasna. 2012. *Costs and Consequences: Unplanned Explosions and Demilitarization in South-east Europe.* Special Report No. 18. Geneva: Small Arms Survey.

Lucas, Sébastien. 2012. 'MBDA is Building a Munitions Demilitarization Capability in France.' Proceedings from the Military Green 2012 conference, 19–20 June, Brussels.

MBDA. 2011. 'MBDA to Set Up Industrial Capability for the Demilitarization of Complex Munitions.' Press release. 25 November.
   <http://www.mbda-systems.com/mediagallery/news-files/PR_2011-11-25_EN-1-650.pdf>

Mescavage, Gary. 2010. 'Implementation of Design for Demil (DFD) in the Joint Services.' Presentation made at the 18th Annual Global Demilitarization Symposium and Exhibition, Tulsa, 17 May. <https://tpm.dac.army.mil/events/Docs/2011GDS/GS-A_10.pdf>

Meyer, Wilfried and Frank Winkler. 2012. 'GD-OTS/SAB Mobile Demil Equipment.' Presentation made at the NATO Maintenance and Supply Agency conference on Mobile Equipment for Ammunition Demilitarization, Capellen, Luxembourg, 31 May.

MSIAC (Munitions Safety Information Analysis Center). 2006. Review of Demilitarization and Disposal Techniques for Munitions and Related Materials. Brussels: North Atlantic Treaty Organization. <http://www.rasrinitiative.org/pdfs/MSIAC-2006.pdf>

Nammo. 2012. 'Small Arms Survey Questionnaire for Industrial Demilitarization Contractors.' Unpublished questionnaire.

NAMSA (North Atlantic Treaty Organization Maintenance and Supply Agency). 2009. *Proposal to Albania and United States Department of State Bureau of Political Affairs Office of Weapons Removal and Abatement for the Destruction of Surplus Ammunition Stocks in Albania.* December. Capellen, Luxembourg: NAMSA.

NATO (North Atlantic Treaty Organization). 2010. *Manual of NATO Safety Principles for the Storage of Military Ammunition and Explosives (AASTP-1: Edition 1, Change 3).* Brussels: NATO.

NIAG (North Atlantic Treaty Organization Industrial Advisory Group). 2010. *Final Report of NIAG SG.139 Study on NATO Industrial Capability for Demilitarization and Disposal of Munitions.* 13 November. Unpublished document.

Nordquist, Tyrone, Randall Cramer, and Ryan Williams. 2009. 'Teamwork Is the Key to Better Understanding of OB/OD Emissions.' *JOCG Demil Express*, Vol. 26. Fall. <https://tpm.dac.army.mil/events/Docs/DemilExpress/Vol26.pdf>

Park, Jason, John Eng, and George Garrard. 2011. 'An Update of Policy and Legislation as it Pertains to the Disposal/Demilitarization of Ammunition & Explosives in the DND/CF.' Presentation made at the RTO-MP-AVT-177 Symposium on Munition and Propellant Disposal and Its Impact on the Environment, 17–20 October, Edinburgh.

Perala, Reijo. 2001. 'NAMMO BUCK GmbH, Germany Awarded 3-Year Contract for Demil of BL-755 Cluster Bombs'. *JOCG Demil Express*, Vol. 11. Spring. <https://tpm.dac.army.mil/events/Docs/DemilExpress/Vol10.pdf>

—. 2002. 'Nammo Creates Demil Division.' *JOCG Demil Express*, Vol. 10. Fall. <https://tpm.dac.army.mil/events/Docs/DemilExpress/Vol10.pdf>

Peske, Tom. 2010. 'Crane Army Disposes of White Phosphorus Ammunition.' *JOCG Demil Express*, Vol. 27. Spring. <https://tpm.dac.army.mil/events/Docs/DemilExpress/Vol27.pdf>

Peugeot, Frédéric. 2009. 'The Conventional Ammunition Stockpile Reduction & Destruction Problematic.' Presentation made at the First RASR Workshop, Zagreb, Croatia, 5–7 May. <http://www.rasrinitiative.org/pdfs/workshop-1/RASR-Stockpile-Reduction.pdf>

Raftery, Brian. 2007. *Innovative Approaches for Recycling Munitions.* Presentation made at the 15th Annual Global Demilitarization Symposium and Exhibition, Reno, Nevada, 15 May. <http://www.dtic.mil/ndia/2007global_demil/GeneralSessionTuesday/T0850Raftery.pdf>

—. 2008. *Conventional Ammunition Demilitarization (Demil): A Growing Challenge.* January–March. <http://asc.army.mil/docs/pubs/alt/2008/1_JanFebMar/articles/38_Conventional_Ammunition_Demilitarization_%28Demil%29_--_A_Growing_Challenge_200801.pdf>

RTO (Research and Technology Organization). 2010. *Environmental Impact of Munition and Propellant Disposal: Final Report of Task Group AVT-115.* AC/323 (AVT-115) TP/274. Neuilly-sur-Seine: RTO, North Atlantic Treaty Organization.
<http://ftp.rta.nato.int/public//PubFullText/RTO/TR/RTO-TR-AVT-115///$$TR-AVT-115-ALL.pdf>

Schmit, Steven. 2009. 'Commercial Demilitarization of Explosive D Projectiles: A Demil R&D Success Story.' *JOCG Demil Express*, Vol. 25. Spring. <https://tpm.dac.army.mil/events/Docs/DemilExpress/Vol25.pdf>

SEESAC (South Eastern and Eastern Europe Clearinghouse for the Control of Small Arms and Light Weapons). 2004. *SALW Ammunition Destruction: Environmental Releases from Open Burning (OB) and Open Detonation (OD) Events.* Belgrade: SEESAC.
<http://www.seesac.org/uploads/studyrep/Environmental.pdf>

Sina, Shkëlqim. 2011. 'Financial Support to Destruction of Surplus Weapons and Munitions.' Presentation made at the Centre for Security Cooperation (RACVIAC)–Pula Conference, May.

Small Arms Survey. 2012. 'Unplanned Explosions at Munitions Sites.' 19 October.
<http://www.smallarmssurvey.org/weapons-and-markets/stockpiles/unplanned-explosions-at-munitions-sites.html>

Spreewerk Lübben GmbH. 2012. 'Small Arms Survey Questionnaire for Industrial Demilitarization Contractors.' Unpublished questionnaire.

Stalker, David. 2011a. 'Design for Demilitarization (Including an Introduction to Design for the Environment).' Presentation made at the RTO-MP-AVT-177 Symposium on Munition and Propellant Disposal and Its Impact on the Environment, 17–20 October, Edinburgh.

—. 2011b. 'Future Options for Disposal of Energetics.' Presentation made at the RTO-MP-AVT-177 Symposium on Munition and Propellant Disposal and Its Impact on the Environment, 17–20 October, Edinburgh.

Temple, Tracey and Geoff Hooper. 2011. 'Managing the Environmental Effects of Insensitive Munitions Compositions: Air, Land and Water.' Presentation made at the RTO-MP-AVT-177 Symposium on Munition and Propellant Disposal and Its Impact on the Environment, 17–20 October, Edinburgh.

Thompson, George. 2007. 'Web-Based MACS Emissions and Health Risk Assessment Modules.' *JOCG Demil Express*, Vol. 22. Fall.
<https://tpm.dac.army.mil/events/Docs/DemilExpress/Vol23.pdf>

— and Jacqueline Holkum. 2011a. 'An Overview of the U.S. Demil, Range, "Green" and Other Munition Management Capabilities.' Presentation made at the RTO-MP-AVT-177 Symposium on Munition and Propellant Disposal and Its Impact on the Environment, 17–20 October, Edinburgh.

— and Jacqueline Holkum. 2011b. 'Automated and Web-based Munition Analytical Compliance Suite (MACS).' Presentation made at the RTO-MP-AVT-177 Symposium on Munition and Propellant Disposal and Its Impact on the Environment, 17–20 October, Edinburgh.

—, George Kevin Kennedy, and Tyrone Nordquist. 2004. 'Integrated Munitions Analytical Compliance Suite (MACS).' *JOCG Demil Express*, Vol. 16. Fall.

Towndrow, David. 2010. 'NAMSA's Involvement in the Demilitarization of Cluster Munitions 1996–2010.' Presentation made at the 18th Annual Global Demilitarization Symposium and Exhibition, Tulsa, 12 May. <https://midas.dac.army.mil/Symposium/2010/10_Proceedings/B2_Towndrow.pdf>

—. 2011a. 'Demilitarization Developments in NATO.' Presentation made at the 19th Global Demilitarization Symposium and Exhibition, Sparks, Nevada, 18 May.

—. 2011b. 'NAMSA and Its Role in Demilitarization.' Presentation made at the RTO-MP-AVT-177 Symposium on Munition and Propellant Disposal and Its Impact on the Environment, 17–20 October, Edinburgh.

—. 2012. 'Third NATO Trust Fund Project in Albania: Fourth Periodic Report, October–December 2011.' Albania Surplus Ammunition Demilitarization Trust Fund Project. Unpublished report.

TRZK (Tehnički remontni zavod Kragujevac). 2012. 'Small Arms Survey Questionnaire for Industrial Demilitarization Contractors.' Unpublished questionnaire.

UNDP (United Nations Development Programme) and Threat Resolution Ltd. 2004. *Bosnia and Herzegovina Small Arms and Light Weapons Ammunition Demilitarization Feasibility Study*. September. Sarajevo: UNDP. <http://www.undp.ba/upload/publications/SALW%20Feasibility%20Study.pdf>

UNECE (United Nations Economic Commission for Europe). 2009. European Agreement concerning the International Carriage of Dangerous Goods by Road ('ADR'). As applicable from 1 January 2011. ECE/TRANS/215, Vols. I–II. Geneva: UNECE.

—. 2011a. 'Globally Harmonized System of Classification and Labelling of Chemicals (GHS).' 4th edn. <http://www.unece.org/trans/danger/publi/ghs/ghs_rev04/04files_e.html>

—. 2011b. 'UN Recommendations on the Transport of Dangerous Goods: Model Regulations.' 17th edn. <http://www.unece.org/trans/danger/publi/unrec/rev17/17files_e.html>

UNEP (United Nations Environment Programme). 1989. Basel Convention on the Control of Transboundary Movements of Hazardous Wastes and Their Disposal. Châtelaine, Switzerland: UNEP. 22 March. <http://www.basel.int/Portals/4/Basel%20Convention/docs/text/BaselConventionText-e.pdf>

United States. 2004. National Emission Standards for Hazardous Air Pollutants from Hazardous Waste Combustors. US Code of Federal Regulations, Title 40, Part 63, Subpart EEE. 40CFR63.1200. July.

UNODA (United Nations Office for Disarmament Affairs). 2011a. *International Ammunition Technical Guideline: Glossary of Terms, Definitions and Abbreviations*. IATG 01.40. <http://www.un.org/disarmament/convarms/Ammunition/IATG/docs/IATG01.40-Glossary_and_Definitions%28V.1%29.pdf>

—. 2011b. *International Ammunition Technical Guideline: Demilitarization and Destruction of Conventional Ammunition*. IATG 10.10. <http://www.un.org/disarmament/convarms/Ammunition/IATG/docs/IATG10.10-Demilitarization_and_Destruction%28V.1%29.pdf>

—. 2011c. *International Ammunition Technical Guideline: Quantity and Separation Distances*. IATG 02.20, 1st edn. <http://www.un.org/disarmament/convarms/Ammunition/IATG/docs/IATG02.20-Quantity_and_Separation_Distances(V.1).pdf>

USDA (United States Department of the Army). 2011. 'Ammunition and Explosives Safety Standards.' Washington, DC: USDA.

USEPA (United States Environmental Protection Agency). n.d. 'Summary of the Resource Conservation and Recovery Act.' <http://www.epa.gov/regulations/laws/rcra.html>

Van Baalen, Mark and Peter Honey. 2011. *Final Report of NIAG SG.139 Study on NATO Industrial Capability for Demilitarization and Disposal of Munitions*. Presentation made at the RTO-MP-AVT-177 Symposium on Munition and Propellant Disposal and Its Impact on the Environment, 17–20 October, Edinburgh.

Voice of Russia. 2012. 'Russia to Upgrade Its Munitions Storage Facilities.' 2 February. <http://english.ruvr.ru/2012/02/02/65200403.html>

Voie, Øyvind. 2011. 'Risk Assessment Tools for Management of Contaminated Sites—Source Characterization, Fate and Transport (AVT-197).' *Final Report of NIAG SG.139 Study on NATO Industrial Capability for Demilitarization and Disposal of Munitions*. Presentation made at the RTO-MP-AVT-177 Symposium on Munition and Propellant Disposal and Its Impact on the Environment, 17–20 October, Edinburgh.

Walsh, Marianne, Michael Walsh, and Charles Collins. 2011. 'Remediation of a Military Training Range Contaminated by White Phosphorus Ordnance.' Presentation made at the RTO-MP-AVT-177 Symposium on Munition and Propellant Disposal and Its Impact on the Environment, 17–20 October, Edinburgh.

Walsh, Michael, et al. 2011. 'Explosives Residues on Military Training Ranges.' *Final Report of NIAG SG.139 Study on NATO Industrial Capability for Demilitarization and Disposal of Munitions*. Presentation made at the RTO-MP-AVT-177 Symposium on Munition and Propellant Disposal and Its Impact on the Environment, 17–20 October, Edinburgh.

Wilkinson, Adrian. 2006. 'The Three Ds: Disposal, Demilitarization, and Destruction of Ammunition.' In Stéphanie Pézard and Holger Anders, eds. *Targeting Ammunition: A Primer*. Geneva: Small Arms Survey.

Williams, Ryan. 2010. 'JOCG OB/OD Emissions Factor Review Protocol.' *JOCG Demil Express*, Vol. 27. Spring. <https://tpm.dac.army.mil/events/Docs/DemilExpress/Vol27.pdf>

Wright, Jeff, Jeff Lee, and Larry Gunter. 2011. 'US Army Missile Recycling Overview.' Unpublished presentation for the RTO-MP-AVT-177 Symposium on Munition and Propellant Disposal and Its Impact on the Environment, 17–20 October, Edinburgh.

Zaugg, Mark, et al. 2007. 'GD-OTS and EBV EEC Unveils New CBU Demil Line.' *JOCG Demil Express*, Vol. 21. Spring. <https://tpm.dac.army.mil/events/Docs/DemilExpress/Vol21.pdf>

ACKNOWLEDGEMENTS

Principal author

Pierre Gobinet

Emergency personnel at the United Nations offices which were devastated by a bomb blast in Abuja, Nigeria, August 2011. © Afolabi Sodtunde/Reuters

'Infernal Machines'
IMPROVISED EXPLOSIVE DEVICES

10

INTRODUCTION

Shortly after 6 p.m. on 17 February 1880, Stepan Khalturin lit a fuse in the cellar of the Russian tsar's Winter Palace in St Petersburg. Around 15 minutes later, the fuse initiated 145 kg of explosives that the carpenter had smuggled into the palace on behalf of the revolutionary group, The People's Will. The resulting explosion killed and injured around 50 people, many of them servants.

The People's Will was well aware that the bombing would endanger ordinary workers—the very people the group professed to be trying to liberate—but deemed the casualties acceptable if Tsar Alexander II was killed. 'It will kill 50 without a doubt', said one of the plotters. 'It is better to put in more dynamite so they don't die in vain, so it definitely gets him.' The sacrifice was futile, though, as the Russian monarch was not in the dining hall when the bomb exploded because his guest was late for dinner (Radzinskiĭ, 2005).

This was the first mass-casualty attack carried out using high explosives and detonators, technology that had only been invented around a decade earlier by Alfred Nobel. The Swedish industrialist had devised a way to stabilize nitro-glycerine in the form of dynamite and to detonate it using small charges of less stable explosives. These technological breakthroughs had incalculable benefits for the mining and construction industries, but also put hitherto unimaginable destructive power in the hands of small groups and individuals. Fin-de-siècle anarchists seized on this democratization of violence, using the power of high explosives to carry out spectacular bombings with the aim of intimidating their enemies and inspiring followers.[1]

In the days of the anarchists, bombs were referred to as 'infernal machines'; now they are less colourfully known as improvised explosive devices (IEDs). With the addition of various prefixes, this term covers an extremely wide range of explosive devices, from letter bombs to suicide vests, as well as trucks and boats laden with explosives. IEDs have become the principal weapon for insurgents who are fighting superior military forces. They have also become a significant cause of civilian casualties.

This chapter surveys the range of IEDs utilized today, the tactics used to deploy them, the resulting civilian casualties, and efforts to mitigate the threat. Its key findings are:

- IEDs killed and injured at least 13,000 civilians in 44 countries in 2011, according to open-source reporting. The actual toll is probably higher and more research is needed to assess the overall impact that IEDs have on communities, development, and governance.
- Globally, the ratio of non-fatal civilian IED injuries to deaths was approximately 3:1 in 2011.
- The vast majority of civilian IED casualties occurred in Afghanistan, Iraq, and Pakistan in 2011.
- It is possible to make it harder for militants to source the materials most commonly used to make the large IEDs that are responsible for the majority of civilian casualties, but such measures are difficult to implement, especially in the worst-affected countries.

- Militant Sunni Islamist groups are responsible for the overwhelming majority of civilian casualties inflicted in IED attacks. This is largely attributable to their use of large IEDs and indiscriminate tactics.

The chapter begins by providing an overview of the various types of IEDs and the contexts in which they are used. It then examines the available information on the impact of IEDs on civilians and assesses the types of weapons and tactics that are responsible for the majority of casualties. It continues by looking at efforts to mitigate the threat of IEDs with a particular focus on counter-proliferation, and concludes with reflections on the current challenges facing efforts to reduce IED proliferation.

A TYPOLOGY OF IEDS

Militant Sunni
Islamists are
responsible for most
civilian casualties in
IED attacks.

By definition, all IEDs contain a main charge of explosives. Much like military and commercial explosive specialists, improvised-bomb makers typically use a relatively inert explosive that can be handled safely for their main charge. These are initiated by a small charge of a more sensitive primary explosive that detonates readily. The most common type of detonator (also known as blasting cap) consists of a small metal tube filled with a primary explosive, such as mercury fulminate, which is initiated by an electrical charge. IEDs that use such detonators require one or more batteries to supply the necessary power. The activation mechanisms (switches or triggers) on these IEDs consequently involve various ways of completing an electrical circuit.

The complexity of IEDs increases with size. A larger device requires multiple detonators or detonating cord to ensure the whole of the main charge—which is generally divided into multiple sub-charges—detonates simultaneously. Also known as det/primer cord, detonating cord consists of a flexible, plastic tube that wraps around a core of high explosive and can be cut to length as required. High-explosive booster charges are needed in IEDs whose main charges cannot be initiated by detonators (such charges are known as 'cap-insensitive'). Bomb makers often add fragmentation (commonly referred to as shrapnel) such as ball bearings, nails, and bolts to their devices to increase lethality. The typology presented here classifies IEDs according to their switch or activation system.[2]

Time-delayed

Time bombs remain a staple IED due to their simplicity. These can be as crude as a burning fuse that gives the bomber time to reach safety. While this might seem old-fashioned, the system is still used. For example, Norwegian right-wing extremist Anders Breivik used a cannon (or visco) fuse to initiate a vehicle bomb containing 950 kg of explosives in Oslo on 22 July 2011. Used in commercial fireworks displays, cannon fuses consist of a core of black powder wrapped in layers of string and nitrocellulose, a combination that burns at around 1 cm per second. They are considered ineffective for many types of IED as they burn with a visible flame and emit smoke. Nevertheless, they are often used in improvised hand grenades and pipe bombs, which are employed in significant numbers in some areas, notably northern Nigeria.

The next level of sophistication involves the use of an analogue clock or kitchen timer. A metal contact is attached to a clock hand or a timer's rotating mechanism, so that it will eventually reach another contact, thus completing a circuit and activating the device. Digital clocks and timers are also used, including the clock or countdown functions on mobile telephones. Tapping into the device's circuit board requires a degree of electrical proficiency.

Victim-operated

Victim-activated or -operated IEDs (VOIEDs) include a range of devices, such as mail bombs that function when opened, improvised mines that explode when someone steps on them, and booby traps that are activated by other means. In their simplest and most common form, VOIEDs are activated when a person, vehicle, or animal applies sufficient pressure to push together two metal contacts or to press a button that allows an electrical current to flow to a detonator embedded in a main charge of explosives. Such devices are known as pressure-plate IEDs.

Pressure-release IEDs or explosive booby traps are typically similar in their operation: by removing weight from the device, a victim causes two metal contacts to come together, thereby completing an electrical circuit. For example, bombers set devices with one contact weighed down by an object that a victim might be tempted to pick up.

VOIEDs can also be initiated by tripwires. These can be as basic as using a clothes peg on the end of a wire to hold electrical contacts apart. When the victim pulls the wire, the clothes peg snaps shut, completing the circuit. More sophisticated VOIEDs include tilt switches or other forms of anti-tampering mechanisms. These can involve a metal ball bearing that rolls down a plastic tube when it is tilted and then completes a circuit. Passive infrared sensors are another sophisticated way of triggering VOIEDs.

Command-operated

IEDs that are operated from a distance are generally known as command-operated IEDs (COIEDs). They are often used in ambushes since they allow militants to detonate a pre-emplaced device at the precise time a target moves into the target area. At their simplest level, these can be the same as tripwire devices, but with the bombers pulling the wire when they want to detonate the device. Electrical cables can be used to the same effect, with the bomber completing the circuit from a distance. Both types are known as command-wire IEDs.

> IEDs operated from a distance are known as command-operated IEDs (COIEDs).

Radio- or remote-control devices are another common form of COIED. Car alarms, garage door openers, remote control toys, mobile telephones, and two-way radios have been adapted to this purpose. This type of IED is vulnerable to electronic countermeasure systems that prevent initiation signals from reaching the device; when effective, these systems can force the insurgents to revert to more primitive types of initiation, including command wires or victim-operated systems.

Suicide bomber-operated

The IEDs used in suicide bombings are forms of command-operated devices as bombers initiate them at a time of their choosing, generally using a switch that completes an electrical circuit. These IEDs sometimes involve switches designed to actuate the device if the bomber is killed by defensive counter-fire. This is done with some form of 'dead man's switch' or a remote-control trigger operated by a handler with visual oversight of the attack. The latter system can also be used to activate the device if the bomber has second thoughts about completing the mission.

The devices used in suicide bombings are typically referred to as body- or person-borne IEDs (PBIEDs) when used by bombers who approach their targets on foot. Suicide vehicle-borne IEDs (SVBIEDs) involve a driver who steers a vehicle laden with explosives towards a target; this approach tends to utilize civilian cars, minibuses, and trucks, but boats have also been used.

PBIEDs usually consist of a vest containing one or more high-explosive charges covered in outward-facing fragmentation. While these devices are generally worn inconspicuously under normal clothing, some bombers have responded

A policeman examines the remains of a vehicle used in a suicide bomb attack on the home of a colleague in Quetta, Pakistan, April 2011.
© Naseer Ahmed/Reuters

to improved security by developing new ways of concealing PBIEDs. In 2011, for example, a series of Afghan offi-cials were assassinated by suicide bombers who had concealed IEDs in their turbans, knowing their headwear would not be searched. Similarly, female and child suicide bombers are widely presumed to have been used in Iraq because they attracted less suspicion and, in the case of women, because they were less likely to be searched by members of the security forces, who are predominantly men (Rubin, 2009).

Al Qaeda and its affiliates have developed IEDs that are specifically designed to pass undetected through airport security, disguised as shoes and various carry-on items such as beverages and disposable cameras. More recently, the Yemen-based affiliate Al Qaeda in the Arabian Peninsula managed to get an IED on board an airliner in the underwear of a would-be suicide bomber and on cargo aircraft inside the toner cartridges of printers (BBC News, 2010). None of these efforts have been successful.

SVBIEDs allow for the covert delivery of larger charges into a target area as the explosives can be concealed in the vehicle. Covertness is often a secondary consideration when SVBIEDs are used to attack well-defended targets. In such cases, the vehicles tend to be laden with explosives and driven as fast as possible towards the objective. Gunmen are sometimes tasked with overwhelming or distracting security personnel so the SVBIED can get closer to the primary target.

Improvised explosive projectiles

Although not classified by their activation mechanism, improvised explosive projectiles are an important category of IED. They consist of any improvised standoff weapon that fires an explosive charge towards a target. They include direct-fire weapons such as improvised shoulder-launched rockets and rifle grenades, but more commonly take the form of indirect-fire (parabolic-trajectory) weapons, specifically improvised mortars and artillery rockets. Such weapons are generally directed against targets that are far away or in well-defended positions that cannot be effectively engaged with direct fire.

The Provisional Irish Republican Army (PIRA) used improvised mortars against security forces facilities in Northern Ireland, where the weapons were sometimes referred to as 'barrack busters'. A multiple-launch version was also used to bring down military helicopters (Geraghty, 1998). More recently, Palestinian militants based in the Gaza Strip regularly fired improvised artillery rockets known as 'Qassams' (after a militant cleric) into Israel. Videos released by militants in Iraq and Syria show that they have fabricated similar weapons (Ansar al-Islam, 2011; Stratfor Global Intelligence, 2012).

> IRAMs are among the most effective improvised indirect-fire weapons deployed to date.

The effectiveness of improvised rockets is limited as they typically have less powerful motors and warheads than military equivalents and are significantly less accurate. Palestinian militants have fired several thousand Qassams into Israel since 2001, killing 15 civilians up until the end of September 2012, according to the Israeli government (Israel MFA, n.d.).

While militants favour factory-produced artillery rockets over their home-made counterparts, there is still an improvised element in most of the militant attacks involving the former, which are designed to be launched in barrages by vehicle-mounted launchers. Militant groups rarely have military launchers and thus improvise their own. This can be as crude as laying the rocket on a suitably inclined piece of ground, a procedure that does nothing to improve accuracy and heightens the danger to civilians in the vicinity of the target. To mitigate the threat of a rapid military response, militants often use time-delay mechanisms so that they can leave the scene before the rockets are launched.

Among the most effective improvised indirect-fire weapons deployed to date are improvised rocket-assisted mortars or munitions (IRAMs), which the US military has described as a signature weapon of Iranian-backed Iraqi militant groups (JIEDDO, n.d.b). Sometimes referred to as 'flying IEDs', these are cylinders filled with approximately 100 kg of explosives and attached to 107 mm artillery rocket motors. Starting in November 2007, they were periodically fired in intense barrages from the back of civilian trucks over short ranges at US bases in Iraq. While IRAMs were exclusively used against US military targets in Iraq and no attacks have been recorded in that country since US forces withdrew at the end of 2011, they could potentially cause high civilian casualties if used against populated areas. This may have happened in Syria in early 2013, where government forces used similar weapons (Chivers, 2012a).

Other characteristics

IEDs can also be defined by other characteristics, including the type of target they are designed to engage. Anti-personnel IEDs are generally comparatively small and/or contain fragmentation; anti-armour IEDs are either large or focus their energy. The latter include shaped charges, platter charges, and explosively formed projectiles or penetrators, all of which fire metal liners towards their target from varying standoff distances. These are all directional IEDs that are not designed to be buried in the ground. Anti-personnel IEDs can also be directional. These tend to consist of a metal box filled with explosives and a layer of fragmentation on the open side, which is placed facing the target. They are sometimes referred to as improvised claymores, after the US military's M18 directional anti-personnel mine. Both anti-armour and anti-personnel IEDs can be either VOIEDs or COIEDs.

THE IMPACT OF IEDS

Weapons of asymmetric war

The term 'IED' was popularized by the use of vast numbers of improvised explosive devices during the recent conflicts in Iraq and Afghanistan. IEDs became the primary weapon for insurgents in these conflicts due to the asymmetric nature of the battle between irregular forces and the world's best-equipped and most technologically advanced militaries. All the same, IEDs are not new and are used by most insurgent groups currently operating around the world. Open-source reporting suggests that around 60 per cent of violent actions by non-state actors involve IEDs (AOAV, 2012, p. 24).

IEDs are used by most insurgent groups operating around the world.

Cheap and easy to construct, IEDs allow lightly armed and barely trained militants to engage far better-equipped security forces. They help tip the balance in an asymmetric conflict by enabling insurgents to inflict casualties without exposing themselves. IEDs also hamper the mobility of security forces as they have to conduct time-consuming sweeps for concealed devices and are weighed down with equipment such as metal detectors, electronic countermeasure systems, and robots. In addition, the security forces may have to use more heavily armoured vehicles with limited off-road capabilities, thereby restricting their ability to patrol rural areas and allowing the insurgents to establish and maintain control over territory.[3]

The shadowy nature of IED warfare can sap the morale of security forces far more effectively than conventional fighting. Soldiers operating in high-threat environments have to bear the strain of knowing they could be attacked at any moment. They face sudden death or life-changing injuries, with limb amputations being a particularly common result of IED attacks. Security forces that suffer casualties and are unable to engage their elusive adversaries have been known to vent their frustrations on local civilians, thereby undermining efforts to engage communities in the counter-insurgency effort. While this is more often a problem among ill-disciplined forces, even highly trained NATO soldiers have been known to fire randomly when attacked (Meo, 2008; Will, 2012). The threat from suicide bombers can also limit interaction between security forces and locals.

IEDs are the primary tool for strategic attacks on critical infrastructure. Oil and gas pipelines are particularly vulnerable and carry a key source of foreign revenue for many states. Insurgents looking to put pressure on governments also target mobile telephone networks, railway lines, bridges, electricity grids, and tourist resorts. Such actions disrupt commerce, limit communication, and undermine confidence in the authorities.

Civilian casualties

While many insurgent groups claim to target only combatants, civilians are often the victims of their IEDs. There is no single body of definitive figures of civilian casualties caused by IEDs around the world. That said, the NGO Action on Armed Violence has set up the Explosive Violence Monitoring Project (EVMP) to track civilian casualties caused by IEDs and explosive military ordnance around the world. The EVMP stresses that its database is populated using English-language media reporting and offers a useful indicator of the scale and pattern of explosive violence, rather than a comprehensive survey of all such incidents.[4]

It is also particularly difficult to assess injuries caused by IEDs as the figures reported by the media are often vague and do not detail the severity of the wounds, which can range from relatively minor lacerations to life-changing disfigurement and disability. More serious injuries have a considerable impact on societies, as caring for the victims can put a significant strain on families and health systems. Modern prosthetic limbs, for example, cost thousands of dollars. In 2012, the Iraqi Ministry of Health estimated that the annual demand for new prosthetic limbs hovered around 20,000 and that more than 72,750 had been distributed over an unspecified timeframe. These figures include demand from people who have suffered amputations due to all causes, not just IEDs (Al-Shumosy, 2012).

There has been increased reporting on traumatic brain injuries resulting from IED blasts. Medical research has also found that large numbers of IED survivors could suffer from an Alzheimer's-like condition called chronic traumatic encephalopathy later in life (Mooney, 2012). While the condition is normally associated with athletes who have received repeated head injuries, it can be caused by a single IED blast. The psychological trauma of IED attacks is even harder to gauge but is likely to be considerable.[5]

The EVMP data shows that 3,352 civilians were killed and another 9,827 injured by IEDs in 44 countries in 2011. According to the data, the ratio of non-fatal injuries to deaths for that year is approximately 3:1 globally, with variations by context. In Afghanistan, the fatality rate was higher, with 1,301 non-fatal injuries and 829 deaths, yielding a ratio of about 3:2; in Iraq, there were 4,295 non-fatal injuries and 1,127 deaths, or a ratio of roughly 4:1. With more than 5,400 casualties in 2011, Iraq has been the worst-affected country in recent years, according to EVMP data. The US military has estimated that 21,000 civilians were killed and 68,000 injured by IEDs in Iraq from 2005 to 2010 (Vanden Brook, 2011).

After Iraq, the countries where civilians have been most heavily affected by IED usage in recent years are Afghanistan and Pakistan. IED attacks in these three countries accounted for 74 per cent of the total number of civilian

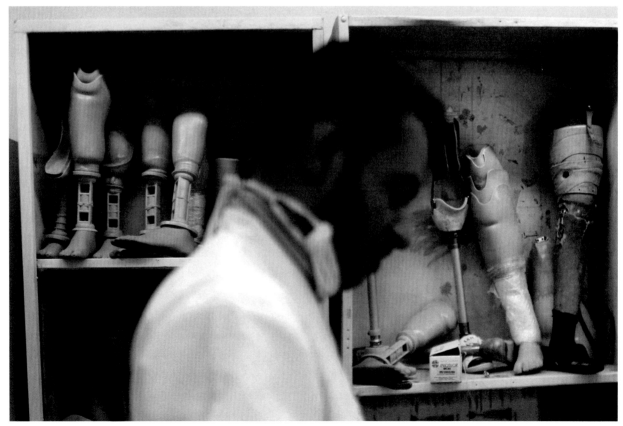

A technician works at a prosthetics factory in Baghdad, Iraq, where the numerous war-related injuries have created a high demand for the aids, December 2011.
© Mario Tama/Getty Images

Figure 10.1 **EVMP record of IED casualties (injured and killed) by country, 2011**

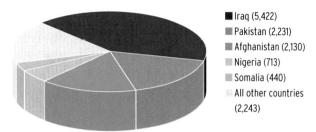

- Iraq (5,422)
- Pakistan (2,231)
- Afghanistan (2,130)
- Nigeria (713)
- Somalia (440)
- All other countries (2,243)

Source: EVMP 2011 dataset provided to the authors by Action on Armed Violence, 2012

casualties recorded by the EVMP in 2011 (see Figure 10.1). The fourth and fifth worst-affected countries are Somalia and Nigeria, which together suffered 9 per cent of total casualties. In all the top five countries, militant Sunni Islamist groups are either the only or primary users of IEDs.

These figures reflect a degree of under-reporting, especially in intense conflict zones where researchers and journalists struggle to record all the IED attacks that take place every day, often in remote and dangerous areas. The Afghan figures, for example, can be compared to those released by the United Nations Assistance Mission in Afghanistan (UNAMA), which is more systematically gathering data on civilian casualties through an extensive network of sources (UNAMA, 2012). It reported that 967 civilians were killed and 1,586 injured by IEDs in 2011. Even though these figures do not include the casualties caused by IEDs used in suicide attacks, they are around 20 per cent higher than the EVMP's figures of 829 killed and 1,301 injured. Another 431 civilians were killed in suicide attacks, according to UNAMA, although not all by IEDs as the perpetrators sometimes used firearms as well as bombs.[6]

The IED toll may be even higher than UNAMA's reporting suggests. According to declassified military statistics, 3,843 civilians were killed or injured in IED attacks carried out by anti-government elements in Afghanistan in 2011. This figure is 80 per cent higher than the one recorded by the EVMP using open sources.[7] By comparison, 252 Coalition military personnel were killed by IEDs in Afghanistan in 2011, accounting for slightly more than half of all hostile deaths of those forces (iCasualties.org, n.d.).[8]

IEDs also have a wider socio-economic impact on communities. Normal life in parts of Afghanistan has been significantly disrupted, with locals unable to tend their fields and orchards or travel on roads, which consequently cuts them off from schools, medical facilities, and markets (see Box 10.1). The same threat deters investment and aid projects, while greatly increasing the expense of any development work that is undertaken as aid workers and officials have to take restrictive and expensive security precautions.

Some militant groups deliberately try to restrict the development of communities, thus making them less supportive of the government and more vulnerable to subversion. The most striking example of this was a series of attacks on the international community and NGOs in Iraq starting in 2003. The first attack came in Baghdad on 19 August 2003, when an SVBIED targeted the Canal Hotel, which had been converted into the United Nations headquarters, killing more than 20 people, including Special Envoy Sergio Vieira de Mello (Power, 2008). While one of the key figures behind the bombing later testified that it was revenge for the UN Security Council's imposition of sanctions on Iraq during the 1990s and for the special envoy's role in the secession of East Timor and Bosnia and Herzegovina, it was part of a wider pattern of attacks that appeared to be designed to intimidate the international community and aid groups. Further attacks on the UN and the International Committee of the Red Cross persuaded both organizations to pull their foreign personnel out of Iraq by the end of October 2003, depriving the country of their resources and expertise.

Box 10.1   Life in the IED zone

The most prolific IED usage in Afghanistan has occurred in parts of Helmand and the agricultural districts of western Kandahar. Kandahar city, the former Taliban locus of control, is targeted with suicide attacks in addition to IEDs. Sixty per cent of the 20,866 IEDs encountered in Afghanistan in 2011 were in Helmand and Kandahar.[9] Interviews conducted for the Small Arms Survey in Helmand and Kandahar with a Taliban commander, tribal elders, farmers, law enforcement personnel, and a female activist confirmed IEDs as the most hazardous insurgent weapon, particularly because strikes often resulted in multiple casualties. Interviewees described the day-to-day IED threat as greater in volatile rural areas, particularly on unpaved roads, although they also noted the unpredictability and severity of suicide attacks in urban areas.

The chances of survival are reduced for victims of multiple-casualty incidents as health care facilities are overwhelmed by both the number of wounded and the serious nature of their injuries. A doctor working in Kandahar said that the hospital did not have sufficient beds to handle the casualties caused by major IED attacks, such that some victims had to be accommodated on the floor. He added that people in rural areas risked dying of blood loss because of a lack of local first-aid facilities.

IEDs can have a devastating impact on Afghan families, especially if multiple family members are killed or injured in a single incident. A female activist described how more than 20 women and children were killed and injured when a bus carrying her relatives to a wedding struck an IED. A tribal elder recalled an incident in which a family was killed when their vehicle hit an IED and then relatives travelling to pay respects were killed and injured in precisely the same way.

Locals said that moving from rural areas to district centres or provincial capitals placed them at the greatest risk of triggering an IED. Facilities in villages are often non-existent, so the associated reluctance of rural people to travel restricts their access to health care, education, and government. Pointing out that the threat of an attack was greatest around military convoys and government facilities, locals reported that they avoided government facilities. Feelings of insecurity were also reported in markets and other public spaces, particularly in those close to government facilities. Farmers and elders complained that IEDs restricted access to agricultural land and markets and that grazing livestock were also at risk.

A local policeman noted that the insurgents warned people not to travel at night, left indicators such as circles of stones, or blocked access to alert locals as to the presence of IEDs. Yet, as an elder stated, the number of IEDs and the wide area in which they are planted mean that locals are still at risk, as are outsiders who visit the area. Insurgents sometimes trigger IEDs unintentionally, underlining the irresponsible deployment of the weapons.

A police chief reported that, despite the fears of IED explosions, some local people were involved in IED fabrication and placement, for example by smuggling fertilizer from Pakistan to Afghanistan. One doctor recounted that he had treated bomb setters who were injured during a premature detonation, saying they were naïve and inexperienced locals who had been recruited by the Taliban. Other interviewees affirmed that the Taliban recruited youths to plant IEDs.

The Taliban commander interviewed refused to take responsibility for civilian casualties inflicted by IEDs. Although he acknowledged that some civilians had been killed, he suggested this was their own fault as they had ignored warnings about the placement of IEDs on certain roads. He said the Taliban's top-level religious guidance committee had issued a *fatwa* (ruling) allowing the use of VOIEDs, but that Taliban leader Mullah Mohammed Omar had also issued directives to avoid harming civilians with the devices. He added that no attempts to negotiate an end to IED usage could take place while the Coalition forces had freedom of movement.

A tribal elder underscored that residents were afraid to demonstrate against IED usage as this would imply that they were protesting against the Taliban and cooperating with the government. He said that locals who expressed such dissent could be added to insurgent hit lists.

Indiscriminate weapons and tactics

The likelihood of civilian casualties is greatly increased by the use of indiscriminate types of IEDs as well as disregard for civilians on the part of the bombers. All IEDs represent potential threats to civilian life and livelihoods, but some types are fundamentally more dangerous than others. COIEDs are among the least indiscriminate as they are designed to be triggered only when the intended target is in the target area and attacks can be aborted if civilians are at risk.

Time-delay IEDs are less precise weapons than COIEDs. A bomb may have been planted to target a specific individual who is normally in a certain place at a certain time, but a slight change in routine can mean the explosion misses the intended victim and inflicts unintended casualties. Some militants plant time-delay IEDs and then provide a warning so that the authorities can evacuate the threatened area, thereby demonstrating their capabilities, causing disruption, and damaging property. It also means the militants will be taken seriously when they call in future warnings, even if they have not planted a device.

However, this tactic can go wrong. One notorious example is the vehicle-borne IED (VBIED) that was set to detonate in the Northern Irish village of Omagh on 15 August 1998. The militant Irish nationalists responsible for the device telephoned warnings to journalists from around 40 minutes before the device was set to explode, but the wrong area was evacuated and 29 people were killed (BBC News, n.d.b).

Most VOIEDs are even less discriminating. While various militant groups around the world have deployed VOIEDs, they have been used on an unprecedented scale in the current conflict in Afghanistan (see Figure 10.2). In its mid-year 2011 report, UNAMA noted that 13,000 of the 20,000 IEDs cleared over a 12-month period had been analysed and 69 per cent (8,970) were VOIEDs, with 90 per cent of those (8,073) involving pressure plates (UNAMA, 2011, p. 2). Extrapolating this ratio to the entire sample would suggest that, of the 20,000 IEDs deployed by insurgents, at least 12,000 were pressure-plate VOIEDs. UNAMA also found that most pressure-plate IEDs contain approximately 20 kg of explosives, meaning the victims have little chance of survival, and the majority that had been analysed by the UK's Defence Exploitation Facility would be activated by 10 kg of pressure, the weight of very young child (UNAMA, 2011, pp. 2, 16).

Afghan insurgents have at times tried to mitigate the threat to civilians by advising locals to avoid areas where IEDs have been emplaced, typically by distributing 'night letters' around communities. These might inform locals of areas to avoid or warn them against travelling at night. A UN Mine Action Service (UNMAS) official told the Small Arms Survey that there was considerable regional variation in the extent to which insurgents were trying to mitigate civilian casualties, which probably reflected the varying levels of interaction between local insurgent groups and communities.[10]

Sometimes Afghan insurgents use arming devices that allow them to switch pressure plates on only when targets are in the area. Some VOIEDs also incorporate simple ways to regulate the amount of pressure required to activate them so they will only detonate when a Western soldier weighed down with equipment steps on them—as opposed to lighter locals.[11] Nevertheless, Coalition counter-IED officers told the Small Arms Survey that they are not seeing a significant increase in attempts to reduce civilian casualties through the use of safety devices on VOIEDs.[12]

UNAMA has repeatedly stated that it considers pressure-plate IEDs equivalent to military landmines as they are equally indiscriminate. Nevertheless, there are significant differences between Afghan VOIEDs and landmines. The former represent a less persistent threat as most are made using home-made explosives, which are rendered inert as they degrade over time; they also are generally triggered by electrical circuits that rely on batteries, which run out of power.[13] In contrast, modern anti-personnel landmines have non-electrical initiation mechanisms and more stable, factory-made explosives that ensure they continue to function for years.

The widespread use of batteries and other metal components also makes IEDs easier to find than modern military landmines, which

Figure 10.2   IEDs in Afghanistan by switch type, 2011

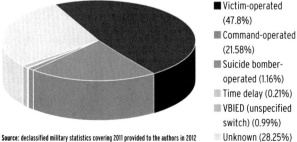

- Victim-operated (47.8%)
- Command-operated (21.58%)
- Suicide bomber-operated (1.16%)
- Time delay (0.21%)
- VBIED (unspecified switch) (0.99%)
- Unknown (28.25%)

Source: declassified military statistics covering 2011 provided to the authors in 2012

are usually made with as few metal parts as possible to make them more difficult to detect. However, in response to the increased use of metal detectors by foreign military forces, Afghan insurgents have developed ways of reducing the metal content in their IEDs. For example, some now use carbon rods taken from inside batteries as their electrical contacts. These conduct electricity but do not have a metal signature (JIEDDO, 2011). IED emplacers also bury the batteries to make them harder to detect.

A more sophisticated solution began to emerge in southern Afghanistan in 2010, in the form of copies of the Soviet PMN anti-personnel landmine. The casings for these IEDs were made using a plastic extrusion machine. Like the real PMN, they have no electrical components and thus represent a more persistent threat than most pressure-plate IEDs; unlike military mines, the copies do not have arming mechanisms, making them more dangerous to transport, handle, and neutralize (Wright and Binnie, 2010).

While the deployment of minimal- and no-metal VOIEDs makes them as hard to find as military landmines, if not harder, the process of clearing IEDs is also complicated by their irregular nature. Explosive ordnance disposal technicians know at what depth they will encounter military landmines and how to disarm the mass-produced weapons. Under international law, they should only be buried in clearly marked areas. In contrast, every IED potentially represents a unique challenge that can be more dangerous and time-consuming to disarm.[14] The dangers are also greatly increased by the practice of adding additional anti-tampering mechanisms to IEDs, such as pressure-release, photo-sensitive, and tilt switches that activate the devices when they are moved.

Like command-operated devices, suicide IEDs ostensibly give their operators an opportunity to abandon their attacks if they cannot reach their intended targets or if they risk inflicting undesired casualties. Indeed, some groups have described suicide bombers as their equivalent of military precision-guided munitions, with the human operator

A pressure plate initiator, recovered in Kandahar, 2012. Carbon rods from batteries are used to prevent the device from being located by metal detectors.
© Joanna Wright

Figure 10.3 **Civilian IED casualties in Afghanistan, by switch type, 2011**

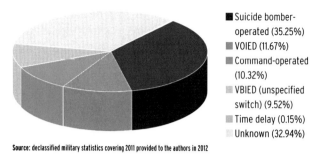

■ Suicide bomber-
operated (35.25%)
■ VOIED (11.67%)
■ Command-operated
(10.32%)
■ VBIED (unspecified
switch) (9.52%)
■ Time delay (0.15%)
■ Unknown (32.94%)

Source: declassified military statistics covering 2011 provided to the authors in 2012

replacing the sophisticated guidance technology.[15] Such arguments belie the unreliability
of suicide bombers, who are often under considerable psychological strain and frequently
make mistakes, such as initiating their devices
too early or in the vicinity of civilians.

The unreliability of suicide bombings is
reflected in the civilian casualties they inflict
in Afghanistan, where attacks that deliberately
target ordinary civilians are relatively rare.

According to the declassified military statistics, PBIEDs and SVBIEDs accounted for 35 per cent of civilian casualties
in Afghanistan in 2011. In contrast, VOIEDs accounted for just 12 per cent of civilian casualties (see Figure 10.3).[16]

The risk of civilian casualties in suicide IED attacks is heightened by their use in busy places, where bombers
typically have a better chance of closing on their targets by blending in with locals. The risk of civilian casualties is
also elevated in such attacks because of the use of larger amounts of explosives; this threat is particularly associated
with the use of VBIEDs and SVBIEDs, which are usually designed to deliver large quantities of explosive to a target.
The EVMP data shows that in 2011 vehicle bombs were most frequently used to target military and security forces
facilities, but civilians represented 67 per cent of the resulting casualties. It also shows that vehicle bombs inflicted
nearly ten times the number of civilian casualties as roadside IEDs and attributes that rate both to the relatively large
amount of explosives they carry and to their frequent use in populated areas (AOAV, 2012, p. 25). Declassified military
statistics reveal that, in Afghanistan, VBIEDs and SVBIEDs were used in just over 1 per cent of attacks but caused 25
per cent of civilian IED casualties in 2011.[17]

While there are no available figures showing a clear trend towards larger VBIEDs, it is likely that militants are
using more explosives in an attempt to overcome defensive measures adopted by their targets. Such measures include
the use of more heavily armoured vehicles and the erection of blast barriers around facilities. What is clear is that the
use of indiscriminate IEDs and tactics are responsible for the overwhelming majority of civilian casualties. EVMP data
indicates that around 26 per cent of the 13,179 civilian IED casualties in 2011 were inflicted in incidents in which the
military, security forces, or non-state armed groups were the intended targets. At the same time, 35 per cent of civilian
IED casualties were caused by attacks that deliberately targeted civilians (the intended targets of the remaining 39 per
cent were not reported).[18]

Targeting civilians

Non-state armed groups routinely target civilians. Most see political leaders, civilian officials, and informers who are
involved in efforts to suppress their activities as legitimate targets. They also typically try to silence other types of
civilians whom they perceive to be a threat—including critics in their own communities—using violence or intimidation. While such attacks are often highly targeted, they can cause high casualty rates when IEDs are used. The most
devastating such attack was the attempt to assassinate Benazir Bhutto when she returned from self-imposed exile to
Pakistan on 18 October 2007. A suicide bomber killed at least 130 people and injured more than 400 by detonating
his explosives during her procession through Karachi that day. Two months later, more than 20 people died in the
suicide bombing that killed her on 27 December 2007 (BBC News, 2007).

Lower-level IED attacks on civilian opponents happen frequently in Pakistan, with tribal elders being popular targets as the militants attempt to supplant traditional forms of social organization with their own Islamist system. For example, there have been a series of suicide bombings at *jirgas*, the councils of Pashtun tribal leaders. The targeted tribal groups were attempting to mobilize resistance to the militants, knowing that attacks that deter them from holding *jirgas* threaten their system of social and political organization.[19]

There are also extremist groups and individuals who deliberately target ordinary civilians who have no involvement in countering militancy. IEDs—especially large ones—are the ideal weapons for carrying out these types of indiscriminate attacks. Such actions are generally intended to draw attention to the bombers' cause, avenge a perceived injustice, instil fear in the targeted population, undermine confidence in the security forces, influence government policy, or provoke retaliatory action that helps mobilize a certain community. Sometimes the motive is unclear. Members of the right-wing group Nuclei Armati Rivoluzionari were convicted of the 2 August 1980 bombing at the main railway station in Bologna, Italy, in which 85 people died, but it was never established what they hoped to achieve by killing civilians (BBC News, n.d.a). Similarly, the motive behind the 11 April 2011 bombing of the Minsk Metro in Belarus remains unclear (Sweeney, 2012).

Mass-casualty attacks have been carried out by actors with various cultural, religious, and political backgrounds. Norwegian right-wing extremist Anders Breivik, for example, stated that he carried out his VBIED and shooting attack in Norway in an attempt to publicize his anti-immigration ideology and inspire others to take up the cause (Breivik, 2011). Timothy McVeigh claimed he was avenging the bungled 1993 assault on the Branch Davidians (a sect with which he was not affiliated) when he detonated a VBIED that killed 168 people in Oklahoma City on 19 April 1995 (BBC News, 2001).

Criminals generally use IEDs to attack rivals or law enforcement officials.

Criminals who use IEDs generally employ them in highly targeted attacks to kill rivals or law enforcement officials, but there have been instances of them carrying out mass-casualty incidents. The Colombian drug lord Pablo Escobar is suspected of ordering the bombing of an airliner on 27 November 1989, which killed 110 people. A few days later, on 6 December 1989, a VBIED killed 52 people when it detonated outside the Administrative Department of Security headquarters in Bogotá, Colombia (Bowden, 2001).

While criminals and right-wing extremists have sporadically carried out mass-casualty bombings targeting civilians, militant Sunni Islamists have been overwhelming responsible for such attacks in recent years. The worst-affected countries are Iraq and Pakistan. According to the EVMP dataset, 462 (or 41 per cent) of the 1,127 fatalities caused by IEDs in Iraq in 2011 occurred as a result of attacks that deliberately targeted civilians. In Pakistan, the figure was 233 (or 39 per cent) of the 604 killed by IEDs (AOAV, 2012). While the EVMP does not attribute responsibility for attacks, a Small Arms Survey review of the incidents shows that militant Sunni Islamist groups either claimed or were held responsible for all the attacks that deliberately targeted civilians in Iraq.

The picture in Pakistan is complicated by the presence of both ethnic Balochi and Sunni Islamist groups that have claimed or been held responsible for attacks on civilians. The close correlations between Pakistan's religious and ethnic identities and political allegiances can also make it difficult to determine the motives behind attacks. Nevertheless, the EVMP recorded only 13 fatalities in attacks targeting civilians in Balochistan province; 11 of these victims died in an SVBIED attack that was probably carried out by Sunni extremists. Pakistan also has a long history of sectarian violence, which has claimed more lives in recent years as extremists have increasingly turned to mass-casualty IED tactics.[20]

Militant Sunni Islamists were also responsible for at least 86 per cent of the fatalities caused by IED attacks that targeted civilians in countries other than Iraq and Pakistan (AOAV, 2012). Some of the attacks were primarily aimed at non-Muslims, such as the suicide bombings at a Coptic church in Egypt on 1 January 2011 and Moscow's Domodedovo airport on 24 January 2011. Nevertheless, in most incidents Muslims—often members of non-Sunni sects—were targeted. It is consequently clear that the overwhelming majority of civilian IED casualties—whether intentional or otherwise—are being inflicted by militant Sunni Islamists and the majority of the victims are Muslims.[21]

SOURCES OF IED COMPONENTS AND CONTROLS

Bomb makers are hindered when acquiring materials becomes harder, riskier, and costlier.

It is extremely difficult to prevent insurgents from making and deploying IEDs because explosives can be synthesized from everyday materials that are difficult to control. However, it is possible to increase the logistical burden on bomb makers by forcing them to shift to materials that are harder, riskier, and more expensive to acquire, or that have to be transported over longer distances and in smaller batches, that require more complex processing, or that are less powerful when they are turned into explosives.

It stands to reason that, if deprived of resources, insurgents and terrorists would be limited to building fewer or smaller IEDs. They would thus produce fewer large devices—which are among the primary causes of civilian casualties—and instead be forced to adopt more discriminating targeting methods. This section looks at the various sources of explosives and efforts to control them.

Military explosives and recycled ordnance

IED makers have made extensive use of military explosives, whether in the form of plastic explosives such as Composition-4 (C-4), which consists of RDX explosive combined with a plasticizing agent, or munitions that are adapted for use in IEDs. Military-grade plastic explosives are desirable weapons for insurgents and terrorists as they are designed to be safe to handle, easy to use, and highly adaptable. They are also tightly controlled, so one of the primary ways they have traditionally found their way to non-state actors is through state sponsorship.

State sponsorship

The best-recorded example of a state supplying militants with plastic explosives was the provision of Czechoslovakian SEMTEX to the PIRA by Col. Muammar Qaddafi's Libya. Used sparingly to make booster charges and small IEDs for targeted assassinations, this explosive greatly increased the capabilities of PIRA bombers. Although more than 25 years old, small amounts of SEMTEX continue to be used in bombings carried out by the militant Irish nationalist groups that reject the peace process that ended the PIRA's campaign of violence (IMC, 2009).

Iran has also been accused of providing explosives to various militants, including the Shia radicals responsible for a series of mass-casualty SVBIED attacks in Lebanon in 1982 and 1983 (Crist, 2012). These militants were subsequently incorporated into Hezbollah, which remains the world's most powerful non-state armed group thanks largely to continued Iranian support.

Iran tried to replicate its success in Lebanon by arming Shia militants in Iraq after the US-led invasion in 2003. US forces found large quantities of Iranian weaponry in caches used by groups such as Asaib Ahl al-Haq and Kataib Hezbollah, including Iranian-made C-4. The United States holds the Qods Force—the external operations arm of the Islamic Revolution Guards Corps—responsible for arming and training these groups (Schroeder and King, 2012; USDOT, 2008a; 2008b; 2009). Tehran also appears to see IED attacks as a deniable way of striking back at its adversaries.

In 2011–12, Iranian and allied Hezbollah agents were accused of involvement in bombing conspiracies in Azerbaijan, Bulgaria, Cyprus, Georgia, India, Kenya, Thailand, and the United States (Levin, 2012).

The Pakistani military's Directorate of Inter-Services Intelligence (ISI) is another organization that is regularly accused of supporting non-state armed groups in an effort to weaken regional rival India and establish a friendly regime in neighbouring Afghanistan. In India, the use of RDX is widely seen as evidence that the ISI supported the perpetrators, on the basis that they could not have obtained the military explosive from other sources (Ghosh, 2000). In the most notable incident, the Indian authorities claimed ISI-trained militants used RDX that had been smuggled into India from Pakistan in the 11 July 2006 Mumbai train bombings, which killed more than 180 people (BBC News, 2006). India has not, however, released compelling evidence of official Pakistani involvement and Islamabad denies the allegations.

The international community has responded to the plastic explosive threat with the 1991 Convention on the Marking of Plastic Explosives for the Purpose of Detection, which has been signed by 147 states (UNGA, 1991). This dictates that all plastic explosives made in signatory states must include detection taggants—volatile chemicals that slowly evaporate from the explosive and can be detected by either trained sniffer dogs or specialized air-sampling machines. This makes it far harder for terrorists to use powerful plastic explosives to bomb targets that have these types of security measures in place, most notably airliners. Iran remains a conspicuous non-signatory state, meaning that its domestically produced explosives need not include taggants, making them more of a threat to international security if they proliferate.

> Pakistan's ISI is regularly accused of supporting non-state armed groups.

States have also sought to use diplomatic pressure to curb state-sponsorship of non-state actors. Probably the most prominent diplomatic effort is the US State Department's list of state sponsors of terrorism. Designated states are subject to US sanctions that include a ban on arms exports and controls on the export of dual-use items that could significantly enhance their military capability or the ability to support terrorism. But Pakistan has not been blacklisted by the United States and Iran has shown no sign of changing its policies even though it has been on the list since 1984 (Bozorgmehr, 2012). The international community has only sanctioned one state—Libya, from 1992 to 1999—for its involvement in terrorism.

Looting arsenals

State sponsorship is not the only way for militants to source military explosives; they also take advantage of the looting of arsenals after the collapse of a state's military structures and recycle explosive ordnance that has proliferated through other means. There have been two major proliferation events, in the last decade in Iraq and Libya, and a third is in progress in Syria. In 2003 the Iraqi military essentially disintegrated after it was defeated by US-led forces, leaving many arms storage facilities unguarded and vulnerable to looting. Coalition forces proved incapable of securing, destroying, and recovering much of this weaponry, which fuelled the resulting insurgency that continues today (Center for Public Integrity, 2008).

In one of the most significant proliferation incidents, 342 tonnes of HMX, RDX, and PETN high explosives disappeared from the Al-Qaqaa weapons facility south of Baghdad, according to the International Atomic Energy Agency, which had inspected and sealed the site shortly before the invasion (UNSC, 2004). Iraqi insurgents have testified that the looted explosives were used to increase the power of IEDs and the area around the Al-Qaqaa facility became a stronghold for militant Sunni Islamists known as the 'Triangle of Death' (Streatfeild, 2011). A similar proliferation event took place in Libya in 2011, when the existing military structures collapsed during the conflict that led to the overthrow and death of Qaddafi (Daragahi, 2011).

Weaponry was flowing out of Libya even before Qaddafi's demise. Nigerien soldiers intercepted an arms-smuggling convoy on 12 June 2011 and seized 640 kg of SEMTEX and 435 detonators, as well as firearms, although two of the vehicles escaped (Tele Sahel, 2011). The Nigerien authorities suspected that the arms had been destined for Al Qaeda in the Islamic Maghreb, which has long maintained a presence in northern Mali (RFI, 2011). An Algerian newspaper reported in June 2012 that soldiers in Mauritania had captured 300 kg of explosives and detonators smuggled in from Libya after a clash with suspected militants of the same group (Echourouk El Youmi, 2012). The Algerian authorities seized more than a tonne of explosives between July 2011 and February 2012 (UNSC, 2012, p. 20).

While plastic explosives are particularly useful IED components, bomb makers operating in conflict zones also recycle all sorts of explosive ordnance to make their weapons. This can be done either by extracting the explosives from munitions and repackaging them or by replacing the fuses in munitions so their contents can be detonated as part of an IED. In the wake of the invasion of Iraq, one of the most common types of IED used by insurgents consisted of an artillery shell with its fuse removed and replaced with a detonator attached to some form of activation mechanism. Military munitions were so plentiful that VBIEDs were made by loading vehicles with artillery shells, tank rounds, mortar bombs, and rocket warheads.

Bomb makers operating in conflict zones recycle explosive ordnance to make weapons.

Military landmines require no alteration to be turned into effective victim-operated weapons. Insurgents, however, often modify them with new activation mechanisms to allow them to be command-operated, either for discriminating roadside IEDs attacks or as part of an SVBIED. They are also sometimes rigged with an offset pressure plate that is activated by the wheel of a vehicle, which triggers a mine emplaced so that it will explode under the vehicle's crew compartment. While anti-personnel landmines contain only small amounts of explosive, which makes them of little use as a source of explosives, insurgents use them as a way of initiating larger VOIEDs.

Islamist militants also take fuses from hand grenades and use them to initiate suicide bombs by attaching them to a length of detonating cord leading to the main charge. Once the safety pin is removed, these operate as 'dead man's' switches that can activate the IED even if the suicide bomber is killed by security forces.

Military munitions have been adapted in the same way in Afghanistan, where the various armed factions that have been fighting since the late 1970s have been supplied with vast quantities of weaponry by the Soviet Union, the United States, Pakistan, and other states. While much of this ordnance is so old and degraded that it can no longer be used reliably as its designers intended, some of its parts can still be of some use as IED components. Videos released by militant Sunni Islamist groups show them extracting the explosive from shells and replacing it with home-made explosive, probably in the belief that the fragmentation from the shells will make the resulting IED more lethal (Jundullah Studio, 2009).

Arms caches are not the only source of military munitions that can be used in IEDs. Militants will recycle explosive remnants of war such as unexploded artillery shells and landmines. One of the legacies of the extensive use of artillery by Soviet counter-insurgency operations in Afghanistan in the 1980s is that unexploded shells continue to be salvaged by locals and sold to insurgents.[22] There have been claims that militants have been able to recycle munitions dating back to the early 1970s. Egypt's Interior Ministry released a statement saying that some of the explosives used in a series of bombings that targeted tourists in the Sinai Peninsula on 7 October 2004 had been recovered from military ordnance left over from the country's wars with Israel, the last of which took place in 1973 (Nasrawi, 2004).

The only way to reduce the threat of old military ordnance being reused in IEDs is a concerted effort to identify and clear arms caches and explosive remnants of war. Such an approach showed signs of success in Iraq by 2008, when insurgents were making more use of home-made explosives. The scale of this cottage industry was demonstrated when a militant explosive factory blew up in Mosul in January 2008, levelling a block of the northern city. Towards the end of 2011 the militant Iraqi Sunni Islamist group Ansar al-Islam released a video called *Inexhaustible Weapons*, which shows how the group was overcoming its growing difficulties in sourcing arms by fabricating its own (Ansar al-Islam, 2011).

Commercial explosives

When military explosives are unavailable, commercial explosives are a viable substitute for IED makers as they are similarly reliable, powerful, and safe to handle. Used for mining, road construction, and demolition, these types of explosives are generally subject to strict government regulation. Nevertheless, insurgents and terrorists have managed to source them in significant quantities.

Commercial detonators make it easy to construct IEDs that are activated by an electrical circuit, while detonating cord is particularly suited for the construction of large devices, such as VBIEDs, whose multiple sub-charges must explode simultaneously. Other types of commercial explosive are also used as booster charges to detonate large quantities of comparatively inert home-made explosives. Like military plastic explosives, some forms of commercial explosives are particularly suitable for making suicide-bombing vests, as the resulting devices are powerful yet small enough to conceal under an individual's clothes.

Militants sometimes steal commercial explosives. The Basque separatist group Euskadi Ta Askatasuna (ETA) has carried out some of the most high-profile explosives heists. In September 1999, it stole more than eight tonnes of Titadyn (a type of dynamite used in mining) as well as detonators and detonating cord from a factory in Brittany, France (Expatica, 2005). ETA members stole

BIAFO detonating cord packaging (without lot or batch number) recovered from an IED in Khowst province, Afghanistan, 2010. © Joanna Wright

another 1.6 tonnes of Titadyn from an explosives factory near Grenoble, France, in March 2001 (Tremlett and Goldenberg, 2001).

While the ETA threat has led Spain to introduce some of the tightest controls on explosives in Europe, militant Sunni Islamists were still able to obtain a sufficient amount of stolen mining explosive to build ten bombs that they left on trains heading into central Madrid on 11 March 2004. The subsequent explosions killed 191 people (Tremlett, 2004). They also had enough left over to blow themselves up as the police raided their safe house.

The Goma-2 ECO explosives and detonators used to make these devices came from a former miner in the north-western region of Asturias. While it is unclear precisely how he managed to obtain the explosive from supposedly secure facilities, Spanish Civil Guard officers later told a parliamentary inquiry that small quantities of explosives are regularly stolen in Asturias, where it was generally used for illegal land development (Giles, 2004).

For many countries, the diversion of commercial explosives is a very serious problem.

Other countries have a far more serious problem with the diversion of commercial explosives. Indian government documents obtained by the *Sunday Express* in 2007 show that 86,899 detonators, 52,740 m of detonating cord, 419 kg of gelatin sticks, and 20,150 kg of slurry explosives were stolen in 2004–06 (Sarin, 2007b). In October 2011, the *Indian Express* cited government documents as saying that 218,624 detonators, 3,500 m of detonating cord, 1,907 kg of ammonium nitrate-based explosives, and 16.58 tonnes of emulsion matrix (a slurry that needs to be sensitized before it can be detonated) had been stolen from the beginning of 2010 until July 2011 (Sarin, 2011). These quantities suggested widespread corruption in the supply chain.

While Indian officials believe much of the stolen material was channelled to illegal mining operations, they said some of it could have been acquired by militant groups, including the Maoist militants who operate in several Indian states (Sarin, 2011). The commercial explosive Neo Gel 90 has also been used in mass-casualty attacks, including the multiple bombings in Jaipur on 13 May 2008, which killed more than 70 people and were claimed in the name of the Indian Mujahideen (Rediff, 2008). Large quantities were also diverted to the Liberation Tigers of Tamil Eelam in Sri Lanka. In a particularly notable haul, the Sri Lanka Navy intercepted a boat carrying 61,000 detonators that had been made in Hyderabad in January 2006 (Sarin, 2007a).

Pakistan appears to have similar issues with the diversion of commercial explosives. While it is difficult to assess the scale of the problem, it is clear that militants operating in Pakistan's tribal areas and neighbouring Afghanistan have access to large quantities of commercial detonators, which are used in a significant proportion of the thousands of IEDs deployed every year. They also have access to substantial quantities of detonating cord. Videos released by Al Qaeda and other militant Sunni Islamist groups based in Pakistan's tribal areas have shown large quantities being used in the construction of IEDs. One video released by the Pakistani Taliban shows two alleged informers being wrapped in detonating cord and blown up—an unusual execution method that suggests the militants had an ample supply of the material (JTSM, 2010).

Afghanistan has no explosives manufacturers and has regulations to control the importation and distribution of explosives. These regulations are, however, so complicated and difficult to enforce that they encourage users who could legitimately obtain explosives to turn to the black market to avoid the corruption of the official system.[23]

Nevertheless, there are suspicions that many of the detonators used in IEDs are coming from Pakistan, which has two explosives manufacturers: Biafo Industries and the Wah Nobel Group of Companies (Cahn, 2009). Militants have been able to obtain products made by both companies. A significant quantity of plastic explosive wrapped in Wah Nobel packaging can be seen in an Afghan Taliban video released in 2012 (Al-Emarah Jihadi Studio, 2012). Emmulite and Wabox explosives made by Wah Nobel have also been recovered in Afghanistan (JIEDDO, 2011).

A roll of Biafo detonating cord can be seen in an Islamic Movement of Uzbekistan video showing the construction of an SVBIED that was used to attack a security forces checkpoint in Pakistan's tribal areas on 18 August 2009. The packaging of a used roll of Biafo detonating cord was also found in an IED that failed to function in Afghanistan. The roll did not have the requisite lot number, date of manufacture, or foreman's signature, suggesting it was either produced before Pakistan tightened explosives controls or had not been subject to the standard monitoring process at the Biafo factory.

Both Biafo and Wah Nobel insist they adhere closely to Pakistan's tight rules governing the production, storage, sale, and transportation of explosives. Nonetheless, both have been implicated in cases where these rules have been flouted. A senior Pakistani police officer told journalists in March 2010 that two men had been arrested in possession of 260 kg of Wah Nobel explosives that they were smuggling from the company's factory to militants in the Northwest Frontier Province (now called Khyber Pakhtunkhwa Province), who intended to use it to make suicide-bombing devices. As is often the case in Pakistan, it is unclear if the investigation made any progress (APP, 2010).

Authorities temporarily suspended Biafo's licence and shut down its factory in November 2009, after police intercepted a consignment of 58.5 tonnes of explosives that was being illegally shipped to a mine in Pakistan's Balochistan Province (Abbasi, 2009b; Khan, 2009). The company was allowed to resume operations the following month, after paying a fine (Khan, n.d.). Yet the police reportedly stopped another consignment of Biafo explosives that was being illegally transported to another mine in Balochistan in August 2011 (Ismaeel, 2011).

> Demand for explosives from unlicensed mining operations creates black markets that can be used by militants.

Pakistani newspaper reports published after the November 2009 seizure suggested the illegal transfer of commercial explosives was commonplace in the country, but the authorities were doing little to counter it (Abbasi, 2009a; Khan, 2009). As in India, a strong demand for explosives from unlicensed mining operations apparently exists in Pakistan, creating a black market that militants can tap into to source IED materials. These explosive-trafficking networks may also supply Afghanistan's illegal mining sector, aspects of which are tied to militants based in Pakistan's tribal areas (DuPee, 2012).

Commercial explosives products also appear to be widely available in the Middle East. Syrian insurgents have said that detonators generally cost them around USD 2, making IEDs cost-effective weapons as the price of black market small arms ammunition soared due to demand (Chivers, 2012b).

While there appears to be a strong correlation between illegal mining, the diversion of commercial explosives, and their use in IEDs, there are significant challenges in regulating the informal mining sector. This is especially the case in Afghanistan and Pakistan, where small mining operations are scattered over vast and remote areas that often lack infrastructure and government control (World Bank, 2003).

Home-made explosives

When insurgents and terrorists are unable to source sufficient quantities of military or commercial explosives, they turn to home-made explosive (HME), which can be synthesized from a wide range of precursors.

High explosives

The most sophisticated bomb makers with access to the right chemicals are capable of making military- or commercial-grade explosives. For example, Al Qaeda bomb makers have synthesized PETN, which is used in a variety of explosives and munitions. The main charge in the shoe bomb that Richard Reid attempted to detonate on a transatlantic flight on 22 December 2001 was made from PETN (Belluck and Chang, 2001). The Yemen-based Al Qaeda in the Arabian Peninsula has also used PETN in IEDs that were specifically designed to be undetectable by airport security, including the one that Umar Farouk Abdulmutallab smuggled on to a transatlantic airliner in his underwear on 25 December 2009 (USDC, 2010). The device failed to function as intended.

Al Qaeda has also used hydrogen peroxide to make explosives. While there are numerous examples of militants using peroxide-based explosives such as TATP for improvised detonators, Al Qaeda operatives in Europe and the United States began using hydrogen peroxide to make the main charges in their IEDs from 2005. The only attacks successfully carried out with peroxide-based main charges were the 7 July 2005 London suicide bombings, which killed 52 people and the four bombers (BBC News, 2011). Hydrogen peroxide was the intended main IED precursor in bombing conspiracies thwarted in Germany in September 2007, the UK in August 2006, and the United States in September 2009.[24]

These and other conspiracies have prompted calls for further restrictions to be placed on the concentration of hydrogen peroxide that can be sold to the general public (Esposito and Sandholm, 2009; *Metro*, 2011). So far, the response has been limited to a ban on passengers carrying liquids through airport security and awareness campaigns to educate vendors about the risks of hydrogen peroxide and other HME precursors, to urge them to 'know their customers', and to encourage them to report suspicious behaviour (DHS, n.d.; Home Office, 2012). However, the European Union (EU) is working on regulations to control common HME precursors. Under the proposed legislation, a licence would be needed to buy hydrogen peroxide with a concentration of more than 12 per cent (EC, 2010).

Ammonium nitrate fertilizer

By far the most common precursor used to make IEDs around the world is ammonium nitrate-based fertilizer, although other substances can be used as well (see Box 10.2). This is readily available in large quantities, affordable, and generally easier to process into explosives than other types of fertilizer, making it an attractive option for bomb makers who are looking to construct numerous or large IEDs.

Various measures have been introduced in an attempt to control access to detonable ammonium nitrate fertilizer. In the early 1970s, the extensive use of the substance in militant Irish nationalist IEDs prompted the UK government to introduce new regulations under which only vetted licence holders may purchase fertilizers containing more than 79 per cent ammonium nitrate in Northern Ireland (Hansard, 1972).

Box 10.2   The Haqqani Network and potassium chlorate

Potassium chlorate is relatively easy to turn into a main-charge explosive but is only used to make a small percentage of the IEDs deployed in Afghanistan. Nevertheless, it should be given more consideration than the usage statistics suggest because it is used by the Afghan militant faction known as the Haqqani Network (JTSM, 2010). Together with foreign allies such as the Islamic Jihad Union, the Haqqani Network is responsible for a large number of suicide bombings–often involving very large SVBIEDs–that cause civilian casualties.

For example, the Islamic Jihad Union claimed responsibility for an SVBIED attack in Khowst on 28 December 2008, saying it had killed many foreign soldiers. Footage from a security camera shows that the bomber actually triggered his device as a group of school children was walking past; 14 of the children died (JTSM, 2009).

The Haqqani Network is based in the Pakistani tribal area of North Waziristan and operates mainly in Paktia, Paktika, and Khowst provinces on the Afghan side of the border. It has also been held responsible for many of the suicide bombings in Kabul, which accounted for more than 93 per cent of civilian casualties in the capital in 2011.[25]

There is no industrial requirement for potassium chlorate in Afghanistan, so Coalition officers presume the Haqqani Network sources it in Pakistan, where it is used in match factories.

The Joint IED Defeat Organization (JIEDDO) responded to the threat from potassium chlorate-based HME in July 2012, when it called on the private sector to submit proposals on ways to make it harder to turn the compound into explosives. It also asked for improved ways of detecting and neutralizing potassium chlorate-based HME (FBO, 2012).

Tighter regulations were imposed on ammonium nitrate in England, Wales, and Scotland in 2003. Because the UK agricultural sector is one of the most intensive users of ammonium nitrate fertilizers in the world, a licensing regime was deemed undesirable (NaCTSO, n.d.). Instead, every batch of fertilizer with more than 80 per cent ammonium nitrate (28 per cent nitrogen by weight) has to pass a detonation resistance test, after which it can be sold without restriction (OPSI, 2003).

The EU introduced stricter controls in June 2009. The legislation bans the sale of ammonium nitrate containing more than 28 per cent nitrogen that had not been specifically formulated to make it harder to turn into explosives and subject to detonation resistance tests. It also stipulated that only registered farmers and other legitimate downstream users could purchase ammonium nitrate with a nitrogen content of more than 16 per cent (EC, 2009). These regulations raise significant barriers to would-be terrorists, but enhanced monitoring is needed, as the case of Anders Breivik shows (see Box 10.3).

One initiative that could help address the problems with IED precursors is Program Global Shield. The pilot scheme began in November 2010, with more than 70 countries participating, and the World Customs Organization approved it as a long-term programme in June 2011. Participating governments share information to identify illegal shipments of materials that could be used to make IEDs. By June 2012, the initiative had prompted 41 seizures of chemical precursors, totalling more than 126 tonnes (DHS, 2012).

However, imposing restrictions on who can purchase ammonium nitrate fertilizer is completely unworkable in developing countries whose governments do not have the resources to monitor and regulate their large agricultural sectors effectively. Some states that are facing a significant threat from IEDs have instead decided to completely ban the sale of ammonium nitrate-based fertilizers.

Box 10.3   Raising barriers: lessons from the Breivik case

Although Norway typically adopts EU legislation even though it is not a member state, it did not pass the new regulations regarding ammonium nitrate into law until November 2011 (DSB, 2012). However, Anders Breivik appears to have been under the impression that the regulations had already been adopted when he began his preparations to build a VBIED a year earlier.

According to his own account, he rented a farm so that he could register as an agricultural business and obtain a farmer identification number that would allow him to purchase calcium ammonium nitrate fertilizer with a nitrogen content of 27 per cent (CAN-27), which he believed was the most suitable precursor available to him. In fact, these steps were unnecessary and, as he subsequently realized, he could have obtained ammonium nitrate fertilizer with a nitrogen content of 34 per cent in Norway at that time. Nevertheless, he purchased 3,000 kg of CAN-27 and used it to make the 950 kg of explosives that he loaded into a rented van to create the VBIED that he detonated in Oslo on 22 July 2011 (Breivik, 2011).

Breivik's success in turning CAN-27 into explosives does not mean that reducing the nitrogen content of ammonium nitrate is futile. His misapprehension about the ease with which he could obtain suitable fertilizer in Norway at that time increased the logistical and financial burden on his project. He rented a farm and acquired the additional equipment and chemicals he required to process and sensitize his CAN-27 and to make another type of explosive for the booster charges he needed to ensure his relatively stable main charge would detonate. According to his own account, it took him around 80 days to make his explosives and the processes he used exposed him to more personal danger and risk of exposure than if he had worked with a higher concentration of ammonium nitrate.

Breivik's case also demonstrates that the regulation of HME precursors would be more effective if they were supported by a vigorous monitoring regime. He ordered a significant quantity of aluminium powder from an online chemist based in Poland, claiming he would use it in boat paint. The Norwegian Customs Service informed the Norwegian Police Security Service (PST) about the purchase on 3 December 2010, but no further action was taken (Brenna, Grøttum, and Ravndal, 2012). If this information had been cross-checked with his large fertilizer order it should have raised suspicion as aluminium powder is a well-known ammonium nitrate sensitizer. According to the PST report on whether it could have prevented Breivik's attack, the security service was not tracking fertilizer purchases at that time. Even if it had known about the fertilizer, the PST would have been unable to cross-check his December 2010 aluminium powder and May 2011 CAN-27 purchases because it does not keep records for more than four months.

For example, Afghanistan's government introduced a ban on ammonium nitrate fertilizer in January 2010. It soon became apparent, however, that Afghanistan's porous borders were seriously limiting the ban's effectiveness. Security forces began intercepting large shipments of ammonium nitrate that were being smuggled into the country; 435 tonnes were seized in the first seven months of 2012 (Jaffe, 2012). In one of the largest reported seizures, 10 tonnes of ammonium nitrate were found in Kabul in April 2012 (Al Jazeera, 2012).

A Pakistani smuggler told a reporter in May 2010 that he was part of an operation that was bribing officials to send convoys carrying up to 85 tonnes of ammonium nitrate fertilizer into Afghanistan twice per week (Rodriguez, 2010). If this was the case, it would suggest there is strong demand for Pakistani fertilizer from Afghan farmers, as estimates have put the annual amount of fertilizer used in Afghan IEDs at around 200 tonnes (Jaffe, 2011). Indeed, large quantities of fertilizer were being imported into Afghanistan before the ban because the country could not meet domestic demand. Pakistani fertilizer has long been a popular option as it is subsidized, meaning that traffickers can make higher profits by selling it in Afghanistan (Emerging Asia, 2009). The director of JIEDDO, Lt. Gen. Michael Barbero, said in December 2012 that more than 85 per cent of IEDs used against Coalition forces in Afghanistan contained HME, and that about 70 per cent of those (60 per cent of the total) were made from ammonium nitrate fertilizer coming in from Pakistan (Garamone, 2012).

Of Afghan IEDs, 85 per cent contain home-made explosives.

Pakistani officials have disputed these claims, saying that Afghanistan's other neighbours produce large quantities of fertilizer, some of it easier to turn into explosives than the Pakistani equivalent, which is calcium ammonium nitrate fertilizer with a nitrogen content of 26 per cent (CAN-26) (Fatima Group, n.d.). Produced in two factories, Pakistani CAN-26 is generally freely traded in the country but was banned in November 2009 in certain parts of Khyber Pakhtunkhwa to prevent militants from using it (Shah, 2011).

Pakistani security forces have also tried to prevent ammonium nitrate fertilizer from being moved into the militant stronghold of North Waziristan and other tribal areas since 2009. This has proved problematic as it is difficult to distinguish between different types of fertilizer, which has led security forces to seize them all, alienating farmers in the process (Abbot, 2012; Yusufzai, 2012).

While US officials concede that only around 0.5 per cent of Pakistan's CAN-26 output is diverted to produce IEDs in Afghanistan, they have been pushing Islamabad to do more to control ammonium nitrate fertilizer, with Congress threatening to freeze USD 700 million in aid unless Islamabad took more action in December 2011 (Anthony and Nauman, 2011; JIEDDO, n.d.a). The United States has offered to pay Pakistan's factories to include a dye in their CAN-26. This would make it easier for security forces to distinguish the dangerous fertilizer from more inert types. The Fatima Group, which operates both of Pakistan's CAN-26 factories, said it was prepared to introduce this initiative in December 2011 (Hasan, 2011). Nevertheless, in congressional testimony on 20 September 2012, Lt. Gen. Barbero confirmed that this had not happened (NewsStand, 2012).

Some figures suggest that, in the absence of Pakistani cooperation, the ammonium nitrate fertilizer ban in Afghanistan has had no impact on the insurgency. Figures released by JIEDDO show that Afghan and foreign security forces encountered 16,600 IEDs in the first seven months of 2012, a slight increase compared to the same period in 2011 (Jaffe, 2012). While this increase suggests the fertilizer ban has had no impact, it is probably costing the insurgents more money to maintain this level of IED usage. Anecdotal evidence suggests the price of ammonium nitrate has increased in Pakistan's tribal areas where it has been banned; this hike would presumably be passed on to Afghan consumers. According to one Pakistani report, a bag of CAN-26 cost PKR 1,400 (USD 15) in Bannu in Khyber Pakhtunkhwa, but PKR 2,400 (USD 25) in neighbouring North Waziristan due to the expense of smuggling—a difference of more than 70 per cent (Yusufzai, 2012).

Nevertheless, many officials have concluded that the efforts to reduce insurgent access to ammonium nitrate in Afghanistan have had limited results. Former JIEDDO director Lt. Gen. Michael L. Oates said the ammonium nitrate ban 'has had little to no impact on the flow of precursor materials'.[26] Having initially called on Pakistan to follow Afghanistan's example and ban ammonium nitrate fertilizer, the team that monitors the UN sanctions on Al Qaeda and the Taliban concluded in its October 2012 report that this would not be feasible (UNSC, 2012).

Knowledge proliferation

There is a debate surrounding the threat posed by the proliferation of IED knowledge. On the one hand, there is evidence to suggest that some groups and even individuals can acquire the knowledge needed to make and deploy IEDs successfully without any coaching. On the other hand, this process can be accelerated by direct instruction from external experts and the proliferation of information.

The PIRA provides a clear example of self-acquired IED knowledge. It began building simple IEDs in the early 1970s, but gradually developed increasingly sophisticated devices over the following decades with little or no external training. This was an evolutionary process in which the militants and security forces were constantly trying to develop new ways of countering one another.

The same process has been seen in more recent conflicts, with IED cells in Afghanistan developing ways to overcome the latest countermeasures. This can be an extremely localized process as a cell adjusts to the different procedures

Syrian brothers making home-made explosives for the Free Syrian Army in Ma'ar Shamarine village, near Idlib, Syria, January 2013. © Ghaith Taha/Reuters

followed by a new foreign military unit that has rotated into its area. It can involve adopting less sophisticated technology. For example, if the security forces operating in a certain area have been equipped with effective electronic countermeasure systems, then the local IED cell might start using command wires or pressure plates rather than radio-control devices. An UNMAS official described Afghan IEDs as living organisms that were constantly adapting to their environment.[27]

The IEDs typically encountered by Coalition forces in Iraq were more advanced than the ones seen in Afghanistan. This has been attributed to the Arab country's better-educated population and access to more sophisticated technology. Many Iraqis also had appropriate skills, having spent years repairing and improvising electrical and mechanical equipment in the face of shortages experienced during years of UN sanctions.[28]

Afghan IEDs have been described as living organisms, constantly adapting to their environment.

While IED cells evolve their devices and procedures according to environmental demands, there is some evidence that militant groups are passing on their knowledge. The PIRA, for example, supposedly trained ETA bomb-makers (Cragin et al., 2007, p. 71). Three Northern Irish men were arrested in Colombia in 2001 on suspicion that they were former PIRA members who had been hired to train rebels from the Revolutionary Armed Forces of Colombia (FARC) to make and use improvised mortars.[29] A former member of Al Qaeda has claimed that Hezbollah trained some of the Al Qaeda operatives who were involved in the 7 August 1998 attacks on the US embassies in Kenya and Tanzania (NYT, 2000). The militant Sunni Islamist training camps that were established in Afghanistan under Taliban rule in the 1990s attracted individuals from numerous countries and militant groups, some of whom would return home to pass on the lessons they had learned.

There has also been a history of militaries and intelligence agencies training allied militant groups. Various Arab states supported the Palestinian groups that carried out airliner hijackings and other attacks in the 1970s.[30] Western intelligence agencies supported Pakistan's efforts to train Afghan insurgents in the 1980s. The Pakistani military continued this policy into the 1990s to support militants who were fighting Indian security forces in Kashmir. The Iraqi insurgency may have benefited from some of the training that Saddam Hussein's intelligence services provided to non-state actors before the US-led invasion in 2003 (Jehl, 2004). It seems likely that members of Iraq's subsequently disbanded intelligence service joined the insurgency and passed on relevant skills, although the extent of their influence remains unclear. At the same time, Iranian and Hezbollah operatives were passing on skills as well as weaponry to Iraq's militant Shia groups.

There is also a debate surrounding the role of the Internet in the proliferation of IED knowledge. Much of the information available on the Internet is amateurish or rehashed versions of documents that have been available for years, such as the *Anarchist Cookbook*. In recent years Al Qaeda and its affiliates have put more sophisticated IED manuals and video tutorials online to encourage their followers to carry out independent attacks. At the same time, sympathizers are compiling multiple sources into online encyclopaedia collections that are updated as more information becomes available. There are also Internet forums where would-be bomb makers can ask apparently more-experienced individuals direct questions (UNSC, 2011, paras. 67–70).

Nevertheless, experts are still generally sceptical about the effectiveness of online IED training because even the most thorough and accurate instruction materials typically need to be supported by practical training or experimentation. This view has been corroborated by Syrian insurgents who have said they found some useful IED-related information on the Internet, but that it took time to perfect the techniques and adapt them to the environment (Chivers, 2012b). In its April 2011 report, the team that monitors the UN sanctions on Al Qaeda and the Taliban noted that it knew of 'no successful attack by perpetrators trained only online' (UNSC, 2011, para. 68).

This situation soon changed. On 28 April 2011, two IEDs exploded in a tourist café in Marrakesh, Morocco, killing 17 people. The authorities identified the bomber as a man who used the Internet to learn how to build explosive devices after his attempts to join militant Sunni Islamists in Iraq and Chechnya failed (Morocco News Board, 2011). Less than two months later, Anders Breivik detonated his VBIED in Oslo. According to Breivik's account, he received no external instruction, but instead undertook considerable Internet research. He stated that he found much of the available material to be unhelpful and even misleading, but by filtering the available information he nevertheless managed to acquire the knowledge he needed to build a viable VBIED.

CONCLUSION

This chapter has established that VOIEDs with no arming mechanisms represent a significant threat to civilians as they are indiscriminate weapons. The threat is especially great in Afghanistan, where these types of IEDs are used most prolifically. However, their usage will probably decline after the withdrawal of foreign forces in 2014.[31]

The IEDs that are responsible for the most civilian casualties around the world are the ones that deliberately target civilians in mass-casualty attacks, as well as VBIEDs that are used in areas frequented by civilians. An obvious way to reduce this threat is to restrict access to the materials commonly used in the more dangerous types of IEDs. Such measures include the disposal of military ordnance and the regulation of commercial explosives that can be used to make powerful, yet concealable, suicide bombing vests and booster charges for large VBIEDS made using HME.

These measures, however, cannot be effectively enforced in the countries that suffer most from IEDs due to corruption, lack of capacity, and porous borders. More research is needed to find out if overly complicated regulations and the practice of bribing officials to obtain licences are fuelling black market demand. If so, it may be possible to improve licensing systems so that it is easier for legitimate users to obtain explosives legally. While this may seem counterintuitive, it would shrink the black market and improve oversight, thereby restricting militant access to explosives.

Limiting access to common HME precursors can help increase the logistical burden on bomb makers, but such measures have to be weighed against the cost of regulation and the impact they have on agriculture, commerce, and industry. Such measures are significantly less practical in developing countries with agrarian societies.

Nevertheless, there is still scope for more international cooperation on monitoring HME precursors and other potential IED components. More countries could join Program Global Shield and Pakistan could accept the US offer to finance the dying of its CAN-26 to make it easier for security forces on both sides of the border to identify it, thereby allowing less dangerous fertilizer to reach farmers.

Given that the greatest IED threat to civilians comes from militant Sunni Islamists, a campaign to raise awareness in Muslim countries could have merit, especially if supported by respected Islamic scholars and clerics. This would highlight the impact that militant Sunni Islamist IED attacks are having on civilians and condemn the use of indiscriminate weapons and tactics. It would be more successful if it were supported by a concerted effort to gather more definitive data on civilian IED casualties, while the identification of the perpetrators of attacks through transparent investigations would undermine the conspiracy theories behind which militant Sunni Islamist groups hide.

If the long-running campaign to stigmatize land mines and cluster munitions has been the most effective way of reducing their usage—as claimed by the NGOs involved—then the stigmatization of mass-casualty weapons and tactics may also prove to be the most practical way of reducing civilian IED casualties. ◼

LIST OF ABBREVIATIONS

C-4	Composition-4
CAN	Calcium ammonium nitrate
CJTF	Combined Joint Task Force
COIED	Command-operated improvised explosive device
ETA	Euskadi Ta Askatasuna
EU	European Union
EVMP	Explosive Violence Monitoring Project
FARC	Revolutionary Armed Forces of Colombia
HME	Home-made explosive
IED	Improvised explosive device
IRAM	Improvised rocket-assisted mortar/munitions
ISI	Inter-Services Intelligence (Pakistan)
JIEDDO	Joint Improvised Explosive Device Defeat Organization
MRAP	Mine-resistant ambush-protected
NGO	Non-governmental organization
PBIED	Person-borne improvised explosive device
PIRA	Provisional Irish Republican Army
PKR	Pakistani rupee
PST	Police Security Service (Norway)
SVBIED	Suicide vehicle-borne improvised explosive device
UNAMA	United Nations Assistance Mission in Afghanistan
UNMAS	United Nations Mine Action Service
VBIED	Vehicle-borne improvised explosive device
VOIED	Victim-operated improvised explosive device

ENDNOTES

1   Militant anarchists carried out numerous bombings in various European countries and, to a lesser extent, the United States in the late 19th and early 20th century.

2   See, for example, Multi-National Corps–Iraq (2008).

3   The US Department of Defense, for example, procured thousands of mine-resistant ambush-protected (MRAP) vehicles of various types to safeguard its soldiers in Iraq. However, these vehicles lacked the mobility needed for Afghanistan's rough roads, so the Department issued a requirement for an MRAP all-terrain vehicle in 2008 (FBO, 2008). The competition was won by Oshkosh, which has since delivered more than 6,000 such vehicles at a unit cost of up to USD 500,000 (Clark, 2009).

4   EVMP 2011 dataset provided to the authors by Action on Armed Violence, 2012.

5   The US Health Services Research and Development Service has noted that—due to their exposure to IEDs—veterans of the conflicts in Afghanistan and Iraq suffer higher rates of post-traumatic stress disorder, traumatic brain injury, and other forms of trauma than veterans of previous conflicts (HSR&D, 2009). The authors were unable to find any research on the psychological impact of IEDs on civilians.

6   Suicide attacks involving both firearms and explosives have been carried out in Afghanistan since the 14 January 2008 attack on the Serena Hotel in Kabul.

7   Declassified military statistics covering 2011 provided to the authors in 2012.

8   These casualties include foreign military personnel participating in Operation Enduring Freedom Afghanistan, but not Afghan security forces.

9   Declassified military statistics covering 2011 provided to the authors in 2012.

10   Author interview with UNMAS official, New York, 27 September 2012.

11   Author interview with Combined Joint Task Force (CJTF) Paladin officer, Kandahar, September 2012.

12   Author interviews with commander and deputy operations officer, CJTF Paladin, Bagram, September 2012.

13   Author interview with deputy commander, CJTF Paladin, Bagram, September 2012.

14   Author interview with the deputy commander of CJTF Paladin, Bagram, September 2012.

15 This analogy is made in a Taliban document on suicide bombing titled *Omar's Missiles*, a reference to the movement's leader, Mullah Mohammed Omar (Taliban–Islamic Emirate of Afghanistan, n.d.).

16 It is likely that VOIEDs caused more than 12 per cent of the casualties as pressure-plate devices probably accounted for a proportion of the fatalities in the 'unknown' category.

17 Declassified military statistics covering 2011 provided to the authors in 2012.

18 The percentage was arguably slightly higher as the EVMP recorded a suicide bombing outside an Iraqi police station on 18 January 2011 as an attack on combatants even though it is highly likely that the prospective recruits who were queuing outside the facility were the intended targets. The explosion inflicted 217 civilian and no police casualties.

19 Author interview with a senior member of the Analytical Support and Sanctions Monitoring Team established to support UN Security Council Resolution 1267 concerning Al Qaeda and the Taliban, New York, 28 September 2012.

20 This is reflected in the trajectory of the Sunni extremist group Lashkar-e-Jhangvi, which primarily carried out firearms attacks after its formation in the mid-1990s, but has been held responsible for a number of mass-casualty suicide bombings since 2005, including an attack on Barelvi Muslims in Karachi's Nishtar Park on 11 April 2006, which killed more than 50 people (Rana, 2009).

21 The regular IED attacks on Shia Muslims in Iraq are presumed to be part of Al Qaeda in Iraq's strategy of inciting retaliatory violence against Sunni Muslims in the hope of mobilizing support for its cause. This view has been expressed by numerous US officers. Author telephone interview with Lt. Gen. Michael L. Oates (ret.), former director of the US military's Joint IED Defeat Organization (JIEDDO), October 2012.

22 Author interview with deputy commander, CJTF Paladin, Bagram, September 2012.

23 Author interview with a member of the Analytical Support and Sanctions Monitoring Team established to support UN Security Council Resolution 1267 concerning Al Qaeda and the Taliban, New York, 28 September 2012.

24 News coverage provides details of the 2007 Sauerland Cell case, the 2006 plot to blow up an airliner with chemicals such as hydrogen peroxide, and a 2009 plot in the United States to detonate hydrogen peroxide bombs (Musharbash, 2009; BBC News, 2009; Meyer and Susman, 2009).

25 Declassified military statistics covering 2011 provided to the authors in 2012.

26 Author interview with Lt. Gen. Michael L. Oates (ret.), former director of JIEDDO, New York, 2 October 2012.

27 Author interview with an UNMAS official, New York, 27 September 2012.

28 Author interview with the deputy commander, CJTF Paladin, Bagram, September 2012.

29 The men were known associates of the PIRA and two were suspected members of the group's 'engineering division'. They were convicted for travelling on false passports and it was not proved in court that they were training the FARC.

30 Libya, Iraq, South Yemen, and Syria were the first to be designated by the United States as state sponsors of terrorism in 1979 for their support of Palestinian militant groups.

31 Author interview with Lt. Gen. Michael L. Oates (ret.), former director of JIEDDO, New York, 2 October 2012. Oates also noted that IEDs would continue to be used against Afghan security forces, which are more vulnerable than Coalition forces.

BIBLIOGRAPHY

Abbasi, Ansar. 2009a. 'Criminal Neglect in Checking of Explosives.' *News* (Karachi). 15 November.
   <http://pakfungama.blogspot.co.uk/2009/11/criminal-neglect-in-checking-of.html>

—. 2009b. 'Explosives Factory Closed as Ministry Finally Wakes Up.' *News* (Karachi). 14 November.

Abbot, Sebastian. 2012. 'Farmers Angry at Counterterror Tactic in Pakistan.' Associated Press. 14 September.
   <http://www.guardian.co.uk/world/feedarticle/10437767>

Al-Emarah Jihadi Studio. 2012. 'Who Are the Agents?' 30 May.

Al Jazeera. 2012. 'Afghanistan Claims Explosive-Material Haul.' 21 April. <http://www.aljazeera.com/news/asia/2012/04/201242171758450787.html>

Al-Shumosy, Chasib Latif Ali. 2012. 'Iraqi Ministry of Health Program to Support Mines Victims.' PowerPoint presentation made at the 2012 session of the Group of Experts established by the Tenth Annual Conference of the High Contracting Parties to Amended Protocol II of the Convention on Certain Conventional Weapons. Geneva, 24 April.
   <http://www.unog.ch/80256EDD006B8954/(httpAssets)/1DDB4820E28C064DC12579F1005531BB/$file/Iraq_IEDs+2012.pdf>

Ansar al-Islam. 2011. 'Inexhaustible Weapons.' Video. November.

Anthony, Augustine and Qasim Nauman. 2011. 'U.S. Lawmakers Freeze $700 Million to Pakistan, Ties Strained.' Reuters. 13 December.
   <http://www.reuters.com/article/2011/12/13/us-pakistan-usa-idUSTRE7BC0QI20111213>

AOAV (Action on Armed Violence). 2012. *Monitoring Explosive Violence: The EVMP Dataset 2011.* March.
   <http://www.aoav.org.uk/changing-policy/the-impact-of-explosive-weapons-2/explosive-violence-monitoring-project-2>

APP (Associated Press of Pakistan). 2010. 'Pakistan Police Say Seized Explosives Were to Be Used to Make Suicide Jackets.' BBC Monitoring International
    Reports. 16 March. <http://www.accessmylibrary.com/article-1G1-221404905/pakistan-police-say-seized.html>

BBC (British Broadcasting Corporation) News. 2001. 'Profile: Timothy McVeigh.' 11 May. <http://news.bbc.co.uk/1/hi/world/americas/1321244.stm>

—. 2006. 'Pakistan "Role in Mumbai Attacks."' 30 September. <http://news.bbc.co.uk/1/hi/5394686.stm>

—. 2007. 'Benazir Bhutto Killed in Attack.' 27 December. <http://news.bbc.co.uk/1/hi/world/south_asia/7161590.stm>

—. 2009. 'Three Guilty of Airline Bomb Plot.' 7 September. <news.bbc.co.uk/2/hi/uk_news/8242238.stm>

—. 2010. 'Al-Qaeda Offshoot Claims Cargo Bombs.' 5 November. <http://www.bbc.co.uk/news/world-middle-east-11703355>

—. 2011. '7/7 Inquests: Coroner Warns over Bomb Ingredient.' 1 February. <http://www.bbc.co.uk/news/uk-12337575>

—. n.d.a. '1980: Bologna Blast Leaves Dozens Dead.' <http://news.bbc.co.uk/onthisday/hi/dates/stories/august/2/newsid_4532000/4532091.stm>

—. n.d.b. '1998: Dozens Die in Omagh Bombing.' <http://news.bbc.co.uk/onthisday/hi/dates/stories/august/15/newsid_2496000/2496009.stm>

Belluck, Pam and Kenneth Chang. 2001. 'Shoes Were a "Homemade Bomb," F.B.I. Agent Says.' *The New York Times*. 29 December.
    <http://www.nytimes.com/2001/12/29/national/29INQU.html?pagewanted=all>

Bowden, Mark. 2001. *Killing Pablo: The Hunt for the World's Greatest Outlaw*. New York: Atlantic Monthly Press.

Bozorgmehr, Najmeh. 2012. 'Iran Hosts Islamic Resistance Festival.' *Financial Times*. 5 September.
    <http://www.washingtonpost.com/world/iran-hosts-islamic-resistance-festival/2012/09/05/cfbdebe4-f785-11e1-8253-3f495ae70650_story.html>

Breivik, Anders Behring. 2011. *2083: A European Declaration of Independence*. Self-published.
    <http://www.fas.org/programs/tap/_docs/2083_-_A_European_Declaration_of_Independence.pdf>

Brenna, Jarle Grivi, Eva-Therese Grøttum, and Dennis Ravndal. 2012. 'Derfor Mener PST de Ikke Kunne Fanget opp Breivik.' *Verdens Gang* (Oslo).
    16 March. <http://www.vg.no/nyheter/innenriks/22-juli/artikkel.php?artid=10079185>

Cahn, Dianna. 2009. 'Bomb-Makers Being Targeted by Coalition Forces in an Increasingly Prolific IED War.' *Stars and Stripes*. 25 November.
    <http://www.stripes.com/news/bomb-makers-being-targeted-by-coalition-forces-in-an-increasingly-prolific-ied-war-1.96746>

Center for Public Integrity. 2008. 'Failure to Secure Weapons in Iraq.' 10 December.
    <http://www.publicintegrity.org/2008/12/10/6290/failure-secure-weapons-iraq>

Chivers, C. J. 2012a. 'Syrian Forces' Improvised Arms: Desperate Measures, or Deliberate Aid?' *The New York Times*. 18 October.
    <http://atwar.blogs.nytimes.com/2012/10/18/syrian-forces-improvised-arms-desperate-measures-or-deliberate-aid>

—. 2012b. 'Syrian Rebels Hone Bomb Skills to Even the Odds.' *The New York Times*. 18 July.
    <http://www.nytimes.com/2012/07/19/world/middleeast/syrian-rebels-hone-bomb-skills-military-analysis.html?hp>

Clark, Colin. 2009. 'Oshkosh Wins $1B MATV Deal.' DoDBuzz. 30 June. <http://www.dodbuzz.com/2009/06/30/matv-decision-likely-tuesday/>

Cragin, Kim, et al. 2007. 'Sharing the Dragon's Teeth: Terrorist Groups and the Exchange of New Technologies.' RAND Corporation.
    <http://www.rand.org/content/dam/rand/pubs/monographs/2007/RAND_MG485.pdf>

Crist, David. 2012. *The Twilight War: The Secret History of America's Thirty-Year Conflict with Iran*. New York: Penguin Press.

Daragahi, Borzou. 2011. 'Libya Rebels Seize Kadafi Arms Depot.' *Los Angeles Times*. 29 June.
    <http://articles.latimes.com/2011/jun/29/world/la-fg-libya-weapons-20110629>

DHS (United States Department of Homeland Security). 2012. 'Readout of Secretary Napolitano's Visit to France and Belgium.' 22 June.
    <http://www.dhs.gov/news/2012/06/22/readout-secretary-napolitanos-visit-france-and-belgium>

—. n.d.. *Bomb-Making Materials Awareness Program (BMAP): Private Sector User Guide*. <http://www.hsdl.org/?view&did=689411>

DSB (Directorate for Civil Protection of Norway). 2012. *Proposal of Regulation and Control of Access to Ammonium Nitrate: An Assessment*. 15 June.
    <http://www.dsb.no/Global/Publikasjoner/2012/Rapport/DSB_report_ammonium_nitrate.pdf >

DuPee, Matthew. 2012. 'Afghanistan's Conflict Minerals: The Crime–State–Insurgent Nexus.' *CTC Sentinel*, Vol. 5, No. 2, pp. 11–14. February.
    <http://www.ctc.usma.edu/posts/afghanistans-conflict-minerals-the-crime-state-insurgent-nexus>

EC (European Commission). 2009. Commission Regulation (EC) No. 552/2009. *Official Journal of the European Union*. L164/7. 22 June.
    <http://eur-lex.europa.eu/LexUriServ/LexUriServ.do?uri=OJ:L:2009:164:0007:0031:en:PDF>

—. 2010. Proposal for a Regulation of the European Parliament and of the Council on the Marketing and Use of Explosives Precursors. COM/2010/0473
    FIN. Brussels. 20 September. <http://eur-lex.europa.eu/LexUriServ/LexUriServ.do?uri=COM:2010:0473:FIN:EN:PDF>

Echourouk El Youmi (Algeria). 2012. 'Mauritanian Forces Clash with Al-Qa'idah, Arrest Guide, Seize Explosives.' BBC Monitoring International
    Reports. 17 June. <www.accessmylibrary.com/article-1G1-293644043/mauritanian-forces-clash-al.html>

Emerging Asia. 2009. *Afghanistan's Fertilizer Market: Reliant on Imports from Neighboring Countries*. 18 January.
    <http://www.emerging-asia.com/wp-content/uploads/2010/09/Afghanistan-Fertilizer-Market-Emerging-Asia-Whitepaper-January-20091.pdf>

Esposito, Richard and Drew Sandholm. 2009. 'Easy Sales of Peroxide Questioned in Beauty Parlor Bomb Plot.' ABC News. 20 October.
    <http://abcnews.go.com/Blotter/senator-calls-tighter-restrictions-peroxide/story?id=8872597#.UGRf5mj3CoQ>

Expatica. 2005. 'Five ETA Terrorists Jailed for Dynamite Robbery.' 30 June.

<http://www.expatica.com/news/local_news/five-eta-terrorists-jailed-for-dynamite-robbery--21536.html>

Fatima Group. n.d. 'Sarsabz Calcium Ammonium Nitrate (CAN) Fertilizer.' Accessed 7 November 2012.

<http://www.fatima-group.com/fatimafertilizer/can.php>

FBO (Federal Business Opportunities). 2008. 'Mine Resistant Ambush Protected (MRAP) All Terrain Vehicle (M-ATV).' W56HZV-09-0115. 13 November.

<https://www.fbo.gov/index?s=opportunity&mode=form&id=d9ad87ddc80db9d8bd4c39f777cb7230>

—. 2012. 'Rapid Development of Methods to Defeat Potassium Chlorate Based IEDs.' BAA-JIEDDO-12-03. 25 July.

<https://www.fbo.gov/index?s=opportunity&mode=form&tab=core&id=8638652f26c20ba717578bd88fe3a0a5>

Garamone, Jim. 2012. 'More Effort Needed to Counter IEDs, General Says.' American Forces Press Service. 14 December.

<http://www.defense.gov/News/NewsArticle.aspx?ID=118804>

Geraghty, Tony. 1998. *The Irish War: The Hidden Conflict between the IRA and British Intelligence.* Baltimore: Johns Hopkins University Press.

Ghosh, Srikanta. 2000. *Pakistan's ISI: Network of Terror in India.* New Delhi: APH Publishing Corporation.

Giles, Ciaran. 2004. 'Dynamite Smuggling Investigated before March 11 Train Bombing, but Trail Turned Cold.' Associated Press. 21 July.

Hansard. 1972. 'Northern Ireland (Control of Explosives).' 5 June.

<http://hansard.millbanksystems.com/commons/1972/jun/05/northern-ireland-control-of-explosives>

Hasan, Saad. 2011. 'Fertiliser or Bomb?: Fatima Group Says Its Product within Accepted Standards.' *Express Tribune* (Karachi).16 December.

<http://tribune.com.pk/story/307331/fertiliser-or-bomb-fatima-group-says-its-product-within-accepted-standards/>

Home Office. 2012. *Coroner's Inquests into the London Bombings of 7 July 2005: Review of Progress.* London: Home Office. May.

<http://www.homeoffice.gov.uk/publications/counter-terrorism/inquest-7-7-progress-report?view=Binary>

HSR&D (Health Services Research and Development Service). 2009. 'Emerging Evidence: Operation Enduring Freedom/Operation Iraqi Freedom (OEF/OIF).' Washington, DC: United States Department of Veterans Affairs. Updated 30 December.

<http://www.hsrd.research.va.gov/news/emerging_evidence/oef_oif.cfm#.UO1Crnggvap>

iCasualties.org. n.d. 'Operation Enduring Freedom.' Accessed 14 January 2013. <http//icasualties.org/OEF>

IMC (Independent Monitoring Commission). 2009. *Twenty-First Report of the Independent Monitoring Commission.* London: Stationery Office. 7 May.

<http://www.official-documents.gov.uk/document/hc0809/hc04/0496/0496.pdf>

Ismaeel, Tariq. 2011. 'Illegal Movement: Two Trucks Carrying Explosives Seized.' *Express Tribune* (Karachi). 28 August.

<http://tribune.com.pk/story/240811/illegal-movement-two-trucks-carrying-explosives-seized/>

Israel MFA (Ministry of Foreign Affairs). n.d. 'Victims of Palestinian Violence and Terrorism since September 2000.' Accessed October 2012. <http://www.mfa.gov.il/MFA/Terrorism-+Obstacle+to+Peace/Palestinian+terror+since+2000/Victims+of+Palestinian+Violence+and+Terrorism+sinc.htm>

Jaffe, Greg. 2011. 'To Stop Afghan Bombs, a Focus on Pakistani Fertilizer.' *Washington Post.* 26 November. <http://www.washingtonpost.com/world/national-security/to-stop-afghan-bombs-a-focus-on-pakistani-fertilizer/2011/11/23/gIQAg6j0wN_story.html>

—. 2012. 'Ammonium Nitrate Fertilizer Is Being Smuggled into Afghanistan for IEDs.' *Washington Post.* 27 September.

<http://www.washingtonpost.com/world/national-security/in-afghanistan-ied-key-component-ammonium-nitrate-fertilizer-is-being-imported-from-pakistan/2012/08/18/60edeb16-e92e-11e1-936a-b801f1abab19_story.html>

Jehl, Douglas. 2004. 'Inspector's Report Says Hussein Expected Guerrilla War.' *The New York Times.* 8 October.

<http://www.nytimes.com/2004/10/08/politics/08intel.html?_r=0>

JIEDDO (Joint Improvised Explosive Device Defeat Organization). 2011.'Victim Operated Improvised Explosive Device (VOIED) Recognition Guide: Afghanistan, 1st edn.' <https://www.jieddo.mil/content/docs/VOED%20Guide_Final_v1.1.pdf>

—. n.d.a. 'HME Profile: Calcium Ammonium Nitrate (CAN-26).' <https://www.jieddo.mil/content/docs/JIEDDO_HME_Tri-fold_v3.pdf>

—. n.d.b. 'IED Profile: Improvised Rocket-Assisted Munitions (IRAM).' <https://www.jieddo.mil/content/docs/JIEDDO_IED_Tri-fold_v3sm.pdf>

JTSM (*Jane's Terrorism and Security Monitor*). 2009. 'Unravelling Haqqani's Net.' 30 June.

—. 2010. 'Af-Pak IED Supply Lines.' 3 August.

Jundullah Studio. 2009. 'Martyrdom Operation in North Waziristan.' Video. July.

Khan, Iftikhar. 2009. 'Mystery Surrounds Seizure of Explosives in D.G. Khan.' *Dawn* (Karachi). 12 November.

<http://archives.dawn.com/archives/37863>

—. n.d. 'Private Explosives Factory's Licence Restored.' *Dawn* (Karachi). <http://archives.dawn.com/archives/80489>

Levin, Sandy. 2012. 'Letter Urging EU Council to Designate Hezbollah as a Terrorist Organization.' 21 September.

<http://levin.house.gov/letter-urging-eu-council-designate-hezbollah-terrorist-organization>

Meo, Nick. 2008. 'Afghanistan: The Night I Was "Killed in Action" by a Taliban Ambush.' *Daily Telegraph.* 18 October.

<http://www.telegraph.co.uk/news/newstopics/onthefrontline/3223963/Afghanistan-The-night-I-was-killed-in-action-by-a-Taliban-ambush.html#>

Metro (London). 2011. 'July 7 Families: Limit Supply of Bomb Chemical.' 10 March.
<http://www.metro.co.uk/news/857791-july-7-families-limit-supply-of-bomb-chemical>

Meyer, Josh and Tina Susman. 2009. 'Denver Man Charged in Alleged Terrorist Bomb Plot.' 25 September.
<http://articles.latimes.com/2009/sep/25/nation/na-terror-plot25>

Mooney, Brenda. 2012. 'Single IED Blast Can Cause Degenerative Brain Condition.' *US Medicine*. 26 June.
<http://www.usmedicine.com/neurology/single-ied-blast-can-cause-degenerative-brain-condition.html>

Morocco News Board. 2011. 'Suspected Bombers Arrested.' 5 May. <http://www.moroccoboard.com/news/5226-morocco-suspected-bombers-arrested>

Multi-National Corps–Iraq. 2008. *Counter IED Smart Book*. September.
<http://www.scribd.com/doc/36113212/GTA-90-10-046-Counter-IED-Smartbook-Iraq-USA-2008>

Musharbash, Yassin. 2009. 'Sauerland Cell Testifies: Jihadists Describe Hatred of US as Reason for Terror Plot.' Spiegel Online. 12 August.
<http://www.spiegel.de/international/germany/sauerland-cell-testifies-jihadists-describe-hatred-of-us-as-reason-for-terror-plot-a-642047.html>

NaCTSO (National Counter Terrorism Security Office). n.d. 'Secure Your Fertiliser.' Accessed 29 January 2013. <http://www.secureyourfertiliser.gov.uk>

Nasrawi, Salah. 2004. 'Egypt Says Palestinian Plotted Sinai Attacks.' *Boston Globe*. 26 October.
<http://articles.boston.com/2004-10-26/news/29204052_1_taba-hilton-ras-shitan-car-bomb>

NewsStand. 2012. 'U.S. Frustrated by Pakistan's Lack of Help in Combating Fertilizer Smuggling.' *Inside the Army*. 24 September.

NYT (*The New York Times*). 2000. 'Excerpts From Guilty Plea in Terrorism Case.' 21 October.
<http://www.nytimes.com/2000/10/21/nyregion/excerpts-from-guilty-plea-in-terrorism-case.html>

OPSI (Office of Public Sector Information). 2003. The Ammonium Nitrate Materials (High Nitrogen Content) Safety Regulations. Statutory Instrument:
No. 1082, 9 April. <http://www.legislation.gov.uk/uksi/2003/1082/pdfs/uksi_20031082_en.pdf>

Power, Samantha. 2008. *Chasing the Flame: Sergio Vieira de Mello and the Fight to Save the World*. New York: Penguin Press.

Radzinskiĭ, Ėdvard. 2005. *Alexander II: The Last Great Tsar*. New York: Free Press.
<http://books.google.co.uk/books/about/Alexander_II.html?id=qrFoAAAAMAAJ>

Rana, Amir. 2009. 'Enemy of the State—Lashkar-e-Jhangvi and Militancy in Pakistan.' *Jane's Intelligence Review*, Vol. 21, No. 9, pp. 14–19.

Rediff (Mumbai). 2008. 'Neogel-90 Not RDX Used in Jaipur Blasts.' 15 May <http://www.rediff.com/news/2008/may/15rajblast.htm>

RFI (Radio France Internationale). 2011. 'Niger Army in Pursuit of Suspected AQLIM "Traffickers" after 12 June Arms Find.' BBC Monitoring International
Reports. 15 June. <http://www.accessmylibrary.com/article-1G1-258987723/niger-army-pursuit-suspected.html>

Rodriguez, Alex. 2010. 'Pakistani Smugglers Supplying Afghan Bombmakers.' *Los Angeles Times*. 1 May.
<http://articles.latimes.com/2010/may/01/world/la-fg-pakistan-fertilizer-20100501>

Rubin, Alissa. 2009. 'How Baida Wanted to Die.' *The New York Times*. 12 August.
<http://www.nytimes.com/2009/08/16/magazine/16suicide-t.html?pagewanted=all>

Sarin, Ritu. 2007a. 'Explosive Theft: Everyone Admits Problem, No Work on Solution.' *Indian Express*. 8 October.
<http://www.indianexpress.com/news/explosive-theft-everyone-admits-problem-no-work-on-solution/225874/0>

—. 2007b. 'Stolen, No Trace: Tonnes and Tonnes of Explosives.' *Indian Express*. 7 October.
<http://www.indianexpress.com/news/stolen-no-trace-tonnes-and-tonnes-of-explosives/225516/0>

—. 2011. 'Alarm Bells Ring Yet Explosives Get Stolen by the Stockpile.' *Indian Express*. 24 October.
<http://www.indianexpress.com/news/alarm-bells-ring-yet-explosives-get-stolen-by-the-stockpile/864457/0>

Schroeder, Matt and Benjamin King. 2012. 'Surveying the Battlefield: Illicit Arms in Afghanistan, Iraq, and Somalia.' In Small Arms Survey. *Small Arms
Survey 2012: Moving Targets*. Geneva: Small Arms Survey.
<http://www.smallarmssurvey.org/fileadmin/docs/A-Yearbook/2012/eng/Small-Arms-Survey-2012-Chapter-10-EN.pdf>

Shah, Sabir. 2011. 'The Chemical Compound Can Be Used to Make Explosive Devices and to Serve Humanity at the Same Time.' *News* (Karachi).
23 September. <http://www.thenews.com.pk/Todays-News-13-9048-The-chemical-compound-can-be-used-to-make-explosive-devices-and-to-
serve-humanity-at-the-same-time>

Stratfor Global Intelligence. 2012. 'Syrian Rebels Use Homemade Rockets (Raw Footage).' Video. 27 December.
<http://www.youtube.com/watch?v=ymBFUMfdI48>

Streatfeild, Dominic. 2011. 'How the US Let Al-Qaida Get Its Hands on an Iraqi Weapons Factory.' *Guardian*. 7 January.
<http://www.guardian.co.uk/world/2011/jan/07/iraq-weapons-factory-al-qaida-us-failure>

Sweeney, John. 2012. 'Belarus: Were Executed Minsk Metro Bombers Framed?' BBC News. 30 July. <http://www.bbc.co.uk/news/world-19012541>

Taliban–Islamic Emirate of Afghanistan. n.d. *Omar's Missiles*.

Tele Sahel (Niger). 2011. 'Niger Army Seizes Explosives Haul in Country's North.' 13 June. BBC Monitoring International Reports.
<http://www.accessmylibrary.com/article-1G1-258898250/niger-army-seizes-explosives.html>

Tremlett, Giles. 2004. 'Spanish Police Foil New Railway Bomb Attack.' *Guardian*. 3 April. <http://www.guardian.co.uk/world/2004/apr/03/alqaida.spain>

— and Suzanne Goldenberg. 2001. 'Eta "Sold Hamas Bombers Dynamite".' *Guardian*. 19 June. <http://www.guardian.co.uk/world/2001/jun/19/israel>

UNAMA (United Nations Assistance Mission in Afghanistan). 2011. *Midyear Report 2011: Protection of Civilians in Armed Conflict*. Kabul: UNAMA. July. <http://unama.unmissions.org/Portals/UNAMA/Documents/2011%20Midyear%20POC.pdf>

—. 2012. *Annual Report 2011: Protection of Civilians in Armed Conflict*. Kabul: UNAMA and Office of the High Commissioner for Human Rights. February. <http://unama.unmissions.org/Portals/UNAMA/Documents/UNAMA%20POC%202011%20Report_Final_Feb%202012.pdf>

UNGA (United Nations General Assembly). 1991. Convention on the Marking of Plastic Explosives for the Purpose of Detection ('Montreal Convention'). 1 March. <http://treaties.un.org/doc/db/Terrorism/Conv10-english.pdf>

UNSC (United Nations Security Council). 2004. *Annex: Letter Dated 25 October 2004 from the Director General of the International Atomic Energy Agency Addressed to the President of the Security Council*. S /2004/831 of 25 October. <http://www.un.org/ga/search/view_doc.asp?symbol=S/2004/831>

—. 2011. *Eleventh Report of the Analytical Support and Sanctions Implementation Monitoring Team Established Pursuant to Security Council Resolution 1526 (2004) and Extended by Resolution 1904 (2009) concerning Al-Qaida and the Taliban and Associated Individuals and Entities*. S/2011/245 of 13 April. <http://www.un.org/ga/search/view_doc.asp?symbol=S/2011/245>

—. 2012. *Twelfth Report of the Analytical Support and Sanctions Implementation Monitoring Team, Submitted Pursuant to Resolution 1989 (2011) concerning Al-Qaida and Associated Individuals and Entities*. S/2012/729 of 1 October. <http://www.un.org/ga/search/view_doc.asp?symbol=S/2012/729>

USDC (United States District Court for the Eastern District of Michigan). 2010. *United States of America vs. Umar Farouk Abdulmutallab*. Indictment. 6 January. <http://graphics8.nytimes.com/packages/pdf/us/20100106-abdulmutallab.pdf>

USDOT (United States Department of the Treasury). 2008a. 'Treasury Designates Individuals and Entities Fueling Violence in Iraq.' 16 September. <http://www.treasury.gov/press-center/press-releases/Pages/hp1141.aspx>

—. 2008b. 'Treasury Designates Individuals, Entity Fueling Iraqi Insurgency.' 9 January. <http://www.treasury.gov/press-center/press-releases/Pages/hp759.aspx>

—. 2009. 'Treasury Designates Individual, Entity Posing Threat to Stability in Iraq.' 2 July. <http://www.treasury.gov/press-center/press-releases/Pages/tg195.aspx>

Vanden Brook, Tom. 2011. 'IEDs Kill 21,000 Iraqi Civilians 2005–2010.' *USA Today*. 12 January. <http://usatoday30.usatoday.com/news/world/iraq/2011-01-12-1Aied12_ST_N.htm?csp=34news&utm_source=feedburner&utm_medium=feed&utm_campaign=Feed%3A+usatoday-NewsTopStories+(News+-+Top\+Stories)>

Will, The (San Francisco). 2012. 'JTF Soldiers on Rampage, Raze Vehicles, Houses, over 50 Persons Killed.' 8 October. <http://thewillnigeria.com/politics/16528.html>

World Bank. 2003. *Republic of Pakistan: Mineral Sector Development Policy Note*. 20 November. <http://siteresources.worldbank.org/PAKISTANEXTN/Resources/pdf-Files-in-Events/Mineral-Sector/MSPN.pdf>

Wright, Joanna and Jeremy Binnie. 2010. 'Explosive Reaction: Afghan Insurgents Make IED Adjustments.' *Jane's Intelligence Review*. 12 August.

Yusufzai, Mushtaq. 2012. 'Fertile Explosives.' *News on Sunday* (Karachi). 5 February. <http://jang.com.pk/thenews/feb2012-weekly/nos-05-02-2012/dia.htm>

ACKNOWLEDGEMENTS

Principal authors

Jeremy Binnie and Joanna Wright

Contributors

Afghan colleagues, who cannot be named for security reasons

An arms dealer shows his wares, the prices of which rose dramatically when civil war broke out in neighbouring Syria. Beirut, Lebanon, 2012. © Marwan Tahtah

Price Watch
ARMS AND AMMUNITION AT ILLICIT MARKETS

11

INTRODUCTION

In the run-up to the withdrawal of NATO-led troops—scheduled for the end of 2014—prices for illegal arms in Afghanistan have soared dramatically. The price for an AK-47 rifle tripled during 2012. As an Afghan civilian explained, 'People are saying security will collapse, or soldiers will join warlords or the Taliban, so we need something to protect our families when there's a crisis' (Petty, 2012).

The prices of illicit firearms and their relation to security dynamics have attracted interest among journalists and researchers for some time. In Afghanistan, for example, the recent price increase spurred speculation that the security situation in the country would soon deteriorate. Analysts also argue that prices provide an indication of arms availability, 'demonstrating whether or not they can be easily obtained' (Karp, 2002, p. 65). Statistical analysis has even suggested that lower Kalashnikov rifle prices lead to an increased risk of civil war (Killicoat, 2007, p. 258).

Despite continued coverage of arms prices, analysis has been constrained by the difficulties inherent in gathering information from illicit markets. Most research has relied on second-hand data, often prices quoted in media reports. The fact that data collectors generally cover different locations and periods of time—while speaking to different sources—further hampers the comparability of the data. Information on prices for illicitly sold ammunition is particularly scarce.

This chapter seeks to advance current knowledge through a preliminary analysis of price data collected by the Small Arms Survey between February 2011 and September 2012. This initiative relied on field-based researchers, NGOs, and other informants with direct access to arms dealers. They collected prices on a monthly basis for both arms and ammunition sold at open-air and underground illicit markets in Lebanon, Pakistan, and Somalia. Consistent with previous research, surveyed arms dealers and observers identified a series of factors that help to explain variations in the price of arms and ammunition, including political unrest, activities of armed groups, and official corruption. While recognizing the plurality of these factors, the chapter focuses on the following two questions, drawing primarily from the quantitative data gathered over the 20-month period:

- Do prices of arms and ammunition exhibit similar variations over time and across locations?
- Is there a relationship between local security-related conditions and the prices of illicit arms and ammunition?

The main findings include:

- Within each surveyed location—Lebanon, Pakistan, and Somalia—the prices of arms and ammunition generally exhibited similar trend lines.
- Ammunition prices in Lebanon were strongly correlated with reported conflict casualties in neighbouring Syria.
- Behind the generic 'Kalashnikov' label hides a variety of models with very different price tags. When different Kalashnikov variants are available, those chambered for the 7.62 × 39 mm cartridge are much less expensive than models that use the more recent 5.45 × 39 mm round.

- In addition to calibre, determinants of weapons prices include their condition, the country of manufacture, and the type of stock (such as wooden or folding)—yet reliable information on some of these features is often hard to obtain from arms dealers.
- Local perceptions and beliefs associated with particular models also influence arms prices.
- Technical characteristics and local perceptions seem to play a lesser role in determining ammunition prices, resulting in smaller price ranges for ammunition than for arms.

Arms prices typically increase dramatically in the early stages of conflict.

This chapter has three sections. The first reviews available literature and presents chapter methodology, data sources, and limitations. The second section summarizes the main trends and observations emerging from the data on arms and ammunition prices in the three locations, examining whether the two are correlated. The third section identifies some of the factors that appear to affect price levels, with a particular focus on local security conditions. Unless otherwise noted, this chapter draws on investigative and narrative reports submitted by the Survey's data collectors in the three countries under review; Annexe 11.1 provides the raw data collected between February 2011 and September 2012.

UNDERSTANDING ARMS PRICES

Small arms prices have attracted considerable interest from researchers, economists, and policy-makers. This section reviews current knowledge and presents the data collection process used for this chapter. It also discusses challenges involved in gathering such information, noting the resulting limitations in the data.

Current knowledge

In places where data on weapons stockpiles and transfers is non-existent, illicit market prices are relied on to provide an indication of how difficult it is to obtain arms (Karp, 2002, p. 65; Chivers, 2010, p. 381). The most significant quantitative study to date compares Kalashnikov rifle price data across countries, using a supply and demand model.[1] It finds that several supply-side factors influence arms prices, noting that:

- The more effective a country's regulations,[2] the higher weapons prices will be.
- Countries with more porous borders tend to have lower weapons prices. [. . .]
- [Rises] in the military spending of neighbouring countries tend to reduce weapons prices in a particular country [. . .].
- [A surfeit of] weapons in post-conflict environments keep[s] prices low and contribute[s] to the risk of conflict throughout the region for some time after the conflict has ended (Killicoat, 2007, pp. 257–58).

Another particularly significant finding from this study is that 'cheaper weapons prices lead to an increased risk of civil war, independently of other conflict risk factors' (Killicoat, 2007, p. 258). This suggests that monitoring arms prices has utility from an early warning perspective, with low prices being among the factors that should raise the alarm about a possible outbreak of conflict.

Research also notes that, once a war has begun, 'the relationship between weapons prices and the intensity and duration of conflict takes on a different dynamic', with arms prices typically increasing dramatically in the early stages of conflict (Killicoat, 2007, p. 270). Indeed, observers have noted that rising arms prices in Afghanistan, Syria, and Iraq could reflect 'rising expectations of violence in the future' (Petty, 2012; Chivers, 2012a; Barr, 2007). In markets fuelled by conflict-driven demand, high and rising prices reflect an expectation that the security situation will continue to deteriorate.

In post-conflict settings, prices for military rifles tend to plummet. The FN FAL rifle, for instance, sold for just USD 500–800 in Libya in February 2012, a sharp decrease when compared with the thousands of dollars it was worth at the height of the 2011 conflict (Spleeters, 2012a, pp. 16–17). After conflict, more concealable weapons, such as pistols and the associated ammunition, tend to be sold at inflated prices. Also in Libya in February 2012, the FN Browning HP pistol sold for USD 2,400–3,200, and a 9 × 19 mm cartridge cost more than USD 6, even though these items were hardly in demand during the 2011 civil war (Jenzen-Jones, 2013, p. 3; Spleeters, 2012a, p. 17).

Despite continued interest in the prices of illicit arms, many questions remain unanswered. While the Killicoat study finds that several 'supply-side' factors affect arms prices, it also notes that 'all proxy measures for motivation proved insignificant for explaining weapons prices' (Killicoat, 2007, p. 266). The tested proxies included lagged income growth, the proportion of young men in the population, civil war onset, and homicide rates (p. 264). This means that existing models do not help explain what motivates individuals to buy weapons.

The inherent difficulties of gathering systematic information from illicit markets represent a second set of limitations. The available comparative studies have relied on second-hand data—often prices as quoted in media reports—which can fail to capture important information such as the precise type of weaponry, the quantities traded, the location of the transaction, and the characteristics of the trading parties (Killicoat, 2007, p. 272). These limitations make the comparison of arms prices over time and across settings particularly challenging.

> Prices for military rifles tend to plummet in post-conflict settings.

Data on the prices of weapons other than Kalashnikov rifles is rather scarce, despite their importance. As a Lebanese arms dealer explained in 2010:

> I know there is a real problem on the streets right now not just because of the machine guns but because I am selling so many RPG [rocket-propelled grenade] launchers. People only buy grenades when they think war is coming. An RPG isn't really a weapon you use to protect your house, but everyone is buying them anyway. Not good (Prothero, 2010).

Similarly, there is little, if any, available information on prices for illicitly sold ammunition, with a few recent exceptions.[3] Anecdotal evidence suggests that scarcity of specific types of ammunition makes the associated weapons unpopular and less used.[4] Yet there is insufficient data to confirm this hypothesis.

The data collection process

This chapter analyses arms and ammunition price data collected in the framework of a pilot project initiated in February 2011. The project was designed to gather information at open-air and underground illicit markets on a regular basis, with the purpose of generating average monthly prices that can be compared over time. Monthly price data covering the period February 2011–September 2012 forms the basis for the analysis presented in this chapter.

The project focused on three locations with known, active illicit or informal arms markets where adequate access to dealers could be established:

- In Lebanon, which lacks open-air arms markets such as those found in Pakistan and Somalia, underground arms dealers sell a variety of items working from home or on the street.[5] The dealers consulted as part of this study operated in the Bekaa Valley and South Beirut (see Map 11.1).
- In Pakistan, the project monitored the markets of Darra Adam Khel and Bara in the Federally Administered Tribal Areas (FATA) (see Map 11.2). These arms markets are known not just for their trade in industry-made weapons, but also for their vibrant local 'craft' industry, which is capable of reproducing most industrial models of arms (Shinwari and Malik, 2004, pp. 10–11; SPADO, 2005, pp. 21–22).[6]

- In Somalia, the project focused on Mogadishu, including the infamous Bakara market, which was under the control of the Al Shabaab insurgency until the August 2011 offensive by the Somali Transitional Federal Government (TFG) (Cadde, 2011; UNSC, 2012, para. 27; Zimmerman, 2011) (see Map 11.3).[7] Following this operation, most Al Shabaab forces fled Mogadishu and the TFG seized control of Bakara market, while Bakara arms dealers went underground and transferred to another part of the capital.

The three locations have in common the fact that demand was affected by local or nearby conflict during the period under study. Somalia has faced recurrent internal conflict since the early 1990s, and fighting between soldiers of the TFG and the African Union Mission in Somalia (AMISOM) on the one side and Al Shabaab and other insurgents on the other was intense for most of 2011 and 2012 (Cadde, 2011; UNSC, 2012, para. 27; Zimmerman, 2011). The surveyed markets in Pakistan are located in particularly volatile regions of the country,[8] as well as near the border with Afghanistan. Although Lebanon did not face armed conflict during this time, fighting erupted in neighbouring Syria in March 2011 and escalated throughout the period under review (VDC, 2012). Syrians have reportedly been crossing the border to Lebanon to purchase arms since the beginning of the conflict (Alami, 2011; Blanford, 2012; Qassem, 2012).

One of the aims of the project was to create a data collection process that would address some of the above-mentioned limitations. For this purpose, the project relied on

Map 11.1 **Case study: Lebanon**

Map 11.2 **Case study: Pakistan**

Map 11.3 **Case study: Somalia**

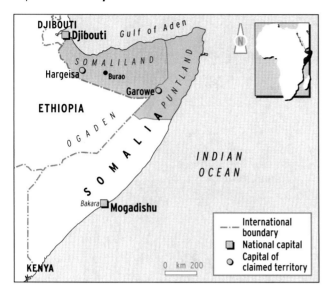

individuals and institutions with established access to arms sellers in the selected illicit markets. The data collectors included, in no particular order, a local NGO, a journalist, and vetted local contacts and informants with experience collecting information from the surveyed markets. Common working principles guided the data collection process. Specifically, the data collectors:

- inquired about prices of weapons for sale with a minimum of two local dealers on a regular basis, preferably twice per month;

- reported monthly minimum and maximum prices for preselected weapons and corresponding ammunition that were sold by local sellers;

- monitored available Kalashnikov variants in each location, distinguishing them by calibre (7.62 × 39 mm or 5.45 × 39 mm) and by any other features (such as condition or type of stock);

- tracked prices for other available equipment, which consisted primarily of other military rifles of NATO calibre (5.56 × 45 mm and 7.62 × 51 mm), pistols, general-purpose machine guns, heavy machine guns, and their associated ammunition; and

- asked dealers to identify any market changes and possible reasons behind them.

The Small Arms Survey then entered monthly minimum and maximum prices for each weapon model and ammunition type in a central database. Weapons and ammunition were generally sold in US dollars (USD) in both Lebanon and Somalia. In Pakistan, the rupee (PKR) was used at the markets and PKR values were kept for the analysis of trends. When arms and ammunition prices for Pakistan are provided in USD for comparative purposes, average monthly exchange rates were used for the conversion.

In all three countries, the data collected typically referred to amounts to be paid for small transactions, usually involving one or very few weapons. Typical customers included local individuals and businessmen acquiring weapons and ammunition for self-defence, protection, and other purposes; some probably acted as intermediaries or resellers of small quantities of weapons, such that some of the sold arms may have ended up with armed groups or other organizations. Regardless of the end user and use, the prices reviewed here do not refer to large, wholesale purchases. While this chapter provides unit prices to allow for comparisons, it should be noted that cartridges were usually sold in packages of 10 in Pakistan, 50 in Lebanon, and 30 to 100 in Somalia.

Caveats

Despite efforts to standardize methodology, full comparability of data across locations remains elusive. In Pakistan, the data collectors visited different dealers every month; in Lebanon and Somalia, they regularly contacted dealers with whom they were already acquainted. Even in the context of a single location, different sources sometimes provided

An arms dealer repairs a Kalashnikov rifle at his shop in Landikotal, Pakistan's Federally Administered Tribal Areas, December 2012. © Shahid Shinwari/Reuters

conflicting information. In Mogadishu, for instance, the Survey worked with a total of five data collectors, each of whom consulted different sellers. Two of these data collectors provided reports for most of the 20-month period under study, yet the other three were not as reliable and were occasionally tasked only with cross-checking specific information. At times, the main two data collectors provided contradictory information, especially with respect to Kalashnikov-pattern rifles (7.62 × 39 mm variants) and 7.62 × 39 mm ammunition, with significant discrepancies in the prices of these items after the TFG offensive of August 2011. As a result, analysis of Mogadishu data in the chapter relies on reporting by one data collector who seemed the most reliable based on cross-checking of information, his responses to probing questions, and the depth of his narrative reports, as well as his ability to provide evidence such as photos of the materiel sold.

In Pakistan and Lebanon, where the Survey relied mainly on one data-collecting individual and organization, cross-checking was undertaken mainly through peer review and the checking of other sources.[9] Lastly, in the case of Lebanon, local authorities' crackdown on dealers and rising tensions in Syria made regular consulting with sellers more difficult, with the result that the data collector provided incomplete reports between February and September 2012.[10]

Another challenge lay in distinguishing between weapon types based on limited information provided by dealers. This was particularly true for Kalashnikov-pattern rifles (7.62 × 39 mm variants), which dealers priced on the basis of different criteria in each location. In Pakistan, for instance, different price ranges applied based on whether the rifle was

Table 11.1 Average prices per unit, USD, February 2011–September 2012

Country	Lebanon		Pakistan				Somalia	
			Industry-made		Locally crafted replicas			
Types of weapon and ammunition	Weapon	Ammunition	Weapon	Ammunition	Weapon	Ammunition	Weapon	Ammunition
Pistols								
Browning/9 × 19 mm	2,008	1.10						
Makarov/9 × 18 mm			888	0.60	70	0.20	1,681	2.60
Military rifles								
AK-47 and AKM variants/7.62 × 39 mm	1,606	1.20	1,205	0.60	148	0.20	731	0.60
AK-74/5.45 × 39 mm			2,899	1.50	205	0.30		
AKS-74U/5.45 × 39 mm	4,073	1.50						
FN FAL variants/7.62 × 51 mm	972	0.70						
M16 variants/5.56 × 45 mm	2,847	0.90	3,334	0.30	289	0.20		
General-purpose machine gun								
PKM pattern/7.62 × 54R mm	3,984	0.70					6,808	0.70
Heavy machine gun								
108 mm							7,995	0.50

Notes: All prices reflect the average of monthly prices for the period February 2011–September 2012, with the exception of locally and industry-made Makarov pistols and 9 x 19 mm ammunition in Pakistan (March 2011–September 2012), and the Makarov pistol and 9 x 19 mm ammunition in Somalia (October 2011–September 2012). Average ammunition prices are rounded to the nearest tenth to avoid false precision. For Pakistan, PKR prices were converted using average monthly exchange rates.

Source: Annexe 11.1

Russian-, Chinese-, or locally made—and based on its condition (unused or second-hand). In Lebanon, Russian Kalashnikovs were sold at a different price than were Bulgarian, Chinese, and East German variants, which were all grouped into the same price range. In Somalia, the condition and the type of stock (wood or folding) affected prices. These inconsistent price groupings resulted in broad price ranges in all three locations for Kalashnikov-pattern rifles (7.62 × 39 mm variants).

To allow for comparative analysis over time and across locations, this chapter uses the average price per month (calculated as [minimum price + maximum price]/2) as the unit of analysis. This fails to capture the broad ranges for generic weapon models, such as Kalashnikov-pattern rifles (7.62 × 39 mm variants). The chapter separates Pakistan's locally crafted firearm replicas from industrial products, given that industrially produced weapons cost up to ten times more than the craft equivalents (see Table 11.1). Significantly, weapons are also distinguished by calibre; this point is especially important with respect to Kalashnikov rifles, since the AK-74 series is chambered for 5.45 × 39 mm ammunition, whose availability may differ from that of original 7.62 × 39 mm cartridges used in the AK-47 and AKM models.

ARMS AND AMMUNITION PRICES

This section provides a general overview of the arms and ammunition prices collected by the Small Arms Survey between February 2011 and September 2012. It focuses on a limited set of weapons and ammunition types in each location, such as Kalashnikov variants and other locally available military rifles. One type of pistol in each country and, where available, general-purpose machine guns and heavy machine guns are included for comparison purposes (see Table 11.1). After identifying the main patterns and trends in the data, the section explores the relationship between the prices of arms and those of ammunition.

Weapons prices

Challenges in interpreting Kalashnikov prices

Local perceptions of weapons can have an impact on prices. Prices collected for Kalashnikov variants chambered for 5.45 × 39 mm ammunition—such as the AK-74 and AKS-74U— were significantly higher than those of 7.62 × 39 mm Kalashnikov variants (see Table 11.1). In Pakistan, based on average prices over the 20-month period, the more modern AK-74 sold for more than twice the price of 7.62 × 39 mm Kalashnikov models, almost reaching the price of an M16. In Lebanon, the AKS-74U is also more than twice as expensive as 7.62 × 39 mm Kalashnikov variants. As a shortened but less accurate version of the AK-74, the AKS-74U has a high price tag that may reflect local perceptions of this particular weapon. Indeed, it is referred to as the 'Bin Laden' on the Lebanese markets, a reference to photographs and videos of Osama Bin Laden featuring the rifle (see Table 11.2).[11] As a result, its price can exceed that of NATO-calibre weapons such as the M16, which is usually more expensive than original 7.62 × 39 mm Kalashnikov-pattern rifles. Local perceptions of the more common Kalashnikov models can also have an impact on prices. In Syria in 2012, the uprising 'bred a set of popular mythologies into the minds of the men,' including the belief that Russian-made Kalashnikovs have 'diamonds' in the barrel (Spleeters, 2012b). At the time, these Russian models were being sold for twice the price of the Bulgarian variants.

It is important to note that a wide variety of arms fall under the 7.62 × 39 mm Kalashnikov category, resulting in significant price ranges. In September 2012, in Pakistan, the price for reportedly Russian-manufactured 7.62 × 39 mm Kalashnikovs ranged from about USD 760 for a second-hand model to almost USD 1,900 for a new, unused rifle—a price ratio of 1:2.5. Meanwhile, local replicas sold for just USD 140. The range of prices in Lebanon for the same month was narrower, with rifles presented as Russian-made selling for USD 1,750–1,800 compared with the USD 1,400 asked for reportedly Bulgarian, Chinese, and East German variants. In Mogadishu, data collectors reported higher prices for folding-stock variants of 7.62 × 39 mm Kalashnikovs than for their wooden-stock equivalents.[12]

Taken together, these varying and sometimes wide ranges provide further illustration of the limitations of comparing generic 'Kalashnikov' prices across settings, especially when the models concerned are not clearly described. This chapter partly addresses this concern by distinguishing Kalashnikov variants by calibre. The condition and country of production, as well as popular conceptions around particular weapons, appear to be additional criteria that influence prices. Yet, as outlined above, such information is difficult to gather in a reliable and systematic fashion, partly because dealers often provide false information in order to obtain the best possible price, or because they group different types in a similar price range according to local criteria.

The source of the weapon may also affect prices. In Mogadishu, arms that had leaked from government sources were usually sold at a lower price than similar models smuggled from Yemen or Puntland, presumably due to the additional transport costs.[13] An outstanding question is that of the reliability of locally produced weapon replicas in Pakistan. Virtually all original, factory-manufactured models, including automatic firearms, are copied and sold for a tenth of the price, yet little is known about their actual capabilities and use.

Table 11.2 Selected nicknames of weapons sold at illicit markets

Model	Nickname (country of use)	Notes
Makarov pistol	Dabanacas (Somalia)	In Somali, 'Dhabano' refers to cheeks, and 'Cas' means 'Red'. The nickname, which can be translated as 'red-cheeked', seems to refer to the red plastic pieces embedded on either side of the pistol's stock.
7.62 × 39 mm Kalashnikov variants	Circle 11 (Lebanon) Rocket (Lebanon)	Both names refer to factory markings visible on the rifles. The number 11 inscribed in an oblong circle corresponds to the Polish Lucznik (formerly F.B. Radom) factory marking. 'Rocket' appears to refer to the Russian Izhevsk factory marks featuring a triangle and arrow.
5.45 × 39 mm Kalashnikov variants	Kalakov (Pakistan)	Appears to be used as a generic term for 5.45 × 39 mm Kalashnikov variants, such as the AK-74. Not to be confused with 'Krinkov', a name that was apparently devised by Afghani Mujaheddin during the Soviet invasion of Afghanistan in the 1980s and that refers specifically to the AKS-74U.
AKS-74U	Bin Laden (Lebanon)	The name harks back to the former Al Qaeda leader's frequent video appearances with the rifle visible in the background (Chivers, 2010, p. 383).
Locally produced Kalashnikov replicas	TT-Kof* (Pakistan)	A combination of 'TT' in reference to the Tokarev TT pistol and 'Kof' for 'Kalashnikov'. The use of 'TT' seems to derive from the fact that the TT-Kof rifle fires pistol ammunition.

Note: * Prices for the TT-Kof rifle in Pakistan are not analysed in this chapter.

Source: Reina (2012); confidential author correspondence with data collectors, February 2011-September 2012

Top photo: A Makarov pistol, nicknamed 'Dabanacas' (meaning red-cheeked), alongside some khat, Hargeisa, Somaliland, 2010. © Jonah Leff

Middle photo: A video image of Osama Bin Laden with an AKS-74U rifle, June 2001. © AFP/TV grab

Bottom photo: An AK-74 pattern rifle, referred to as a 'Kalakov,' at Bara market, in Pakistan's Federally Administered Tribal Areas, 2012. © SPADO

Degrees of volatility

In order to measure the extent to which arms prices varied over time and across locations and types, a 'coefficient of variation'[14] (CV) was calculated for each weapon model. The CV value expresses price volatility, or the extent to which the price of a weapon for each month differed from its average price over the entire study period. Higher scores express higher volatility.

The average CV score across weapon models and locations, and over the study period, was 0.17 (see Table 11.3). The most volatile prices were those of the FN FAL in Lebanon and 7.62 × 39 mm Kalashnikov variants in Somalia (CV=0.33), while prices for locally produced replicas of the M16 in Pakistan varied the least (CV=0.04). Prices for military weapons varied more markedly than those of handguns: military rifles and machine guns scored 0.18 and 0.19 on average, respectively, compared with just 0.13 for pistols. Location also matters: volatility of arms prices was lower in Pakistan (0.13) than in Lebanon (0.19) and Somalia (0.22).

As might be predicted, a single weapon model can experience varying degrees of volatility in different locations. This is the case, for instance, for 7.62 × 39 mm Kalashnikov variants, which scored 0.12 in Pakistan, 0.19 in Lebanon,

Table 11.3 **Volatility of arms prices, February 2011–September 2012**							
Rank	Location	Type	Model	Number of months of data analysed	Average price in transaction currency*	Standard deviation	Coefficient of variation
1	Lebanon	Military rifle	FN FAL	16	972	320	0.33
2	Somalia	Military rifle	Kalashnikov (7.62 × 39 mm variants)	20	731	238	0.33
3	Somalia	Machine gun	DShK	20	7,995	2,205	0.28
4	Pakistan	Military rifle	Locally manufactured AK-74	20	18,313	4,029	0.22
5	Lebanon	Military rifle	Kalashnikov (7.62 × 39 mm variants)	16	1,606	312	0.19
6	Pakistan	Military rifle	AK-74	20	261,250	50,507	0.19
7	Somalia	Pistol	Makarov	12	1,681	307	0.18
8	Lebanon	Machine gun	PKM	16	3,984	675	0.17
9	Lebanon	Military rifle	AKS-74U	16	4,073	682	0.17
10	Lebanon	Pistol	Browning	16	2,008	317	0.16
11	Pakistan	Military rifle	Locally manufactured Kalashnikov (7.62 × 39 mm variants)	20	13,250	1,957	0.15
12	Pakistan	Pistol	Locally manufactured Makarov	19	6,316	837	0.13
13	Lebanon	Military rifle	M16	16	2,847	372	0.13
14	Pakistan	Military rifle	Kalashnikov (7.62 × 39 mm variants)	20	108,450	13,309	0.12
15	Somalia	Machine gun	PKM	20	6,808	765	0.11
16	Pakistan	Military rifle	M16	20	299,625	32,406	0.11
17	Pakistan	Pistol	Makarov	19	79,842	4,646	0.06
18	Pakistan	Military rifle	Locally manufactured M16	20	25,900	1,083	0.04
Average							**0.17**

Notes: * Prices are listed in USD for Lebanon and Somalia and in PKR for Pakistan. CV values are rounded to the nearest hundredth and are listed in descending order.

Source: Annexe 11.1

Figure 11.1 **Weapons prices in Lebanon, USD, February 2011–September 2012**

■ Browning pistol   ■ 7.62 × 39 mm Kalashnikov variants   ■ AKS-74U   ■ FN FAL   ■ M16   PKM

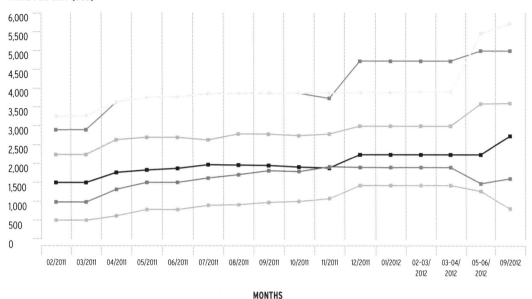

PRICE PER UNIT (USD)

MONTHS

Source: Annexe 11.1

and 0.33 in Somalia (see Table 11.3). While this may sound intuitive, it is significant in that it shows that the prices for illegal weapons depend more on local dynamics than on a single 'global' market.

Perhaps less intuitive, and more significant, is the finding that different weapons in the same location experienced varying levels of price volatility (see Table 11.3). In Lebanon, not only were volatility scores inconsistent across models, but price trends for some weapons also seemed to diverge. The most striking divergence is the collapse in the price of the FN FAL between May and September 2012, while prices for other weapon models continued to increase or remained stable (see Figure 11.1).

In summary, in the studied markets, the prices of weapons belonging to the same category (for instance, military rifles) can follow different and sometimes conflicting trajectories in a single location. Moreover, prices for long, automatic, or 'military-style' weapons appear to have fluctuated more than those of handguns. Previous research has shown that supply factors such as the effectiveness of a country's regulatory system, the military spending of neighbouring countries, and border porosity help in determining the prices of Kalashnikov rifles (broadly defined) across countries (Killicoat, 2007, p. 257). The evidence reviewed here suggests that additional factors may influence the prices of arms, and that their impact on different types of arms varies.

Ammunition prices

Calibre matters

This section examines prices for the types of ammunition corresponding to the above-mentioned weapons. The surveyed ammunition includes rounds that originated in the former Eastern bloc (9 × 18 mm, 7.62 × 39 mm, 5.45 × 39 mm, 7.64 × 54R mm, 12.7 × 108 mm) as well as cartridges of NATO standard (9 × 19 mm, 7.62 × 51 mm, 5.56 × 45 mm).

Prices for Kalashnikov rifle ammunition were higher for the newer types, with 5.45 × 39 mm rounds (for use in the AK-74 series) more expensive than the original 7.62 × 39 mm cartridges (used in AK-47 and AKM models). In Lebanon, the former was 25 per cent more expensive than the latter; in Pakistan, the newer rounds cost more than twice as much as the older variety (see Table 11.1). NATO 7.62 × 51 mm (for the FN FAL) and 5.56 × 45 mm (for the M16) were cheaper than Kalashnikov rounds in both Lebanon and Pakistan. AK-74 rifles and their ammunition appear to be unavailable in Somalia.

Ammunition for pistols was particularly expensive in Somalia, much more so than any other calibre reviewed here. A single 9 × 18 mm cartridge in Mogadishu cost USD 2.60 on average (see Table 11.1). In comparison, pistol ammunition cost USD 1.10 in Lebanon and USD 0.60 in Pakistan—prices that are more consistent with those of other locally available ammunition.

Table 11.4 Volatility scores for ammunition prices, February 2011–September 2012

Rank	Location	Model	Number of months of data analysed	Average price in transaction currency*	Standard deviation	Coefficient of variation**
1	Lebanon	7.62 × 51 mm	16	0.70	0.34	0.48
2	Lebanon	7.62 × 54R mm	16	0.70	0.30	0.44
3	Lebanon	5.45 × 39 mm	16	1.50	0.49	0.32
4	Lebanon	5.56 × 45 mm	16	0.90	0.29	0.31
5	Lebanon	7.62 × 39 mm	16	1.20	0.35	0.29
6	Somalia	7.62 × 54R mm	20	0.70	0.15	0.22
7	Pakistan	9 × 18 mm	19	52.20	9.54	0.18
8	Somalia	7.62 × 39 mm	20	0.60	0.10	0.18
9	Lebanon	9 × 19 mm	16	1.10	0.16	0.15
10	Pakistan	7.62 × 39 mm	20	55.50	6.64	0.12
11	Pakistan	Locally manufactured 5.56 × 45 mm	20	17.30	1.98	0.11
12	Pakistan	5.45 × 39 mm	20	131.80	13.96	0.11
13	Somalia	12.7 × 108 mm	20	0.50	0.04	0.09
14	Pakistan	5.56 × 45 mm	20	30.10	2.63	0.09
15	Pakistan	Locally manufactured 9 × 18 mm	19	18.40	1.41	0.08
16	Somalia	9 × 18 mm	12	2.60	0.17	0.06
17	Pakistan	Locally manufactured 7.62 × 39 mm	20	19.30	0.98	0.05
18	Pakistan	Locally manufactured 5.45 × 39 mm	20	25.90	1.15	0.04
Average						**0.19**

Notes: * Prices are listed in USD for Lebanon and Somalia and in PKR for Pakistan. Average ammunition prices are rounded to the nearest tenth to avoid false precision.

** CV values are rounded to the nearest hundredth.

Source: Annexe 11.1

Technical characteristics appear to have less impact on the prices of ammunition than on those of arms. Reported prices for ammunition often consisted of single values, not ranges. If price ranges were provided for ammunition, they were usually much narrower than price ranges for associated weapons.[15] This suggests that, while design, year, country of production, and type of stock are important features in determining the price of a weapon, fewer factors seem to affect the price of ammunition. Further research and more precise identification of ammunition sold at illicit markets is needed to confirm this finding, however, as smaller price ranges for ammunition may simply reflect a more homogenous supply.

More consistent trends

Calculating coefficients of variation for ammunition prices makes it possible to measure the extent to which ammunition prices varied from month to month in relation to the average price. As a result, CV values are comparable not only across types of ammunition, but also with the CV values for weapons prices.

Overall, ammunition prices seem to have been roughly as volatile as arms prices, with an average CV score of 0.19 compared with 0.17 for arms (see Tables 11.3 and 11.4). Yet, at each location, volatility scores for ammunition prices were more consistent than those of arms prices. The five most volatile prices relate to ammunition in Lebanon, whose average CV value is 0.33—significantly higher than the 0.19 average score for Lebanese arms prices. In contrast, ammunition prices show an average CV score of 0.14 in Somalia and 0.10 in Pakistan, both of which are therefore less volatile than the prices of arms in the same locations. Ammunition for long, automatic firearms scored highest with a 0.20 CV average, compared with just 0.12 for pistol ammunition.

Figure 11.2 **Arms and ammunition price trends in Lebanon, Pakistan, and Somalia, February 2011–September 2012**

LEBANON

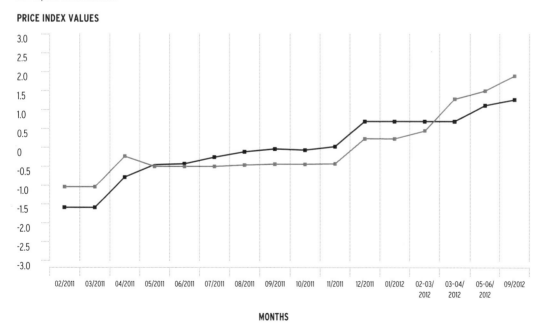

Note: Correlation: R=0.87; P<0.001.

Source: Annexe 11.1

PAKISTAN

■ Weapons ■ Ammunition ■ Local weapons ■ Local ammunition

PRICE INDEX VALUES

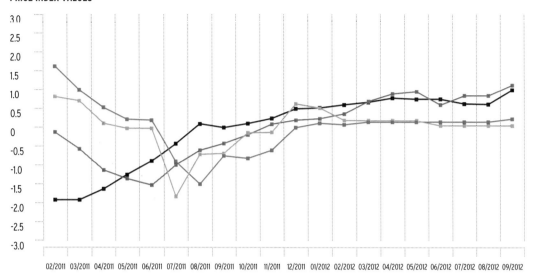

MONTHS

Note: Correlation, industry-made: R=0.77; P<0.001. Correlation, locally made: R=0.75; P<0.001.

Source: Annexe 11.1

SOMALIA

■ Weapons ■ Ammunition

PRICE INDEX VALUES

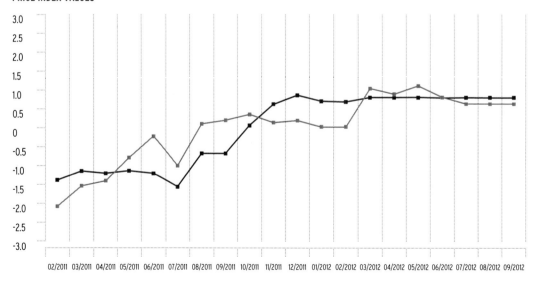

MONTHS

Note: Correlation: R=0.84; P<0.001.

Source: Annexe 11.1

Arms and ammunition prices generally followed similar trends. Figure 11.2 compares arms and ammunition prices across settings using standardized indices. These weapons and ammunition indices were calculated by (1) translating monthly price values for each type of ammunition and weapon model into standardized Z scores, and then (2) calculating the average monthly Z score for all weapons and ammunition surveyed in each location.[16]

Analysis of standardized indices shows that arms and ammunition prices usually evolved in the same fashion and that they were statistically correlated in all three locations (see Figure 11.2). One exception involves the prices of industry-made ammunition in Pakistan between February and June 2011, which decreased while the prices of arms increased. This appears to be the result of the sharp decline in the price of only one type of ammunition, the 5.56 × 45 mm. During the same period, prices for the other three types of ammunition surveyed in Pakistan either remained stable or increased slightly. Overall, arms and ammunition prices in Pakistan were still statistically correlated, although to a lesser degree than in Lebanon and Somalia. In Pakistan, the evolution of prices for industry-made arms and cartridges differed from those of the locally made materiel.

Does the price of ammunition influence that of arms?

Qualitative research has suggested that the availability of ammunition in an area affected by conflict may have an impact on the popularity and use of the corresponding weapons. Interviews with fighters, for instance, revealed that combatants do not care for, and sometimes even dispose of, weapons for which ammunition cannot easily be found locally.[17] Translated into pricing analysis, with other things held constant, this should entail that, when ammunition is cheap, available weapons that chamber it should be in higher demand, and therefore more expensive. At the same time, locally available weapons that use scarcer and more expensive ammunition should experience lower demand and should therefore be cheaper.

Arms and ammunition prices were statistically correlated in the three surveyed locations.

For this theory to be tested in ideal conditions, one would need to compare the prices of locally available weapons that have similar capabilities but that use distinct calibres of ammunition. While the weapons studied in this chapter all have distinct features and capabilities, the four different types of military rifles under consideration—namely 7.62 × 39 mm Kalashnikov variants, AK-74 variants, the M16, and FN FAL variants—provide a reasonable basis for comparison. Indeed, these rifles use four different calibres of ammunition and, although their design, accuracy, and range vary, they share several common features. Most important, all four weapons are individual combat rifles and can fire rounds automatically.

The data collected for this study makes it possible to compare average arms and ammunition prices for Kalashnikov rifles and associated 7.62 × 39 mm ammunition with those of other common rifles across several locations. In the surveyed markets of Lebanon and Pakistan, the M16—chambered for 5.56 × 45 mm ammunition—is considered one of the automatic weapons in highest demand, together with 7.62 × 39 mm Kalashnikov variants. The data includes the 'generic' AK-74 for Pakistan and the AKS-74U for Lebanon, both of which are associated with 5.45 × 39 mm ammunition. In Mogadishu, the market for military rifles is dominated by 7.62 × 39 mm Kalashnikov variants. FN FAL variants and their distinct 7.62 × 51 mm ammunition can be found in other parts of Somalia, however, namely in Puntland and Somaliland, for which partial price information was collected. FN FAL rifles were also available in Lebanon.

Based on the data reproduced in Table 11.5, the hypothesis of 'the cheaper the ammunition, the more expensive the military rifle' seems to apply only partially. In Puntland, where the 7.62 × 39 mm round is cheaper than the 7.62 × 51 mm cartridge, 7.62 × 39 mm Kalashnikov-pattern rifles tend to be more expensive than FN FAL variants. In

Table 11.5 Average arms and ammunition prices for five military rifles of different calibre, in USD

	Eastern bloc					NATO			
	7.62 × 39 mm Kalashnikov variants	7.62 × 39 mm	AK-74	AKS-74U	5.45 × 39 mm	FN FAL variants	7.62 × 51 mm	M16	5.56 × 45 mm
Lebanon	1,606	1.20		4,073	1.50	972	0.70	2,847	0.90
Pakistan	1,205	0.60	2,899		1.50			3,334	0.30
Somalia: Puntland	682	0.80				491	1.30		
Somalia: Somaliland	677	1.00				677	1.00		

Note: The five rifle types are followed by the ammunition for which they are chambered. Average prices are for the periods February 2011–September 2012 for Lebanon and Pakistan, October 2011–April 2012 for Puntland, and October 2011–September 2012 for Somaliland. Average ammunition prices are rounded to the nearest tenth to avoid false precision.

Source: Annexe 11.1

Somaliland, where ammunition for both calibres sells at similar prices, both FN FAL and Kalashnikov variants sold at around USD 680. Prices in Lebanon and Pakistan are much less conclusive. As noted earlier, both the AK-74 variants and 5.45 × 39 mm rounds are more expensive than 7.62 × 39 mm Kalashnikov variants and their cartridges in both countries. The same applies to NATO-standard rifles in Lebanon, with the M16 and 5.56 × 45 mm rounds selling at

Figure 11.3 7.62 × 51 mm ammunition and FN FAL rifle price trends in Lebanon, February 2011–September 2012

■ FN FAL   ■ 7.62 × 51 mm

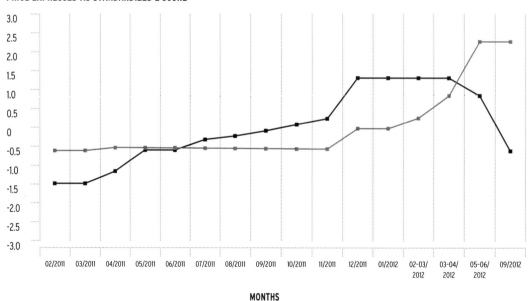

PRICE EXPRESSED AS STANDARDIZED Z SCORE

MONTHS

Note: A standardized Z score indicates by how many standard deviations an observation is above or below the average. Expressing price values as Z scores preserves the overall trend line and makes it possible to compare the prices of arms with those of ammunition on the same scale.

Source: Annexe 11.1

higher prices than the FN FAL and its 7.62 × 51 mm ammunition. Comparisons between what appear to be the most commonly sold models seem to hold better, however. Compared to 7.62 × 39 mm Kalashnikov variants, the M16 rifle was more expensive and its ammunition cheaper than its Eastern bloc equivalent in both Lebanon and Pakistan.

An examination of trends should also help in understanding the impact of ammunition prices on those of arms. If the hypothesis of 'the cheaper the ammunition, the more expensive the military rifle' holds true, in case of a decrease (or increase) in ammunition prices, one would expect an increase (or decrease, respectively) in the price of the associated arm. The available data does not suggest that changes in ammunition prices systematically affect corresponding arms prices. The information reviewed above shows that, in each studied location, the prices of arms and ammunition generally followed similar paths over time (see Figure 11.2). This important finding does not necessarily contradict the hypothesis of an effect of ammunition prices on those of weapons, however. When weapons and ammunition prices vary in similar ways, they may be driven by the same external factors, such as conflict-driven demand.

Examining cases where prices varied both markedly and unusually yields interesting results. As discussed above, in Lebanon ammunition prices were particularly volatile and generally followed patterns exhibited by arms prices. Yet prices for some specific military rifles and associated ammunition followed opposite paths. The price of the 7.62 × 51 mm cartridge, for instance, initially experienced several months of stability, increased significantly between November 2011 and June 2012, and then remained stable and high in September 2012 (see Figure 11.3). Although the price of the FN FAL—which is chambered for this type of ammunition—increased until December 2011, it stayed stable and subsequently decreased in May–June 2012, before collapsing again in September 2012.

Figure 11.4 **5.56 × 45 mm ammunition and M16 rifle price trends in Lebanon, February 2011–September 2012**

■ M16 ■ 5.56 × 45 mm

PRICE EXPRESSED AS STANDARDIZED Z SCORE

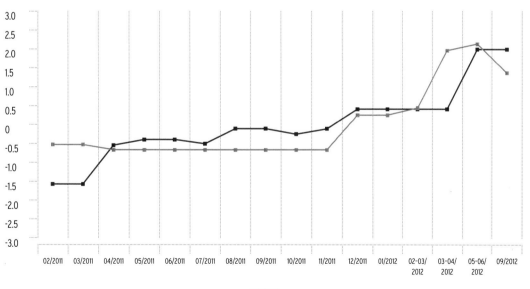

MONTHS

Note: A standardized Z score indicates by how many standard deviations an observation is above or below the average. Expressing price values as Z scores preserves the overall trend line and makes it possible to compare the prices of arms with those of ammunition on the same scale.

Source: Annexe 11.1

Numerous factors could explain this sudden drop in FN FAL prices. A war reporter suggests, for instance, that more abundant supplies of the rifle in neighbouring Syria during the same period may have contributed to stabilizing and decreasing prices in Lebanon.[18] Reports also indicate that 7.62 × 51 mm ammunition was particularly scarce and expensive in neighbouring Syria, reaching USD 3 per cartridge and making FN FAL rifles 'useless' to fighters (Spleeters, 2012b). This provides additional support for a link—even if anecdotal—between ammunition scarcity in the region on the one hand and the fall in FN FAL prices in Lebanon on the other. Interestingly, demand for this rifle seems to have declined in favour of other military rifles for which ammunition prices were decreasing. As Figures 11.3 and 11.4 illustrate, in March–April 2012, at the time the price of the FN FAL was collapsing, that of the M16 began to increase. In other words, FN FAL buyers might have opted to buy other rifles to compensate for the increase in FN FAL ammunition prices.

Overall, the evidence of an effect of ammunition prices on that of the corresponding weapon is mixed. Counter-examples are easy to find, and where a relationship appears to exist, other factors may also intervene. Yet some observations made here are worthy of further investigation. When the most commonly available military rifles—such as 7.62 × 39 mm Kalashnikov variants and the M16 in Lebanon and Pakistan—are expensive, corresponding ammunition prices tend to be low. Similarly, in cases where several military rifles of different calibre are available, unusual changes in the prices of ammunition can correspond with a reversal in the price trend of the corresponding arm, as was the case with 7.62 × 51 mm and the FN FAL rifle in Lebanon.

A Syrian rebel fighter holds an FAL rifle, Aleppo, Syria, August 2012. © Muhammed Muheisen/AP Photo

PRICES AND SECURITY-RELATED CONDITIONS

This section examines the relationship between the prices of arms and ammunition and local security-related conditions, in particular situations of instability and insecurity. The objective is to better grasp the extent to which illicit arms and ammunition prices are connected to local events. Local security conditions are considered using several data sources. First, the data collectors who monitored prices also submitted narrative reports that relate which factors arms dealers and other informed individuals identified as drivers of market shifts. Second, the section compares price data with available quantitative information on local conflict intensity.

Notes from the field

Narrative reports from data collectors propose a series of factors that local dealers and other informants cited when explaining price variations. Table 11.6 provides a summary of these observations, organizing them according to the supply and demand framework used in Killicoat (2007, p. 264). While it is beyond the scope of the chapter—and beyond the possibilities of the collected data—to measure and test each of these factors against price trends, these notes from the surveyed locations are useful in further refining our understanding of local supply and demand for arms and ammunition and in identifying paths for future quantitative research.

> Local security concerns were primary motivations for purchasing arms and ammunition.

Although the 'means/income' component was not directly mentioned by local sources, the decreasing value of the PKR was cited as contributing to an increase in the price of foreign-made weapons in Pakistan. In identifying primary motivations for purchasing arms and ammunition, data collectors often cited local security events, such as nearby fighting, and political tensions surrounding elections or political appointments. Anticipated security events—such as the prospective intervention of foreign troops in Somalia—reportedly played a role as well. Lastly, in Pakistan, some seasonal trends appear to affect prices. The tradition of celebratory shooting during Ramadan and Eid reportedly increases ammunition prices; in addition, the Taliban's winter break decreases demand while the traditional spring offensive stimulates it again.

Changes in or events related to the regulatory regime also appear to have played an important role in determining prices in the three locations. Local government initiatives to shut down markets or track down dealers were repeatedly presented as leading to increased prices in the three locations, as were efforts to monitor and control borders more closely in Lebanon and Pakistan. A programme by local authorities to buy back automatic weapons in Pakistan reportedly contributed to an increase in their prices. In Somalia, the Al Shabaab insurgency appeared to set limits on the prices of certain types of ammunition that were sold at the Bakara market and that were becoming expensive to procure.

The factors in red in Table 11.6 relate to the prices of specific types of arms and ammunition, as opposed to prices in general. Since the Killicoat study focuses exclusively on one type of arm, the Kalashnikov rifle broadly defined, it does not address several of these factors. Yet they confirm some of the observations made above. Although not reported by the data collector, press reports indicated that sabotaged military rifle ammunition was introduced in Syria in an attempt to weaken the Syrian opposition (Chivers, 2012b). Such a practice may help explain the decreasing prices in neighbouring Lebanon of certain weapon models and ammunition types in March–April 2012. Finally, narrative reports suggest a number of factors may influence ammunition prices in Somalia, including fighting in Yemen—a country where Somali dealers appear to procure part of their ammunition—as well as leakage from AMISOM and TFG holdings.

Table 11.6 Local supply and demand factors, as reported by data collectors			
Components	**Factors identified in Lebanon**	**Factors identified in Pakistan**	**Factors identified in Somalia (Mogadishu)**
Income/means		• Falling value of the PKR (+)	
Motivation	• Political tensions in Lebanon (+) • Unrest in Syria (+) • Militarization of conflict in Syria (+) • Free Syrian Army demand shifts to more sophisticated weapons, (-) for common models, (+) for sophisticated models	• Fighting between Pakistan Army and Taliban in Pakistan (+) • Fighting across the border in Afghanistan (+) • Celebratory shooting during Ramadan and Eid, (+) for ammunition • Self-defence (+) • Spring and traditional Taliban offensive (+) • Winter (-) • High price of M16 linked to lower ammunition price, (+) for M16 • Arrival of new models on the market, (-) for old models	• Expectation that Ethiopia will intervene militarily in Somalia (+) • Al Shabaab orders dealers to arm themselves to defend Bakara (+) • Rearming of clan leaders due to their exclusion from the parliamentary elections (+)
Regulatory	• Tightened border controls (+) • Seizure by the Lebanese Navy of a ship carrying weapons reportedly destined for Syria (+) • Pursuit of dealers by authorities (+)	• Borders tightly monitored by authorities (+) • Closure of Bara and other nearby markets by authorities (+) • Buyback by local authorities (+) • Markets reopened, (-) especially for locally crafted weapons	• AMISOM and TFG crackdown on markets (+) • Al Shabaab flee from Mogadishu (-) • Prices for certain types of ammunition at Bakara market are controlled by Al Shabaab (-)
Supply costs	• Saturation of the Syrian market (-) • Syrian soldiers sell weapons to the opposition and to Lebanese dealers (-) • Smuggling of arms from Syria into Lebanon (-)		• Defeated Al Shabaab combatants flee and sell their arms (-) • Fighting in Yemen, (+) for ammunition • TFG receive large amounts of ammunition (-) • New deliveries of Kalashnikovs and RPGs smuggled from Yemen (-) • AMISOM troops sell ammunition in exchange for mobile phone credit (-) • TFG exchange ammunition for khat or sell it for income due to non-payment of salaries (-)

Notes: Supply and demand components in the first column are taken from Killicoat (2007, p. 264). The symbol (+) indicates that a factor was reported to increase prices; in contrast, (-) reflects that a factor led to a decrease in prices. Factors in red relate to the prices of specific types of arms and ammunition, as opposed to prices in general, which appear in black.

Sources: data collectors' monthly narrative reports, February 2011–September 2012

Do prices correlate with conflict intensity?

The three locations reviewed in this chapter have in common their proximity to armed conflict. These conflicts are internal, as in Somalia; external, as for Lebanon (Syria); or both internal and external, as for Pakistan (Afghanistan). Because these conflicts were either starting or already active when the collection of arms prices for this chapter began, it is not possible to examine whether cheaper prices lead to an increased risk of war.

While quantitative data capturing conflict intensity levels is not available for Somalia, one key event during the research period is worth highlighting given the study's focus on markets in Mogadishu. In August 2011, following the TFG and AMISOM offensive, Al Shabaab withdrew most of its troops from the capital. Following this development, the insurgents mainly carried out 'hit-and-run' operations in Mogadishu (Cadde, 2011); subsequently, they faced increasingly determined opposition from Kenyan and Ethiopian forces and aligned Somali militias in several parts of the country (UNSC, 2012, para. 27). As noted in Table 11.6, local sources explained that the withdrawal of Al Shabaab from Mogadishu and its markets—and the associated decrease in local conflict-driven demand—contributed to stabilizing prices after several months of sustained price increases. Figure 11.2 appears to confirm these interpretations, with arms prices in particular stabilizing after December 2011.

Statistics on conflict casualties and events, although imperfect, provide a basis for measuring the intensity of the conflicts in Pakistan and Syria. Monthly data on fatalities in Syria is available from the Violations Documentation Center, which keeps an account of battle-related deaths among civilians, 'non-civilians', and regime forces. The organization recorded more than 30,000 such deaths between March 2011 and September 2012 (VDC, 2012). Monthly figures show

Bakara market, ten days after Islamist extremist Al Shabaab militants who had controlled the area withdrew abruptly from the capital, Mogadishu, Somalia, August 2011. © John Moore/Getty Images

Figure 11.5 **Fatalities in Syria vs. arms and ammunition price trends in Lebanon, February 2011–September 2012**

■ Reported fatalities (Syria)   ■ Ammunition (Lebanon)   ■ Weapons (Lebanon)

PRICE INDICES AND CASUALTIES EXPRESSED AS STANDARDIZED Z SCORES

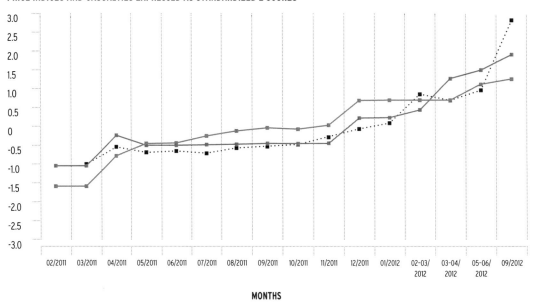

MONTHS

Notes:

Correlation: Syria fatalities and Lebanon weapons price index: R=0.81; p<0.001.

Correlation: Syria fatalities and Lebanon ammunition price index: R=0.93; p<0.001.

When price data covered two months, the average of the corresponding two months of fatality data was used. A standardized Z score indicates by how many standard deviations an observation is above or below the average. Expressing values as Z scores preserves the overall trend line and makes it possible to compare indicators of armed violence with the prices of arms and ammunition on the same scale.

Source: price data: Annexe 11.1; Syria fatality data: VDC (2012)

a rapid and continuous increase in conflict fatalities starting in November 2011, with levels peaking in August and September 2012. This spike followed stable fatality levels from March to October 2011.

Strikingly, the Syria fatality trend line closely follows the evolution of both arms and ammunition prices in Lebanon. This finding lends credence to previous observations that, in some contexts, rising arms prices reflect an expectation among the local population that the security environment will deteriorate (Barr, 2007; Chivers, 2012a; Petty, 2012). The particularly strong statistical correlation between fatalities and ammunition prices suggests that ammunition prices may be an even better indicator of such expectations (see Figure 11.5).

The relationship between arms and ammunition prices and conflict intensity in the FATA and neighbouring Khyber Pakhtunkhwa (KPK) province of Pakistan is much less conclusive. As noted above, prices in Pakistan were the least volatile, or fluctuated the least compared to their average value, compared to the prices in the two other locations studied. Available data on conflict intensity seems highly inconsistent from month to month. Figure 11.6 compares weapons and ammunition price indices for Pakistan with 'terrorism-related' fatality levels derived from the South Asian Terrorism Portal (SATP, 2012); it also reflects the number of security incidents in FATA and KPK reported by the local media and assembled by Delve Solutions (2012).

The 'spiky' patterns of armed violence in Pakistan are clearly different from the more steady arms and ammunition price trend lines, showing no statistical correlation. While this finding appears to contradict the above findings from

Figure 11.6 **Armed violence in KPK and FATA vs. arms and ammunition price trends in Pakistan, February 2011–September 2012**

■ Terrorism fatalities   ■ Violent incidents   ■ Weapons   ■ Ammunition

PRICE INDICES AND ARMED VIOLENCE INDICATORS EXPRESSED AS STANDARDIZED Z SCORES

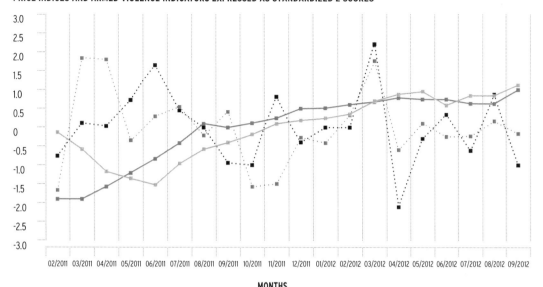

MONTHS

Note: A standardized Z score indicates by how many standard deviations an observation is above or below the average. Expressing values as Z scores preserves the overall trend line and makes it possible to compare indicators of armed violence with the prices of arms and ammunition on the same scale.

Source: price data: Annexe 11.1; terrorism-related fatalities: SATP (2012); violent incidents: Delve Solutions (2012)

Lebanon, the two situations need to be put in context. Price monitoring in Lebanon began as tensions started rising in Syria; they could therefore be expected to increase as the conflict intensified. On the contrary, tensions and instability in the FATA and KPK province of Pakistan preceded the price data collection period. If comparable pricing data had been available for the years reaching back to 2001 and the beginning of conflict in neighbouring Afghanistan, the analysis might have produced different results.

CONCLUSION

This chapter uses unpublished time-series data gathered in multiple locations in three countries to revisit and build upon existing knowledge on arms and ammunition prices at illicit markets. It shows that difficult research conditions at illicit markets do not preclude the creation of a regular data-collection system or the application of basic controls to improve the quality of data.

A careful review of gathered information shows that arms prices depend on a greater set of variables than ammunition prices, including their technical features, local symbolism associated with particular models, and the availability and price of the associated ammunition. In some cases, sudden, unusual shifts in ammunition prices corresponded with a reversed shift in the price of the associated military rifles. Variations in the prices of different types of ammunition also appear to be more consistent, and thus more predictable, than trends in arms prices.

An arms dealer who began trading at the age of ten at his stall in Bakara market, Mogadishu, Somalia, June 2006. © Hannah Allam/Getty Images

Data limitations constrain the analysis of the relationship between illicit arms and ammunition prices and local security conditions. Yet available information shows a clear link between illicit market prices in Lebanon and conflict deaths in Syria. The particularly strong correlation between ammunition prices in Lebanon and fatalities of the first 19 months of the conflict in Syria provides additional evidence of the value of monitoring ammunition prices. In this context, at least, prices for ammunition appear to be a significant indicator of local insecurity, especially during the outbreak of war. Yet available reporting from conflict zones has tended to neglect this important piece of the puzzle, focusing on prices for the most common weapons instead.

The chapter illustrates that a focus on prices for 'Kalashnikov' rifles is fraught with limitations, a finding that may be especially relevant to researchers and reporters. Due to the large number of weapon models possibly falling under this label, the price range tends to be relatively broad. These weapons are priced and sold based on local preferences and criteria rather than on precise technical features that would enable their identification. Monitoring a more diverse selection of arms and, importantly, the corresponding ammunition promises to generate a richer analysis of illicit markets and of their linkages with local insecurity. ◼

ANNEXE

Annexe 11.1

Arms and ammunition prices in Lebanon, Pakistan, and Somalia, monthly averages

Lebanon prices (per unit, in USD)

Year	Month	Weapons						Ammunition					
		Browning	7.62 × 39 mm Kalashnikov variants	AKS-74U	FN FAL	M16	PKM	9 × 19 mm	7.62 × 39 mm	5.45 × 39 mm	7.62 × 51 mm	5.56 × 45 mm	7.62 × 54R mm
2011	February	1,500	975	2,900	500	2,250	3,250	0.80	0.77	0.77	0.50	0.77	0.46
	March	1,500	975	2,900	500	2,250	3,250	0.80	0.77	0.77	0.50	0.77	0.46
	April	1,750	1,300	3,625	600	2,650	3,625	1.30	0.83	1.45	0.52	0.73	0.53
	May	1,825	1,500	3,750	775	2,700	3,750	1.00	1.00	1.45	0.51	0.73	0.50
	June	1,875	1,500	3,750	775	2,700	3,750	1.00	1.00	1.45	0.51	0.73	0.50
	July	1,950	1,600	3,875	875	2,650	3,875	1.00	1.00	1.45	0.51	0.73	0.50
	August	1,950	1,700	3,875	900	2,800	3,875	1.00	1.00	1.50	0.51	0.73	0.50
	September	1,950	1,800	3,875	950	2,800	3,875	1.00	1.05	1.50	0.51	0.73	0.50
	October	1,925	1,775	3,875	1,000	2,750	3,875	1.00	1.05	1.50	0.51	0.73	0.50
	November	1,900	1,925	3,750	1,050	2,800	3,875	1.00	1.05	1.50	0.51	0.73	0.50
	December	2,250	1,900	4,750	1,400	3,000	3,875	1.10	1.50	1.50	0.70	1.00	0.70
2012	January	2,250	1,900	4,750	1,400	3,000	3,875	1.10	1.50	1.50	0.70	1.00	0.70
	February–March	2,250	1,900	4,750	1,400	3,000	3,875	1.10	1.65	1.50	0.80	1.05	0.80
	March-April	2,250	1,900	4,750	1,400	3,000	3,875	1.30	1.90	1.55	1.00	1.50	1.05
	May-June	2,250	1,450	5,000	1,250	3,600	5,500	1.20	1.67	2.00	1.50	1.55	1.05
	September	2,750	1,600	5,000	775	3,600	5,750	1.32	1.32	3.00	1.50	1.32	1.50

Pakistan prices (per unit, in PKR)

Year	Month	Weapons							
		Makarov	7.62 × 39 mm Kalash-nikov variants	AK-74	M16	Locally manufac-tured Makarov	Locally manufac-tured 7.62 × 39 mm Kalash-nikov variants	Locally manufac-tured AK-74	Locally manufac-tured M16
2011	February	n/a	90,000	157,500	225,000	n/a	18,500	25,000	26,500
	March	72,500	85,000	160,000	225,000	5,500	18,500	25,000	26,500
	April	72,500	87,500	175,000	250,000	5,500	15,000	25,000	26,500
	May	72,500	90,000	200,000	275,000	5,500	12,500	25,000	26,500
	June	72,500	95,000	217,500	300,000	5,500	12,500	25,000	26,500
	July	72,500	107,500	260,000	300,000	5,000	12,500	18,500	24,000
	August	80,000	107,500	285,000	300,000	4,750	12,000	17,000	22,500
	September	80,000	105,000	272,500	300,000	5,750	11,500	16,000	25,000
	October	81,500	105,000	272,500	305,000	5,750	11,500	15,000	25,000
	November	81,500	107,500	265,000	320,000	6,500	11,500	15,000	25,000
	December	83,000	109,000	275,000	332,500	7,000	12,500	16,500	26,000
2012	January	83,000	107,500	275,000	340,000	7,000	12,500	16,500	26,500
	February	83,000	117,500	285,000	320,000	7,000	12,500	15,750	26,500
	March	83,000	117,500	300,000	320,000	7,000	13,000	15,750	26,500
	April	83,000	120,000	305,000	325,000	7,000	13,000	15,750	26,500
	May	83,000	120,000	300,000	325,000	7,000	13,000	15,750	26,500
	June	83,000	122,500	305,000	315,000	7,000	13,000	15,750	26,500
	July	83,000	122,500	305,000	300,000	7,000	13,000	15,750	26,500
	August	82,500	122,500	305,000	300,000	7,000	13,000	15,750	26,500
	September	85,000	130,000	305,000	315,000	7,250	13,500	16,500	26,000

				Ammunition			
9 × 18 mm	7.62 × 39 mm	5.45 × 39 mm	5.56 × 45 mm	Locally manufactured 9 × 18 mm	Locally manufactured 7.62 × 39 mm	Locally manufactured 5.45 × 39 mm	Locally manufactured 5.56 × 45 mm
n/a	48	123	34	n/a	19	28	20
34	48	123	34	19	19	28	20
37	48	123	27	19	19	28	15
37	48	123	25	19	19	28	14
37	48	113	25	19	19	28	14
49	48	118	27	13	16	28	14
50	50	120	29	17	19	25	16
50	54	120	29	17	19	25	16
50	55	120	31	18	19	25	19
55	55	125	32	18	19	25	19
57	56	125	32	19	20	26	20
57	56	130	32	19	20	26	19
60	58	130	31	19	20	25	18
60	63	140	31	19	20	25	18
60	63	150	31	19	20	25	18
60	63	155	31	19	20	25	18
60	63	150	28	19	20	25	17
60	64	150	30	19	20	25	17
60	64	150	30	19	20	25	17
60	64	150	33	19	20	25	17

Somalia prices (per unit, in USD)

Year	Month	Weapons				Ammunition			
		Makarov	7.62 × 39 mm Kalashnikov variants	PKM	DShK	9 × 18 mm	7.62 × 39 mm	7.62 × 54R mm	12.7 × 108 mm
2011	February	n/a	400	6,000	4,250	n/a	0.32	0.40	0.40
	March	n/a	415	6,250	5,050	n/a	0.41	0.49	0.41
	April	n/a	425	5,750	6,000	n/a	0.44	0.53	0.40
	May	n/a	475	5,750	6,000	n/a	0.49	0.58	0.45
	June	n/a	490	5,750	5,500	n/a	0.52	0.63	0.50
	July	n/a	450	5,200	5,000	n/a	0.47	0.53	0.44
	August	n/a	600	6,500	5,750	n/a	0.56	0.65	0.52
	September	n/a	600	6,500	5,750	n/a	0.58	0.66	0.52
	October	1,150	550	7,250	9,000	2.50	0.65	0.60	0.53
	November	1,150	675	7,750	10,000	2.50	0.65	0.60	0.50
	December	1,425	900	7,500	10,250	3.00	0.67	0.60	0.50
2012	January	1,400	925	7,250	9,750	2.75	0.63	0.58	0.50
	February	1,825	925	7,250	9,700	2.50	0.63	0.58	0.50
	March	1,825	975	7,350	9,700	2.50	0.68	0.80	0.55
	April	1,900	975	7,350	9,700	2.50	0.68	0.80	0.53
	May	1,900	975	7,350	9,700	2.50	0.68	0.90	0.53
	June	1,900	965	7,350	9,700	2.75	0.65	0.90	0.50
	July	1,900	965	7,350	9,700	2.75	0.63	0.85	0.50
	August	1,900	965	7,350	9,700	2.75	0.63	0.85	0.50
	September	1,900	965	7,350	9,700	2.75	0.63	0.85	0.50

Puntland prices (per unit, in USD)

Year	Month	Weapons		Ammunition	
		7.62 × 39 mm Kalashnikov variants	FN FAL variants	7.62 × 39 mm	7.62 × 51 mm
2011	October	600	465	0.75	1.25
	November	700	475	0.80	1.25
	December	650	500	0.80	1.30
2012	January	650	500	0.80	1.30
	February	725	500	0.80	1.25
	March	725	500	0.80	1.25
	April	725	500	0.80	1.25

Somaliland prices (per unit, in USD)

Year	Month	Weapons		Ammunition	
		7.62 × 39 mm Kalashnikov variants	FN FAL variants	7.62 × 39 mm	7.62 × 51 mm
2011	October	625	600	1.00	0.50
	November	625	600	1.00	1.00
	December	700	650	1.00	1.00
2012	January	660	650	1.00	1.00
	February	700	720	1.00	1.00
	March	700	850	1.00	1.00
	April	670	700	1.00	1.00
	May	670	650	1.00	1.00
	June	690	670	1.00	1.00
	July	700	680	1.20	1.20
	August	675	650	1.00	1.00
	September	710	700	1.00	1.00

LIST OF ABBREVIATIONS

AMISOM	African Union Mission in Somalia
CV	Coefficient of variation
FATA	Federally Administered Tribal Areas
KPK	Khyber Pakhtunkhwa
PKR	Pakistani rupee
TFG	Transitional Federal Government of Somalia
USD	United States dollar

ENDNOTES

1   The demand side of the model was adapted from Brauer and Muggah (2006).

2   This study used global indices of government effectiveness and democratic accountability to measure governments' regulations generally and, by extension, their ability to implement small arms control legislation (Killicoat, 2007, pp. 264, 266).

3   See, for instance, Chivers (2012a); Jenzen-Jones (2013); and Wepundi et al. (2012, p. 59).

4   See Chivers (2012a); Florquin and Pézard (2005, pp. 54–55); Greene (2006, p. 3); Spleeters (2012b).

5   See Blanford (2011); Ibrahim (2008); Prothero (2010); and Qassem (2012).

6   For a documentary on the Darra arms market, see Vice (2009).

7   From November 2011, the project began collecting prices in Burao, Somaliland. In Puntland, data was also gathered over several months. Unless indicated otherwise, Somali prices in this chapter refer solely to data collected in Mogadishu, however.

8   See SATP (2012).

9   See, for instance, Alami (2011) and Qassem (2012).

10   Only four reports were received during that period, providing price averages for late February–early March, late March–early April, late May–early June, and September 2012.

11   See also Chivers (2010, p. 383).

12   Confidential author correspondence with data collectors, September 2012.

13   Confidential author correspondence with a data collector, December 2012.

14   The coefficient of variation in this case is the standard deviation (from the average price) divided by the average price.

15   In Pakistan, for instance, the typical monthly price range for 5.45 × 39 mm ammunition stayed within one per cent of its average price. In contrast, the price range for the AK-74 rifle (chambered for 5.45 × 39 mm ammunition) reached eight per cent beyond its average value. Confidential author correspondence with data collectors, February 2011–September 2012.

16   A standardized Z score indicates by how many standard deviations an observation is above or below the average. Indices take into account the price values of all the weapons and ammunition listed in Table 11.1, with the exception of the Makarov pistol and associated 9 × 18 mm cartridge in Somalia, for which data was incomplete (covering only 12 months). For Pakistan, different indices were calculated to distinguish the prices of factory-made arms and ammunition from those of locally crafted materiel.

17   See, for instance, Chivers (2012a); Florquin and Pézard (2005, pp. 54–55); Spleeters (2012b).

18   Author correspondence with Damien Spleeters, freelance journalist, November 2012.

BIBLIOGRAPHY

Alami, Mona. 2011. 'As Arab Spring Continues, Black Markets Boom.' Al Jazeera. 14 May.
   <http://www.aljazeera.com/indepth/features/2011/05/201151410154606644.html>

Barr, James. 2007. 'The Kalashnikov Index.' Setting the Desert on Fire. Blog. 12 February.
   <http://desertonfire.blogspot.fr/2007/02/kalashnikov-index.html>

Blanford, Nicholas. 2011. 'As Syrian Uprising Escalates, Business Booms for Lebanon's Arms Dealers.' Time. 22 May.
   <http://www.time.com/time/world/article/0,8599,2073315,00.html#ixzz29wN5ccPM>

—. 2012. Arms Smuggling between Lebanon and Syria. Unpublished background paper. December. Geneva: Small Arms Survey.

Brauer, Jurgen and Robert Muggah. 2006. 'Completing the Circle: Building a Theory of Small Arms Demand.' Contemporary Security Policy, Vol. 27, No. 1. April, pp. 138–54.

Cadde, Aweys. 2011. 'TFG and AMISOM Battle Al-Shabaab in Mogadishu.' Somalia Report. 6 September.
   <http://www.somaliareport.com/index.php/post/1516/TFG_and_AMISOM_Battle_Al-Shabaab_in_Mogadishu>

Chivers, C. J. 2010. The Gun. New York: Simon and Schuster.

—. 2012a. 'Arming for the Syrian War: Do Soaring Prices Predict Escalating Conflict?' At War Blog. The New York Times. 17 July.
   <http://atwar.blogs.nytimes.com/2012/07/17/arming-for-the-syrian-war-do-soaring-prices-predict-escalating-conflict/>

—. 2012b. 'Syrians Place Booby-Trapped Ammunition in Rebels' Guns.' The New York Times. 19 October.
   <http://www.nytimes.com/2012/10/20/world/middleeast/syrian-government-booby-traps-rebels-ammunition.html?hp&_r=1&&pagewanted=print>

Delve Solutions. 2012. Chronology of Security Events in KPK and FATA, February 2011–September 2012. Unpublished background paper. Geneva: Small Arms Survey.

Florquin, Nicolas and Stéphanie Pézard. 2005. 'Insurgency, Disarmament, and Insecurity in Northern Mali, 1990–2004.' In Nicolas Florquin and Eric Berman, eds. *Armed and Aimless: Armed Groups, Guns, and Human Security in the ECOWAS Region*. Geneva: Small Arms Survey, pp. 46–77.

Greene, Owen. 2006. 'Ammunition of Small Arms and Light Weapons: Understanding the Issues and Addressing the Challenges'. In Stéphanie Pézard and Holger Anders, eds. *Targeting Ammunition*. Geneva: Small Arms Survey, pp. 1–13.

Ibrahim, Alia. 2008. 'Fearing a War, Lebanese Prepare by Buying Up Arms.' *Washington Post*. 24 April.
<http://www.washingtonpost.com/wp-dyn/content/article/2008/04/23/AR2008042303433.html>

Jenzen-Jones, Nic. 2013. *The Headstamp Trail: An Assessment of Small-calibre Ammunition Found in Libya*. Working Paper No. 16. Geneva: Small Arms Survey.

Karp, Aaron. 2002. 'Red Flags and Buicks: Global Firearm Stockpiles.' In Small Arms Survey. *Small Arms Survey 2002: Counting the Human Cost*. Oxford: Oxford University Press.

Killicoat, Philip. 2007. 'What Price the Kalashnikov? The Economics of Small Arms.' In Small Arms Survey. *Small Arms Survey 2007: Guns and the City*. Cambridge: Cambridge University Press.

Petty, Martin. 2012. 'Insight: Afghans Turn to AK-47, Fearing Taliban Return or Civil War.' Reuters. 17 December.
<http://www.reuters.com/article/2012/12/18/us-afghanistan-guns-idUSBRE8BH00Y20121218>

Prothero, Mitchell. 2010. 'Lebanon's AK Index May Be Pointing to War.' *National*. 3 February.
<http://www.thenational.ae/news/world/middle-east/lebanons-ak-47-index-may-be-pointing-to-war>

Qassem, Qassem. 2012. 'Arms to Syria: Theft, Entrapment, and Tampering.' Alakhbar English. 31 October. <http://english.al-akhbar.com/print/13217>

Reina, Pilar. 2012. *Examples of Nicknames for Arms Sold at Illicit Markets*. Unpublished background paper. Geneva: Small Arms Survey.

SATP (South Asian Terrorism Portal). 2012. 'Fatalities in Pakistan Region Wise: 2012.'
<http://www.satp.org/satporgtp/countries/pakistan/database/fatilities_regionwise2012.htm>

Shinwari, Naveed Ahmed and Salma Malik. 2004. *A Situation Analysis of SALW in Pakistan and Its Impact on Security*. Islamabad: Community Appraisal and Motivation Programme.

SPADO (Sustainable Peace and Development Organization). 2005. *The Prevalence and Impacts of Small Arms and Light Weapons in North-West Frontier Province and Federally Administered Tribal Areas (FATA) of Pakistan*. Peshawar: SPADO.
<http://www.spado.org.pk/researchandpublications_small_arms.htm>

Spleeters, Damien. 2012a. *The FAL Rifle in Libya: During and after the 2011 Conflict*. Unpublished background paper. Geneva: Small Arms Survey.

—. 2012b. 'Guerrilla Country.' *Foreign Policy*. 15 October.
<http://www.foreignpolicy.com/articles/2012/10/15/Guerrilla_Country_Syria_Jebel_Zawiya>

UNSC (United Nations Security Council). 2012. *Report of the Monitoring Group on Somalia and Eritrea Pursuant to Security Council Resolution 2002 (2011)*. S/2012/544 of 13 July.

VDC (Violations Documentation Center in Syria). 2012. Online database. Accessed 13 January 2013. <http://vdc-sy.org/index.php/en/>

Vice. 2009. 'The Gun Markets of Pakistan.' <http://www.vice.com/the-vice-guide-to-travel/the-gun-markets-of-pakistan>

Wepundi, Manasseh, et al. 2012. *Availability of Small Arms and Perceptions of Security in Kenya: An Assessment*. Special Report No.16. Geneva and Nairobi: Small Arms Survey and Kenya National Focus Point on Small Arms and Light Weapons.
<http://www.smallarmssurvey.org/fileadmin/docs/C-Special-reports/SAS-SR16-Kenya.pdf>

Zimmerman, Katherine. 2011. 'Al Shabaab's Withdrawal from Mogadishu.' Critical Threats. Washington, DC: American Enterprise Institute. 7 August.
<http://www.criticalthreats.org/somalia/zimmerman-shabaab-retreat-mogadishu-august-7-2011>

ACKNOWLEDGEMENTS

Principal author

Nicolas Florquin

Contributors

Nicholas Blanford, Jonah Leff, Sustainable Peace and Development Organization (SPADO), Ryan Murray, Pilar Reina, Delve Solutions, and Robin Gut

Soldiers guard captured arms, said to be the largest seizure of drug-cartel weapons in the country, Reynosa, Mexico, November 2008. © Gregory Bull/AP Photo

Captured and Counted

ILLICIT WEAPONS IN MEXICO AND THE PHILIPPINES

12

INTRODUCTION

The sprawling collection of weaponry seized in the border town of Reynosa, Mexico, could easily have been mistaken for the arsenal of a well-equipped infantry battalion: hundreds of assault rifles, sub-machine guns, pistols, grenades, and grenade launchers arranged in eight rows that ran the entire length of the Mexican Army's spacious press room (AP, 2008). The massive cache—discovered during the pursuit of a high-ranking drug cartel member in November 2008—is illustrative of Mexico's thriving black market in small arms and light weapons, which is dominated by the country's powerful and well-financed drug-trafficking organizations (DTOs). Fuelled by billions of dollars in drug revenue each year, the cartels are among the best-funded non-state armed groups in the world.

There is little disagreement that the arsenals built with these funds are vast, but their precise composition and the sources of their contents are subjects of much debate. Do the DTOs have the 'wealth and armies of nations', as some claim?[1] Does their wealth afford them access to weapons that are unavailable to armed groups of lesser means? Are there notable differences between the weapons acquired by the profit-motivated Mexican DTOs and those obtained by groups that have ideological or political ambitions and operate in other countries? This chapter attempts to answer these and other questions through data-driven analysis of illicit small arms and light weapons in countries affected by low-intensity armed conflict and high-intensity organized criminal violence.

The chapter is the second instalment of the Small Arms Survey's multi-year study on illicit small arms and light weapons. The purpose of the study, launched in 2012, is to improve public understanding of illicit small arms and light weapons through the compilation and analysis of hitherto unused or under-utilized data from official (government) sources. During the first phase of the study, reported in the *Small Arms Survey 2012*, the Survey analysed data on illicit small arms, light weapons, and rounds of light weapons ammunition in three high-intensity armed conflict zones: Afghanistan, Iraq, and Somalia.[2]

The focus of the current phase is on illicit weapons in countries affected by high-intensity organized criminal violence and low-intensity armed conflict. To this end, the Survey collected data on illicit weapons seized in Mexico, which is home to some of the largest and most powerful organized criminal syndicates in the world, and in the Philippines, where several ideologically, politically, and religiously motivated armed groups are active. During the third phase of the study, the Survey will examine illicit weapons in countries affected by high- and low-intensity criminal violence that is primarily unorganized in nature (individually motivated and interpersonal violence).

The main findings from this chapter include:

- Armed groups in Mexico and the Philippines have acquired few, if any, technologically sophisticated light weapons, such as portable missiles.
- Nearly 90 per cent of illicit rifles seized in the Philippines were US-designed models.[3]

- Despite their vast wealth, armed groups in Mexico do not possess the full array of light weapons available to governments and some state-sponsored armed groups.

- The data suggests that some firearms identified as 'weapons of choice' of drug traffickers in Mexico are not as widespread as commonly assumed. These include .50-calibre rifles and 5.7 mm × 28 mm pistols, which combined account for fewer than 1 per cent of all seized firearms studied.

- The data provides little clarity on the proximate sources, age, condition, and intrastate and international movements of illicit weapons. More data on these aspects would significantly improve public understanding of black market weapons in Mexico and the Philippines.

TERMS AND DEFINITIONS

Some firearms identified as 'weapons of choice' are not as widespread as assumed.

For the purposes of this chapter, 'illicit small arms and light weapons' are defined as weapons that are produced, transferred, held, or used in violation of national or international law. The chapter uses the term 'illicit' rather than 'illegal' to include cases of unclear or contested legality. The term 'small arms' (alternatively, 'firearms') refers to the following items:

- revolvers and self-loading pistols;
- rifles[4] and carbines;
- shotguns;
- sub-machine guns;
- light and heavy machine guns; and
- accessories and ammunition for small arms.

The term 'light weapons' refers to:

- mortar systems of calibres of 120 mm or less;
- hand-held, under-barrel, and automatic grenade launchers;
- hand grenades;
- recoilless guns;
- portable rocket launchers, including rockets fired from single-shot, disposable launch tubes;
- portable missiles and launchers, namely anti-tank guided weapons (ATGWs) and man-portable air defence systems (MANPADS);
- landmines;
- improvised explosive devices (IEDs); and
- accessories and ammunition for light weapons.

These definitions are consistent with the Small Arms Survey's practices and with usage of these terms during the first phase of the illicit weapons project.[5] Thus, unless otherwise specified, data compiled and analysed in this chapter includes illicit small arms, light weapons, and ammunition.[6] The term 'Kalashnikov-pattern rifles' is used to refer to the numerous models of automatic and semi-automatic rifles that are manufactured in different countries but that are all modelled on the original AK series rifles produced in the former Soviet Union and later in the Russian Federation.

The definition for 'armed conflict' is borrowed from the Armed Conflict Dataset developed by the International Peace Research Institute, Oslo, and the Uppsala Conflict Data Program. The dataset defines 'armed conflict' as 'a contested incompatibility which concerns government and/or territory where the use of armed force between two parties, of which at least one is the government of a state, results in at least 25 battle-related deaths' (UCDP, 2012, p. 1). Armed conflicts are further divided into 'minor' conflicts with 'between 25 and 999 battle-related deaths in a given year' and 'wars', which are defined as conflicts with 'at least 1,000 battle-related deaths in a given year' (p. 9).

The focus of the first report from this study was illicit weapons in 'wars' or high-intensity armed conflicts. This chapter assesses illicit small arms in minor (low-intensity) armed conflicts and high-intensity organized criminal violence through case studies on the Philippines (low-intensity armed conflict) and Mexico (high-intensity organized criminal violence). Data on weapons seized in Mexico and the Philippines is also compared to findings from the first phase of this study.

The definition for high-intensity organized criminal violence used in this chapter is derived from the definition of 'organized criminal group' in the United Nations Convention against Transnational Organized Crime. As defined in the Convention, an organized criminal group is:

> *a structured group of three or more persons, existing for a period of time and acting in concert with the aim of committing one or more serious crimes or offences established in accordance with this Convention, in order to obtain, directly or indirectly, a financial or other material benefit* (UNODC, 2000, p. 5).

By extension, organized criminal violence is violence perpetrated by groups that fit that description and, for purposes of this chapter, countries affected by high-intensity organized criminal violence are those in which at least 1,000 people are killed by organized criminal groups annually.

The data covers more than 5,200 small arms, light weapons, and rounds of their ammunition.

ANALYSING THE DATA

The datasets on illicit weapons used in this chapter consist of the following:

- **Data on Mexico-bound weapons seized at the US border.** The data, which was obtained under the United States Freedom of Information Act, reflects the seizure of 141 small arms and light weapons, as well as nearly 80,000 rounds of small-calibre ammunition reportedly bound for Mexico that were seized at the US ports of exit from January 2009 to July 2011.[7] Most of the records identify the type, model, calibre, destination country, and quantity of seized items. The data includes all types of 'seizures'—that is, instances when the US government takes physical possession of merchandise that is prohibited, restricted, undeclared, unreported, or smuggled (USCBP, 2004, pp. 13–14). While most of the seizures took place in response to actual or suspected substantive violations, not all of the items were necessarily bound for the drug cartels.

- **Data on weapons seized in Mexico.** The data covers the seizure of more than 5,200 small arms, light weapons, and rounds of light weapons ammunition as reported by the Secretaría de la Defensa Nacional (SEDENA), the department that oversees the Mexican Army and Air Force.[8] The seizures occurred between January 2009 and August 2012. Most of the weapons were found in arms caches, confiscated from detainees, or recovered after armed engagements with DTOs or other criminals. While the individuals and organizations from whom the weapons were seized are not always identified, contextual information in the source documents suggests that most of the weapons were recovered from DTOs and their affiliates.[9]

- **Data on weapons seized in the Philippines.** This dataset was compiled from online summaries of seizures published by the Philippine Information Agency, the Armed Forces of the Philippines, and the Philippine Army, Air Force, and National Police. The summaries include data on approximately 1,000 small arms, light weapons, and rounds of light weapons ammunition, along with more than 100,000 rounds of small-calibre ammunition.

To supplement these datasets, the Survey obtained aggregate data from the Government of Mexico, along with similar data published by the US Bureau of Alcohol, Tobacco, Firearms and Explosives (ATF). Additional sources of data and information include interviews with Mexican, Philippine, and US government officials, and reports by researchers from the United Nations, governments, and private institutions.

ILLICIT SMALL ARMS AND LIGHT WEAPONS IN MEXICO

Drug trafficking has affected Mexico for decades, but the violence associated with this trade has metastasized into a large-scale national security crisis in recent years. Many of the organizations that control this trade have thousands of members and exercise influence over large swaths of territory. The Sinaloa 'Federation' is among the largest drug-trafficking entities in the world. It controls the western half of Mexico's drug markets and routes. On the Caribbean coast resides its enemy-turned-ally, the Gulf Cartel, which competes for influence with the third major DTO, Los Zetas. Founded by former members of the military, Los Zetas is known for paramilitary tactics, bold engagements with government forces, and brutality.

The DTOs use illicit small arms and light weapons in pursuit of several organizational objectives. At the tactical level, illicit weapons are used to protect drug shipments, drug traffickers, and revenue generated through narcotics sales, which is often transported back to Mexico as large bundles of currency. At the strategic level, drug traffickers use small arms and light weapons to seize and maintain control over drug supply routes and to defend themselves, while also intimidating and weakening rival cartels and Mexican security forces. At the grand strategic level, cartels use illicit weapons to create a climate of fear and intimidation that is conducive to drug trafficking and greater accumulation of power (Bouchard, 2011, p. 3).

Data on the seizures studied reveals that the vast majority of the weapons seized in Mexico were firearms, which account for approximately 80 per cent of the weapons

Table 12.1 **Illicit weapons recovered by the Mexican military, 2009–12**		
Weapon category	**Quantity**	**Percentage of total**
Firearms*	4,200	80%
Grenades and grenade launchers**	985	19%
Rockets	16	<1%
Mortar systems and rounds	10	<1%
RPG launchers and rounds	7	<1%
Improvised explosive devices	2	<1%
Landmines	0	0%
Recoilless rifles and rounds	0	0%
Portable missiles (MANPADS and ATGWs)	0	0%
Total	**5,220**	**100%**

Notes:

* Includes all firearms and major accessories for firearms.

** This category includes hand grenades, projected grenades and launchers, rifle grenades, and other (unspecified) grenades, but not rocket-propelled grenades or launchers.

Source: Small Arms Survey (2012c)

studied. Grenades and grenade launchers were the second most frequently seized items, accounting for approximately 19 per cent of recovered weapons. Rockets, mortars, and rocket-propelled grenades (RPGs) were also seized, but in much smaller quantities. Table 12.1 summarizes the items seized by category.

Small arms

Illicit small arms in Mexico range from bolt-action hunting rifles to heavy machine guns. The most visually striking are the ornate assault rifles and pistols seized from cartel leaders, which are often gold- or silver-plated and feature elaborate engravings of cartel insignias. Valued at up to USD 30,000 each (García, 2010), these weapons are symbols of the excess—in violence, cash, and power—associated with the illicit drug trade in the Americas.

The surreptitious and opaque nature of arms trafficking to and within Mexico precludes a definitive accounting of illicit firearms. However, data on seized and trafficked weapons provides a sense of the size and composition of Mexico's black market, including the weapons acquired and used by drug-trafficking organizations.

Data provided by the Government of Mexico indicates that authorities recovered more than 306,000 illicit firearms and 26 million rounds of ammunition in Mexico from late 1994 to mid-2012. These figures include seizures by the military and police forces, and weapons voluntarily surrendered as part of an amnesty programme sponsored by SEDENA. Seizures account for most of the recovered weapons (see Table 12.2).

While the percentage of illicit firearms and ammunition in Mexico reflected in this data is unclear, other metrics, including estimated trafficking from the United States, suggests that only a small fraction of illicit weapons are recovered

Gold-plated, diamond-encrusted weapons, confiscated by the army during counter-drug operations, Zapopan, Mexico, May 2010. © AP Photo

Table 12.2	**Illicit firearms and ammunition recovered by the Mexican government, 1994–2012**		
Category			**Quantity**
Firearms	Seized by military and police	Long guns*	133,579
		Handguns	119,660
		Total	253,239
	Voluntarily forfeited		53,115
	Total		**306,354**
Ammunition	Seized by military and police		25,601,297
	Voluntarily forfeited		485,246
	Total		**26,086,543**

Note: * Long guns include sub-machine guns, shotguns, rifles, carbines, and machine guns.

Source: written response from the Government of Mexico to questions submitted by the Small Arms Survey, September 2012

each year. In 2009, William Hoover, then assistant director for field operations at ATF, estimated that the number of firearms illicitly transported into Mexico across the US border on a daily basis was 'probably in the hundreds' (USDOJ, 2009). Based on this claim, which is significantly more conservative than other estimates,[10] the illicit trade in firearms is likely to be at least 100–200 units per day, or 35,000–70,000 units each year. Given that the United States is not the only source of illicit weapons in Mexico, the total number of trafficked firearms is likely to be higher, although ambiguities in available data preclude a precise estimate. Regardless, the data suggests that the 20,000 to 30,000 weapons seized annually in recent years represent only a fraction of illicit weapons in Mexico, and that firearms trafficked into Mexico from abroad equal or exceed the number of weapons seized by Mexican authorities each year.

An army soldier catalogues seized weapons in a warehouse at the Secretary of the Defence headquarters in Mexico City, Mexico, April 2009.
© Eduardo Verdugo/AP Photo

Types and models of illicit small arms

According to US and Mexican officials, Mexican DTOs have sought various types of firearms over the past ten years. Whereas .38-calibre handguns were the 'weapon of choice' for the cartels in the late 1990s, 'they now have developed a preference for higher quality, more powerful weapons, such as .223 and 7.62 × 39 mm caliber rifles, 5.7 × 28 caliber rifles and pistols, and .50 caliber rifles' (USDOJ, 2009, p. 11). The increased demand for rifles is evident in aggregate data on seized weapons provided by the Mexican government. Prior to 2007, Mexican authorities seized roughly 50 per cent more handguns than long guns annually. Since then, seizures of long guns—and the ratio of seized long guns to handguns—have increased dramatically. By 2010, long guns accounted for more than 63 per cent of seized firearms (see Figure 12.1).

These figures are consistent with data on individual seizures compiled for this study. Of the firearms studied that were seized in Mexico from 2009 to 2012, approximately 72 per cent were long guns—rifles, shotguns, sub-machine guns, machine guns, and unspecified 'long guns'—the vast majority of which were rifles. Pistols were the next most commonly recovered items, accounting for more than 19 per cent of seized firearms. Shotguns and revolvers made up 6 per cent and 4 per cent of seized weapons, respectively. Machine guns and sub-machine guns were also recovered in Mexico, but in much smaller quantities.

Interestingly, the ratio of long guns to handguns seized at the US border is roughly similar to that of long guns to handguns seized in Mexico. Of the 139 firearms reportedly bound for Mexico and seized at the US border from January 2009 to July 2011, approximately 75 per cent were rifles, shotguns, and machine guns. The ratio of handguns to other firearms seized at the border is also similar to the ratio of handguns seized in Mexico, accounting for 24 per cent of seized firearms (vs. 28 per cent for firearms seized in Mexico). Table 12.3 summarizes this data.

The data also provides some insight into the models of illicit firearms in Mexico, corroborating some commonly held assumptions and calling others into question. Several of the firearms frequently referred to by government officials and journalists as 'weapons of choice' for DTOs and other unauthorized end users in Mexico were indeed recovered in comparatively large quantities in the seizures studied. These include Kalashnikov-pattern and AR-15 variant assault rifles, .38 Super pistols,[11] and 9 mm pistols. Kalashnikov-pattern rifles alone accounted for at least 19 per cent of all seized firearms identified by model or calibre, and more than 30 per cent of seized rifles. Models identified in the

Figure 12.1 **Illicit firearms seized in Mexico, 2000-10**

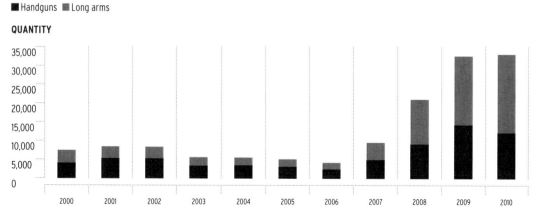

■ Handguns ■ Long arms

QUANTITY

Source: author correspondence with the Government of Mexico, 11 September 2012[12]

Table 12.3   Illicit firearms destined for and seized in Mexico, by type

Seized weapons*	Seizures in Mexico (January 2009–July 2012)		Seizures at US ports (January 2009–July 2011)	
	Quantity	Percentage	Quantity	Percentage
Pistols	817	19%	31	22%
Revolvers	183	4%	3	2%
'Short arms'	194	5%	n/a	n/a
Rifles	1,967	47%	97	70%
Shotguns	269	6%	7	5%
Sub-machine guns	60	1%	0	0
Machine guns	9	<1%	1	<1%
'Long arms'	700	17%	n/a	n/a
Unspecified	1	<1%	0	0
Total	**4,200**	**100%**	**139**	**100%**

Note: * As identified in the source document.

Sources: Small Arms Survey (2012c); USCBP (2011)

data include Norinco's MAK-90 and the WASR series (WASR 10) of semi-automatic rifles, the latter of which are frequently included in lists of 'weapons of choice' of the DTOs (Dudley, Schmitt, and Young, n.d.; Freedman, 2011). AR-15 variants accounted for most of the remaining rifles identified by model. Of the 251 seized AR-15s, at least 14 were identified as models produced by the US company Bushmaster; these weapons are also included in lists of firearms seized in Mexico (Dodge, 2009; Freedman, 2011; HCFA, 2008, p. 91).

The prevalence of .38 Super and 9 mm pistols is also consistent with previous reports on illicit weapons in Mexico. In fact, 9 mm and .38-caliber pistols—including at least 121 .38 Super pistols—were the most commonly seized handguns. Together, pistols identified as '9 mm', '.38 caliber', and '.38 Super' account for approximately 45 per cent of seized handguns studied that were identified by model or calibre. Nine-millimetre firearms were also the most frequently seized handguns along the US border and were seized at almost the same rate as in Mexico. Together, pistols that were identified as 9 mm or .38 calibre account for 35 per cent of the pistols and revolvers seized at the border.

Far fewer sub-machine guns and machine guns were seized. Most sub-machine guns identified by model were Uzi or Uzi-pattern guns. Other models and brands identified in the data include MP-5 and Intratec. No sub-machine guns are listed in the data on weapons seized at the US border. Data on the few machine guns seized in Mexico is vague. Only two are identified by model, one of which is a Minimi-pattern light machine gun recovered in San Luis Potosí. The one 'machine gun' seized at the US border during this time period was a Browning .30 calibre, a World War-II era gun that is produced in several countries and in various configurations, including a semi-automatic version made for the civilian market. Whether the Mexico-bound gun seized at the border was a civilian variant is not clear. Table 12.4 contains a list of firearms recovered during the seizures studied.

Table 12.4 Illicit firearms recovered in Mexico, by model, January 2009–August 2012

Seized weapon category	Type, model, and calibre*	Quantity	Percentage
Handgun	Pistol, 9 mm	217	18%
	Pistol, .45 calibre	127	11%
	Pistol, .38 Super	121	10%
	Pistol, .22 calibre	116	10%
	Pistol, .38 calibre	114	10%
	Revolver, .38 Special	64	5%
	Revolver, .22 calibre	52	4%
	Pistol, .25 calibre	44	4%
	Revolver, .357	24	2%
	Pistol, .32 calibre	23	2%
	Pistol, 5.7 × 28 mm	17	1%
	Revolver, .32 calibre	13	1%
	Revolver, .44 calibre	12	1%
	Revolver, .38	11	<1%
	Other/unspecified	239	20%
	Total/percentage of all seized firearms	**1,194**	**28%**
Machine gun	7.62 mm, unspecified	3	33%
	Minimi-pattern	1	11%
	7.62 × 39 mm, unspecified	1	11%
	7.62 × 51 mm, unspecified	1	11%
	.50 calibre	1	11%
	Other	2	22%
	Total/percentage of all seized firearms	**9**	**<1%**
Other	'Long guns'***	701	100%
	Total/percentage of all seized firearms	**701**	**17%**
Rifle	.22 calibre, various	729	37%
	Kalashnikov-pattern rifle	614	31%
	AR-15-pattern rifle	251	13%
	.30-.30, .30-.06	78	4%
	7.62 × 39 mm, unspecified	48	2%

▶

Seized weapon category	Type, model, and calibre*	Quantity	Percentage
	M1 Carbine	18	<1%
	G3-pattern rifle	13	<1%
	.50-calibre rifle**	10	<1%
	M16 and M4	7	<1%
	FAL-pattern rifle	4	<1%
	Other/unspecified	195	10%
	Total/percentage of all seized firearms	**1,967**	**47%**
Shotgun	12-gauge, unspecified	172	64%
	16-gauge, unspecified	28	10%
	20-gauge, unspecified	26	10%
	.410, unspecified	24	9%
	Other/unspecified	19	7%
	Total/percentage of all seized firearms	**269**	**6%**
Sub-machine gun	9 mm, unspecified	28	47%
	Uzi and Uzi-pattern	17	28%
	Intratec, 9 mm	4	7%
	MP-5	3	5%
	Other	8	13%
	Total/percentage of all seized firearms	**60**	**1%**
Total seized firearms		**4,200**	**100%**

Notes:

* As identified in the source document.

** Includes one firearm of unidentified calibre labelled 'Barett'.

*** Includes one unspecified 'firearm'.

Source: Small Arms Survey (2012c)

The data raises questions about other common claims, including references to .50-calibre sniper rifles as 'weapons of choice' of the cartels, a term that is also used to refer to the ubiquitous Kalashnikov- and AR-15-pattern rifles.[13] This categorization implies that .50-calibre rifles are frequently encountered and widely deployed,[14] an impression that is reinforced by the prominent display of large-calibre firearms during Mexican government press conferences on seized caches. However, .50-calibre rifles comprise a very small percentage of the seized weapons studied. Of the more than 3,200 firearms seized by SEDENA that are identified by model or calibre, only ten .50-calibre rifles are listed (fewer than 0.5 per cent of all seized firearms).

It should be noted that the data does not contradict claims that the DTOs are actively seeking and acquiring .50-calibre rifles, or that these weapons pose a significant threat. The DTOs used these rifles during several engagements with Mexican military and police units, including a firefight in which two soldiers were killed and another incident in which DTO members fired at a military helicopter with the rifles (Cabrera Martínez, 2012; *El Universal*, 2010). The data does suggest, however, that .50-calibre rifles are not encountered as frequently as implied in many media reports.

Similarly, the number of seized 5.7 mm × 28 mm pistols identified in the data is lower than expected given frequent references to them as 'weapons of choice' for the DTOs.[15] This type of pistol is often referred to as *mata policía* (cop killer) because of its reported ability to penetrate the body armour worn by police (Tucker, 2011). Of the 996 handguns seized by the Mexican military that were identified by model or calibre, only 17 (fewer than 2 per cent) had a calibre of 5.7 mm × 28 mm.

Finally, the data reveals striking differences between the types and models of illicit firearms seized in Mexico and those seized in countries studied during the first phase of this project.[16] Whereas the vast majority of illicit firearms recovered from arms caches in Iraq were Kalashnikov-pattern rifles (Small Arms Survey, 2012a, p. 321), these weapons comprised less than a third of illicit firearms identified by model or calibre that were recovered in Mexico. Other notable differences include the prevalence of handguns in Mexican caches, and of machine guns in Iraqi caches. Pistols and revolvers were recovered from arms caches in Mexico at more than five times the rate of handguns found in caches in Iraq.[17]

The data provides less insight into other key issues, such as whether the seized firearms are fully automatic or semi-automatic—a key point of contention in the ongoing debate over the role of the US domestic firearms market in Mexico's illicit firearms trade. Many military rifles are designed as selective-fire weapons, which allow the user to switch between fully automatic and self-loading (single-shot) modes of operation. Civilian variants of these weapons are widely available in the United States, but generally only in self-loading configurations. US and Mexican officials claim that the latter type of rifle is popular with DTOs, and US authorities have documented the smuggling—or attempted smuggling—of hundreds of semi-automatic Kalashnikov- and AR-15-pattern rifles from the US to Mexico in recent years.[18]

> Cartels are willing to pay a premium for a 'true military-grade Colt firearm'.

Others contend that most firearms used by DTOs, such as selective-fire rifles, are sourced from the Mexican government, Central America, and international arms networks (La Jeunesse and Lott, 2009; Kuhn and Bunker, 2011). While many of the studied seized rifles that are identified by model are semi-automatic weapons commonly sold in the United States, it is not clear whether these models constitute the majority of seized rifles given the infrequency with which seized rifles in the sample were identified by mode of fire. Their share of the broader population of illicit weapons is also unclear.

The seizure data also identifies a handful of craft-produced firearms. These references are consistent with other accounts of illicit weapons in Mexico, including reports of counterfeit Colt M16 rifles, at least 41 of which were reportedly recovered from December 2006 to July 2009. According to a 2010 US government report obtained by the Survey, the markings on the counterfeit rifles were 'very crude'. The rifles had no serial numbers, the markings contained misspellings, and the placement of the 'crudely forged' Colt symbol was inconsistent (USDOJ, 2010, pp. 2–3). ATF identified two possible reasons for producing the counterfeit rifles: first, because cartels are willing to pay a premium for a 'true military grade Colt firearm' and, second, because, as weapons issued to Mexican law enforcement, they facilitate the impersonation of police officers and military personnel (p. 8).

There are also numerous media references to conversion of illicit semi-automatic rifles into automatic rifles by the DTOs, but little hard data supports these assertions.[19] When queried about these references, the Mexican government indicated that authorities do not keep statistics on the percentage of seized firearms that have been converted to automatic weapons. A US government official interviewed for this report confirmed the seizure of converted firearms, but did not indicate how frequently they are seized.[20]

Data on the age of the illicit small arms in Mexico is also sparse. Few records of the seized weapons list the date of manufacture. However, there is some data on the 'time-to-crime' of US weapons diverted to Mexico, which provides a sense of how long seized weapons were on the black market. 'Time to crime' refers to the time between 'the first retail sale of a firearm and a law enforcement recovery of that firearm during a use, or suspected use, in a crime' (USDOJ, 2011, p. 6). Data provided by the Mexican government of weapons traced from 2006 to 2012 indicates that 'the time from the legal sale until their seizure can be anywhere from two weeks to a decade'.[21]

In recent years, the US Justice Department has published data on the time-to-crime of weapons purchased by traffickers who are specifically affiliated with the DTOs. The time-to-crime of long guns purchased by one trafficking ring ranged from 26 days to more than three years, with a median time of a little less than 1.5 years (OIG, 2010, p. 39). Guns bought by straw purchasers[22] monitored during the ill-fated Operation Fast and Furious had times-to-crime of as little as one day, according to the US Justice Department (US House of Representatives, 2012a, p. 1280).[23]

Sources of illicit small arms

Identifying the sources of illicit firearms using open-source information is an extremely difficult task. Many models of firearms are produced under licence in several countries and are widely exported. A US-designed M16 rifle could have come from the United States or from one of dozens of countries in Central America or elsewhere that have imported

A bullet-riddled police car parked with vehicles seized at crime scenes; '39' being a police code for 'death', in Ciudad Juárez, Mexico, September 2010. © Reuters

the rifles. The markings on seized weapons often identify the importing country or at least the country of manufacture, as well as the serial number, but these markings are rarely included in publicly available data. Even when this information is available, using it to trace a particular weapon to its proximate source requires access to documentation that is rarely made available to the public.

This lack of data and documentation precludes a definitive assessment of the sources of illicit weapons in Mexico and elsewhere. It also helps to explain the intractability of the ongoing debate over the sources of illicit firearms in Mexico. On one end of the spectrum are estimates that 90 per cent or more of these weapons are acquired in the United States, primarily from retail gun stores and gun shows (CBS News, 2009; Levi, 2009). These estimates appear to be based on data on firearms trace requests submitted by the Mexican government to the US government, which are not necessarily representative of all seized firearms, let alone all illicit firearms in Mexico. Some analysts explicitly note these data gaps. In a 2009 report, the US Government Accountability Office (GAO) concludes that '[o]ver 90 percent of the firearms seized in Mexico and traced over the last 3 years have come from the United States' (USGAO, 2009, p. 15).[24] Yet GAO also concedes that the data is incomplete; only firearms submitted for tracing to the United States by the Mexican government are reflected in the estimate, not all firearms seized in Mexico. Other references to the 90 per cent figure are less nuanced.[25]

Other analysts contend that firearms diverted from the US civilian market constitute only a small fraction of weapons used in crimes in Mexico—'probably around 17 percent', according to Fox News (La Jeunesse and Lott, 2009).[26]

An assault rifle and bundles of pesos and dollars seized from an alleged financial operator for the Zetas drug cartel, Mexico City, Mexico, June 2012.
© Alexandre Meneghini/AP Photo

Proponents of this position often claim that most firearms acquired by the DTOs are machine guns and automatic rifles that are illegal for civilians to purchase and sell in the United States. These weapons, they claim, include fully automatic M16, AK series, G3, and FAL assault rifles, as well as M249 and M60 machine guns (Kuhn and Bunker, 2011). These weapons are reportedly acquired from the Mexican military and police, poorly controlled government stockpiles in Central and South America, and the international arms market (La Jeunesse and Lott, 2009; Kuhn and Bunker, 2011).

A careful analysis of the ATF's 2012 report on traces of firearms recovered in Mexico sheds some light on this debate, including ambiguities and gaps in the data that call into question both the high- and low-end estimates. The ATF report includes data on 99,691 firearms seized from 2007 to 2011 that Mexico sought to trace with assistance from the US government, or approximately 65 per cent of the 154,943 firearms reportedly seized by Mexican authorities in this time period (USDOJ, 2012).[27] Little is known about the remaining firearms, including why the Mexican government did not submit data on them for tracing. Several reasons may explain why data on a particular firearm is not sent to ATF. In some cases, the weapon is clearly not of US origin. In other cases, bureaucratic obstacles and staffing limitations hinder submission of trace requests (USGAO, 2009, p. 16). It is not clear which of these reasons, or combination of reasons, are applicable to the roughly 55,000 firearms not submitted for tracing.

Of the 99,691 firearms that were submitted for tracing, ATF was able to confirm that 51,267 were manufactured in the United States, and that an additional 16,894 were imported into the US by federal firearms licensees. In other words, at least 68,161 (68 per cent) of the traced firearms were either of US origin or entered the United States at some point. This data is presented in Table 12.5.

Of the 68,161 US-sourced firearms recovered, ATF was able to trace 27,825 to retail purchases in the United States. An additional 1,461 were traced to foreign entities, such as governments, law enforcement organizations, or dealers. This data is summarized in Table 12.6.

Thus, ATF was able to account for at least 29,286 of the 99,691 firearms submitted for tracing, of which at least 27,825 were diverted from the US domestic market at some point. Little can be said definitively about the remaining 70,405 firearms. It is likely that many of the 38,875 untraceable firearms identified by ATF as 'US-sourced' were trafficked to Mexico from the United States, but without additional information it is impossible to determine how many. Similarly, while many of the 12,260 weapons identified as 'non-US-manufacture[d]' and not traced to a US entity may

Table 12.5 **Firearms recovered in Mexico and submitted to ATF for tracing, 2007–11**		Number of firearms	Percentage of traced firearms
Source country			
United States	Manufactured in the United States	51,267	51%
	Imported into the United States	16,894	17%
	Total	68,161	68%
Undetermined	Non-US manufacturer	12,260	12%
	Undetermined country of origin	19,270	19%
	Total	31,530	32%
Total		**99,691**	**100%**

Source: USDOJ (2012)

Table 12.6 **US-sourced firearms recovered in Mexico and submitted to ATF for tracing, 2007–11**		
Trace results*	**Total**	**Percentage of US Sourced Traces**
Traced to a retail purchaser in the United States	27,825	41%
Traced to a foreign country	1,461	2%
Unable to determine a purchaser	38,875	57%
Total	**68,161**	**100%**

Note: * As identified in the source document.

Source: USDOJ (2012)

never have entered the United States, ATF notes that even these weapons may have been 'legally imported into the US' before making 'their way to Mexico by legal or illegal means' (USDOJ, 2012, p. 6).

Despite its limitations, the data is useful in assessing the high- and low-end claims about the flow of illicit firearms from the United States to Mexico. Many of the high-end estimates (90 per cent) appear to be misinterpretations or misrepresentations of data on successful traces conducted by ATF, which, as noted above, reflects only a small percentage of all seized weapons.[28] For this estimate to be accurate, at least 90 per cent of the 31,530 firearms identified by ATF as being from 'undetermined countr[ies] of origin' and 90 per cent of the 38,875 US-sourced weapons for which ATF was 'unable to determine a purchaser'—along with 85 per cent of the roughly 55,000 firearms not submitted for tracing to ATF—would have to be sourced from the United States. While not inconceivable, there is insufficient publicly available, empirical evidence to support these claims.

An example of a low-end estimate is Fox News' claim that 17 per cent of crime guns in Mexico come from the United States (La Jeunesse and Lott, 2009). The claim is based on ATF trace data for 29,000 firearms recovered at crime scenes in Mexico in 2007 and 2008.[29] According to Fox News, 11,000 of those firearms were submitted for tracing. ATF successfully traced 6,000 of them, 90 per cent of which (5,114 firearms) came from the United States. The other 23,886 weapons, according to Fox News, '*could not* be traced to the US' (La Jeunesse and Lott, 2009, emphasis added).

This claim is problematic for two reasons. First, all that is known about the firearms not submitted for tracing is that they *were not* traced back to the United States, not that they *could not* have been traced to a US source if they had been submitted to ATF. Second, the authors fail to note that simply because a trace request is unsuccessful does not necessarily mean that the weapon in question was not trafficked from the United States. As explained by ATF in its 2012 report, traces fail for a variety of reasons, including incomplete trace request forms, obliterated serial numbers, incomplete record-keeping by retail sellers, and the age of the seized firearm (USDOJ, 2012, p. 7). Thus, the fact that the trace request was unsuccessful reveals very little about the seized weapon. Without more detailed information about the untraced and untraceable weapons, little can be said definitively about these weapons, including their origins. Given these ambiguities, the low-end estimates do not appear to be supported by existing data either.

A related claim is that the DTOs—having the 'wealth and armies of nations'—are able to obtain 'large lots of weaponry on the transnational black market' and therefore do not need to 'trifle with paperwork at US gun stores' (La Pierre, 2009). There is little doubt that the DTOs have acquired firearms, including light machine guns and automatic rifles, that are not readily available in the United States (Stewart, 2011a). Photographs of seized weapons confirm their acquisition, but open-source evidence, including US government trace data described in this chapter, suggests that the DTOs and their suppliers also frequently obtain guns from US sources.

As noted above, the US government traced 27,825 firearms seized in Mexico from 2007 to 2011 to retail purchasers in the United States. An additional 38,875 'US-sourced' firearms were also seized but were untraceable due to one or more of the reasons identified above. If the data on successful traces is any indicator, thousands of these untraceable weapons were probably also acquired in the United States.

The underlying notion that DTOs prefer the international black market because of the paperwork associated with obtaining small arms in the United States is also problematic. It is the vast, semi-autonomous network of traffickers that supplies the cartels with weapons that deals with the necessary paperwork, not the cartel leadership. Dozens of brokers and straw purchasers acquire and funnel firearms to the cartels, usually in small batches. As evidenced by the many individuals arrested for trafficking firearms to Mexico in recent years,[30] the profit[31] earned on each firearm purchased exceeds the perceived risk of legal prosecution, not to mention the modest effort required to fill out the necessary paperwork and deliver the firearm to the broker.

Furthermore, there is often considerable paperwork associated with the diversion of military-grade weapons from state stockpiles. UN reports on intercontinental diversions of small arms reveal the complexity of these transactions once the deals are finalized. To conceal their cargo and deceive export control and customs officials, traffickers set up complex, multinational networks of shell companies, obtain and submit false documentation, and arrange circuitous routing for the transfers. Such transfers often involve multiple parties located in different regions of the world and take months to arrange.[32] In aggregate, the administrative burden of acquiring firearms piecemeal through straw purchases may exceed that of fewer, larger international shipments, but this burden is not borne by the DTO alone; it is diffused throughout the trafficking chain.

In conclusion, while data gaps preclude a complete accounting of the sources of illicit firearms in Mexico, available data suggests that the US civilian market is a significant source of weapons. Whether firearms trafficked from the United States constitute the majority of illicit weapons in Mexico is unclear and will remain so until the vast majority of seized weapons are traced and more and better data on the models, countries of manufacture, and proximate sources of seized weapons is made available.

Mexican authorities have seized hundreds of illicit light weapons.

Light weapons

In recent years, Mexican authorities have seized hundreds of illicit light weapons, including hand grenades;[33] under-barrel, hand-held, and automatic grenade launchers; RPGs; directional, command-detonated anti-personnel mines (Claymore type); and anti-tank rockets in single-shot, disposable launch tubes. Data on weapon seizures from 2009 to 2012 published by SEDENA and compiled by the Small Arms Survey includes more than 1,000 light weapons and rounds of light weapons ammunition, the majority of which were hand grenades and 40 mm grenades for grenade launchers (Small Arms Survey, 2012c). Types of grenades seized include fragmentation, smoke, flash-bang, gas, and practice grenades. Notably, approximately half of all identified hand grenades were described as 'inert' or 'practice' grenades. In recent years, US authorities have seized dozens of these grenades, which are smuggled into Mexico and converted into craft-produced (live) grenades for use by DTOs (ADPS, 2009; Myers, 2011).[34] According to the Mexican government, the craft-produced grenades are made from grenade bodies similar to those used in M26A2, M67, and MKII grenades, which are reportedly purchased in souvenir shops in the United States.[35]

Seventy-three grenade launchers were also seized, along with roughly two dozen rockets, rocket launchers, and RPGs. All but four of the grenade launchers identified by calibre were 40 mm; the four remaining launchers were 37 mm. Most of the launchers were described as *aditamento lanzagranadas*, an apparent reference to under-barrel

Table 12.7	Illicit weapons seized by the Mexican military, 2009-12		
Weapon category	**Weapon type/calibre***	**Quantity**	**Percentage**
Grenades	Grenade, hand	374	37%
	Grenade, projected, 40 mm	267	26%
	Grenade, projected, other/unspecified	26	3%
	Grenade, unspecified	245	24%
Grenade Launcher	Grenade launcher, 40 mm	50	5%
	Grenade launcher, 37 mm	4	<1%
	Grenade launcher, other/unspecified	19	2%
Improvised explosive devices		2	<1%
Mortars and mortar rounds	Mortar rounds, 60 mm	10	<1%
Recoilless rifles and rounds		0	0%
Portable missiles	Man-portable air defence systems	0	0%
	Anti-tank guided weapons	0	0%
Rockets	Rockets and rocket launchers, 66 mm	3	<1%
	Rockets, other/unspecified	5	<1%
	Rocket launcher, other/unspecified	8	<1%
	Rocket-propelled grenade launchers	5	<1%
	Rocket-propelled grenades	2	<1%
Total		**1,020**	**100%**

Note: * As identified in the source document.

Source: Small Arms Survey (2012c)

grenade launchers such as the US M203. The 37 mm launchers could be flare launchers, which are reportedly converted to fire 40 mm grenades by criminals in Mexico (USDOJ, 2010, p. 6). At least one multiple grenade launcher and at least three craft-produced grenade launchers were also seized. Little is known about the 23 seized rockets and rocket launchers; only nine of them were identified by model or calibre, and none was identified by country of manufacture. Four of the 15 rocket launchers were identified as RPG-7s. Three of the rockets identified by calibre were 66 mm, which is the same calibre as the US-designed M72 light anti-tank weapon—a rocket known to be in the arsenals of the DTOs. The two IEDs identified among the weapons studied were seized in Sinaloa. Table 12.7 summarizes this data.

The data is largely consistent with other accounts of illicit light weapons in Mexico.[36] In a written response to a query from the Small Arms Survey, the Mexican government provided the following list of examples of light weapons acquired by criminal groups:

- Russian-made RPG-7s;
- US-made light anti-tank weapon rockets;
- 60 mm mortars;
- 'Claymore' mines;
- C-4 plastic explosives;
- K200, M406, and M433 projected grenades manufactured in South Korea and the United States; and
- other fragmentation, smoke, tear gas, and craft-produced grenades.[37]

According to the Mexican government, an analysis of the physical characteristics and condition of recovered weapons, along with information received from law enforcement agencies in other countries, indicates that a 'significant number' of weapons and military explosives seized in Mexico come from regional surplus stockpiles of weapons acquired in the 1980s and 1990s. Equally important, the Mexican government does not report having seized any MANPADS, ATGWs, machine guns of calibres greater than 12.7 mm, artillery rockets, or anti-tank mines.[38]

The bomb reportedly contained 20 pounds of explosives laced with three-inch drywall screws.

Additional types and models of light weapons identified in photographs and other accounts of weapons seized from DTOs include PG-7V and PG-7M RPG rounds; M79 and M203 grenade launchers; various projected, rifle, and hand grenades; and at least one AT-4 infantry rocket. In recent years, the DTOs have constructed various IEDs. In a car bomb attack in Juárez in 2010, one of the cartels used a wounded man dressed as a police officer as bait to attract first responders. When a doctor and a police officer approached the man, the cartel detonated the IED with a cell phone, killing the wounded man, the doctor, the police officer, and a bystander. The bomb reportedly contained 20 pounds of explosives laced with three-inch drywall screws (Esposito, 2010).

The data suggests that at least some DTOs have access to relatively large quantities of certain types of light weapons and ammunition, but not the full array of light weapons available to the 'armies of nations', as is sometimes claimed. There are no references to seized MANPADS, anti-tank guided missiles, anti-tank mines, or artillery rockets in the data studied. Indirect fire weapons are limited to a handful of 60 mm mortars, and there is no evidence of widespread acquisition of latest-generation infantry rockets. Thus, while formidable, the arsenals of light weapons acquired by criminal groups in Mexico are not the equivalent of those of state actors.

In some respects, illicit light weapons acquired by the DTOs are also more limited than the weapons acquired by non-state groups in other regions. Armed groups in Iraq, Lebanon, the Russian Federation (Chechnya), Somalia, Sri Lanka, and Syria have inventories of light weapons that are more varied and technologically sophisticated than those acquired by DTOs in Mexico.[39] Light weapons seized from illicit arms caches in Iraq, for example, include anti-tank mines, 120 mm mortars, artillery rockets, advanced IEDs, and limited numbers of anti-tank guided weapons, first- and second-generation MANPADS, and advanced anti-armour rockets (Small Arms Survey, 2012, pp. 322–29).

There are several possible explanations for the DTOs' comparatively limited arsenal. One is that, tactically, they simply do not need some of these weapons, including anti-tank missiles or rockets with tandem high explosive anti-tank (HEAT) warheads. Rival DTOs generally do not drive heavily armoured vehicles, and publicly available data suggests that the Mexican army does not have any armoured vehicles with modern reactive armour. High-powered rifles, RPGs, and grenade launchers are adequate for the vehicles most frequently targeted by the DTOs. Thus, the absence of these types of weapons in the cartels' arsenals may say little about their capacity to acquire them.

This explanation is less convincing when applied to other types of light weapons, including MANPADS. As mentioned above, no surface-to-air missiles are listed in the summaries of the seized caches studied, and there is little additional evidence of illicit acquisition or use of MANPADS by the DTOs. The few media references to illicit surface-to-air missiles in Mexico are either unsubstantiated or demonstrably erroneous. Most recently, five 'anti-aircraft missiles' reportedly recovered from an arms cache in Coahuila (Prensa Latina, 2012) were actually RPGs, as revealed by photographs of the seized items.

In a written correspondence with the Small Arms Survey, the Mexican government confirmed that it has no evidence of illicit acquisition of anti-aircraft missiles, guided rockets, or machine guns of calibres greater than .50 by the DTOs. According to the government, attacks on aircraft to date have been perpetrated with firearms of calibres ranging from 7.62 mm to .50 BMG.[40] While these weapons are capable of shooting down aircraft, they lack the range and accuracy of dedicated anti-aircraft weapons, such as MANPADS. Whether and to what extent the DTOs are actively seeking these weapons is unclear. As noted below, there is some anecdotal evidence of active DTO interest in procuring MANPADS, but this evidence is extremely limited.

In 2009, David Díaz Sosa, a Mexican national acting on behalf of a representative of the Sinaloa cartel, attempted to purchase a Stinger missile and other weapons from undercover US agents. A US agent involved in the case claimed that, when Díaz Sosa was inspecting weapons assembled by ATF as part of the operation, he said he 'was not interested in that particular Stinger missile' because it was 'a couple years old'. Instead, 'they were interested in a new one', according to the agent (USDC Arizona, 2011, p. 18). It is unclear whether this attempt was part of a broader, systematic effort by the Sinaloa cartel to acquire MANPADS, or whether other DTOs have engaged in similar efforts. The DTOs' need for such weapons is presumably less pressing than armed groups facing large-scale counter-insurgency air operations, but the potential tactical and strategic value is significant, and no weapon currently in their arsenals is an adequate substitute for MANPADS.

> No weapon currently in DTO arsenals is an adequate substitute for MANPADS.

Given their potential utility, why have the DTOs not acquired MANPADS and modern infantry rockets? Regarding MANPADS, one possible explanation is that the perceived benefits are lower than potential costs, which extend beyond the high price tag of the weapons themselves. Because of the terrorist threat posed by MANPADS, they are closely tracked by intelligence agencies worldwide. Their acquisition by the DTOs, which are already widely viewed as a serious regional security threat by US authorities, could prompt greater action against the cartel by US military, law enforcement, and intelligence agencies. While some DTOs have reportedly sought to increase US involvement in Mexico through attacks on US targets,[41] they must be careful not to go too far, as illustrated by aggressive action against the Guadalajara cartel following their brutal execution of an agent of the US Drug Enforcement Administration in 1985 (Stewart, 2011b). As one US government official noted: 'The cartels are smart enough to know that if they acquired weapons that can be used in terrorism, they would likely attract a lot of unwanted attention from the US Defense Department.'[42]

Supply-side dynamics are another possible explanation for the apparent absence of MANPADS in DTO arsenals. A decade-old global counter-MANPADS campaign has significantly reduced the world's inventory of surplus and poorly secured missiles, and most exporters apply special controls to transfers of MANPADS. As a result, it is extremely difficult for non-state groups to acquire MANPADS in most regions of the world, including the Americas. Lending credence to this theory is the seizure of craft-produced weapons from cartel members, which suggests that at least some members have had difficulty acquiring sufficient quantities of more commonplace light weapons, let alone MANPADS. Particularly notable is the seizure of dozens of craft-produced under-barrel grenade launchers and components for hundreds of craft-produced hand grenades[43] from DTOs in recent years.

As noted above, approximately half of the 374 seized hand grenades studied were described as 'inert' or 'practice' grenades, which US authorities claim are often converted into live grenades. When queried about this practice, the

Mexican government indicated that it has seized at least 500 craft-produced ('artisan') grenades in recent years.[44] Given that craft-produced grenades are likely to be less reliable than their factory-built counterparts, it seems unlikely that DTOs or their suppliers would go to the trouble of acquiring the various components and assembling the grenades if they had consistent and unfettered access to conventional grenades.

The conversion of 37 mm flare launchers into grenade launchers is another sign that access to illicit light weapons may be more limited than commonly assumed, at least for some criminal groups. According to a 2010 US government report, Mexican authorities seized at least 34 counterfeit grenade launchers in 22 seizures from 2007 to 2009. The counterfeit launchers were reportedly made from the trigger housing of 37 mm Cobray flare launchers, which are 'easily purchased from a variety of locations', including on the Internet, 'for a retail price of approximately $550' (USDOJ, 2010, p. 6). According to the Mexican government, the converted launchers are used to fire 40 mm rounds—mainly K200, M406, or M433 grenades manufactured in South Korea and the United States.[45]

As noted above, the US government believes that production of the counterfeit launchers may be motivated by the large profit margins resulting from low supply and high demand. ATF observes that '[a]ctual military weapons are extremely difficult for the DTOs to acquire, and they are willing to pay top dollar for them' (USDOJ, 2010, p. 8). Regardless of their motivation, the procurement of craft-produced weapons is another example of how even the best-funded non-state groups do not have the same access to light weapons as the 'armies of nations'.

Authorities seized at least 34 counterfeit grenade launchers from 2007 to 2009.

ILLICIT SMALL ARMS AND LIGHT WEAPONS IN THE PHILIPPINES

Many insurgent groups are engaged in low-intensity armed conflict in the Philippines. Some of them have been fighting against the government for decades. This is the case with the New People's Army (NPA)—the armed wing of the Communist Party of the Philippines—which was founded in 1969 and engages in complex raids and other guerrilla operations using a variety of weapons and explosives. There are also several Islamist-oriented insurgent groups, of which the most widely known are the Abu Sayyaf Group (ASG) and the Moro Islamic Liberation Front (MILF). Both operate in the southern islands of the archipelago.

Illicit small arms and light weapons in the Philippines range from craft-produced shotguns to 81 mm mortar systems. As in other countries, the quantity of illicit small arms and light weapons available in the Philippines is difficult to assess. The Philippine government estimates that there were approximately 610,000 'loose' firearms in the country as of 2012. This figure, which is considerably higher than previous estimates, includes handguns and rifles but not machine guns or firearms with calibres larger than 7.62 mm.[46] There are no comparable publicly available estimates regarding the number of illicit light weapons.

Given this chapter's focus on low-intensity armed conflict, the small arms holdings of the best-known insurgent groups—the ASG, MILF, and NPA—are of particular interest.[47] A review of existing literature provides a sense of the size of these groups and their estimated holdings, along with baseline estimates of the types and models of weapons in their arsenals. Estimates vary, but most accounts indicate that none of the groups has large reserves of weapons. Table 12.8 summarizes recent estimates of the membership, holdings, and types of small arms and light weapons for the three most prominent insurgent groups.

Data compiled from summaries of weapons seized by Philippine authorities sheds additional light on the types, models, quantities, and end users of illicit small arms and light weapons, including weapons acquired by insurgent

Table 12.8 Estimated holdings of small arms and light weapons by insurgent groups in the Philippines

| Group | Members | Weapon types* | | Estimated holdings of 'firearms' |
		Data compiled by the Small Arms Survey**	Other sources	
Communist Party of the Philippines–New People's Army	5,760–7,260	Revolvers (.22 calibre, .357 Magnum, .38 calibre); pistols (9 mm, .38 calibre, .45 calibre); rifles (.22 calibre, M16, M15, M14, M653, M2, M1, AK-47, craft-produced); shotguns (12-gauge, craft-produced); sub-machine guns (Thompson, Ingram, Uzi-style, craft-produced); machine guns (5.56 Ultimax, .30 calibre Browning Automatic Rifle); mortars (60 mm); grenade launchers (M203, M79, craft-produced); grenades (hand, projected, rifle, craft-produced); RPGs; landmines (Claymore, improvised); IEDs	Revolvers (.357 Magnum); pistols (.22 calibre, 9 mm, .38 calibre, .38 Super, .40 calibre); rifles (.22 calibre hunting rifles, AK-47, AR-18, AR-15, M16, M14, M4, M2 and M1; M1903); shotguns (factory-manufactured and craft-produced); sub-machine guns (Thompson; M10; Uzi); machine guns (M2, M60; M1918 BAR); mortars; grenade launchers (M203); hand grenades; RPGs (RPG-2); land-mines (craft-produced command-detonated); IEDs	5,694–6,050
Moro Islamic Liberation Front	11,000–11,769	Pistols (.45 calibre); rifles (M16, M14, M2, M1, M653); mortars (60 mm); grenade launchers (M79, M203, craft-produced); RPGs; IEDs	Pistols (.45 Colt and .38 Smith & Wesson); rifles (M16, M14, M4, M2, M1, AR-15, FN FAL, Kalashnikov-pattern, .50 calibre); machine guns (M60, M2, .60 calibre); mortars (60 mm and 81 mm); grenade launchers (M79, M203); RPGs (RPG-2)	7,700–8,170
Abu Sayyaf Group	400–500	Rifles (M653, M16, M14, M4, M2, M1, FAL); machine guns (Minimi); mortars (60 mm); RPGs (B40)	Various types of handguns; rifles (Colt M4, M16A1, M16A2, M14, M1 Garand); machine guns (M60, Ultimax light-duty models, heavy-duty .30- and .50-calibre models); mortars (60 mm, 81 mm); grenade launchers (M203); recoilless rifles (M18, M67); RPGs (RPG-2, B40)	300

Notes:

* As identified in the source document.

** Models listed in the table do not necessarily reflect all models of seized weapons studied.

Sources: IHS Jane's (2010); Chalk et al. (2009, pp. 42, 58); Santos et al. (2010); Small Arms Survey (2012d)

groups. Of the approximately 1,000 seized small arms, light weapons, and rounds of light weapons ammunition studied, more than two-thirds were firearms. Grenades and grenade launchers accounted for approximately 13 per cent of seized items, followed by landmines (12 per cent) and IEDs (3 per cent). Rockets, RPGs, recoilless rifles, and mortars were also seized, but in much smaller quantities. Together, the latter four categories of light weapons account for less than 4 per cent of all seized items—in sharp contrast to the thousands of mortar rounds, RPGs, and recoilless rounds recovered from arms caches in Iraq and Afghanistan (Small Arms Survey, 2012, pp. 317–36). No MANPADS

New recruits to the New People's Army undergo training, Mindanao, Philippines, July 2009. © Jonas Gratzer/Lightrocket/Getty Images

or ATGWs were identified. The types of weapons seized and their corresponding share of all weapons studied is presented in Table 12.9.

Most of the data on the seizures studied for this chapter identifies the end user (or suspected end user) of the seized weapons. Disaggregating the data by end user reveals that most of the weapons were seized from the insurgent groups in Table 12.8, with the New People's Army accounting for the vast majority of seized weapons. Combined, these three groups accounted for more than 80 per cent of the seized light weapons and ammunition, and nearly all of the landmines and RPGs. Other illicit end users include suspected members of a political clan, drug trafficking groups, fishermen, gun dealers and gun store owners, militias associated with insurgent groups, and unspecified 'communist terrorists', 'criminal elements', and 'private armed groups'.

End users of the illicit small arms studied were more diverse than end users of light weapons. Most handguns and craft-produced firearms were seized from users other than the three main insurgent groups, whereas the vast majority of rifles—most of which were identified as military rifles—were seized from insurgents. Notably, all of the recoilless rifles and nearly half of the mortars and machine guns, were reportedly seized, not from the insurgent groups listed above, but from 'the Ampatuans'—members and supporters of a powerful political family in the province of Maguindanao. The weapons were found in boxes buried in a vacant lot next to houses reportedly owned by senior members of the clan (Cinco, 2009; Roque, 2009).

Table 12.9 Illicit weapons seized by the Philippine government, 2007–12

Weapon category	Percentage of total
Firearms	69%
Grenades* and grenade launchers	13%
Landmines	12%
IEDs	3%
Mortar systems and rounds	2%
RPGs and rounds	1%
Anti-tank rockets and recoilless rifles	<1%
MANPADS and ATGWs	0

Note: * This category includes hand grenades, projected grenades, rifle grenades, and other (unspecified) grenades, but not RPGs.

Source: Small Arms Survey (2012d)

Small arms

As noted above, firearms were the items most frequently recovered by authorities in the seizures studied. A total of 690 firearms were recovered, most of which were rifles. Nearly half of the seized rifles were identified as M16s or craft-produced M16s. Several dozen older-model US-designed semi-automatic rifles were also seized, including the Vietnam-era M14 and the M1 Garand, which was first fielded in the 1930s. Pistols and revolvers were also recovered in comparatively large quantities; together, they account for approximately 30 per cent of all seized firearms. Forty-five-calibre pistols were the most commonly seized handgun, followed by .38-calibre revolvers. The remaining firearms consisted of shotguns (7 per cent), sub-machine guns (2 per cent), and machine guns (2 per cent). A detailed listing of the seized firearms is provided in Table 12.10.

Craft-produced firearms being manufactured by gunsmiths in an illegal workshop, Danao, Philippines, July 2012. © Erik De Castro/Reuters

The data is largely consistent with existing accounts of the types and models of illicit small arms in the Philippines. Nearly all of the models and makes of firearms identified in the data are also identified in other sources, including assessments of armed group arsenals in Table 12.8.[48]

Also consistent with previous assessments is the prevalence of US-designed firearm models, which contrasts sharply with the thousands of Soviet-designed Kalashnikov-pattern and SKS rifles, and PK series machine guns recovered from arms caches in Afghanistan, Iraq, and Somalia. Nearly all of the seized rifles were of US design, with M16s, M14s, and M1s being the most numerous. Combined, US-designed rifles accounted for at least 88 per cent of all rifles, and approximately 96 per cent of all rifles identified by model or country of manufacture. Notably, the ratio of US- to Soviet-designed rifles is a nearly perfect inverse of the ratio of US and Soviet firearms in Iraq, where 90 per cent of all seized rifles studied—and 99 per cent of those identified by model—were Kalashnikov-pattern or SKS rifles (Small Arms Survey, 2012, p. 321). Further underscoring the dominance of US-designed rifles (and hence their ammunition), four of the remaining non-US rifles had been converted to fire M16 ammunition. Only five Kalashnikov-pattern rifles were recovered during the seizures.

The frequent seizure of craft-produced firearms is also consistent with previous accounts of insurgent holdings. Craft-produced firearms have long been an integral part of the illicit trade in firearms in the Philippines. The *paltik* (craft-produced) handgun 'has been locally produced since 1928' (Quilop, 2010,

Table 12.10 Illicit firearms seized in the Philippines, 2007–12

Type	Model/calibre*	Quantity
Firearm (unspecified)	Various	11
	Improvised	6
	Total	**17**
Pistol	.45 calibre	74
	9 mm	9
	Improvised	6
	.38 calibre	4
	Other/unspecified	10
	Total	**103**
Revolver	.38 calibre	51
	Improvised	22
	.22 calibre	19
	.357 calibre	5
	Other/unspecified	2
	Total	**99**
Shotgun	Improvised	23
	12-gauge	5
	Unspecified	20
	Total	**48**
Rifle	M16	192
	M14	60
	Garand (including M1)	56
	Carbine, unspecified	20
	M653	11
	Improvised	9
	.30 calibre, various	8
	M2	8
	AK-47	5
	.50 calibre	4
	Other/unspecified	22
	Total	**395**

Type	Model/calibre*	Quantity
Sub-machine gun	Uzi and Uzi-type	4
	Ingram, 9 mm	3
	Thompson, .45 calibre	2
	KG-9	1
	Improvised	3
	Total	**13**
Machine gun	Browning automatic rifle, .30 calibre	4
	M60	4
	Ultimax	3
	Minimi-pattern	1
	Heavy machine gun, .50 calibre	1
	HK 11	1
	Other/unspecified	1
	Total	**15**
Total		**690**

Note: * As identified in the source document.

Source: Small Arms Survey (2012d)

p. 244). Since then, craft producers in the Philippines, including those working for the MILF and other armed groups, have developed the capacity to produce a wide array of other firearms, including 'cheap replicas' of Armalite assault rifles and Uzi-, Interdynamic- (KG-9), and Ingram-brand sub-machine guns, along with accessories such as silencers (Quilop, 2010, p. 244; IHS Jane's, 2010, p. 3).

The continuing influence of this tradition is evident in the data on seized weapons. Ten per cent of seized firearms were identified as craft-produced.[49] This ratio of craft-produced to conventional firearms is significantly higher than in Afghanistan, Iraq, Mexico, and Somalia.[50] Approximately half of the 69 seized craft-produced firearms were handguns, with shotguns accounting for most of the remaining weapons. Several craft-produced military firearms were also seized, including copies of M16 rifles and Ingram and Thompson sub-machine guns.

Light weapons

More than 300 light weapons and rounds of light weapons ammunition were recovered during the seizures reviewed. Grenades and grenade launchers were the most common category of light weapon seized, accounting for 40 per cent of the seized weapons. Nearly all of the seized grenade launchers were identified as US-designed under-barrel M203 or hand-held, single-shot M79 launchers. No seizures of automatic grenade launchers were reported. Hand and projected grenades (spin-stabilized and rifle grenades) were recovered in roughly equal numbers. Not surprisingly, all of the spin-stabilized grenades identified by model were for M203 launchers.

The seized IEDs ranged from devices constructed using 60 mm and 81 mm mortar rounds to a five-foot-long pipe bomb weighing 45 kilograms. Some of the seized IEDs were designed for non-military purposes. For example, in November 2007, police seized six 'bongbongs' from a fishing boat in Vigan City on the South China Sea. Components used in the IEDs include dedicated explosives-related items, such as C-4 plastic explosives and blasting caps, along with a variety of household items, such as an alarm clock, 9-volt batteries, fishing line used as tripwire, and ball bearings.

Anti-personnel mines were also seized in comparatively large quantities. At least half were craft-produced mines, most of which were found in an NPA explosives factory in March 2011. Summaries of the seizures provide few details about the style or composition of the mines. Most are identified as 'Claymores', which are presumably versions of the US-designed directional fragmentation mine fielded in the 1950s. Claymore mines can be employed as command-detonated weapons (controlled role), meaning that they are detonated by the operator rather than the victim, or as victim-actuated weapons (uncontrolled role). The data contains little descriptive information about the seized anti-tank mines.

The remaining light weapons identified in the data include 17 mortars and mortar rounds, 13 RPG launchers and rounds, and four 'bazookas' allegedly recovered from the Ampatuan political clan. Nearly all of the RPGs and RPG launchers were seized from—or surrendered by—members of the ASG, MILF, and NPA. The make and model of most seized RPGs and launchers are not specified. The one exception is a B-40 recovered in April 2010 from an Abu Sayyaf camp. The B-40 is a variant of the first-generation Soviet RPG-2, which was first fielded in the late 1940s. According to IHS Jane's, the MILF also uses the RPG-2, reportedly producing its own launchers (IHS Jane's, 2010, p. 3).

Data on the seized 'bazookas' is unclear. Of the four seized items, two are described simply as 'bazookas', a term that is often used to refer to any man-portable recoilless gun. The third item, a '57RR baby bazooka', is probably a US-designed M18 recoilless rifle, a World War II-era system that was reportedly ineffective as an anti-tank weapon but widely used against personnel. The Chinese military produced a copy called the Type 36, which was exported to the Viet Cong during the Vietnam War. The fourth item is referred to as a '90 recoilless rifle', which could be a reference to the 90 mm US M67 recoilless rifle, another older system that was widely deployed by US forces in Vietnam and is currently in the Philippine Armed Forces' inventory. Table 12.11 provides a detailed summary of light weapons seized by Philippine authorities.

The seized weapons include few, if any, technologically sophisticated systems. There are no references to ATGWs or MANPADS in the summaries of the seizures analysed, nor is there any mention of modern automatic grenade launchers, anti-tank rockets, or technologically advanced accessories for these weapons, such as computerized fire control systems or thermal sights.

The data also suggests that illicit light weapons in the Philippines, including light

Table 12.11 **Light weapons seized in the Philippines, 2007–12**		
Type	**Model***	**Quantity**
Grenade, hand	Various/unspecified	45
Grenade, rifle	Unspecified	28
Grenade, projected	M203 rounds	22
Grenade, craft-produced	Improvised grenade	1
Grenade, unspecified	Various/unspecified	16
Grenade launcher	M203	7
	M79	5
	Craft-produced	2
IEDs	IEDs	33
Landmines, anti-personnel	Claymore, including craft-produced copies	43
	Unspecified	13
Landmines, anti-tank	Unspecified	10
Landmines, unspecified	Craft-produced	56
Mortar system and rounds	60 mm	9
	81 mm	6
	Various/unspecified	2
RPG launcher	Unspecified	3
RPG round	Various/unspecified	10
Recoilless rifle	Various/unspecified	4
Total		**315**

Note: * As identified in the source document.

Source: Small Arms Survey (2012d)

Table 12.12 Comparison of small arms and light weapons recovered from non-state armed groups in Afghanistan, Iraq, Mexico, and the Philippines

Weapon category	Percentage of seized weapons studied			
	Afghanistan (2006–08)	Iraq (2008–09)	Mexico (2009–12)	Philippines (2004–12)
Mortar systems and rounds	37	57	⊲1	2
Grenades and grenade launchers*	29	7	19	13
Recoilless rifles and rounds	13	2	0	⊲1
RPG launchers and rounds	13	10	⊲1	1
Firearms	4	12	80	69
Landmines	4	7	0	12
IEDs	1	5	⊲1	3
Rockets in disposable launchers	⊲1	⊲1	⊲1	0
Portable missiles (MANPADS and ATGWs)	0	⊲1	0	0

Note: * This category includes hand grenades, project grenades, rifle grenades, and other (unspecified) grenades other than RPGs.

Sources: Small Arms Survey (2012a; 2012c; 2012d)

weapons acquired by insurgent groups, differ in key ways from light weapons in high-intensity armed conflict. Table 12.12 compares small arms and light weapons seized in the Philippines with weapons seized in Afghanistan, Iraq, and Mexico. As illustrated in the table and explained in the *Small Arms Survey 2012,* the majority of weapons recovered from caches in Iraq and Afghanistan were light weapons and their ammunition, which accounted for more than 88 per cent of the seized weapons studied in Iraq and 96 per cent of seized weapons in Afghanistan. In contrast, most small arms and light weapons seized in the Philippines were firearms.

Particularly notable are the differences in the quantity of indirect fire weapons (such as mortars) seized in Iraq and Afghanistan vs. those seized in the Philippines. Only a handful of mortar systems and mortar rounds were identified in the Philippines seizures studied, and several of them were converted into IEDs rather than used as designed. The quantity and type of seized mortars and RPGs is consistent with other accounts of armed groups and their weapons. According to Santos, '[t]here have been no reports of the Philippine security forces ever having come under attack by NPA units using either mortars or rocket-propelled grenades'. Santos et al. attribute the absence of such attacks to 'a lack of ammunition' (Santos et al., 2010, p. 271). Previous accounts also indicate that the types of mortars and RPGs are limited to 60 mm and 81 mm mortars, as well as first-generation RPG-2s; there is no mention of 120 mm mortars or more modern RPGs.

Sources of small arms and light weapons

The data on the weapons seized in the Philippines contains little specific information on the country of origin and proximate source of the seized weapons. To fill these gaps, information was obtained from the Philippine government and collected from existing literature, including assessments by the Small Arms Survey, IHS Jane's, and the RAND Corporation, all of which identify several sources of illicit weapons and ammunition for insurgent groups.

These reports indicate that military and police depots are sources of illicit weapons and ammunition.[51] Weapons stockpiled by—or intended for—Philippine security forces are acquired by armed groups and other unauthorized end users in a variety of ways. Some are looted from overrun outposts and taken from security forces captured or killed in battle (PCTC, n.d., p. 7). Others are reportedly stolen or diverted from depots and stockpiles. In one particularly brazen incident, NPA members donned police uniforms, walked into a police station, and simply helped themselves to weapons and ammunition (Quilop, 2010, p. 242).

Diversion is often more subtle and is sometimes facilitated by corrupt or sympathetic government officials or members of government-sponsored civilian militias composed of relatives and former members of insurgent groups, according to IHS Jane's (2010, p. 3). Some weapons intended for security forces are also reportedly diverted shortly after import. According to Quilop, arms dealers acting on behalf of local governments order more weapons than are needed by the agency and then sell the excess weapons on the black market (Quilop, 2010, p. 242).

Craft production is another source of illicit small arms and light weapons in the Philippines, although the extent of this production—and the utility of the weapons produced—is difficult to assess. As noted above, there is a long tradition of craft production of firearms that continues to some extent today, although the quantity of craft-produced weapons has declined in recent years, according to the Philippine government.[52] Some insurgent groups have reportedly developed the capacity to produce a variety of small arms and light weapons. Several analysts claim that the MILF is able to produce semi-automatic and automatic firearms, M79 grenade launchers, and RPG-2 launchers (IHS Jane's, 2010; Chalk et al., 2009, p. 42).

Philippine soldiers carry light weapons seized following a massacre in Maguindanao Province, Philippines, December 2009. © Jeoffrey Maitem/Getty Images

There is a sub-group of paltik firearms that the Philippine government considers 'high quality (class A)'.[53] However, the quality of most craft-produced weapons is reportedly low. Commenting on craft-produced guns, a Philippine government official explained that '[t]hese weapons are useable but do not last very long' and that, in some cases, 'the ammunition for which the firearm is designed does not fit properly, or the gun misfires and injures the user'.[54] IHS Jane's describes the quality of the MILF's light weapons as 'questionable', noting that 'some sources clai[m] that the only weapon that the MILF can successfully produce is the crude RPG-2' (IHS Jane's, 2010).[55]

Finally, weapons are reportedly shipped to armed groups by sympathizers located abroad. The Philippine government confirmed that these shipments are often large but did not provide any additional information.[56] An undated government report on arms trafficking notes that Philippine nationals living abroad are a major external source of illicit weapons, and particularly of 'the more sophisticated and high powered firearms' (PCTC, n.d., p. 5). The report notes that the weapons are smuggled into airports and maritime ports with assistance from corrupt officials. Other modes of delivery reportedly include door-to-door shipments of commercial goods and international aid (p. 4). The report cites data on weapons seized at Ninoy Aquino International Airport from 1991 to 1999, suggesting that the information is quite dated. Whether the methods and routes highlighted in the report are still used is unclear.

CONCLUSION

Data on weapons seized in Mexico and the Philippines sheds important light on illicit weapons in these and other countries studied as part of this project. The data presented here suggests that most illicit weapons in Mexico and the Philippines are firearms. This contrasts sharply with previously compiled data on weapons seized in Iraq and Afghanistan, where illicit light weapons and light weapons ammunition were overwhelmingly more common than firearms (Small Arms Survey, 2012a).

The types of light weapons most frequently acquired by armed groups in the five countries also varied significantly. Whereas RPGs and mortars constituted the bulk of seized light weapons in Iraq and Afghanistan, hand grenades and 40 mm grenade launchers were the most commonly recovered light weapons in Mexico and the Philippines. There are also notable differences in the models and provenance of illicit weapons in the countries studied, with US and European designs constituting most of the seized weapons in the Philippines and Mexico, and Soviet- and Chinese-designed systems accounting for most weapons seized in Afghanistan, Iraq, and Somalia.

Illicit small arms and light weapons in the five countries studied are also similar in several ways. Among the most notable similarities is the apparent absence of latest-generation light weapons. There is no evidence that any armed groups in the countries studied have acquired the most recently fielded MANPADS or ATGWs, and groups in Mexico and the Philippines have acquired few, if any, portable missiles. Other advanced light weapons are also scarce. There is no mention of thermobaric or tandem HEAT infantry rockets, or light weapons (that is, mortars or automatic grenade launchers) equipped with computerized fire control systems, or thermal weapon sights. Armed groups in Iraq have acquired some of these systems, namely tandem HEAT RPGs, but only in very small quantities.

Another similarity is the widespread acquisition and use of craft-produced weapons. In Mexico, the DTOs have acquired craft-produced shotguns, rifles, hand grenades, and grenade launchers. In the Philippines, craft-produced weapons include handguns, rifles, shotguns, sub-machine guns, RPG launchers, grenades, grenade launchers, and landmines. In Iraq and Afghanistan, craft-produced launchers for artillery rockets are common. Uniting all of these countries is the increased use of IEDs, which are now prevalent among non-state groups worldwide (IMPROVISED EXPLOSIVE DEVICES). Iraq has seen the most—and the most sophisticated—IEDs, but that may change in the coming years as more groups acquire the skills and experience required to build and deploy them effectively, and as they adapt to government counter-IED efforts.

These comparisons highlight several common misperceptions and oversimplifications regarding illicit small arms and light weapons. The first is the tendency to associate the AK-47 assault rifle and the RPG-7 with the global black market in small arms and light weapons. While these weapons are widely available on many local and regional black markets, they are not the dominant illicit weapons in every country. In Mexico and the Philippines, US and European models[57] are much more common than in Afghanistan, Iraq, and Somalia. These differences are largely explained by the apparent reliance by armed groups on local and regional sources of weapons.

Second, data collected as part of this study suggests that another common assumption—that most illicit weapons are supplied by international 'merchants of death' such as Viktor Bout—is not accurate, at least with regard to the five countries studied to date. While specific data on proximate sources is scarce, evidence suggests that sympathetic governments in neighbouring states, remnants of looted stockpiles, or the country's own security forces serve as the largest sources of illicit weapons for armed groups in the contexts studied to date. In all five case studies, nearly all of the models identified in the data are available either in country or in neighbouring states, and many have been available for decades. International arms brokers do provide weapons to armed groups and other unauthorized end users, but their contributions appear to be comparatively limited.

These observations have clear implications for policy-makers. The illicit weapons that are acquired and used most frequently in the countries studied are technologically simple systems that are readily available in the region and often have been around for decades. Armed groups in these countries have acquired few if any latest-generation portable missiles and other technologically sophisticated weapons, and it is unclear whether and to what extent they are attempting to acquire them. These findings underscore the need for strong controls on *all* small arms and light weapons, not just the newest and most sophisticated models. Similarly, while large international shipments of weapons arranged by global arms traffickers continue to fuel conflict, the slow leakage of weapons from domestic and regional sources is often the more pressing threat. Identifying these sources and strengthening controls is at least as important as chasing the 'merchants of death'. ▪

LIST OF ABBREVIATIONS

ASG	Abu Sayyaf Group
ATGW	Anti-tank guided weapon
ATF	United States Bureau of Alcohol, Tobacco, Firearms and Explosives
DTO	Drug-trafficking organization
GAO	Government Accountability Office
HEAT	High explosive anti-tank
IED	Improvised explosive device
MANPADS	Man-portable air defence system
MILF	Moro Islamic Liberation Front
NPA	New People's Army
SEDENA	Secretaría de la Defensa Nacional
RPG	Rocket-propelled grenade

ENDNOTES

1   See LaPierre (2009).

2   See Small Arms Survey (2012a, pp. 312–54).

3   Note that the weapons are of US design but may have been produced or sourced in countries other than the United States.

4   This category includes all military and civilian rifles, including assault rifles.

5   See Small Arms Survey (2008, pp. 8–11; 2012a, pp. 314–15).

6   Parts for small arms and light weapons are not included in the datasets. For the Small Arms Survey's definition of 'parts' and 'accessories', see Small Arms Survey (2012a, pp. 243–46).

7   The data reflects seizures by officials from US Customs and Border Protection, US Immigration and Customs Enforcement, and the US Border Patrol. Author telephone interview with US Customs and Border Protection official, July 2012.

8   Summaries of caches seized by SEDENA are the only relatively comprehensive source of detailed, disaggregated data on weapons seized in Mexico. Consequently, it is extremely difficult to account for possible selection biases in the source data.

9   Mexican and US officials have stated that 'most guns trafficked into Mexico are facilitated by and support operations of Mexican DTOs' (USGAO, 2009, p. 22). See also US Embassy in Mexico (2010, p. 4). The US Government Accountability Office did note, however, that a 'small number' of firearms trafficked from the United States are for 'hunters, off-duty police officers, and citizens seeking personal protection' (USGAO, 2009, p. 23).

10   The Brady Center notes: 'Estimates of the guns flowing into Mexico from the U.S. are as high as 2,000 guns every day' (Brady Center, 2009, p. 7).

11   The .38 Super is a .38-calibre round that was first developed in the 1920s. According to IHS Jane's, it is more powerful and more accurate than the .38 automatic even though the two rounds have the same dimensions (Ness and Williams, 2007, p. 32).

12   The information in the table was taken from a graph titled 'Armas decomisadas en México (1990–2011)'.

13   See, for example, US House of Representatives (2012b, p. 72).

14   See USDOJ (2009, p. 11).

15   See, for example, Harris (2009) and Tucker (2011).

16   See Small Arms Survey (2012a, pp. 319–22, 331–33, 338–39).

17   Twenty-eight per cent of all firearms recovered from caches in Mexico were handguns, whereas pistols and revolvers comprised only 5 per cent of firearms recovered from caches in Iraq. See Small Arms Survey (2012, p. 320).

18   See, for example, USDC Southern District of Texas (2011a; 2011b; 2012) and Dodge (2012).

19   See AP (2009).

20   Written response from the Government of Mexico to questions submitted by the Small Arms Survey, September 2012, and author telephone interview with a US government official, November 2012.

21   Written response from the Government of Mexico to questions submitted by the Small Arms Survey, September 2012.

22   Many firearms trafficked to Mexico from the United States are acquired by 'straw purchasers'—individuals who purchase firearms for someone else while falsely claiming that they are the 'actual transferee/buyer of the firearm(s)' on ATF firearms transaction forms. See, for example, USDC Eastern District of California (2011).

23   Operation Fast and Furious was a multi-year investigation into an extensive network of arms traffickers accused of supplying firearms to Mexican DTOs. During the course of the investigation, which began in October 2009, at least 40 suspects purchased more than 2,000 firearms worth approximately USD 1.5 million. Hundreds of the weapons were later recovered at crime scenes in Mexico, including firearms purchased by individuals whom law enforcement officials had identified as suspects. For more information on this operation, see OIG (2012, pp. 103–418) and Small Arms Survey (2012a, pp. 57–60).

24   A 2005 ATF report also references possible illicit transshipment of foreign-sourced firearms through the United States. Citing an unconfirmed Mexican intelligence report, the ATF identifies Port Langley, British Columbia, as the 'landing point' for Kalashnikov-pattern rifles from former Eastern bloc states, Kosovo, and Serbia. The weapons are reportedly trafficked through Arizona, California, and Texas and are eventually delivered to Mexico (Price, 2005, p. 21).

25   See Farley (2009) for examples of less nuanced statements made by US and Mexican officials.

26   Kuhn and Bunker also estimate that 17 per cent of 'weapons currently acquired by the Mexican cartels' come from US domestic weapons sources. It is not clear what is meant by 'weapons'—that is, whether their estimate includes all weapons or just firearms, or how they arrived at so precise an estimate given the limitations of open-source data (Kuhn and Bunker, 2011, p. 818).

27   According to data provided by the government of Mexico, Mexican authorities seized 154,943 firearms from December 2006 to 23 August 2012. Of those firearms, 99,691 were traced through 'e-trace'; 68,161 of those were manufactured in the United States or brought to Mexico from the United States (written response from the Government of Mexico to questions submitted by the Small Arms Survey, September 2012). ATF provides the same figures, suggesting that the two datasets are comparable even though the Mexican government's data covers six additional months.

28   See also Cook, Cukier, and Krause (2009).

29   These figures differ from the trace data released by ATF in 2012. It is unclear what accounts for these differences.

30   See, for example, Dodge (2012); USDC Southern District of Texas (2011a; 2011b; 2012); and USDC Eastern District of California (2012).

31   Anecdotal data on trafficking suggests that straw purchasers are often paid about USD 50–200 per weapon. See, for example, US Court of Appeals (2011, p. 11) and USDC Southern District of Texas (2008).

32   See Small Arms Survey (2008, pp. 112–53).

33   Data provided to the Small Arms Survey by the government of Mexico indicates that Mexican authorities seized and collected 15,673 grenades from 1994 to 2012; of these, 13,917 were seized by the military and police and 1,756 were voluntarily forfeited as part of a weapons collection programme. Included in this total are projected, military-style fragmentation, craft-produced, smoke, and tear gas grenades.

34   Written response from the Government of Mexico to questions submitted by the Small Arms Survey, September 2012.

35   Written response from the Government of Mexico to questions submitted by the Small Arms Survey, September 2012.

36   See, for example, McCaffery (2009) and Johnson (2009).

37   Written response from the Government of Mexico to questions submitted by the Small Arms Survey, September 2012.

38   Written response from the Government of Mexico to questions submitted by the Small Arms Survey, September 2012.

39   See Small Arms Survey (2012a, pp. 313–55; 2012b).

40   Written response from the Government of Mexico to questions submitted by the Small Arms Survey, September 2012.

41   For an example involving the Juárez cartel and the Barrio Azteca gang, see Stewart (2010).

42   Author telephone interview with US government official, November 2012.

43   See Myers (2011).

44   Written response from the Government of Mexico to questions submitted by the Small Arms Survey, September 2012.

45   Written response from the Government of Mexico to questions submitted by the Small Arms Survey, September 2012.

46   Author telephone interview with a Philippine government official, October 2012. Previous estimates were not only significantly lower but also included additional types of weapons. Data obtained by Quilop indicates that, as of 2005, there were 321,685 'loose' firearms, meaning weapons acquired by armed groups and criminals but also citizens who have not registered their firearms (Quilop, 2010, p. 234).

47   Several additional armed groups are active in the Philippines. For a description of these groups, see Santos et al. (2010, pp. 260–418).

48   See IHS Jane's (2010, p. 3); Quilop (2010, p. 237); and Chalk et al. (2009, p. 58). The few exceptions include AR-18 rifles and .60-calibre and M2 .50-calibre machine guns, none of which are identified in the accounts of the seizures studied.

49   This figure includes four firearms converted to fire a different calibre.

50   This assertion is based on the description of the seized firearms in the source documents. It is possible that additional firearms were craft-produced but not identified as such in the source document. See Small Arms Survey (2012a).

51   See PCTC (n.d., p. 6) and IHS Jane's (2010, p. 3). Research for this study indicates that a 'significant number of small arms and light weapons are seized on the battlefield' (author telephone interview with a Philippine government official, October 2012). Former insurgents have also identified the Philippine military as a source of arms and ammunition; see Quilop (2010, p. 242).

52   One interviewee indicated that '[c]raft-produced guns account for a small fraction of loose weapons, roughly around 2 per cent' (author telephone interview with a Philippine government official, October 2012).

53   Author telephone interview with a Philippine government official, October 2012. The official further explained: 'During the administration of the late President Corazon Aquino [1986–1992], the government allowed the registration of paltik weapons for legal use. This is no longer allowed and all previously registered paltik weapons must be surrendered to the government.'

54   Author telephone interview with a Philippine government official, October 2012.

55   Quilop uses similar language when describing anti-personnel mines and bombs produced by the MILF (Quilop, 2010, p. 244).

56   Author telephone interview with a Philippine government official, October 2012. See also Santos et al. (2010, p. 356).

57   Note that the weapons are of US and European design but may have been produced or sourced elsewhere.

BIBLIOGRAPHY

ADPS (Arizona Department of Public Safety). 2009. 'MISTIC Task Force Investigators Seize 23 Military Grade Grenade Casings and Arrest Three Suspects.' 18 November.

AP (Associated Press). 2008. 'Mexico Seizes Hundreds of Drug-cartel Weapons in Record Raid.' 7 November.

—. 2009. 'Mexico's Weapons Cache Stymies Tracing.' 7 May.

Bouchard, Michael. 2011. 'Statement of Michael R. Bouchard, Retired Assistant Director, Bureau of Alcohol, Tobacco, Firearms and Explosives, Concerning Operation Fast and Furious and Related Firearms Trafficking and Straw Purchases Issues.' Washington, DC: House Committee on Oversight and Government Reform, United States House of Representatives. 30 June.

Brady Center (Brady Center to Prevent Gun Violence). 2009. *Exporting Gun Violence: How Our Weak Gun Laws Arm Criminals in Mexico and America*. March.

Cabrera Martínez, Javier. 2012. 'Atacan con "monstruos" SSP de Los Mochis.' *El Universal* (Mexico). 6 March.

CBS News. 2009. 'Joint Press Conference with President Barack Obama and President Felipe Calderón of Mexico.' Transcript. 16 April. <http://www.whitehouse.gov/video/Obama-Calderon-Joint-Press-Conference#transcript>

Chalk, Peter, et al. 2009. *The Evolving Terrorist Threat to Southeast Asia: A Net Assessment*. Santa Monica, CA: RAND Corporation.

Cinco, A. F. 2009. 'Army Uncovers Ammo Arsenal in Maguindanao.' Philippine Information Agency. 7 December.

Cook, Philip, Wendy Cukier, and Keith Krause. 2009. 'The Illicit Firearms Trade in North America.' *Criminology and Criminal Justice*, Vol. 9, No. 3, pp. 265–86.

Dodge, Angela. 2009. 'Firearms Trafficker Sentenced.' Houston, TX: United States Attorney's Office Southern District of Texas. 27 March. <http://www.justice.gov/usao/txs/1News/Archives/Archived%20Releases/2009%20March/032709Gutierrez_print.htm>

—. 2012. '21-Year-Old Houston Woman Sentenced for Straw Purchasing Firearms.' McAllen, TX: United States Attorney's Office Southern District of Texas. 31 August.

Dudley, Steven, Rick Schmitt, and Rick Young. n.d. 'Gunrunners: Investigating the Saga of the WASR-10, an AK-47 Knockoff and Weapon of Choice for Mexico's Cartels.' PBS Frontline. <http://www.pbs.org/wgbh/pages/frontline/gunrunners-mexico/>

El Universal (Mexico). 2010. 'Reportan nueva balacera en centro de Apatzingán.' 9 December.

Esposito, Richard. 2010. 'Mexican Drug Cartels' New Weapon in Border War: The Car Bomb.' ABC News. 12 August.

Farley, Robert. 2009. 'Obama Claims 90 Percent of Guns Recovered in Mexico Come from U.S.' Politifact. 16 April.

Freedman, Dan. 2011. 'High-powered Weapons Prized by Mexican Cartels.' Hearst Newspapers. 30 May.

García, Jacobo. 2010. 'El museo del narco mexicano.' *El Mundo*. 8 January.

Harris, Byron. 2009. 'Texas Is Arming Mexican Drug Cartels.' WFAA-TV (Dallas/Fort Worth). 13 March.

HCFA (House Committee on Foreign Affairs). 2008. 'Hearing before the Subcommittee on the Western Hemisphere of the Committee on Foreign Affairs.' Serial No. 110–170. Washington, DC: HCFA. 7 February.

IHS Jane's. 2010. 'Divide and Rule: Controlling the MILF's Fractured Factions.' *Jane's Intelligence Review*. June.

Johnson, David. 2009. 'The Merida Initiative.' Testimony before the Subcommittee on State, Foreign Operations, Related Programs of House Committee on Appropriations, Washington, DC. 10 March. <http://www.state.gov/j/inl/rls/rm/120225.htm>

Kuhn, David and Robert Bunker. 2011. 'Just Where Do Mexican Cartel Weapons Come From?' *Small Wars & Insurgencies*. 29 November.

La Jeunesse, William and Maxim Lott. 2009. 'The Myth of 90 Percent: Only a Small Fraction of Guns in Mexico Come from US.' Fox News. 2 April.

LaPierre, Wayne. 2009. 'US Freedoms not to Blame for Mexico's Drug War.' CNN. 26 March.

Levi, Michelle. 2009. 'Mexico: U.S. Supplies 90% of Cartel's Guns.' CBS News. 12 April.

McCaffrey, Barry. 2009. 'Narco-Violence in Mexico: A Growing Threat to U.S. Security.' Chapel Hill, NC: American Diplomacy. January. <http://www.unc.edu/depts/diplomat/item/2009/0103/comm/mccaffery_mexico.html>

Myers, Amanda Lee. 2011. 'Mexico Says US Man Smuggled Grenade Parts.' Associated Press. 7 September.

Ness, Leland and Anthony Williams, eds. 2007. *Jane's Ammunition Handbook 2007–2008*. Coulsdon: Jane's Information Group.

OIG (Office of the Inspector General). 2010. *Review of ATF's Project Gunrunner*. 1-2011-001. Washington, DC: OIG, United States Department of Justice. November.

—. 2012. *A Review of ATF's Operation Fast and Furious and Related Matters*. Washington, DC: OIG, United States Department of Justice. September.

PCTC (Philippine Center on Transnational Crime). n.d. *Illicit Trafficking and Manufacturing of Firearms: Philippine Context*. Quezon City, Philippines: PCTC.

Prensa Latina. 2012. 'Arsenal with Anti Aircraft Rocket Seized in Mexico.' 17 September.

Price, Adam. 2005. *Firearms Trafficking to the United Mexican States through Arizona: Project Iron River*. Phoenix: Phoenix Field Division, United States Bureau of Alcohol, Tobacco, Firearms and Explosives. September.

Quilop, Raymund Jose. 2010. 'Small Arms and Light Weapons in the Philippines: Possession, Demand, Supply, and Regulation (Overview).' In Soliman Santos et al., pp. 231–57.

Roque, Pat. 2009. 'Philippine Troops Raid Homes of Massacre Suspects.' Associated Press. 4 December.

Santos, Soliman, et al. 2010. *Primed and Purposeful: Armed Groups and Human Security Efforts in the Philippines*. Geneva: Small Arms Survey.

Small Arms Survey. 2008. *Small Arms Survey 2008: Risk and Resilience*. Cambridge: Cambridge University Press.

—. 2010. *Small Arms Survey 2010: Gangs, Groups, and Guns*. Cambridge: Cambridge University Press.

—. 2012a. 'Surveying the Battlefield: Illicit Arms in Afghanistan, Iraq, and Somalia.' In Small Arms Survey. *Small Arms Survey 2012: Moving Targets*. Cambridge: Cambridge University Press.

  <http://www.smallarmssurvey.org/fileadmin/docs/A-Yearbook/2012/eng/Small-Arms-Survey-2012-Chapter-10-EN.pdf>

—. 2012b. 'Guided Light Weapons Reportedly Held by Non-state Armed Groups, 1998–2012.' Geneva: Small Arms Survey. September.

  <http://www.smallarmssurvey.org/fileadmin/docs/M-files/armed-groups-guided-missiles.pdf>

—. 2012c. 'Analysis of Data on Illicit Weapons Compiled from Documents Published by Mexico's Secretaría de la Defensa Nacional, 2009–12.' Geneva: Small Arms Survey.

—. 2012d. 'Analysis of Data on Illicit Weapons Compiled from Documents Published by the Philippine Government, 2004–12.' Geneva: Small Arms Survey.

Stewart, Scott. 2010. 'Mexico: The Struggle for Balance.' Stratfor. 8 April. <http://www.stratfor.com/weekly/20100407_mexico_struggle_balance>

—. 2011a. 'Mexico's Gun Supply and the 90 Percent Myth.' *Stratfor*. 10 February.

—. 2011b. 'The Buffer Between Mexican Cartels and the U.S. Government.' *Stratfor*. 17 August.

Tucker, Will. 2011. 'Photo Gallery: The Top Ten Favorite Guns of the Mexican Drug Cartels.' *Texas on the Potomac*. 15 July.

UCDP (Uppsala Conflict Data Program). 2012. *UCDP/PRIO Armed Conflict Dataset Codebook*.

  <http://www.pcr.uu.se/digitalAssets/118/118670_codebook_ucdp_prio-armed-conflict-dataset-v4_2012.pdf>

UNODC (United Nations Office on Drugs and Crime). 2000. United Nations Convention against Transnational Organized Crime and the Protocols Thereto.

  <http://www.unodc.org/unodc/en/treaties/CTOC/index.html>

USCBP (United States Customs and Border Protection). 2004. *Customs Administrative Enforcement Process: Fines, Penalties, Forfeitures and Liquidated Damages*. February.

—. 2011. Documents obtained in response to a Freedom of Information Act request filed by the Small Arms Survey and the Federation of American Scientists for 'a copy of all records from the Seized Asset and Case Tracking System (or current equivalent database) of outbound seizures of firearms and other weapons and military equipment seized at the US Border from January 1, 2009 to July 1, 2011'. Received on 29 September.

US Court of Appeals (United States Court of Appeals, Tenth Circuit). 2011. *United States of America* vs. *Erika Denise Garcia*. March 28.

USDC Arizona (United States District Court for the District of Arizona). 2011. *United States of America* vs. *Jorge De Jesus-Casteneda*. Transcript. 20 April.

USDC Eastern District of California (US District Court for the Eastern District of California). 2011. *United States of America* vs. *Ernesto Salgado-Guzman et al*. Indictment. 3 November.

USDC Southern District of Texas (United States District Court for the Southern District of Texas). 2008. 'Brownsville Man Sentenced to Prison for Firearms Trafficking.' 2 October.

—. 2011a. *United States of America* vs. *Alberto Rueda-Cabrera*. Indictment. 20 December.

—. 2011b. *United States of America* vs. *Saul Salazar et al*. Indictment. 17 March.

—. 2012. *United States of America* vs. *Andrew Joshua Guerrero*. Indictment. 14 February.

USDOJ (United States Department of Justice). 2009. 'Law Enforcement Responses to Drug Cartels.' Statement of William Hoover and Anthony P. Placido before the United States Senate Committee on the Judiciary Subcommittee on Crime and Drugs. 17 March.

—. 2010. 'Mexico: Counterfeit Colt M16A2 Rifles and M203 Grenade Launchers.' Washington, DC: Office of Strategic Intelligence and Information, Bureau of Alcohol, Tobacco, Firearms and Explosives. 12 March.

—. 2011. *ATF Firearms Tracing Guide*. ATF Publication 3312.13. November.

—. 2012. *ATF Mexico Trace Data: Calendar Years 2007–2011*. 12 March.

US Embassy in Mexico (Embassy of the United States in Mexico City, Mexico). 2010. 'Mexico Weapons Trafficking: The Blame Game.' Cable. 09 Mexico 2952. 2 July.

USGAO (United States Government Accountability Office). 2009. *US Efforts to Combat Arms Trafficking to Mexico Face Planning and Coordination Challenges*. GAO-09-709. Washington, DC: USGAO. June.

US House of Representatives (United States House of Representatives). 2012a. *Fast and Furious: The Anatomy of a Failed Operation (Part 1 of 3)*, app. I, pt. 3 of 3, Exhibit 217. 31 July.

—. 2012b. *Fatally Flawed: Five Years of Gunwalking in Arizona*. Report of the Minority Staff. 12 January.

ACKNOWLEDGEMENTS

Principal author

Matt Schroeder

INDEX

S